THE BEST OF *BUSINESS ECONOMICS*

THE BEST OF *BUSINESS ECONOMICS*

HIGHLIGHTS FROM THE FIRST FIFTY YEARS

By

National Association for Business Economics

Edited by

Robert Thomas Crow

palgrave
macmillan

THE BEST OF *BUSINESS ECONOMICS*

First published 2016 by
PALGRAVE MACMILLAN

Palgrave Macmillan in the UK is an imprint of Macmillan Publishers Limited, registered in England, company number 785998, of Houndmills, Basingstoke, Hampshire, RG21 6XS.

Palgrave Macmillan in the US is a division of Nature America, Inc., One New York Plaza, Suite 4500, New York, NY 10004-1562.

Palgrave Macmillan is the global academic imprint of the above companies and has companies and representatives throughout the world.

Hardback ISBN: 978–1–137–57250–9
E-PUB ISBN: 978–1–137–57252–3
E-PDF ISBN: 978–1–137–57251–6
DOI: 10.1057/9781137572516

Distribution in the UK, Europe and the rest of the world is by Palgrave Macmillan®, a division of Macmillan Publishers Limited, registered in England, company number 785998, of Houndmills, Basingstoke, Hampshire RG21 6XS.

Library of Congress Cataloging-in-Publication Data

The best of Business economics : highlights from the first fifty years / National Association of Business Economics; edited by Robert Crow.
pages cm
Includes bibliographical references.
ISBN 978–1–137–57250–9 (hardback : alk. paper)
1. United States—Economic policy. 2. United States—Economic conditions—1945– 3. Economics—United States. 4. Business—United States. 5. Managerial economics—United States. I. Crow, Robert, editor. II. National Association for Business Economics (U.S.), issuing body. III. Business economics (Cleveland, Ohio)

HC103.B44 2015
330.973—dc23 2015027014

A catalogue record for the book is available from the British Library.

CONTENTS

Introduction xvii
Robert Thomas Crow

PART I 1965–1974 **1**

1. A New Look at Monetary and Fiscal Policy (1967) 3
Paul A. Volcker
Although the recent past amply demonstrates the temptation for policy makers to discount the complications that today's actions may create for tomorrow, it would be a serious mistake to confine policy makers to a fixed monetary rule. Part of our recent difficulties stemmed from underlying developments in financial markets, such as the liberalization of institutional lending, that weakened the "availability effects" of monetary policy. For the longer run, actions are needed to make financial markets more evenly responsive to monetary policy.

2. The Role of Money in Economic Activity: Complicated or Simple? (1969) 9
Edward M. Gramlich
The FRB-MIT model focuses on monetary factors, with structural relationships which highlight their transmission to the real economy. These are the cost of capital channel (capital goods, housing, consumer durables and state and local spending), the net worth of consumers and credit rationing. Money proves to be important, but with lags long and variable. An extensive econometric model is found more helpful than a single equation.

3. Econometric Model Building for Growth Projections (1969) 19
Lawrence R. Klein
The Wharton Model is extrapolated for 24 quarters with appropriate assumptions. The problems involved in specifying a fresh model for long range forecasting are then outlined, including "endogenizing variables" such as government spending. Attention is drawn to the less precise performance in predictions of the long run. Skepticism is expressed concerning deceptively smooth and free hand extrapolations.

4. Presidential Address: The Challenge to Our System 31
Alan Greenspan
Concern is expressed about the extent of government intervention. Yet government has a role to play, e.g. in industrial pollution. But there are problems.

A law of fiscal constituencies is formulated: the growth rate of benefits to constituent groups tends to exceed the fiscal dividend. Grave questions remain about the fiscal outlook in coming years.

5. The Social Significance of Environmental Pollution (1970) 39
Barry Commoner
Environmental pollution is not an incidental by-product. Rather, it is an intrinsic feature of the very technology developed to enhance productivity. This technology is so imbedded in the agricultural and industrial production processes that the required change would involve serious economic dislocations. The author contends that the problem is so serious that these dislocations must be confronted.

6. The Productivity Slow-Down (1971) 47
John W. Kendrick
The slowdown in productivity since 1966 is due to: (1) the decline in R&D expenditures in relation to GNP; (2) the accelerated growth of the labor force, particularly in the youngest age groups; (3) the acceleration in price-inflation which has diverted resources to mitigating its unfavorable consequences; (4) social tendencies which have reduced the power of material goals and the work-ethic among a small but growing proportion of the population, particularly in the younger age-brackets.

7. Why Productivity Is Important (1973) 59
Geoffrey H. Moore
Productivity growth has played a key role in insuring higher real wages and in combating inflation over the last quarter of a century. These facts and others relating to productivity are documented as the relation of hourly compensation, productivity and unit labor costs is sketched, and the relation of the latter to total costs, prices and profits is outlined. Future real economic growth without inflation will depend on high rates of productivity growth.

PART II 1975–1984 **65**

8. *Presidential Address*: NABE and the Business Forecaster (1975) 67
Robert G. Dederick
Despite some success, economists, on the whole, have been sadly lacking in foresight, and have not provided their managements with advanced warning of the distressing situation into which the economy was drifting. Granted that the usual cyclical developments have been overwhelmed by explosive, structural shifts, it is doubtful that accuracy will be achieved upon a return to economic equilibrium. Accuracy was not present in earlier periods of equilibrium. Further, economists have tended to predict the unimportant and not the important. Explanations for the profession's forecasting failures are reviewed, and the point made that the relationships have been emphasized rather than the facts. A course of action for NABE is suggested.

9. Thoughts on Inflation: The Basic Forces (1975) 75
Gottfried Haberler
In a clear and concise fashion, the basic principles involved in inflation are reviewed. The author distinguishes three types of inflation: classical demand

inflation, cost or wage push inflation, and shortage inflation stemming from special factors. Each type is analyzed and suggestions made as to how it can be treated. Special emphasis is placed on cost or wage push inflation and from what causes it arises. The spectrum of opinion on the part played by unionization in wage push inflation is reviewed. Finally, various anti-inflation policies are examined and some international aspects of inflation touched upon.

10. The Practical Use of Economic Analysis in Investment Management (1975) 85
Edmund A. Mennis
Economic analysis can be most effective if it is fully integrated into the investment decision process. Here, the investment decision process is described. Specific uses of economic analysis in the various parts of the process are detailed, examples are given, and certain caveats provided.

11. *Presidential Address*: On Human Welfare (1979) 95
Albert G. Matamoros
As important as it is continuously to assess our role as business economists, I think it is equally imperative that we step back, from time to time, and examine still broader issues. Today I want to raise some questions regarding the extent to which economic policies and the consequent actions of the agencies of government during the past 15 years have contributed to the human condition. It is not only appropriate, but I think mandatory, that, as social scientists, we be concerned for man's welfare and his destiny.

12. Company Total Factor Productivity: Refinements, Production Functions, and Certain Effects of Regulation (1981) 105
Douglas L. Cocks
The current concern over the lack of productivity growth in the US mandates certain actions by companies. One of these actions is the measurement of productivity for individual firms. This chapter presents some refinements in the measurement of Total Factor Productivity (TFP) at the firm level. In addition, alternative methodologies are investigated with the result that these alternatives yield consistent results. The chapter also demonstrates two applications of the TFP model to empirical investigations relevant to public policy issues: the impact of regulation on measured productivity and estimation of production functions for the firm. One interesting empirical result is that, given the necessary input data, the negative effects of regulation on productivity can be demonstrated through the TFP model.

13. *The Adam Smith Address*: Conservatives, Economists, and Neckties (1983) 121
Herbert Stein
One might expect Adam Smith to be the patron saint of economists of all ideologies. He was the father not only of a particular idea of how the economy works but also of the idea that there is an economic system. Moreover, some of his ideas about how the system works are incorporated in all kinds of economics, from extreme left to extreme right. Any economist teaching the history of economic thought would start with Adam Smith. But the wearing of Adam Smith neckties is not uniformly or randomly distributed among economists. Only economists who are, loosely, called conservatives wear it.

14. Economics from Three Perspectives (1982) 129
Marina v. N. Whitman
This chapter is based on a talk Dr. Whitman gave at Notre Dame University. In it, she shares some of her personal views on the various roles economists play in society, the need for greater interaction among academic, government and business economists and the evolution of the role of corporate economists at General Motors Corporation.

15. *The Adam Smith Address*: Was Adam Smith a Monetarist or a Keynesian? (1984) 137
Charles P. Kindleberger
I give this talk the foregoing title (a) because it is the Adam Smith Lecture and (b) because I want to hold forth on Keynesianism and monetarism. It is evident, however, that to put the matter as a choice between a single pair of alternatives is fallacious. Adam Smith was and is under no compulsion to fall exclusively into one category or the other.

PART III 1985–1994 **149**

16. *The Adam Smith Address*: The Effect of Government on Economic Efficiency (1987) 151
George J. Stigler
This chapter examines the effects of governmental policies upon the efficiency of the economy, including both traditional governmental areas (such as justice, defense, and environmental protection) and the vast and growing share of governmental programs aiming to redistribute income. A proposed principle of legitimacy states that every action set by a legislature represents a social judgment that society is better off for that action. Thus all governmental policies are by hypothesis utility-increasing for the nation. Any costs of (say) a redistribution of income are less than the benefits. National output as presently measured can and usually will fall when a new redistribution of income is instituted, because it is costly to redistribute income. Is this trend in governmental policy likely to be reversed, perhaps by a general movement toward deregulation? The author's answer to this question is calculated to restore the claim that economics is the dismal science.

17. *The Adam Smith Address*: On the Structure of an Economy (1988) 161
James M. Buchanan
Economic choices are made by many buyers and sellers as they participate in many markets for many goods and services. "The Economy" is best described by the structure (the rules) within which these market choices take place. Efforts to reform the pattern of results observed in an economy should be directed exclusively at this structure; attempts to modify directly the outcomes or results of market process within structures are based on fundamental misunderstanding.

18. Rethinking International Trade (1988) 171
Paul Krugman
In the past decade, many economists are rethinking their historic belief in free trade. The theory of comparative advantage is being supplemented by a theory of increasing returns, i.e., the advantages of specialization per se. While the new

theory may strengthen the arguments for free trade, it also alters recommended government trade policy. Subsidies may tilt competition in favor of a high return domestic industry, giving it a head start and a persistent advantage. While this new trade theory may not always be effective, it does change free trade from a dogma to a reasonable rule of thumb in an imperfect world.

19. *The Adam Smith Address*: The Suicidal Impulse of the Business Community (1989) 181
Milton Friedman
Corporations often promote policies adverse to their own best interests. In the political arena, business has a short time horizon that differs from its approach in long-term corporate planning. Examples are given of business attitudes toward protectionist tariffs, tax and regulatory policy, fixed exchange rates, corporate contributions, and budget and trade deficits. Corporations, acting in a climate that considers government action a cure for all problems, are contributing to the destruction of a free market economy rather than shoring up its foundations.

20. A Guide to What Is Known about Business Cycles (1990) 189
Victor Zarnowitz
This chapter reviews the common core of the pervasive and persistent nonseasonal fluctuations that have characterized modern capitalist economies. But much diversity also exists, and the differences between cycles before and after World War II are discussed. Some reasons for these changes are offered. Finally, a brief comment considers the various theories advanced to explain "the" cycle, and the difficulty of so doing because cycles are not all alike.

21. Some Financial Perspectives on Comparative Costs of Capital (1991) 203
J. Fred Weston
Empirical studies of international cost of capital comparisons have taken two related forms. One is to compare weighted average costs of capital (WACC) for samples across economies. Sample WACC comparisons may be subject to error because the cost of capital measures may not be applied to appropriate definitions of operating cash flows whose qualities, time-growth patterns, and risk may differ. Comparisons of riskless rates such as yields on government securities ignore relevant risk differences. No financially derived competitive advantage is likely to exist with: (1) no net tax or subsidy differences, (2) capital market and economic integration.

22. Health Insurance Derivatives: The Newest Application of Modern Financial Risk Management (1993) 213
James A. Hayes, Joseph B. Cole, and David I. Meiselman
This chapter discusses the derivatives revolution in financial and other markets, emphasizing the gains in market efficiency and innovation by reducing transaction costs and promoting new product development. Health insurance futures and options, a natural extension of the derivatives revolution, will be trading at the Chicago Board of Trade in 1993. In addition to an overview of the structure of the health insurance futures contract, an example is given of a long hedge by an insurance company to protect itself from unexpectedly higher claims payments.

PART IV 1995–2004 **221**

23. *The Adam Smith Address*: An Ambitious Agenda for Economic Growth (1996) 223
Murray Weidenbaum
Two undesirable ways to achieve faster economic growth are to adopt an easy monetary policy or just cut tax rates. A better way is to deal with structural defects that depress productive capacity and productivity through structural reform. Budget cuts should aim to shift emphasis from programs that encourage consumption to those that encourage investment, review subsidy programs, avoid funding programs to offset problems caused by regulation, and privatize activities that belong in the private sector. Tax reform also should encourage saving, and regulatory costs should be reviewed in light of the benefits derived. Slow growth is not susceptible to a quick cure, but an extensive array of expenditure, tax and regulatory reforms can shift the US economy to a higher growth path.

24. *The Adam Smith Address*: Capitalism and Its Discontents (1998) 231
Michael J. Boskin
A review of episodes in economic and intellectual history indicates the superiority of a limited government market economy over the alternative models of economic organization. The siren calls of pundits, politicians and even some economists in favor of: Communist central planning during the Great Depression; market socialism after World War II; and, more recently, massive welfare states and/or extensive government micromanagement of markets each ran afoul of their own problems and comparisons to the limited government (based on sound criteria) capitalist model. The limited government capitalist model, once again under attack from those who would greatly expand the role of government, needs its defenders, as the alternative models have proven historically, intellectually and practically bankrupt.

25. Protecting Against the Next Financial Crisis: The Need to Reform Global Financial Oversight, the IMF, and Monetary Policy Goals (1999) 243
Henry Kaufman
Recent distress in world financial markets has underlined the need for supervising and regulating financial institutions and markets on a global basis. A new institution, in addition to the International Monetary Fund (IMF) and the World Bank, is required to set forth a code of conduct to encourage reasonable financial behavior and to supervise risk-taking. It also should be empowered by member governments to harmonize minimum capital requirements, to establish uniform trading, reporting and disclosure standards, and to monitor the performance of institutions and markets under its purview. The IMF should be able to demand policy changes in anticipation of problems. Securitization and the development of financial derivatives have liberalized granting of credit, requiring steeper interest rates to end a period of excessive monetary expansion. Monetary policy also should be concerned with asset inflation as well as price inflation.

26. How the Economy Came to Resemble the Model (1999) 255
Alan S. Blinder

Over the years, economists have spent much effort to modify the capitalist, perfect-competition, profit-maximizing model of classical microeconomics to fit reality. Thus, it is ironic that in recent times reality has been approaching the classical model. This is due only in part to the persuasive talents of economists, and not all of this change is necessarily an improvement. Among the factors contributing to the reversion to the classical model are the failure of socialism, alignment of managerial and shareholder interests, focus on shareholder value, decline of labor union power, changes in financial markets, global competition, and changes in regulatory practices.

27. *The Adam Smith Address*: What Would Adam Smith Say Now? (2000) 271
Henry Kaufman

The breadth and depth of Adam Smith's thought over 200 years ago still provide powerful lessons today. Were he present, he would applaud much of what has transpired in the organization of economic life, particularly in the US economy and its thrust toward individual achievement and relatively free markets for goods and services, capital, and labor. However, he would also be deeply troubled by recent trends toward consolidation, particularly in the financial sector, and the emergence of "too-big-to-fail" as an argument for government to weaken the discipline of markets.

28. Information Technology and the U.S. Productivity Revival: A Review of the Evidence (2001) 279
Kevin J. Stiroh

Aggregate, industry, and firm level studies all point to a strong connection between information technology (IT) and the US productivity revival in the late 1990s. At the aggregate level, growth accounting studies show a large and growing contribution to productivity growth from both the production and the use of IT. At the industry level, industries that produce or use IT most intensively have shown the largest increases in productivity growth after 1995. At the firm level, IT-intensive firms show better performance than their peers, and several specific case studies show how IT improves real business practices. This accumulation of evidence from a variety of studies suggests a real productivity impact from IT.

29. *Presidential Address*: Understanding Inflation: Lessons from My Central Banking Career (2002) 291
Harvey Rosenblum

Economic theory—much less modeling based on historical data—has a difficult time keeping up with structural change in the contemporary economy. Anecdotal evidence and a feel for the economy based on experience are likely to be as important as theory-based modeling in making real-time policy decisions on the control of inflation and the stability of the economy. Many of the phenomena to be understood are microeconomic in nature. While much has been learned about effective stabilization policy over the past forty years, economists still have a long way to go before inflation can be understood and managed.

30. Managing Exchange Rates: Achievement of Global Re-Balancing or Evidence of Global Co-Dependency? (2004) 305
Catherine L. Mann
Long-term global economic health requires that external imbalances and the internal imbalances that support them be corrected by both the United States and its trading partners. The current path of external imbalances appears to be unsustainable, but relying on exchange rate adjustments is unlikely to suffice as long as there is a co-dependency of structural characteristics and policy choices between the United States and its trading partners. There is a real possibility that the entanglements created by this co-dependency cannot be undone by anything short of a global economic crisis.

PART V 2005–2015 **319**

31. *The Adam Smith Address:* The Explanatory Power of Monetary Policy Rules (2007) 321
John B. Taylor
Over the past 20 years, the use of monetary policy rules has become pervasive in analyzing and prescribing monetary policy. This chapter traces the development of such rules and their use in the analysis, prediction, and stabilization of national economies. In particular, rules provide insight into eras in which monetary policy was not effective as well as when it was, such as the persistence of the ongoing "Great Moderation." The chapter stresses "the scientific" contributions of rules, including their insight into fluctuations of housing construction and exchange rates, as well as into the term structure of interest rates.

32. *The Adam Smith Address:* Adam Smith and the Political Economy of a Modern Financial Crisis (2008) 335
Michael Mussa
Financial crises have occurred periodically for hundreds of years, and Adam Smith had important insights into their causes. Although by no means all that we know about such crises has been derived from Smith, it is interesting and important to reflect on what he did know and how ignoring his warnings about the creation of excess liquidity has contributed to the current crisis. In addition to the complexity of contemporary finance and the role of central banks and other regulatory institutions, a major difference between Smith's day and ours is the emergence of "moral hazard" as an important policy issue and its corollary, "immoral results." It is important to realize that the risks of financial crisis, moral hazard, and immoral results cannot be avoided by financial and accounting gimmicks, and that there is no substitute for adequate capital in the creation of liquidity.

33. Underwriting, Mortgage Lending, and House Prices: 1996–2008 (2009) 355
James A. Wilcox
Lowering of underwriting standards may have contributed much to the unprecedented recent rise and subsequent fall of mortgage volumes and house prices. Conventional data do not satisfactorily measure aggregate underwriting standards over the past decade: the easing and then tightening of underwriting, inside and especially outside of banks, was likely much more extensive than

they indicate. Given mortgage market developments since the mid-1990s, the method of principal components produces a superior indicator of mortgage underwriting standards. We show that the resulting indicator better fits the variation over time in the laxity and tightness of underwriting. Based on a vector auto-regression, we then show how conditions affected underwriting standards. The results also show that our new indicator of underwriting helps account for the behavior of mortgage volumes, house prices, and gross domestic product during the recent boom in mortgage and housing markets.

34. The Impact of the Housing Market Boom and Bust on Consumption Spending (2010) 377
Jeremy A. Leonard
While econometric evidence for the United States has consistently shown that increases in real estate wealth induce additional consumption, it does not directly speak to the effect of a substantial decrease in real estate wealth. This chapter examines the real estate wealth-consumption relationship over the past half century with a particular focus on the sharp decline in 2006–2008, and finds that the wealth effect in the recent down market is significantly larger than in an up market. Additionally, wealth changes seem only to affect consumption of services and nondurable goods; there is virtually no impact on durable goods consumption.

35. *The Adam Smith Address*: Macroprudential Supervision and Monetary Policy in the Post-Crisis World (2010) 393
Janet L. Yellen
Until two years ago, it was believed that the financial system as a whole was self-correcting and that modern tools of stabilization policy—monetary policy in particular—were sufficient to prevent severe economic contractions. We now know that we need a robust system of regulation and supervision that will recognize and prevent financial excesses before they lead to crisis, while at the same time maintaining an environment conducive to financial innovation. This address traces the causes of the crisis and the role of the Dodd-Frank Act in providing a framework for preventing recurrence. It then describes what must be done to identify emerging systemic financial risk, the tools and implementation of macroprudential financial supervision that must be developed, and the role of coordination between monetary policy and macroprudential supervision. Prevention of crises will not be easy—particularly because it will be necessary to walk a tightrope between prevention of catastrophe and keeping too tight a hold on the financial system.

36. *The Adam Smith Address*: Nightmare on Kaiserstrasse (2011) 407
Kenneth Rogoff
The overhang of debt (private and surging public) is perhaps the principal reason why recessions following financial crises are so deep and lasting. Frequently, a wave of international financial and banking crises is followed by a wave of sovereign defaults. This is the case of the Eurozone crisis today. How might a sovereign debt default of, say, Greece affect the Eurozone? The nightmare scenario is a complete unraveling of the euro. The euro can still be saved, but perhaps only with the weaker countries undergoing major restructuring of their sovereign debt.

37. *The Adam Smith Address*: Financial Services and the Trust Deficit: Why the Industry Should Make Better Governance a Top Priority (2013) 413

Roger W. Ferguson, Jr.

The US economy, while recovering, is still feeling lingering effects of the 2008 financial crisis and the recession that followed. Although government has acted to prevent a future recurrence, much needs to be done—particularly in corporate governance of financial firms. Currently, there is a pervasive lack of trust in the financial industry, which will be difficult to undo. Nonetheless, finance is so important that it is critical that trust be restored. This is particularly true in an era in which planning for retirement is inadequate, and financial literacy is increasingly important. This implies a critical role for a financial services industry whose guidance can be trusted. This trust must be built through appropriate corporate governance on the part of all stakeholders, and specific recommendations are advanced for bringing this about.

38. US Economic Prospects: Secular Stagnation, Hysteresis, and the Zero Lower Bound (2014) 421

Lawrence H. Summers

The nature of macroeconomics has changed dramatically in the last seven years. Now, instead of being concerned with minor adjustments to stabilize about a given trend, concern is focused on avoiding secular stagnation. Much of this concern arises from the long-run effects of short-run developments and the inability of monetary policy to accomplish much more when interest rates have already reached their lower bound. This address analyzes contemporary macroeconomic problems and proposes solutions to put the US economy back on a path toward healthy growth.

PART VI Feature Articles **437**

39. *Focus on Industries and Markets*: Electric Power Transmission and Distribution Equipment (2011) 439

David A. Petina, Michael Murphy, and Andrew C. Gross

The US electrical grid must be upgraded, and there is a strong debate about the characteristics of the next-generation electrical network. However, slow growth of electricity usage, among other factors, means that the demand for transmission and distribution (T&D) equipment is growing slowly also. Within the T&D equipment sector, switchgear and transformers are still the dominant segments, but sales of meters are growing rapidly in response to increased demands for security, safety, and connectivity. Six firms hold about 40 percent of the T&D equipment market share, selling to electric utilities, nonutility industrial firms, commercial firms, and residential customers. Foreign trade is also important in this industry, with the United States running a substantial trade deficit.

40. *Focus on Statistics*: Initial Results of the 2012 Economic Census (2014) 455

Robert P. Parker

The initial results of the 2012 Economic Census are being released and will continue to be released until mid-2016. It provides detailed industry and geographic data used by businesses, researchers, and government policy makers. It provides the detailed data used to benchmark the Index of Industrial Production and the Producer Price Index, and to prepare input-output accounts and quarterly GDP. The Census Bureau uses the data to benchmark most of the Census Bureau's annual, quarterly, and monthly economic surveys and this benchmarking maintains the reliability of these sample surveys. The 2012 Economic Census is essentially the same as 2007 census.

41. *Economics at Work*: Economics at the American Chemistry Council (2014) 469

Thomas Kevin Swift

This chapter examines the role of the economics team at the American Chemistry Council, a major trade association representing the leading companies in the business of chemistry. The history of the team, its organization, its role in providing good statistics, monitoring and forecasting business conditions, conducting policy analysis, and thoughts on managing professionals are presented.

INTRODUCTION

> "If all the economists were laid end to end, they'd never reach a conclusion."
> George Bernard Shaw

In 1959, the National Association of Business Economists—now the National Association for Business Economics (NABE)—was formed. In 1965, its Governing Council decided to create a professional journal, *Business Economics*. This collection of articles commemorates *Business Economics'* 50th anniversary. It is an attempt to pull together the best from each decade of those 50 years.

Business Economics was intended by its founders as a *professional* journal, not an academic one. Throughout its history, although editorial policies have changed from time to time, this intent has been consistent.[1] Its focus has been on what is useful to economists working in business rather than on advancing economic science. Often, however, an article will be useful *and* advance economic science—so much the better. Excerpts from *Business Economics'* current instructions to authors reflect the journal's consistent intent:

> "To be considered for publication, there must be a clear statement of how and why the analysis and information presented in the paper are important to business. That is, articles must pass the 'So what?' test."
>
> "*Business Economics* readers are professionals, managers, and researchers in organizations of all sizes and kinds, primarily in North America. Their interests—improving their performance on the job and using economics in the workplace—shape what *Business Economics* editors look for in reviewing submissions."

A horseback guestimate is that about 1,200 regular articles have appeared in *Business Economics* over its 50-year history. This implies an immense job of screening and evaluation to select the 3 percent or so that will actually be published. To do this, the Editorial Board and feature editors were recruited into five teams—one per decade—to select the best articles. However, *Business Economics* over the years has some traits that permitted some screening so that the teams would not have to review every article.

In 1986, NABE inaugurated the Abramson Award for the outstanding paper published in *Business Economics* in the preceding year. That year, it also inaugurated the Adam Smith Award for "leadership in the profession and the application of economic principles and knowledge in the workplace and policy arenas." Upon receiving this award, the recipient gives an address that is subsequently published in *Business Economics*. Thus, for 1986 to 1999, only the President's Address articles, the Adam Smith Award articles, and the Abramson Award articles were considered. In 1999, winners of the competition for the Mennis Award were added; and in 2014 NABE inaugurated the Lifetime Achievement Award for Economic Policy, the presentation of which is accompanied by an address by the recipient. These awards provided a means of screening the articles to be considered. Although some outstanding articles that have proven to be more valuable through the test of time than they appeared to be initially may have been lost in this process, it seemed like a reasonable way to make selections.

However, "best" in economics—as in art—is a slippery concept. In what sense is Bach better than Beethoven, or vice versa? What about Mozart and Tchaikovsky? Hence, the George Bernard Shaw quote above. Few articles were consensus choices; most were by plurality. Finding a consensus on the best economics articles is not unlike corralling a hatful of mice.

Even though it was possible to limit the population from which the selections were made, selecting was still a demanding, time-consuming job, and I would like to acknowledge those who took on this task. They are as follows:

Roger C. Bird
Oral Capps
Glenn R. DeSouza
William C. Dunkelberg
Robert A. Eisenbeis
Elinda Fishman Kiss
Andrew C. Gross
J. Paul Horne
Parul Jain
Douglas J. Lamdin
Lynn O. Michaelis
Gerald L. Musgrave
Francis H. Schott
Nancy D. Sidhu
Thomas F. Siems
James F. Smith
Charles Steindel
Christopher M. Swann
T. Kevin Swift
Diane C. Swonk

Although the content of *Business Economics* is quite varied, the overwhelming number of the articles selected for this volume concern the environment in which firms do business rather than the role of economics within the firm or the how economics should be practiced in business. The latter concern is often addressed in a feature entitled "The Business Economist at Work" or "Economics at Work" that appears in many issues. Other features are "Focus on Statistics" and "Focus on Industries and Markets." One example of each of these features is included in this volume.

There is a great deal of wisdom and inspiration in the articles that have been selected. Some are uniquely relevant to the time in which they were written. Most, however, still speak to economists and those who use economics in their work. I hope that this volume will be a source of information and inspiration to these readers.

Robert Thomas Crow
Editor, *Business Economics*
2015

Note

1. An article on the history of *Business Economics* appears in the October 2015 issue.

PART I

1965–1974

CHAPTER 1

1967

A NEW LOOK AT MONETARY AND FISCAL POLICY

Paul A. Volcker, Chase Manhattan Bank

The simple fact of the matter is that I cannot detect—out of all the welter of commentary on 1966—an agreed doctrine emerging on the delicate job of managing prosperity.

There is, I think, a wide consensus on two basic points.

- First, nearly everyone agrees that fiscal policy needs to play a more effective role than has been evident in the past two years.
- Second, the point has been well made—particularly by one of NABE's past presidents and a colleague and mentor of mine, William F. Butler—that success in fine tuning the economy is utterly dependent on accurate forecasting. In its absence, the policy-maker too often will be leaning against a non-existent wind—or he can begin leaning only after a gust has already blown him off balance.

Hindsight vs Foresight

I agree with the consensus on those points. But I find them of decidedly limited usefulness in terms of practical guidance for the policy-maker in business or government. Take the fiscal policy question. In retrospect, it is amply clear that taxes should have been raised in early 1966. But at the time, I was not exactly deafened by the pleas of professional economists for action along those lines.

That contrast between hindsight and foresight—even when the basic economic principles are widely understood—is hardly surprising to a group of business economists. We deal regularly with the uncertainties surrounding business decision-making in a complex world—and we are well aware that there are, quite properly, more ingredients in nearly all decisions than a question of economic judgment. I would only point out that the political setting is still more difficult, particularly in so sensitive an area as tax and expenditure policy, and we cannot assume that fiscal policy will always be unerringly in tune with our needs.

I do not mean to be defeatist. The fact that the Administration is pushing hard for a tax increase now, and with a great deal of professional and business support, seems to me evidence of progress. In particular, I believe the President and his advisers are quite right in recognizing that to wait until all the evidence is in—to wait until the business expansion has already reached the point of adding further fuel to the inflationary pressures—would be to wait far too long. Yet, clear as the need seems to me, prospects for action are obscured by the entirely legitimate related questions of spending policy, as well as by the doubts as to whether tax action is premature, or excessive or necessary at all.

The difficulties of fine tuning fiscal policy are obviously related to forecasting problems. Something in the mystique that still surrounds central banking—plus some real elements of greater flexibility—have made monetary policy less vulnerable to the charge of resting on weak forecasts. But the lags in policy impact are clearly there. So long as they are, so is the forecasting problem.

The combination of policy lags and forecasting errors assure that it will always be possible, in looking at the past record, to find specific instances of when it would have been better to have done nothing—or to have followed a fixed rule—than to have done what was in fact done. Plenty of examples can be found in the past two years. And these examples have, I suspect, provided a more sympathetic audience for those who favor a mixed rule, whether of the monetary or the fiscal variety.

I would myself concede that the recent period has amply demonstrated the strong temptation for policy makers—in their impatience to deal with today's fires—to underestimate the lags in policy transmission, and to discount too heavily the possible complications that today's action is creating for tomorrow. But I remain a very long way from wanting to put blinders on the policy makers by confining them to a fixed monetary policy rule. In fact, recent experience provides an exceptionally clear demonstration of how violently liquidity preferences may shift in response to expectations or other factors, and how quickly and massively an established process of financial intermediation can be distorted. These seem to me precisely the kind of economic phenomena that cannot be dealt with satisfactorily within the framework of some *a priori* judgment as to a desirable rate of increase in some single monetary or credit variable.

Caution Needed

My conclusions are these: I have some hope that we have learned to be more alert and courageous in the use of restrictive fiscal measures. At the same time, I hope we have learned to be more cautious in driving either fiscal or monetary policies to an extreme, without recognizing the lags at work. But these lessons lead to intangible—and possibly impermanent—changes in policy attitudes. They provide no set formula for managing prosperity, and no guarantee against a repetition of problems in financial markets akin to those of 1966.

The situation last year was abnormal in one respect. The economy is rarely called upon to absorb so rapid—and so poorly estimated—a military buildup. But in another, and even more fundamental, respect it was presumably not so abnormal: a basic aim of economic policy is clearly to make full employment the norm. So long as that is the target, instances seem sure to arise in which the strength of demand pressures will be misjudged; fiscal restraint will be applied too late or not at all; and the monetary authorities will be left with a sharp dilemma, seemingly caught between the twin evils of underwriting inflation through excessive doses of credit or of pursuing restraint to the point of demoralizing capital markets, with distorting and unpredictable repercussions for the real economy.

The seeming absence of much middle ground between those extremes in 1966—and potentially again in 1968—is partly a reflection of the degree to which fiscal policy is out of tune. But I suspect that some underlying developments in financial markets over a period of years also help to account for the sharpness of the dilemma. Without attempting to list or analyze the relevant changes in detail, I would point to such developments as the negotiable CD and the Eurodollar market, more aggressive and imaginative competition for other varieties of time money and savings among banking and savings institutions, the relatively liberal administration of official interest-rate ceilings on bank deposits during the first half of the 1960s, a greater flexibility in portfolio policies by institutional lenders and liberalization of self-imposed or official restrictions on institutional lending policies. The net effect was to increase markedly the elasticity and fluidity of credit markets. A more perfect market was created, in the sense that changes in demand and supply were reflected more fully through interest rates and less through changes in credit availability.

An economist is inclined to look upon improved market performance as an unmitigated blessing. During the early 1960s, the kinds of developments to which I am referring contributed very significantly to the growth and balance of the economy. But from the viewpoint of those called upon to apply a restrictive credit policy, a more perfect market also generated drawbacks.

In particular, the early moves toward restraint were reflected more in higher interest rates—and less in reduced availability—than seemed either politically or economically tolerable. The economic problem arose because of the relative inelasticity of spending with respect to interest rates—at least in the short run and in those sectors of the economy that were the source of greatest concern. I find no evidence from recent experience to cast doubt on the prevailing view that it is the availability effects of monetary policy that count most heavily in terms of effective short-run restraint on business. With these availability effects weakened, the real economy had become less quickly and predictably responsible to traditional Federal Reserve controls operating primarily through bank reserves.

The obvious answer seemed to be to push restrictive policies harder, at the expense of still higher rates. And in time this approach did expose some very basic institutional rigidities. Many savings institutions, dependent on borrowing short but locked into long-term assets acquired earlier at lower rates, were simply unable to keep pace with the increases in market rates. Disintermediation found its way into our vocabulary, and this indeed triggered strong availability effects.

The trouble was that the appropriate dosage of this strong medicine proved difficult to prescribe and control, and the side effects were serious. The resulting dislocations and imbalances in the credit markets quickly fed back into the real economy.

In attempting to even out the impact on financial markets and moderate the rate pressures, while maintaining effective restraint, the authorities manipulated what instruments of selective control they had readily at hand—notably interest-rate ceilings, selective adjustments in reserve requirements, and by September 1966, the more direct approach of spelling out for the banks what type and how much lending was appropriate.

In somewhat cavalier fashion, I would sum up this episode as a piecemeal and unplanned effort to improve the linkages between Federal Reserve action and economic reaction. Intense restraint was certainly achieved. But I think it also fair to conclude that, in pushing the credit and capital markets close to the point of paralysis, effective control over the degree of restraint was lost.

Edge of Urgency

I have reviewed this familiar ground in some detail because I believe a very similar dilemma for monetary policy could arise again, and the authorities seem little more equipped to deal with it. In fact, there are serious complicating factors growing directly out of the experience a year ago. Inflationary expectations and real cost pressures are more solidly entrenched. Lenders and borrowers alike have understandably wanted to restore liquidity to insulate themselves as best they can from a repetition of 1966; faced with a business slowdown, the Fed had little choice but to meet those liquidity desires through a fresh outpouring of bank credit. Prolongation of that process as business picks up has obvious inflationary dangers. But how can the process be stopped when there is a ballooning deficit to be financed, when the market is hyper-sensitive to any restraint, and when memories of the near chaos of August 1966 are fresh in mind?

All this is what puts the edge of urgency on the current proposal to raise taxes. It is also this prospect that seems to be leading some money market observers to a conclusion that we must, almost inexorably, move toward direct credit controls if the tax bill fails, and maybe if it doesn't. The argument is insidiously simple. Monetary restraint, applied strongly enough to be effective in the short run, will risk a repeat of the 1966 distortions and crisis atmosphere. The kind of ad hoc selective measures taken in 1966 provide no protection. But, on the other hand, we cannot permit inflation to be unchecked. Ergo, we need to develop a more effective system of direct controls.

This is not the place for a philosophical discussion about the inadequacies of direct controls. More immediately to the point, there are some practical considerations that cast into doubt the usefulness of direct controls as a means of meeting our problems.

We had a taste last year of the way controls, applied piecemeal and selectively, can distort markets and have perverse effects on expectations and psychology. We do not have the kind of clear national emergency that in the past has been the only justification for more comprehensive controls. And, even if these powers did exist, it is not apparent how an apparatus of controls designed to restrain the private market could redress an imbalance so clearly arising in the federal sector.

I earlier indicated my belief that the kind of problem we faced in 1966 will not prove unique. Partly for that reason, I would resist the thought that "controls are all right—after all we are in a war." And I feel certain that the policy makers in Washington do not want to see the great experiment of the New Economics give way to a network of direct controls.

Limits to Monetary and Fiscal Policy

For the longer run, all of us could list many specific actions that might improve the performances of financial markets—and at the same time make them more evenly and predictably responsive to monetary policy. My personal list would include such broad and complex matters as measures to improve the liquidity of the mortgage market—and to strengthen the weaker links in our structure of savings institutions.

I would also include a new look at the Federal Reserve discount window in an effort to break down what seems some overly rigid attitudes on the part of both member banks and the Federal Reserve concerning its use—a matter under close official examination. I would certainly undertake a careful reappraisal of the role that interest rate ceilings should play—if any at all. I would hope, too, that private lenders and borrowers have learned to maintain better control over their forward commitments.

But most of all I believe the fundamental lesson of the past two years has been to reemphasize what we already knew: there are limitations on the ability of monetary and fiscal policy to keep the economy moving ahead at a steady and fully employed pace. I do not want to underestimate the real achievements of the past two years. But I believe that they also illustrate that we have not yet learned how to reconcile full employment with price stability. And that is a difficulty that arises more in labor markets than in money markets.

Note

Originally published in *Business Economics*, Vol. 3, No. 1 (Fall 1967), pp. 29–31.

CHAPTER 2

1969

THE ROLE OF MONEY IN ECONOMIC ACTIVITY: COMPLICATED OR SIMPLE?

Edward M. Gramlich, Board of Governors of the Federal Reserve System

A hot dispute currently rages as to the importance of money in influencing economic activity. But we would be wrong to think this a new controversy. Indeed, it is a very old controversy which has been with us for decades. Money was all-important in classical models of the economy but much less so in Keynesian models which gained predominance in the Great Depression and continued into the postwar period. Lately, however, there has been a strong revival of interest in monetary phenomena and this revival has led to the current heated dispute on the importance of money.

The main reason for differences of opinion on the importance of money has been the difficulty in obtaining convincing empirical evidence concerning the sensitivity of aggregate demand to monetary and fiscal forces. Historical evidence suggests that autonomous monetary forces such as gold discoveries and reserve requirement decisions played a major role in the inflation of 1900–1910, the Great Depression, and the contraction of 1936–1937. These findings are buttressed by the one equation studies of Friedman-Meiselman, Andersen-Jordan, and others of the monetarist persuasion, which have invariably found monetary, variables to be much more important than fiscal variables in explaining subsequent movements in GNP. On the other hand, the evidence from the large econometric models—the Wharton School model, the OBE model, the Michigan model, and the Brookings model—is that monetary forces are rather unimportant in influencing total demand.

The FRB-MIT econometric model originated in this controversy. The project has been under the joint direction of Frank de Leeuw at the Board and Professors Franco Modigliani of MIT and Albert Ando at Penn, the latter two of whom were spurred on in an attempt to resolve their inconclusive interchange with

Friedman-Meiselman in the 1965 *American Economic Review*. The aim of the project was to build a model which, though not necessarily larger than most other existing models, would focus more intensively on monetary forces and the way they affect the economy. We used an econometric model because we wanted above all to explain the structure of the relationships involved in the transmission of monetary influences to the real economy. We felt that the US economy is so complex, with such a large number of important relationships, so many different monetary and fiscal policy instruments having such diverse effects and such complicated and variable time lags, that a simple, cheap one equation approach could not possibly do justice to the problem.[1]

Three Channels

A basic difference between our model and other large-scale econometric models is that we have incorporated additional channels through which monetary forces affect economic activity. All models have what we call a cost-of-capital channel, by which interest rates affect investment in real capital. In our model this cost-of-capital influence works on plant and equipment investment, on housing, on investment in consumer durables, and on the construction expenditures of state and local governments. No other model includes the latter influence, and most other models do not spell out the other three cost-of-capital influences as completely and consistently as our model does. Thus even for the cost-of-capital channel we think our model makes a considerable advance over other models in determining the quantitative importance of monetary forces. I might add that our model shows a stronger monetary influence through the cost-of-capital channel than other models do.

A second channel of transmission of monetary forces is through the net worth of consumers. An important link in this mechanism is the stock market: interest rates on long-term bonds influence the rate at which the stock market capitalizes dividend payments; this dividend-price ratio determines the value of common stock in net worth; and net worth is one of the factors which influences consumption. The wealth channel works very much the way Professor Milton Friedman has described monetary policy as working. It is very powerful in both the short and long run, and we think it makes great progress in reducing the monetary controversy to one where we can argue about the specific values of coefficients rather than about the basic structure of macroeconomic systems. For these reasons, we think that finding this channel to be a significant vehicle for transmitting monetary influences has been another important contribution of our model.

A third channel of monetary transmission is credit rationing. Rationing may be defined to include all cases where interest rates alone do not clear financial markets, such that lenders are forced to equate demand and supply by rationing funds. By all odds, the most prominent example of this rationing in the present day US economy is in the mortgage market, which is the only rationing effect we have had any success in identifying. The combination of sluggish deposit rates at thrift institutions and constraints on the lending behavior of these institutions means that when market interest rates rise, deposits flow out of thrift institutions, force mortgage credit rationing, and depress housing starts. It is likely that there are other traces of credit rationing in our economy, possibly working through commercial loans and inventory investment, but as yet we have not been able to confirm the importance of these other types of rationing in affecting final demand. To the extent our rationing channel is important, however, it again reduces the debate to specific values of coefficients rather than the structure of macro systems.

When we simulate our model to determine policy multipliers, we find monetary influences to be appreciably more powerful in influencing final demand than is found by other large-scale econometric models. By way of illustration, the three-year GNP multiplier for a maintained change in bank unborrowed reserves (implemented by open-market operations) is very small for the Michigan model, about 3 for the Wharton School model, about 8 for the Brookings model, and about 20 for our model. This is true even though the corresponding three-year GNP multipliers for government expenditures in the various models are quite similar: 2.5 for the Michigan model, 2.9 for the Wharton model, 2.7 for the Brookings model, and 2.4 for our model. Thus money has a powerful influence in our model, both absolutely and in relation to the fiscal influence. Our conclusions are still not classical because we find the intermediate run effects of monetary policy to be less than those predicted by a simple quantity theory of money and because we find significant intermediate run effects of fiscal policy. But, the conclusions are at least more classical than the results of other large-scale models—a finding which should please monetarists.

There is another way in which our model reaches conclusions pleasing to at least some monetarists. We find the lags on monetary policy to be long and variable. Of the three-year multiplier for open-market operations referred to above, a simulation done for recent years indicates that only 5 percent of the response in GNP is achieved in the first quarter, 10 percent by the second quarter, 20 percent by the third quarter, and 30 percent by the fourth quarter. It is not until the second year following the policy change that the major impact of these policies is felt. Although these long lags do not make it impossible to use monetary policy as a stabilization device, especially against persistent cyclical swings such as the Vietnam War buildup period, neither do they imply that it will be easy to "fine-tune" the economy by monetary operations.

The Long Lags

There are many reasons for the long lags. The first is that we find investment and consumption responding to long-term rates of interest rather than short-term rates. Plant and equipment expenditures respond to the corporate bond rate and stock prices, housing responds to the mortgage rate, consumer durables respond to a proxy for the consumer credit rate, and state and local construction responds to the state and local rate. Thus even though the Fed can bring about prompt changes in bill rates and free reserves, it takes much longer to influence the rates that actually determine investment because of the sluggishness of these long-term rates.

The second reason for the long monetary lag is the decision lag of investors. It takes firms time to order and purchase capital goods once interest rates have changed, it takes homeowners time to alter house purchases once mortgage rates have changed, it takes state and local governments time to float bonds and build schools once state and local rates have changed. Offsetting these delays are the influences of credit rationing generated by short-run disequilibria in financial markets. If the credit rationing channel were more important in our model, we would find monetary influences to operate more quickly.

The lags for monetary operations are variable as well as long. The main cause of the variability lies in the nonlinear price-wage sector, according to which a given change in real output and employment demand will have much less of an impact on prices if the economy is at low levels of capacity utilization and high levels of unemployment than if the economy is in a tight capacity range. In addition, initial order backlogs, corporate profits, capital stocks, interest rates, stock prices, and tax rates all work in one way or another to make the monetary lag variable. This lag variability does not necessarily make monetary influences less predictable, for all initial levels and tax rates would be known in advance. However, it does conform to the intuitive feelings of most people that in an economy as complex as ours, it would be most surprising if responses to monetary policy followed a constant schedule every time.

Just as we feel that our project has narrowed the monetary debate by showing that monetary forces can be important in a large-scale econometric model, an analytical technique the monetarists generally do not favor, the study by Leonall Andersen and Jerry Jordan in last November's *St. Louis Bank Review* has made numerous statistical improvements over previous correlation studies purporting to show the exclusive influence of money on economic activity. Instead of using correlation coefficients and discrete lags, Andersen-Jordan have used multiple regressions with flexible distributed lags. Instead of representing fiscal policy by actual government expenditures and receipts, Andersen-Jordan have adjusted these totals for cyclical movements in real income and prices so as to remove possible simultaneous equations bias which could work against fiscal policy.[2] And instead of using money as the independent monetary variable, Andersen-Jordan have gone some way toward making monetary influences more exogenous by using the monetary base.

Fiscal Policy Still Important

Thus, although for reasons I will indicate below I am not basically in sympathy with the one equation approach, the Andersen-Jordan results are interesting and suggestive and deserving of careful attention. Unfortunately for those of us who believe either in fiscal policy or the quantity theory of money, however, Andersen-Jordan still find that fiscal policy has virtually no effect on economic activity and that monetary policy has impacts about twice as great as would be predicted by a simple quantity theory. Just to spell this out more clearly, the St. Louis model is asserting that as long as the central bank did not allow the money supply to change, the Vietnam War, the 1964 tax cut, the surtax, and the investment credit all would have had no effect on aggregate demand. At the same time, simple open market operations unaccompanied by fiscal policy have remarkably powerful effects.

The advantage of a one equation technique such as Andersen-Jordan's is that if the economy really is too complicated to understand, it may be useful simply to compare inputs such as money and outputs such as GNP. It could be, for example, that monetary influences are so mysterious and elusive that they cannot be captured even by complicated econometric models. Monetary influences may work through channels model-builders have not yet discovered or been able to estimate, or they may work on some components of final demand sometimes and other components other times. Either way, the effect of money on final output may be more regular and predictable than its effect on any component of final output. We might wonder at this juncture, however, why the monetary influences that are so mysterious and elusive as to defy econometric model-builders would follow GNP with a constant and short lag, which is what Andersen-Jordan have found in their statistical results.

Some Drawbacks

At the same time, there are several disadvantages to the Andersen-Jordan one equation approach as it compares to econometric models. The first objection has been alluded to already—the inherent simplicity of the one equation model. Everybody would agree that our economy is much more complicated than one equation, as indeed it is more complicated than one hundred equations. Any model, whether one or one hundred equations, necessarily simplifies things by aggregating behavioral units, omitting variables, including error terms, and other devices. The appropriate degree of disaggregation to strive for in model-building is at bottom a matter of taste in which the benefit of increasing the structural richness of the model is traded off against the cost of increasing the complexities of the relationships, including more mysterious feedbacks, increasing the problems of data management, and being less up-to-date. Thus I will not make the unfounded accusation that a one equation model is too simple to use—many people have a justifiable preference for simple models—but we should recognize that the one equation approach foregoes an awful lot of structural richness.

To get some idea of the specific nature of this objection, I will state some of the propositions that are *assumed* to be true in the Andersen-Jordan model. Since GNP is a function of the adjusted monetary base, the full employment surplus, and a time trend only, fluctuations in all other exogenous forces are assumed to have only random effects on the economy. Fluctuations in exports, strikes, changes in initial stocks of capital and debt, demographic movements, changes in foreign or raw materials, prices, and changes in defense orders all have only random effects on aggregate demand. All do have effects in our model.

Since total Federal expenditures were used as an independent variable, the composition of these expenditures between defense purchases, compensation of employees, interest payments, unemployment benefits, social security payments, grants-in-aid to state and local governments, foreign aid payments, and post office subsidies did not matter. All of these types of spending are assumed to have exactly the same effects. All have different effects in our model.

Similarly, indirect taxes, which may even raise current dollar GNP to the extent that they cause higher prices, are treated the same as personal taxes and corporate taxes, which would certainly lower GNP. A corporate tax decrease is treated the same whether it is brought about by rate reductions, the investment credit, or accelerated depreciation provisions.[3] Our model treats all of these tax provisions differently.

On the monetary side, since we are dealing with the monetary base adjusted for liberated reserves, we must assume that a given adjusted base has the same impact on GNP whether reserve requirements are at present levels or twice as high. We must assume that changes in ceiling rates on time deposits, discount rates, the introduction of certificates of deposits, and rate differentials between thrift institution deposits and market instruments all have had no effect on the real economy. We do not need to make these assumptions in our model. In each of these and many other areas, an econometric model can specify relationships the way they should operate, as our model has tried to do, but the one equation model because of its very simplicity must ignore the problems.

Impact on Specific Sectors

A second objection concerns the almost total absence of structural information which comes out of the one equation approach. Even if the relationship between monetary variables and GNP were close and predictable, which has not been documented by Friedman-Meiselman, Andersen-Jordan, our model, or any other study, the obligation of monetary authorities, business forecasters, and research economists would extend beyond knowing *what* will happen to GNP if we alter monetary policy. We want to know how it will happen, when it will happen, and what we look at to make sure it is happening. We must worry about the fate of specific sectors—what will happen to unemployment rates and the balance of payments, whether savings and loan institutions will go bankrupt, how many new homes will be built, whether state and local governments will be able to sell securities. Our model gives answers to all of these important questions and the one equation approach does not.

The econometric problem associated with this structural agnosticism involves the complete avoidance of use of prior information in obtaining statistical estimates. As any casual observer of the economics profession knows, lately the computer has fostered a tremendous boom in applied econometrics. It is now quite easy to put some data together, run them through a statistical program, get results, and write them up. Such an atmosphere encourages lack of caution—caution in making sure you fulfill all the assumptions econometrics' textbooks say are necessary, caution that you have enough data that you really are explaining structure and not simply some few observations, and caution that you have investigated all implications of your results and are sure these results are internally consistent and consistent with any available, prior information. Virtually all econometric models leave something to be desired on these grounds and ours is no exception. We have unreliable coefficients, unusual feedbacks and inconsistencies, and other defects. In fact, suspicion of these defects is what encourages many people to favor simple models in the first place.

But the virtues are not all on one side. The trouble with a simple model is that it ignores so much useful structural information. For example, we know that GNP equals consumption plus investment plus government spending. Thus if government spending rises, GNP will rise the same amount unless something else rises or falls. We have orders statistics and are reasonably sure that there are lags in the investment process because we can trace response patterns first through orders and then through final expenditures. We are reasonably sure that disposable income affects consumption but that the investment credit does not. In all of these cases a model can take advantage of the many things we do know about the economy and build them in rigorously—knowledge about identities, lags, the mathematical form of relationships, and what variables should or should not be included in various equations. In all of these cases a one equation approach takes its chances, ignoring prior information and having no checks on internal consistency.

We may then want to examine the internal consistency of the Andersen-Jordan one equation model. This model says first of all that the response of GNP to money is greater than the quantity theory would predict, with the whole process operating by the end of four quarters. This means that the entire response of consumption, investment, housing, unemployment, and prices has been completed within four quarters. Short-term rates have responded completely, long-term rates have responded completely, business firms and state and local governments have responded completely, the multiplier reaction on consumption is over, these impulses have worked through unemployment rates and raised or lowered prices to their new level, and velocity has overadjusted—all within four quarters.

The Andersen-Jordan model shows a coefficient on current government expenditures substantially less than unity. Since government spending is part of GNP, this coefficient means that a rise in government spending is accompanied by a large decline in other components of final demand. For this to happen, there must be some combination of a very low multiplier and prompt "crowding out" of other expenditures through the financial sector. The first possibility implies a very low marginal propensity to consume. In fact, the most likely conjecture is that the short- and long-run MPC is negative (or marginal savings rates are in excess of 100%). Such a conjecture would simultaneously explain the weird positive short- and long-run coefficients for tax revenues.

How Much Elasticity?

The second possible explanation for Andersen-Jordan's results is the interest-inelasticity of demand for money or the monetary base. If this demand is insensitive to interest rates, fiscal policy can only increase interest rates and "crowd out" other expenditures. This explanation flies in the face of a countless number of empirical studies showing substantial interest sensitivity of the demand for money and/or near money, including, interestingly enough, the PhD thesis of one Jerry Jordan.[4] Which incarnation are we to believe?

I do not mean to carp at the Andersen-Jordan results, which I have already admitted are suggestive and interesting. When they imply propositions as startling as the above, however, disagreeing with new economists and quality theorists alike, I think Andersen-Jordan have an obligation to tell us more about how their model works. Could they, for example, provide other reduced-form equations for interest rates, consumption, investment, unemployment rates, and prices just so we can follow the process, see exactly what is happening, and decide whether we believe it?

A further defect of the Andersen-Jordan approach has already been thoroughly debated by de Leeuw-Kalchbrenner and Andersen-Jordan in this April's *St. Louis Review,* and I will only summarize the issues. Just as it is not convincing evidence that money determines GNP if really GNP is determining money, so it is not convincing that the monetary base determines GNP if GNP really determines the monetary base. Thus in any regression of GNP on monetary variables we must make sure the monetary variable is exogenous, for if it is not, one equation results will not tell us any more than that the coefficients are meaningless. As de Leeuw-Kalchbrenner have shown, if the Fed really takes un-borrowed reserves as exogenous, the Andersen-Jordan equations give radically different, and to many people much more credible, results. Now both taxes and expenditures matter, money matters less, and the lags seem to be much longer. In fact, the policy multipliers are now quite close to those of our model. Thus our decision as to the fundamental properties of the macro system apparently hinges on what is the exogenous monetary variable.

If the Fed has regularly used any one monetary variable as a policy target, nobody has discovered what this variable is. The more likely possibility is that the Fed has followed targets on some variables some of the time and other variables other times. In addition to the money supply and the monetary base, free reserves and interest rates have been commonly proposed and probably often used as Federal Reserve target variables, a proposition argued even by observers at the Federal Reserve Bank of St. Louis.[5] If either one of these variables really were the target, moreover, it would be closer to the truth to use unborrowed reserves as the exogenous monetary variable, thus favoring the de Leeuw-Kalchbrenner view. The Andersen-Jordan response that you can only use one side of the base identity misses the point completely—you should use whatever side the Fed uses—as does their regression attempting to show that the central bank offsets borrowed reserves. We get a perfectly satisfactory answer to that regression just by looking at bank behavior. Whatever one thinks is the exogenous monetary variable, therefore, we would all agree that to say the basic properties of the macro system depend on what is exogenous, which we do not know, is a very unsatisfactory way to leave the question. In the last analysis the Andersen-Jordan regressions have raised more questions than they have answered. In fact, if the 1965 pattern repeats its-self, this will stimulate somebody else to build an econometric model to get to the bottom of these issues.

The discussion thus far has centered on what the two models can tell us about monetary policy and the way it influences economic activity. But since the topic of this conference is forecasting, we still may want to ask how the two models compare as forecasting devices.

Forecast Errors

The one quarter standard error for the FRB-MIT econometric model is $2.4 billion for current dollar GNP. This error gradually increases as we try to forecast more into the future. We can predict GNP two quarters ahead with a standard error of $4.0 billion and four quarters ahead with an error of $7.1 billion. After that, due to the inherent stabilizing properties of the model, our standard error of forecast stays in the $8 to $9 billion range for two-three years and is only about $15 billion for periods as long as ten years.

We can compare this with the one quarter forecast errors produced by Andersen-Jordan, which average about $4.1 billion for one quarter ahead. We notice that these errors are larger than those of the FRB-MIT model for two quarters ahead. In other words, our model can in a sense see twice as far ahead with the same clarity. Andersen-Jordan have provided no forecast errors further ahead than one period, but since their model has no obvious stabilizing properties, I think we would expect it to drift off much more rapidly than does ours and be substantially worse in longer-run forecasting.

If you don't care about long-run forecasting, you may inquire whether it is worth the effort to add ninety-nine equations merely to reduce the one quarter forecast error by $1.7 billion. My answer is to turn the tables on Andersen-Jordan and confront them with a model even simpler than theirs which works almost as well in short-term forecasting. Let me propose a model where current dollar GNP grows by exactly 1.42 percent per quarter, quarter in, quarter out. This model is not as good in business cycles, but over the 1952–1968 period it would nevertheless have predicted current dollar GNP one quarter ahead with a standard error of only $5.4 billion, closer to the Andersen-Jordan one quarter standard error than theirs is to that of the FRB-MIT model. Thus if we want real simplicity, let's go to my 1.42 percent model. It doesn't even have any variables to worry about.

Conclusion

The motivation for our project was the feeling that monetary forces influenced the economy in complicated ways, but not so complicated as to defy statistical analysis. We have attacked the problems using an econometric model which embodies all of the prior structural information at our disposal and investigates each of the linkages in the causal chain statistically. For each statement we make about the properties of the macro system, we can point to the responsible coefficients and tell what statistical tests were made to give the results.

We find that monetary policy is quite important, but by no means the only force influencing aggregate demand. Fiscal policy also matters, as do exports, population, and a host of other exogenous variables. In addition to having a powerful influence, monetary forces are found to operate with a long and variable lag, which at least raises the possibility that using short, constant lags will be inadequate.

We are confronted with a simple one equation model which gives the appearance of working very well. It says that only money matters, that money matters by twice as much as the quantity theory would have predicted, with very short lags, and that fiscal policy does not matter at all. These conclusions are sufficiently alarming that they should be investigated, especially when the conclusions do not stand up to different yet entirely reasonable assumptions as to what is exogenous. And on inspection, we find that one equation may not forecast so well either. For one quarter ahead it beats a very naive model by only \$1.3 billion and loses to our model by \$1.7 billion.

I do not deny that econometric models have problems. This is still a very early stage in their development, they are complicated and costly, and their implications are not easily understood. The last year has been a chastening experience for all models, ours included, even though for many years before this they have worked tolerably well. Thus while I admit that our econometric model is complicated, costly, and presently leaves much to be desired, I think you should be quite wary before succumbing to the wiles of our low-cost competitor. It may very well be that monetary forces are complicated enough to defy even simple models.

Acknowledgments

The views expressed herein are my own and do not reflect those of the Federal Reserve Board. I thank John Kalchbrenner, Frank de Leeuw, and Harvey Galper for their helpful comments on this chapter.

Notes

Originally published in *Business Economics*, Vol. 4, No. 4 (September 1969), pp. 21–26.

1. There are several write-ups of our model. De Leeuw and I have published articles in the *Federal Reserve Bulletin* for January, 1968, and June, 1969, Harold Shapiro and Robert Rasche have an article in the May, 1969, *American Economic Review*, and Ando and Modigliani have one in the May, 1969, *American Economic Review*.
2. Andersen-Jordan assented to the price adjustment after a comment by de Leeuw and John Kalchbrenner.
3. Andersen-Jordan did try to answer to these defects by using the full employment budget surplus weighted for differential demand impacts. In fact, they used weights provided by me. But even though it is better to use a weighted surplus than an unweighted surplus, there are many defects with a weighted surplus as compared with an econometric model. The values of the weights depend on how the model works, relevant time dimensions, and, for taxes, whether reductions or increases are brought about by rate changes or incentive features—all questions which cannot be solved satisfactorily no matter what weights are used.
4. See J. L. Jordan, "The Market for Deposit-Type Financial Assets," UCLA PhD thesis, 1969.
5. An article by Michael Keran and Christopher Babb, two colleagues of Andersen and Jordan, in the June, 1969, *St. Louis Review* argues at length that free reserves is "the most reliable indicator of monetary policy" (John Wood's phase).

CHAPTER 3

1969

ECONOMETRIC MODEL BUILDING FOR GROWTH PROJECTIONS

Lawrence R. Klein, University of Pennsylvania

Emphasis in much recent work on macroeconometric model building has been placed on short-term forecasting. This is by no means a misguided activity, but it leaves undone another task of great importance to the users of econometric output. There is an evident need for longer-term analysis, capable of providing projections ahead for a decade or more. Just as many users find it essential to look ahead for the next few months or for periods up to two or three years, others find it essential, for their purposes, to look ahead for much longer stretches of time.

It is reasonable to ask whether short-term models might in fact be used for longer-term analysis, as well, by simply projecting them several short periods into the future. It would be a great economy of effort if we could, indeed, use one overall model simultaneously for short and long-term analysis. Attempts at extrapolating a short-term model into the future for a decade or more is one approach to the problem of growth projection, and this lead will be considered. In following this lead, however, deficiencies in the approach will become evident, and we shall be led to consideration of an alternative research strategy, namely the idea of building a specialized long-term model which is better designed for applicability to growth projections.[1]

Normally, the Wharton Model is extrapolated ahead every quarter for 8 quarters. On occasion we have extrapolated for 10–12 quarters, but it is only recently that we have considered long-range extrapolations of 5 or more years, up to a maximum of 25.

Long-Term Extrapolation of Short-Term Models

Given the budgetary practices of government, a forecast ahead for one year (by smaller time units preferably) covers a sensible period for which it is possible to deal with econometric forecasting on a scientific basis. In the case of Wharton Model forecasts, we feel comfortable with the projection of the first four quarters. It is necessary, however to look ahead even further in order to gain an impression of the economy's expected *time path*. This accounts, roughly, for our interest in two-year, or eight-quarter, forecasts.

Dropping scientific aspirations, though, we can form longer-term forecasts and judge the adequacy of existing models in growth analysis. First, let us consider a six-year forecast that is currently being studied by members of the Wharton Econometric Forecasting Unit. In extrapolating the Model ahead for 24 quarters, major assumptions must be made about government policies, and careful attention must be paid to trend variables such as labor force, productivity increase, and length of the work week. The particular six-year projection is designed so that unemployment is held near to 3–4 percent over the course of the next six years. Similarly, short-term interest rates are not allowed to fall below 4.5 percent.

Any forecast for a period as far ahead as five to six years must make some specific assumptions about the termination of the war in Viet Nam, demobilization, and a return to more of a peace time economy. Hopefully, these considerations should be relevant to short-run forecasts of less than two years' duration. In the six-year extrapolation of the Wharton Model, it is assumed that a peace settlement is reached by January 1, 1970, and that the first quarter of that year is the beginning of a modest decline in government military expenditures and demobilization. On a gradual basis, defense spending is assumed to be reduced by $5.0 billion in

Wharton-EFU model, selected variables

	1969.1	*1969.2*	*1969.3*	*1969.4*	*1970.1*	*1970.2*	*1970.3*	*1970.4*	*1971.1*	*1971.2*	*1971.3*
Consumer Expenditures	559.2	565.8	575.6	583.8	594.2	602.0	612.4	622.3	631.3	640.9	649.4
Fixed Capital Formation	99.2	100.3	100.1	100.2	100.3	101.9	102.4	103.8	105.2	107.1	108.6
Residential Non-farm Construction	32.5	32.0	32.2	31.9	32.1	32.6	35.4	38.0	39.6	40.5	42.1
Inventory Change	5.7	6.9	8.7	8.1	6.8	7.2	6.3	6.9	6.5	6.3	6.6
Net Exports	0.6	3.2	2.8	2.9	3.0	3.3	3.1	3.1	3.1	3.4	3.6
Government Expenditures	206.4	210.1	215.2	219.0	221.1	222.9	224.7	226.5	228.3	231.9	234.3
GNP	903.6	918.2	934.7	946.0	957.4	970.0	984.2	1,000.5	1,014.1	1,030.0	1,044.6
GNP (1958 $)	724.0	728.0	733.6	735.9	738.9	741.6	747.2	753.8	758.6	764.0	769.6
Price Deflator	124.8	126.1	127.4	128.6	129.6	130.8	131.7	132.7	133.7	134.8	135.7
Profits Before Tax	90.1	92.2	95.5	94.5	94.1	96.2	98.4	98.9	98.0	100.6	103.7
Unemployment Rate (percent)	3.5	3.4	3.7	3.5	3.7	4.0	4.1	3.9	3.8	3.8	3.9

1958 prices, while the number of persons under arms is assumed to fall by 340,000 persons. Although the assumed cut in defense spending appears to be small, it is accompanied by a substantial demobilization. This changed "mixture" in composition of the military establishment is meant to reflect the view that officers will prevail on the civilian government to provide them with new hardware and R & D for further developments. These requests follow a period of preoccupation with an irritating war.

Fiscal Assumptions

To compensate for the reduced amount of military activity, taxes are assumed to be cut by elimination of the surcharge—a reduction to 5 percent on January 1, 1970, and complete elimination by July 1, 1970. This is the present Administration position, apart from the war situation. We have also programmed elimination of the investment tax credit from April, 1969. Although military spending is programmed to be cut after the first quarter of 1970, total government expenditures are assumed not to fall. The growth in state and local expenditures plus added civilian expenditures at the federal level keep the constant dollar total rising after the cessation of hostilities, first by \$0.2 billion per quarter (annual rate), then by \$0.4 billion, and then by \$0.6 billion. In addition, there is an assumption that normal growth will continue in social security contributions and in transfer payments.

Population trends are assumed to continue over the six years; world trade is projected on its course of secular growth; and monetary policy is assumed to be somewhat eased after the financial burden of the war is lessened. Even so, interest rates stay at a level as high as 4.5 percent (short-term) or 5.5 percent (long-term).

The outcome of this intermediate length projection is a hesitating phase of demobilization and transition to peace; whereupon the economy quickly regains its regular growth trajectory. It is a well balanced growth, but all prices do not rise uniformly. Prices related to services grow steadily (20% over six years), but some

Six-year projection (billions of dollars)

1971.4	*1972.1*	*1972.2*	*1972.3*	*1972.4*	*1973.1*	*1973.2*	*1973.3*	*1973.4*	*1974.1*	*1974.2*	*1974.3*	*1974.4*
660.9	670.8	681.1	690.0	701.6	712.7	723.9	733.8	746.3	758.2	770.1	780.0	792.9
110.1	112.4	114.8	116.5	117.9	120.1	122.7	124.5	126.0	128.3	131.2	133.3	134.8
43.4	44.2	44.6	46.2	47.4	48.2	48.6	50.3	51.5	52.3	52.9	54.6	55.9
7.4	6.8	7.3	6.5	7.7	8.3	8.1	7.5	7.6	8.3	9.0	7.1	8.0
3.5	3.6	3.8	3.8	3.7	3.6	4.0	4.2	4.3	4.1	4.4	4.5	4.5
239.7	243.6	247.4	251.1	254.8	258.6	262.3	266.1	270.0	274.0	277.9	281.9	285.9
1,064.9	1,081.3	1,099.1	1,114.2	1,133.2	1,151.5	1,169.7	1,186.5	1,205.8	1,225.3	1,245.7	1,261.5	1,282.0
778.9	785.4	791.6	797.3	805.4	812.8	818.4	824.3	831.7	839.4	846.3	851.7	859.8
136.7	137.7	138.8	139.7	140.7	141.7	142.9	143.9	145.0	146.0	147.2	148.1	149.1
105.3	105.8	109.3	112.2	113.3	113.4	116.8	120.2	120.9	120.8	124.5	127.3	128.0
3.6	3.5	3.5	3.6	3.5	3.3	3.3	3.4	3.3	3.1	3.0	3.2	3.0

durable goods' prices rise much more slowly (13% over six years). The peace pause lasts for less than two years and is not expected to develop into a recession such as the one we had after the Korean War.

It is interesting to note that if the economy can continue to grow at full employment for a number of years, tax revenues come in quite strongly, while transfer payments are restrained; therefore the budget deficit withers away. It builds up in the transition period and then declines. If the solutions were projected at full employment for a few more years, budget balance and a surplus would gradually be reached. We have noticed this result in 15–25 year simulation projections of the Model. This is an eventual "fiscal dividend."

In order to project the Wharton Model ahead for six years, it was necessary to make strong assumptions about the growth of the self-employed, government employment, productivity, and labor force. These exogenous assumptions have a strong influence on the unemployment rate. Also, the equations for nonmanufacturing hours worked per week have strong downward trends. This variable tends to get far out of line in connection with rising wage rates in the solution. To keep the solution pattern in balance for long periods, it is necessary to make frequent adjustments to some of the equations; otherwise their solutions drift over 24 quarters. This is not much of a problem in one or two-year extrapolations, which are the primary objective of a system like the Wharton Model.

A special assumption of this programmed solution is that residential construction (including mobile homes, recorded under consumer outlays on automobiles and parts) will be a strong trend growth sector, reaching price-corrected levels in excess of current outlays by about 40 percent in six years.

This particular model has been solved dynamically for 15- and 25-year periods ahead. These solutions have been generated under both deterministic and stochastic conditions. A short-term forecasting model may be useful in giving longer-run information, but it must be handled very carefully and adjusted, so as to keep it on track. It is a useful start, but is only an expedient substitute for a genuine long-run model.

Specification and Characteristics of a Long-Run Model

A more satisfactory approach to the problem of long-range forecasting is to build a fresh model specifically designed to exhibit the processes of economic growth. A self-evident prerequisite for such a research project would be the preparation of a data base that, itself, incorporates a long span of economic growth. Some parameters of simple models that are known to be capable of generating dynamic growth trends could conceivably be estimated from short samples of recent data. Also, recent cross sections samples could be used to estimate some typical parameters of a growth model, for it is often argued that cross section based relationships come closer to picturing long-run than short-run patterns. But without a long-run data base, there is limited possibility for testing the accuracy of growth models by their ability to interpret observed trends. In addition, some socio-economic processes that tend to get overlooked in short-run business cycle analysis will not show up in recent short-run data samples, and must be based on observations from a longer time span. In general, we shall be shifting variables from an exogenous (short-run) category to an endogenous (long-run) category in building a growth model.

To be quite pragmatic, a growth model should be estimated at least on a sample that goes back as far as 1929, only because the official national income and product accounts of the US Department of Commerce begin from that date. A sample period beginning in 1919 would, in many respects, be better, but there are difficulties in reconstructing a complete set of national accounts for the 1920s.[2] In any event, whether the sample period begins with 1919 or 1929, a long range study designed for growth projections should be based on annual data. It is extremely difficult, but not impossible, to extend quarterly series as far back as the 1930s and 1920s, but one should not be pre-occupied with very short-run fluctuations, especially those associated with inventory cycles, in such analysis, and annual data would seem to be better suited to the task.

For some purposes, it is possible to construct annual data series as far back as 1890 or 1900, but these would mainly serve small models and be limited in the types of variables that could be projected.[3] On a somewhat rougher plane, decade accounts can be estimated for the period since the Civil War. Rudimentary models can be estimated from these long-run statistics.[4] The decade data smooth out more than short-run inventory cycles; they eliminate the classical business cycle.

It has been remarked that a long-run model ought to "endogenize" a number of variables that are now placed in the exogenous category. These are, especially, variables connected with government fiscal and monetary policies and demographic magnitudes. In some short-run econometric models, the expenditure and financial decisions of state and local governments are placed partly in the endogenous category. This is all the more compelling for a long-run model. The principal expenditure magnitudes for state and local governments are for education and highways. These, in turn, depend on the human and automobile populations, both of which should be explained by the model. The automobile stock is generated by consumer expenditures on cars and a depreciation relationship. These are both endogenous processes. The whole matter of modeling demography is a major issue to be explained below.

As far as state and local revenues are concerned, they are generated by the income and asset bases of the population, given the tax laws. Financial decisions on the issuance of state and local securities are tied to interest rates and other money market phenomena determined in the monetary part of a model.

Federal Spending

Federal expenditures are of at least three basic types: (1) national defense; (2) discretionary civilian expenditures; (3) non-discretionary civilian expenditures. For the most part, defense expenditures are exogenous. They have changed in character enormously in this century and have been determined under quite different criteria in each of the post-war governments from Presidents Truman to Nixon. It seems best to leave these in the exogenous category for long-term analysis. Non-defense expenditures can be made according to specific programs that any administration decides (with Congressional support) to carry out. These discretionary expenditures, such as crop support programs, Medicare, social insurance extension, public works, and the like are also exogenous. But much of government outlay is associated with population growth and the normal development of filling the country's needs. These should be explained by population and income variables. Taxes and many transfer payments will be related to income and activity bases according to the prevailing laws. Short-run models already contain such relationships, and it is nothing new to include them in longer-run models.

The "endogenized" government sector depends significantly on demographic characteristics, as do other economic processes, such as house construction, consumer expenditures, and labor force development. A major part of the widening of the endogenous sector of a model for long-run analysis will be associated with population growth in its various dimensions.

In the first place, total population must be projected. Following the original suggestion of Valavanis-Vail, we can form the identity

$$N_t = N_{t-1}\,(1 + b_t - d_t + i_t)$$

N_t = population at t

b_t = birth rate

d_t = death rate

i_t = net immigration rate.

The econometric problem, therefore, is to explain birth, death, and immigration rates. These are likely to depend on rates of income growth, international income differentials, and trends.

Total population projections are not, however, adequate for the growth problem. The age composition is significant for education demands; the age and sex composition is needed for determining labor force participation rates; the age, sex, and race composition for unemployment and its effects on wage rates; and finally marriage or household formation rates for housing demand. Some of these demographic variables are largely exogenous, while others have an appreciable element of endogeneity.

Econometricians have largely neglected careful consideration of demographic processes, but they are in an excellent position to interrelate social and economic factors that determine population dynamics.[5]

The distinctive features of a long-run growth model may show up in ways other than the transference of variables from the exogenous to the endogenous category, together with the addition of new explanatory equations. Some variables and types of equations are likely to be modified as we focus attention from the short to the long run. Inventory equations may be consolidated with fixed investment, or if left as separate equations, they may be simple transaction relationships between stock holding and production. In wage determination equations, the influence of short-run labor market conditions (unemployment ratio) may be downgraded, and the relationship of wage changes to productivity changes may dominate the wage equation in the long run. Other dimensions of unemployment, such as its demographic composition, may be more important than the overall level of unemployment in the long run.

In the original mathematical formulations of the Keynesian theory of employment, it was artificially declared that a short-run period was being considered in which the stock of capital could be taken as given. On this basis, the production function of the model was expressed as a simple bivariate relationship between labor input and total output. This is surely an unsatisfactory specification of the model, even for the short run, because nonzero investment is capable of being estimated from the propensity-to-invest function, and this could not be consistent with a given and fixed stock of capital. In the short or the long run, it is essential to have both labor and capital inputs in the aggregate production function. It is plausible to consider a concession to the idea of the use of a capital variable for short-run analysis by modifying the variable from K to uK, where u is an index of the rate of utilization of capital facilities. In the long run, we can smooth the typically cyclical variable u, by fixing it at some constant level, either unity or just below unity. The production function in a long-run model should therefore depend on both labor and capital as inputs, and if it is at all possible, the capital variable should be corrected for quality change. Instead of the usual measure,

$$K_t = K_0 + \sum_{i=1}^{t} (I_t - D_t)$$

where

K_t = stock of capital at end of period t
I_t = gross investment of period t
D_t = capital consumption of period t

we can use the "vintage" measure,

$$K_t = \sum_{i=0}^{\infty} V(i) I'_{t-1}$$

or more specifically,

$$K_t = \sum_{i=0}^{\infty} \lambda^i I'_{t-1} \qquad 0 < \lambda < 1$$

These measures weight investment i periods ago with the coefficient V (i) or λ^i. The "vintage" type measure is one possible device for taking care of technical change, but a productivity trend, specific if available, should be considered as an additional variable for the long-run production function.

Input-Output Linkage

Input-output analysis is mainly valuable as a tool for long-run research into the structure of technology of an economy. Its principal use is to show the industrial composition of output at projected levels of activity, but it is not a good device for actually projecting the overall activity levels. A fruitful linkage can potentially be made between an input-output and a macro-econometric model made by using the latter to project the level of aggregate activity—final demand for input-output analysis—and the former to translate this volume of total activity into separate industry activities. To do this, it would be necessary to allocate total final demand among separate industries. A formal linkage between an input-output and a macromodel is made in the Brookings Model.[6] In the same way that input-output is linked to a short-run model in that study, it could also be linked to a longer-run macro model of the type we have in the present chapter.

To review the linkage technique used in the Brookings Model volume, we can outline the procedure as follows. For each sample time period, a vector of gross output can be multiplied by the input-output matrix to obtain a series of final demand

$$(I - A)X_t = F_t.$$

Each element of F_t (one time series for each sector) can be regressed on *relevant* items of GNP that are explicitly determined as variables in the corresponding macro model

$$F_t = f(gnp_{1t}, \ldots, gnp_{nt}).$$

The arguments gnp_{jt} are components of GNP that are included among the dependent variables of the macro model. A simultaneous determination of the elements gnp_{jt}, F, and X_t comes out as part of the complete model solution and, in effect, shows how $(GNP)_t$ is distributed among the components of F_t and finally X_t. In long run analysis, it may not be desirable to keep the elements of $(I-A)$ fixed. For projection purposes they can be altered along trends or according to *a priori* pieces of information about the impact of technology.

Precision of Long-Range Projections

There are two views about the relative accuracies of short- and long-range forecasting. The dominant view, and one to which I strongly subscribe, is that error accumulates the further ahead one tries to look, and on these grounds alone, one should expect to turn in a less precise performance in predicting long-rather than short-run phenomena.

The other view is that smooth regularities reveal themselves more clearly in the long run than in the short run. Long-run predictions should be less likely to be strongly affected by singular near-term events and should be more correct, on average. Without prejudging the issue of long versus short-run prediction, but indicating the reliability of long, smooth, extrapolations, Herman Kahn, in debating the issue on *the outlook* for the year 2000, has declared:[7]

> Simplistic prediction, by graphing on the right kind of paper—log, semi-log, or linear—and then drawing straight lines or straight curves, is an extraordinarily good way to predict a rate of change of a technology that already has a history of change.

Confidence in simple, smooth and bold interpretations of history is typical of many of the contributions to the above-cited symposium on the twenty first century. I find these thought speculations fascinating as literature, but I have little confidence in their accuracy.

All econometric-based systems of prediction, whether for short or long periods in the future, are subject to statistical error, but there are two major sources of error in long-range prediction that make this variety inherently less accurate. One major source of imprecision is error accumulation in dynamic systems, the other is lack of knowledge about exogenous events.

The principal source of dynamics in econometric models comes about from the lag structure—the need to use historical values of endogenous variables in order to project their present and future values. In historical studies, we treat lag values as known observations, but in trying to depict the future, we must determine successive lagged inputs from the immediately preceding predictions, and these are subject to error. This can be readily illustrated in the simplest possible dynamic model. A single equation with one parameter and one lag can be written as

$$y_t = \propto y_{t-1} + e_t$$

and has the extrapolation solution

$$y_{T+j} = \propto^j y_T + \sum_{i=1}^{j} \propto^{j-i} e_{T+i}$$

for periods 1, 2,..., j beyond historical observations 1, 2,..., T. In this formulation, e_t stands for error at period t. A statistical sample for t = 1, 2,..., T provides a basis for the estimation of $\propto = a$. If we use only the estimated relationship for extrapolation, the forecast of y_t at T+j will be obtained from

$$y^f_{T+j} = a^j y_T$$

The error accumulation, $\sum_{i=1}^{j} \propto^{j-i} e_{T+i}$ as well as the deviation of "a" from $\propto$ is going to affect the precision of the forecast. The further into the future that the forecast is pushed, the more error accumulation we obtain from $\sum \propto^{j-i} e_{T+i}$. This whole argument can be generalized into large systems of simultaneous dynamic relations of the type that we deal with in economics.[8]

Kahn vs. Klein

A slight extension of the simple first-order autoregressive relationship enables us to show the significance of the other error in long-range economic prediction. If the basic equation is written as

$$y_t = \propto y_{t-1} + \beta x_t + e_t$$

the extrapolation solution is

$$y_{T+j} = \propto^j y_T + \beta \sum_{i=1}^{j} \propto^{j-i} x_{T+i} + \sum_{i=1}^{j} \propto^{j-i} e_{T+i}$$

At period T+j, there is not only an error accumulation from the term with random disturbances $\sum \propto^{j-i} e_{T+i}$, but also the possibility of another source of error from the cumulative term $\beta \sum \propto^{j-i} x_{T+i}$. If the future values of exogenous variables x_{T+i}, i=1,2,..., j are not known with precision at t=T, we shall have additional error in the extrapolation. Exogenous variables are infrequently known in advance with a great deal of certainty, but they are much more firmly known for short than for long periods ahead. Major exogenous variables are government policy decisions on fiscal and monetary affairs, some of which are committed or well laid out for future periods up to one year and occasionally longer. They are not known for the next decade. These variables are so important in econometric models, and in economic life; we know so little about them for the year 2000 that it seems clear to me that we must be making very imprecise economic judgments. My view of the structure of an economy, its dynamics, and its exogenous components, leads me to be very skeptical of any long-range forecast, and especially of those that are deceptively smooth and simple in continuing the free-hand extrapolation of historical trends. For these reasons I reject the entire philosophical approach illustrated by Herman Kahn's remarks quoted above, and also the view that is in some sense, easier to predict the long-than the short-run future.

I do not intend to present a counsel of despair with regard to long-range forecasting. I fully realize the need to plan ahead according to the best judgments that can be made in advance on the basis of prevailing materials, but I do think that the size of the task in long-range modeling should be fully recognized and that we should be prepared to commit larger errors than those involved in short-run forecasting.

Notes

Originally published in *Business Economics*, Vol. 4, No. 4 (September 1969), pp. 45–50.

1. Long-range solutions of the Wharton Model programmed by Paul Gretzinger of Boise Cascade Corporation have been important in forming a base case for the projections discussed in this chapter. Suggestions from additional discussions with Dr. Louise Curley of Scudder, Stevens and Clark and Mrs. Mary Virginia Bowden of New York

Life Insurance Company were used in the present projections. Mr. Mitsuo Saito of the Wharton-EFU provided invaluable programming assistance and economic analysis.

2. In my earliest macroeconometric model building studies, I did try to build a data base back to 1919. See L. R. Klein, *Economic Fluctuations in the United States, 1921–1941* (New York: John Wiley, 1950). In later studies, I pushed the starting date up to 1929 because this is the starting date of the official US national income accounts. See L. R. Klein and A. S. Goldberger, *An Econometric Model of the United States, 1929–1952* (Amsterdam: North-Holland Publishing, 1955). At present, Bert C. Hickman and Robert Coen of Stanford University are constructing a new US model based on data from 1919, and are preparing a complete and detailed set of accounts spanning the 1920s, 1930s, and the post-World War II era.
3. See L. R. Klein and R. Kosobud, "Some Economertics of Growth: Great Ratios of Economics," *Quarterly Journal of Economics,* LXXV (May, 1961), 173–198. M. Morishima and M. Saito, "A Dynamic Analysis of the American Economy, 1902–1952," *International Economic Review,* 5 (May, 1964), 125–164.
4. S. Valavanis-Vail, "An Econometric Model of Growth, U.S.A., 1869–1953," *American Economic Review,* Supplement, 45 (May, 1955), 208–221.
5. Many hypotheses about these interrelationships are to be found in R. A. Easterlin, *Population, Labor Force, and Long Swings in Economic Growth* (New York: National Bureau of Economic Research, 1968).
6. F. M. Fisher, L. R. Klein, and Y. Shinkai, "Price and Output Aggregation in the Brookings Econometric Model," *The Brookings Quarterly Econometric Model of the United States*, ed. by J. Duesenberry, et al. (Chicago: Rand, McNally, 1965).
7. Herman Kahn, "Toward the Year 2000: Work in Progress," *Daedalus* (Summer, 1967), 939–940.
8. See L. R. Klein, *An Essay on the Theory of Economic Prediction* (Helsinki: The Academic Bookstore, 1968).

CHAPTER 4

1971

PRESIDENTIAL ADDRESS: THE CHALLENGE TO OUR SYSTEM

Alan Greenspan, Townsend-Greenspan & Co., Inc.

Since our profession came of age, we have been content to examine the structure of our business system, develop models, econometric and otherwise, and project its dynamics. But, we have always assumed that the system's fundamental nature could be taken as a given. In our long-term projections, we have automatically presumed that the business system would essentially be free enterprise, profit-motivated and technically progressive. This assumption has led us to project continued growth in productivity in the 3 percent per year range and an economy which tended toward a noninflationary full employment level.

If economists have taken growth for granted, it is perhaps not surprising that this view has been embraced by almost everyone else. This has led to the implicit belief that it is possible to tamper indiscriminately with our economic system, making patchwork adjustments here, and imposing controls there, without affecting our rising productivity and standard of living. I believe that we have reached the point where we can no longer afford this view.

Having been in the forecasting profession for more than 20 years, I am most reluctant to assert that perceived trends inevitably trace some predetermined course. Nonetheless, it is difficult to avoid the conclusion that the rapidly expanding economic role of government, if not reversed, will fundamentally change the nature of our system. I recognize that there are wide differences of opinion, even within our profession, regarding the appropriate role of government with our economic system. There are few of us, however, who would maintain that there is not some point at which government intervention eventually become government control of the economy, at which point we have moved, by definition, to a socialist, or quasi-socialist system.

We may disagree on whether the development of government intervention is so gradual as to cause no disruption in the transition, or whether there is a point of discontinuity in the development process followed by an acceleration toward a controlled economy. What concerns me is that I suspect the latter is the actual case. If so, the developments over the next five years will materially affect the direction and nature of the American economy perhaps for decades to come.

The System and the Problem

On the first level, our difficulties stem from the tendency these days to identify the source of our problems, real or imagined, with the functioning of our system. Some government control or government programs is then immediately advocated to come to grips with supposed problems. In one sense it is understandable that once a specific problem is identified, then a straightforward engineering-type solution appears to be the best answer. If inflation is rampant, is not the most sensible solution to come directly to grips with the problem and regulate wages and prices?

On the other hand, if there is anything that economics teaches, it is that engineering solutions are inherently self-defeating in a complex, interrelated economic structure. There are secondary and tertiary effects from all government actions. Problems do not disappear by fiat, they merely become displaced. This was the great insight of the early classical economists as they viewed the effects of the Mercantilism of their day. Even today there is dramatic evidence of the economic superiority of free economies. The remarkable advance of the essentially free enterprise West German economy compared with that of East Germany is as dramatic an example of the fruits of freedom as one could probably devise. Yet, the fault-finding continues unabated.

Our system is now criticized because certain segments of our society—the blacks, the Mexican Americans, the Indians—have not yet achieved parity with the remainder of the society. And yet, even the lowest income segments of our economy enjoy standards of living which would put them among the upper strata in most nations of the world. The average American Negro, for example, enjoys a standard of living slightly above that of the average Briton.

We are told that our society is racist, suppressing our minorities and forcing them into ghettos. One can scarcely deny that racial prejudice exists in this country or for that matter in most of the rest of the world. It is perhaps the most extraordinary tribute to a free economic system, that despite intolerance, competitive economic pressures not only induce even the intolerant to hire blacks and other minority groups, but owing to our heavy capital investment, marginal labor productivity is such that the average black factory worker in the US ranks with the elite of Western European workers in real income terms.

Answering Back

What is most regrettable is the extent to which this anticapitalist propaganda goes unanswered. One reason, of course, is that a large segment of our society believes the accusations are at least partially true. Even when people reject the specifics of the attacks on our free enterprise system, many still believe that *somehow* our system is not functioning appropriately. Why an economy and a society which has developed by far the highest standard of living in history is now philosophically on the defensive covers a much broader issue of political and moral philosophy than is our immediate focus.[1] However, the ramifications of the belief that despite its success there is something basically wrong with our system have given the green light to all those who are looking to find problems with the American society and economy. The attractiveness of the "action-solution" is perhaps nowhere more apparent than in the seemingly innocuous area of "consumer protection."

Certainly, no one can be against the notion that food should be pure, automobiles safe, or breakfast cereals nutritious. But, one may seriously question the contribution of those particular consumer advocates who arbitrarily set criteria for the purity of meats or the safety of buses which just manage to be a shade higher than industry is then able to effectively meet. Of course, nothing is ever safe in an absolute sense nor are foods ever 100 percent pure. It is always possible to devise a standard which certain products just fail to meet. But the choice of the standard is peculiarly related to the existing state of technology. We are never told, for example, that an automobile is an inferior product because it cannot fly, nor are we told that television sets are inferior because they do not work indefinitely without repair.

There is no better way to undermine any institution than to set a standard for it which by its nature or the current state of the art is unachievable. In fact, I would submit that when, and if, the arbitrary standards of the consumer advocates are eventually met, you will find not applause at the system's success, but another revision in the standard, upped now one full notch to make it again unattainable in the then existing state of affairs.

Too many self-styled protectors of the consumer downgrade brand names, advertising, and hence the competitive struggle for product identity. This is the greatest protection for the consumer and the basic force for product quality. If you have any doubts, go shopping in the Soviet Union where the consumer ostensibly is fully protected from the greed of the capitalist system.

While I believe that most of the alleged difficulties of our society are more imagined than real, there are, nevertheless, severe problems which require our close and thoughtful attention. The area of industrial pollution is certainly one.

For years many companies have been using our rivers, our waterways and our atmosphere as cost-free depositories for their industrial wastes. This has amounted to an implicit subsidy offset on the companies' income statements by the failure to register an appropriate cost item for disposal. Moreover, one may legitimately ask whether the rights of other individuals in the society are being violated by industrial pollution. Doubtless a full costing of production and disposal will require greater capital costs. Here, however, we are calling upon the proved technological capabilities of American industry to solve the problem. I have no doubt that if sensibly handled in the appropriate time context our industrial waste difficulties can largely be resolved.

As our population continues to grow and our technology changes, more exasperating problems certainly will arise. However, they need be nothing more than a challenge to our ingenuity.

Methodology the Key

What concerns me is not the nature of the problems which must inevitably emerge in a growing society, but our methodology in dealing with them. The temptation of expediency per se perhaps could be dealt with through rational persuasion, but unfortunately our system has developed a political mechanism which has elevated expediency to a politically profitable level.

Government solutions have been fostered by the cynical recognition that in a society characterized by "one man, one vote," and a skewed income distribution, the taxing of the rich to finance payments, direct or indirect, to the not so rich can corral more votes than it loses.

This principal, first put into practice in the 1930s, has become almost a subconscious political calculation in appealing to the American electorate.

A corollary of this principle, recognized only in recent years, is that favors, once given, cannot easily be retracted.

There is, in effect, a ratchet which allows such programs to expand, but never to retrench. Whether or not a particular program actually solved the problem to which it was addressed has become of minor moment.

Fiscal Constituents

We now have 23 million receiving Social Security checks. Approximately 40 million are receiving some form of veterans benefits. Another 11 million are receiving public assistance. Nearly 10 million obtain physicians services under Medicare. The list continues and is extensive. If President Nixon's new welfare proposals become law, an additional 13 million will be added to the welfare rolls. To be sure, there is a good deal of overlapping; many recipients receive payments under two or more programs. The unduplicated totals, however, have been rising very rapidly. The various groups are now being formalized into what we may call fiscal constituencies, that is, individuals receiving payment in cash or in kind on a continuing basis under an ongoing federal program. While it's the rare politician who will outwardly acknowledge his vote-getting techniques, most are acutely aware of their fiscal constituencies.

In years past we tended to classify Americans into loose groupings: the elderly, the indigent, the white, the black, the worker, the capitalist. But to a surprising degree, patriotism acted as a congealing force. The development of the fiscal constituent as a major issue of governmental policy during the 1960s has brought us to the edge of a budgetary crisis and concurrently, and not independently, to the edge of social divisiveness.

Until approximately a decade ago, only the Agriculture Department, Veterans Administration and Social Security Administration had substantial fiscal constituencies. Most government departments—Defense, Justice, Commerce, etc.—had only general and diffuse relationships to the broad sector of our citizenry. There was, of course, the emergent Military-Industrial complex which President Eisenhower identified as he was leaving office. But here the problem was mixed. This complex operated in the context of a broad generalized national interest. And clearly, the voter constituency or the ratchet effect was not generally applicable. (Certainly, the evidence of the last couple of years indicates the lack of political power of the Military-Industrial complex in maintaining its programs.)

So long as government functions are general and citizens have a diffuse relationship with the government, the fiscal constituency problem is of limited significance. But as soon as strong association with specific programs emerge, the pressure on the Congress and on the Administration to expand these programs becomes overwhelming. The issue becomes singularly clear when even a small, seemingly limited, program is under attack. The most famous case of recent days is the inability to eliminate our so-called tea-tasters. What we are, of course, saying is that the interests of a very limited group are highly concentrated on a specific program and their political vote far outweights the politically weighted vote of all other elements in the society upon whom the cost is distributed. So long as the so-called fiscal dividend, that is, the normal growth of tax revenues at existing tax rates, is adequate to meet the expansion in these programs, the process does not appear to induce disequilibrium. However, the rate of expansion of fiscal constituency programs appears to have finally become larger than the fiscal dividend.

In a sense, we may formulate a law of fiscal constituencies: namely, the growth rate of benefits to constituent groups tends to exceed the fiscal dividend.

Conflict and Polarization

A corollary of this proposition is that benefits ultimately increase to a level which strains the tax-raising capacity of the system. This in turn leads to a rationing of benefits among the various fiscal constituencies, inducing a confrontation for the limited funds available. At first, it appears that the confrontation is between the constituencies and the government. However, it later becomes clear that the government is merely an intermediary. This inevitably leads to direct conflicts between constituencies and to the polarization of societal groups. Gone is the communion of interests and the sense of unity which kept the nation together.

Until recently the burgeoning constituency programs have largely been a problem for the developers of the federal budget. The numbers are now beginning to move beyond the realm of priority juggling and program restraint. Priorities imply the expansion of one program and the curtailment of others. In the last year or two, new programs have been able to be squeezed into the budget largely at the expense of severe contractions in the military establishment. However, further reductions in the Pentagon budget are bound to be small. Were it not for the ratchet effect, we might expect the increase in ongoing programs to be offset by reductions in older, seemingly less desirable domestic programs. But if we are unable to do away even with the tea-tasters, the potential leverage from priority substitution is surely limited.

Presumably we will struggle through the fiscal 1972 budget aided by further cuts in military expenditures and some reductions in areas with weak fiscal constituencies, that is, space programs, the SST, etc. The yawning deficit will be curbed, in part at least, by scattered tax increases.

But what of fiscal '73 and beyond?

By then the new welfare program, if passed, should be adding at least an additional $5 billion to the federal budget and perhaps as much as $8 billion. The increases in Social Security, Medicare, veterans benefits, etc., presumably will continue on trend. Savings coming out of the military and space programs are by then likely to be negligible. Thus, budgetary expenditures could very well be increasing at a rate far exceeding the fiscal dividend. How then can the gap be closed? On the tax side, pressure to obtain higher levies through possibly a value-added tax or other new levy will obviously become pressing. Can we seriously expect the President to ask for higher income taxes so soon after the enactment of the Tax Reform Act of 1969?[2]

I will not go into the obvious problems of attempting to finance substantial deficits for series of years. The inflationary implications and the international monetary consequences are readily evident. Ultimately, the budget must be brought into balance, but implicit in that process is going to have to be some major changes in the way we handle our fiscal-political apparatus.

Reversing the Trend

The growing tendency of Congress and the Executive to develop and expand programs for specific constituencies without regard for their aggregative budgetary effects must be reversed. Perhaps the mushrooming budget can be held in check by requiring Congress to pass not only individual revenue and expenditure items, but on a total revenue and expenditure control authorization as well. This alone may not be wholly successful in stemming the spending tide but it could be a first step leading to a repeal of the law of fiscal constituencies.

I suspect there are few groups in this country who are more aware of the virtues of a free competitive capitalist system than business economists. As a group, we are especially conscious of the critical necessity of maintaining a rational, far-sighted economic policy. The years immediately ahead are bound to be ones of serious social-fiscal confrontation. Many of you will be in the forefront of the debates which will ultimately determine the direction of the economic and political structure of our society. There will continue to be exceptional pressure from many quarters to resolve our problems by short-term expedients. Politically, the easiest course is always to fight symptoms, rather than causes. There will be the usual call for "temporary" controls to confront some particular economic imbalance. Controls which themselves induce other imbalances make the intervention difficult to unwind. We have already seen the beginnings of this process in our balance of payments programs.

The road of short-term expediencies has full economic regimentation at its end. Should we reach that point, our political freedoms become jeopardized. It will be a great tragedy if this comes to pass.

It is clear that we can no longer blithely assume everything will work out for the best. There are a number of developing trends which, if not diverted, can only lead to erosion of our freedoms, both economic and political. I do not believe, however, that there is some fatalistic necessity for what is happening. These are man-made problems and they are reversible by men in positions of influence and authority.

Notes

Originally published in *Business Economics*, Vol. 6, No. 1 (January 1971), p. 3.

1. For a definitive treatise on this broader issue see Ayn Rand, *Capitalism: The Unknown Ideal,* (The New American Library, Inc., New York, 1967).
2. While a tax increase for fiscal 1973 may conceivably solve that year's problems, additional tax rate increases could be required for fiscal 1974. In fact, unless altered, it is possible for the *rate* of increase in budgetary expenditures to so exceed the rate of growth of taxable income as to require *annual* increases in overall tax rates or new types of taxation.

CHAPTER 5

1970

THE SOCIAL SIGNIFICANCE OF ENVIRONMENTAL POLLUTION

Barry Commoner, Washington University in St. Louis

It is now a commonplace that environmental pollution is a major public concern. The immediate reasons for this concern are not difficult to detect, for they assail our senses every day: our eyes smart with smog; our ears throb with the noise of automobiles, aircraft and construction tools; we are assailed by the odors of polluted waters and the sight of mounting heaps of rubbish.

Less apparent than the fact of pollution is what can be done about it. The problems are enormous in size. Cities are running out of places to dump garbage and a lake as large as Erie has been nearly totally polluted. The problems are bewildering in complexity: if we expand sewage treatment facilities, we only intensify the pollution due to rotting masses of algae; if we incinerate garbage, we intensify air pollution; if we attempt to control smog by means of exhaust devices which reduce waste fuel emission, we worsen the pollution due to nitrogen oxides.

Why has a society which is so enriched by the progress of technology now become so impoverished in the quality of the life which that technology supports? What lessons can be learned from the environmental crisis that might help us survive it?

My thesis is as follows: Environmental pollution is not to be regarded as an unfortunate, but incidental, byproduct. It is, rather, an intrinsic feature of the very technology which we have developed to enhance productivity. Our technology is enormously successful in producing material goods, but too often is disastrously incompatible with the natural environmental systems that support not only human life, but technology itself.

Moreover, these technologies are now so massively embedded in our system of industrial and agricultural production that any effort to make them conform to the demands of the environment will involve serious economic dislocations. If, as I believe, pollution is a sign of major incompatibilities between our system of productivity and the environmental system that supports it, then, if we are to survive we must successfully confront these economic obligations, however severe and challenging to our social concepts they may be.

A Complex Machine

The environment makes up a huge, enormously complex living machine—the ecosphere—and every human activity, including technology depends on the integrity and proper functioning of that machine. This machine is our biological capital, the basic apparatus on which our total productivity depends. If we destroy it, our most advanced technology will come to naught and any economic and political system which depends on it will founder. Yet, the major threat to the integrity of this biological capital is technology itself.

One example is that much of our present water pollution problem is not due to inadequate utilization of the present technology of sewage disposal, but rather to the very success of that technology. Present sewage treatment procedures were designed to relieve the burden of organic wastes on the self-purifying biological system of surface waters, by converting these wastes to supposedly innocuous inorganic products, such as nitrate and phosphate. This sewage-treatment system is quite successful in achieving its aim. It is failing, however, because its inorganic products are themselves reconverted to organic materials by the green plants that participate in the aquatic biological system, thereby frustrating the initial aim of the treatment process. This accounts for much of the mass of rotting algae which fouls the water and beaches of Lake Erie.

Another example is the matter of air pollution due to automotive exhaust fumes. This problem originates with the production of nitrogen oxides by gasoline engines. Released to the air these oxides, upon absorption of sunlight, react with waste hydrocarbon fuel to produce the noxious constituents of smog. This problem is the direct outcome of the technological *improvement* of gasoline engines: the development of the modern high-compression engine. Such engines operate at higher temperatures than older ones; at these elevated temperatures the oxygen and nitrogen of the air taken into the engine tend to combine rapidly, with the resultant production of nitrogen oxides.

Smog Control

The present smog control technique—reduction of waste fuel emission—by diminishing the interaction of nitrogen oxides with hydrocarbon wastes, enhances the level of airborne nitrogen oxides. In the air nitrogen oxides are readily converted to nitrates, which are then brought down by rain and snow to the land and surface waters. There they add to the growing burden of nitrogen fertilizer, which is an important aspect of water pollution. A recent study shows that in the heavily populated Eastern section of the country the nitrate content of local rainfall is proportional to the local rate of gasoline consumption. Thus, the modern gasoline engine is itself responsible for most of the smog problem and for an appreciable part of the pollution of surface waters with nitrate.

As a final example, we may look at the current status of the insecticide problem. Recent reports from Asia, Africa, and Latin America show that, with awesome regularity, major outbreaks of insect pests have been *induced* by the use of modern contact-killing insecticides, because such insecticides kill the natural predator and parasitic insects which ordinarily keep the spread of insect pests under control. At the same time there is now increasing evidence that synthetic insecticides are responsible for declining populations of birds and fish. Because of such hazards, and the still poorly understood danger to man, DDT has just been banned in Sweden, and its official registry is being withdrawn in Michigan and other states.

These examples illustrate the point that major problems of environmental pollution arise, not out of some minor inadequacies in our new technologies, but because of the very success of these technologies. This raises an important question about new technology: Does it pay? Whether we ask this question in the direct language of profit and loss, or in the more abstract language of social welfare, it is crucial. For, sooner or later, every human endeavor—if it is to continue—must pass this simple test: Is it worth what it costs?

It might appear that this question has already been answered. After all, power companies are eager to build plants for nuclear fuels rather than fossil ones; farmers rapidly adopt new insecticides, fertilizers, and machines. Apparently their cost accounting tells them that the new technologies yield the best available margin between income and costs. I should like to suggest, however, that these calculations are not complete—that certain costs have not yet been taken into account.

For example, what are the true costs of operating a coal-fired power plant in an urban area? The obvious costs—capital outlay, maintenance, operating costs, taxes—are well known. But we have recently discovered that there are other costs and have even begun to put a dollar value upon them.

We now know that a coal-burning power plant produces not only electricity, but also a number of less desirable things: smoke and soot, oxides of sulfur and nitrogen, carbon dioxide, a variety of organic compounds, and heat. Each of these is a *non*-good and costs someone something.

Some of these costs can be converted to dollar values. The US Public Health Service estimates the overall cost of air pollution at about $60 per person per year. A reasonable assessment of the overall costs of air pollution to power production from fossil fuels is about one-third. This means that we must add to the cost of such power production, for each urban family of four, about $80 per year—an appreciable sum relative to the annual bill for electricity.

Social Costs

The *hidden* costs of power production, such as air pollution, are *social* costs; they are met, not by a single producer, but by many *consumers.* To discover the true cost of electric power we need to look for, and evaluate, all the hidden, social costs represented by environmental pollution—the dirty linen, so to speak. These hidden costs degrade the biological capital—pure air—on which the lives and livelihood of the people depend.

These hidden costs are a serious challenge to the social value of our new technology and the economic system which is based upon it. The economic consequences of the hidden costs of environmental pollution due to modern technology are not trivial. It has been calculated that if the US paper industry were required to meet present water-pollution standards, the industry would need to spend $100 million for each of ten years—reducing the industry's profit by one-third for ten years. The total cost of bringing water pollution control up to present standards has been calculated at $100 billion over the next 10–20 years. The total economic loss from air pollution has been estimated at $11 billion annually. In certain industries these sums may represent amounts which are so large relative to profits as to constitute a serious threat to the industry's stability—if it were required to pay the full bill for the hidden costs of operation.

How can we account for this pervasive relationship between technology and pollution? One answer to this question is that at least some of the environmental failures which are so characteristic of modern technologies are the end result of a response to economic pressure.

The Holstein Cow

To illustrate: For many years, dairy farming in New York State has been based on a particular breed, the Holstein cow. This animal was well suited to the small-scale irregular terrain of the local pastures. At the same time, the Holstein cow helped considerably to maintain the capital investment represented by the farmer's pasture land, for its wastes contributed to the organic content of the pasture soil, maintaining its fertility in a natural manner. This was an ecologically balanced system capable of maintaining, indefinitely, a given level of productivity in the form of milk, and exacting little or no social cost in the form of pollution.

However, the rate of economic return from this system of dairying is low, relative to competitive forms of investment of the land and capital involved. Naturally the farmers were interested in ways of increasing the direct financial return from their dairy operations. This has taken the form of scientific efforts to breed a new strain of Holstein, capable of increased yields of milk per unit of feed. These efforts have met with success, and New York dairies now have available to them such high-yield Holstein breeds. However, the new Holstein breeds are not only more productive, they are also considerably larger and heavier than their forebears. The new Holstein cows are not very good at negotiating their hilly pastures—and are therefore unable, in that environment, to obtain sufficient nutrition by their own efforts. This biological difficulty can be solved—by an *economically* acceptable solution—by bringing the feed to the cow, which is then confined to a feedlot.

Thus, the Holstein has become a kind of highly productive milk machine. But this machine, like other forms of technology breaks the natural cycle of environmental processes. For now the cow no longer deposits its waste usefully over the pastures, but drops it instead in a restricted feedlot. Here, the waste constituents, such as nitrogen, can no longer become naturally incorporated into the soil. Instead, they overburden the soil's assimilatory capacity and nearly all of the nitrogenous material leaches through the soil into surface waters—where it becomes a pollutant.

At the same time, the pasture lands, now deprived of the organic matter of the cows' wastes, begin to decline in their fertility. Their productivity can be maintained by using inorganic fertilizer, which is now so cheap and easily spread as to compete favorably with manure. But while this expedient is an effective way to maintain the immediate productivity of the land, it does so at the expense of a major *social* cost—added pollution of surface waters.

This same situation is operating on a larger scale in recent changes in English agriculture, a good deal of which was based in the past on the kind of balanced animal-pasture operation that was characteristic of dairy farming in New York State. However, in recent years, the economic demand for increased agricultural productivity has begun to separate the livestock from the land. In the East of England, where the terrain is suitable to intensive, heavily fertilized grain production, feed is produced. This is shipped to the West, where concentrated livestock operations have been established, many of them in so-called "animal machines" which constrain the animals in small stalls, where they are fed and their manure removed by endless belts. So, the once naturally integrated and non-polluting agricultural system has been disrupted—with the result that the West of England is faced with pollution from concentrated animal wastes, while in the East there is a water pollution problem due to excess fertilizer.

This kind of new agricultural technology has been adopted on a massive scale in the United States. Because of the development of feedlot techniques, the United States is confronted with a huge waste disposal problem—which is considerably greater than the human sewage which we are attempting to handle with grossly inadequate treatment. The result is predictable—massive, still unresolved, pollution problems exist in all the surface waters of the Midwest.

Chemical Fertilizers

As a necessary concomitant to this development, the United States had been forced to adopt, on an equally massive scale, chemical fertilization of the land, which is now deprived of the natural organic fertility of the animal wastes. In the period 1945–1968, the use of nitrogen fertilizer in the US increased about 14-fold. This vast change has occurred for sound economic reasons. Since 1945 the cost of farm labor, land, and machinery has risen about 50–60 percent; but in that time the cost of fertilizer has *declined* about 25 percent. Moreover, intensive use of fertilizer, especially of nitrogen, provides a quick return on the farmer's investment; a fertilizer investment made in the spring is quickly reflected in the return obtained from the crop in the fall. Certain government policies have intensified this effect. For example, the establishment of the Land Bank system has encouraged farmers to grow more crop on less land. This can be accomplished by very intensive use of nitrogen fertilizer and in many places in the Midwest the density of corn plants grown per acre, for example, has been markedly increased.

These agricultural problems most directly reveal our dependence on the natural systems which constitute the environment. These examples also show explicitly that environmental pollution is due to the violation of the integrity of natural environmental systems and illustrate the seriousness of the immediate social costs of the resultant pollution. However, these agricultural problems also illustrate a much graver consequence of technological intrusions on the environment—a threat to the very survival of the biological systems which sustain us. For example, one consequence of our increasing dependence on the massive use of inorganic nitrogen fertilizer may be the loss, perhaps irretrievably, of certain species of soil microorganisms which in nature sustain the fertility of the soil by converting the nitrogen of the air to soil organic nitrogen. If this should happen, any effort to restore the dwindling organic content of the soil and return to a balanced soil-water system will become difficult, and in some areas impossible. We would then be *forced* into increasing dependence on inorganic fertilizer, with its attendant water pollution; like a drug addict, we would be "hooked" on a continued self-destructive course.

Insect Control

We face a similar crisis in the control of insects. It is becoming increasingly clear that we will soon need to abandon our reliance on synthetic insecticides and restore the natural control of insect pests by their insect enemies. However, as the massive use of persistent insecticides—such as DDT—continues, some species of these useful insects may face extinction, so that biological control may be difficult, and perhaps impossible, to re-establish. We would then be forced to rely on synthetic insecticides—"hooked" on them. In each of these cases, the new technology has not, in fact, yielded an unequivocal improvement in the ratio of productivity to cost of production because of the pervasive social cost of the resultant environmental disruption: pollution, and perhaps ultimately, our very survival.

There seems to me to be a faith, now common in our society, that a technological advance which results in an improvement in the yield of a particular desired product is an undiluted social good. In a sense, this faith is justified. The modern automobile, or the nuclear reactor, is indeed a technological triumph. In each is embodied the enormous insights of modern physics and chemistry, and the exquisite skills of metallurgy, electronics, and engineering. Our success is in the construction of these machines; our failure is in their operation.

We have already paid a large price for such illusions. Because of them we have become *unwitting* victims of environmental pollution. Most of the technological affronts to the environment were made, not out of greed, but ignorance. We produced the automobile that envelops our cities in smog—long before anyone understood its harmful effects on health. We synthesized and disseminated new insecticides—before anyone learned that they also killed birds and might be harmful to people. We produced synthetic detergents and put billions of pounds into our surface waters—before we realized that they would not be degraded in disposal systems and would pollute our water supplies. For a number of years we spread radioactive fallout across the globe—before we learned that the resulting biological risks made it too dangerous to continue. We have unwittingly killed thousands of sheep in testing our chemical weapons and have triggered unanticipated earthquakes with our nuclear tests. We have, in sum, blindly assaulted the integrity of the environmental systems that support us, and unwittingly risked our very survival.

New Attitudes

If we are to succeed as inhabitants of a world increasingly transformed by technology, we need to reassess our attitudes toward the natural world on which our technology intrudes. For in the eager search for the benefits of modern science and technology, we have become enticed into a nearly fatal illusion: that we have at last escaped from the dependence of man on the rest of nature.

The truth is tragically different. We have become, not less dependent on the balance of nature, but more dependent on it. Modern technology has so stressed the web of processes in the living environment at its most vulnerable points that there is little leeway left in the system. And time is short; we must begin now, to learn how to make our technological power conform to the more powerful constraints of the living environment. To succeed we shall need to re-examine not only the nature of technology, but also its relation to our economic system.

Note

Originally published in *Business Economics*, Vol. 5, No. 1 (January 1970), pp. 70–73.

CHAPTER 6

1971

THE PRODUCTIVITY SLOW-DOWN

John W. Kendrick, The George Washington University

Ever since 1966, there has been a pronounced slow-down in the rate of productivity growth in the American economy. The significance of this development has passed largely unnoticed, even by the nation's economists who have tended to attribute it to the 1966–1969 retardation in the rate of economic growth generally, and to the 1969–1970 recession. As I shall demonstrate in this chapter, the productivity slow-down is much greater than has occurred in past periods of slow economic growth, and appears to be primarily the result of other unfavorable socio-economic developments of the past four or five years. If this is so, it is a matter of concern to all of us to determine the negative forces at work so that they may be corrected before too much damage has been done to the actual and potential performance of the US economy.

The Definition and Significance of Productivity Advance

Most people are acquainted with the familiar "output per manhour" measure of productivity. This is a useful measure, since labor is the most important type of resource and "input" into the production process, as reflected in the fact that about three-fourths of the national income represents compensation for labor services. But a more sophisticated and meaningful measure is "total factor productivity" which relates output to all the associated resource inputs, human and nonhuman. That is, in addition to labor, the input measure includes natural resources and man-made capital goods—the structure, equipment, and inventory stocks that enhance the productivity of labor. When output rises in relation to total input, this means that productive efficiency has risen and that there has been a net saving achieved in the use of all resources per unit of output. Such increases in total factor productivity primarily reflect advances in the technology and organization of production, although in the short-run they also reflect changes in rates of utilization of labor and capital resources.

In Table 6.1, it will be seen that output per manhour in the US private economy 1948–1969 went up at an average rate of 3.2 percent a year, compared with an increase in total factor productivity of 2.3 percent a year, on average. The difference is due to the fact that there was a substantial increase in the machinery, equipment, and other non-human resources per worker. But since it is economically desirable to conserve natural resources and capital as well as labor per unit of output, the total factor productivity is especially meaningful. Incidentally, the measures are confined to the private economy, which comprises 85 percent of the total, since there are not yet adequate measures of governmental outputs and productivity.

During the same period, 1948–1969, output as measured by the gross national product (deflated to eliminate the effects of price change—the "real GNP") has risen by about 4 percent a year in the private economy, on average. Thus, productivity advance has accounted for well over half of total economic growth. Further, population has risen by 1.5 percent a year since 1948—about as fast as total factor

Table 6.1 Total and partial productivity ratios

Private Domestic Economy and Manufacturing Sector Percentage Rates of Change, 1948–1969, by Subperiods.

	Subperiods					
	1948–1969	*1948–1953*	*1953–1957*	*1957–1960*	*1960–1966*	*1966–1969p*
Private Domestic Business Economy						
Real Product	3.9	4.6	2.5	2.6	5.2	3.4
Real Product per Unit of: Total Factor Input	2.3	2.8	1.9	2.3	2.9	1.1
Labor-Weighted Manhours	2.9	3.5	2.6	2.9	3.2	1.6
Unweighted manhours	3.2	4.1	2.7	2.6	3.6	1.9
Capital	0.3	0.3	−1.2	0.3	1.8	−1.0
Capital/Labor Ratio	2.4	3.2	3.8	2.6	1.3	1.0
Total Manufacturing						
Real Product	4.1	6.0	1.1	1.2	6.5	3.4
Real Product per Unit of: Total Factor Input	2.3	2.9	1.5	2.0	3.2	1.4
Labor	2.8	3.3	2.1	2.5	3.5	2.3
Capital	0.4	0.9	−2.1	0.2	3.1	−2.3
Capital/Labor Ratio	2.6	1.9	3.6	2.6	1.7	4.8

inputs. Thus, advances in total factor productivity have accounted for about *all* of economic progress, as measured by real GNP per capita. Obviously, continued significant economic progress, and the associated increases in levels of living in the United States depend on continuing significant increases in productivity.

In recent years, some voices have been raised to question the desirability of the goals of economic growth, and of the technological progress that lies behind productivity advances. Some of these are the voices of the small but vociferous radical left, who see this as another means of weakening our system. But many of the critics are genuinely concerned about the increasing pollution and other environmental problems associated with economic expansion.

The consensus of concerned and informed observers seems to be that the answers to the environmental deterioration lies in diverting an increasing proportion of output to pollution abatement and other means of improving the environment, rather than in slowing or halting economic progress. This may mean a somewhat slower growth in the physical volume of goods, but it would be offset by a corresponding improvement in the quality of life. In any case, the rate of economic growth is not set by government edict. It emerges as a result of the decisions regarding work versus leisure, and consumption versus saving and investment, by the myriad households, business firms, and governmental units that comprise our free economy. And whatever the growth-rate that emerges as the net impact of the myriad relevant decisions, it is only rational to strive to achieve the increases in real GNP with less than proportionate increases, or actual decreases, in the resources used in production.

The obvious rationale is that the resources all have alternative uses—the increasing leisure associated with fewer hours worked per year, in the case of laborsaving innovations; more consumption rather than saving and investment, in the case of capital-saving innovations; and conservation for recreative or future use rather than using-up by this generation, in the case of innovations that reduce natural-resources usage per unit of output. Or, to put it the other way around, whatever the volume of resources we decide to utilize, we can get a higher output by increasing productivity. And it is my firm impression that the vast majority of Americans desire rising real incomes—judging from union demands and the search by individuals for better pay, the saving habits of individuals who seek to increase their property incomes, and the continued pressures on governments at all levels to provide more and better services.

This is apart from the other benefits of increasing productivity—to help eliminate poverty, to help broaden our national security base, and foreign aid, trade, and investment programs, and to help offset inflationary pressures of rising wage-rates and interest or profit rates.

With regard to the role of productivity in helping offset inflationary pressures, if productivity had continued to rise at its average trend rate after 1966, the general price level would have been almost 6 percent lower at the end of the year 1960—assuming the same rate of increase in total money demand. Under the same assumption, the GNP in 1970 would have been about $60 billion higher than it was. And the cumulative loss in GNP over the four-year period 1966–1970 because of the productivity slow-down was close to $120 billion. This sum could have made a big contribution toward reversing deterioration of the natural environment, financing the income maintenance program to eliminate poverty in this country, and left over enough to have financed completion of the SST development if Congress had been venturesome enough to assume the risks!

The Productivity Record since 1948

In addition to the rates of change in the productivity ratios for the entire period 1948–1969, Table 6.1 shows the rates of change for subperiods measured between peaks of the five business cycles which occurred during the 21-year period. It can be seen that there was considerable variation in rates of change of real product and productivity over the subperiods. These variations, sometimes referred to as "long-swings," are quite usual, and have been evident in US economic history for at least the past century. They generally reflect changes in intensity of final demand from one cycle to the next, but may also reflect variations in the net impact of more fundamental growth forces.

During the first subperiod 1948–1953, output increased at an average annual rate of 4.6 percent, and the total and labor productivity ratios likewise rose at well above-average rates. During the next two subperiods between 1953 and 1960, output and the productivity ratios showed marked deceleration in growth, associated with declining rates of utilization of plant capacity and of the labor force. The following subperiod 1960–1966 showed the fastest rates of increase of all in real product and total factor productivity. Whereas the rate of increase in output per unit of labor input was only moderately above the secular rate, the output/capital ratio showed a marked acceleration prior to the "mini-recession" of 1967.

The last subperiod 1966–1969 registered a deceleration in growth of real product, but not down to the low rates of the 1953–1960 periods. Yet the total and labor productivity ratios showed the lowest rates of increase of all the subperiods, and the output/capital ratio fell at a 1 percent a year average rate. The unemployment ratio actually dropped somewhat between 1966 and 1969, although there may have been some decrease in the intensity with which employed labor was utilized. Whereas the rate of utilization of capacity in manufacturing declined, the rate of decreases was no greater than that which occurred between 1953 and 1957, when productivity advance was much stronger. This suggests that the decline in productivity was due chiefly to a weakening in the secular forces that promote productivity advance, which we examine below.

This interpretation is reinforced by a look at the percent changes in preliminary estimates of real product and output per manhour in 1969 and the recession year of 1970. Between these two years, there was an increase of only 0.9 percent in real private product per manhour. This small increase was approximately offset by a significant drop in real product per unit of capital input, so that total factor productivity showed no gain at all. This contrasts with experience during the four previous post-war recessions, when both productivity measures showed close to their normal secular rates of advance, based on annual averages. Yet the recent economic contradiction was relatively less severe than the first three post-war contractions and only moderately more pronounced than the 1960–1961 contraction (see

Table 6.2 Productivity in the US private economy and related variables
Percentage Changes in Recession Years Since 1948.

	Percentage Changes			*Percentage Point Changes*	
	Total Factor Productivity	*Real Product Per Manhour*	*Real GNP*	*Ratio of Civilian Employment to Labor Force*	*Ratio of Utilization of Mfg. Capacity*
1948–1949	2.5	3.2	0.1	−2.1	−9.5
1953–1954	2.2	2.5	−1.4	−2.6	−10.7
1957–1958	2.2	3.2	−1.2	−2.5	−7.6
1960–1961	2.3	3.5	2.0	−1.2	−2.1
1969–1970p	–	0.9	−0.4	−1.4	−7.1

Table 6.2). Since the poor productivity performance is due only in part to cyclical forces, this re-enforces the interpretation that there has been a weakening in secular forces underlying productivity advance. Before trying to specify the possible areas of weakness in recent years, we review briefly the basic determinants of productivity change.

Causal Forces

The forces behind economic growth generally, and productivity advance in particular, are very complex. Of fundamental importance are the basic values and institutions of a society, as they affect material goals and incentives, attitudes toward work, and propensities to save and invest. In looking at causes of productivity advance, of especial importance as a proximate determinant are "intangible investments" designed to increase and diffuse the practical knowledge which increases the productive efficiency of the tangible factors of production.

Chief among intangible investments are outlays for research and development, and for education and training. Basic research, which accounts for less than 10 percent of total R&D is designed to increase knowledge generally. The scientific and other potentially practical portion of the stock of knowledge is drawn upon in applied research, and development of new and improved products and processes which reduce unit real costs of production, and improve the variety and quality of consumer goods. Upon commercial application, the cost-reducing innovations (including new and improved procedures goods) act directly to increase productivity. The development and production of new and improved consumer goods are reflected directly in measures of real product and productivity to only a limited extent. But introduction of new products indirectly exerts an important influence on productivity through the "learning curve" effect. That is, productivity tends to advance rapidly during the phase of rapidly increasing production of new goods. The exponential trend of productivity is thus due in part to the continuous invention and introduction of new products.

Intangible investments in education and training are closely interrelated with R&D investment. The increase in general and technological knowledge enriches the content of education and training. Conversely, education is necessary to produce the scientists, engineers, and business managers who make the inventions and innovations, and training is required to teach the workforce generally how to operate the increasingly complex technology.

The key roles of research, development, education, and training have been recognized and elucidated by Nelson, Mansfield, Denison, and other economists who have analyzed the process of economic growth.[1]

Denison, for example, estimated that during the period 1929–1962, of the increase in real product in the United States not accounted for the growth of tangible factor inputs (unadjusted for quality change), 40 percent was due to education and training, and about 35 percent was due to the increase in knowledge, resulting largely from R&D and learning by doing.[2] Most of the remaining increase in productivity he viewed as resulting from economies of scale and increasing effectiveness of man-hours worked due to reductions in the length of the average workweek.

Actually, it is difficult to disentangle the effects of increased knowledge and education and training, since the income-enhancing effect of the latter (as estimated by Denison) would have been less without the continuous technological progress which has upgraded the quality of labor required in production processes. Regardless of the issue of the relative contributions of advance in productive knowledge as compared with its diffusion, however, there is a large measure of agreement among growth economists that these two factors together are the chief proximate determinant of productivity advance.

Intangible Investment Trends

In Table 6.3 below, in addition to the gross private domestic (tangible) investment now included in GNP, we show the chief categories of intangible investment. Although not identified as "investment" in the official GNP accounts, most economists now use that term to include all outlays, intangible as well as tangible, that enhance income—and output—producing capacity for future years. It has been estimated that the rate of return on education, based solely on its income-enhancing effect, is comparable to that in industrial plant and equipment.[3] While it is more difficult to estimate the return on research and development, economic specialists in that area believe that the rate of return in R&D is above that on other types of investment. A recent study concluded: "Although what we know about the relationship between R&D and economic growth is limited, all available evidence indicates that R&D is an important contributor to economic growth and productivity; (and) ...the United States is probably underinvesting in civilian sector R&D from a purely economic growth/productivity point of view."[4] In the table, we also include one-half of medical and health care expenditures, which enhance income producing capacity by increasing longevity, decreasing time lost due to illness, and possibly by increasing vitality. Also included are relatively small amounts spent for labor mobility, which is required to adapt to and promote technological advance and other dynamic forces affecting economic structure.

Table 6.3 Tangible and intangible investments in relation to GNP (billions of current dollars, and percentages)

	1929	*1948*	*1957*	*1966*	*1969*
Gross national product	103.1	257.6	441.1	749.9	931.4
Gross private domestic tangible investment	16.2	46.0	67.8	121.4	139.8
Gross intangible investment	15.7	45.0	92.7	197.8	269.0
Research & development	0.25	2.4	10.3	22.3	26.2
Education & training	11.0	30.8	61.4	136.6	188.5
Health & mobility	4.4	11.8	21.1	38.9	54.3
Percentages of GNP:					
Gross private domestic tangible investment	15.6	17.9	15.4	16.2	15.0
Gross intangible investment	15.2	17.5	21.0	26.4	28.9
Research & development	0.24	0.9	2.3	3.0	2.8
Education & training	10.7	12.0	13.9	18.2	20.2
Health & mobility	4.3	4.6	4.8	5.2	5.8

The striking fact that emerges from the table is the strong and steady growth of intangible investment as a percent of GNP over the past 40 years (1929–1969), in contrast to a relatively constant proportion devoted to tangible investments in structures, machinery and equipment, and inventory stocks. Tangible and intangible investments were each little more than 15 percent of GNP in 1929; 40 years later, intangible investment had almost doubled relatively, to about 29 percent, almost twice the tangible investment proportion of 15 percent in 1969. The increase in the intangible investment ratio was more pronounced after World War II than before.

Changes in Causal Forces since 1966

During the most recent subperiod 1966–1969, there have been significant changes in composition of investment. The ratio of R&D to GNP, which had shown by far the most rapid rate of increase over most of the period, topped out at 3 percent in the mid-1960s (1963–1967) and thereafter declined, to 2.8 in 1969, continuing to 2.7 and 2.6 in 1970 and 1971 according to preliminary estimates of the National Science Foundation.[5] This relative decline is of particular significance in view of the germinal nature of R&D and its presumed above-average rate of return. It is one factor in the 1966–1970 deceleration in productivity advance.

It should be observed, however, that the decline in the R&D ratio was due to cutbacks in the Federally-financed portion, particularly that part related to military procurement, which presumably has less productivity significance. The industry financed portion rose from 1.0 percent of GNP in 1966 to 1.1 percent in 1970. But even for the industry-financed portion, this represents some retardation in the relative rate of increase. And the ratio is expected to level off at 1.1 percent in 1971, according to the preliminary NSF R&D estimates, assuming a GNP for 1971 of at least $1,050 billion.

Medical and health care outlays have accelerated somewhat in relation to GNP, but this reflects in part the expansion of medicare, and probably has less productivity significance than the other types of investment.

The major category of outlays for education and training showed a further relative increase from 1966 to 1969, and again in 1970. But there are several qualifications that are important. In the first place, this was the period of the bulge of enrollments in colleges and universities. Many observers believe that on average there has been a decline in the quality of instruction delivered by the institutions of higher education, not to mention the adverse effects on learning of the wave of campus disruptions. Further, there has been a trend away from the hard sciences and engineering, accentuated in the last couple of years by the rising unemployment of scientists and engineers due to the cut-back in Federal support of R&D.

Estimates of formal and informal training programs of industry are rough, but they do indicate a further increase since 1966, more or less in proportion to the accelerated growth of the labor force. It is important to remember that from 1966 to 1970, the labor force was increasing by an average of 1.75 million a year, compared with an average of less than one million a year during the preceding decade. Also significant is the fact that most of the large increase was coming in the younger age brackets. Since "learning by experience," while not amenable to measurement, is an important aspect of labor productivity in addition to formal education and training, it is apparent that the average experience of the labor force has been declining along with its average age, tending to offset productivity-enhancing forces. This is probably another significant factor in the slow-down in productivity since 1966.

Values and Institutions

Finally, we come to the underlying values and institutions of our society which obviously have an important bearing on levels and changes of productivity. Unfortunately, this is an area in which it is difficult or impossible to quantify the relationships. So my comments will be more qualitative, and inevitably reflect subjective judgments.

With regard to values, we have already referred to the increasing questioning, particularly by youth, of the material goals of American society. As we become wealthier, the added value of further increases in real income and wealth per capita may seem to diminish. Certainly, the spread of the hippie culture, and the alarming increase in use of drugs, is a tangible manifestation of changing attitudes and values. Further, the increased activity and influence of the radical left has undoubtedly had a disruptive and divisive effect. Although we cannot quantify the net impact of these social tendencies, it seems probable to me that they have had some effect on productivity advance, although it is probably still relatively minor.

With regard to institutions, I do not see any major net impact of the slow changes that have been taking place. There is, however, one major economic development that began in 1966 and has continued until recently which may well have had an adverse effect on productivity—that is the marked acceleration in the pace of price inflation. This has had a somewhat disruptive effect in various markets, and has required a larger volume of resources to be devoted to attempts to mitigate its unfavorable consequences. As one example, the regulated industries have had to apply much more frequently to the regulatory bodies for increased rates or prices, in order to preserve adequate rates of return on investment. The manhours spent in preparing and hearing these cases have increased greatly, although the absolute numbers are not large. But the complexity of almost all price, wage-rate, and other income determinations has also increased, requiring increasing amounts of time and effort to be devoted to what is essentially a non-productive activity. The effect on productivity is negative, although we cannot measure its extent.

Summary and Outlook

The slow-down in productivity advance since 1966 appears to have been only partially the result of a mild retardation in economic growth 1966–1969, and the contraction of 1969–1970. Among the more fundamental forces affecting productivity which have become less favorable since 1966, I singled out four for special comment: (1) the decline in R&D expenditures in relation to GNP, which has reduced the rate of increase in new knowledge and know-how embodied in men and capital goods; (2) the accelerated growth of the labor force, particularly in the youngest age-brackets, which has reduced the average age and experience of workers; (3) the acceleration in price-inflation, which has diverted resources to mitigating its unfavorable consequences; and (4) social tendencies, which have reduced the power of material goals and the work-ethic among a small but growing proportion of the population, particularly in the younger age-brackets.

Other social scientists would undoubtedly suggest other factors, or give somewhat different emphasis to the factors I have mentioned. But if my diagnosis is accepted as having some validity, what is the prognosis and prescription for the years ahead?

First, it is clear that a continuation of the current economic recovery, which seems assured at least through 1971 and 1972, will bring with it substantial gains in productivity as unutilized capacity is reduced. In the first quarter of 1971, real product per manhour in the private economy increased by 3.3 percent over the first quarter 1970, and 5.3 percent over the previous quarter, according to estimates of the Bureau of Labor Statistics. The important point to watch is whether the gains are as big as those experienced in the past in the same phases of recovery. If not, it will be evidence that the more basic forces continue to be less favorable than in earlier periods.

In recent quarters, evidence has also accumulated of a slowing in the rate of price inflation, which may well continue for another year or more. But it is unlikely that the rate of price advance will return to the 2 percent a year rate experienced before 1966 unless the rate of increase in money wage-rates falls back closer to the rate of increase in output per manhour—which seems unlikely if unemployment declines as expected in 1971–1972. Actually the pace of inflation may well begin to accelerate again in 1972, given the strong economic recovery which is the administration goal. Indeed, the problem of achieving reasonable price stability at full employment has not yet been solved, and remains to plague us in the future.

Better Prospects for R&D

The decline in R&D as a percent of GNP has probably run its course. The Science Advisor to the President, Dr. Edward David, recognizes the tragic waste of resources involved in the rising unemployment of scientists and engineers, and has proposed measures to reverse the trend. The President's Budget for 1972 calls for an almost one billion dollar increase in Federal funds for R&D. Industry spending will also probably accelerate during the current recovery. And an improving job market for scientists and engineers will tend to encourage more young people to major in science and engineering. The important thing for the longer-term future is that a more rational and consistent Federal Government science policy be formulated and implemented. Such a policy is now being developed in the Office of Science and Technology.

Similarly, it is essential that outlays for education and training continue to increase relatively. An ultimate objective of our society should be that no one should be denied the education of which they are desirous and capable. This is an important aspect of eliminating poverty, and widening opportunity for all, as well as increasing productivity. Prospects in this area appear favorable.

Regarding values, in a free society these emerge from the experiences and dialogue of its members. It appears to me to be incumbent upon those of us who are molders of public opinion, both in and out of government and the professions, to stress the importance of productivity advance and economic progress for the future of this and the other nations of the world, as I attempted to do earlier in the chapter. We must also answer the arguments of the critics who decry the "materialism" of America. These critics fall into three main groups. First, there are those of the radical left who would weaken and revolutionize our system and presumably substitute some form of communist totalitarianism. I believe the great majority of Americans have the good sense to try to preserve the democratic institutions that permit continuing, peaceful evolution toward community objectives. Besides, Marx was the materialist par excellence, but there is no evidence that communism is achieving material advance any more effectively than predominantly free enterprise economies.

There is a second group of critics who would emphasize spiritual, cultural, aesthetic and other "higher" values than materialistic ones. The answer here is that widening the material base is a prerequisite to expanding cultural and other "nonproductive" activities. Those of us who believe in economic progress do so precisely because we believe also in the higher values which it makes possible of realization. Although in passing, I would remark that the productive, inventive, and innovative activities involved in economic progress often elicit the highest creative talents of which man is capable. And as someone said, man is seldom so harmlessly engaged as in economic pursuits!

Finally, there is the third group of critics whose alternative to "materialistic," productive activities seems to be chiefly the mindless pursuit of short-term pleasure, as typified by the hippie, drug culture. There, the need is for moral guidance, to help them distinguish short-term from long-term interest. I do not see signs of any religious revival, or moral renaissance in America. But I do believe that people learn from their own experiences, even if they refuse to profit from that of the race. Further, the lack of a secure material base would tend to limit the expansion of the hippie approach to life. I would guess that this will eventually wane.

In sum, although I do not pretend to be a social forecaster, I believe the negative social trends in our society tend to be self-limiting—particularly as we see more clearly their dangers, and leaders of public opinion speak out more clearly for positive, basic values and objectives.

The Productivity Commission

In conclusion, I note the creation last year of a National Commission on Productivity by President Nixon. Although slow in getting started, the Commission is developing positive recommendation for improved productivity performance in the years ahead. The Commission plans to sponsor a national conference this fall to discuss papers relating to major areas of importance for productivity advance—including techniques for improving efficiency in Federal, state, and local governments. The Commission will, of course, go far beyond the several areas I have noted as contributing to productivity advance.

This is a most hopeful development, since it is the first time that an official body has made a comprehensive review of all the significant factors affecting productivity from a policy-oriented view-point. It is to be hoped that after the Commision's report, a permanent agency will be established to continue this function. So many governmental measures affect productivity, that it is important that a single agency consider them from this angle. It should be of real assistance in getting back on the productivity growth-path, and avoiding slow-downs in the future such as that of the past five years.

Notes

Originally published in *Business Economics*, Vol. 6, No. 4 (September 1971), pp. 7–13.

1. See R. Nelson, M. Peck, and E. Kalachek, *Technology, Economic Growth and Policy.* Washington, DC: The Brookings Institution, 1967; Edwin Mansfield, *The Economics of Technological Change.* New York: W. W. Norton, 1968; Edward F. Denison, *The Source of Economic Growth in the United States and the Alternatives Before Us.* New York: Committee for Economic Development, 1962.
2. Denison, *The Source of Economic Growth in the United States and the Alternatives Before Us,* Table 32, p. 266.
3. Gary Becker, *Human Capital.* New York, National Bureau of Economic Research, 1964.
4. "A Review of the Relationship Between Research and Development and Economic Growth/Productivity." National Science Foundation, Office of Economic and Manpower Studies, January 1971 (preliminary), pp. 5 and 13.
5. See *National Patterns of R&D Resources,* March 1971. The estimates were furnished the author by NSF for the present use.

CHAPTER 7

1973

WHY PRODUCTIVITY IS IMPORTANT

Geoffrey H. Moore, National Bureau of Economic Research and Stanford University

In recent months productivity has almost become a household word in view of the wider understanding that (1) long-term growth in productivity is a key to greater real income, and (2) productivity gains enhance the prospect for containing inflation. What are the facts underlying these propositions?

Productivity Trends and Real Income

Over the long run, the growth in real wages in the private sector—that is, hourly compensation adjusted for changes in purchasing power—has been nearly the same as the growth in output per manhour. Both rose at an average rate of nearly 3 percent per year during the past two decades. As a result, by the fourth quarter of 1972, production per hour in the private sector was nearly double its 1950 level, and real wages per hour also had nearly doubled.

In the latter half of the 1960s, when inflation accelerated and productivity growth slackened, growth in real wages also slowed. Productivity growth fell from 3 percent a year during 1950–1965 to about 2 percent during 1965–1969; meanwhile, increases in real hourly wages fell from a 3 percent rate to about 2.5 percent. Recently, however, there has been a turnaround. Productivity rose sharply in 1971 and 1972 and so did real earnings.

These recent changes reflect one of the most important results of the effort to control inflation and to spur economic expansion—the rise in workers' real earnings. The spiraling inflation of 1965–1969 increased the average wage, but most of the increase was eaten up by increases in prices. During 1970 and early 1971 anti-inflation policies began to pay off—the rate of increase in the Consumer Price Index fell below 4 percent, and productivity and real earnings began to rise. Finally, during the past year the rate of price inflation has fallen still farther, while productivity and real earnings have had their best growth in years.

Clearly, productivity increases become translated into real earnings gains.

Productivity Change and Employment

It is often thought that one of the dangers of productivity increases is that they automatically lead to layoffs. The increase in real earnings per worker would not help much if fewer people were employed. This view is based in part on the belief that with a given increase in output, the larger the increase in productivity the smaller the increase in employment. There is nothing wrong with this arithmetic, but happily the economy does not generally work that way.

Studies of various industries, by the Bureau of Labor Statistics and the National Bureau of Economic Research, indicate that there is no general tendency for rapid productivity improvement to reduce employment growth. Many industries, such as air transportation and radio and TV, have experienced high productivity growth, large output increases and expanded employment. One reason is that a rise in productivity can reduce costs and prices, stimulate demand and output, and thereby create more jobs, not fewer. In farming, on the other hand, where productivity growth has been outstanding, employment has declined. The process can work either way, and there seems to be no simple rule.

Productivity, Costs, and Prices

Productivity—or output per manhour—affects the price level through its influence on unit labor costs. When wage increases exceed productivity increases, labor costs per unit of output rise.

Over the last quarter-century, that is what has happened. Hourly compensation in the corporate sector increased at an average rate of 5 percent per year (see Chart 7.1).[1] Productivity gains averaged 3 percent. Hence, unit labor costs increased 2 percent per year. However, there was substantial variation about these averages. In many years the gains in productivity greatly exceeded 3 percent; in others there was virtually no increase. On the other hand, the rate of increase in compensation was much steadier, year in and year out. As a result, unit labor cost changes have been extremely sensitive to productivity changes. The years in which productivity increased the most are those in which unit labor costs rose the least, or actually fell, and vice versa (compare the two top lines in the chart). During the present expansion, the upsurge in productivity growth has been a major force retarding labor cost increases despite the continued rise in wages.

Since labor costs are a major proportion of total costs of production in the corporate sector as a whole, labor cost movements have dominated those of total costs. Price movements have not been as volatile as those of labor and total costs, but the largest increases in prices have usually occurred when costs rose the most, which is also when productivity rose the least.

The greater stability of prices than of costs, and the important influence of productivity change upon cost changes implies that productivity and corporate profits are closely related. For example, the most rapid increases in profits per unit of output occurred in 1950–1951, 1955, 1959, the early 1960s, and during 1971–1972. These are just the points when productivity gains were the greatest. Virtually every movement in the top line of the chart (output per manhour) is reflected in the profits line.

While the factors that explain these relationships are complicated, productivity has obviously played a critical role in the movements of prices, costs and profits. In the past 25 years, there have been only 3 periods when the price level, as measured for the corporate sector of the economy, rose less than 2 percent per year (Table 7.1). In each of these periods (1949–1950, 1953–1955, 1959–1966), productivity rose about 4 percent. The rest of the time, when prices rose faster, the productivity growth rate was around 2.5 percent or less. Wage increases in each of the periods of relative price stability were about equal to productivity growth, that

Table 7.1 Rates of change in productivity, costs, and profits during periods of rapid and slow inflation, nonfinancial corporations

	Average Rate of Change Per Year[a]							
Periods When Implicit Price Deflator Rose Less than 2% Per Year	*Implicit Price Deflator*	*Output Per Manhour*	*Compensation Per Manhour*	*Unit Labor Costs*	*Unit Nonlabor Costs*	*Total Unit Costs*	*Unit Profits*	*Real Compensation[b] Per Manhour*
IV 1950–I 1953	3.7	2.7	7.7	5.0	4.0	4.7	0.5	3.0
IV 1955–IV 1958	3.1	1.7	5.7	4.1	7.3	4.8	−4.9	3.3
III 1966–I 1972	3.1	2.6	6.7	4.1	5.8	4.5	−5.3	2.3
Average, 3 Periods	3.3	2.3	6.7	4.4	5.7	4.7	−3.2	2.8
III 1949–III 1950	0.3	4.6	3.6	−0.9	6.3	0.5	0.2	4.7
II 1953–III 1955	1.0	4.2	4.5	0.5	4.3	1.3	1.5	4.4
I 1959–II 1966	0.8	3.7	3.8	0.1	1.0	0.3	4.0	2.5
Average, 3 Periods	0.7	4.2	4.0	−0.1	3.9	0.7	1.9	3.9
II 1972–IV 1972	1.5	5.1	6.2	1.1	0.4	0.9	7.2	2.8

[a]Based on percentage changes over four-quarter spans, dated in the terminal quarter of the span.

[b]Compensation per manhour deflated by the consumer price index. The rates of change in the consumer price index, for the periods given above, are: 4.6, 2.4, 4.4, 3.8 (av.); −1.0, 0.2, 1.4, 0.2 (av.); 3.3.

Source: Bureau of Labor Statistics.

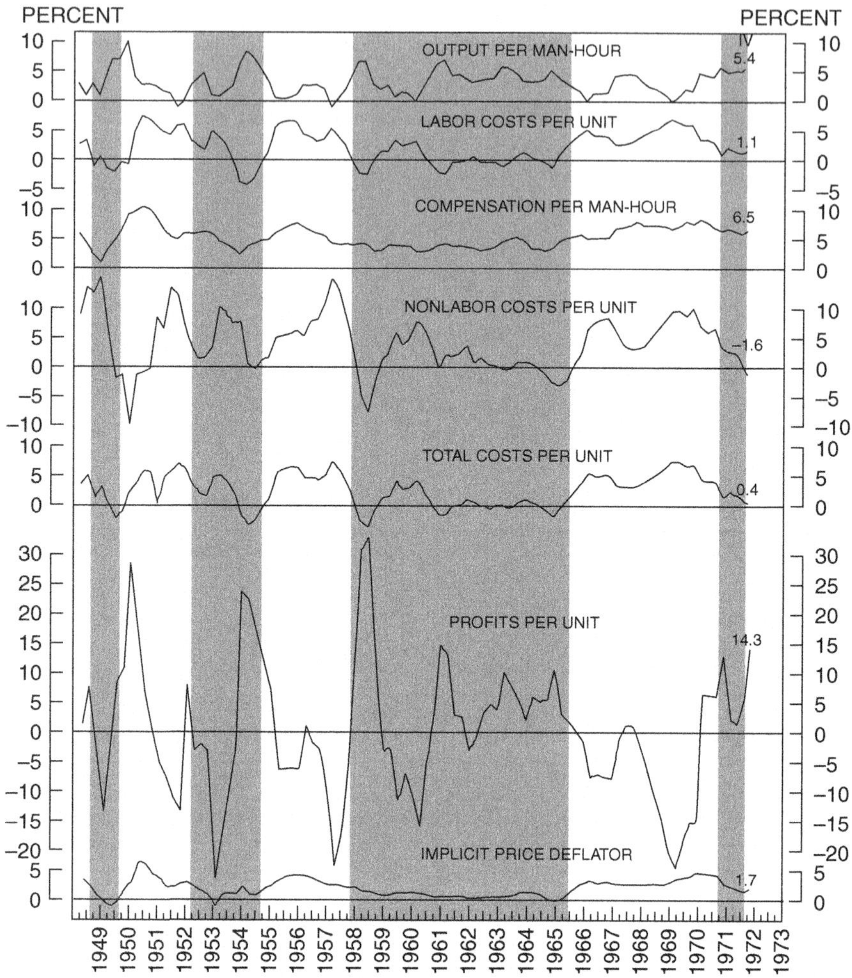

Chart 7.1 Productivity and related measures, nonfinancial corporations, percent change from same quarter a year ago.

Shaded areas represent periods when the implicit price deflator for the corporate sector rose less than 2 percent per year.

Source: Bureau of Labor Statistics.

is, 4 percent per year, and this virtually stabilized costs of production. Although wages rose faster—6–7 percent per year—in the periods of rapid inflation, this did not help *real* wages, because prices also rose faster. In short, wage and productivity increases of around 4 percent per year were associated with little inflation in prices and substantial gains in real wages.

The lesson is clear that productivity growth has helped to insure less inflation and higher real wages without adversely affecting overall employment. The record justifies the view that if we are to look forward to an era of real economic growth without inflation, we would be well advised to seek high rates of productivity growth.

Notes

Originally published in *Business Economics*, Vol. 8, No. 3 (May 1973), pp. 28–31.

1. The corporate sector data are used in Chart 7.1 and Table 7.1 instead of the more comprehensive data for the total private or private nonfarm sectors because corporate profits can be distinguished from other nonlabor payments (depreciation, interest, rental income, and indirect taxes). As the chart shows, the cyclical behavior of unit profits is altogether different from that of other nonlabor payments. The corporate data, by the same token, also permit one to compute total costs per unit of output and hence to compare the movements of costs and prices.

PART II

1975–1984

CHAPTER 8

1975

PRESIDENTIAL ADDRESS

NABE AND THE BUSINESS FORECASTER

Robert G. Dederick, The Northern Trust Co.

Of all the phenomena that have mystified me over the years—and there have been many—one of the most cryptic is the Presidential Address delivered at annual meetings of professional societies—and some not so professional societies. Two questions invariably come to mind on those, fortunately, rare occasions when I am confronted with the Presidential Address issue: First, why is a society president, who presumably has been busy throughout his term holding down both this nonpaying job and a paying one, subjected to the burden of composing a farewell sermon? And, second, why is a paying audience of his peers, who presumably have come to the Annual Meeting to add either to their store of knowledge or to their store of pleasure, subjected to the burden of listening to his farewell sermon? Thus far, I have failed to come up with a satisfactory answer to either query. There is a widely accepted explanation, of course, to the effect that society presidents would not be society presidents if, before fading into limbo, they were not capable of preparing a statesmanlike set of remarks suitable for consumption by fellow members of the lodge. Oh, if only it were so! But you and I—and especially I—know that it is not. No, I suspect that the actual rationale is something closer to the following: Society presidents are forced to give Presidential Addresses as partial penance for their various misdeeds while in office, and Society members are forced to hear Presidential Addresses as partial penance for being foolish enough to vote such miscreants into office.

Nonetheless, unfortunate or not, the tradition exists. And, indeed, much to my—and, no doubt, to your—sorrow, it even lives on in such a supposedly enlightened organization as the National Association of Business Economists. In our own case, though, thus far there is no evidence that great harm has been done. On the contrary, an evening spent reading past Presidential Addresses shows them to have been of a high order of quality. But those were the famous exceptions which prove the Dederick rule, and econometricians have told us that exceptions cannot persist indefinitely. You are now about to learn that even econometricians can eventually be right.

First, though, a quotation—not, I hasten to assure you, from Lewis Carroll, but instead from that most distinguished of economists, Arthur Burns:

> "You could sit around and listen to these professional colleagues of mine, and they debate whether the price level at the end of the year will be rising 7 or 8 percent. And no one ever knows what he is talking about." (Testimony before the Joint Economic Committee, August 6, 1974.)

And now another, this from a second well known authority, the business economist's number one competitor, *Business Week*:

> "A case can be made that businessmen have come to rely altogether too heavily on economic forecasts that are not related to the real world of commerce and industry. The wise man is better advised right now to follow his instincts, stay attuned to his markets and customers, and not pay too much attention to the forecasters." (*Business Week*, March 9, 1974.)

These quotes—and others that I could give as well, some regrettably from members of my own management—suggest that the present must not be a cheerful time for economists. And such is, in fact, the case. Indeed, as an article in the *New York Times* recently put it, "economists are suffering a severe recession of confidence nowadays, perhaps even a failure of faith."[1]

Now, the question is, why are we so gloomy? And the answer, as the quotes imply, lies in this particularly painful truth: The characteristic that has set us apart from other mortals all these postwar years—our ability to predict with some degree of confidence the future economic implications of current developments—has now become subject to serious question. In other words, the public has ceased to believe in our prescience. Even more importantly, so, too, have we. And with good reason, for the truth is that any honest appraisal of our recent forecasting record can and does yield only one conclusion: Our presumed special powers notwithstanding, we have been badly—and sadly—lacking in foresight.

To be sure, our efforts have not been a complete disaster, even this year, which—again to quote *Business Week*—will in some circles be remembered as "the year the forecasters blew it."[2] After all, we did predict that the direct impact on production of the energy crisis would be neither severe nor long lived, and we did predict that inflation would be pronounced. Looking back earlier into the decade, we foresaw that the New Economic Policy of 1971 would be temporarily successful—or at least appear so—and we also foresaw some of the problems that controls would ultimately beget. But, with this said, the fact still remains that almost without exception we utterly failed in the most important forecasting assignment of all: We did not provide advance warning to our managements of the distressing situation into which the US economy has drifted over the past several years.

Economic Disequilibrium

Now, of course, it is a genuine question whether any mortal could have been expected to foresee the current sad state of the economic union. After all, the last few years have been an extraordinary phase in the course of world economic history. The American economy has been subjected to a series of shocks—Vietnam, dollar overvaluation and dollar devaluation, weather vagaries, controls and decontrols, the OPEC oil blow, not to mention the famous anchovy disappearance—and these disturbances have thrown it deep into disequilibrium in a world which has been similarly discombobulated. And a world in disequilibrium is not one in which it is easy for anyone—economists included—to forecast accurately.

As we're all aware, our short-term predictions are cyclically oriented, concerned with emerging balances and imbalances rather than with fundamental, secular changes. Ordinarily this approach, while limited, is adequate for the task. But the present is not an ordinary time, for this is a period when conventional cyclical developments have been overwhelmed by the explosive structural shifts.

Moreover, another and related practice of ours, the tendency to think in terms of the margin and, thus, in relatively small increments, also has let us down. This time the increments have instead been massive—beyond the bounds of our conventional dynamics. In consequence, we have a succession of forecasting failures, including this one of my own: As 1974 began, I felt for no very good reason that inflation would be even more serious than conventional forecasting techniques were suggesting. So what did I do? I tacked an extra percentage point onto my GNP deflator—a differential that appeared daring at the time but that in the end proved to be completely meaningless. I simply was unable to think in terms sufficient to match the scale of the new realities.

Now, presumably states of disequilibrium do not last forever, and today's distortions will become tomorrow's textbook fodder. And, when equilibrium returns, we shall be back to the good old days when economists were, if not kings, at least princes. Thus, we need only suffer through the current aberrational stage in silence—hoping against hope that our employers will do the same—and eventually we shall once again be paragons of accuracy.

Or shall we? I doubt it.

The Earlier Forecasting Record

I take this negative position not because I don't expect equilibrium eventually to be restored—it always has been—but because in my view we never *were* paragons of accuracy. This is heresy to be sure; even *Business Week* asserts that we were "extremely good" in the second half of the sixties and "accurate" in 1970, 1971, and 1972.[3] And *everybody* knows, of course, that prior to the Vietnam War, that is, back when equilibrium did prevail, we were invariably on target. Maybe so, but that's not the way I remember it. In fact, I recall a rather steady stream of errors. Now, some of you are perhaps thinking that my recollection may only encompass my own forecasts—that perhaps I was being wrong while the world was being right. Well, that may be part of it—I refuse to discuss the matter on grounds of executive privilege—but, just to make certain, I spent an evening reviewing the findings of old NABE annual forecast surveys. Believe me, they did not make for happy bedtime reading.

As I interpret history, we tended to overestimate the economy's vigor in years of slow growth and to underestimate it in years of rapid growth. Moreover, even on those rare occasions when the forecast numbers tended to be nearly identical with the actuals, we did not always impart to the public the true *feel* of the economy. And isn't it the feel which really counts? Perhaps the most noteworthy example in this respect is our pre-1971 effort. To be sure, we foresaw sluggish growth and moderate inflation for that year; but what we did not foresee were both the events which would produce the numbers that we forecast and the implications for the vital industrial sector of the economy. In other words, we predicted the unimportant but not the important. And, as for periods encompassing cyclical turning points, at those times we tended to be hopelessly divided. Some of us were right, to be sure, but others of us were wrong.

But, enough! There is no point in flagellating ourselves further; others will do that for us. No, the relevant questions now are these: (1) What is the explanation for our chronic failure to forecast as well as we and our employers would like? (2) What, if anything, can NABE do to improve our accuracy?

Forecast Error Explanations

As regards the explanation for our mistakes, it has several aspects—or, at least, several that are commonly enumerated. And you know them as well as I.

Inadequate data are one problem, of course. If you are misinformed about the extent of capacity utilization in one year and the extent of inventory accumulation in the next, the odds would suggest that you will yourself misinform others about what lies out in the future.

The growing role of government in the economy is also deservedly singled out for censure. If you don't know what Pennsylvania and Constitution Avenues will suddenly decide to do, how can you know what Main and Wall Streets will do in response?

Still another culprit is said to be inadequate economic theory, by which is meant theory that insufficiently or deficiently explains economic phenomena and thus makes it impossible accurately to forecast their implications. Frequently this inadequacy is attributed to the fact that economic theory is narrowly based, failing to incorporate the insights of other disciplines. If you don't know what it is that makes Washington and Peoria react as they do to a given set of stimuli, it won't do you any good to know what these stimuli might be.

And finally—and helping to explain the inadequacy of economic theory—there is the problem of our inadequate factual knowledge of the economy's inner workings, including the impact of international influences. Our traditional national income accounts framework is deficient in this respect; it can conceal more than it exhibits, as evidenced most recently by the utter failure of at least the conventional GNP aggregates to portray the widespread vigor of the vast industrial sector earlier this year. And input-output analysis, which was supposed to fill in the gaps, has let us down even harder. Witness its abject inability to handle the impact of the oil shortage. As for flow of funds analysis, either we don't know how to use it or it doesn't really offer much that is useful.

In sum, we don't forecast the future very well, because we really don't know very much about the present—both in a factual way and with respect to the theory which unifies and rationalizes the facts. And this is not just a feature of today's atypical environment but a chronic problem, because there is a constant tendency for the facts to change, thereby depleting our already limited intellectual capital. The present differs from the past only in the rate of speed at which the facts have recently been changing.

The Fundamental Problem

This, then, is the proximate—and conventional—explanation for our distress. But I think that something more fundamental also is at work, which goes far to explain our lack of knowledge. As I see it, we don't know very much about the present, because we don't really make very much of an effort. We simply haven't been doing our homework on the economy, diverting our attention elsewhere. And, by *we,* I mean both economists in general and business economists in particular.

As a group, economists have concerned themselves much less with studying the economy *per se* than with studying economic relationships. In particular, the emphasis in recent years has been on econometric model building—on attempting to quantify relationships among economic statistics—rather than on determining what statistics are needed to depict the economy's workings and then accurately developing these statistics. I am not denigrating what econometricians have done—that would be nonsense—but I am suggesting that probably they have overdone it at the expense of more beneficial alternatives. Silk purses cannot be made out of sows' ears even by a computer. Moreover, econometric forecasting carries with it a special difficulty of its own, not, to be sure, of its own making but of its users' making. In view of the complexity of the model making and model remaking process, too often we allow various models—and model makers—to do our thinking for us. Increasingly, one or two publicly distributed models actually have tended to yield what becomes the standard forecast, as the rest of us have merely tinkered with the inputs and the printouts in order to differentiate our own products. And tinkering has usually proven to be not enough.

Forecasters have not only tended to look elsewhere in the methodological sense—emphasizing relationship at the expense of facts—but even with respect to the facts themselves. One great economic development of recent years has been the internationalization of business and finance. But how much attention have we really devoted to the domestic impact of trends in the so-called *foreign* sector? Embarrassingly little. And, of course, the other great development—the shift from a shortage of demand to a shortage of supply—was overlooked until it was perhaps closer to its end than to its beginning. Again our attention was directed elsewhere.

So much for economists in general. What of business economists in particular? What have we been contributing to the state of the forecasting art? In my view, not much.

Despite the fact that most macro forecasts are made by business economists—and that in presenting his forecast the business economist typically is held to a much more rigorous standard than his academic counterpart—what I have said about economists as a group applies even more strongly to us. Let me hasten to add, though, that I do not believe we should be specially criticized on this score. To me, it is inevitable that our contributions to general business forecasting knowledge will be limited. The typical business economist is required to be macro oriented, applying his training and knowledge to analyzing the impact of external economic developments on his own firm. Thus, he has neither the manhours nor the incentive to do much original research on the aggregate economy. This is not to say that developments in the economy as a whole aren't extraordinarily important to his firm—how can you predict the micro without first knowing the macro? But this is to say that in the macro area he is much less likely to be a toolmaker than a tool user. To the extent, therefore, that direct progress is made in resolving our broad forecasting deficiencies, it will probably have to come not from us but from the outside, that is, from non-business economists.

A Recommendation for NABE

All of which brings me to my second question: "What can the National Association of Business Economists do to improve macro economic forecasts?" If you agree with me that the need for improvement is great, you also will agree, I think, that NABE should involve itself in this crucial area. And, of course, we are in fact already doing so in a limited way, via our program of publications, annual meetings, seminars, and—beginning this winter—workshops. But these are primarily communications devices—means of transmitting information, rather than means of developing new information. We need to do more—much more—in my opinion, than simply to serve as a communications vehicle. Therefore, I want to end these remarks with two modest proposals.

First, I suggest that NABE—contrary to its long-standing refusal to take public positions on public policy matters—actively support efforts to encourage increased Federal spending on government statistical programs. To me, the need here is self-evident. The nation simply cannot risk a repeat of the statistical reporting fiascoes of recent years. And, if NABE can do something to prevent such a repetition, we would be derelict if we allowed old taboos to stand in the way.

Second, I suggest that NABE conduct an award competition, a contest which would call both for the solicitation of papers designed to improve economists' forecasting ability and for the granting of generous cash prizes to those participants deemed to have made the most outstanding contributions. The contest would be open to anyone who believes that he can improve our knowledge of how the economy operates—whether his paper be strictly economic or canted toward the sociological, political, psychological, technological, or whatever is left. And, in order to provide a strong inducement for individuals to participate, the awards would be large—totaling, say, $20,000 annually over a three-year period, $10,000 annually to each year's winner and $10,000 spread among several runners-up each year. To review the papers, a panel of economists from academia, business, and government would be established—with the panel members to be paid for their efforts. While an attempt would be made to finance the contest by soliciting funds from institutional members and other outside sources, NABE itself would stand ready to tap its treasury to whatever extent is deemed necessary to make the financial incentives meaningful.

I fully recognize that this second proposal would be no small commitment. We have only recently reached our long-sought goal of a reserve fund equivalent to one year's expenditures. Now, if the proposal were to be accepted, we would be taking the risk of reducing our assets by as much as one-half over a mere three-year period. Moreover, the effort might be to little avail; we're all aware that scholarship cannot be programmed to produce near-instant results on demand. Nonetheless, in my view, some such effort is well worth making, and some such risk is well worth taking.

The National Association of Business Economists is celebrating its fifteenth anniversary this year. Since 1959 the organization has grown in many ways, until today it stands as a mature professional society. NABE owes this progress to its members, many of whom have given of their time and effort, all of whom have given at least their financial support. Now business economists themselves are in need of help, their stock of intellectual capital badly decimated, their credibility badly tarnished. Under such circumstances, it behooves NABE to come to the aid of the profession in whatever ways that it can, perhaps not in those forms which I have suggested—I offer them more as stimuli to thought than as panaceas—certainly, though, via one or more alternatives. We can't do much perhaps, but I am convinced that we must do something—for the good of ourselves, our employers, and the public at large.

Notes

Originally published in *Business Economics*, Vol. 10, No. 1 (January 1975), pp. 7–11.

1. Wade Green, "Economists in Recession," *New York Sunday Times Magazine*, 5/12/74.
2. "Theory Deserts the Forecasters," *Business Week*, 6/29/74.
3. Ibid.

CHAPTER 9

1975

THOUGHTS ON INFLATION: THE BASIC FORCES

Gottfried Haberler, American Enterprise Institute

So much has been written and is currently being written on inflation that it is impossible to read everything and say anything that has not been said before. The best I can do under these circumstances is, I believe, not to comment on current events but to go back to basic principles which are often lost sight of in daily work, although they are frequently a better guide for things to come than minute description of current events and the extrapolation of recent trends.

I take it for granted that inflation is a monetary phenomenon in the sense that there has never been a serious inflation without an increase in the quantity of money and that inflation cannot be stopped or reduced to a tolerable level without restrictions on monetary growth. It is only slightly less obvious to me that inflation has to be stopped, if we wish to assure for the long pull a reasonable rate of economic growth and employment, and that continuing high inflation would eventually undermine our free enterprise system.

This proposition is not generally accepted; in fact, it is often rejected implicitly, sometimes even explicitly, by some leaders of the economic profession. But let me restate it in a more analytic (less normative) form. If inflation is not stopped, it will tend to accelerate and eventually become intolerable. The reason is well known: gradually money illusion is eroded, more and more people expect prices to go on rising and take steps to protect themselves by stepping up their demands. Unions press for higher wages, other pressure groups escalate their demands, interest rates rise and so on. This does not mean, however, that any creeping inflation must inexorably become a trotting and then a galloping one. I still cannot believe that the Federal Reserve will permit that to happen. What it does mean is that expected and anticipated inflation loses its stimulating effect unless it is allowed to accelerate unexpectedly and that at a later stage slowing down the rate of inflation has the same depressing effect on economic activity as stopping it altogether would have had earlier. This is, I believe the real meaning of stagflation: We have reached a stage of the process where an attempt to slow down the rate of inflation, or merely to reduce the rate of its acceleration, is bound to produce some slack and unemployment. If we do not act to curb inflation now, we would merely postpone the day of reckoning. Those who clamor for expansionary measures now in the midst of a two-digit inflation because we already experience some slack, simply close their eyes to the virtual certainty that if we follow their advice in a year's time the rate of inflation will be still higher and the pains of stopping inflation correspondingly greater.

Types of Inflation

In a sense monetary restraint is not only a necessary but also a sufficient condition for preventing or halting inflation—in the sense namely that any inflation, however caused, can be stopped or prevented by sufficiently tight money. Let me distinguish three types of inflation: (1) *Classical demand inflation*, monetary expansion in excess of what is needed to match the flow of real goods and services. The new money may be used to finance investment in the private sector and/or to finance a government deficit. This is what Keynes (in his *Treatise on Money*) called "profit inflation." (2) Cost or wage-push inflation due to union pressure and monopoly pricing; Keynes' "income inflation." (3) The so-called *new* inflation caused by real shortages such as a crop failure, the oil embargo and oil price rise imposed by OPEC, the disappearance of the anchovies off the coast of Peru and other factors depressing real GNP, either by reducing output or by worsening the international terms of trade. The different forces causing inflation often operate concurrently, but sometimes it is possible to find periods where the one or the other clearly dominates the picture.

Each of these different types of inflation can be stopped by monetary restraint, but the side effects will, of course, be different. For brevity I consider only short term side effects, primarily generalized effects on overall employment and output, mentioning sectoral side effects and long term effects on the rate of growth only in passing.

Demand Inflation

I now proceed to analyze the three cases. For demand inflation monetary restraint is the specific cure, especially if it involves the private sector. But even if demand inflation stems from a government deficit, it can be prevented or stopped by monetary policy. If money remains tight the budgetary deficit must be financed in a non-inflationary fashion by *borrowing from the public*. In that case it drives up interest rates and *crowds out* private investment. There are other methods of curbing a government deficit inflation. The deficit can be eliminated by raising taxes or by cutting government outlays. As far as the short run effect on overall employment and activity is concerned, there is probably not much to choose between the three methods—borrowing from the public, raising taxes or cutting expenditures. But the effects on specific sectors and on long run growth will differ, although they are not easy to evaluate; the outcome will depend among other things on the types of taxes that are raised and the expenditures that are cut.

Shortage Inflation

Before taking up the highly controversial but to my mind crucially important and pervasive cost or wage push inflation, I turn to the third type of inflation that is caused by shortages of important commodities, sharply driving up their prices. The surge of inflation in 1973 and 1974 is widely supposed to have been due to a large extent to three *special factors*—a poor crop, the oil price rise and the devaluation of the dollar (leaving out the anchovies). Tight money could have prevented the overall price level from rising, it is conceded, but only by driving down prices other than those of food, fuel and of imports; this surely would have caused a recession.

There is some truth in this analysis, but in my opinion the importance of the special factors has been greatly exaggerated.

The three special factors have in common that they imply a decrease in real GNP, or more precisely in the aggregate supply of goods and services. The enormous increase in the oil import bill by some $20 billion dollars a year means that we have to export so much more and forego other imports to pay for the oil; this reduces available supplies. The decrease in agricultural production constitutes a reduction of real GNP and, in addition, a substantial internal transfer of income from the urban population to the farmers. The depreciation of the dollar was necessary to eliminate a fundamental disequilibrium in the balance of payments. When the dollar was overvalued we had an external deficit, which permitted us to supplement domestic production by larger imports and smaller exports, in other words, we *lived beyond our means*. When the imbalance was corrected by the depreciation of the dollar we had to *tighten our belts* a little bit. The improvement of the current balance from 1972 to 1973 by over $10 billion can be regarded as a rough measure of that effect on aggregate supply. In addition there may have been a slight deterioration in the terms of trade over and above that caused by the rise in oil prices.

The total decrease in supplies caused by the three factors in a trillion dollar economy is, however, quite small, about 2 percent or a little more. It follows that if there had been no other sources of inflation—demand-pull and/or cost-push—in other words, if in the absence of the three *special factors* the price level would have remained stable—the shortfall of real GNP, of aggregate supply due to the operation of the three special factors would account for only a small rise in the price level, probably about 2 percent. The rest of the actual price rise must be attributed to the other sources of inflation. But whatever the magnitudes of the effect in question, it remains true in principle that in an economy with rigid money wages even a mild attempt at deflating the rest of the economy to compensate for the price rise of fuel, food and imports would produce some unemployment. An internal transfer of income from the urban population to the farmers would, in the presence of rigid wages and prices, have the same deflationary effect.

Wage Push

I now come to the second type of inflation, the cost or wage push inflation or *price-wage-price spiral*. This is an analytically and politically very difficult and controversial subject, but in my opinion an extremely important matter.

At the outset it should be observed that in a competitive economy with flexible wages and prices there would be no such thing as a cost or wage-push. Cost or wage-push inflation implies monopolies, or more generally absence of competition. I shall concentrate on labor monopolies, that is on labor unions. But what is said about the relation between inflation and labor monopolies holds in principle also of other monopolies. In my opinion, however, other monopolies or oligopolies, except in the public utility area, are of much lesser importance.[1]

What is of great importance, however, are the many ways in which government regulations, restrictions and subsidies keep or push prices up (or alternatively the political pressure groups which force the government to act as it does). In all too many cases where private producers are unable to organize themselves in effective monopolies, the government steps in and, in effect, makes them behave like a monopoly.[2] This can be achieved in many different ways: by import restrictions, including the imposition of anti-dumping or countervailing duties on imports, export subsidies, farm price supports, government-guaranteed loans to producers to prevent a fall in livestock prices, so called *voluntary* export restrictions forced on foreign producers of textiles, steel, and other commodities, regulation of wellhead prices of natural gas,[3] high minimum wages which cause unemployment among underprivileged workers, etc., Hendrik Houthakker[4] and Thomas Moore have presented a long list of such cases and evaluated their impact. But let me now concentrate on labor unions.

First a word on the attitude of economists. I believe that the majority of economists who have addressed themselves to the problem have reached the conclusion that in many democratic countries labor unions have become a major threat to price level stability. But there are some curious inversions of opinion. While one would expect conservative, laissez-faire economists to attribute to unions a share of the blame for inflation and socialist economists to take the opposite position, we find that monetarists, such as Milton Friedman, Harry Johnson, and their numerous followers here and in Great Britain absolve the unions of any responsibility for inflation. The conservative maverick British politician, Enoch Powell, takes the same position. On the other hand the left-wing economist, now Lord Balogh, thinks that British labor unions are largely responsible for the inflation, and many other socialist economists share his view.

In this matter I find myself on the opposite side of the fence from my monetarist friends. But let's not exaggerate the disagreement. There is agreement that a wage-push inflation, too, requires permissive monetary policy. There is also agreement that the recent militancy of unions in many countries is largely a consequence of prolonged inflation and that the upsurge of inflation in 1973 and 1974 was a demand inflation aggravated by shortages. It was *not* triggered by a wage explosion. On the contrary unions were taken by surprise as everybody else was and were surprisingly slow to react. There is, furthermore, agreement that a sudden increase in monopoly power of labor and business would push up the price level. This happened as Milton Friedman has pointed out on a large scale during the early years of the New Deal. The Wagner Act, AAA and NRA greatly strengthened the monopoly power of unions and fostered business monopolies. As a consequence an abnormally large part of the sharp increase in money GNP—aggregate expenditure—which occurred from 1933 to 1937 went into prices and a correspondingly small fraction into output and employment so that at the next cyclical peak in 1937 unemployment was still at the very high level of over 14 percent of the labor force. This was indeed an extreme case of a monopoly and wage push inflation in the midst of high unemployment.

What then is the disagreement about? It is this: Monetarists say there is no such thing as a *continuous* push on wages and costs by unions. When the monopoly or market power of unions is increased—as was the case in the early 1930s—there is a once-for-all increase in wage costs. Union wages will be higher, but if the monetary authorities stand firm, a new equilibrium will be established presumably with a greater spread between union and non-union wages.

Applied to the present situation monetarists will say—although I have not seen it spelled out in so many words—that there has recently been no increase in monopoly power similar to what happened in the early 1930s. Therefore, monetarists are optimistic: If monetary-fiscal policy is gradually tightened, unions will moderate their wage demands. It is acknowledged that a certain amount of transitional unemployment will be necessary to bring that about. But that would be the case, monetarists say, even if there were no unions. As far as the United States in particular is concerned, monetarists point out that only about 25 percent of the labor force is unionized and that this percentage has shown no tendency to go up.

This appraisal is, I am afraid, much too optimistic and complacent with respect to the United States and even more so for Great Britain and some other industrial countries. It is true that there have been no additional legal immunities and privileges granted to unions since the early New Deal. But it does not follow that there was no increase in the *monopoly* or *market* power of unions. There have been important changes in public policy and attitudes which have given the unions much more power than they used to have. For one thing, more liberal unemployment benefits and welfare payments make it much easier for unions to hold out in long strikes. It is no exaggeration to say that the government to a large extent finances strikes. (In some states even the strikers themselves are eligible for unemployment benefits, if the strike lasts longer than a set number of weeks.)

That only some 25 percent of production workers are unionized is misleading for two reasons: First, higher union wages obtained by threat of strike spread more or less rapidly to the rest of the labor force. Non-union firms are under pressure to match union wage increases for workers of similar skills; and, for reasons of maintaining morale and efficiency and to prevent unionization, employers find it necessary not to let the spread between union and nonunion wages and between wages of workers of different skill become too large. The second reason why the persisting low percentage of unionized labor is misleading, is that unionization has spread to groups that were not organized before—to public employees and officials in all levels of government—teachers, firemen, policemen, civil servants, and so on. It is undoubtedly true that these developments have been greatly stimulated, if not originally initiated, by inflation. But these changes are here to stay, even if inflation were reduced to a tolerable level.

The relentless push for higher wages is highlighted by the fact that it seems now to continue even in periods of unemployment. Recent mild recessions have only slowed down but not stopped the rise in money wages, and there are many cases on record of individual industries where despite substantial unemployment wages have been pushed up. If we add to this the innumerable government sponsored restriction and price boosting schemes and the mounting claims of the government itself on the economy, one is led to regard inflation as a method of reconciling and scaling down inconsistent claims on the national product advanced by various pressure groups.

Although this way of looking at inflation is not incompatible with monetarism, monetarists often reject it. They believe that a tolerable amount of unemployment for a not too lengthy period would be sufficient to induce unions and other pressure groups to moderate their demands. Some anti-monetarists take an equally relaxed position. James Tobin clearly sees the problem, but says complacently, "there are worse methods of resolving group rivalries and social conflicts than inflation." The inflation method has the great advantage that it works "blindly, impartially and nonpolitically,"[5] Tobin seems to visualize a steady, non-accelerating rate of inflation that keeps unemployment permanently at a lower level than would be possible with stable prices. But it is difficult to believe that the various pressure groups would not raise their monetary claims when they see their expectations again and again frustrated by inflation. This dilemma is being increasingly recognized. That is why we hear so much of social compacts and tax concessions to induce unions and possibly other pressure groups to moderate their demands.

On the other side there are pessimists such as George Terborgh and Friedrich Lutz. In a recent powerful paper Terborgh argued that monetary and fiscal policy, unaided by "other measures" of wage control, cannot cope with inflation, because they would create a socially intolerable amount of unemployment. He is alarmed, rightly in my opinion, that profits in real terms (after elimination of the inflationary element) are at a very low level and concludes that the distribution of personal incomes must be shifted "in favor of its nonwage components." He hints that this can be done only by some sort of wage restraints. But he ends on a rather pessimistic, if not fatalistic note: "There is at present nothing in sight to stop the wage explosion" which is now in progress.[6]

Lutz, too, believes that tight money does not prevent price increases any more but produces unemployment on top of inflation. The only way to solve the inflation problem would be to dissolve the pressure groups and make the economy more competitive. But only a strong government could do that and democracy is likely to perish in the process.[7]

Anti-Inflation Policies

In a recent book[8] I expressed the view that Lutz's pessimism was exaggerated. To illustrate that monetary restraint can only lead to stagflation, Lutz referred to what happened in the United States in 1969–1970. I pointed out that, although the recession was quite mild, inflation was reduced from about 6 percent in 1969 to 4 percent in 1970 and 3.3 percent in 1971. But now in the midst of a two-digit price inflation and a two-digit wage explosion I am no longer so sure that the pessimists are wrong. How can the wage rise be reduced to a level of, say, 5 percent that is compatible with stable prices? If, miraculously, inflation could be reduced first to 2–3 percent, unions would presumably moderate their wage demands correspondingly. But how can inflation be reduced when wages go up by over 12 percent? Indexing of wages or of anything else, whatever its long run merits, is of no help in an acute emergency—and the present situation can hardly be described differently. The same must be said, I am afraid, of cutting government expenditures. Although highly desirable in the longer run, it can hardly be done fast enough to make a substantial contribution to the fight against inflation now or next year. But there can be no doubt that in a broad anti-inflation package a firm program of cutting government expenditures would play a very useful psychological role to restore confidence.

Another part of an effective anti-inflation policy should be, as recently proposed by Hendrik Houthakker and Thomas Moore, a determined effort to overhaul the many policies by which the government restrains competition and props up prices burdening the great mass of consumers for the benefit of various small pressure groups. I am afraid, however, that this too is not likely to show quick results in the fight against inflation.

Money surely has to be kept tight and precipitate relaxation at the first sign of slack should be avoided. I do believe, however, that another fast-acting anti-inflationary medicine is needed. The only one I can think of is additional taxation, not for the purpose of financing additional expenditures, but to siphon off excess spending power. A tighter fiscal policy than can be achieved by waiting for government expenditures to be cut would have a favorable effect on capital and credit markets and would permit a relaxation of monetary policy and thus bring down interest rates. Raising additional government revenue would become all the more important, if taxes are reduced for low incomes and if billions of dollars are spent, as now seems likely, for public service employment. That taxes can be raised in many different ways could be turned to good use in negotiating an anti-inflation package with organized labor.

None of the measures mentioned so far solves the wage dilemma. It is politically impossible to have wage controls without price control and the whole system of controls has been thoroughly discredited.[9] Without the cooperation of organized labor any anti-inflation policy, whether it uses monetary or fiscal policy, would probably produce a socially and politically intolerable amount of unemployment; in fact, to be successful, it would have to rely on the wage-dampening effect of unemployment. By pointing out this danger it should be possible to get the cooperation of union leaders. They surely are aware of the dangers of inflation and the threat that inflation poses to the jobs is uppermost in their minds. Mr. I. W. Able, President of the United Steel Workers, was reported to have warned that unless labor moderates its wage demands, the economy might "go to hell." In working out an anti-inflation program with the unions concessions in the tax area could be very useful.

But some temporary increase in slack and unemployment, in one word, a recession, hopefully a mild one, is the price we have to pay for stabilization. This burden can be reduced, but not entirely avoided, by union cooperation.

There are economists who believe that a properly designed anti-inflation policy which relies more on fiscal and less on monetary policy can achieve a smooth transition to stable prices. They point to the fact that in Germany the hyperinflation after World War I, as well as the repressed inflation after World War II, could in the end be quickly stopped without causing a recession.[10] In fact, in both cases stabilization was followed by rapid expansion.

This argument overlooks the essential difference between the present inflation and the two cases mentioned. The post World War I inflation in Germany, France, and other European countries was a typical demand or profit inflation with wages lagging behind prices. Such an inflation is easy to stop with monetary and fiscal policies without serious side effects on employment. After World War II, on the other hand, tight controls had suppressed the symptoms of inflation, but strangled economic activity in the process. When in 1948 the money overhang was eliminated by the monetary reform, Ludwig Erhard abolished, at one stroke, the controls. Naturally, the economy reacted by rapid and sustained expansion.

Our present inflation is entirely different; it has by now become a cost inflation. This is often described by saying that "excess demand has been squeezed out of the system"—a very misleading description; for aggregate demand in the sense of total monetary expenditure is still excessive, that is, grows faster than output. What has been squeezed (not *squeezed out*, but reduced excessively) is profits—a fact which is obscured by the inflationary distortion of the profit figures. This type of inflation is much more intractable than either a pure demand inflation or a repressed inflation.

Some International Aspects of Inflation

In conclusion let me say a few words, mainly from the American standpoint, about some international aspects of inflation. I have discussed inflation as an internal, homemade, American problem. However, the alarming acceleration of inflation of the last two years has been conspicuously international in character. The money managers in many countries have made good use of this fact. They have, if I may repeat what I have said elsewhere, blamed other countries and anonymous international markets for what has happened, as if the inflation bacillus had flown in from outer space. The truth is that despite its international character inflation can be stopped only by national policies in each country.

But can a single country conquer its inflation unless its principal trade partners go along? In other words, is it possible for any one country to become or remain an island of price stability in an inflationary world? The short answer is with fixed exchanges, no, with flexible exchange rates, yes. Let me elaborate a little.

Obviously it is easier for a large country than for a small one to get out and to stay out of an inflationary world trend. For the United States I have no doubt that we could go it alone, if necessary. Suppose we were able sharply to reduce the rate of inflation. All those countries—some twenty of them—which still peg to the dollar more or less rigidly and routinely would have the choice either to disinflate along with us or to let their currencies depreciate. Probably quite a few would go along, but others would find it difficult to keep in step and would prefer to let their currencies depreciate (either cleanly and openly or dirtily, disguised by controls). If inflation continues in the outside world or if our inflation rate comes down faster than in most other countries, the dollar will appreciate because our trade balance will improve and foreign capital, including oil money, will be attracted. The improvement in the trade balance is an inflationary factor, but thanks to floating, the appreciation of the dollar would contain and neutralize the inflationary impact of rising exports.

This statement requires, however, a small qualification. Because the dollar is still the world's foremost reserve currency—foreign central banks and other official institutions hold close to $70 billion as reserves—there is a theoretical possibility that we might be subjected to inflationary pressures from abroad. Suppose many countries find it difficult to restrain their inflation and get into balance of payments troubles. They could then be tempted to use their dollar reserves to finance their deficits (our surplus)—and alleviate thereby their own inflation. In other words, they might take the opportunity to *re-export* the inflation to us which we had *exported* to them when we had our large deficits. The potential threat would be greater, if the monetary gold price were raised to conform to the free market level and if the United States were called upon to finance other countries' oil deficits by accepting their gold, by liberal foreign lending through swaps, *special oil facilities* arranged by the IMF, IBRD or any other of the innumerable international organizations.

The danger is, however, hypothetical and remote. We have not yet solved our inflation problem and if and when we do dollar holdings will become more attractive. The largest foreign dollar holders are not likely to go on a spending spree.

To put the problem in proper perspective let me add one further observation. If this contingency ever arises, it would not be the consequence of a malfunctioning of floating exchange rates, but on the contrary the result of an attempt to prevent the floating system from working. Collectively foreign dollar holders have it in their power, for a period of time, to stabilize the dollar exchange rate.

I repeat, the danger that we will be put under serious inflationary pressure from abroad is remote. But this does not mean that there is nothing to worry about in the world economy. Far from it. There are many highly dangerous trouble spots. To mention only two, the deepening economic crisis of Great Britain and Italy is a frightening development.

But let us mind our business first. If we can regain stability we give a good example to others and we will be in a better position to help them.

Notes

Originally published in *Business Economics*, Vol. 10, No. 1 (January 1975), pp. 12–18.

1. This is discussed at greater length in my book, *Economic Growth and Stability: An Analysis of Economic Change and Policy* Los Angeles, Nash Publishing Co. 1974, pp. 112–116.
2. It is, of course, not claimed that the government-sponsored restriction and price maintenance schemes operate exactly as well organized producer monopolies would. What these public policies have in common with private monopolies is that they restrict output, raise prices above the competitive level and make them rigid downward.

3. This particular policy resembles a monopsony rather than a monopoly, because it keeps the price below the competitive level in the interest of a certain group of consumers. But it restricts output and has, therefore, on balance an inflationary effect.
4. "A Positive Way to Fight Inflation," *Wall Street Journal*, July 30, 1974.
5. See his presidential address, "Inflation and Unemployment," *American Economic Review*, 1973, p. 13.
6. George Terborgh, *Control of Home-Grown Inflation,* Machinery and Allied Products Institute. Washington, DC: MAPI 1974 (Mimeographed). Two important recent monographs take the same position. Emerson P. Schmidt, *Union Power and the Public Interest.* Los Angeles: Dutton. 1973; W. H. Hutt *The Strike-Threat System: The Economic Consequences of Collective Bargaining*, New Rochelle, NY: Mises Institute, 1973.
7. Friedrich Lutz, "Dilemmasituationen Nationsler Anti-inflations politik" in 25 Jahre *Marktwirtschaft in der Bundesrepublik Deutschland.* Stuttgart 1972.
8. *Op. cit.,* p. 116.
9. But if inflation continues we can be sure that the clamor for imposition of general price and wage controls will again become very strong and perhaps irresistible. Too many legislators, economists and journalists have still not learned their lesson. They are unaware or ignore the fact that the country which has the lowest inflation rate—West Germany—has strongly resisted the temptation to impose any price or wage controls, even under the government of the Social Democratic Party.
10. See for example, J. K. Galbraith, "Inflation: A Presidential Catechism," *The New York Times Magazine*, September 15, 1974.

CHAPTER 10

1975

THE PRACTICAL USE OF ECONOMIC ANALYSIS IN INVESTMENT MANAGEMENT

Edmund A. Mennis, Security Pacific National Bank

The use of economic analysis in investment management has grown considerably in recent years. I believe further significant expansion lies ahead as financial analysts develop greater skills in economic analysis and these analyses are integrated more into the investment decision process. Prior to a discussion of the practical uses of economic analysis, however, the purposes of financial analysis need to be considered.

Objective of Financial Analysis

The ultimate objective of financial analysis is the determination of appropriate investments for portfolios with properly defined risk and return characteristics. This objective is often obscured because many organizations and financial analysts participate in only a part of the decision-making process. The functions of both security research and portfolio management are not necessarily performed in every investment organization. Financial analysis is itself a specialized world, and many other specialists provide services to those engaged in investment analysis and management. Economists ordinarily operate on the periphery of the investment decision process and rarely are an integral part of it. Only in large organizations can most of these specialists be housed under one roof. Therefore, an overview of the investment decision process leading to the ultimate objective of selecting investments for a portfolio may clarify the areas in which the economist can make a contribution.

The Investment Decision Process

Exhibit 10.1 outlines a fully integrated approach to portfolio management that we have found most effective. This approach divides the investment decision process into three broad areas: inputs for investment decisions, policy decisions applicable to all portfolios managed and finally decisions and actions applied to each particular portfolio managed.

The box on the left portion of the chart indicates the types of information needed for policy decisions and effective portfolio management. The basis of this information is projections of the economic environment, both long- and short-term, in which investment decisions will be made. From these projections, expectations for long- and short-term interest rates are derived, which really require consideration of the whole fixed-income sector of the financial markets. The economic projections also provide the basis for estimates of corporate profits. These profit estimates, in turn, are used to estimate earnings of the various stock-market averages, such as the Standard & Poor's and the Dow Jones Industrials. The application of appropriate multiples to these averages provides value estimates for the stock-market averages, against which current prices can be compared. Finally, the economic projections and expectations for the fixed-income and equity sectors of the securities markets are essential inputs for the industry studies and company analyses prepared by security analysts where earnings and their valuations are key elements.

The center box on the chart indicates the policy decisions that must be made. These decisions are the guidelines established for all of the portfolios under management. Usually they are made by a committee or by senior investment executives, although some decisions may be delegated to the individual portfolio manager. The first policy decision is the determination of the probable future economic environment and the expected path of the financial markets, both near and long term. This decision involves a review of the economic and securities-markets projections and alternatives submitted by the staff. Second, the objectives for various types of portfolios managed must be considered, particularly if the accounts are large in number and varied in objectives. The third area of policy decisions is portfolio diversification. Portfolio assets may be broadly classified into riskless assets with a known fixed return, investments with a fixed contractual return and investments with a variable return. Ordinarily, we are concerned with portfolios that contain short-term debt instruments, bonds and stocks, although other types of investments may be included in appropriate categories. Given the assessment of the economic and market environment, the returns expected from alternative investments, the time horizon for investment and the risk that can be assumed for various types of accounts, investment policy can then be established with respect to asset selection and portfolio distribution among riskless assets, fixed-income securities and variable income securities. Finally, within the equity portion of the portfolio, the diversification by industry or economic sector categories should be determined.

The box on the right side of the chart indicates the functions performed by the individual portfolio manager. Utilizing the inputs and direction provided to him, he should first formulate objectives and risk assumptions for each account he manages.

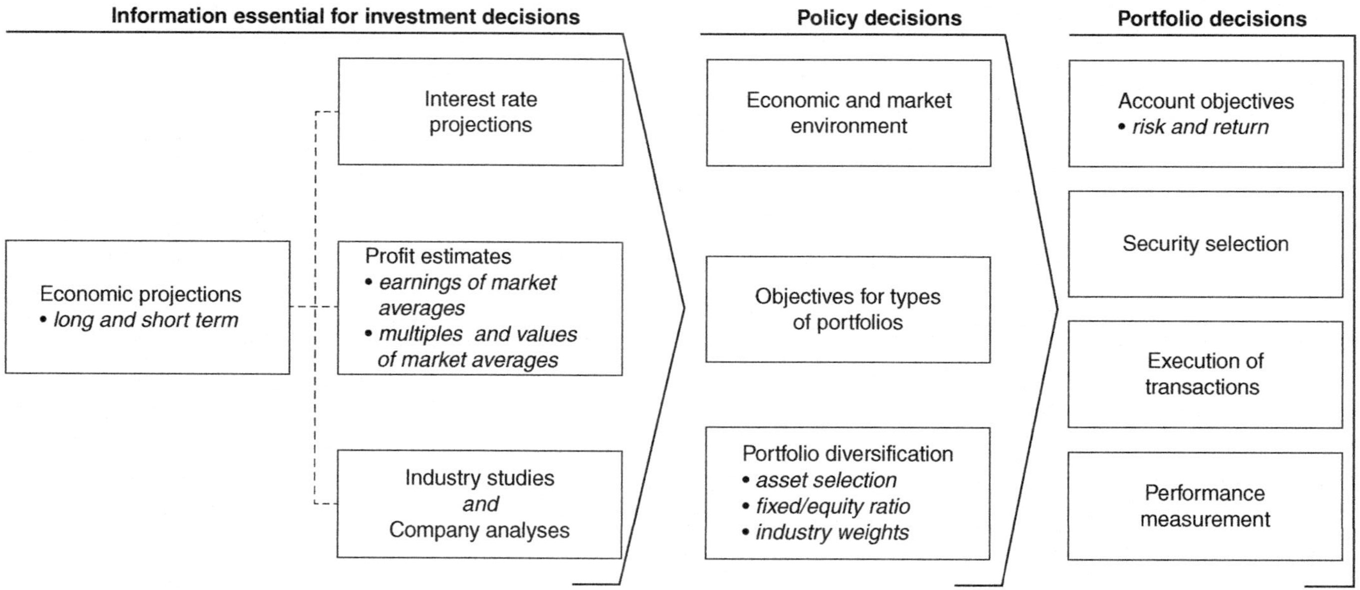

INSTITUTIONAL INVESTMENT MANAGEMENT DEPARTMENT SECURITY PACIFIC NATIONAL BANK

EXHIBIT 10.1 The investment decision process.

Within the portfolio diversification guidelines given, he should then select and time the purchases and sales of investments for the portfolio. He is also responsible for supervising the execution of these transactions. The final step in the process is the monitoring of portfolio decisions in order to ascertain whether the objectives of the individual accounts have been achieved.

Individual versus Institutional Investment

Institutional investing involves management problems different from those of managing relatively small individual portfolios. Institutions manage large sums of money, many accounts with varying investment objectives, or both. Requirements for managing institutional portfolios are, therefore, much more complex than for small individual portfolios. Moreover, the kinds of securities that institutions can purchase differ from those available to the individual investor. Many areas of fixed-income investment are either not open to individual investors or the expense to participate is prohibitive. On the other hand, the large amounts that institutions have to invest and requirements of marketability and liquidity limit the number and kinds of stocks that an institution can purchase.

The resources available to institutions are normally large, requiring a substantial staff of economists, analysts and portfolio managers, together with computer and other facilities needed for a large investment operation. An organizational structure must be established that will blend together the professional talents of these many people in order to achieve successful investment results. The organization must have flexibility to adjust to changing economic and market conditions and also the perspective to manage many kinds of portfolios in a complex economic and market environment. Finally, and most important, an institution must develop a system of controls that will insure uniformity of performance for the various accounts managed within the differing portfolio objectives that exist.

Although economic input should not be ignored in managing individual portfolios, the complexity of institutional investment requires greater use of economic analysis and gives such analysis its broadest scope. Therefore, this chapter will discuss economic analysis in the framework of institutional rather than individual investment.

Economic Projections

Investment is ultimately the purchase of economic performance. Therefore, economic assumptions are needed for several purposes. They indicate the environment in which investments are made. They point up the profitability of alternative investment media. Industry and company earnings are affected by the economic environment, both domestic and international, in which they operate as well as by particular sectors of economic activity. Assumptions about the economy are important in projecting corporate earnings. These broad general uses of economic projections indicate the form and content of the economic inputs needed for investment.

First, however, let me state my conviction that the best use of an economist is *not* the production of neat statistical tables covering national income account data, industrial production, prices, profits, and interest rates. As financial analysts, we have a tendency to be preoccupied with numbers and to expect that quantification somehow equals accuracy and precision. More important than the numbers are the qualitative evaluation and assumptions that precede their preparation.

In this connection, the economist's role might be compared to that of a skilled taxicab driver. When you arrive at Los Angeles International Airport and you wish to go to the Hotel Biltmore downtown, the taxi driver's job is to get you there quickly, safely and as inexpensively as possible. His job is not to take you to the Beverly Hilton, nor to persuade you that your destination is Disneyland.

The point of this analogy is that, prior to any quantification of the economic outlook, certain assumptions have to be made, and these are best made jointly with the economist, or at least discussed with him. These assumptions may vary from time to time, and they are critical to the results he will provide you. For example, what is the current cyclical status of the economy and how does it compare with or differ from previous cycles? What will government fiscal and monetary policy be? What will be the dimensions of the energy program and what will be its timing? What are your general expectations for consumer and business spending? What will corporations do about inventories and prices? What significant changes might occur in the international picture that could affect the domestic economy? In this interchange of ideas, both the investment manager and the economist contribute to each other.

When these assumptions are agreed upon, the economist-taxi driver can then tell you their economic implications. We have found it useful at this stage to set forth in qualitative terms not just one path for the economy near term but at least three possible paths. For each path we outline possible monetary and fiscal policies, inflation and unemployment rates, prices, consumer and business spending actions, business inventory changes and construction spending. The investment policy committee then considers, with the economist, any adjustments deemed necessary to these assumptions and assesses the probability of each economic alternative. Then the economist prepares the statistical quantification of these assumptions. These short-term projections for the next four to six quarters are used as the basis for deciding on portfolio strategy and also determining the near-term attractiveness of individual securities for inclusion in the portfolio.

In addition to preparing economic assumptions and statistical data for the next four to six calendar quarters, it is strongly recommended that longer term projections be made, say for a period three to five years out from the current period. These long-term projections are most useful to permit evaluation of the longer term investment climate, as well as to consider broad investment alternatives and the returns to be received from them. In addition, these projections are used as the basis for preparation of earnings trends for industries and companies. The same techniques and alternatives used in preparing short-term assumptions can be applied to the longer term projections as well.

What are the specific items we estimate after the initial assumptions have been agreed upon? At a minimum they include gross national product and its components in both current and constant dollars, personal income, disposable personal income and personal savings, the unemployment rate, the Federal Reserve Board index of industrial production and its major components. Other useful economic data include automobile production and sales, construction activity, business spending plans and a projection of price indexes, such as the major components of the wholesale price index and the consumer price index, as well as the GNP deflator.

Financial Flows

After the broad economic projections are prepared, their implications for interest rates can be estimated. Interest rate projections are used in investment management for a variety of purposes, the most obvious of which is the determination of the relative attractiveness of bond versus stock investment. Both long- and short-term rates do have an impact on the stock market. In addition, the level of short-term rates will indicate the risk-free return obtainable on any cash reserves held in an account. Interest rate projections are also useful in evaluating the shares of financial enterprises and of non-financial industries such as utilities that are sensitive to movements in interest rates. Bond yields may also be compared with yields available from stocks where current income is an investment consideration.

What interest rates should be projected? We have found it helpful to project both long- and short-term rates, and to predict them for both the long- and short-term economic estimates that we have prepared. The rates we use are those for Moody's seasoned AAA bonds, AA new issue utilities, Bond Buyers index, Treasury bills, commercial paper and the prime rate. Estimates for the levels of these rates will also require the discipline of reviewing the yield spreads between these types of securities for internal consistency.

Even more interesting analyses in the financial area can be made based on the flow-of-funds information provided by the Federal Reserve System. These data indicate the flow of funds by economic sector and also by type of instrument and give useful insights into the structure of the mortgage market, business borrowing, government borrowing, and household lending. The capability of doing detailed analyses such as those so ably prepared by Salomon Bros, and Bankers Trust Company may well be outside the capability of most investment organizations. On the other hand, the work of others can be used and modified in order to obtain further helpful insights into the financial environment.

Corporate Profits

One of the most important analyses that the economist can prepare and the most valuable contribution he can make to the investment process is to provide estimates of corporate profits and interpret the impact of macroeconomic developments on the outlook for profits. Of course, the profits data in the national income accounts are not particularly reliable nor directly comparable to earnings as reported by corporations to shareholders. Nevertheless, the exercise required to prepare estimates for this profit series can give considerable insight into price changes, non-labor costs, labor productivity and compensation, taxes, the impact of policy decisions on profits and the trend of profits related to gross national product. Although not especially reliable, the national income account profits series recently did focus the attention of financial analysts on the significance of inventory profits, the importance of FIFO and LIFO inventory policies and the quality of corporate earnings.

Such an overall view can provide most useful insights into the economic factors that will impact the earnings of particular industries and companies. These aggregate profit estimates, as I have indicated earlier, can be used in preparing estimates of the earnings for the various stock market indexes, which in turn can be used to prepare value ranges and estimates for stock prices.

International Environment

Another area where the economist can make a significant contribution is in the analysis of the international environment; that is, the economies of major industrialized countries and the possible impact of changes in these economies on American corporations and American security prices. This analysis should not only cover the United States and foreign balance of payments, but also trends in production, prices, interest rates, and labor costs abroad. Such analysis is useful in evaluating the potential competition of American companies or the operations of their international subsidiaries. Changes in our balance of payments may result in restrictions on foreign investment; changes in interest rates and currency fluctuations may impact international money flows and the overseas earnings of American companies. Finally, investment is becoming more international in scope, with securities of foreign companies finding a place in United States portfolios, and a substantial flow of foreign investment funds may come to the United States. Such a flow could have an important impact on our securities markets.

The kind of economic research in the international field may differ from that done for the domestic economy. Lack of available data or staff may preclude comprehensive analysis, but foreign periodicals and statistical reports can be helpful. In addition, much useful information can be provided by reports and personal contacts with research organizations and banks, both in the United States and abroad. This information should be integrated into the preparation of economic assumptions and also be provided to the research staff to assist them in the evaluation of their industries and companies.

Caveats

Certain caveats should be kept in mind in the preparation and use of economic assumptions. The primary purpose of this type of analysis is to determine what the probable path of the economy *will* be, not what it *should* be. The economist in an investment organization is not advising for either corporate or government policy, and his views on what should be done may be of interest but are of limited importance. His most valuable contribution is his assessment of the probable outcome of particular assumptions that are agreed upon beforehand.

Secondly, economic projections should be monitored and reviewed on a continuing basis, not changed only at calendar intervals. Forecasting quarterly or semiannually may result in following clearly wrong assumptions for a considerable period of time to the detriment of investment judgments. A significant change in final demand, such as occurred in the fall of 1974, clearly calls for a reappraisal of the economic outlook. A drought or an oil embargo are also unpredictable variables that must be immediately evaluated. Flexibility and willingness to change are vital if economic analysis is to have any value.

A third suggestion is that, when economic projections are prepared and agreed upon, they be used uniformly throughout the organization at the policy and analytical level. Only in this way can uniform investment decisions be reached and uniform and consistent results be achieved for your clients.

Certain cross-checks may be useful in order to determine whether economic assumptions are being followed or, alternatively, whether the information from the staff suggests a modification of the economic outlook. One is to aggregate corporate profits by companies and industries and compare the totals with profits estimates prepared by the economist. Another cross-check is to aggregate sales and earnings of companies by economic sectors, such as consumer durables, non-durables and services, capital investment, construction, interest sensitive, and energy related. These aggregates may be compared with the expectations for that economic sector in order to determine whether internal consistency has been achieved.

Uses of Economic Analysis

Although the previous comments have suggested areas where economic analysis may be useful and woven into the investment decision process, it may be helpful to conclude with a few more specific illustrations.

Can economic analysis and forecasting be helpful in predicting the stock market? Although ultimately stock prices reflect the earnings trends of companies and, therefore, economic analysis may assist in indicating the trend in stock prices, predicting the shorter term movements of stock prices from economic data may not always be successful. In the first place, non-economic forces—political, psychological, and social—may have a more immediate impact on stock prices. Secondly, economic data are frequently revised and current information is not always reliable, which provides a somewhat uncertain base from which to predict the immediate future with confidence. Thirdly, stock prices are a leading indicator of business activity, so that you need to predict business conditions accurately and sufficiently far ahead to anticipate the future path of the stock market. Some success has been achieved in relating certain economic variables to stock prices, such as interest rates, the money supply, profits, industrial production, and inflation and unemployment rates. However, these factors are not consistently successful and the relationship may vary from cycle to cycle. Consequently, relying on economic data or projections alone is not likely to lead to successful short-term stock market forecasting.

An area where economic inputs can be more useful is in the determination of portfolio diversification. As I have indicated earlier, the economist together with the investment manager can prepare alternative economic assumptions and the expected returns for riskless assets, intermediate- and long-term bonds and common stocks consistent with each of these economic alternatives. The investment policy committee or the portfolio manager can then decide the risk premium necessary to induce the shift of funds from riskless assets into either bonds or stocks. Historical risk premiums can be examined and tempered by either the economic assumptions or judgment of the conditions of the securities markets and the types of accounts managed. With this information available, probabilities can be assessed of achieving each economic alternative and of achieving more-than-required returns from bonds and stocks. The results will then indicate the probabilities of superior performance in each market and assist in selecting the appropriate portfolio mix. The advantage of this approach is that it makes explicit the assumptions made in determining the appropriate portfolio mix, taking into account the economic alternatives, the expected returns from alternative investments and the risk premiums required to shift investments from riskless assets.

Another use of economic analysis at the policy level is determining equity diversification by industry. We have divided the 500 stocks in the S & P index into 40 industry groupings and classified these industries into appropriate economic sectors. Depending upon the outlook for each economic sector, the weighting of that group of industries in the S & P index and the expected relative market performance for that group of stocks, we can decide whether we are willing to expose the portfolio to the specific risk of either a heavier or lighter weighting than the market weighting in that particular sector.

Economic analysis and projections are also useful to the analyst in preparation of industry and company studies. Economic projections, either in total or for certain special sectors of the economy, can be very helpful guides in making estimates of sales volume and in estimating changes in factors affecting costs and prices and, therefore, profit margins. With his broader perspective, the economist can evaluate the economic and political forces affecting price and wage trends, productivity, tax changes, interest costs and other factors that influence corporate profitability.

Conclusion

Economic analysis can be most effective if it is fully integrated into the investment decision process. The economist has a broader perspective and an analytical training similar to that of the financial analyst. He can provide a most useful understanding of the environment in which companies operate, both domestically and internationally. He can explain the impact of alternative economic policies. He can contribute to the understanding of financial markets. He can view investments from a *macro* approach rather than the *micro* approach of the analyst, who is preoccupied with individual company data. His contribution can be significant if organized and used properly. He can be an important member of the investment team rather than an occasional contributor of economic information. I commend to you a greater use of his important services.

Note

Originally published in *Business Economics*, Vol. 10, No. 4 (September 1975), pp. 38–44.

References

1. Sidney Cottle, Mennis, Edmund A., and Schuelke, Mary, "Corporate Earnings—Long Term Outlook and Valuation" and Mennis, Edmund A. and Cottle, Sidney, "Corporate Earnings—Short Term Outlook and Valuation," *Financial Analysts Journal*, vol. 27, no. 4, (July–August 1971), pp. 22–25 and 50–64.
2. Edmund A. Mennis, "Economics and Investment Management," *Financial Analysts Journal*, vol. 22, no. 6 (November–December 1966), pp. 17–23.
3. Edmund A. Mennis, "An Integrated Approach to Portfolio Management," *Financial Analysts Journal*, vol. 30, no. 2 (March–April 1974), pp. 38–46 and 86.
4. Edmund A. Mennis, "Forecasting Corporate Profits," a chapter in Methods *and Techniques of Business Forecasting*, ed. William F. Butler, Robert A. Kavesh, and Robert B. Platt (Englewood Cliffs, NJ: Prentice-Hall, 1974), pp. 517–542.
5. Edmund A. Mennis, "The Survey and the Financial Analyst," *Survey of Current Business*, vol. 51, no. 7, part II, July 1971 (Washington, DC: Government Printing Office), pp. 126–128.
6. Roy E. Moor, "Portfolio Economics," *The Bankers Magazine*, vol. 157, no. 3 (Summer 1974), pp. 66–73.
7. Roy E. Moor, "Aggregate Profits vs. Company Profits," *Business Economics*, vol. VII, no. 1 (January 1972), pp. 67–69.
8. Robert B. Platt, "Forecasting Industry Profits," *Business Economics*, vol. IX, no. 1 (January 1974), pp. 47–50.
9. Gary Wenglowski, "Industry Profit Forecasting," *Business Economics*, vol. VII, no. 1 (January 1972), pp. 61–66.

CHAPTER 11

1979

PRESIDENTIAL ADDRESS

ON HUMAN WELFARE

Albert G. Matamoros, Armstrong Cork Co.

Before preparing my remarks for today's meeting, I reviewed the titles of all the Presidential Addresses delivered at Annual NABE Meetings. Almost without exception, they have dealt, quite appropriately, with the role of the business economist. Last year, in New Orleans, Frank Schott developed the rationale for a program of continuing education that would be designed to keep the business economist on top of the latest developments within the profession with the objective of strengthening individual effectiveness. The year before, Peter Max made common sense appeal to business economists to become more concerned with and involved in the allocation processes within their organizations. The broader role of the business economist in helping to lift the level of economic literacy was set forth by Gil Heebner in his Presidential Address in 1976.

As important as it is continuously to assess our role as business economists, I think it is equally imperative that we step back, from time to time, and examine still broader issues. Today I want to raise some questions regarding the extent to which economic policies and the consequent actions of the agencies of government during the past 15 years have contributed to the human condition. It is not only appropriate, but I think mandatory, that, as social scientists, we be concerned for man's welfare and his destiny. Albert Einstein, who was born 100 years ago, held that this concern, "ought to be at the center of scientific inquiry and endeavor."

I think of human welfare as being comprised of several components: individual freedom, justice, participative democracy, esthetics, peace within and among individuals, and, of course, economic well-being.

It is this last-mentioned component of human welfare, economic well-being, that has been the focal point of analysis and prescription by the welfare economists.

This is not to suggest that business economists have not been concerned with the conditions which determine the total economic welfare of our world and national communities. But while we have been addressing ourselves to the outlook for interest rates, automobile demand, housing starts and the role of the business economist, the welfare economist has been grappling with, to use the words of Oscar Lange, "the problem of maximization of total welfare." Moreover, while the business economist has been testifying before Congressional committees on individual bills and sometimes narrow issues on an *ad hoc* basis, the welfare economist has been influencing the formulation of basic policies.

Who have been the principal contributors to welfare economics? Evan Bitsaxis in a book entitled *Welfare Versus Freedom,* identifies Vilfredo Pareto as the "brain," Pigou "the pioneer," John Maynard Keynes, "the giant," Joan Robinson, Kenneth Arrow, Abram Bergson, I. M. D. Little, Paul Samuelson, "the analysts," John Hicks, "the skeptic," John Kenneth Galbraith, "the iconoclast," and "the composer," William J. Baumol. You will recall that, following Pareto, much of the theory of welfare economics derived from the basic notion that, in society, if one person is better off, and no one is worse off, welfare is enhanced. This, of course, posed the problem of the inter-personal comparability of utility. Lange argued that the total welfare of a community "has to be defined not as the sum of the utilities of the individuals (a scalar quantity) but as a vector." Bergson, too, was worried about the problem of welfare maximization insofar as it involves the measurement of utility losses by some and utility gains by others. As John C. Harsanyi put it in an article in the *Journal of Political Economy* in 1955, Bergson was troubled with "the naive concept of social welfare as a sum of intuitively measurable and comparable individual cardinal utilities." He, Bergson, argued for a more general concept of a social welfare function, "defined as an arbitrary mathematical function of economic (and other social) variables, of a form freely chosen according to one's personal ethical (or political) value judgments." P. A. Samuelson went one step further in his "Aspects of Public Expenditure Theories" appearing in *Review of Economics and Statistics,* November 1958, where he observed that "given a social welfare function, and given the absence of all technological and taste externalities, and given universal constant returns to scale, there would be needed only one type of public policy—redistributive transfers."

The Central Government

An enhanced role for the central government is at the heart of most of the prescriptions written by the welfare economists. The State as the "ethical observer" or the "impartial referee" should have as its paramount concern the correction of inequality in income and wealth. Abba Lerner in his *Economics of Control, Principles of Welfare Economics,* published in 1944, minces no words when he says, "we shall assume a government that wishes to run society in the general interest and is strong enough to override the opposition afforded by any sectional interest." While Lerner by that time had come to the view that private enterprise ought to be preserved, he nevertheless held that under conditions of imperfect competition or monopoly, there was no other alternative but to collectivize. He made the case for nationalizing industries where perfect competition is clearly impossible and specifically in those instances where marginal costs are below average costs. He thought it possible, indeed even desirable, that public and private enterprises compete in the marketplace with all guided by the requirement that they equate price and marginal cost.

Central to the thought of the welfare economist is the notion that there are individuals insightful enough to arrive at a social welfare function and beneficent enough to prescribe the appropriate policies. Running through the literature of welfare economics is the suggestion that if the purpose of policy is to maximize welfare, then some constraints on individual choice are required. At the same time, the recurring emphasis is not on efficiency in production or how we could produce more with our existing resources but rather on how we can more equitably distribute the fruits of production.

The results of the policies, the roots of which lie deep in the theories of welfare economics are so glaring they are recognized by all of us, by members of Congress on both sides of the aisle, and, indeed, by observers on both sides of the Atlantic. Most obvious has been the growth of government, not only in absolute and relative dollar terms, but even more importantly as an intrusive force impinging on private property rights and individual freedoms. Most tragically, the "benefits" deriving from attempts at the redistribution of money income and the establishment of agencies and programs designed to protect us from ourselves have fallen far short of the associated money and psychic costs.

The most apparent cost has been escalating inflation which, in the words of Martin J. Bailey in an article entitled "The Welfare Cost of Inflationary Finance" appearing in the *Journal of Political Economy* (1956) is a tax on the holding of cash balances, a cost which is fully analogous to the welfare cost (or "excess burden") of an excise tax on a commodity or productive service. Bailey establishes that the theoretical analysis of the welfare cost of open inflation is a reasonably straightforward extension of the theory of the welfare cost of an excise tax. In a more recent analysis, "The Welfare Cost of Permanent Inflation and Optimal Short-Run Economic Policy" (NBER Working Paper No. 201, September 1977), Martin Feldstein concludes, as had Bailey, that "inflation imposes an implicit tax on money balances." Feldstein challenges those economists who have argued that the welfare loss of fully anticipated inflation is so small that there is a strong case for using expansionary macroeconomic policy to lower unemployment rates even if this results in a permanent increase in the rate of inflation. Treating the unemployment-inflation tradeoff question as a dynamic optimization problem, Feldstein concludes, "If a temporary reduction in unemployment causes a permanent increase in inflation, the present value of the resulting future welfare costs may well exceed the contemporary shortrun gain."

Turning for a moment to what I have referred to as the psychic costs associated with the proliferating programs rooted in the theories of welfare economics, I am impressed by observations made by William J. McGill, President, Columbia University, just about a year ago. In an address entitled "Simple Justice and Existential Victims," McGill points out that "Many of our current social policies seem to me not directed toward the goal of a productive society offering maximum opportunity for self-realization. They are directed instead at alleviating a wide range of perceived grievances and perceived tensions via increased benefits, special legal protections, and improved social services. The cost of policy is measured, not in money alone, but in exaggerated forms of dependency." He goes on to say, "We must begin to devise social policies and concepts of public need that are genuinely humane to those genuinely in want, but that are not also so attractive as to foster uncontrollable growth of the victimization phenomenon . . . Under great political pressure, we have tended in recent years to overprovide, ignoring the danger of increasing numbers of dependent, neurotic victims."

Welfare Payments

I believe that as economic policies, the laws of our land and social practice encourage the growth in the number of "existential victims," depending for their support on an ever shrinking proportion of the productive public, the threat to America's potential to survive becomes ever more ominous. The division between producers and nonproducers is clearly deepening. As economists, we observe that the ratio of transfer payments to total personal after-tax income has climbed sharply in the past ten years. The wage-earning man on the street, without benefit of the relevant data, has a feeling his pocket is being picked. It is no mystery why a tax rebellion was born in California, where, on average, income maintenance payments per person run about 30 percent above the national average.

For all state and local governments, expenditures on public welfare are approaching $35 billion, up from less than $15 billion in 1970. Federal outlays for public welfare at the beginning of this decade were something over $10 billion; today they are almost $50 billion. Add to this another $95 billion in Social Security and Railroad Retirement payments in the fiscal year ended September 30, 1978, and we arrive at total Federal outlays for income security of close to $150 billion, compared to a little over $60 billion in fiscal 1973.

As a percent of total Federal outlays, expenditures on income security stood at 32 percent in fiscal 1978. This contrasts with the 23 percent of budget outlays for national defense in the same year. Remember, the $150 billion paid out for income security last year does *not* include roughly $50 billion spent for health, education and other welfare.

Over the past five years, that is, from fiscal 1973 to fiscal 1978, the fastest growing major components of the income security spending category have been Social Security payments, up almost twofold during the period ($46 billion to more than $90 billion) and Medicare outlays, almost triple (from something over $9 billion to more than $25 billion). At the end of that same period, despite dramatic growth in civilian employment during recent years, there were roughly three working persons for every one receiving Old Age Survivor and Health Insurance benefits. And herein lies the seeds of a potentially dangerous distinction.

When the economy was growing vigorously in real terms from the early 1960s to 1973, there was no loud outcry against Great Society programs. As the economic pie grew larger, it seemed appropriate to many, indeed compassionate, to serve a larger slice to the disadvantaged. But the pie shrank in 1974 and 1975, and, despite three years of recovery and expansion since, during which large annual additions to employment have been made, the growth of real product simply has not been fast enough to keep pace with a proliferation of transfer payments. Here are just a few more numbers to illustrate my point. Between 1969 and 1973 (peak to peak), real disposable personal income per capita rose almost 16 percent. Five years later, in 1978, real disposable personal income per capita stood scarcely more than 9 percent higher, and the principal impetus to the overall growth of personal after-tax income was given by transfer payments themselves.

Frustration and irritability on the part of the producing public as they perceive their piece of the pie not getting any larger, while the non-producer appears to be receiving more generous slices has found expression in taxpayers' revolts all around the nation. At the same time, the disadvantaged have seen that which the right hand of government gives taken away by the sinister left hand of inflation. Observe how the Administration's budget, calling for modest restraint in social programs, has brought forth protests from big city mayors and minority spokespersons.

And both groups, producers and non-producers alike, have much about which to complain. Here is just one example of how one segment of the disadvantaged has actually lost ground in the past few years. From 1967 to 1977, the number of black families with incomes of $10,000 and over (in constant 1977 dollars) jumped from 43 percent of all black families to almost 48 percent. The number of black families with incomes over $15,000 rose almost 75 percent in that period.

Impressive?—Yes! But wait. In 1977 more than half of all black families still had incomes under $10,000. What Bureau of the Census numbers reflect is that upper-income productive black families have moved up the economic ladder faster during the past decade than lower-income black families. Moreover, in 1977, the median income of black families was 57 percent of the median income of white families, representing a decline from 61 percent in 1970 and reversing the improving tendency of the last half of the 1960s.

There is little doubt that, as our economy suffers reverses during the next several months, unemployment rises, I believe to 8 percent by the middle of 1980, inflation persists at or near current levels, and real after-tax income per person declines persist, the voices of producers and nonproducers alike will become louder and perhaps even strident.

In these circumstances, pity the poor policymakers. Any attempt to counteract economic weakness later this year and in 1980, either by fiscal or monetary policy initiatives, will surely give the "kiss of death" to any real hope of bringing down the secularly rising rate of inflation and might well prompt the unwilling holders of US dollars abroad to unleash a new assault on our currency. On the other hand, the absence of attempts to stimulate a stagnating economy will produce predictable pressures from union leadership and spokespersons for the poor.

As a new decade dawns, what advice will the economists have for the policymakers? Will the long parade of experts appearing before Congressional committees produce the same prescriptions that have been found wanting in the past? Even as the invisible hand is being rediscovered, I think it's safe to predict that the same old "new" welfare economists will prescribe liberal doses of Federal spending for public job programs and public works. They will seek greater progressivity of the individual income tax structure and higher rates on those obscene corporate profits, while seeking to redress the inequities they would hold as inherent in last year's liberalization of the capital gains tax.

At the same time, some of us here today will make yet another trip to the Hill to enumerate the compelling reasons why Federal spending and the budget deficits should be reduced. We will develop the rationale for further incentives to private capital formation. Some of us may even be so enterprising as to produce our own comprehensive program involving such key ingredients as welfare reform, a private jobs program, a drastic revision of Social Security, and a legislative limitation on the growth of Federal spending.

In presenting their positions, business economists and welfare economists will have more in common than meets the naked eye. Down deep, both will be motivated by a genuine concern for lifting the level of economic well-being. But both groups, if they perform as they have in the past, will make the same mistakes that have been observed in the past insofar as they confuse means and ends.

D. M. Winch, in a book published in 1971 entitled *Analytical Welfare Economics* observes that "The inability of welfare economists to devise and agree on rigorously formulated solutions to the pressing problems of policy should not, however, blind us to the fact that all problems of economic policy are problems of economic welfare. If attention is focused only on achieving means, while the shifting relationships between means and ends are overlooked, the diverse tools of economic policy may be misused. The commonly evoked targets of full employment and stable prices are not goals, they are means. To think of choosing among alternative mixes of incompatible means by value judgment is nonsense. Value judgments are the basis of objectives; the choice of appropriate means to achieve a given end is the task of analysis."

When I reread materials that I have prepared in the past, I am struck by my own obsession with means, that is, alternative economic policy tools. But I am not alone among my business economist brethren in my failure to elaborate a theory of economic welfare.

Is Welfare Economics The Answer?

In the absence of a "new" theory, intellectuals in Europe and the United States, painfully aware that the floodtide of welfare economics has drowned initiative and incentives, is eroding human dignity and is choking individual freedoms, are rediscovering the doctrine of the "old" liberalism. The stir that has been created by this process has been brought to the attention of the general public by the press. The most recent article in the business press, of which I am aware, appears in the October 1, 1979 edition of *Forbes* Magazine. It is a rather good account of the new interest in Friedrich von Hayek.

Whether the floodtide of welfarism is really turning is, of course, difficult to ascertain. Eugene Genovese will only concede that the "American Left finds itself temporarily in disarray." He went on to say during a symposium on capitalism, socialism and democracy, held by the American Enterprise Institute last year that the Right relies on "Madison Avenue philosophers or, better, some Parisian equivalents." Arthur Schlesinger, Jr. observes wryly that "one is glad to know that French intellectuals are rediscovering the wheel." He concludes, "But let no one, in his excitement, assume that back-to-Hooverism, whether Herbert's or J. Edgar's, is the road to democracy."

While I find the disparagements of those who have been left high and dry as the tide of welfarism and socialism recede to be of little substance, I am concerned with what I believe to be a widely held view among the converts to the "Old-Time Religion," that they can have the best of both worlds. One final quotation from the aforementioned symposium, "The more efficient the economy becomes through capital intensive investment, the fewer people are needed to produce the same goods. In principle, however, if the system is healthy, it should have momentum enough to initiate new enterprises and jobs. It is up to us not to interfere with this health. Since the welfare state is going to be with us for the foreseeable future, it would be advisable if the economy were left otherwise free and productive enough to pay the cost of welfare. This is obviously a problem of delicate management, and it remains to be seen whether it can be brought off without our sliding into a form of *de facto* bureaucratic socialism." (William Barrett, Professor of Philosophy, New York University) I believe that the unanimity expressed in the March 1979 Annual Report of the Joint Economic Committee endorsing "conservative" solutions to public problems was possible only because some, and perhaps most, of the members hold that same view. I think an Administration official, Jerry J. Jasinowiski, expressed the "best of all worlds" point of view in a speech last month when he said, "Now we must admit openly that conscious management of demand via public expenditures, taxes, and control over credit is a necessary, but not sufficient activity in addressing the problems of the 1970's and 1980's."

What I see then as the two most probable paths into the future for the Free World's developed economies are (1) the establishment of institutional arrangements that restore and enlarge the freedom of markets, competition, entry and choice in consumption as well as employment. In this kind of world, "the major threats to individual freedoms would be seen to stem from concentrations of political and economic power, whether in the hands of the State, of bureaucrats, of firms, or of private citizens." Moreover, "Laws (would be) prospective and never retrospective in their effect, since their intention is to influence current and future choices and not to punish ...for past decisions registered in ignorance of the subsequent coercive intervention,..., laws would be known and certain, to the maximum extent attainable, so that individuals are in a position accurately to predict the decisions of the courts....laws would apply with equal force to all individuals without exception or discrimination—including those who govern." This new world would be characterized by "monetary constitutionalism," the illegality of closed or union shop arrangements, the vigorous enforcement of antitrust laws and the extension of such laws to unions (Charles K. Rowley and Allan T. Peacock, *Welfare Economics: A Liberal Restatement,* 1975).

Path #2 would see the developed economies of the Free World moving toward what Heilbroner describes as the third and final stage of capitalism. You are all familiar with his view that, having passed through the "dog eat dog" stage and now leaving the welfare phase, we are moving into the planning stage, where, presumably, the allocative process is to be arranged by big government, big business and big labor.

I am not going to conclude my remarks here today with a prescription of economic policies or institutional arrangements that would serve us best in the years ahead, but I do want to make a few suggestions to the business economists of the world. Those of us who have studied the economic history of the United States and the history of economic thought recognize that, whether we regard economics as a science that is pure or one that is normative, or both, there is nothing new under the sun. Resources have always been scarce in relation to human needs. So my suggestions are these:

1. Our principal concern as social scientists should be for the maximization of economic welfare.
2. We should bear prominently in mind that economic welfare is but one ingredient of a wider concept of welfare including individual freedom and the quality of life.
3. We must be careful not to confuse ends with means, inside our firm or in dealing with matters of broad public policy.
4. As former NABE President, Peter Max, reminded us, our principal contribution to our firms is contributing constructively to the optimization process, and I would add that optimization is the principal contribution our organizations can make to the maximization of economic welfare.
5. In carrying out Dr. Heebner's injunction to help promote the cause of economic education, we must ourselves understand and be able to articulate, not only the economic process itself, but its rationale as well.
6. To follow up on Dr. Schott's appeal for programs of continuing education for the business economist, I should propose courses in the history of economic thought for those who have not had that enriching experience.
7. Business economists should be at the forefront of economic policy formulation, for it is clear that new initiatives and a longer-term perspective are required at the national level. In this regard, may I further suggest reading, or rereading, Charles Schultze, *The Public Use of Private Interest,* and Albert Sommers, "Ends and Means in the 1980's," appearing in the September 1979 edition of the Conference Board's publication, *Across the Board.*

The business economist has many roles, as they have been elaborated by my predecessors on occasions like this during recent years. We also have many concerns with which to grapple. The business economist must analyze the movement and make short-term forecasts of macroeconomic variables, consider political, social and technological developments in assessing long-range developments and must decide what all of that implies for the organization that pays the salary. The business economist must be the spokesperson for the market system, for the profit motive, and in my own situation, for my company in the investment community. The business economist must advise departments of government and, of course, make innumerable speeches.

At the same time, the business economist must be concerned with such mundane things as annual operating budgets, and in some instances, with general management and administrative matters. The business economist must be concerned with the never-ending need to "keep up" professionally.

But in all these roles, we business economists should never forget that, as social scientists, our overriding concern must be for human welfare in its broadest sense. Our task is to demonstrate that, in the market process, the probability of welfare maximization is higher than in alternative processes.

Note

Originally published in *Business Economics*, Vol. 15, No. 3 (May 1980), pp. 53–58.

CHAPTER 12

1981

COMPANY TOTAL FACTOR PRODUCTIVITY: REFINEMENTS, PRODUCTION FUNCTIONS, AND CERTAIN EFFECTS OF REGULATION

Douglas L. Cocks, Eli Lilly and Company

Recently there has been much concern and discussion over the performance of overall productivity in the US economy. One important aspect of this productivity issue is the development of an understanding of the total productivity characteristics of individual economic units. To generate this understanding it is necessary that these units have techniques for measuring productive results. Furthermore, such measurements may be useful in assessing part of the impact of public policy on the individual economic unit.

It is the purpose of this paper to update and refine the measurement methodology of total factor productivity (TFP) at the firm level. In addition, alternative methodologies will be applied in order to assess the empirical sensitivity of the methodologies. As case studies, this paper also provides two examples of the way TFP measures may be applied to public policy issues. Utilizing analyses on the cost of regulation, the first application is an attempt to assess the impact of regulation on firm TFP. The second application is to use TFP relationships to generate empirical estimates of a firm's production function. Production function estimates may be useful in determining the extent to which economies of scale exist at the firm level. The existence of scale economies may have important implications for certain public policy issues.

Total Factor Productivity Measurement Methodology: A Summary

In an earlier chapter, the author adapted a methodology for measuring TFP at the firm level.[1] The methodology was based on evolving measurement techniques used by the Department of Commerce's Bureau of Economic Analysis for measuring the TFP of US nonfinancial corporations. The measurement technique

Table 12.1 Total factor productivity relationships

$O_t = S_t/PI_t - PGS_t/PGPI_t - RDEP_t - RTx_t$

$L_t = MH_t$

$$C_t = .75\sum_{t=1}^{n} GS_t + .25\sum_{t=1}^{n} NS_t$$

$$\sum_{t=1}^{n} GS_t = \sum_{t=1}^{n} \left(GI_{it} - R_{it}\right)/P_{it}$$

$$\sum_{t=1}^{n} NS_t = \sum_{t=1}^{n} \left(GS_{it} - D_{it}\right)/P_{it}$$

$OI_t = O_t/O_b$

$LI_t = MH_t/MH_b$

$CI_t = C_t/C_b$

$TFI_t = s_1LI_t + s_cCI_t$

$TFPI_t = OI_t/TFI_t$

Definitions

O_t	Real output in year t, t—1963, 1964,..., 1978
S_t	Net sales in year t, t—1963, 1964,..., 1978
PI_t	Corporate price index in year t, t—1963, 1964,..., 1978
PGS_t	Purchased goods and services in year t, t—1963, 1964,..., 1978
$PGPI_t$	Purchased goods and services price index in year t, t—1963, 1964,..., 1978
$RDEP_t$	Real depreciation in year t, t—1963, 1964,..., 1978[a]
RTx_t	Real indirect business taxes in year t, t—1963, 1964,..., 1978[b]
L_t	Labor input in year t, t—1963, 1964,..., 1978
MH_t	Total manhours in year t, t—1963, 1964,..., 1978
C_t	Capital input in year t, t—1963, 1964,..., 1978
GS_t	Gross capital stocks in year t, t—1963, 1964,..., 1978
NS_t	Net capital stocks in year t, t—1963, 1964,..., 1978
GI_{it}	Gross investment in category i of buildings and equipment in year t, t—1963, 1964,..., 1978
R_{it}	Retirement of category i of buildings and equipment in year t, t—1963, 1964,..., 1978
P_{it}	GNP price deflator of category i of buildings and equipment in year t, t—1963, 1964,..., 1978
D_{it}	Straight line depreciation for category i of buildings and equipment in year t, t—1963, 1964,..., 1978. (Based on 85% of Bulletin F services lives.)
OI_t	Index of real output in year t, t—1963, 1964,..., 1978
O_b	Real output in base year
LI_t	Index of labor input in year t, t—1963, 1964,..., 1978
MH_t	Total manhours in base year
CI_t	Index of capital input in year t, t—1963, 1964,..., 1978
C_b	Real capital input in year t, t—1963, 1964,..., 1978

continued

Table 12.1 Continued

Definitions	
TFI_t	Index of total factor input in year t, t—1963, 1964,...,1978
s_l	Factor share of labor. (Ratio of total compensation to the sum of total compensation and income before taxes—five-year average 1973–1977.)
s_c	Factor share of capital. (Ratio of income before taxes to the sum of total compensation and income before taxes—five-year average 1973–1977.)
$TFPI_t$	Index of total factor productivity in year t, t—1963, 1964,...,1978

[a,b]See D. L. Cocks, "The Measurement of Total Factor Productivity for a Large U.S. Manufacturing Corporation," (cited in note 1) for the calculation of real depreciation and real indirect business taxes, p. 9.

developed allows a direct comparison of the firm's productivity performance with that of some "average" in the total economy. Table 12.1 provides a summary of the methodology that was developed and reported previously.

The most difficult aspect of TFP measurement is deriving an estimate of the capital input. The previous analysis utilized the firm's plant and equipment accounting system, known as the Asset Depreciation Range, in conjunction with the Internal Revenue Service's Bulletin F, and individual price deflators from the National Income Accounts to estimate the real capital stocks of the firm.

One of the primary functions of the earlier productivity study was to provide a demonstration of the way these data sources could be matched.[2] Once the capital input is determined the measurement of an index of total factor productivity is relatively straightforward.

Firm Total Factor Productivity Measurement: Update and Refinements

This article provides three possible methodological refinements to the work reported earlier.[1] The first of these relates to the measurement of the labor input. In many cases in productivity measurement, labor is implicitly assumed to be homogeneous. However, it is generally recognized that this is not necessarily a valid assumption and the heterogeneity of these inputs should be taken into account. One of the methodological refinements offered in the present chapter is the application of a technique that broadly recognizes the heterogeneous nature of labor inputs.

The second methodological investigation concerns the expansion of the kinds of inputs considered for TFP measurement. Studies of TFP generally deal with just two basic factors of production—capital and labor. However, production includes more discrete inputs, and these may be inputs where certain of the productivity enhancing aspects occur before they enter the individual firm's production operations. One of the more obvious of these is purchased goods and services and the present analysis investigates one way to treat these as a specific input.

Two Measurement Devices

In the history of TFP measurement methodology, two measurement schools have evolved. One school includes the work of such economists as Denison and

Kendrick.[3] The other school is exemplified through the work of Jorgenson and Grilliches who have worked with what are known as Divisia indexes.[4] In one sense the distinction between these two schools is empirical. This study utilizes both techniques on a single set of data in order to assess the empirical significance of differences between the two for measurement at the firm level.

Table 12.2, Column (1) shows the estimates of the index of TFP of Eli Lilly and Company (excluding recent acquisitions) for the years 1963 through 1978. These numbers are based on the methodology outlined in Table 12.1 with 1975 serving as the base year for all elements in the model. The factor weights, s_1 and s_c, are determined as defined in Table 12.1 in which total compensation and income before taxes are based on a five-year average for the years 1973 through 1977.

Table 12.2, Column (2) provides an estimate of firm TFP where labor is not considered to be totally homogeneous. By utilizing the definition and classification

Table 12.2 Indexes of total factor productivity (1975 = 100)

	Methodological Approach				
Year	*TFP Index Original Methodology*[a] *(1)*	*TFP Index Labor Treated Heterogeneously (2)*	*TFP Index Purchased Goods and Services as Input (3)*	*TFP Index Divisia Methodology (4)*	*US Private Domestic Economy*[b] *(5)*
1963	14.9	15.6	16.3	15.4	82.4
1964	13.9	14.5	14.8	14.3	85.5
1965	15.4	16.2	15.5	15.9	88.7
1966	17.3	18.1	16.9	17.9	91.2
1967	18.4	19.2	17.1	18.9	92.4
1968	26.2	27.1	23.5	26.6	95.1
1969	31.6	33.3	28.8	32.1	95.3
1970	30.8	31.4	27.8	31.0	95.0
1971	34.2	34.7	30.6	34.3	97.1
1972	45.6	45.5	39.6	45.8	100.3
1973	73.6	74.0	66.3	73.8	102.3
1974	104.5	105.1	104.9	104.8	99.4
1975	100	100	100	100	100
1976	97.5	96.9	95.1	97.	104.4
1977	106.1	105.2	103.1	106.1	105.8
1978	112.9	111.8	103.2	112.9	n.a.
Compound Rate of Growth[c]	17.8%	17.3%	17.2%	17.5%	1.6%

[a]As contained in D. L. Cocks, "The Measurement of Total Factor Productivity for a Large U.S. Manufacturing Corporation," *Business Economics*, 9 (September 1974), pp. 7–20.
[b]American Productivity Center, *Productivity Perspectives* (Houston: American Productivity Center, Inc.), p. 11. (Data derived from J. Kendrick and E. Grossman, "Recent Trends and Cycles in Productivity," to be published.)
[c]Calculated by linear regression using all data points fit to the following form: $\ln Y_n = \ln Y_0 + n\ln(1+r)$, where the antilog of ln(1+r) is one plus the growth rate.

scheme developed by the Equal Employment Opportunity Commission, the various reports submitted to this agency can be used to estimate the proportion of employees in selected employment classifications. For the purposes of this analysis, three major EEOC classifications of employees were selected—(1) managers, officials, and professionals; (2) technicians and sales workers; (3) office, clerical, craft, operatives, laborers, and service workers. These classifications are somewhat arbitrary, but the educational and background characteristics of the groupings are sufficiently internally consistent so that these may not be an unreasonable categorization for the present purpose. The EEOC reports from which the data used here were derived provided a history back to 1966 and the 1966 proportions were applied to the prior years. These reports cover a substantial proportion of the total number of employees for the firm that serves as the example in this study.

The three proportions of employees that were derived were applied to the total number of employees to get the number of employees in each classification. These were then weighted by the average compensation in each category in the base year selected—again 1975. This is consistent with standard economic theory.

Symbolically, the index of labor input that is shown in Table 12.1 becomes:

$$LI_t = \sum w_i N_{it} / \sum w_i N_{ib}, \tag{12.1}$$

where LI_t is the index of labor input, w_i is the average compensation for each category of employees, N_{it} is the number of employees in each employee group in year t, and N_{ib} is the number of workers in each category in the base year.

From an empirical standpoint this methodological refinement has relatively little impact as can be seen by comparing Columns (1) and (2) of Table 12.2. This results from the fact that there was little difference within the company studied in the rate of change in the numbers of employees in each classification over the time period of data availability. The simpler assumption of labor homogeneity for TFP measurement is more or less reasonable or unreasonable depending upon relative changes in the composition of the labor force.

Table 12.2, Column (3) shows the yearly indexes with purchased goods and services treated as a separate input. In this case purchased goods and services has its own share in which the denominator of the ratio to determine the individual shares is the sum of total compensation, income before taxes, and the value of purchased goods and services. Again, these shares are calculated on the basis of a five-year average for 1973 through 1977.

Symbolically, the model outlined in Table 12.1 would be amended as shown below to account for purchased goods and services as an input.

$$RPGS_t = PGS_t / PGPI_t, \tag{12.2}$$

$$PGSI_t = RPGS_t / RPGS_b, \tag{12.3}$$

$$TFI_t = s_1 LI_t + s_c CI_t + s_{pg} PGSI_t. \tag{12.4}$$

where PGS_t, $PGPI_t$, LI_t, and CI_t are as defined in Table 12.1. The weights s_1, s_c, and s_{pg} are defined in the preceding paragraph. $RPGS_t$ and $RPGS_b$ are real purchased goods and services in years t and b respectively, and PGSI is the index of purchased goods and services input in the given year. As indicated by comparing Columns (1) and (3) in Table 12.2, the inclusion of purchased goods and services as an input has the effect of only slightly dampening the TFP index numbers. The compound rate of growth is less than 1 percent per year less when purchased goods and services are treated as an input.

Comparison with Overall Economy

For comparison with measures of TFP in the overall economy, Table 12.2, Column (5) includes some recent estimates of US total productivity made by Kendrick. Even though the methodologies are not necessarily the same, the comparison provides an order of magnitude assessment of the difference between the company and an average of the total economy. For Eli Lilly and Company the compound growth rate in total productivity over the 15-year period is almost 18 percent when using the original methodology. With purchased goods and services treated as an input the compound growth is 17.2 percent. For the years 1963 through 1977 the growth rate of US TFP is 1.8 percent.

Some economists feel that the most appropriate methodology for measuring TFP is the Divisia Index approach. This has generated a discussion in the literature on productivity measurement over the relative merits of the traditional approach compared to the Divisia method.[5] To test the sensitivities of empirical estimates relative to methodology, the present study offers estimates of firm productivity measurement using both methodologies.

A recent seminar on TFP measurement conducted by Teleglobe Canada provides a very useful and compact summary of the Divisia methodology.[6] Werner outlined a Divisia model that is applicable at the firm level.[7] Utilizing many of the symbols already presented, the following relationships outline the Divisia methodology:

$$\Delta P = \Delta O / \Delta I, \tag{12.5}$$

$$\Delta O = O_t / O_{t-1}, \tag{12.6}$$

$$\Delta I = \left(K_t / K_{t-1}\right) S_{k_t} \left(L_t / L_{t-1}\right) S_{l_t}, \tag{12.7}$$

$$S_{k_t} = .5\left(Y_{k_t} + Y_{l_{t-1}}\right), \tag{12.8}$$

$$S_{l_t} = .5\left(Y_{l_t} + Y_{l_{t-1}}\right), \tag{12.9}$$

$$Y_{k_t} = P_{k_t} K_t / E_t, \tag{12.10}$$

$$Y_{l_t} = P_{l_t} L_t / E_t, \tag{12.11}$$

$$E_t = P_{k_t} K_t + P_{l_t} L_t, \tag{12.12}$$

$$P_{k_t} = (IBT_t + D_t) K_t. \tag{12.13}$$

The terms shown above have the following definitions:

ΔP	Yearly change in total factor productivity
ΔO	Yearly change in output where output is determined in the manner shown in Table 12.1
O_t	Output in year t
ΔI	Yearly change in weighted factor inputs
S_{k_t}	Factor weight of capital in year t
S_{l_t}	Factor weight of labor in year t
Y_{k_t}	Capital's share of total factor payments
Y_{l_t}	Labor's share of total factor payments
E_t	Total factor payments in year t
P_{k_t}	Price of capital in year t
IBT_t	Income before taxes in year t
D_t	Reported depreciation in year t
K_t	Real capital stock in year t, derived in the manner shown in Table 12.1

Terms with $t - 1$ subscripts have the same definitions as the subscript t terms but are lagged one year. Since these measurements of TFP are in terms of changes, these can be transformed into index numbers with any year designated as 100.

In addition to the measures already discussed, Table 12.2, Column (4) shows the Divisia TFP estimates. The primary difference between the two methodologies is in the factor weights. With the Divisia approach, the weights are a kind of "moving average." Whereas with the methodology outlined in Table 12.1, the weights are an average that centers around the selected base year of 1975. As can be seen from the table there is essentially no empirical difference in the results for the firm analyzed. The annual compound growth rates in TFP are 17.8 percent and 17.5 percent for the original method and the Divisia approach respectively.

TFP Application 1: The Impact of Regulation on Productivity

There has been much interest recently in determining the impact of regulation on the economy. This interest precipitated the Business Roundtable's study of the cost of regulation in which the public accounting firm of Arthur Andersen and Co.

was asked to develop consistent techniques and procedures for determining the regulatory costs associated with six agencies—EPA, OSHA, FTC, EEO, DOE, and ERISA.[8] These costs were ascertained for 48 firms and the firm used as the example in this study was one of those firms.

Subsequent to the Business Roundtable study, Eli Lilly and Company assembled and audited in an identical manner data concerning the cost of regulation associated with the Food and Drug Administration as it relates to human pharmaceuticals.

One of the important things about the Arthur Andersen studies is that the methodology that was developed is one which attempts to determine the "incremental costs" of regulation. The methodology does not suggest that the goals of the regulations investigated should be eliminated. Rather, the firms were asked to determine, judgmentally, the additional costs of complying with the regulations promulgated and interpreted by the regulatory agencies beyond the costs that would be necessary to achieve the objectives of the regulations. In other words, the firms were asked to assess the difference in compliance costs they would incur in achieving the legislative-regulatory objectives as opposed to the ways that are mandated by the agencies. This difference is the "incremental cost" of regulation. The procedures that were developed to determine costs were systematic and consistent so that the results could be audited and related across all the firms investigated.

These accounting costs do not capture all of the true economic costs of regulation. Specifically, what is required is an assessment of what society gains in terms of certain social benefits but must give up in productivity with the regulatory structure that exists. These productivity losses are the social costs that are associated with regulation.

An important aspect of the TFP methodology outlined here and the incremental costs determined in the cost of regulation studies is that these can be married to provide an estimate of the loss in productivity associated with the current regulatory structure—specifically because of the "incremental cost" definition used.

Entering Regulatory Costs in the Model

There are three points at which the cost of regulation estimates of the company serving as an example here can feed into the TFP model. The incremental costs were determined for one year—1977 in the Business Roundtable study and 1978 for the study of FDA costs of regulation.[9] In addition, the costs were grouped into three main categories—purchases of goods and services, labor costs by various classes of labor, and capital expenditures. By applying these cost areas to output, labor input, and capital input it is possible to determine the index of TFP without the effect of regulation. Comparing this estimate with an estimate from the preceding productivity calculations provides a measure of the degree of foregone productivity.

Purchased goods and services is one of the components of the value-added concept of output that is used in the TFP methodology discussed above. The cost of regulation studies' estimates include the value of the incremental purchases of goods and services. These represent an unnecessary reduction in value added and therefore cause the level of output to be less than would be the case if there had not been the extra regulatory burden. The following shows the adjustment to output that eliminates the effect of the extra regulation:

$$O_t = S_t / PI_t - (PGS_t - PGSR_t) / PGPI_t - RDEP_t - RTx_t. \quad (12.14)$$

All of the terms in equation (12.9) are as defined in Table 12.1 with the exception of $PGSR_t$ which is the dollar value of the regulatory induced purchases of goods and services.

For the labor input the incremental costs of regulation suggest that there were more labor inputs in place than were necessary to produce the firms output in a given year. The Arthur Andersen methodology accounted for the incremental labor costs of various categories of labor that were directly related to the labor categories used in the previous calculation of labor input for the firm in this study. Dividing the total incremental costs for each category of labor by the corresponding average total compensation for that category yields an estimate of the number of workers in each category that were unnecessary. Applying the labor input weights that were previously used provides an estimate of the extra labor inputs resulting from regulation. The index of labor input as shown in equation (12.1) would be adjusted as follows:

$$LI_t = \sum w_i (N_{it} - NR_{it}) / \sum w_i N_{ib}. \quad (12.15)$$

The NR_{it} term is the number of regulation induced employees.

Regulatory Costs on Capital

The calculation of the regulatory burden on the capital input is rather straightforward. Since the costs of regulation were determined in the year that is the last year of the productivity estimates, the capital costs ascertained in the Arthur Andersen numbers are a direct and equal reduction in both gross and net stocks. This is because there is no depreciation for investments made in the last year of the TFP estimates. Symbolically the adjustments are as follows:

$$GS_t = (GI_{it} - R_{it}) / P_{it} - GI_{rt} / P_t, \quad (12.16)$$

$$NS_t = (GS_{it} - D_{it}) / P_{it} - GS_{rt} / P_t. \quad (12.17)$$

GI_{rt} and GS_{rt} are the regulation induced incremental capital costs and as stated above are equal. The Arthur Andersen methodology did not account for incremental capital costs by ADR equipment classes so these capital costs were deflated by a single price deflator—P_t. The price deflator chosen was the one associated with the largest category of equipment in real dollar terms as determined from the TFP estimates.

Table 12.3 Selected effects of regulation on measured total factor productivity

Regulation Status	*1978 TFP Index*	*% Δ 1978 TFP Index Without Regulation Vs. With Regulation*	*% Δ TFP Index 1978 over 1977 Without Regulation Vs. With Regulation*
With Regulation	111.8	—	6.3
Without Regulation	118.5	6.7	12.6

The obvious effect of the preceding adjustments is to raise the level of output and to lower the level of both the labor and capital inputs. This in turn has the effect of raising the measured index of TFP. Table 12.3 presents the measured effects on productivity of the regulations covered in the two cost of regulation studies. (Based on the methodology in which purchased goods and services are not treated as an input, adjusting for this definition of the incremental costs of regulation the 1978 index of TFP rises from 111.8 to 118.5 or 6.7%.)

Another way of looking at the effects of the incremental costs of the selected regulations is to calculate the yearly percentage change in TFP of 1978 over 1977. Table 12.3 indicates that the yearly increase in productivity in 1978 was 6.3 percent with regulation and would have been 12.6 percent without the effects of regulation that were determined from the cost of regulation studies. A word of caution is necessary concerning this comparison. The effects of the extra regulation are contained in the elements that go into the calculation of the index of TFP for 1977. A valid comparison probably requires a calculation of the rate of growth in the index of TFP between *the* year in which there were no regulatory effects and the year in which the extra costs of regulation are assessed—in this case 1978. Growth rates with and without regulation could then be compared. The difficulty is that yearly estimates of the costs of regulation were not possible and it is arbitrary to designate a year in which regulatory effects were essentially nonexistent. Notwithstanding this caveat, if the incremental costs of regulation measured for this firm had not been incurred in 1978, there would have been a one-time doubling in the percentage increase in TFP for that year.

The regulatory effects that are reflected in Table 12.3 are really just the tip of the iceberg. First, the study only covers seven regulatory agencies and the coverage of FDA regulation is not complete because it focuses on the pharmaceutical part of FDA regulation and the FDA affects other activities of the firm that serves as the analytical example. In addition there are other regulatory agencies that impact firms—the Internal Revenue Service and the Securities Exchange Commission stand out as prime candidates. Including all possible regulatory agencies would surely increase the measured negative impact of regulation on productivity.

Second, this study simply assesses the impact on measured productivity. There are many subtle effects that cannot be determined through the measures employed here. There are such things as the diversion of management attention to the problems that arise in dealing with regulation. There is also the loss of entrepreneurial insight and spirit that can be dampened by the drudgery and vagaries of regulation. In a high technology firm like the one studied here, regulation can divert the attention of the scientific workforce which could eliminate valuable scientific insight for areas that could improve productivity.

All of this suggests that the measured effects of regulation shown in Table 12.3 are the minimum impact. That these are the minimum effects, and that these effects are as discernible as they are, would strongly suggest the true total effect of regulation has to be quite substantial.

TFP Application 2: Production Functions at the Firm Level

With the methodology that has been developed in this and the earlier analysis, it is possible to use the derived data to make preliminary production function estimates for the firm. It is recognized that the 15-year span of data limits the number of degrees of freedom, but an empirical investigation of the production characteristics of the firm may reveal certain tentative relationships.

Empirical estimates of production functions have primarily concentrated on the Cobb-Douglas and constant elasticity of substitution (CES) specifications.[10] To a certain extent the appropriate specification is an empirical issue, therefore the present analysis investigates both forms.

The well known Cobb-Douglas production function has the following form:

$$O = AL^{a}K^{b}, \tag{12.18}$$

where

O physical output,
A positive constant generally representing technology and other "productivity enhancing" factors,
L real labor input,
K physical capital input,
a,b parameters.

A major characteristic of the Cobb-Douglas production function is that it is homogeneous of degree (a + b). In most theoretical discussions of the Cobb-Douglas production function the function is constrained to be linearly homogeneous where (a + b = 1).[11] From an empirical standpoint an estimate of the value of (a + b) provides an assessment of the returns to scale. A value of $(a + b < 1)$ indicates decreasing returns to scale; $(a + b = 1)$ indicates constant returns to scale; and, $(a + b > 1)$ represents increasing returns to scale.[12]

In order to estimate the production function using multiple linear regression, the production function is usually transformed by taking the natural logarithms of both sides of the equation where:

$$\ln O = \ln A + a\ln L + b\ln K. \tag{12.19}$$

Utilizing the data for real output, real labor, and real capital from the TFP calculations, the following regression provides an estimate of the Cobb-Douglas production function for Eli Lilly and Company for the period 1963–1978:

$$\ln O = -42.86855 + 1.31939 \ln L + 2.09583 \ln K. \qquad (12.20)$$
$$(0.708) \qquad (3.463)$$
$$(R_2 = .957) \quad (F = .501) \quad (d = .896)$$

The significance of the R^2 is judged by the F-ratio and the significance of the regression coefficients is assessed by t-tests which are shown in parentheses under the coefficients. The Durbin-Watson d-statistic is included as a test for serial correlation.

The Cobb-Douglas production function estimated in equation (12.16) indicates fairly substantial economies of scale because the sum of the parameters (a + b) is 3.415. The signs of each of the parameters A, a and b are consistent with economic theory.[13] However, the model is not robust as indicated by the low F value and the insignificance of the labor variable. In addition, the Durbin-Watson statistic is indeterminant in testing for serial correlation.

Besides the Cobb-Douglas production function, the most widely investigated production relationship is the constant elasticity of substitution (CES) production function. This function is felt to be a more general representation of productive activity in which the Cobb-Douglas is a special case. The general expression of the CES production function is the following:

$$O = A\left[aK^{-r} + (1-a)L^{-r}\right]^{-u/r} \qquad (12.21)$$

where O, A, K, and L have the same theoretical and empirical definitions as the previous Cobb-Douglas function; a represents a capital intensity variable, r is a function of the elasticity of substitution between capital and labor, and u represents the degree of economies of scale. When u = 1, the production function indicates constant returns to scale and directly relates to the Cobb-Douglas form as a special case.[14]

The estimation of the CES production function is not as straight forward as the Cobb-Douglas form, but estimating techniques have been developed. The approach used here is one suggested by Bodkin and Klein.[15] The procedure involves two steps where two separate regression equations are estimated. The first step involves the estimation of an equation which has the following form:

$$\ln(p_k/w) = \ln\left[a/(1-a)\right] - (r+1)\ln(K/L), \qquad (12.22)$$

where a and r are the parameters indicated in equation (12.17): p_k is the price of capital which is the annual return on equity; w is the price of labor calculated as average total compensation; K and L represent real capital and labor respectively as measured previously. Equation (12.22) is a logarithmic transformation of the marginal productivity relationship based on cost minimization as suggested by standard economic theory.[16]

Linear regression of equation (12.22) provides estimates of $a/(1 - a)$ and $(r + 1)$ as regression coefficients. By plotting values for a and $\ln [a/(1 - a)]$ graphically, it is possible to determine an approximate value for $\hat{a}$ when the value of $\ln [\hat{a}/(1 - \hat{a})]$ is given from the estimate of the regression coefficient. The value of $\hat{r}$ is directly derived from the value of the regression coefficient $(\hat{r} + 1)$.

The second step of the procedure is to use the estimates of a and r to form the equation:

$$\ln O = \ln A - (u/\hat{r}) \ln [\hat{a}K^{-\hat{r}} + (1 - \hat{a})L^{-\hat{r}}] \tag{12.23}$$

where all terms are identical to those in equation (12.4) and $\hat{a}$ and $\hat{r}$ are the estimated parameters indicated in equation (12.5). Using linear regression applied to equation (12.23) it is then possible to estimate A and u.[17]

From the data developed for Eli Lilly and Company, the regression estimate of equation (12.23) is as follows:

$$\begin{aligned} &\ln\left(p_k / w\right) = -.98983 - .31945^{(K/L)}. \\ &\left(R^2 = .473\right) \quad \left(F = 12.654\right) \end{aligned} \tag{12.24}$$

As outlined above, equation (12.24) allows the determination of values for $\hat{a}$ and $\hat{r}$: $\hat{a}$ = .284 and $\hat{r}$ = −1.31945. Using these values, $\hat{a}K^{-\hat{r}}$ and $\left(1 - \hat{a}\right)L^{-\hat{r}}$ can be determined in order to derive yearly values for the $\ln [\hat{a}K^{-\hat{r}} + (1 - \hat{a})L^{-\hat{r}}]$ term in equation (12.23). This allows a linear regression estimate of equation (12.23) which for the firm under investigation has this result:

$$\begin{aligned} &\ln O = -63.57161 - 5.75343 [\hat{a}K^{-\hat{r}} + (1 - \hat{a})L^{-\hat{r}}] \\ &(R^2 = .918) \qquad (F = 156.739) \end{aligned} \tag{12.25}$$

In order to investigate the degree of economies of scale, it is necessary to determine a value for $\hat{u}$ in equation (12.23). The regression coefficient determined in equation (12.25) is $\hat{u}/\hat{r}$. Since $\hat{r}$ was estimated in step one of the two-step procedure $\hat{u}$ is directly derived from the empirical formulation contained in equation (12.23).

$$\hat{u}/\hat{r} = -5.75343 \tag{12.26}$$

the value for $\hat{r}$ as determined above is −1.601; therefore,

$$\begin{aligned} &-\hat{u} = \hat{r}\left(-5.75343\right) \\ &U = 7.59136 \end{aligned}$$

As with the Cobb-Douglas formulation the CES production function suggests economies of scale for the firm under investigation over the period 1963 through 1978. That economies of scale exist may stem from certain characteristics of the economic environment in which the firm operates. This is an environment that could be characterized as a dynamic, technologic crucible that is the result of a great amount of research and development.[18] Continuing product innovation and process innovation at the firm level may be the cause of the shifting short-run production function that is indicated by the index of TFP. The production functions suggest that the technological environment may be generating "natural" increasing returns to scale. This is, of course, an important consideration in several contexts relative to public policy. However, it must be pointed out that any interpretation of the production function relationships is very tentative due to the limited number of observations available.

Summary and Conclusions

The issue of productivity has caused justified concern in recent years. Organizations like the American Productivity Center in Houston, Texas have arisen to focus much needed attention on the productivity problem. A thrust has been to make companies aware of the importance of productivity improvement and to make firms aware of the need to measure productivity and institute programs that will generate improvement. It has been one of the primary purposes of this chapter to demonstrate that several total factor productivity measurement methodologies are available for company level use. However, for the firm used as an example in the analysis, there were essentially no empirical differences in results when alternative methodologies were used.

The second purpose of the chapter is to suggest ways in which productivity measurements can be applied to public policy issues. Analysis illustrates through the use of explicit studies of the incremental cost of regulation how productivity measures may be used to empirically demonstrate that productivity is directly affected by regulation. Relative to the measured productivity of the firm that serves as the example for this paper, the regulatory impact on productivity may not seem that great. However it must be kept in mind that if the regulatory environment created by a sample of agencies can cause this slowing in the rate of growth in productivity within high technology industries, it is eating at the heart of the source of productivity improvement for all industries. This suggests that if the negative impact of regulation is even as perceptible as it is for the firm that serves as an example in this study, then its impact may be stronger for firms that are not in industries that have high technological opportunities.

Another example of the way in which the TFP measures may be applied to aspects of public policy issues is given in the empirical assessment of economies of scale for the firm.

Note

Originally published in *Business Economics*, Vol. 16, No. 3 (May 1981), pp. 5–14.

References

1. D. L. Cocks, "The Measurement of Total Factor Productivity for a Large U.S. Manufacturing Corporation," *Business Economics*, 9 (September 1974), pp. 7–20.

2. Ibid., p. 12.
3. E. F. Denison, "Some Major Issues in Productivity Analysis: An Examination of Estimates by Jorgenson and Grilliches," *Survey of Current Business,* 49 (May 1969), pp. 1–27; J. W. Kendrick, *Postwar Productivity Trends in the United States* (New York: National Bureau of Economic Research, 1973).
4. D.W. Jorgenson and Z. Grilliches, "The Explanation of Productivity Change," *Review of Economic Studies,* 34 (July 1967), pp. 249–282.
5. Denison, "Some Major Issues in Productivity Analysis," pp. 1–27; Jorgenson and Grilliches, "The Explanation of Productivity Change," pp. 249–282.
6. M. Werner, ed., *Total Factor Productivity: Symposium 1* (Montreal: Teleglobe Canada, 1977).
7. M. Werner, "An Integrated Total Factor Productivity-Financial Based Corporate Planning Model," in M. Werner, ed., *Total Factor Productivity: Symposium 1 (Montreal: Teleglobe Canada, 1977).*
8. Arthur Andersen & Co., *Cost of Government Regulation Study for the Business Roundtable* (Chicago: Arthur Andersen & Co., March 1979).
9. So that the effects of the cost regulation of both studies could be determined for one year, 1978, the Business Roundtable numbers were inflated by appropriate price index numbers to reflect 1978 dollars.
10. R. G. Bodkin and L. R. Klein, "Nonlinear Estimation of Aggregate Production Functions," *Review of Economics and Statistics,* 59 (February 1967), pp. 28–44.
11. A. C. Chiang, *Fundamental Methods of Mathematical Economics* (St. Louis: McGraw-Hill, 1967), pp. 373–374.
12. E. Mansfield, *Microeconomics: Theory and Applications,* 2nd Ed. (New York: W. W. Norton, 1975), pp. 144–147.
13. Chiang, *Fundamental Methods of Mathematical Economics,* pp. 373–374.
14. M. Brown and A. H. Conrad, "The Influence of Research and Education on CES Production Relations," in M. Brown, ed., *The Theory and Empirical Analysis of Production* (New York: National Bureau of Economic Research, 1967), pp. 343–344.
15. Bodkin and Klein, "Nonlinear Estimation of Aggregate Production Functions," op. cit., pp. 28–44.
16. Ibid., p. 33.
17. Ibid.
18. For a discussion of additional economic significance of the pharmaceutical industry's technological base and its implicit relationship to firm productivity see, D. L. Cocks, "Product Competition and the Dynamic Elements of Competition in the Ethical Pharmaceutical Industry," in R. B. Helms, ed., *Drug Development and Marketing* (Washington, DC: American Enterprise Institute, 1974), pp. 225–254.

CHAPTER 13

1983

THE ADAM SMITH ADDRESS

CONSERVATIVES, ECONOMISTS, AND NECKTIES

Herbert Stein, American Enterprise Institute and University of Virginia

I am honored to be invited by the National Association of Business Economists to deliver the first Adam Smith Address. I hope that the series will be long and successful.

It seems to me highly appropriate that the Association of Business Economists should give this series the name of Adam Smith. It was Adam Smith two centuries ago who attested to the intelligence and effectiveness of businessmen in utilizing the nation's economic resources to meet the desires of the population. And if we can assume, as I suppose we can, that business economists supply the intelligence of business then Adam Smith's tribute to businessmen is also a tribute to business economists. Of course, Adam Smith did not think that everyone who aspires to be a businessman or, by association, a business economist, is a person of great capability. He relied upon the market to weed out the ones who were not, so that survival would be a certificate of quality. Since you are all survivors here you can regard yourselves as certified by Adam Smith.

It is well known that Adam Smith was suspicious of meetings of businessmen, and, if he had ever heard of a business economist he would have been suspicious of their meetings also. He thought that they never got together for lunch or other social occasions without conspiring to raise prices or otherwise defraud the consumer. But Adam Smith wrote that before he knew about the income tax. He didn't know that businessmen and business economists get together now not to do business but to enjoy a deductible lunch or golf weekend.

I do not, however, intend to say much about Adam Smith today. Instead my talk today is inspired by the Adam Smith necktie. I do not want to talk about how they are made or about their commercial success. I want to talk about who wears them and why.

One might expect Adam Smith to be the patron saint of economists of all ideologies. He was the father not only of a particular idea of how the economy works but also of the idea that there is an economic system. Moreover, some of his ideas about how the system works are incorporated in all kinds of economics, from extreme left to extreme right. Any economist teaching the history of economic thought would start with Adam Smith. But the wearing of Adam Smith neckties is not uniformly or randomly distributed among economists. Only economists who are, loosely, called conservatives wear it. For example, Milton Friedman wears it but Paul Samuelson does not.

Adam Smith would also have a claim to be one of the patron saints of conservatives. At least as commonly viewed today one of the main elements in conservative doctrine is the need to minimize the power and responsibility of the State. Certainly Adam Smith did more than any other person to demonstrate the folly of state intervention in economic life. So one would expect other conservatives, and not only economists, to wear the Adam Smith tie. But in my observation they do not.

There are exceptions. Edwin Meese, Counselor to President Reagan, is not an economist but he does wear the Adam Smith tie. In fact, it is reported that he has cushions in his office made of the Adam Smith necktie material. I have sometimes wondered what it is about Adam Smith that endears him to Mr. Meese. Perhaps it is Smith's statement that there is a great deal of ruin in a nation, which must certainly be a comfort to a counselor to a President.

So what I want to talk about is why conservative economists wear the Adam Smith tie but other conservatives and other economists do not. That is, I want to talk, first, about the differences between conservative economists and other conservatives and then, about the differences between conservative economists and other economists—other than wearing the tie, of course.

The relation between conservative economists and noneconomist intellectual conservatives ranges from indifference to hostility. In fact, until recently the typical American intellectual conservative ignored economics. If you read the writings of the leading people, like Russell Kirk or Peter Viereck, you will have difficulty in learning what they thought about any of the issues that engage economists.

Clinton Rossiter's excellent study of conservatism in America contains in its index 37 references to Edmund Burke and 2 to Adam Smith, 23 references to Russell Kirk and one each to Frank H. Knight, Henry Simons and Milton Friedman. It contains no reference to inflation, unemployment, taxes or budgets.

That was written in 1962. Since then conservative intellectuals, perhaps because they feel themselves closer to power, have become more interested in economic policy, but no less disdainful of conservative economics and economists. I will give three examples.

The first is George F. Will, who is my ideal and with whom I agree 99 percent of the time. Yet he has a suspicious attitude toward economists and specifically toward Adam Smith. In one of the columns reprinted in his recent book, *The Pursuit of Virtue and Other Tory Notions,* Will tells the story of Adam Smith going out for a walk in his garden in his dressing gown and absent mindedly ambling 15 miles away. A student of Adam Smith assures me that the story is apocryphal, but Will's telling it reveals his belief that there was something not quite right with Adam Smith. And what was wrong with Adam Smith was that "he assumed that the aim of social life is to increase the consumption of goods and services." "He argued that individual self-interestedness, when given ample scope, can produce this result and guarantee social harmony." Again quoting, "The theory makes government seem merely coercive and barely necessary."

In other words, Adam Smith and the generations of economists descended from him, and especially those who now wear his necktie, have a materialistic and vulgar view of society. They think that the objective of society is to serve the desires of individuals, whatever they are, all desires being equally worthy. This objective is most efficiently met by the unhampered play of self-interest in a free market. To paraphrase, economists see no need for anything but the free market because they do not appreciate the higher things of life.

A similar position is taken by my friend, the Godfather of the neoconservatives, Irving Kristol. His reservations are already apparent in the title of his collected essay, *Two Cheers for Capitalism*. Perhaps oversimplifying a little, capitalism gets only two cheers, and not three, because it is only efficient, and not good, or noble, or beautiful, or something else. Kristol also finds the root of the problem in Adam Smith. He quotes Smith asking, "What can be added to the happiness of man who is in health, who is out of debt, and has a clear conscience?" And Kristol answers: "But if you believe that a comfortable life is not necessarily the same thing as a good life, or even a meaningful life, then it will occur to you that efficiency is a means, not an end in itself. Capitalist efficiency may then be regarded as a most useful precondition for a good life in a good society. But one has to go beyond Adam Smith, or capitalism itself, to discover the other elements that are wanted."

My third example is George Gilder, whose *Wealth and Poverty* was for at least a year the conservative politician's bible. In a way he takes up Kristol's challenge, and gives capitalism not two cheers, but four. Like Kristol he finds the conventional economists' justification for capitalism, that it is efficient, inadequate. But he believes that there is much more to be said for capitalism and especially for capitalists. The capitalist in Gilder is not a pawn in the invisible hand, doing good to others unknowingly and unintentionally. Instead he is an active, purposeful and therefore moral doer-of-good. The evidence of this is that the capitalist puts forth his resources for the sake of an uncertain future return. By this test, of course, the bettors at Las Vegas get high marks also. In any case, Gilder rescues capitalism from the charge of immorality by also rejecting the defense of the free market made by Adam Smith and the economists who followed him.

More generally, the intellectual conservatives reject the thinking of conservative economists as being inadequate on the moral, ethical or cultural scale. We—for I consider myself to be one of those benighted creatures—regard all wants as equal, not recognizing some to be better or more valuable than others. We are like Oscar Wilde's cynic, who knows the price of everything and the value of nothing. Being satisfied with the preferences of individuals, we extol a system which meets those preferences.

Moreover, the system we extol is worse than indifferent to the relative qualities of values. It rewards and encourages certain base values—material consumption—and certain rather pedestrian or even low personality traits—prudence, calculation, competitiveness, and selfishness. The intellectual conservatives start with the proposition that some values are more valuable than others and therefore better deserve being met. They go beyond that, at least they frequently do. They think they know what the better values are. They think that the quality of these values is revealed by tradition. And they believe that some authority is needed to promote these values and see to it that they are served.

It is precisely at this point—the identification of the hierarchy of values and the need for an authority to effectuate them—that conservative economists find themselves most in disagreement with other conservatives. Some economists in their enthusiasm for the neatly ordered economic model they have constructed may have gone too far in talking as if economics is the end of life. But more serious economists have not. This is especially clear in the writings of Frank H. Knight. Since Knight was the teacher of Milton Friedman, George Stigler and Allen Wallis, one can validly regard him as the father of modern conservative American economics. Knight emphasized that economics, like other sciences or would-be sciences, has to abstract from some aspects of the real world and concentrate on others. Economics assumes that wants, resources, and technology are given and it studies how the economy works and how it should be organized on that assumption. Economists do not believe that wants are really given, either in the sense that they are unchangeable or in the sense that all wants are to be considered equally valuable. How wants are changed, and which wants are most valuable, are legitimate subjects for inquiry. They are not the subjects of economics. The conclusions of economics, whether positive or normative, are contingent upon this condition. Despite this self-imposed limitation, economics has proved to be useful, both as description and as guide.

Economics does not deny the point of its conservative critics that consumers' preferences are not the final determinant of what is good, true or beautiful. But conservative economists tend to be very skeptical about the claim of anyone, including conservatives, to be the arbiter of what is good. And most of all, they resist the notion that cultural or moral values, however well recommended they come, should be imposed by coercion.

The classic statement of this position of economists is found in an essay by Friedrich Hayek, the Nobel-Prize winning economist. Professor Hayek does not call himself a conservative. Indeed, the essay I am about to quote is called "Why I Am Not a Conservative." Yet there is no doubt that within the spectrum of economists he is a conservative. By all the tests of positions on economic policy which conventionally distinguish liberals from conservatives Hayek is one of the most conservative. I do not know whether he wears the Adam Smith tie. But I was present when he laid a wreath on the tomb of Adam Smith. (This was, of course, some years after Smith died.) It is a sign of the depth of their difference from other conservatives that Hayek and other economists whom we all call conservative, like Milton Friedman, insist on calling themselves liberals, or "old-fashioned liberals" or libertarians.

The quotation I want to read from Hayek is this: "There are many values of the conservative which appeal to me more than those of the socialists; yet for a liberal the importance he personally attaches to specific goals is no sufficient justification for forcing others to serve them. To live and work successfully with others requires an intellectual commitment to a type of order in which, even on issues which to one are fundamental, others are allowed to pursue different ends."

"It is for this reason that to the liberal neither moral nor religious ideals are proper objects of coercion, while both conservatives and socialists recognize no such limits. I sometimes feel that the most conspicuous attribute of liberalism that distinguishes it as much from conservatism as from socialism is the view that moral beliefs concerning matters of conduct which do not directly interfere with the protected sphere of other persons do not justify coercion. This may also explain why it seems to be so much easier for the repentant socialist to find a new spiritual home in the conservative fold than in the liberal."

The key words here are "proper objects of coercion." What Hayek calls the liberal and I call the conservative economist does not deny that moral, religious, or cultural values are proper objects of concern. He denies that they are proper objects of coercion. He does not deny the right of anyone to try to influence others to his own view of these matters. And of course there are elaborately developed processes of communication—through education, literature, art, religion—by which some people are always trying to influence the values of others. But he is deeply suspicious of efforts to coerce individuals into the observance of principles of conduct except, as Hayek says, where necessary to safeguard "the protected sphere of other persons."

This matter on which the conservative economists and other conservatives differ is highly conspicuous and serious today. The prominence of social issues in the national discourse and political struggle—issues like abortion, pornography, prayer, sexual practice—is evidence of division within the Nation about acceptable modes of behavior in areas usually considered private. It is also evidence of the desire or willingness of many conservatives to invoke the authority of the state to "correct" this behavior. Even from the standpoint of what Hayek calls the liberal and what I call the conservative economist, these are hard issues. It is hard to tell where Hayek's exception for interference with the rights of others applies. And in a society where government does much, it is hard to tell what coercion is. For example, is the government's refusal to pay for something coercion? But despite these difficulties of interpretation a difference of leaning between conservative economists and many other conservatives on this issue is clear.

I would hope that discussion would narrow this difference. Economists could be more explicit in recognizing the limitations of their discipline and accepting the relative worth of different goals and values as legitimate objects of concern, even if they are not the concerns of economics. Other conservatives could be more cautious about asserting their claim to be the final arbiters of values and especially about the role of the State in determining and enforcing values.

I want to turn now from the distinction between conservative economists and other conservatives to the distinction between conservative economists and other economists. I confine myself to economists within what I call the mainstream. The mainstream dominates the economics profession and also, although not quite to the same extent, nonprofessional discussion of economic issues. The views of the mainstream include the largest part of the range of economic policy options among which choices will be made in, say, the next 10 or 20 years, although that is not necessarily true if we look 50 years ahead.

The limits of the mainstream are not precisely definable. I think of it as ranging from, say, Friedman to, say, Tobin. It excludes Marxists and Anarcholibertarians. It includes all past Presidents of the American Economic Association, with the possible exception of Galbraith, who would not thank me if I did include him in the mainstream. It includes all members of the President's Council of Economic Advisers of the past 30 years. Although there has been no census taken, I would be surprised if the mainstream did not include 95 percent of all economists.

Reading the popular press makes it clear that each economist like every child who's born alive is either a little liberal or else a little conservative. The press knows, for example, that the American Enterprise Institute is a conservative think-tank and the Brookings Institution is a liberal think-tank. Some economists think of themselves as difficult to classify, but popular opinion finds few economists difficult to classify, even when they are not wearing neckties.

The positions which distinguish these mainstream conservatives from the mainstream liberals are well known. By and large, conservatives are suspicious of government intervention in the market, they are opposed to what they call fine-tuning, they are particularly adverse to what are commonly called incomes policies, they place relatively more emphasis on price stability and relatively less on unemployment, relatively more on efficiency and growth and relatively less on income redistribution. Anyone can expand or elaborate this list.

These differences in practical terms—in terms of what is actually being proposed—are so much smaller than the differences which noneconomists associate with the words liberals and conservatives that they seem to be of an entirely different kind. They are not the differences between the Gulag Archipelago and anarchy. They are differences of degree within a fairly narrow range.

The differences are not mainly the result of differences of economic analysis. Conservatives do not differ from liberals because they have different estimates of the interest elasticity of the demand for money or of the tax rate elasticity of the supply of savings. The reverse is more likely to be true. They have the elasticity estimates they do because they are conservatives or liberals.

To some extent the differences are aesthetic. There are some economists who are fascinated by the beauty of the picture of an economic system endowed by nature and running optimally down the grooves of time as long as it is untouched by human hands. Others love the idea of the sophisticated and compassionate government planner playing the instruments of economic policy to produce a harmony of growth, stability and equity. They especially love it if they dream of themselves as the organist.

There is some narrow political element in the differences. Economists like to participate in the political process. To participate it is necessary to join. And once joined the economist becomes committed to a line of policy and especially policy argument—not insincerely but naturally. They are liberals because they are Democrats and not Democrats because they are liberals.

How much do these differences within the present range of policy discussion matter? How much difference does it make whether Federal government spending as a percentage of GNP rises to 25 percent or falls to 21 percent, whether the budget is balanced or runs deficits equal to 2 percent of GNP, whether the Nation's water is 99 percent pure or 98 percent pure, whether social security is indexed to wages or prices, whether the inflation rate is stabilized at 10 percent, 6 percent, or 2 percent, whether the standard deviation of the quarterly money supply around its average path is 1 or 5 percent? The simplest answer is that we do not know for sure. Probably these are important but not critical differences. They do not entail radical differences in our social system or way of life. They are important—worth the attention that the country, including economists—pay to them. But they are not the differences between disaster and utopia.

There is, however, another, more apocalyptic, way of looking at all this. Today's policy issues are not the end of the road. They are part of an historical process in which one argument, one way of thinking and one decision leads to another. What we have to be concerned with is where the current steps lead us in the end. This is a way of looking at the matter which is especially impressive to conservatives and which is best suggested by the title of Hayek's book, *The Road to Serfdom*. Each step towards more government control, however apparently innocuous in itself, reinforces a trend which makes further steps more probable, if not inevitable. Little by little, without any decision to change the system, we have gone in about 50 years from a Federal government spending 3 percent of GNP to one spending 24 percent. We have increased the number of major Federal regulatory agencies from 15 to 55 in the same period. Eisenhower's gentle exhortation to labor unions to restrain wage increases led, in about 13 years, to Nixon's mandatory, comprehensive wage-price freeze. Each step must be resisted and if possible repulsed before the process reaches a point at which it is irreversible and irresistible.

There are, of course, replies to this argument. Although government is bigger than ever the private sector is also bigger than ever and the American people on the whole are freer than ever. We are not necessarily on a straight road to serfdom or anywhere else. As Colin Clark said in another connection, every pig that grows up to be a hog does not grow up to be an elephant. The expansion of government that began with F. D. Roosevelt was slowed down and absorbed in a growing private economy in the time of Eisenhower. The expansion that began with Kennedy is being slowed and digested within the free system in the regime of Reagan.

In fact, liberals have their own version of the road to serfdom, which is different from Hayek's. In their version the failure of government to try actively to meet the public's demands for stability, security and equity leads finally to popular revulsion against the system and a flight to Big Brother. In this view, for example, Franklin Roosevelt was the savior of the free system, not its enemy.

Which of these scenarios for the road to serfdom is more realistic or probable is hard to say. There is, in my opinion, force to both of them. Careless acceptance of the growth of government by an indifferent public led by power seeking politicians and alienated intellectuals is a danger. But so is popular resentment against the neglect of real problems out of subservience to doctrinal purity. Each of these dangers may be more real at one time and less real at another. In my opinion, the danger of excessive government has in recent years been the more serious, and the reaction now under way in the Reagan Administration is proper. But is important that the other danger be kept in mind.

There is much room for constructive cooperation between those economists who wear the Adam Smith tie and those other mainstream economists who do not. They have a common interest in trying to find ways to solve the nation's real economic problems that do not threaten freedom. Although the tendency on both sides to promise a free lunch—policies that are all benefits and no costs—is unfortunate, I do not believe that economic policy is a zero-sum game. In other words, I believe it is possible to find policies that both sides would recognize as yielding a net benefit from their standpoint. We will have a better chance of finding those policies and getting them adopted if those who wear the tie and those who do not will try to listen to each other rather than concentrate on leading cheers for their own team.

Note

Originally published in *Business Economics*, Vol. 18, No. 1 (January 1983), pp. 5–9.

CHAPTER 14

1982

ECONOMICS FROM THREE PERSPECTIVES

Marina v. N. Whitman, General Motors Corporation

Economists, Corporate and Otherwise

Twenty years' varied experience as a professional economist has provided me with the basis for some broad, perhaps even unique, perspectives on the different roles economists play in society. I have toiled in all three vineyards—academia (University of Pittsburgh), government (Council of Economic Advisers) and now business (General Motors), and found the soil fertile in each—though perhaps conducive to different varietals.

My current position as Vice President and Chief Economist of the General Motors Corporation also gives me a vantage point for viewing, as well as an opportunity for shaping, the evolving role of the corporate economist. Because General Motors has one of the largest and most diversified corporate economics staffs, and has long been a leader in recognizing the contributions economists can make to successful corporate performance, I think the changes occurring at GM provide some valuable insights into the future role of the corporate economist.

In what follows I shall try to compare and contrast, from these vantage points, the roles of academic, government and business economists, and indicate the substantial changes I foresee in the traditional role of the corporate economist—changes which should promote greater interaction, cooperation and understanding among academic, government and business economists and, I hope, between academia, government and business as well.

Academic, Government and Business Economists: Some Differences and Some Common Bonds

There are readily observable differences among the professional economists who inhabit these three environments. The casually-dressed, absent-minded professor contrasts sharply with the starched, pinstriped corporate economist. Government economists who don sport coats and corduroys in the office but show up for meetings in vested suits may have found the golden mean. The costumes reflect, as they usually do, more fundamental differences in the roles played by academic, government and business economists and in the preferences, prejudices, and personalities of those who are attracted to these respective roles.

Basic versus Applied Research

Economists in all three branches of the profession are, by and large, fundamentally research oriented. Perhaps economics attracts those with an inquisitive nature; and then, too, we are all products of our training. The research orientation results also from the nature of the complex issues economists study, and the fact that we seem to know so frustratingly little about these complex phenomena.

While this research orientation is a strong common bond among economists, specific research interests vary substantially among those in the academic world, government and business. Academic economists are primarily interested in basic research—the development and testing of new theories and new models. Government and, even more so, corporate economists are primarily concerned with applied research—the application of currently accepted theory and verified empirical evidence to the resolution of pressing problems facing the government agency or business enterprise. Obviously, society needs both, and benefits from an efficient division of labor.

Timing

Academic economists tend to have relatively long research horizons and generally do not face the pressing deadlines that are the operating norms for government and business economists. This difference, of course, reflects a fundamental distinction between basic and applied research. Among the most prized attributes of the academic researcher are originality and thoroughness—the ability to generate new hypotheses and the tenacity to assemble and organize data in meaningful and rigorous tests of those hypotheses. A successful government or business economist, by contrast, is one who can grasp and deal with the essence of a complicated problem quickly and on the basis of inevitably incomplete and inadequate information. Here, as elsewhere, resources are limited and tradeoffs are unavoidable. Thoroughness is also important in government and business research, but there is nothing more useless than an analysis completed the day after your CEO has testified, or a White House policy decision has been reached.

Because of the significantly different research time horizons, we are always sensitive to "temporal shock" when interviewing a recent graduate who has just spent a year—or two or three—completing a dissertation. Explaining to such a graduate that a similar question might have to be researched and analyzed in three weeks, or even three days, often elicits expressions of puzzlement, disbelief, or utter dismay.

Specialist versus Generalist

The academic economist typically specializes in one or two relatively specialized branches of economics. For example, except for occasional forays into the introductory course or intermediate micro or macroeconomics courses, my teaching and research were both focused on a particular sub-specialty: the theory of international trade and finance. There is no such luxury for most government or business economists. If Adam Smith is correct, that the division of labor is limited by the extent of the market, I can assure you that there is a very small market in government or business for such a narrowly specialized focus.

Opportunities for specialization are somewhat greater in government than in business because of the larger size of the government market and the existence of numerous specialized public agencies and institutions such as the Federal Reserve System and the International Monetary Fund. However, at the Council of Economic Advisers, I began to learn what it means to be a generalist. As a member of that three-person body in the early 1970s, "my" share of the economic policy universe included not only international economic developments and policy but also price and wage developments, including the US wage-price control program, human resource development programs, environmental policies, issues related to regulated industries, and a variety of industry studies ranging from agriculture to transportation.

In business one does specialize in a certain sense, along industry lines rather than by economic specialty. Working for GM, my major focus of concern is, of course, the motor vehicle industry. But, the worldwide dimensions of this industry are so extensive that the term generalist has taken on new meaning for me. In the course of a day, I may have to address such diverse issues as car and truck (and locomotive) sales forecasts, interest rate trends, an antitrust suit, the private and social costs and benefits of a safety regulation, the future course of exchange rates, differences in US-Japanese labor costs, and the impact on the Corporation of a balanced budget amendment.

Individual versus Collective Achievement

The academic's work tends to be highly personal, at least in economics, where large group research projects are the exception rather than the norm. The end product is the researcher's own, as are the plaudits or the brickbats. Indeed, the entire university experience—as a student in the classroom, faculty member in the library, scientist in the laboratory—is focused on individual learning. In that sense, the university is the last frontier of individualism. In sharp contrast, government and business economists are members of much more collectivist institutions. Government agencies must reconcile their differences, and corporations must reach a consensus among their numerous central office staffs and operating divisions. As a result, achievements are almost invariably collective, and the ability to listen, interact, persuade and compromise is much more important to success in government and business than in academe, where professional reputations are honed on originality and sometime burnished by intransigence.

Constituencies

The academic economist is free to analyze behavior or welfare optimization at any chosen level—the world economy, a single nation, or a particular factor of production such as labor or capital. The government or business economist, on the other hand, apparently has a particular constituency as the primary frame of reference. But, in fact, the "government" or the "company" does not really represent a single, monolithic point of view or set of needs. There are often as many competing views on a particular issue within a government agency or a large corporation as there are professors in an economics department. Thus, for the government or business economist the constituency is neither clearly defined nor freely chosen. Even at the CEA, where we told ourselves that the relevant frame of reference is always the national economic welfare, the definition of that elusive concept was inevitably tempered by the ideology, the preferences, and the political commitments of a particular President.

The business economist also has the complex task of reconciling the firm's private interests with the larger interests of the society of which it is a part. (Though not everyone would agree, I would argue this is also a major challenge for government economists.) Corporate strategies that are at variance with the public interest, though they may sometimes offer short-run advantages, are not likely to be viable in the long run. Economists' training in analyzing ultimate as well as immediate welfare effects gives them a special ability, as well as responsibility, to address these conflicts, many of which have surfaced in the last decade or two under the broad rubric of "corporate social responsibility" or "corporate governance."

Doing versus Managing

In academia, good teaching and research are rewarded with promotion and increased opportunities for more specialized teaching and additional research. In government and business, good performance as an analyst leads to promotion and increasing management responsibilities. As one rises through the ranks in government or business, one must rely more and more upon other people's work rather than one's own. Thus, increasingly one who has been trained for and has a natural inclination for research analysis, becomes a manager of other analysts. As an academic, I *did* things (wrote an article, delivered a lecture); as an executive, I spend much of my time directing and expediting the work of others, and then "marketing" the product of their analysis both inside and outside the Corporation.

Insider versus Outsider

The academic economist enjoys the "academic freedom" to speak his or her mind, and to be publicly critical of economic policy. This is not only a freedom, it is a responsibility and a necessity for maintaining an effectively functioning economy and a free society. The economist working inside government or business has less latitude in public commentary. Comments by government or business economists, unlike those from academic economists, are generally attributed to their particular agency or corporation. The government or business economist must therefore be sensitive to the implications of public statements on a particular issue for many other aspects of his institution's activity.

Because the government or business economist is an insider, on the other hand, he or she has opportunities to effect constructive change not available to the outsider. Considerable and prolonged internal discussion typically precedes a significant public statement or course of action taken by a government agency or private business. During this internal review process the government or business economist has an opportunity to argue for more constructive policies and, at times, effect significant change.

Both public and private criticism are essential to the effective functioning of our democratic, capitalist society. If one is lucky, as I have been, there can be the opportunity to do both during the course of a professional lifetime. But one can not do both effectively at the same time—public criticism of one's own institution is bound to reduce drastically one's effectiveness in influencing opinion and helping to shape policy internally. Thus, the complementary roles played in society by academic, government and business economists represent an effective specialization of essential tasks.

Economics at General Motors

As the discussion above suggests, there seems to be an efficient division of labor among academic, government and business economists. But, for this division of labor to bear fruit, there must also be markets where their specialized products can be exchanged. There has been and still is too much isolation among academic, government and business economists—too little exchange. I think one of the major reasons I was asked to head the Economics Staff at General Motors is because I was seen as someone who could help develop this needed "market for ideas" not only among academic, government and business economists, but among academia, government and business as well.

I interpret my role at GM as an ambassador for mutually beneficial exchange among the various elements of the total society of which General Motors is a part. I help interpret the economic realities of the world for GM and of GM for the world. This role is becoming increasingly important with the growing complexity and interdependencies among all aspects of society. There is virtually nothing General Motors does today that is not in some way affected by public policy.

To bridge the gap between business and society at large requires the development of an economics staff which can shoulder the heavy two-way traffic such a bridge must bear. This is one of my major goals at General Motors. I can, perhaps, best describe our efforts to achieve this goal by reviewing the development and overall structure of the Economics Staff at General Motors, and some of the more significant changes that have occurred recently.

There have been some very prominent economists at General Motors over the years who have risen to high positions in the Corporation. Donaldson Brown (Vice Chairman), Albert Bradley (Chairman), C. E. Wilson (President), F. G. Donner (Chairman), Ernest Breach (Vice President and Group Executive), were all GM economists at various points in their careers.

The current Economics Staff at General Motors traces its origins to a Social and Economic Relations section started in 1946. A Business Research Staff reporting to the President and Chief Executive Officer was created in 1948. Andrew Cort, widely known for his work on hedonic price indices and General Motors cost-of-living allowance formula, was in charge of the Industrial Economics section of this staff. Numerous reorganizations occurred over the years, and Henry Duncombe was named Chief Economist in 1972. He then became the first Vice President for Economics in 1974.

Since I joined General Motors after Mr. Duncombe's retirement in 1979, the Economics Staff has been expanded and reorganized to provide for a better integration of the forecasting, policy analysis and planning functions that are increasingly essential to successful business performance.

General Motors Economics Staff currently has over 70 members, located in New York and Detroit, plus two European specialists based in London. The staff has three basic functions—economic forecasting, public policy analysis and strategic planning.

The economic analysis and forecasting groups monitor both general economic conditions and motor vehicle markets in North America and overseas, with increasing emphasis on the faster growing (though smaller) foreign markets. Short-term cyclical and long-run trend factors are both analyzed. The cyclical analysis has about a two-year time horizon and focuses on such cyclical factors as business inventories, consumer debt levels and capacity utilization. The longer-run analysis emphasizes demographic and productivity trends, energy costs, exchange rates and competitive cost positions. The cyclical analysis provides important input into the corporation's product scheduling function as well as the financial forecasts. The longer-term analysis assists future product and facilities planning.

These groups utilize both econometric techniques and judgmental analysis. Econometric models facilitate the massive data processing requirements and the evaluation of different economic scenarios and alternative policy assumptions. The use of econometric models also imposes a measure of objective discipline and internal consistency on the forecast. However, raw model output as well as the basic assumptions underlying this output must be subjected to judgmental analysis. Because of the growing importance of planning flexibility into the firm's operations in the face of a highly uncertain and volatile economic outlook, GM is increasingly stressing the development of alternative future business scenarios rather than single point forecasts. This approach is also consistent with the fact that our economist's tool kit equips us far better to make conditional statements about the future ("if a particular policy is followed, then the following results are likely to occur") than unconditional forecasts ("the unemployment rate will average 'x' percent in 1983").

The primary purpose of economic policy analysis is to assist General Motors' management and other staff groups in the systematic review and formulation of public policy positions. International policy analysis monitors political and regulatory developments which affect General Motors' foreign operations and new offshore capital investment decisions.

This analysis is becoming increasingly important with the "world car" concept and the rapid internationalization of product planning and marketing strategies. We also track developments in international trade relations (e.g., import restraints, local production and export requirements, reciprocity, etc.), GATT negotiations and other developments affecting our worldwide trading and operating position.

The analysis of domestic policy issues ranges from regulatory reform, antitrust, labor and social responsibility issues to governmental tax and expenditure policies. This group conducts private and social cost-benefit analyses, analyzes the sales, employment and income effects of proposed public policies and explores alternative means of achieving social objectives at reduced cost.

An energy analysis group, recently added to the Economics Staff, monitors trends in energy demand, supplies and prices and evaluates alternative fuel developments. US energy policies, such as contingency planning for supply disruptions and emergency allocation procedures, are also reviewed by this group.

The Corporate Strategic Planning group is the most recent addition to the Economics Staff. This group evaluates alternatives future business scenarios, analyzes fundamental industry success factors, and works closely with operating groups to develop and implement strategic business management techniques and processes. These analyses are used to assist in the formulation and consolidation of the five-year business plans of the Corporation and its divisions and in the identification of new business opportunities, such as the GM-Fanuc joint venture with a Japanese firm recently established to engage in robotics manufacturing in Michigan. Finally, Strategic Planning also provides computer-based support systems for evaluating and monitoring alternative strategic decisions.

Strategic planning is an ideal complement to the business forecasting and policy analysis activities. The forecasting and policy analysis efforts provide important inputs into the business plans and overall corporate strategy. In turn, the interaction with corporate strategic planners sharpens the analytical focus of the forecasting and policy analysis activities, and insures their effective integration into strategic decision making.

Integration and Bridge Building

Integration rather than size is the most distinguishing feature of General Motors Economics Staff. Many corporations undoubtedly perform these forecasting, policy analysis and strategic planning functions, but not usually within a single staff. However, to perform these functions adequately increasingly demands their effective integration, which we are seeking at General Motors. The increasing impact of government policies and regulations on the business environment requires that analysis of socio-political processes, goals and criteria be effectively integrated into product forecasts and corporate planning.

As I noted earlier, I see my current role as an economic bridge-builder between General Motors and the society in which it operates. The growing importance of socio-political factors in successful business planning also demands full participation and greater interaction among academic, government and business economists in the "marketplace of ideas."

My staff and I are participating in this marketplace, on an increasing scale. During the last two years, General Motors has conducted a series of "academic seminars" in which a small group of GM executives visits college campuses to discuss critical industry issues with broad societal implications. These seminars bring our most important concerns to the attention of academia, and provide us with outside feedback which assists our internal policy reviews and decisions. On occasion, we also invite outside experts to Detroit to discuss an important issue of mutual interest.

We participate very actively in numerous studies of the motor vehicle industry being conducted in academia or the government. I have also encouraged members of my staff to attend professional meetings, present papers and publish articles in referred journals whenever possible. I also encourage direct interaction among individual members of my staff with any academic or business economist interested in issues affecting our industry.

These are some of the efforts General Motors has mounted to increase the interaction among business, academia and government. In the future, we will take advantage of every opportunity to enhance this interaction in the firm belief that an open exchange of ideas on important public policy issues is essential to informed public policy and the rational pursuit of both public and private goals.

The greater integration of business forecasting, policy analysis and strategic planning and an expanded exchange of ideas among academic, government and business economists together offer new opportunities for the reconciliation of public and private long-run interests, the maximization of social and economic well-being, and a challenging and productive future for economists, whatever uniform they wear.

Note

Originally published in *Business Economics*, Vol. 18, No. 1 (January 1983), pp. 20–24.

CHAPTER 15

1984

THE ADAM SMITH ADDRESS

WAS ADAM SMITH A MONETARIST OR A KEYNESIAN?

Charles P. Kindleberger, Massachusetts Institute of Technology and Brandeis University

Adam smith, let me start by saying, was a remarkable writer, person, and economist. He was in many ways the real founder of economics, starting our science off in resource allocation, income distribution and a host of similar aspects of microeconomics. Despite a number of interesting passages, such as that on debt, however, he was not distinguished as a macro-economist. The hagiography tends either to ignore his weakness in money and banking, as does Samuel Hollander in *The Economics of Adam Smith*, or to protest that he is much better on the balance of payments [9], or on monetary economics generally [20] than most observers are willing to allow. I yield to none in my admiration for *The Wealth of Nations*—and in fact recommend to students that they, like Bismarck's tariff negotiator for Prussia under the Zollverein, Rudolph Von Delbrück, read the hallowed text each night for half an hour before retiring [8, vol. 1]. But it is helpful for Smith's reputation as a human being to acknowledge that he, like the rest of us, from time to time made a mistake or overlooked a significant aspect of the economy of his day—even on the microeconomic side. I happened to elicit strong protests from two critics at the Glasgow celebration of the bicentenary of *The Wealth of Nations* when I suggested that Adam Smith was totally unaware of the technological changes taking place in the industrial revolution cooking around him [2, 12]. His other slips not recited in my chapter on that occasion include the remark that Dutch merchants are uneasy at being separated from their capital which is why they unload goods from East Prussia in Amsterdam to look at them before shipping them on to Italy—when the real reason was to repack the grain more carefully to prevent it from exploding from spontaneous combustion under the hot Mediterranean sun [28, Book

IV, 422]; or the amateurish and quite unsupported sociology that ascribed French interest in life annuities and tontines to the "fact" that the farmers general (of tax collections and the like) who accumulate wealth are social upstarts, cut off from marrying into the upper classes and too proud to marry their lower-class equals, hence celibate and without heirs [28, Book V, 871–872]. This is the sort of implicit theorizing to which social scientists are always tempted and against which Wesley C. Mitchell warned us at Columbia in the mid-1930s. Some years ago in a book on the terms of trade, I wrote in the introduction that I would thereafter give up empirical work, disheartened that some of our most fascinating results at the three-quarter mark turned out to rest on computing errors. The statement evoked a warm response from professional friends. But the thrust of all this is to assert that Adam Smith is a marvelous economist even when he proves to be somewhat short of outstanding on money and banking.

Keynesianism and monetarism in what follows are used loosely. I am tempted to paraphrase Gilbert's lyric in *Iolanthe* on Liberals and Conservatives by saying that all economists are either Keynesians who believe in expanding investment or government spending to achieve higher employment, or monetarists who want to restrict bank lending and the growth of the money supply to help fight inflation. In some cases it makes a difference when one came into the profession, whether in the 1930s when unemployment was rife, or in the period after World War II of steady growth and reasonably full employment. In a paper a few years ago on Keynesianism versus monetarism in eighteenth- and nineteenth-century France, I lined up John Law, Napoleon I, the Saint-Simonian school, including notably Jacques Laffitte, the Pereire brothers who found the *Crédit Mobilier,* and Michel Chevalier among the Keynesians; the Paris brothers (who won out over John Law), François Mollien, Napoleon's Minister of the Public Treasury, and the Bank of France establishment of the *hautes banques,* including especially Baron James de Rothschild, among the monetarists [19]. For England, a generation after Adam Smith, the big division occurred in the Bullionist controversy between the Currency School, which can broadly be identified with monetarism, and the Banking School, which clung to the quasi-Keynesian belief in the real-bills doctrine that money can be expanded *pari passu* with underlying actual trade transactions. The same issue in Sweden in the mid-eighteenth century had divided the "Hats," who had interests in exports and large-scale business and believed in monetary expansion, from the "Caps," in small business, and to a considerable extent import competing. The Caps ascribed exchange depreciation of the period to excess expansion of the note issue, while the Hats, like the Banking School in England half a century later, attributed it to failures that worsened the balance of payments. A similar debate was pursued over the causes of the German hyperinflation of 1923 between monetarists, like Bresciani-Turroni and Philip Cagan, who ascribed it to the expansionary policies of the Reichsbank, and the balance of payments school including, along with Germans such as Karl Helfferich and Moritz Bonn, such Americans as James W. Angell and John H. Williams, who blamed reparation payments. Outside Europe, the same contentious issue has been met in the Baring crisis of 1890 in Argentina, in which monetarists blamed the changes in Argentine banking laws which led to over-issue, while the Keynesian or balance of payments school pointed to the cutoff of British lending to Argentina, the resultant depreciation of the peso, and the necessity with higher international prices to issue more banknotes to support the price level [35].

Which side of this perennial debate was Adam Smith on? First of all, he was more interested in real than in monetary analysis. There are such folk about today. In his stupendous book on the *World Economy,* Walt Rostow explicitly states that he is unconcerned with monetary or banking developments, believing in the dominance of real factors such as population growth, discovery and technological change, ordered in cycles of various sorts, including the Juglar eight-to-nine-year business cycle, the "stages of growth" and the 50-year Kondratieff cycle [26]. Ronald Coase holds the opinion that institutions, including financial institutions, adapt to real conditions of demand and supply—except in the rare cases that transactions costs are especially high—so that monetary and banking practice and institutions fall passively into place [6]. Schumpeter's *History of Economic Analysis* observes that real analysis dominated economic thought prior to 1600, after which there was an interlude to 1760 in which monetary analysis was considered important, until real analysis, with Turgot and Adam Smith in the lead, took over once more [27, 283].

But Adam Smith thought something about money. Of course. Book I, Chapters IV and V, explain the exchange functions of money that widen the market and hence extend the limits to the division of labor. Book II, Chapter II deals with money as part of the capital of society, and with banking in a general way. There are other scattered passages—the long digression on silver, that on banks of deposit, especially the Bank of Amsterdam, the treatment of the public debt. There is, however, no consistent orderly analysis of money and banking, either in the national or in the international dimension, despite the valiant efforts of a number of writers, in their pious defense of the Master, to find them.

Money is the great wheel, Adam Smith asserts in Book II, presumably a water wheel that powers the system. Banking goes further. If gold and silver money, which circulates in a country and allows the dead stock to be converted into active stock, may properly be compared to a highway, banking provides a sort of "waggon-way through the air" [28, II, 305]. These are Keynesian metaphors—although as Bentham complained, from wheels, water and wagons, one cannot get a clear idea of money and banking that need definition and exemplification [32, 301]. On the other side of this methodological issue, however, I commend the reader to a recent paper by Donald McCloskey on "The Rhetoric of Economics," that maintains that a penetrating metaphor is worth more than a lot of integrals, differentials and matrices, together with scads of a + b. He cites as an illustration "investment in human capital," a Chicago metaphor of Ted Schultz and Gary Becker, which illuminates many issues in the economics of labor, of capital and of education. But the metaphors should be apposite and powerful.

To return to the waggon-way through the air provided by banks and the paper money they issue, a monetarist note creeps in when Smith goes on:

> The commerce and industry of the country, however, it must be acknowledged, cannot be altogether so secure, when they are thus, as it were, suspended on Daedalian

> wings of paper money, as when they travel about on the solid ground of gold and silver. [28, II, 305]

This is the way it goes throughout the great work: passages here that sound monetarist, others there which suggest an interest in expansion. Before going into further detail, let me pause to note that a young English economic historian has recently noted that financial history can be written in four differing modes: first, the orthodox, in which the story line is how the central bank gradually got control of the money supply, developed appropriate policy instruments, and repressed the tendency of the financial system to what Smith called "overtrading"; second, the "heroic," in which great innovations in money and banking give a needed lift to economic growth and development; third, the Populist, with emphasis on how orthodox monetary and banking development have held back the small merchant, small farmer and small industrialist by denying them credit and favoring foreign trade, trusts, and perhaps government; and fourth, the "statist," in which emphasis rests on the development of money and banking to assist government in carrying out its functions, especially the finance of war [17, 1982]. The author of this taxonomy was making a point that the central banks of Argentina, Australia and Canada were all created to help finance governments; the same could be said of the founding of the Bank of England in 1694 during the Nine Years' War, of the Bank of France in 1800 in the Napoleonic Wars, and of the National Bank Act of 1863 in the Union States which helped finance the Union in the Civil War. The orthodox mode of writing helped finance the Union in the Civil War. The orthodox mode of writing financial history fits into the monetarist view of money and banking, the heroic into the Keynesian as I loosely use the term, and the Populist into a frustrated Keynesian viewpoint.

On the domestic front, Smith took an orthodox position insofar as he strongly favored convertibility of bank notes into specie, opposed the issue of banknotes of small dimensions, worried about chains of discount accommodation bills in which A drew on B, B on C, C on D and M or N back on A, each discounting these accommodation bills after an appropriate interval. He applauded the Bank of Amsterdam, although not for the subtle reasons which later led Henry Simon and Milton Friedman to advocate 100 percent reserves against bank deposits in order to frustrate the expansion and contraction of bank money through the money multiplier, but because of its contribution to "money-circulating," or monetizing the economy and pushing back the limits on the division of labor. He opposed overtrading. The ideas of John Law are called splendid but visionary and are said to have contributed to that excess of banking which of late has been complained of both in Scotland and in other places [28, II, 303].

And yet in an earlier passage, he observed that the new banking companies of Scotland of the last 25 or 30 years, that is since about 1750, in almost every considerable town, and even in some country villages, had produced great benefit:

> I have heard it asserted, that the trade of the city of Glasgow, doubled in about fifteen years after the first erection of the banks there; and that the trade of Scotland has more than quadrupled since the first erection of the banks at Edinburgh…

But then he waffles:

> Whether the trade of Scotland in general, or of the city of Glasgow in particular, has really increased in so great a proportion, during so short a period, I do not pretend to know. If either of them has increased in this proportion, it seems to be an effect too great to be accounted for by the sole operation of this cause. That the trade and industry of Scotland, however, have increased very considerably during this period, and that the banks have contributed a good deal to this increase, cannot be doubted. [28, II, 281]

It is worth noting, as it bears on a modern debate, that Smith, like most modern monetarists, believed in regulation of banking. His interest was in the convertibility of bank notes into gold and silver on demand, and the prohibition of the circulation of bank notes of small denomination such as £1 and under. But the emphasis on liberty in other fields of economic endeavor whilst maintaining limitations in money and banking presents philosophical problems for "liberals" with a small "l," or possibly "libertarians." It is a Keynesian position sometimes to want regulation in fields other than money and banking, but to insist on easier entry, more expansion, extension of banking into the provinces, and the like in money and banking. A French monetarist, Louis Wolowski, testifying before the 1867 Inquiry into money and banking pushed by the expansionist (Keynesian) school, kept reiterating that "free trade in banking is free trade in swindling," a quotation ascribed to Daniel Webster. He also pointed out that Richard Cobden, the leader of the fight for free trade and against the Corn Laws in England, had voted three times against crippling amendments to the Bank Act of 1844, a victory for the Monetarist Currency School [24, II, 205, 230, 383]. While Milton Friedman is prepared to deregulate by removing license requirements for all sorts of activities, from brain surgery to teenage automobile driving, leaving the necessary discipline to prevent abuse to the market, he has been outdone by the Austrian school that is ready to throw banking and the issue of money open to all comers [14, 31]. Vaubel regards money as a private, not a public good, even in its function as a standard of measurement (unit of account). He believes that Gresham's law need not operate with competitive monies, provided they are traded with flexible exchange rates among them. He maintains, in fact, that the opposite of Gresham's law will result, that good money will drive out bad as banks compete to have their money accepted. This optimistic view seems to fly in the face of a long record of bank failures from John Law's *Banque Royale* to the recent troubles in Nashville and in Penn Square, Oklahoma. And Vaubel does not consider the objection that if different banks' deposits are traded at varying prices, they cease in effect to be money, if we define money as the one asset fixed in price in terms of itself. Adam Smith is far from such a libertarian stance. In his eyes, regulation of banks is not a violation of natural liberty: "those exertions of the natural liberty of a few individuals, which might endanger the security of the whole society, are, and ought to be, restrained by the laws of all governments, of the most free as well as the most despotical" [28, II, 308].

Further on domestic banking, Smith is generally sharply criticized both by monetarists and by some Keynesians for believing in the real-bills doctrine [4,

519; 21, 337; 20, 195]. This doctrine, held by the Banking School, considered that expansion of the money supply was entirely acceptable if the underlying credit transaction was one backed by a bill of exchange drawn on a sale of merchandise by a bona fide seller on a bona fide buyer, rather than on accommodation bills or promissory notes. This is generally regarded as a complete fallacy. With full employment, expanded credit based on a commercial transaction can lead to higher prices, more credit expansion justified by the higher value of the real goods traded, and hence to a cumulative inflationary process. Moreover the attack on accommodation bills, implicit in Smith's discussion of chains of discounts, and taught to me in the 1930s by my banking teacher, H. Parker Willis, can go too far, as Hawtrey has pointed out [13, 124–125]. But there is a kernel of truth in the real-bills view when there is widespread unemployment. It does not justify Smith on real bills, however, as his general assumption was one of full employment [16, 207]. He never accepted Hume's contention that material advantages may be gained by an economy where money is growing—because of initial unemployment.

On the international front, Smith had an opportunity to accept another of David Hume's positions—that of the price-specie-flow mechanism, but he did not. Viner regards this as one of the foremost mysteries in the history of economic thought, since Smith was well acquainted with Hume and his work, and in fact corresponded with him frequently [33, 97]. In fact Smith went back to an old notion in which each country requires a certain amount of money, and if more is issued than the country requires, it ships it abroad to buy foreign goods. Viner calls this an obsolete model, but it comes close to the monetary approach to the balance of payments today as expounded by Frenkel and Johnson [10] or McKinnon [23]. I must say I find the monetarist model of the balance of payments bizarre. In McKinnon's exposition, for example, if more money is issued than households and businesses want to hold, the money is spent or lent abroad, leading to a deficit that brings domestic demand and supply for money back into balance. In some formulations where capital flows are excluded by assumption, changes in earning and spending are used to adjust the stock of money to some desired level, rather than, as my generation was taught, using money to equilibrate temporary discrepancies between income and expenditure. The monetarist model of the balance of payments seems to have switched money from an instrument to an objective variable, and vice versa with income and expenditure. Moreover, why employ assumptions that put the burden on changes in income and expenditure? For the most part, with a banking system in existence, changes in the desired stock of money are brought about by borrowing or lending.

Eagly and Laidler, as already mentioned, seek to exonerate Adam Smith from the charge that he unduly neglected Hume's balance-of-payments adjustment mechanism, although their defense, however respectful and even dutiful, fails to persuade. Laidler is more successful in his assertion that Smith had an appropriate insight into what is called today world monetarism—how world discoveries of gold and silver set the world price level, and the mechanism by which paper money can replace precious metals with important savings for society in real resources. It must be remembered, however, that Smith is not certain he wants to trust the Daedalian wings of paper money, as contrasted with the terra firma of gold and silver.

Part of Smith's uncertainty about paper money and banking had its origin in the fact that Scottish banking was undergoing a series of significant changes in the years from the early 1760s [4]. The period was somewhat comparable to the present day when deregulation is going forward in banking at a ferocious pace and analysts have a hard time trying to decide what the net effects on the system are going to be of CDs, NOW accounts, SUPER-NOW accounts, credit cards, Euro-currencies, money funds, bank holding companies, and the intrusion of insurance companies, brokerage houses and retail stores into banking and of thrift institutions into industrial lending. The pace from 1763 to 1776 was perhaps not so giddy as that of today, but 1763 was the year both that Adam Smith finished the first draft of *The Wealth of Nations,* revised in two years in France, six in the tiny town of Kirkcaldy in Scotland, and four in London, and of the start of branch banking in Scotland. New bank legislation in 1765 gave rise to a debate, addressed particularly to questions of free entry into banking and the so-called "optional clause," which made it possible for banks to postpone redeeming banks notes for six months after presentation. No sooner had these controversies been settled when the Ayr Bank, founded in 1770, failed in 1772 with £200,000 of notes in circulation and £600,000 of discounts on banks in London which it could not pay. Among the shareholders who lost some or all of their estates because of unlimited liability was the Duke of Buccleugh, Adam Smith's patron. Checkland finds it curious that this failure did not modify Smith's optimistic view of the merit of free entry into (regulated) banking, which he thought would require banks to be circumspect in their own interest [4, 515], a position paralleled today by Vaubel.

What had brought caution to the Scottish banks earlier in the century was the device by which the Bank of Scotland and the Royal Bank of Scotland each accumulated and held supplies of the bank notes issued by the other, ready to present them for specie when the competition got particularly rough. Again in 1774 after the Ayr failure, a unified system of note exchanges was established among all Scottish banks [4, 510]. The rapid rate of institutional change in Scottish banking in this period when *The Wealth of Nations* was being revised perhaps accounts for the lack of a clear line of thought on banking on the part of Smith. It is evocative of the view today that changes in banking and finance are proceeding at too rapid a pace to enable analysts and policymakers to figure out how the system is likely to function under different circumstances, and leading Henry Kauffman, the *New York Times* (May 3, 1983), and others to call for a slowdown of deregulation.

Was Smith a Keynesian or a monetarist? My answer to that fallacious question is not "none of the above" as in some questions based on illegitimate alternatives, but giving him the benefit of the doubt, "both." To be both a Keynesian and a monetarist is the only reasonable position. If it does not emerge with clarity in *The Wealth of Nations,* I believe it to be there concealed behind a film of muddle. For a superior statement of such a balanced position, one should read Henry Thornton's *An Inquiry into the Nature and Effect of the Paper Credit of Great Britain,* published in 1802, a short generation after *The Wealth of Nations.* Thornton was a dedicated philanthropist, an abolitionist regarding slavery, a banker, and a thoughtful student. In an introduction to the 1939 edition of *Paper Credit,* Hayek points out that Thornton is overshadowed by the monetarist Ricardo, but "It is not too much to say that the appearance of *Paper Credit* marked a new epoch in monetary theory." In some respects we have today retrogressed from Thornton's understanding.

Thornton was both monetarist and Keynesian. He thought that Currency School adherents such as Boyd were far too simple in criticizing the Bank of England for overissue. He made allowance in the depreciation of sterling for the effects of bad harvests and of British subsidies to her Continental allies [30, 354]. A monetarist insofar as he drafted the Bullion Report of 1810 with William Huskisson and Francis Horner, he applauded Adam Smith's remark about banks being able in short run to activate the dead stock of the country [30, 175], and regarded bills of exchange as near money. In this his ideas differed sharply from those of the leading monetarist and bullionist of 50 years later, Lord Overstone, who excoriated Colonel Torrens for having briefly regarded anything as money except gold or bank notes which substituted one-for-one for gold. In Torrens' case Overstone's scorn was heaped on him for having flirted with the idea that bank deposits might be money [25, II, 713–717]. Thornton opposed too violent a contraction of Bank of England notes in order to attract gold, believing that it would in fact repel it [30, 122, 153]. He further believed that the Bank of England should act as the lender of last resort in crisis [30, 188], while holding that in normal times the Bank should keep its circulation of notes steady, regardless of fluctuations in its gold stock [30, 67].

I am especially interested in Thornton's views on fixing on a single money aggregate. Bagehot later said *à propos* of M1, M2 and so on:

> Men of business in England do not like the currency question. They are perplexed to define accurately what money is; *how* to count they know, but *what* to count they do not know. (his italics) [1, IX, 319]

In another passage in his early writings on monetary questions, well before the magisterial *Lombard Street* of 1873, Bagehot records a victory of Thomas Tooke, the Banking School leader, over Colonel Torrens of the Currency School on the issue:

> No. Tooke contends that no new purchasers can, under the present law (the Bank Act of 1844), be brought into the market by an undue issue of bank notes, nevertheless other media of interchange can be found, such as bills of exchange and book credits, that will do the work. [1, 256]

But Thornton had made the point in 1802:

> If bills and bank notes were both extinguished, other substitutes for gold would be found. Men save themselves the trouble of counting, weighing and transporting guineas in all the larger operations of commerce ... Credit would still exist, credit in books, credit depending on the testimony of witnesses, or on merely verbal promises. [30, 101]

There is nothing new under the sun. I thought I had done well in attacking the monetarist view that booms can be contained by fixing some money aggregate, arguing:

> Fix any M1 and the market will create new forms of money in periods of boom to get around the limit and create the necessity to fix a new variable, M_j. [18, 58]

by citing John Stuart Mill and the Radcliffe Commission. Thornton was ahead of us all. And if you want a modern illustration of his insight, consider the 1982 stock-market boom in Kuwait, which was financed by the simplest form of "money" creation I can think of, the writing of postdated checks.

The essence is that both monetarism and Keynesianism in their simple formulations are right in their place and wrong if one tries to make too much of them as all purpose weapons. Michel Chevalier was an unreconstructed Keynesian in France in the middle of the nineteenth century, wanting more bank notes, more banks, an end to the monopoly of the Bank of France, and especially the extension of banking into the provinces. On his visit to the United States in the 1830s, however, he changed his spots, sympathizing with Nicholas Biddle of the Second Bank of the United States and criticizing President Andrew Jackson who vetoed the renewal of its charter [5, I, iv, vi]. Chevalier was struck by the resemblances between the attacks on the Bank and the Republican tirades of 1791 and 1792 in his native France which led up to the Reign of Terror [5, I, 72], and went on to say that if one got rid of the Bank, one would plunge the country into commercial anarchy which would end up as political anarchy [5, I, 95]. This goes further than most monetarists today.

More contemporaneously, I find the debate between Temin [29] and Friedman and Schwartz [11], plus the rest of the monetarist school represented in Brunner's *The Great Depression Revisited,* terribly simple-minded. To wrap up the Great Depression of the 1930s in a model in which it is critical whether the IS curve, representing spending (the Keynesian view), or the LM curve, standing for the monetarist explanation, moved first, and to decide upon that basis whether the interest rate moved up or down, is to elevate a useful model in its own place into a fetish at the expense of the complex web of history. Where are the other elements in the intricate mechanism: the fragility of international debts, the seizing up of bank credit in New York as a result of the stockmarket crash and its propagation of the crisis to trade credits and consumer debt, the fall of prices, the debt-deflation process, the appreciation of exchange rates and the like? In *The Great Depression Revisited*, various monetarists finally admitted one international element into a previously purely domestic account of the depression—the Hawley-Smoot tariff act of 1930, although most international-trade models regard tariffs as a force for expansion, not contradiction. In *The Way the World Works,* Jude Wanniski even tries to explain Black Thursday and Black Tuesday, October 24 and 29, 1929 respectively, by the defeat of some low-tariff adherents in a Senate subcommittee on a minor carbide item, somehow foreshadowing the passage of the Hawley-Smoot tariff nine months later, its signing into law by some 40 countries, and the world depression which ensued. This is more than rational expectations: it is second sight. I subscribe to the principle of Occam's razor, that one should use parsimony in explanation, the simplest explanation consistent with the facts. My adherence stops short, however, of trying to explain the great depression with a monetarist model—or a simple Keynesian one for that matter—with or without the addition of the Hawley-Smoot tariff.

One conflict between Keynesians and monetarists worth noting is mentioned *à propos* of Ricardo and his critics by an historian of the debate over the resumption of specie payments in 1819. Keynesianism, states Hilton, partly quoting Winch, achieved its success in the 1930s, when politicians were thoroughly frustrated, by reason of its advocacy of an interventionist philosophy. In 1819, on the other hand, the monetarism of Ricardo appealed to such politicians as Lord Liverpool because it justified inaction [34, 70]. I sympathize with the liberal view that there is a lot of capacity in market economies to recover by themselves, but the notion that government should never interfere, or that all intervention is dysfunctional, is surely an exaggeration. Those who think otherwise would do well to contemplate the German monetary reform of 1948—to my mind the most brilliant feat of social engineering in historical memory—or such governmental successes as Lend-lease in World War II and the Marshall plan.

Government is an art that sometimes calls for deregulation and laissez-faire, sometimes for intervention. The monetarists and the Keynesians are both right—some of the time. The trick for government, or less pejoratively, the art of government, is to decide when and how much to intervene, and when and how rapidly to turn away.

After embarking on the outline of this lecture, I came across an excellent book by Ralph Bryant, *Controlling Money: The Federal Reserve and its Critics,* which, with a somewhat more technical approach, comes close to the position here set forth, that putting the fundamental questions of macroeconomic policy in terms of monetarism versus Keynesianism obscures rather than illuminates the issues. Each is correct, some of the time [22, 110], and to focus on a choice limited to these two positions neglects other highly important issues of monetary policy: viz.

—rules vs discretion
—relations between money and fiscal policies
—preferred macroeconomic policies for reducing inflation
—the interdependence of monetary policy in the United States and that in the rest of the world.

I would modify the list slightly, as Bryant himself might have done if he had developed these themes. In the first place, as earlier noted, the issue of rules versus discretion is implicit in the debate over monetarism versus Keynesianism, monetarism favoring rules, Keynesianism discretion. Secondly, I would like to see the interdependence question broadened from a focus on interest rates or world money supplies to include coordinated exchange rates. But surely Bryant is right that the answer to Keynesiansim versus monetarism is both, each in its time and place.

A simple rule which tells when to change rules is monetarism on trend and Keynesiansim in crisis. Friedman and Schwartz come close to articulating this position when they write about the need for a lender of last resort, using the metaphor that one rock held in place may stave off an avalanche, and quoting Bagehot's *Lombard Street* that a panic is a species of neuralgia and one must not starve it [11,

395]. I am doubtful about the latter metaphor and the therapy recommended, but have no difficulty about the monetary policy implied.

In the 1930s, the *New Yorker* ran a series of cartoons by Gluyas Williams concerning the so-called Skeptics Society, in which a group of frock-coated men would undertake to test aphorisms that loomed large in folklore. One cartoon showed the dignified Skeptics chasing a pig, to decide by scientific experiment whether one could or could not make a silk purse out of a sow's ear. On one occasion, the Society took on two folk-sayings simultaneously. They stood around on a platform while a blind-folded man stood on a board, poised over a precipice, as the Society sought to determine whether "He who hesitates is lost" or it is better to "Look before you leap." But of course both in the proper time and circumstances. Equally Keynesianism and monetarism are both right, as, on the right occasions, are Say's law that supply creates its own demand, and Keynes' law that demand creates its own supply. But not simultaneously, and not inevitably in all circumstances. The tasks of economists is to back off from the Pavlovian responses that make the stock market rise or fall on each Friday's announcement by the Fed of the money aggregates, and to explore what circumstances alter what cases, and how and to what extent.

I believe that Adam Smith, if he were to put his mind to macroeconomic policy today, would agree. He was a superb economist.

Note

Originally published in *Business Economics*, Vol. 19, No. 1 (January 1984), pp. 5–12.

References

1. Bagehot, Walter, *Lombard Street,* reprinted in N. St John-Stevas, ed., *The Collected Works of Walter Bagehot,* vol. ix. London: *The Economist,* 1973.
2. Briggs, Asa, "Comment" on C. P. Kindleberger, "The Historical Background: Adam Smith and the Industrial Revolution," in T. Wilson and A. S. Skinner, ed., *The Market and the State: Essays in Honour of Adam Smith.* Oxford: Clarendon, 1976.
3. Brunner, Karl, ed., *The Great Depression Revisited.* The Hague: Martinus Nijhoff, 1981.
4. Checkland, S. G., "Adam Smith and the Bankers," in A. S. Skinner and T. Wilson, eds., *Essays on Adam Smith.* Oxford: Clarendon, 1975.
5. Chevalier, Michel, *Lettres sur l'Amerique du Nord,* 3rd ed., 2 vols. Paris: Charles Gosselin, 1838.
6. Coase, Ronald H., "The Nature of the Firm," *Economica,* new series, vol. 4(1937), 386–405.
7. ———, "The Problems of Social Cost," *Journal of Law and Economics,* vol. 3 (1969), 1–44.
8. Delbrück, Rudolph von, *Lebenserinnerungen,* 2 vols. Leipsig: Duncker u. Humblot, 1905.
9. Eagley, Robert V., "Adam Smith and the Specie-Flow Doctrine," *Scottish Journal of Political Science,* vol. 17 (1970), 61–68.
10. Frenkel, Jacob and Harry G. Johnson, *The Monetary Approach to the Balance of Payments.* London: George Allen & Unwin, 1975.
11. Friedman, Milton and Anna J. Schwartz, *A Monetary History of the United States, 1867–1960.* Princeton, NJ: Princeton University Press, 1963.

12. Hartwell, R. M., "Comment" on C. P. Kindleberger, "The Historical Background: Adam Smith and the Industrial Revolution," in T. Wilson and A. S. Skinner, eds., *The Market and the State: Essays in Honour of Adam Smith*. Oxford: Clarendon, 1976.
13. Hawtrey, R. G., *Currency and Credit,* 3rd ed. London: Longmans, Green, 1927.
14. Hayek, F. A., "Introduction" to Henry Thornton, *Paper Credit*. London: George Allen & Unwin, 1939.
15. Hilton, Boyd, *Corn, Cash, Commerce: The Economic Policies of the Tory Governments, 1815–1830*. Oxford: Oxford University Press, 1977.
16. Hollander, Samuel, *The Economics of Adam Smith*. Toronto: University of Toronto Press, 1973.
17. Jones, Charles, "The Monetary Politics of Export Economies before 1914: Argentina, Australia, and Canada," a paper presented at the Symposium on "Argentina, Australia and Canada: Some Comparisons, 1870–1950," at the 44th International Congress of Americanists, Manchester, September 8, 1982.
18. Kindleberger, C. P., *Manias, Panics and Crashes: A History of Financial Crises*. New York: Basic Books, 1978.
19. ———, "Keynesianism vs. Monetarism in Eighteenth- and Nineteenth-Century France," *History of Political Economy,* vol. 12 (1980), 499–523.
20. Laidler, David, "Adam Smith as a Monetary Economist," *Canadian Journal of Economics,* vol. 14 (1981) 185–199.
21. Matthews, R. C. O., "Public Policy and Monetary Expenditure," in T. Wilson and A. S. Skinner, eds., *The Market and the State: Essays in Honour of Adam Smith*. Oxford: Clarendon, 1976.
22. McCloskey, Donald N., "The Rhetoric of Economics," unpublished draft article, 1983.
23. McKinnon, Ronald I., *Money in International Exchange: The Convertible Currency System*. London: Oxford University Press, 1979.
24. Ministère des Finance, et al., *Enquête sur les principes et les faits généraux qui régissent la circulation monétaire et fiduciare,* 6 vols. Paris: Imprimerie impériale, 1867.
25. O'Brien, D. P., ed., *The Correspondence of Lord Overstone,* 3 vols. Cambridge: Cambridge University Press, 1971.
26. Rostow, W. W., *The World Economy: History, Theory and Prospect*. London: Macmillan, 1978.
27. Schumpeter, Joseph A., *History of Economic Analysis*. London: George Allen & Unwin, 1954.
28. Smith, Adam, *An Inquiry into the Nature and Causes of the Wealth of Nations*. Cannan, ed. Edwin New York: Modern Library, 1937.
29. Temin, Peter, *Did Monetary Forces Cause the Great Depression?* New York: W.W. Norton, 1976.
30. Thornton, Henry, *An Enquiry into the Nature and Effect of the Paper Credit of Great Britain*. London: George Allen & Unwin, 1939.
31. Vaubel, Roland, "Free Currency Competition," *Weltwirtschaftliches Archiv,* vol. 113 (1977), 435–459.
32. Vickers, Douglas, "Adam Smith and the Status of the Theory of Money," in A. S. Skinner and T. Wilson, eds., *Essays on Adam Smith*. Oxford: Clarendon, 1975.
33. Viner, Jacob, *Studies in the Theory of International Trade*. New York: Harper & Brothers, 1937.
34. Wanniski, Jude, *The Way the World Works*. New York: Basic Books, 1977.
35. Williams, John H., *Argentine International Trade under Inconvertible Paper Money, 1880–1900*. Cambridge, MA: Harvard University Press, 1920.

PART III

1985–1994

CHAPTER 16

1987

THE ADAM SMITH ADDRESS
THE EFFECT OF GOVERNMENT ON ECONOMIC EFFICIENCY

George J. Stigler, University of Chicago

When a professional society names a lecture series after a great person, over the years its members are likely to learn much more about that great person than they really desire to know. You may well have reached this state, so I shall be both brief and slightly irreverent in discharging my duty of referring to our patron saint, Adam Smith.

My subject is the effect of governmental policies upon the wealth and rate of progress of nations, and Smith presented a firm opinion on this important matter:

> "According to the system of natural liberty, the sovereign has only three duties to attend to; three duties of great importance, indeed, but plain and intelligible to common understandings: first, the duty of protecting the society from the violence and invasion of other independent societies; secondly, the duty of protecting, as far as possible, every member of the society from the injustice or oppression of every other member of it, or the duty of establishing an exact administration of justice; and, thirdly, the duty of erecting and maintaining certain publick works and certain publick institutions, which it can never be for the interest of any individual, or small number of individuals, to erect and maintain; because the profit could never repay the expence to any individual or small number of individuals, though it may frequently do much more than repay it to a great society."

In a now-lost manuscript he was even more pithy:

> "Little else is requisite to carry a state to the highest degree of opulence, from the lowest barbarism, but peace, easy taxes, and a tolerable administration of justice."

I shall offer two remarks on these passages. First, it is hard to believe that *any* task, no matter how great its magnitude, is so large that the market cannot deal with it, if it is capable of being dealt with by man. Did not Great Britain in Smith's time leave the governance of India, already a nation of several hundred million beings, to a corporation called the East India Company? Was not the early economic development of Canada entrusted primarily to the Hudson's Bay Company? Second, *à propos* of Smith's assertion of the powerful and beneficial effects of peace, low taxes and tolerable justice, surely there have been societies (the Eskimos may be an example) that have not found these three conditions wholly sufficient to reach the highest degree of opulence.

Dr. Smith and all of his sensible disciples have believed that people would not strive to do anything well unless there were a reasonable measure of agreement between the success of their efforts and the rewards they would receive. That reasonable measure of agreement appears to require an institution of property, a social system to defend the property, and a tax system that does not destroy or reduce intolerably the measure of agreement between effort and reward. Does the immense scope of modern governments impair or reinforce these elementary conditions for sustained human effort?

The Paradox of Legitimacy

I shall begin the discussion of the effects of government on economic efficiency with the examination of an example drawn from American environmental protection policy. Limits have been placed upon the construction of new electrical generating plants such that they will not emit more than prescribed rates of various pollutants. These antipollution requirements, such as scrubbers in smokestacks to reduce sulfurous emissions, increase the cost of producing electricity. With customary national income accounting, any improvement in air quality is not measured or directly included in national product. Hence the efficiency of the economy—its output divided by input—declines. To the extent that purer air improves health or preserves goods, however, it will eventually lead to increases in output and GNP.

The improvement in air quality by controlling emissions of electrical generating plants may be a perfectly sensible policy for society to adopt. Of course, it also might be sensible for the society to obtain better air not by this route but by some other route, such as residential air purification or the more economical reduction of pollutant sources other than electrical generating plants. Whatever the method of improving air quality, here is a case where desirable social action is displayed as a reduction in national income: costs of production of goods rise without a commensurate increase, at least in the present, in measureable output. The example correctly suggests that national income is at times a misleading criterion of economic and social policy. We know that this is a general problem, which arises also in areas such as the measurement of the productivity of research and development expenditures.[1]

This simple textbook example deserves to be made more realistic. All new electrical generating plants in the United States must install air scrubbers in their chimneys to reduce sulfurous emissions, and the requirement is not dropped if the utility burns low-sulfur western coal—a requirement obviously put in at the insistence of the legislators from the eastern, high-sulfur coal areas. Quite naturally the electric utilities have delayed constructing highly expensive new plants as long as possible, so until obsolescence and depreciation finally compel replacement of old plants that antedate the clean air act, these plants are kept in service, and during this period the quality of air around such plants is inferior to what it would be in the absence of the law.

Shall we now conclude that the environmental policy is temporarily perverse because it lowers air quality for a time, and that it is excessively expensive because of the protection of the market for high-sulfur eastern coal?

My answer is that we apparently are not permitted to make such complaints. If a law is passed by the Congress, it presumably expresses the verdict of the nation that conditions will be the better for its passage. Assuming, as I think we must assume, that the Congress is aware of the actual effects of its legislation, then every action—certainly every policy left on the books for decades—represents official judgment that it represents improvement for society as a whole. In our air pollution example, the Congress has implicitly if not explicitly taken the following positions:

—that it was in the nation's interest to protect eastern coal markets and deny benefits of the increased demand for cleaner air to western coal owners;
—that grandfather clauses should allow the continued operation of obsolete electrical generating plants, at least for a considerable period, presumably to avoid immediate and costly closing of many operating plants;
—that eventually the electrical generating industry should emit less pollutants.

I call this interpretation of the meaning of public policy the principle and even the paradox of legitimacy. No matter what law is passed, we can and must find a set of Congressional values that justifies that action: we are simply applying the doctrine of revealed preference to the legislature.

It will seem outrageous to many people that we must by definition attribute an increase in national welfare to every act of the state. Of course one can find mistakes in our past public policies. For example, in retrospect our experiment with prohibition of consumption of alcohol was a mistake recognized even by the legislature that had earlier adopted prohibition. Of course, if prohibition had not been repealed, by the principle of legitimacy it would not have been a mistake. Mistakes are inherent in life because foresight is imperfect, and at the time a mistaken action was taken it did not appear mistaken. *Ex ante,* every public action is expected to be non-mistaken; *ex ante,* the state is infallible.

So every tariff, every rent control statute, every usury law, every tax loophole, every industry handout yields a benefit at least equal to its cost in the eyes of the political authorities. That does not dispense with information and analysis; the political authorities have limited resources and will seek to allocate them in such a way as to yield a maximum benefit, directly to themselves, ultimately to those who have the power to choose the political authorities. A useful role exists for the economist in making calculations of the prospective costs and/or benefits of alternative policies. This role is precisely the one Keynes had in mind, I assume, when he expressed the hope that we would become useful after the fashion of dentists. I cannot believe that he would assign such a role to himself; I suspect he rather fancied himself as a brain surgeon who operated on ideologies.

Our national income accounts value governmental activities at their cost of operation, so every pork-barrel bridge on an untraveled road is valued at cost along with wise and farseeing actions such as NSF grants of money to economists for research designed to eliminate poverty, not least for economists. The growth of functions of government transforms output from goods and services valued by the market to goods and (mostly) services valued by the legislature, the chosen voice of the people.

Redistribution versus Production

Modern governments in the western world devote much of their efforts to the redistribution of income. Such activity is clearly present in the selective taxation of certain classes and the exemption of others, for example, the progressive taxation of personal incomes and the exemptions or the deductions or bonuses given to home owners and present social security recipients. Redistribution is as clearly present in the vast host of welfare programs, such as the aid to families with dependent children, the various medical care programs, and food stamps.

Redistribution is just as dominant in a wide array of regulatory programs. The now-informal quota on Japanese automobiles is designed to support the high wage structure and the stock market values of the domestic automobile industry. Protectionism illustrates the possibility of large income redistributions (the automobile quotas cost consumers billions per year) without ever entering the federal budget or any other governmental account.

The automobile quotas and the current bailouts of inadequate corporate pension funds and insolvent financial institutions amply document the fact that most redistribution programs are not simple transfers from rich to poor. Rather, they are transfers from large numbers of unorganized consumers and taxpayers to smaller, more cohesive, and politically more powerful industrial, geographic or occupational groups.

The Principle of Legitimacy tells us that these are desirable transfers, that is, that one dollar taken from the general consumer and given to a well-paid employee of the merchant marine constitutes a net increase in the utility of the nation. If I challenge this interpretation, all that I will be doing is asserting that George Stigler's tastes are not those of the Congress, and who, besides myself, cares about that? Indeed, even I have become reconciled to the fact that American society does not fully share my preferences.

But if we accept the fact that redistribution programs increase utility of deserving groups more than it injures the utility of the losers, we must simultaneously accept the fact that these programs reduce the aggregate sum of goods and services (excluding the gains in utility) available to the aggregate society. Every redistributive program entails deadweight costs, which are costs that have no counterpart benefits other than the utility gains from redistribution.

If the state takes a dollar from Peter and gives it to Paul, there are three costs to the society that represent no benefit to anyone:

1. The cost of raising and disbursing the dollar. (The agents of the redistribution, say tax collectors and social workers, receive pay that in principle is equal to what they could earn elsewhere, so they do not gain from their activity.)
2. In Peter's futile attempts to escape or reduce the levy upon himself, he engages in acts such as buying less of a taxed commodity. The tax is set to raise the dollar after this attempted avoidance, so the endeavor is wasted effort. Pigou once labeled this as non-revenue-yielding hurt.
3. Paul almost always has to modify his behavior in order to receive the dollar, perhaps by changing his name from George to Paul, perhaps by remaining in a rent-controlled dwelling whose location he would not now freely choose in an unregulated market.

The Principle of Legitimacy tells us that the sum of these deadweight losses is less than the legislature's estimate of the gains from the redistribution of income, but Legitimacy does not tell us that these deadweight losses are small.

In fact the deadweight losses can be much larger than the net income being redistributed. Consider the domestic beet sugar industry, which survives only because import quotas have raised the price of raw sugar in the United States to approximately three times the world market price. We produce about 2.5 million tons of refined sugar from American beets grown primarily in ten states (California, Colorado, Idaho, Michigan, Minnesota, Montana, Nebraska, North Dakota, Texas, and Wyoming—I recite the states to indicate the size of the political coalition involved).

In 1985 the price of a pound of refined sugar was 9 cents on the world market and 30 cents in the United States. The cost of production of a pound of refined beet sugar in the United States was approximately 26 cents, or 17 cents more than the import price. Beet sugar farmers made net rents beyond what they could earn with other crops of about 4 cents a pound. The excess of the domestic cost over cost by importation of 17 cents represents a deadweight loss; these 17 cents represent payments to factors of production that could be producing and earning as much in making other products for us. To these deadweight losses in production we should add the deadweight loss borne by consumers on the additional sugar they would buy at the world price. So the total deadweight loss was about 18 cents, or more than four times the gain from protection per pound to beet farmers.

One need not be an economist to be provoked to ask: Why, to give $1 to beet farmers, need we spend perhaps $4.50 to accomplish the transfer? Why not tax consumers $1.10 and use the 10 cents to cover the cost of mailing checks for $1 to the farmers? Our congressional representatives are not sadists—at least, not all of the time—and I assert that they choose this method of giving income to beet sugar farmers because it is the best they can devise. The obviously much cheaper way of effecting the transfer, by paying cash to the beet farmers not to grow beets, is simply unworkable—a large fraction of the farm population, and some of us city dwellers, would volunteer not to grow sugar beets for fairly modest subsidies. Larger incomes are desired by everyone, so it requires a fairly elaborate and costly system to restrict subsidies to a particular group. Even then one can hardly say that the benefits of the subsidies are pinpointed; possibly one can say that they are log-pointed.

Over the past half century, the rate of growth of gross national product per unit of capital and labor employed has declined (let us call this measured efficiency). Partly that decline is attributable to the failure to include the returns in social welfare from research, safety, environmental and income redistribution policies. Surely another large part of the decrease in measured efficiency is due to the large and still rising deadweight losses incurred in carrying out these social welfare programs.

Deregulation

I do not conceal my lack of admiration for a painfully long list of redistributive measures undertaken by modern governments. Many serve no ethically accepted purpose such as compassion for the needy; indeed, they serve only as recognition of which groups possess or lack political influence.

It is tempting to most economists to propose extensive abandonment of programs and the complete redesign of others. This temptation has been yielded to in some respect by almost every economist for more than 200 years. Tariffs have been nearly unanimously criticized by economists in the English tradition, and other policies also have incurred our disapproval, such as laws setting minimum wage and maximum interest rates.

A decade ago it seemed that the criticism of regulations protective of unneedy groups was at last becoming effective. Airlines and ground transportation, financial industries, important parts of energy industries—all were entering a stage of active deregulation. The New York Stock Exchange, a cartel of almost two centuries' standing, had been forced to give up fixed commission rates, and the early termination of the Civil Aeronautics Board was predictable.

By the beginning of Ronald Reagan's first term, deregulation appeared to be a part of national policy. A Task Force for Regulatory Relief was established and implemented by the appointment of Christopher DeMuth (now President of the American Enterprise Institute) as a senior officer in the Office of Management and Budget. The program was ambitious: it required cost/benefit justification of new regulatory policies, simplification of reporting requirements to government and a comprehensive review of existing policies. The achievements ranged from deregulation of gasoline prices to the abandonment by the federal government of its policy of policing rules of local school boards governing students' clothing and haircuts.

Economists were given much credit for these moves, because we had been criticizing such policies in increasing numbers and with increasing vigor. Yet it is dangerous to say that because A precedes B, therefore A is a cause of B. That form of argumentation would allow me to explain the deregulation movement by the appearance of my book, *The Organization of Industry* (1968), when in fact that book's sale would have been better calculated to explain a poor year for publisher Richard D. Irwin.

Alas, the official deregulatory program had apparently ground to a halt by the end of President Reagan's first term. The environmental programs, OSHA, and a host of other regulations were discovered to have powerful supporters, usually in both political parties. The nationalization of Continental Illinois, the powerful wave of protectionism, and the current regulatory moves in the corporate merger and takeover area are evidences that the growth of government in business has not stopped.

We are entitled to be disappointed, but not to be surprised, by the persistence of governmental intervention in economic life. A school of thought attributes great influence to public opinion in the movements toward or away from laissez-faire. Among the many members of this school one may mention Albert Venn Dicey, John Maynard Keynes, and Milton Friedman. These great men would disagree on many subjects, but they all attribute to the molders of public opinion the decisive influence upon the direction of public policy. The intellectuals—people who dislike both poverty and manual labor—produce tides of opinion so powerful that, in Keynes' famous closing remark in the *General Theory*, "the world is ruled by little else."

If that explanation were adequate, it would behoove us to explain why the intellectuals changed their attitude toward government between, say, 1850 and 1930, a task no one has undertaken. I believe that the number of barbers is governed by the amount of hair people wish to carry on their heads and not the converse, that an exogenous supply of barbers governs hair styles. So also I believe that intellectuals proportion their numbers in each camp to market demand, and in equilibrium Lester Thurow and Murray Weidenbaum will have roughly equal incomes. I am tempted to make a similar statement about Adam Smith and Karl Marx, but it would be true only of their propagandizing roles, not of their scientific contributions to economics, where Marx is to Smith as Death Valley is to Mount Everest.

The explanation for the immense proliferation of redistributive policies in modern states is due, not to a change of opinion, but to a change in circumstances. An agricultural nation such as we were in the first half of the nineteenth century could do very little through the state to redistribute income in favor of the politically powerful groups. A farm economy that exported to European markets where prices of its products were determined could not extort noncompetitive prices from these markets, and there were too few nonfarmers to tax at home. Differential provision of public services to various groups also was hard to devise in a rural setting, although transportation services were a much-sought political plum.

When industrialization created many industries and occupations, the possibilities of income redistribution by political action became numerous and have been exploited. I have no idea of how many thousands of tax and spending preferences and regulatory policies of governments are now in operation. It is a small, diffused and unenterprising special interest group that does not find some accommodation in the political scene.

So I attribute changes in the scope and depth of public regulation of economic life to changes in circumstances, that is, in the opportunities in the political area to improve a group's lot, not to a growth of avarice in the human breast. Not all circumstances lead to increases in public regulation. On the contrary, comfortably established redistribution policies also can be undermined by political or technological developments.

Consider the major inflation in the late 1970s and early 1980s in the United States. By 1985, the Consumer Price Index stood at four times the level of 1953, and in each of the three years 1974, 1979, and 1980 consumer prices rose more than 12 percent. This strong inflation drove interest rates up to unprecedented heights; the three-month Treasury Bill rate was 16.3 percent in May of 1981, and the long-term AAA corporate bond rate reached 14.2 percent in that same year.

That development was quite sufficient to destroy the viability of the entrenched policy of prohibiting interest payments on demand deposits and setting low permissible interest rates on time deposits. The money market funds appeared to seize this opportunity to attract liquid funds away from banks, and interest rate limitations are no longer a significant force in American banking. If we experience a substantial period of price stability, I shall be surprised if the interest rate ceiling did not reappear in some form.

I shall offer just one other illustration of this theme of the dependence of policy on circumstances. The New York Stock Exchange engaged in a tight control of commission rates for more than 150 years, and toward the end of this period with the support of the SEC. By the late 1960s large block transactions among financial institutions (insurance companies, pension funds, and the like) had grown immensely, and their transactions were moving out of the Exchange. The unfixing of commissions on stock trades was compelled more by the new competition than by the writings of economists.

So we shall experience episodes of deregulation as well as episodes of increased regulation, but the relative preponderance of the latter episodes is so great that it is more appropriate to speak of eras of increased regulation and flurries of deregulation. A substantial period within which deregulation is widespread is most uncommon in modern western history. Mancur Olson recommends that a nation should badly lose a major war if it wishes to bring about such a period.

The Economists' Role

In spite of assigning little influence of economists' preachings on actual public policy, I do not believe that economists' influence is negligible. The reconciliation of these views lies in the fact that economists are scientists as well as preachers.

Our science seeks to understand how economic institutions and economic systems work, and no informed person can deny that we have made much progress in this work. To verify this assertion, simply ask an intelligent person unversed in economics to write down the effects of an effective minimum wage on employment of different types of workers, on earnings, on fringe benefits of covered workers, etc. Compare his or her answers to those of a professional economist and you will find that the intelligent layman's answers are shallow and inconsistent and grossly incomplete. That is no reflection on the layman—all of us must be laymen in almost every field of science—but it is testimony that we have made progress in our work.

The traditional manner in which economists opposed special interest policies was to point out their costliness to the community at large, primarily on general theoretical grounds. The tariff was criticized because it caused the nation as a whole to become poorer: we produced commodity X directly when by producing commodity Y for which we had a comparative advantage, we could exchange Y for more X than we could have produced at home. Or we criticized the minimum wage law because it forced some labor into uncovered occupations where it was less productive, or even drove some people out of the labor force.

These analyses were correct and possibly had some effect upon the details of public policy; they may have led to a tariff 2 percent lower or a minimum wage ten cents per hour lower than would otherwise have been established. I would dread the task of measuring such effects, but then I would fear the task of isolating empirically any small effect on economic life. Economic relationships can be extraordinarily complex, and the data to estimate them are sadly deficient in quantity and precision. Nor do the econometricians—surely the most quarrelsome class of economists—help us with their apparent inability to converge upon standard estimation procedures.

The effects of public policies on economic variables, in any event, are an order or two of magnitude larger than those of economists upon public policies, and they can be ascertained with tolerable accuracy. Even my simple example of the costs of protecting beet sugar farmers in the United States illustrates that point. The quantification of the costs and effects of public policies is a rapidly developing branch of economic research, and I believe that it will augment our influence upon public policies.

There is a famous remark by Lord Kelvin that until we measure a thing, our knowledge of it will be meager and unsatisfactory. Measurement need not transform our knowledge, but it assuredly makes it more dramatic and persuasive. If Malthus had said that people multiply faster than wheat, I doubt that he would have made anything like the impact that came from comparing the growths of arithmetic and geometric series.

At least a hundred, and possibly three hundred, quantitative studies of the effects of public policies are appearing each year. I believe that they will increase the public awareness of the costs of public programs, and at least marginally affect the generosity of the programs with grossly excessive deadweight costs.

There is a second type of research in which almost no economist has engaged: the devising of policies that accomplish the income transfers dictated by political power at lower deadweight cost. If we can find such policies, our society will require much less persuasion to adopt them than we now lavish in the attempt to persuade it to abandon the income transfers; after all, there will be a larger pie for everyone to divide.

We have made so few attempts at this sort of efficiency study of the mechanics of public policy that I do not know how to assess our prospects. There are a few efforts at a more rational environmental protection program, including the use of larger units of control to allow more efficient reductions of pollution, but they are only a beginning. I suspect that they are mixed with controversial attempts to reduce the depredations of north central cities, and of soft coal miners and mine owners, and other beneficiaries of the existing programs and thus arouse opposition that could have been avoided. If we devise programs that do not much change the gains of the beneficiaries, however much we deplore their existence, but reduce the deadweight costs, I believe we will attain a much quicker and more complete acceptance of our policy amendments.

Even if we devise much more efficient methods of redistributing income, income redistribution will continue to be the main business of politics. Any group possessing political influence will use that resource up to the margin where it yields no further gains in income. That characteristic is not unique to our political system; it is imbedded in all political systems. Come to think of it, shouldn't the National Association of Business Economists seek the establishment of a federal laboratory in some salubrious spot, the better to study and improve the efficiency of the American economy?

Notes

Originally published in *Business Economics*, Vol. 23, No. 1 (January 1988), pp. 7–13.

1. See Zvi Griliches, "R&D and Productivity: Measurement Issues and Econometric Results," *Science*, July 3, 1987, 31–36.

CHAPTER 17

1988

THE ADAM SMITH ADDRESS
ON THE STRUCTURE OF AN ECONOMY: A RE-EMPHASIS OF SOME CLASSICAL FOUNDATIONS

James M. Buchanan, George Mason University

> *The sovereign is completely discharged from a duty, in the attempting to perform which he must always be exposed to innumerable delusions, and for the proper performance of which no human wisdom or knowledge could ever be sufficient; the duty of superintending the industry of private people, and of directing it towards the employments most suitable to the interest of the society.*
>
> Adam Smith, The Wealth of Nations, Book IV, Chapter. IX, 51 (p. 687, Oxford University Press Edition, 1976).

To those of us who share the view expressed so well by Adam Smith in my frontispiece citation, there is both "good news" and "bad news" in the global political economy of 1988. The "good news" is reflected in the developing recognition that centrally planned economies everywhere remain glaringly inefficient, a recognition that has been accompanied by efforts to make major changes in internal incentive structures. More extensively, throughout the developed and the developing world of nations, the rhetoric of privatization in the 1980s has, occasionally, been translated into reality.

The "bad news" emerges from the United States, where in a single week in early May 1988 two separate stories in the media caught my attention. The first was a report that the Greenspan Federal Reserve Board had returned full circle to the once-abandoned effort at monetary fine tuning. The second was a report that councils well placed in the Democratic Party are increasingly disposed to promote specific and directed governmental intervention into industrial operation. These two stories came on top of the protectionist-mercantilist absurdities abroad in the land, absurdities that seemed excessive, even by presidential election years standards.

These items, along with the formal title of this, The Adam Smith Lecture, prompt me to devote my attention exclusively to a restatement and reemphasis of what I think was Adam Smith's own normative attitude on the structure of a national economy, and, by inference, on his attitude toward political-governmental directions for economic policy. Let me say at the outset, however, that I am not an exegetist, and that my concern is really not what Adam Smith may have said or failed to say. My concern is, instead, with articulating what I think would be a consistent position, for Adam Smith, in the context of the United States political economy in the late 1980s. And you will not, of course, be surprised that I shall exploit yet another opportunity to present my own perspective on political economy generally.

I propose, therefore, to defend the categorical distinction to be made between the structure of an economy and the operation of that economy within such structure. I shall argue that the appropriate domain for political economy, for politically directed reform as well as for discussion and analysis of that reform, is exclusively limited to structure. Efforts directed toward effectuating modifications of results that emerge only from complex interdependencies within structure are misguided, as are all canons of putative advice advanced by pundits who fail to understand the necessary distinction. My argument may be properly interpreted as a restatement of the positive case for *laissez-faire* that Adam Smith might have made had he used this term. Above all else, Adam Smith was a man of prudence, who would never have countenanced those fools of right or left whose caricatures through the decades have reduced a potentially meaningful slogan to polemical absurdity.

I shall proceed as follows. In the next section, I shall offer a precautionary tale about the dangers of terms that seem semantically and didactically useful but that may have the effect of making enlightened understanding more difficult to achieve. Functionalism, the familiar scourge of explanatory analysis in the other social sciences, also works its spell among economists. The third section is devoted to a necessarily foreshortened discussion of the order of an economy, as it operates within its own constraining structure. The next section examines elements of structure and analyzes relationships between structure and operations within structure. In the following section, I argue that elements of structure offer the only appropriate targets for reform. In the final section, I demonstrate how confusion in understanding the distinction between structure and operation-within-structure, between rules of the game and play within the rules, between process and end states, produces misdirected, and ultimately self-defeating, ventures in economic policy. The lecture falls clearly within "constitutional political economy," although, by comparison with some of my other papers, discussion here is concentrated on the structure of the economy rather than on the structure of the polity. In other words, the analysis examines the impact of politics on the economy, both in its positive and normative variants. The analysis does not, at least directly, introduce constitutional politics.

The "Functions" of an Economy

Any economist who was exposed directly to the teachings of Frank Knight at the University of Chicago or indirectly through access to one of the many elementary textbooks that incorporated elements of Knight's introductory monograph, "The

Economic Organization" (1933), is familiar with the listing of the "functions" of an economic order. As initially presented by Knight, these are:

1. establishment of a scale of values;
2. organizing production;
3. distributing final product;
4. making provision for growth;
5. adjusting demand to supply over periods of transition.

This listing is indeed useful, both semantically and didactically. It allows the student to focus on distinguishable categories of the economic interaction process, while continuing to recognize that the process, as it operates, carries out or performs the five functions simultaneously.

I want to suggest, however, that this Knightian introduction to our central subject matter may be misleading because it may be interpreted to imply that "the economy," "the economic organization," or "the economic order," accomplishes the listed functions, whether efficaciously or not, is some purposefully directed sense. If the economy, as such, has an acknowledged function or functions such as the establishment of a value scale, does it not seem to follow that the economy, modeled perhaps as a corporate actor, or perhaps through its politically organized agents, acts in furtherance of the stipulated and functionally defined objective? Should we really be surprised when the state, in its perceived role as helmsman of the national economy, takes upon itself those tasks presumably assigned to it by the economists who purport to understand their own domain of scientific competence?

To interpret the listing in this way is, of course, a mark of misunderstanding and confusion, both of Knight's own purpose in setting it out, and of the whole interaction process that defines the central subject matter of our discipline. Indeed we look to Adam Smith for one of the first explanations of how the economy does "perform" the listed functions without such functions, as such, being within the consciously pursued purposes of anyone, whether the individual participant as buyer or seller in a market or the political agent for such a participant. It becomes functionalist fallacy to impute purpose to "the economy" from the observation that the listed functions are, somehow, carried out. The argument from result to conscious design has been, since the eighteenth century, the argument that the economist must counter. And it is but small exaggeration to say that the core of our discipline embodies the understanding that the observed results of economic process emerge without conscious design while at the same time they describe an order that is amenable to scientific analysis.

The Order of an Economy

I apologize for reemphasizing basic principles of economics that may seem both to insult your intelligence and to be remote from practical relevance. I submit, however, that these principles are ignored, forgotten, or deliberately violated in too much of what passes for learned wisdom in our profession. I submit that many modern economists do not know what they are talking about, or, more charitably, that they talk about a realm of discourse beyond that constrained by the origins and history of their scientific discipline.

Adam Smith laid out the boundaries. We take as our assigned task to understand and to explain how an economy generates patterns of order that incorporate achievement of our objectives without requiring either benevolence on the part of economic actors or explicit direction by political agents. The principle of spontaneous coordination of the market is *the* principle of our discipline. Perhaps the most widely cited statement in *The Wealth of Nations* is that which suggests that we get our supper's meat not from the benevolence of the butcher but from his regard to his own self interest.

The butcher has a private pecuniary interest in having inventories of meat that will meet the demands of buyers. The qualities of desirability and availability take precedence over those qualities that may seem aesthetically superior by the butcher's own standards for the simple reason that the butcher seeks a larger relative share in the overall surplus generated by the nexus of trade and exchange among specialized participants. As we add the baker, the candlestick maker, and all of the other producing specializations in the modern complex economy, we explain the emergence of the set of goods and services that we observe, along with quality and locational characteristics. The butcher, in trying to meet the demands of his buyers, who bring to the market their autonomous demands, along with all other potential and actual producers-suppliers and demanders, establishes the scale or standards of valuation, the first of the listed functions that we discussed earlier. This scale or standard emerges from the whole interaction process; it does not directly enter into the self-interest calculus of any participant. The butcher acts on the basis of strictly localized information concerning the demands of his clientele; the relative evaluation of beefsteak does not emerge as if from a poll of public opinion; it emerges from the set of interdependent choices made by sellers and buyers, each of whom responds directly to the incentives that he or she faces in a localized market setting.

The complex order of a market economy emerges from a large set of interlinked game-like cooperative interactions between individual sellers and buyers, each of whom maximizes his or her utility in the localized setting of choice. No "player" in any of these game-like interactions chooses on the basis of an ordinal ranking of "social states" that describe the possible economy-wide inclusive imputation of goods and services, postexchange. A "social choice" among "social states" (allocations, distributions, value scales) is, therefore, conceptually as well as practicably impossible, so long as any person is allowed to adjust behavior independently in the localized choice setting that is confronted.[1]

Order within Structure

I have reemphasized the familiar proposition that, so long as individual buyers and sellers retain liberties to choose among the alternatives offered for sale and purchase in the separate markets, there can be no economy-wide "choice" of the particularized results of the economic interaction process, as these results might be described in terms of allocations, distributions, or evaluations. This conclusion holds independently of how any such attempted choice may be organized, whether under the auspices of an authoritarian regime or a democratically elected government. The results emerge from the whole set of interdependent choices made by individuals as these choices are constrained by the *structure* of the economy. In its inclusive definition, this structure must incorporate the resource and technology limits that describe the natural environment. These more or less immutable limits are not among my principal concerns here. My emphasis is placed instead on those elements of structure that are subject to purposeful modification and change.

The terminology of game theory is helpful. The structure of an economy describes what we may call the "rules" for the whole complex set of interdependent game-like interactions between and among many players, each of whom acts in pursuit of privately selected purpose. This interpretation of structure as a set of rules directly suggests that, as an individual chooses and acts within the structure, as he or she plays in the inclusively defined game, there is, and can be, no conscious or explicit consideration given to the possible choice among alternative sets of rules. For purposes of rational choice behavior in the economic process, the individual must accept the structure of the economy (the rules) as fixed, as a relatively absolute that is not subject to his or her own privately orchestrated change. For example, the preexchange endowments that are within the recognized entitlements of any person are defined by and in the structure of the economy; such a person cannot, separately and independently, modify these endowments.

A distinction must be made between the individual's influence on the overall results of economy-wide interaction (on allocation, distribution, and evaluation) and the influence on the structure. As noted earlier, the results of economic interaction, within a structure, emerge from the localized private choices made by all participants. Each individual choice must, therefore, affect the aggregate result, even if no person, as chooser, has any conscious sense of his or her own influence on this result.

Again a game analogy will be useful. A player chooses among strategies available under the rules that define the game; any player's choice will affect the solution that emerges from the choices of all the players, but no player "chooses" the solution, as such. By contrast, the rules or structure do not emerge from the within-rules choices made by participants; the structure remains necessarily independent of these direct in-structure or within-rules choices.[2]

The pattern of outcomes or results of the economic interaction process (allocations, distributions, evaluations) depend *both* upon the individualized choices made in the whole set of interlinked exchanges and upon the structure of the economy. I have argued that there can be no effective choice among alternative aggregate results, whether the attempt is made individually or collectively. Only the pattern of results is subject to deliberative change and patterns can be changed only through effective changes in structure, that is, in the set of rules that constrain the exercise of individual choices to be made within the rules. I have noted also that the individual can exercise no influence on the structure of the economy as he chooses separately and independently among the options that he confronts. From this it becomes evident that any choice among alternative sets of rules must be, and can only be, collective. The structure of an economy, the set of constraints that limit the choice options of individuals, that define the feasibility spaces, is *public* in the classic sense. This structure is both nonpartitionable and nonexcludable. Any change in structure must, therefore, impact on all actors in the process, quite independently of how and by whom the collective action is motivated and carried out.

Constitutional Political Economy

The analysis of the working properties of alternative structures of an economy, alternative sets of rules and institutions that serve to constrain the choice behavior of participants within that economy, defines the domain for constitutional political economy in its positive aspects. Until recently, neoclassical economists tended to neglect the necessary interdependence between structure and potentially observable patterns of outcomes of the economic process. This neglect has been largely corrected by the emergence of the set of interrelated research programs summarized under the rubric "the new political economy": law and economics, property rights economics, the new institutional economics, public choice. In each of these research programs, the focus of analysis is the impact of differing structures of incentives on the choice behavior of economic actors and, through this impact, on the pattern of aggregative results in an economy.

The positive exercise must precede any normative judgment on structure, on any part thereof, whether directed at the *status quo* or at any proposed alternative. The only legitimate normative exercise involves institutional-structural comparison. Demonstration of "failure" against some idealized standard (efficiency, justice, liberty) that is not anchored in structural feasibility is irrelevant.

How are alternative structures to be arrayed in the normative exercise? What are the standards for ranking? Answers to these questions call for treatises, but I can be cryptic here, especially because I have written at near-disquisition length elsewhere. (1962, 1975, 1977, 1985, 1988).

There are two, quite separate, responses to these questions that must be countered and shown to be untenable. The first is that which proceeds from the presumption that there is a unique, and agreed-on objective, or objective function, for an economy that allows the working properties of alternative structures to be readily assessed. This direction of response, which continues to dominate the thinking of economists, reflects a carryover from idealism in political philosophy. Politics, inclusively defined, is conceived as the search for the "true," the "good," and the "beautiful," some ideal state of bliss waiting "out there" to be discovered or revealed.

As Adam Smith recognized so clearly, however, there is no agreed-on objective for the participants in an economic nexus, each one of whom seeks only to pursue his or her own privately defined aims (which may or may not reflect narrowly-defined economic interest). Absent such agreement, there is simply no external standard by which alternative structures can be evaluated.

A second response commences from this very fact of individual differences. Each person, as participant in the political-economic nexus, can, presumably, array alternatives of structure as "better" or "worse" in terms of his own subjectively defined interest. From these observed differences among persons, the inference is then drawn that no normative judgment that transcends individual evaluation is possible. Hence, if we differ on the ranking of structural alternatives, we fight; that is, the setting is one of pure conflict, out of which a single structure will emerge that satisfies the winners and coerces the losers.

I suggested above that neither of these responses to the basic normative questions is acceptable. We must reject the presumed existence of an ideal standard, and we must also reject the nihilism implied by the absence of agreement. And at this point it is, I think, important to recognize, and to acknowledge quite explicitly, that in some fundamental sense many of us, as citizens, behave as if the structure of the economic-political order embodies legitimacy, which implies voluntary acquiescence in the coercion of the state without attribution of either omniscience or benevolence to political agents. That is to say, we live with each other neither as nihilists nor idealists. In an empirical, practical sense, we reconcile the absence of an ideal agreed-on standard of evaluation and the implied conflict among individual objectives.

In a more formal exercise, we achieve this constitutionalist stance by the introduction of some means of dampening the potential for disagreement among individuals. Such means is provided in the use of something like a veil of ignorance and/or uncertainty, either conceptually or practicably, in the evaluation of alternative structures or constitutional rules. This device is, of course, familiar, from the works of Rawls (1971), Harsanyi (1956), Buchanan and Tullock (1962), and others.

The task of normative evaluation of alternative structures for an economy to be carried out after the positive exercise of comparison is assigned to individuals who are ignorant or highly uncertain about how the alternatives for structural choice will impact on their own identifiable interest. Such individuals will be led to agree, in their own interest, on structural features that exhibit many of the characteristics of the classical liberal social order.[3] And, the empirically observed acquiescence in the operation of many of the rules that define the existing structure suggests that, for many participants there is implied agreement, even without the carrying through of the formal veil-of-ignorance evaluative exercise.

This contractarian-constitutionalist derivation of the elements of structure for an economy allows us to flesh out, in modern terms, much of Adam Smith's message that was left implicit in his own work. The construction here allows us to derive a regime of "laws and institutions" that offer protection to person and property on a nondiscriminatory basis, that enforce voluntary contracts among persons nondiscriminatorily, that protect the natural liberties of persons to enter into voluntary exchanges, that prohibit restriction on entry into trades, that prohibit agreement on restrictive terms of trade. This listing, which could be extended and elaborated, contains elements of the structure that has come down to us in classical liberalism. Adam Smith was straight-forward in suggesting that, within this broadly defined structure of an economy, there was no legitimate basis for directed interference by political agents.

The listing of constituent elements of structure that might be derived from the contractarian normative exercise can be extended to include, importantly, the political-legal guarantee of predictability in the value of the monetary standard or unit of account in the economy. Historically observed political orders have rarely, if ever, provided this guarantee. (And, indeed, I suspect that this failure in structure offers the basis for much of the discussion at this conference and others of your association.)

The contractarian construction remains necessarily incomplete at critical elements of economic structure. While laws and institutions that protect the liberties of persons to enter and consummate voluntary exchanges command legitimacy directly, what are the limits suggested when voluntary exchanges affect other parties outside the exchange itself? The whole domain of externality, inclusively defined, does not find structural resolution directly in the initial normative exercise. As modern research has indicated, however, structural change that moves toward incentive-compatible imputation of rights may eliminate much of the contractarian ambiguity.

The Purposeless Economy

As my subtitle indicates, this lecture reemphasizes the classical foundations of political economy, and especially as these are reflected in the encompassing vision of Adam Smith. Even Smith, however, is subject to criticism in his selection of the title of his treatise. By calling attention to the *wealth* of nations, Smith may be interpreted as setting up a single-valued criterion by which the functioning of an economy might be measured. As I have noted, a much-preferred title would have been "The Simple System of Natural Liberty," because what Smith demonstrated was that there is no need for us to conceptualize a single overriding or even an agreed-on purpose, aim, or objective for an economy, or for those political agents who may presume to take on the charge of furthering such purpose.

Properly understood, the economy has neither purpose, function, or intent. The economy is defined by a structure, a set of rules and institutions, that constrain the choices of many persons in an interlinked chain of game-like interactions, one with another. For any individual, there are, of course, "better" and "worse" economies, but these evaluative terms translate directly into references to sets of rules or structures. Within any given structure, *laissez faire* becomes the indicated policy stance, and this principle holds quite independently of the normative content of structure itself.

In one sense, there is absolutely nothing new or novel in what I have said in this lecture. But in yet another sense, the implications are revolutionary. The shift of emphasis to structure as the exclusive and only appropriate object for reform, along with implied principle of *laissez faire* applied to operation within structure, relegates to absurdity all proposals for reform supported on arguments from "national purpose," as well as all claims that the economy functions more satisfactorily if it is explicitly guided by presumably omniscient and benevolent political agents.

There are two separate, but related, aspects of the normative argument that I advance. The very definition of the economy as a structure, a set of constraining rules within which individuals seek to achieve their separately determined purposes, makes teleological direction of policy normatively self-contradictory. But alternative structures may be compared, and evaluated, in terms of their abilities to facilitate the accomplishment of the separately determined individual objectives. Because only individuals themselves can know what goals they seek, any direct delegation of authority to choose among structures reduces the information content of the constitutional choice process. The implied policy stance involves *laissez faire* within constitutional structure and consensus in the ultimate choice of structure itself.

No claim is made here that adherence to the normative precepts outlined will resolve all issues. Even within the constitutionalist-contractarian paradigm, differences among individuals may arise both in scientific interpretation-explanation-prediction and in a choice of ultimate moral norms. As noted earlier, many features of the classical liberal position would be predicted to emerge from the contractarian procedural test. But the precise boundaries of the constitutionally chosen structural limits on individual voluntary association, as well as the constitutionally derived definitions of the protected spheres of individuals themselves, cannot be drawn from sources other than as revealed by those who count as members of the body politic.

Let us by all means continue to strive for, and to support, efforts to analyze the structure of the economy, and to seek consensus on means to make this structure more capable of allowing us, as individual participants, to further those separately defined objectives that we seek. Let us, however, guard against allowing intellectual confusion about what an economy is to offer, legitimatizing cover for the efforts of some persons and groups to impose their own purposes on others. Beware of those who pronounce on the economy's purpose.

Acknowledgment

James M. Buchanan is indebted to his colleague, Viktor Vanberg, for helpful comments on an earlier draft.

Notes

Originally published in *Business Economics*, Vol. 24, No. 1 (January 1989), pp. 6–12.

1. This point was central to my early (1954) criticism of Arrow's (1951) extension of his impossibility theorem to apply to the results of market process. Only in writing this lecture did I realize that, although stated quite differently and developed from a differing perspective, Sen's (1976) demonstration of the paradox of the Paretian liberal comes ultimately to the same conclusion.
2. The categorical distinction made here would be modified somewhat if we treat elements of structure as products of an evolutionary process. In this case, choice behavior within a structure might itself modify the development of structure over a sufficiently long period of adjustment. For my purposes, however, the categorical distinction made here serves a didactic function. By separating, both conceptually and analytically, the choices made within rules and the choices made among sets of rules, the appropriate domain of normative political economy may be much more clearly set forth.
3. For more extended discussion, see my paper, "The Contractarian Logic of Classical Liberalism" (1988).

References

Arrow, Kenneth, *Social Choice and Individual Values* (New York: Wiley, 1951).

Buchanan, James M., "Social Choice, Democracy, and Free Markets," *Journal of Political Economy,* LXII (April 1954), 114–123.

Buchanan, James M., *The Limits of Liberty* (Chicago: University of Chicago Press, 1975).

———, *Freedom in Constitutional Contract* (College Station: Texas A & M University Press, 1978).

———, *Liberty, Market and State* (New York: New York University Press, 1985).

———, *Economics: Between Predictive Science and Moral Philosophy* (College Station: Texas A & M University Press, 1988).

———, "The Contractarian Logic of Classical Liberalism" (draft paper prepared for conference, Social Philosophy and Policy Center, Bowling Green University, 1988).

Buchanan, James M. and Gordon Tullock, *The Calculus of Consent* (Ann Arbor: University of Michigan Press, 1962).

Harsanyi, John, "Cardinal Welfare, Individualistic Ethics, and Interpersonal Comparisons of Utility," *Journal of Political Economy,* 63 (August 1955), 309–321.

Knight, Frank H., *The Economic Organization* (Chicago: University of Chicago, 1933, mimeographed).

Rawls, John, *A Theory of Justice* (Cambridge, MA: Harvard University Press, 1971).

Sen, A. K., "The Impossibility of a Pareto Liberal," *Journal of Political Economy,* 79 (November–December 1976), 1406–1407.

Smith, Adam, *The Wealth of Nations* (Oxford: Oxford University Press, 1976).

CHAPTER 18

1988

RETHINKING INTERNATIONAL TRADE

Paul Krugman, Massachusetts Institute of Technology and National Bureau of Economic Research

Economists have a reputation for disagreeing with each other; businessmen and politicians usually imagine that there is an economist on every side of every issue. The reputation is only partly deserved; some of the people who call themselves economists would not be recognized by the professionals as colleagues, and the extent of disagreement is exaggerated by the tendency of the press to report every issue as a debate. Nonetheless, the charge has enough truth in it to make economists self-conscious and highly protective of their few areas of virtually total unanimity.

One of the things that almost all economists agree on is the desirability of free trade. Adam Smith said it; David Ricardo, the great English economist of the early nineteenth century, provided a mathematical justification; and ever since, an understanding of the reasons why international trade is a good idea and free trade is best has been a key part of the professional training of every economist. Probably no other idea so well defines what an economist is: every economist understands Ricardo's theory, and almost nobody else does. Or as the Nobel laureate Paul Samuelson puts it, the concept of comparative advantage that underlies the economist's case for free trade is one of the few ideas in economics that is both important and right without being obvious.

That is, if it is right. For more than a century and a half, the basic analysis of international trade has been one of the great constants in economics. Fashions in macroeconomics come and go, with Keynesians and monetarists alternatively dominating the debate, but the theory of international trade has grown by slow embellishment, not revolution. The international trade theory taught in graduate school in 1975 was more sophisticated, embraced a wider range of possibilities, and was far more mathematical than David Ricardo could have imagined—but its core ideas and conclusions were ones that he would have found familiar.

In the past decade, however, a quiet revolution has occurred in international economics. Out of this revolution has emerged a quite different way of thinking about international trade, one that preserves some of the traditional view but that calls other parts of that view into question. The analysis of trade has not been completely stood on its head—economists are not about to become enthusiastic supporters of import quotas on sugar and footwear—but the simple verities of the traditional free trade position are at least partly removed.

The purpose of this chapter is to provide a quick overview of the new developments in thinking about international trade and of the controversy these developments create for economic policy. The chapter begins at the abstract level, asking how our view of what international trade is about has changed. We then turn to the question of whether and when the new economics of trade can offer a justification of policies that would traditionally have been condemned as protectionist. Finally, we turn to the real-world problem of making trade policy: Can the new thinking really help make policy, or is it something better left in the classroom?

Rethinking Trade

Why does international trade happen? You might have thought that by this time this issue would be settled. Yet for most of the past 150 years economists have systematically offered only a partial answer, emphasizing some of the reasons why trade happens while neglecting other equally valid reasons. The theories of trade offered by economists until recently were never *wrong*—the explanations of trade they offered always were valid, and remain so. The problem, we now recognize, is that they were only partial. There is more to trade than the traditional theories recognized.

The question of why trade happens is for the most part a question of why countries produce different things. Why does Japan produce VCRs while the United States does not? Why does the United States produce wide-bodied jets while Japan does not? Because countries do produce different mixes of goods, the desire of consumers and businesses to use a variety of products gives rise to trade. So the question is why the mixes of goods produced differ.

At a basic logical level, two reasons explain why countries might end up making different things. First, the countries are *different*: They have different relative ability to produce different goods, and therefore they end up specializing in the things they are relatively good at. Second, there are *inherent advantages in specializing*: Countries end up producing different sets of goods, even though they may start out with equal capabilities, because whoever produces more of a good has a cost advantage, which leads their production to expand and that of rivals to contract, until each country ends up with a different set of goods produced.

In the compact jargon of the field, the idea that countries specialize in order to take advantage of their differences is known as the theory of *comparative advantage*; the alternative view, that attributes trade to the inherent advantages of specialization, is known as the theory of trade based on *increasing returns*. What happened in the academic study of trade was that, from about 1820 until 1980, almost all analysis of trade emphasized comparative advantage and ignored increasing returns. It was assumed by most economists, whether in textbooks and classrooms or in real-world policy roles, that all trade reflects the different abilities and resources of countries.

Now it is clear that this view contains a great deal of truth. The fact that Saudi Arabia exports oil, while Brazil exports coffee, is not an arbitrary consequence of the need to specialize. Much and perhaps most of world trade can be explained on the basis of international differences in resources broadly defined: land, mineral deposits, and more important still the stocks of physical and human capital. However, it is equally clear that this story is not complete. The fact that France exports Peugeots to Germany, while importing Volkswagens, is not something one would like to attribute to deep-seated differences in resources. Instead, it reflects the advantages of specialization per se. Because of increasing returns in auto production, neither the French nor the German market is by itself large enough to support low-cost production of the full range of vehicles that consumers would like to buy; Therefore, automakers in the two countries produce somewhat different models, and each is able to find a niche that appeals not only to domestic consumers but to those abroad.

Thoughtful observers of international trade always have understood that there was more to trade than comparative advantage. However, increasing returns are more difficult to place into a mathematically rigorous framework than comparative advantage. For one thing, who will specialize in producing what? When comparative advantage drives specialization, the answer depends upon the underlying resources of the countries; when increasing returns drive it, the answer is more likely to depend on historical accident. (Why do the Swiss make watches? Because they used to make watches, and that gives them an advantage over newcomers.) Furthermore, increasing returns usually are associated with industries in which only a few firms struggle for advantage, situations that are much harder to analyze than the atomistic competition among many small players that is the ruling metaphor for most economic analysis. Because economic analysis tends to follow the line of least mathematical resistance, the traditional approach has been to emphasize country differences, and deemphasize the advantages of specialization per se, as reasons for international trade.

The change since 1980 is that at last increasing returns in trade have been put on a rigorous mathematical footing. The details of that task are beyond what we need to discuss here; the key point is not to try to explain too much. In no way can a theory that incorporates increasing returns explain why Switzerland exports watches, while France exports pens. Instead, the theory must adopt a sort of "statistical mechanics" approach, focusing on overall or average results rather than on the details. We try to predict the volume of trade, and the effects of trade on the overall variety of goods available and the average scale of production; we do not try to predict the exact pattern of international specialization.

The important point for noneconomists about this theoretical development is that it has been successful in an intellectual sense. The new approach to trade has successfully dethroned the theory of comparative advantage from its former position of complete dominance. Economists who used to base all their policy advice on trade on the traditional models are now trying to move to a view that gives weight to the new models as well. This rethinking is still in its early stages, but already a significant rethinking of the foundations of international trade policy is in motion.

Trade Theory and Trade Policy

In the first instance, new trade theory is about how to model trade, not what to do about it; it is about *describing* the world, not *changing* it. What difference does it make for trade policy if a lot of world trade reflects arbitrary specialization to gain economies of scale, not the underlying differences in countries' resources? The answer is, of course, that when one changes the explanation of why countries trade, one also changes the recommended trade policy. This is not to say that free trade is completely discarded as a desirable goal, and that every protectionist idea now becomes intellectually respectable. Indeed, in some respects free trade looks even more desirable than before. However, the case for certain kinds of government intervention in trade also looks better, posing a new dilemma for policy.

Before getting to the new case for government intervention, let's look at why the case for free trade is in a way stronger than before. To see this, we need to understand what the case for free trade was before the new theory. In essence, it was that we should have free trade because free trade allows each country to specialize in doing the things it does relatively well. Each country can engage in activities where its productivity is relatively high (not necessarily higher than that of other countries, if it is even less productive in other activities; what is necessary for gains from trade is only a *comparative* advantage, not an *absolute* advantage in anything). The result is a rise in overall world productivity, which is divided among countries to everyone's benefit. However, the extent of the gains is limited by the amount of difference between countries. If countries are rather similar in their aptitudes, resources, and so on, it is difficult to find much room for gains from freeing up trade between them.

The practical policy issue that this raises is whether it is worth the political effort to seek completely free trade between neighboring countries with similar economies, for example, Canada and the United States, or the countries of the European Economic Community. Traditional economic analysis says that free trade between Canada and the United States is desirable—free trade is always a good thing. But it also says that the benefits of free trade are limited. Conventional estimates of the gain from a US-Canada free trade pact are embarrassingly small, only 1 or 2 percent of national income for Canada and barely noticeable for the United States; the same is true for the gains from the "completion of the internal market" that has been agreed on within Western Europe. Because important political objections exist to such trade liberalization in any case, with Canada worried about losing its national identity, US lumber interests worried about competition, Italy and France worried about the interests of pasta producers and winegrowers, the very smallness of the conventional gains from free trade raises the question of whether they are worth it. If Canadian-US free trade produces only a 1 percent gain in income, while risking turning Canada into an cultural colony of New York and Los Angeles, is this a good choice?

The reason for these small estimates is, however, that traditional theory sees little gain from trade between similar countries in the first place. Because the United

States and Canada, or France and Germany, do not differ much in their resources and technologies, they do not gain much from specializing in what each does best. Indeed, it is hard to say in terms of traditional theory why they do so much trade anyway—why, for example, trade within the European Economic Community accounts for about a third of total world trade.

The increasing returns approach to trade suggests an answer both to why these countries trade so much already, and why more trade may produce more substantial benefits than the more conventional analysis allows. The point is that even similar countries still can gain from the ability to specialize and realize economies of scale. Canada, with a domestic market only one-tenth the size of that of the United States, can achieve higher efficiency and greater variety in its consumption if it is integrated into a unified North American market; the European countries, by "completing the internal market," can produce an economic bloc that offers the same opportunities to rationalize production that North America provides. Instead of producing a half-dozen different types of electrical appliances, or telecommunications equipment, a unified Europe could exhibit the same standardization that the United States does, and thereby help to close the still substantial gap in productivity and standards of living.

So the new approach to trade is in one sense a stronger argument than before in favor of free trade. And it is in this guise that new trade analysis has had its most immediate effect of the real debate over policy. In Canada, the cause of free trade with the United States has been strongly bolstered by the arguments of economists that the advantages of specialization within a free trade area will produce substantial benefits, and particularly by the estimates of Richard Harris of Queen's University that the gains from such a free trade area are several times as large as those estimated by his colleagues on the basis of the traditional theory of trade. Within Europe, the role of increasing returns as a source of gains from a more open internal market have been emphasized in White Papers prepared by the European Commission, and the economists Alasdair Smith and Anthony Venables of the University of Sussex have played a role in quantifying this argument that corresponds to Harris's role in Canada.

So far, so good: the new theory of trade has, in Canada and Europe, strengthened the hand of free trade, not weakened it. But there is a darker side as well. Trade may be even more beneficial than we thought; but the opportunities for governments to manipulate trade, seizing more of the gains from trade for their own countries at other countries' expense, unfortunately also look larger under the new theory than they did under the old.

The New Case for Government Intervention

The traditional case against government intervention in trade, whether through protectionism or subsidies, rests on two basic propositions. First, *a country's industries are competing with each other for resources as much as they are competing with foreigners for sales.* Second, *the free market mechanism directs resources to where they earn the highest return.* The first proposition is one that remains true in spite of the major changes in how we view trade, which is why the new theory does not provide a case for crude protectionism. But the second proposition can no longer be argued as strongly as once it was.

To see why these two propositions matter, consider what happens when a government subsidizes an industry against its foreign competitors. The direct effect of the subsidy is, of course, to give that industry an advantage. However, the industry is not only in competition with foreign rivals for markets; it is in competition with domestic rivals for scarce resources of labor, capital, and so on. When the subsidy causes the lucky industry to expand, it does so by bidding away these resources from other domestic industries, making these industries less competitive. When the economy starts at fairly full employment, as the United States does today, the net effect of the subsidy is not to increase employment of capital and labor, so much as to redistribute resources from other parts of the economy to the favored sector. There is no such thing as a subsidy program that makes the economy as a whole more competitive; the government always is favoring some sectors at the expense of others. And this remains true no matter what the reasons for international trade.

But the second proposition takes the argument a step further, by arguing that the redistribution of resources is always a bad thing. The logic is that markets always will put resources where their return is highest. So a policy that second-guesses the markets, putting resources somewhere else, must reduce their overall earnings net or subsidy. From this comes the standard view of economists that interventionist government policies on trade will always lower, not raise, national income.

Now economists always have known that there are exceptions to this dictum. If markets fail to operate properly, high returns will not be fully exploited. For example, suppose that in some sector a union is able to impose an unusually high wage and prevent additional workers from competing it away. Then this high wage will discourage production in a sector that can yield high returns; a subsidy to this sector will, if not simply absorbed by still higher wages (a big if), raise national income by undoing this distortion. Or suppose that an industry generates special benefits to society that firms cannot capture, say, because of its technological spillovers. Then the free-market allocation of resources will short change these industries, and a government subsidy again will be to the national benefit. As these examples suggest, however, these traditional arguments for government intervention are in the way of exceptions that prove the rule. The normal case is taken to be one in which markets direct all resources to their highest return. If there were obvious high returns in a sector, we would expect resources to rush into that sector until the high returns are competed away. Only under special and hard-to-identify conditions would there be any further role left for the government.

What the new trade theory does is to make it clear that many goods are traded in markets where we cannot count on competition to eliminate high returns. When increasing returns exist, the few firms that get a head start in an industry—or the country that establishes an industry first, and thereby acquires a persistent advantage—may earn higher returns in that industry than its resources could have earned in other sectors. In the jargon of the new trade theorists, some industries may turn out to be *strategic,* offering the possibility of special advantage to those countries that get to specialize in them.

It is one thing to show that some industries are especially worth having. It is something quite different to show that government action can help. What the new trade theorists have shown, however, is that at least in principle the government can indeed tilt competition in favor of a domestic industry, in a way that raises national income at foreigners' expense.

Strategic Trade Policy

The basic idea of strategic trade policy can perhaps best be conveyed by an example. Table 18.1 shows a hypothetical competition between two firms—call them Boeing and Airbus (any resemblance to real firms may be coincidental). Both firms can produce a new aircraft and could do so profitably if it did it alone; but if both try to produce the aircraft, both will lose money. The table illustrates this with a set of hypothetical payoffs.

What will be the outcome of this competition? The answer depends on who moves first. Suppose that Boeing is able to commit itself to produce before Airbus can get started. Then the result will be in the upper right corner of the box: once Boeing is committed to produce, there is no point in Airbus following, so Boeing makes profits and Airbus does not.

But now suppose that Airbus is backed by a government that promises to pay a subsidy of 10 for production, whatever Boeing does. The effect is to change the payoffs to those represented in Table 18.2. Now Boeing knows that even if it starts first, Airbus will still produce—and this makes production unprofitable for Boeing.

Table 18.1 Payoffs in a two-firm competition

	AIRBUS			
BOEING				
	Produce		Don't produce	
		−5		0
Produce	−5		100	
		100		0
Don't produce	0		0	

Table 18.2 Payoffs when one firm receives a subsidy

	AIRBUS			
BOEING				
	Produce		Don't produce	
		5		0
Produce	−5		100	
		110		0
Don't produce	0		0	

The result is to shift the outcome to the lower left corner of the box: Airbus produces, Boeing does not.

Now Airbus's profits partly reflect the government subsidy of 10 that it receives. And profits that come out of government subsidy are simply a redistribution from one set of domestic residents to another. However, in this example, the subsidy is only 10, but Airbus's profits rise from 0 to 110! The subsidy somehow has generated much larger profits than the subsidy itself. These extra profits come from Boeing, not from European taxpayers, that is, they represent gains extracted from another country.

The reason for these extra profits is the *strategic* advantage conveyed by the subsidy. In effect, the subsidy gives Airbus the power of commitment, deterring Boeing from competition. And because this is a strategic industry, in which profits can be made, the government is able, with a clever subsidy policy, to do better than it could under free trade.

This simple example is obviously not realistic, but it does convey the principle of the new arguments. The new trade theory, as we argued, shows that the benefits from free trade probably are greater than we imagined; but it also shows that sophisticated government policies can do better than free trade, to some extent at the expense of other countries.

The political explosiveness of this idea is apparent. Opposition to free trade is widespread, but it lacks an intellectual basis. Political opponents of free trade generally are unable to find respectable economists to back their cause; now that deviations from free trade have a theoretical basis, and one rooted in the latest theory, isn't the way open for economists to appear on both sides of this issue as well?

Well, so far it hasn't happened. The new trade theorists have been very cautious about claiming that their ideas provide a justification for any anti-free trade policies in practice. So to conclude this chapter I need to discuss the sources of caution.

Caution about the New Trade Theory

We've seen that in principle a government subsidy can benefit a country by giving its firms a strategic advantage in a high-return industry. But if this is going to be a basis for policy, we need to deal with real industries and real governments. That is the problem: A policy that works well in a contrived example might not be such a good idea in the real world. Let's look at five reasons why.

First, the example was cooked so that the numbers worked out right. What if Boeing turns out to be efficient enough so that it can produce even in the face of a subsidized Airbus? Then the would-be strategic policy will fail in its deterrent effect, and end up just an ordinary subsidy that costs more than the benefits it yields. So the government needs to be careful in its choice of industries to select—but if, like most governments, it relies on the industries themselves for data, it is not likely to get a disinterested answer.

Second, the response of firms to government policies is not always predictable. Instead of being deterred by a foreign subsidy, a firm might launch into a price war that reduces everyone's profits. Theoretical models of trade policy have shown that a policy that raises national income under one plausible description of how firms behave can reduce it under another, equally plausible description.

Third, a government subsidy may all too easily end up being dissipated by the entry of additional firms trying to take advantage of the subsidy. What started out as a high return sector may, with a government subsidy, become one in which an excessive number of firms depend upon the subsidy to survive—all too familiar an experience with industrial policies around the world.

Fourth, there is the question of foreign response. A subsidy that looks like a good idea in isolation may not look so good if it sets off foreign retaliation that spirals into a trade war.

Finally, and most fundamentally, there is the problem of making sophisticated policy in the real world of government. Suppose that economists can devise clever policies that would benefit a country if applied carefully and in a disinterested way. Can we expect a real government agency—say the US Commerce Department—to be that sophisticated and disinterested? Or won't an alleged strategic trade policy quickly degenerate into a mixture of pork barrel and crude old-fashioned protectionism?

These cautions make even those economists who are most enthusiastic about the new trade theory reluctant to call for its immediate application to real-world policy disputes. Moreover, as industry studies based on the new theory have gradually begun to emerge—on autos, semiconductors, consumer durables, aircraft—they have seemed to justify the caution. While in each case the potential for doing better than free trade seems to be there, the estimates of the *size* of the potential gains appears small, suggesting that the risks of political abuse may weigh more heavily than the strict economics.

Is Free Trade an Idea Whose Time Is Past?

The intellectual structure on which economists have traditionally based their arguments for free trade has been partially torn down and replaced with a more complex structure that leaves more room for dispute and less certainty. This transformation has taken place quietly, however, with little impact on the rhetoric of public debate. Where the new international economics has entered the practical debate, in Canada and Europe, it has been to reinforce, not weaken, the case for free trade.

But will this change? Is the new trade theory about to break the traditional commitment of economists to free trade? The answer appears to be no; the cautions about the applicability of the new trade theory have been taken to heart, and none of the prominent new trade theorists has chosen to become a guru of protectionism.

The new free trade position, however, is not the same as the old. Instead of advocating free trade as part of a blanket endorsement of free markets, today's international economists advocate it as a reasonable rule of thumb in an imperfect world. It is a sad, and somewhat cynical, position. But it is also a realistic one—which may make it stronger than the cheerful free trade faith that used to be economists' stock in trade.

Note

Originally published in *Business Economics*, Vol. 23, No. 2 (April 1988), pp. 7–12.

CHAPTER 19

1989

THE ADAM SMITH ADDRESS
THE SUICIDAL IMPULSE OF THE BUSINESS COMMUNITY

Milton Friedman, Stanford University

As business economists, you straddle two fields: economics and business. Those two fields are not synonymous by any manner of means, as Adam Smith, whose name has been given to this series of lectures, clearly recognized. Adam Smith is correctly and properly regarded as the father of modern economics and particularly of the idea that a free, private market society is capable of combining material prosperity with human freedom. Although that idea has been expressed by others before and since, Adam Smith's two great books, *The Theory of Moral Sentiments* and *The Wealth of Nations,* are the classical works on that theme.

One of Adam Smith's most often quoted statements is, "People of the same trade seldom meet together, even for merriment and diversion, but the conversation ends in a conspiracy against the public." Another of his comments is, I believe, even more relevant to the doctrine that has come to be called "the social responsibility of business." It is brief, pithy and definite: "I have never known much good done by those who profess to trade for the public good." That sentence follows immediately after his famous remark about the "invisible hand."

As a disciple of Adam Smith, who believes that the pursuit of self-interest can be in the national interest, I'm not going to bash business for pursuing its self-interest. A corporate executive who goes to Washington seeking a tariff for his company's product is pursuing his stockholders' self-interest, and I cannot blame him for doing so. As an employee of the stockholders, he has a fiduciary responsibility to promote their interest. If he's made a valid, accurate judgment that a tariff will be in the self-interest of his enterprise, he is justified in lobbying for such a tariff. If he is a principled free trader, his proper recourse is to resign and seek a job where his principles do not conflict with his fiduciary interests. So I don't blame corporate executives who lobby for tariffs. I blame the rest of us for being such fools as to let them exploit us. We're to blame, not them. We're the ones who enact the tariffs.

Evaluating Corporate Self-Interest

My complaint about the business community is very different. It was recently expressed in a book by Paul Weaver called *The Suicidal Corporation*. That book, published a year or so ago, is devoted "to the corporation's war against its own best interest," and that's exactly what I intend to discuss. I am going to argue that corporations, and especially large corporations, seeking to pursue through political means what they regard as their own interests, do not do a good job of evaluating their interest. The policies they pursue and promote are very often adverse to their own interests. That's what I mean by my title, *The Suicidal Impulse of the Business Community*.

The activities involved are not only those of individual corporations and, although less often, of individual businessmen, but equally of their trade associations, which supposedly represent the interest of a broader group and not of individual enterprises within that group. I'm not going to try to demonstrate this on an *a priori* basis. I'm just going to cite some examples that I regard as fairly typical. My general conclusion from observing the way businessmen behave is that they are schizophrenic with respect to time. Corporate officials who consider expanding their own enterprises—putting up a new factory, making new investments in developing trade—tend to look a long time ahead. They plan for 5, 10, 15, or 20 years and take into account the long-run consequences of their behavior. However, when they come into the political arena, the only two groups that are more shortsighted than the business community are Wall Street and Washington. On Wall Street, it's a matter of two hours. In Washington, it's a matter of at most two years between congressional elections, and that's an overstatement. The business community is just about as short-sighted. They tend to look at the short-term impact of what they promote and not at the long-term impact.

I have no satisfactory explanation for why the business community behaves in this suicidal fashion. What I'm stating is an empirical observation that is in need of an explanation. Before I finish, I'll try to suggest some tentative explanations, but I have little confidence that they are satisfactory. Let us proceed to some examples.

Tariffs

I mentioned tariffs. The business community has long promoted protectionism. Yet, I challenge you to name any industry in the United States that over a long period has benefitted from protection. The industry in the United States that has the longest record of protectionism is probably the steel industry. Already in 1791, Alexander Hamilton recommended protection of infant industries, of which the iron and steel industry became one of the earliest to receive protection. His famous *Report on Manufactures* is a brilliant example of sophistry. Hamilton praises Adam Smith to the sky, but argues that his principles do not apply to the United States: the United States is different and it needs protection—a pattern of special pleading that has since been repeated *ad nauseam*. The steel industry, to judge from the continued protection it receives, is apparently still an infant industry. Has the steel industry benefitted from protection? Some decades ago, the steel industry asserted that it was being overwhelmed by a flood of foreign imports and asked for additional protection. They received it, at first in the form of a "target price," and then in the form of import quotas. The main effect was higher wages for their workers, higher costs for the industry, and a continued influx of foreign steel. The firms that benefitted from the tariffs, and are saving the industry, are small mini-mills which in the main have not sought protection. More important, perhaps one can understand US Steel seeking protection. But what about the backing it received from the National Association of Manufacturers? Their members include many users of steel, such as the automobile manufacturers, the manufacturers of home appliances, the machine tool industry, and so on and on. There's little doubt that the restrictions on steel imports harmed the users of steel to a far greater extent than they benefitted the steel producers. Why has NAM typically promoted protectionism? The Chamber of Commerce has occasionally shown more sense, but it is far from guiltless.

Tax Legislation

Let me cite some other examples. Consider tax legislation. In the 1930s, Franklin Delano Roosevelt persuaded Congress to impose a tax on undistributed profits. The business community launched a major campaign against the tax, and even though that was the Roosevelt New Deal era, they were successful in getting it repealed. Yet, if they had supported the undistributed profits tax at that time, I believe that the corporate income tax would long since have been eliminated. What was the undistributed profits tax? It said, if a corporation retains income instead of distributing it to shareholders as dividends, the shareholders avoid paying individual income tax on that undistributed income. That's a major tax loophole. The solution adopted was to impose a tax on undistributed income.

In my opinion, the response of the business community should have been to agree that undistributed income did constitute a loophole but that the right solution was to tax the shareholders, not the corporation. That could be achieved by requiring corporations to attribute undistributed income to individual shareholders and requiring the shareholders to report such income on their individual income tax returns along with dividends. That would eliminate the problem of evasion. It would also make it clear that there is no excuse for double taxation—once to the corporation and once to the individual—as occurred then and occurs now with dividends. Such an approach would have enabled the business community to convert the agitation about undistributed income into a vehicle for getting rid of the corporate income tax.

Let me come to a more recent episode. Before the 1981 reforms, the business community was lobbying for specially favorable treatment for depreciation and investment, including an investment credit. I talked to a number of leading business leaders urging them that that was a bad tactic, that they could do much better for themselves, and for the country as a whole, by lobbying for comprehensive indexation of the tax system against inflation, both the corporate tax and the individual tax. They would end up better off and, in addition, they would not be lobbying just for their own special interest; they could be part of a much broader coalition.

The ordinary taxpayer has little interest in accelerated depreciation or an investment credit; but the ordinary taxpayer is and was very much interested in abolishing "tax creep" and being protected against inflation. I believe you will agree that subsequent experience does not, to say the least, contradict my judgment that the alternative I recommended would have benefitted the business community more than the pursuit of special treatment. However, I was unable to persuade any of the businessmen I talked to.

The current attitude of the business community on the capital gains tax is not very different. Again, it seems to me, their self-interest would be far more effectively promoted by indexation of the base for capital gains, the base of depreciation allowances, interest paid, and so on, than by a temporary cut in the capital gains rate. Yet that is not the position spokesmen for industry have taken. I'm not saying that a capital gains tax is a good thing; it isn't. Fundamentally, I'm in favor of a tax on consumption and not a tax on income at all. From that point of view, I'd like to get rid of the capital gains tax. But the capital gains tax is here, and the failure to index the base is a far more serious defect than taxing gains at the same rate as other income. Moreover, it is consistent with the 1986 tax reform, remedying a defect in that reform, rather than appearing to be a departure from it.

Commercial Banking

Consider a very different and more specific example, the commercial banking industry. At the end of World War II, the commercial banking industry probably accounted for well over two-thirds of all commercial and other credit. It's doubtful today that it accounts for as much as a third. What caused the decline? There is no question that it was the banking industry's insistence, first, on regulation Q; and, second, on fixed exchange rates. Those two elements played a major role in the decline of the commercial banking industry. Money market funds would not exist today if there had been no regulation Q. Regulation Q limited the interest rates that banks could pay. Once inflation started accelerating, market interest rates were driven up, regulation Q interest rates were no longer competitive, and money market mutuals were invented to enable ordinary citizens to share in high interest rates. Given regulation Q, that was a desirable social change. From a broader point of view, it was a waste. Why create a new industry just because there is an arbitrary limit on an interest rate? Had there been no regulation Q, the banks would have done what the mutual market industry does now and that activity would have been part of the banking industry.

Similarly, fixed exchange rates had similar adverse effects on the banking industry. One result of fixed exchange rates was that President Johnson imposed restrictions on foreign lending by American banks, a form of exchange control. By all that's logical, it seems to me the world financial center should be in New York, not in London. It's in London primarily because of the banking industry's support of regulation Q and fixed exchange rates. So far as the leaders of the banking industry are concerned, the only exception was Walter Wriston, who was in favor all along of abolishing regulation Q and floating the exchange rate, long before these changes became discussed, and who predicted the adverse consequences of postponing changes that he regarded as inevitable.

Some two decades ago, I recall testifying before a congressional committee on the issue of exchange rates in a session in which another witness was David Rockefeller. Incidentally, his advisor was Paul Volcker, whom I met on this occasion for the first time. David Rockefeller testified in favor of fixed exchange rates, in direct opposition to Walter Wriston. Ideas do have consequences, to parrot the title of Richard Weaver's book. Consider the present status of Citibank on the one hand and Chase on the other.

Thrift Institutions

The savings and loan industry is another example but almost too easy a shot. The savings and loan industry was destroyed by two factors: (1) the inflation of the 1970s along with regulation Q; (2) federal deposit insurance. Deposit insurance alone would not have destroyed it. After all, deposit insurance was enacted in the middle thirties and there were negligible failures of either banks or S&L's for more than thirty years after that. Why? Because so long as S&L's and banks have a major equity position, their owners have an interest in avoiding failure. Deposit insurance insured depositors but not stockholders. The accelerating inflation of the 1970s, along with regulations limiting what savings and loans and banks could do and what interest rates they could pay, destroyed the net worth of many institutions. If all of an institution's liabilities are insured and it has no net worth, there's no reason for its managers to worry about taking risks. It's heads the institution wins and tails the taxpayers lose. That was the fundamental source of the problem. But consider the more recent period after the industry was already in difficulty, what did the associations of savings and loans lobby for in Washington? They lobbied for weaker regulation, for delay in closing down institutions, all of which simply made the situation worse.

Corporate Contributions

Another easy shot consists of corporate contribution under the guise of social responsibility. Many studies of such contributions all show the same thing.[1] The oil companies contribute to conservation groups that are opposed to exploration for oil and that are engaged full time in bashing the oil industry. The nuclear industry contributes to antinuclear organizations that are engaged in bashing the nuclear industry. Most corporations contribute to universities and business schools, whose faculties are often dominated by fervent opponents of free enterprise and supporters of socialism. It would be a nice exercise, and I hope someone will undertake it, to determine the political affiliations of the corporate officials in charge of allocating corporate contributions—in the public affairs section or the government relations section or some other section in charge of corporate contributions. It boggles the imagination to understand why corporate executives believe it is in the interest of their shareholders to finance activities directed to destroying the foundations of a free market society. Yet there is no doubt that they act as if they did.

Trade and Budget Deficits

Finally, consider the attitude that the business community has taken in recent years to budget and trade deficits. The budget deficits over that period have been a boom to the business community. They have been the only thing that has kept Congress from spending more money and wasting more of the taxpayer's substance. I'm not in favor of deficits. On the contrary, I've been an active sponsor of a balanced-budget/tax-limitation amendment. But without such a constitutional amendment, is there any doubt that any increases in taxes over the past five years would not have reduced the deficit, except perhaps momentarily, but would have simply increased government spending? Nobody can tell me that the Democrats who scream about the budget deficit, from Tip O'Neil before to the present group, are born-again budget-balancers. They have historically been big spenders and they still are. They want more taxes not to balance the budget, but so that they can spend more. For every problem, they have a standard response: "We should be spending more on this, that or the other thing"—whether it's drugs, child care, or whatever—"but we need more taxes to do it." What has been the reaction of the business community? In this respect, I guess Wall Street is worse than any of the rest. They've been screaming, "We need higher taxes to be responsible," as if responsibility involved bigger government.

Again, the same is true of trade deficits. The trade deficit is a sign of American strength because its counterpart is a capital inflow. The Japanese and other foreigners, as well as domestic residents, are investing in the United States because they can get a higher return here than they can elsewhere. Is that a sign of our weakness and their strength or is it the other way around? We have been able to have a higher level of investment than we otherwise could have had because of the capital inflow. But what is the position of the business community? "We must end the trade deficit. We must end the fiscal deficit." Talk about shortsighted policies.

Reasons for Business Actions

I trust I've given you enough examples to show that my complaint is not without some basis. Let me turn to the question of why. I don't really have a satisfactory answer. One reason was stated more than a century ago by General Francis A. Walker. He was an honest-to-God military general who enlisted as a young man in the Civil War, had a brilliant war record, rose in the ranks, was wounded and captured, and after the war was over, was granted what was called the brevet rank of general as recognition of his services. He was also probably the most famous American economist of the nineteenth century. He was director of two censuses, gaining a worldwide reputation for his success in improving their accuracy and coverage, he was a professor at Yale, and the president of MIT, and also a very good economist. In one of his books he wrote, "Few are presumptuous enough to dispute with the chemist or mechanician upon points connected with the studies and labors of his life; but almost any man who can read and write feels at liberty to form and maintain opinions of his own upon trade and money…The economic literature of every succeeding year embraces works conceived in the true scientific spirit, and works exhibiting the most vulgar ignorance of history and the most flagrant contempt for the conditions of economic investigation. It is much as if astrology were being pursued side by side with astronomy, or alchemy with chemistry."[2]

I believe that is part of the reason for the suicidal impulse of the business community. The source for many if not most economic fallacies is that what's true for an individual is almost always the opposite of what's true for the country as a whole. If you as an individual go to the market to buy strawberries, the price of strawberries is fixed and you can buy as many as you want. But suppose everybody suddenly decides to buy more strawberries. There are no more strawberries to buy than before. The quantity is fixed for the time being and the price is variable. Similarly, each one of us thinks we can hold as many pieces of paper of those things called money as we want to. But there's a fixed total of money that's been created by the Federal Reserve System. And so you have a game of musical chairs. If I acquire more cash or deposits, it's at the expense of somebody else. In case after case, the same phenomenon arises. But most businessmen do not hesitate to generalize from the particular to the general, satisfying fully the description of General Walker.

Joseph Schumpeter, in his brilliant and penetrating book, *Capitalism, Socialism and Democracy,* gives a very different, and more subtle, explanation of why "the capitalist order tends to destroy itself." He sums up his reasons in four points, one of which is particularly pertinent to my present topic: "the scheme of values of capitalist society, though casually related to economic success, is losing its hold not only upon the public mind but also upon the 'capitalist' stratum itself."[3] To put this point in different words, none of us is able to free himself from the general climate of opinion in which he operates (to cite a trivial example, that climate requires me to hesitate before letting "himself" stand for "himself or herself"). In the United States, and indeed around the world, that general climate of opinion treats government action as the all-purpose cure for every problem.

I have recently been expressing this in what I call a welfare-state syllogism based on three propositions that are clearly part of the conventional wisdom. *Major premise*: socialism is a failure. Everybody agrees with that proposition about Russia, China, the United Kingdom. *Minor premise*: private enterprise capitalism is the only system that has been able to combine prosperity with human freedom. Again, there is wide agreement with that proposition. *Conclusion*: the United States needs more socialism! The conclusion is a clear logical fallacy yet I am sure that you will agree that it is conventional wisdom. Whatever problem you talk about—child care, drugs, health, oil spills, earthquakes, schooling, productivity, volatility in the stock market—the only solution generally regarded as possible is more government intervention, throwing more money at it, passing more laws, more regulations. Like the rest of us, the business community in general has been exposed all their lives to that climate of opinion. They are graduates of colleges and business schools in which the crucial—and implicitly beneficent—role of government is taken for granted. They are busy running the businesses that they own or that employ them. You cannot expect them to be philosophers and independent thinkers in the social area as well. Though there are some notable exceptions, most of them simply accept the common view. As a result, when any problem arises, their immediate answer is, "Let's go to the government and get it solved." I believe that is probably a major part of the explanation for the suicidal impulses of the business community. But I am far from confident that it is the whole answer.

You people are in a first-hand position to observe the phenomenon I have been discussing. I hope some of you will be induced to investigate it further. It is of the utmost importance for the future of our free society to understand what is happening and why it is happening. Perhaps then, something effective can be done to prevent the business community from fouling its own nest. Even better, perhaps it would be possible to harness the undoubted influence of the business community to shoring up the foundations of a free market economy instead of contributing to their destruction.

Notes

Originally published in *Business Economics*, Vol. 25, No. 1 (January 1990), pp. 5–9.

1. See in particular the publications of the Capital Research Center (Washington, DC).
2. Francis A. Walker, *Political Economy* (New York: Henry Holt & Co., 1887), pp. 29–30.
3. 4th ed. (London: Allen & Unwin, Ltd., 1952), p. 410.

CHAPTER 20

1990

A GUIDE TO WHAT IS KNOWN ABOUT BUSINESS CYCLES

Victor Zarnowitz, University of Chicago

Within the three years 1980–1982, total economic activity in the United States as represented by comprehensive time series on output and employment declined twice, in the first half of 1980 and again between mid-1981 and late 1982. The National Bureau of Economic Research (NBER), a private nonprofit research institution that has pursued impartial studies of the US economy for 70 years, distinguishes two recessions in this short period. Since then, however, for more than seven years real GNP has increased in each quarter except one (1986:2). Other measures of important aspects of aggregate activity (nonfarm employee hours, real personal income and sales, industrial production) also rose almost continuously. This makes the economic expansion that began in 1982:4 the longest in peacetime, according to the NBER monthly chronology of business cycles that goes back to 1854.

This does not mean that all industries and regions flourished during the expansion, although most did. Large parts of US manufacturing suffered severe setbacks from intensified foreign competition, aided by a massive appreciation of the dollar during the otherwise vigorous recovery of 1983–1984. The sharp decline in the price of oil in 1986 depressed the economy of the oil-producing states and contributed to the substantial overall growth slowdown in 1985–1986. Meanwhile some industries, e.g. health and other services, did well throughout the 1980s, not only in expansion but also earlier in recession.

In 1989 a second generalized slowdown developed during this long expansion, marked by declines concentrated mainly in manufacturing and construction. A downturn was widely feared late in the year, but the economy so far has proved remarkably resilient again and the expansion seems to continue, albeit weakly, as of the time of this writing (April 1990).

Defining Business Cycles

These developments illustrate the concept of business cycles consisting of recurrent but not periodic sequences of expansions, downturns, contractions, and upturns in a great number of diverse economic (and even some related "noneconomic") processes. These movements are both sufficiently diffused and sufficiently synchronized to create major fluctuations in total output, employment, real income, and real sales. Many components of these aggregates tend to expand together much of the time, then contract together for some time; their rises overlap substantially and so do their declines. As a result, a substantial timing consensus occurs between the peaks in the fluctuations of the major indicators of general business activity, and the same applies to the troughs.

It is this approximate synchronism that allowed the NBER first to define business cycles (Mitchell 1927, p. 468; Burns and Mitchell 1946, p. 1) and then to identify and date them. The time series on production, employment, etc., that are used directly in constructing the NBER chronology are the "coincident indicators" of business cycles. The series that tend to reach their specific-cycle peaks and/or troughs earlier are the "leading indicators," those whose turning points occur usually later are the "lagging indicators."

Business cycles are characterized by their persistence (numerous indicators show high positive serial correlations) as well as pervasiveness or diffusion (time series representing many different variables show high cyclical conformity or coherence, and are accordingly cross-correlated). Fluctuations of this type accompanied the development of modern capitalism in the Western world, interacting with long-term economic growth that proceeded at varying but generally high rates. The annual NBER chronologies for the United States and Great Britain go back to 1790.

Business cycles vary greatly in duration. The peak-to-peak cycle in 1980–1981 was as short as 18 months; that in 1960–1969, as long as 116 months. Wartime cycles tend to have longer-than-average expansions (the one in the 1960s associated with the Vietnam war was particularly long). The average duration of peacetime cycles in the United States is about four years.

The fluctuations also differ much in amplitude and intensity. Severe depressions can be rapid and short (like the deflationary one of 1920–1921) or painfully protracted (the worst one was the "great contraction" of 1929–1933). Vigorous expansions are mostly long and interrupted by growth slowdowns (e.g, 1949–1953, 1961–1969, 1982–?). But most of the recorded cyclical movements, especially the contractions, have been mild and short. Of course, in any secularly growing economy, expansions must be on the average larger than contractions, and most are also longer. There are some interesting exceptions, however. After the expansion of 1933–1937, total output still failed to exceed the pre-depression peak level of 1929, and two of the recent expansions, 1958–1960 and 1980–1981, were disappointingly weak and short.

Business cycles are longer than the periodic intrayear seasonal movements and much longer and larger than the many erratic fluctuations that are also continually present in most economic indicators. They usually dominate changes in the economy over spans of several years, just as the seasonal and other shorter variations dominate many changes over spans of a few weeks or a few months. The developments across decades are primarily the work of forces of long-term growth (rising population, labor force, capital, and productivity). The different types of fluctuation and growth all interact in varied and subtle ways, which frequently impedes the contemporaneous reading of business cycle signals. In the *ex post* analysis, however, business cycles can be clearly distinguished from other fluctuations that are shorter and as a rule also smaller and less widely diffused.

Main Features of Cyclical Behavior

Employment and output in industries that produce durable goods tend to have large fluctuations that conform well to business cycles, that is, rise with substantial regularity in general expansions and fall in contractions. Inventories of these goods, or at least the change (investment) in them, are also highly cyclical. All this applies to both producer and consumer durables. The amplitudes are much smaller for nondurable goods, and the conformity is often weaker. Services, which are nonstorable, are on the whole dominated by relatively stable growth trends, the deviations from which are small; they have the smallest fluctuations and lowest conformity. In personal consumption expenditures too, durable goods are highly cyclical, nondurables less, and services hardly decline at all in recessions, at least the relatively short and mild ones as observed in recent times.

In many industries, particularly manufacturing of durables, production is largely to order. New orders show large fluctuations that are followed with variable lags by much smaller fluctuations in outputs and shipments. The resulting changes in backlogs of unfilled orders and average delivery lags are also procyclical.

Manufacturers' sales move with greater amplitudes than wholesalers' sales and retailers' sales move least. Production typically fluctuates more than sales, which implies a procyclical behavior of inventory investment. Business fixed investment shows large cycles in percentage terms and high conformity, and so do consumer outlays on durable goods (a type of investment by households), in contrast to the much larger but relatively stable consumption of nondurables and services. Corporate profits have very large cyclical movements exceeding those of any other type of income.

Prices of industrial commodities and raw materials traded in organized auction markets exhibit high sensitivity to business cycles. Wholesale prices used to decline in recessions but in the post-World War II era of persistent inflation they merely rise at a lesser rate, often reacting only with lengthy lags. Retail prices are considerably more "sticky" yet.

Monetary aggregates (M1 and M2) usually trend upward in both expansions and contractions, though often at reduced rates before downturns; absolute declines in these series are rare and mostly associated with major depressions. In contrast, short-term interest rates increase in expansions and decrease in contraction with much regularity and amplitudes that tend to be large relative to their average level in each cycle. Long-term rates show much lower conformity and much smaller amplitudes of cyclical movement.

The "specific cycles" in times series representing different economic variables are distinguished not only by their relative size and correlation with business cycles but also by their timing. One important sequence relates to business investment in plant and equipment and proceeds from commitments such as new capital appropriations and new contracts and orders to realizations such as construction put in place, shipments and installations of machinery, etc. Commitments typically peak months before total output and employment do, that is, they lead at business cycle peaks by substantial intervals, whereas realizations and recorded business expenditures for new plant and expenditures have sizable lags. At business cycle troughs, the gestation and delivery periods are on the whole considerably shorter as the levels of capacity utilization are lower, but investment commitments still tend to lead and expenditures to coincide or lag. Other activities marking the early stages of investment processes include the formation of new business enterprises, new bond and equity issues, and the net change in bank loans to business—and all of these tend to be procyclical and leading.

Consumer confidence indexes, buying plans, and expenditures on housing, automobiles, and durable goods such as furniture and appliances show similar patterns of early timing. New residential building permits and housing starts have particularly long leads. Here the time to build is much shorter than for business investment projects, so that residential investment expenditures themselves show sizable leads. Net changes in mortgage credit outstanding and in consumer installment credit lead as well.

Compared with the overall credit flows, the rates of growth in monetary aggregates tend to have lower conformities and amplitudes and more random variations. They have historically led at business cycle turns by highly variable but on average long intervals.

Among the longest leaders are bond prices (bond yields generally lag), profit margins (ratios of profits to corporate income or sales; also, proxy measures such as the ratio of price to unit labor cost), and broadly defined money supply M2, deflated. Stock prices and total corporate profits have usually somewhat shorter leads. Another important variable that tends to fluctuate procyclically around a rising long-term trend, generally with leads, is average productivity of labor (output per hour).

The variables that measure or reflect the costs of doing business tend to lag at business cycle turns: labor cost per unit of output, interest rates, total outstanding debt, total inventories (inventory investment, which is highly volatile, often leads). When inverted, such series show very long leads: for example, declines in inventories and interest rates during a recession pave the way for an upturn in new orders and then output of materials and finished goods.

Most of the evidence in support of the major relationships and characteristics described above comes from the period after World War II when business cycles moderated (see next section). But little in the earlier available data contradicts the presence of these qualitative features of cyclical behavior, and they appear on the whole to be rather robust. This is certainly true for the sequences of leads and lags among groups of indicators, as illustrated in Table 20.1. The classifications of series in each group were based partially on the prior record, but the method does not assure

Table 20.1 Cyclical timing of leading and lagging indicators, 1885–1982

		No. of B.C. Turns[a]		*Number of Observations*			*Lead(−) or Lag(+) in Months*	
Period *(1)*	*Type of Turn* *(2)*	*Total* *(3)*	*Matched* *(4)*	*Leads* *(5)*	*Coincidences* *(6)*	*Lags* *(7)*	*Mean* *(8)*	*Stand. Deviation* *(9)*
A. Leading Indicators[b]								
1885–1938	Peaks	15	15	15	0	0	−6	5
1948–1982	Peaks	8	8	8	0	0	−10	5
1885–1938	Troughs	16	16	16	0	0	−5	3
1948–1982	Troughs	8	8	8	0	0	−3	2
B. Lagging Indicators[c]								
1885–1938	Peaks	15	15	1	0	14	+6	4
1948–1982	Peaks	8	8	0	1	7	+4	4
1885–1938	Troughs	16	16	1	2	13	+6	5
1948–1982	Troughs	8	8	0	0	8	+10	5

[a]B.C. = business cycle.

[b]For 1885–1938, based on the median timing of a group of seventy-five leading series. For 1948–1982, based on the median timing of a group of twelve leading series.

[c]For 1885–1938, based on the median timing of a group of thirty lagging series. For 1948–1992, based on the median timing of a group of six lagging series.

Sources: 1885–1938: Moore 1950, Table 11. 1948–1982: U.S. Bureau of Economic Analysis, *Business Conditions Digest* (BCD), October 1977, appendix F, and subsequent issues. Taken from Zarnowitz and Moore, 1986, Tables 9.15 and 9.16, with some updating.

the consistency of the results over the entire period. Inspection of detail confirms that the relative timing properties of the indicators remained remarkably consistent over the century covered. On average, the leads at business cycle peaks have become longer and the leads at troughs shorter since 1948 then before, while the opposite shift occurred for the lags (Table 20.1, column 8). These changes can be explained by the shift toward longer business expansions and shorter recessions in the postwar era.

Changes in Expansions and Contractions

The NBER chronology shows that business expansions were on average substantially longer and contractions shorter after World War II than before. Between 1854 and 1938, peacetime expansions had a mean duration of nearly 25 months; the corresponding figure for 1948–1982 is 34 months. The historical contractions averaged 21 months; the postwar contractions, 11 months. Looking at consecutive segments of 4 to 6 cycles each reveals no systematic changes in phase durations prior to the past four decades (Table 20.2). Including the wartime cycles, which have long expansions and short contractions, would only sharpen the contrast between the recent era and earlier times (compare parts A and B of the table). Note that the current expansion, of record length but still presumably under way,

Table 20.2 Average duration of business cycles in the United States, 1854–1982

Period Years, (T to T)[a] (1)	Number of Business Cycles Covered (2)	*Average Measures of Phase and Cycles Durations*[b] Expansion[c] Mean (3)	Expansion[c] S.D. (4)	Contraction[d] Mean (5)	Contraction[d] S.D. (6)	Full Cycle (T to T) Mean (7)	Full Cycle (T to T) S.D. (8)
A. Peacetime Cycles[e]							
1854–1879	4	26	7	27	26	53	31
1879–1897	5	25	7	19	11	44	17
1897–1914	5	22	8	20	5	42	4
1919–1938	5	26	15	20	13	46	16
1948–1982	6	34	15	11	4	46	13
1854–1982	25	27	11	19	13	46	16
B. All Cycles[f]							
1854–1919	16	27	10	22	14	48	19
1919–1945	6	35	26	18	13	53	22
1945–1982	8	45	28	11	4	56	27
1854–1982	30	33	20	18	12	51	22

[a]The years are those of the initial and terminal business cycle troughs (T), according to the NBER monthly chronology of U.S. business cycles.
[b]All means and standard deviations (S.D.) are rounded to full months.
[c]Measured from troughs (T) to peaks (P).
[d]Measured from peaks (P) to troughs (T).
[e]Excludes the expansions during the Civil War, World Wars I and II, the Korean War, and the Vietnam War and the immediately following contractions.
[f]Includes the five wartime cycles listed in note e.
Sources: Moore and Zarnowitz 1986, Tables A.3 and A.5 and text.

is not included; if it were, the observed shift in durations would be somewhat larger still. Recessions have become not only shorter but also much more uniform in length; the expansions, not only longer but also more variable (see columns 4 and 6). The full cycles, however, continued to average 42 to 46 months in peacetime for subsets of the last century, and 48 to 56 months when wartime is included (columns 7–8).

It should be noted that the data available for identifying and measuring the historical business cycles are fragmentary and often weak. Much of the evidence relates to cyclically sensitive sectors and processes. Hence, some of the early fluctuations may have involved only slowdowns rather than absolute declines in total output and employment. If so, the mean durations in those lines of Table 20.2 that include the nineteenth century cycles should be somewhat larger for expansions and smaller for contractions. But this would reduce only moderately the contrast between the pre- and post-1948 durations.[1]

Business contractions tended to be not only much shorter but also much shallower and less diffused in recent times compared with the pre-World War I and

Table 20.3 Selected measures of variability of relative changes and amplitude of cyclical movements in output and prices, 1875–1982

Statistic/Period[a]	*Real Gross National Product (GNP)*			*Wholesale (Producer) Price Index*		
	1875–1918 (1)	*1919–1945* (2)	*1946–1983* (3)	*1875–1918* (4)	*1919–1945* (5)	*1946–1983* (6)
Log differences:						
1. Mean	1.0	0.8	0.8	0.3	−0.2	1.1
2. Stand. dev. × 100	2.4	3.6	1.2	3.3	4.1	2.3
3. Coeff. of variation[b]	2.4	4.8	1.5	11.6	20.5	2.0
Statistic/Period[c]	*1878–1914*	*1920–1938*	*1948–1982*	*1876–1914*	*1920–1939*	*1948–1967*
No. of cycl. movements[d]						
4. Rise	12	4	7	11	4	4
5. Fall	12	5	8	10	5	5
Aver. duration (quarters)[e]						
6. Rise	8.9	11.0	16.3	6.6	8.2	12.0
7. Fall	3.2	6.0	2.6	6.9	8.6	5.0
Aver. amplitude (%)[e]						
8. Rise	17.3	30.1	20.9	12.1	15.4	8.7
9. Fall	−5.1	−14.1	−2.5	−11.8	−21.6	−4.8
Aver. amplitude quarter (%)[f]						
10. Rise	1.9	2.7	1.3	1.8	1.9	0.7
11. Fall	−1.6	−2.4	−1.0	−1.7	−2.5	−1.0

[a]Number of quarterly observations per series: 1875–1918, 175; 1919–1945, 107; 1946–1983, 151.
[b]Ratio, standard deviation divided by mean (line 2 ÷ line 1) in absolute value.
[c]Annual dates of the first and last turning points of the series during each period.
[d]Identified by specific cycle peaks and troughs in the series. Only complete upward and downward movements (called "rise" and "fall," respectively) are counted.
[e]Measured from trough to peak for rises and from peak to trough for falls.
[f]Line 10 = line 8 ÷ line 6. Line 11 = line 9 ÷ line 7.
Source: Balke and Gordon 1986, pp. 788–810. See note 2.

interwar periods. No major depressions like those of 1882–1985, 1920–1921, 1929–1933, and 1937–1938 occurred in the post-World War II era. Of the eight postwar recessions, three (in 1960, 1970, and 1980) were among the mildest on record, while five (1948–1949, 1953–1954, 1957–1958, 1973–1975, and 1981–1982) were relatively severe but much less so than a number of deep depressions in the past.

The evidence in support of this statement comes from a variety of sources and data, and it is believed quite credible although not easily quantifiable. Precise comparisons across long stretches of time are not possible here because of the diversity and evolution of business cycles as well as the data deficiencies that generally increase in the direction of the past. Still, historically business contractions used to be accompanied by declines not only in real indicators of commercial and industrial activity but also in financial and nominal aggregates or indexes: security prices, bonds and shares traded, interest rates, business failures (inverted), bank clearings, commodity and wholesale prices. The evidence from both the real activity indexes and the financial and monetary series tends to confirm the identification and dating of business cycles in NBER studies. Further, all this and other available information (accounts of contemporary observers, diffusion measures) help to compare business cycles and rank expansions by their vigor and contractions by their severity.

Table 20.3 shows that the standard deviations of quarterly log differences in real GNP were twice as large in 1875–1918, and thrice as large in 1919–1945, as in 1946–1983 (line 2, columns 1–3). The contrast between the interwar and postwar volatility of output is even greater in terms of the coefficients of variation, that is, ratios of s.d. to the mean growth rates (line 3). The underlying data may well overstate to some extent the instability in the earliest segment covered, but they are almost certainly adequate to demonstrate that the variability of output was greatest in 1919–1945 and smallest in 1946–1983.[2] Excluding the world-war periods would not change this ranking.

The standard deviations of quarterly changes measure short-term volatility; to compare movements over intermediate periods of varying length that correspond to business cycles and to distinguish between expansions and contractions, we must look at average amplitudes of specific-cycle rises and falls in real GNP. These estimates show that in percentage terms the total trough-to-peak increases in output were on average much larger in 1920–1938 than in either 1878–1914 or 1948–1982 (line 8, column 1–3). Much stronger contrasts are indicated for the peak-to-trough decreases in output, which were very shallow in the postwar cycles and very deep indeed in the interwar cycles (line 9). Taking into account the increase in the duration of expansions and the decrease in the duration of contractions (lines 6 and 7) yields more systematic and symmetric differences. For both rises and falls, the average relative amplitudes of cyclical movement per quarter are by a factor of 2 or more larger in 1920–1938 than in 1948–1982, while the figures for 1878–1914 fall in between (lines 10–11, columns 1–3).

Factors in the Moderation of Business Cycles

The moderation of business cycles in the 1950s and 1960s was clearly an international phenomenon. In Japan, West Germany, France, and Italy extraordinarily long and vigorous expansions occurred and cyclical setbacks assumed for a considerable time the form of retardations of growth rather than absolute declines. One probable reason lies in unique initial conditions: World War II destroyed much of the physical capital in Europe and the Far East but it also created huge backlogs of unsatisfied demand and left behind massive reserves of skilled human resources. As a result, after a restoration of sound currencies and free markets and with US aid, the countries in the renewed capitalist system were ready for an era of Great Reconstruction and enjoyed rapid growth of employment, output, investment, and trade. Recessions reappeared in these economies only in mid-1960s or later, as the rebuilding was completed and the growth rates came down to their normal levels.

These developments suggest the hypothesis that high-growth trends are likely to be associated with less cyclical instability, which finds some support in the US economic record. Thus, in periods when real GNP had a relatively high average annual growth of 3.7 percent (1903–1913, 1923–1929, and 1948–1969), the standard deviations of the growth rates were low (3.7 percentage points overall); in periods of relatively low average growth of 2.6 percent (1913–1923, 1929–1948, and 1969–1981), the corresponding measure of variability was high (7.2 percentage points). It is also notable that the proportion of time spent in contraction increased from 15 percent in 1948–1969, when real GNP grew 3.9 percent p.a., to 24 percent in 1969–1981, when it grew only 2.8 percent (see Zarnowitz and Moore 1986, Table 9.11 and text for more detail).

Economic growth was lower and instability higher in the 1970s and 1980s than in the 1950s and 1960s, but the economy remained resilient and depression-proof by historical standards. The proposed or possible explanations vary greatly. The following factors have probably contributed significantly to the moderation of business cycles, judging from a review of data and literature (Zarnowitz 1989):

1. Shifts in the structure of employment to less cyclical, largely service-producing industries. This includes, up to a point, the increased size of the acyclical government sector.
2. The fiscal automatic stabilizers—procyclical income taxes, countercyclical transfer payments. These devices were most effective in the first half of the postwar period, before the rise in inflation and its distorting effects on progressive taxation of nominal incomes.
3. Smoother functioning of the financial system. Federal deposit insurance prevented general banking panics (but, lately, at high costs to taxpayers and the nation).
4. Some favorable fiscal (mainly tax) policy actions. However, the record of discretionary fiscal policies was very mixed.
5. The rates of change in money supply were more volatile in 1875–1914 and, particularly, 1919–1939 than in 1946–1983, although monetary growth increased and became more variable in the second half of the postwar era. These differences parallel those in output variability. Monetary changes often reflect more than they influence the fluctuations of the economy. The active and passive elements in monetary (and fiscal) policies are both important and intermingled. The net contribution of monetary policy actions is difficult to assess but likely to have been modest and positive.
6. Economic agents gradually realized that business recessions have become shorter and milder, which strengthened their confidence and induced behavior that promoted more stable growth. But expectations change with the trend of events, for example, the rise in inflation and unemployment during the 1970s had the opposite effects.

Cyclical Aspects of Price and Cost Movements

Prices in the United States followed alternating upward and downward trends from the earliest years covered by historical statistics (1789–1800) through 1932. The long upswings lasted 21–25 years, the long downswing varied more, from 12 to 32 years. For example, the trend in prices was up in 1843–1864, down in 1864–1896, up in 1896–1920, and down in 1920–1932. Around these trends, prices usually rose in cyclical expansions and fell in contractions, though this applies more to wholesale prices than to the less sensitive consumer prices. These movements largely canceled each other over long stretches of time, even through 1945 when the inflationary war periods are included (see Table 20.3, line 1, columns 4 and 5). The half-century since 1932, however, witnessed the longest, largest, and most continuous US inflation on record. Business contractions and slowdowns still induced some price-level declines through the early postwar years but none after the mid-1960s (column 6). The recent recessions, then, were no longer associated with any deflation, at most with some disinflation (indeed, inflation accelerated during the contractions in 1974 and 1980, in part as a result of the novel supply shocks—the huge increases in oil prices imposed by the OPEC cartel). The variability of quarterly log differences in prices was much smaller in 1946–1983 than in the earlier periods (lines 2 and 3).

Thus, our age of *reduced* cyclical instability is also an age of *increased* downward rigidity of prices (and, it could be shown, of money wages as well). Yet the classical and still prevailing view among economists is that stickier wages and prices make the economy *more* unstable. This creates a problem but no real contradiction. Depending on the underlying conditions and sources of the shifts in the economy, departures from flexibility may or may not be destabilizing. The main contrast is between the stabilizing potential of flexible relative prices and the destabilizing potential of large movements in the general price level (Zarnowitz 1989b and c).

Major deflations of the past had strong adverse effects. Protracted and anticipated wage and price declines can aggravate demand contractions, and their nonoccurrence in recent times was salutary. But the postwar inflation, associated with the upward tilt in monetary growth, was itself a source of instability. It accelerated in the 1970s and grew increasingly volatile, generated much uncertainty and popular discontent, and led to oscillating, tardy, and excessive policy interventions that had disturbing consequences of their own. Relative price adjustments work best when the general price level is reasonably stable.

A long persistent rise in prices will not stay moderate and will eventually give rise to varying inflationary expectations incompatible with a stable relationship between changes in the price level and changes in real activity (a simple "Phillips curve"). The effects on the economy will depend, among others, on the adjustments of nominal interest rates to the changes in expected inflation. These adjustments have become much prompter and stronger in the latter part of the postwar era than they had been before. They can be stabilizing, up to a point, if permitted by the monetary authorities.

The structural changes that have contributed to the relative stabilization of the economy in recent times are probably also responsible in part for the reduction in the cyclicality of wages and prices. Prices as well as quantities tend to by cyclically less sensitive for services than for goods (Moore 1983, ch. 12). Hence the large rise in the relative importance of services will have had the effect of making the overall cost and prices indexes more sticky.

Growth of labor unions, which was most pronounced in 1933–1953 and halted or even reversed since the mid-1970s, worked in the same direction for some time. Here the medium is the spread of long and staggered union wage contracts, usually with partial indexation.

More generally, technical progress and competition require large investments in human capital that pay off best when employment relations are long-term, maintaining stably rising levels of productivity and real compensation. Growth of career employment in the corporate sector, professions, and government may have resulted in increasing reliance on implicit contracts designed to produce such desired conditions. Similarly, stable prices reduce communication costs to sellers and shopping costs to buyers, which is conducive to explicit or implicit contracts facilitating long-term associations between the transacting parties.

A rise in the perceived probability that the recessions will remain relatively brief and mild may also have increased the downward stickiness of prices in general. Since buyers would see less reason to reduce spending, sellers would see less reason to reduce prices of inputs and outputs.

Some new hypotheses on why wages and prices are "rigid" assume monopolistic competition or oligopoly. Labor productivity is taken to be a rising function of real or relative wages that are therefore kept high ("efficiency wages"). Small deviations from the equilibrium price affect profits only slightly and are therefore not worth correcting, as the individual firm sees it ("menu cost"). The applicability of these ideas is yet to be established. Also, it is not clear that greater market power is what distinguishes the past 40 years from the earlier era.[3]

Procyclical movements in delivery lags help absorb changes in demand. This type of nonprice market clearing can reduce the frequency of price changes under competition or monopoly. If an increase in the weight of production to order and the role of adjustments in delivery periods occurred, it would have made the measured price level stickier.

Concluding Thoughts

In this chapter, I was concerned mainly with the basic concepts and observations that enable us to define and study business cycles. We find that there is an important common core to these pervasive and persistent nonseasonal fluctuations that have long characterized the modern capitalist economies. But there is also much diversity as well as elements of an evolution. Business expansions have become longer on average but quite variable in duration and vigor; contractions shorter, milder, and rather more uniform. Through both good and bad times inflation continued, seemingly endless and inevitable, although some disinflation occurred during or after most recessions and major slowdowns. Deflationary depressions were avoided in the postwar period in all highly developed capitalist economies, but inflationary depressions recurrently plagued many countries of the underdeveloped world.

I suggested some presumed reasons for these changes, concentrating on the US economy.

I could not address the vast subject of business cycle theories here (for one recent survey, see Zarnowitz 1986). But such theories should of course help us understand the salient features of the fluctuations as reviewed in this chapter. The latter, therefore, has certain implications for the theory that are worth spelling out.

Although a model should be as simple as possible, the wider the range of the relevant facts it covers the greater is its claim to validity. There is no way to discriminate effectively among the many theories that address "the" business cycle on the sole basis of this or that of its selected aspects; one must ask of the models that they be reasonably consistent with all or most of the important stylized facts supplied by history.

Monocausal theories, whether the single factor on which they rely is real, monetary, or expectational, cannot do justice to the observed complexity and diversity of business cycles. Indeed, they fare poorly when confronted with the data that cover some violent swings of boom and bust, some extended depressions, and many moderate fluctuations. In recent times, long expansions were interrupted by phases of below-average but still positive growth, which stimulated interest in "growth cycles," defined as the consensus of sequences of expansions and contractions in *trend-adjusted* indicators of aggregate economic activity. The contemporary monocausal models fail to distinguish between business cycles and growth cycles. Meanwhile many empirical studies using various econometric and time-series analytic techniques document the importance of shocks and propagation mechanisms involving real and monetary, demand and supply variables.

In sum, business cycles are simply not "all alike," which inevitably impairs the usefulness of theories that depend on the contrary assumption. This includes prominently the recent "new classical" equilibrium models, whether they work with random shocks to money supply or technology. Earlier theories stressed (1) the instability of investment in fixed capital and the supply of credit, or (2) the fluctuations in monetary growth and price changes, due largely to faulty policy interventions and reactions to them of private agents. These factors probably do play a major role in business cycles with severe contractions. In the more numerous moderate business cycles and the still shorter and milder growth cycles, fluctuations of inventory investment, price-cost differences, and profit margins may well be of greater relative importance.

Notes

Originally published in *Business Economics*, Vol. 25, No. 3 (July 1990), pp. 5–13.

1. When three short and doubtful contractions in the second half of the nineteenth century are treated as slowdowns, the number of business cycles in the period 1854–1919 is reduced from 16 to 13 and the average duration of expansions is increased from 27 to 37 months, but the average duration of contractions is practically unchanged (23 months). The overall conclusions drawn in the text above are not significantly altered. For detail, see Zarnowitz 1981, pp. 493–504, and Moore and Zarnowitz 1986, p. 758.

2. The GNP estimates by Balke and Gordon used in Table 20.3 are based on historical annual series by Gallman and Kuznets and more recent series of the US Department of Commerce. The index of industrial production and trade by Persons and the Federal Reserve System index of industrial production were used as quarterly interpolators for 1875–1918 and 1919–1946, respectively. Recent criticism of traditional pre-World War I data led to new estimates and much debate; for one assessment of the results, see Zarnowitz 1989a.
3. Large corporations setting prices have been around for a long time. The increasing globalization of markets is an important postwar trend that presumably had the net effect of raising the levels of competition and the importance of changes in relative prices and wages.

References

Balke, Nathan S. and Robert J. Gordon. 1986. "Historical Data." In Gordon 1986, Appendix B.

Burns, Arthur F. and Wesley C. Mitchell. 1946. *Measuring Business Cycles.* New York: NBER.

Gordon, Robert J. ed. 1986. *The American Business Cycle: Continuity and Change.* Chicago: University of Chicago Press for the NBER.

Klein, Philip A. ed. 1990. *Analyzing Modern Business Cycles: Essays Honoring Geoffrey H. Moore.* Armonk, NY: M.E. Sharpe, Inc.

Mitchell, Wesley C. 1927. *Business Cycles: The Problem and Its Setting.* New York: NBER.

Moore, Geoffrey H. 1950. *Statistical Indicators of Cyclical Revivals and Recessions.* New York: NBER.

———. 1983. *Business Cycles, Inflation, and Forecasting.* 2nd. ed. Cambridge, MA: Ballinger Publ. Co. for NBER.

Moore, Geoffrey H. and Victor Zarnowitz. 1986. "The Development and Role of the NBER's Business Cycle Chronologies." In Gordon 1986, Appendix A.

Zarnowitz, Victor. 1981. "Business Cycles and Growth: Some Reflections and Measures." In *Wirtschaftstheorie und Wirtschaftspolitik: Gedenkschrift für Erich Preiser.* ed. by W. J. Mückl and A. E. Ott. Passau: Passavia Universitätsverlag.

———. 1986. "Recent Work on Business Cycles in Historical Perspective: A Review of Theories and Evidence." *Journal of Economic Literature* 23 (June).

———. 1989a. "Facts and Factors in the Recent Evolution of Business Cycles in the United States." NBER Working Paper no. 2865 (February).

———. 1989b. "Cost and Price Movements in Business Cycle Theories and Evidence: Hypotheses of Sticky Wages and Prices." NBER Working Paper no. 3131 (October).

———. 1989c. "Cost and Price Movements in Business Cycle Theories and Evidence: Causes and Effects of Observed Changes." NBER Working Paper no. 3132 (October).

———. Forthcoming. *Business Cycles: Theories, History, Indicators, and Forecasts.* Chicago: University of Chicago Press for the NBER.

Zarnowitz, Victor and Geoffrey H. Moore. 1986. "Major Changes in Cyclical Behavior." In Gordon 1986, ch. 9.

CHAPTER 21

1991

SOME FINANCIAL PERSPECTIVES ON COMPARATIVE COSTS OF CAPITAL

J. Fred Weston, University of California at Los Angeles

Much has been written on whether firms in some countries have a lower cost of capital than firms in other countries. This chapter first reviews the cost of capital measurement methodologies employed in prior studies of financially derived competitive advantage (FDCA). The problems with these studies motivate use of an alternative methodology based on widely accepted models of asset pricing in the literature of financial economics.[1]

The Analytics of FDCA Measurement

One major challenge confronting measurement procedures is whether the samples of firms being compared have similar technology and product market opportunities. Otherwise differences may arise from nonfinancial characteristics rather than financial. In addition to distinguishing between operational and financial sources of competitive advantage, other difficult measurement problems also must be resolved.

The traditional approach to making comparisons of the cost of capital for firms is the weighted average cost of capital (WACC) method measured by:

$$k = \text{WACC} = K_b(1-T) + K_s(1-L) \tag{21.1}$$

where k = WACC = weighted average cost of capital, K_b = cost of debt, K_s = cost of equity, T = corporate tax rate, L = debt at market value divided by value of a firm (V).

In implementing the WACC method it is also traditional to employ a discounted cash flow (DCF) procedure. The combined DCF/WACC method poses difficult measurement problems, as suggested by Table 21.1. The first issue is whether to use

Table 21.1 Measurement of component costs of capital

I. Before Tax or After Tax
   1. Corporate taxes
   2. Personal taxes
   3. Capital gains taxes
   4. Deductibility of payments
   5. Deductions in measuring taxable income
   6. Tax administration policies and practices

II. Cost of Debt
   1. Government vs. corporate
   2. By debt ratings
   3. Default probabilities
   4. Short-term vs. long-term
   5. Unsecured vs. secured
   6. By industry?
   7. Samples of firms?
   8. Risks of firms
   9. Product-market mixes
   10. Financial leverage ratios
   11. Coverage of financial charges
   12. Institutional vs. individual holders
   13. Growth rates of firms
   14. Covenants of borrowing arrangements
   15. Maturity structure of debt
   16. Duration patterns of assets and claims

III. Cost of Equity
   1. Level of risk-free rate
   2. Slope of Security Market Line
   3. Systematic factors affecting equity risk
   4. Growth rates of assets, earnings, etc.
   5. Models of time-growth patterns of cash flows
      a. No growth
      b. Constant growth
      c. Alternative constant growth rates
         (1) Economy
         (2) Industry
         (3) Firms
      d. Periods of super or sub-growth
   6. Alternative cash return or dividend patterns
   7. Internal vs. external equity financing
   8. Treatment of flotation costs

IV. Time Frame of Measurements
   1. Historical
   2. Current
   3. Anticipatory
   4. Average

before-tax or after-tax measures. The correct procedure is to start with comparable before-tax operating cash flows, then compare the ratios of the capitalized values to the after-tax cash flows. Differences in types of taxes, kinds of deductions, and administrative policies and practices are reflected in the before-tax and after-tax calculations.

Measuring the cost of debt must take into account a wide variety of factors to establish comparability in samples across countries. The measurement problems are even more difficult for cost of equity comparisons. The time framework for measurements also poses dilemmas. Theory requires that the analysis be forward looking—based on expectations. The available data are mainly historical.

More problems are confronted in calculating the weights. Previous studies of the costs of capital across countries have mainly used historical book weights. But it is an error not to take market values into account. In practice, managements for different combinations of reasons may have some target range as an objective. These subtleties are difficult to encompass in large scale studies.

To illustrate the nature of the difficulties, we shall describe the problems of measuring the cost of equity capital in the DCF/WACC approach. In concept, the cost of equity is the appropriate yield to maturity, k, that equates the expected cash flow streams to the observed price in Equation (21.2).

$$P \equiv V \equiv \frac{CF_1}{(1+k)} + \frac{CF_2}{(1+k)^2} + \frac{CF_3}{(1+k)^3} + \cdots + \frac{CF_n}{(1+k)^n} \qquad (21.2)$$

where $P \equiv V$ = price or value, CF = the expected cash flows to equity at each date, k = the cost of equity capital.

Prices for publicly traded firms can be observed. The operating cash flows to equity are the expected cash flows for some planning horizon. But the expected cash flows can take a variety of time patterns. Some studies of FDCA assume that the cash flows in the numerator are constant and continue to perpetuity. Under this assumption the cash flows are priced by Equation (21.3).

$$P = (CF_0) / k \qquad (21.3)$$

Such studies solve Equation (21.3) for k and use the earnings-price ratio or the dividend-price yield as the measure of the cost of equity capital. Other studies of the cost of capital across countries make less restrictive assumptions about the pattern of cash flows. A model erroneously called the "standard finance valuation model" assumes that the cash flows in the numerator of Equation (21.2) are measured by earnings (E) or dividends (D) and grow at a constant rate, g. The resulting valuation expression is Equation (21.4).

$$P = E / (k - g) \qquad (21.4)$$

The earnings-price ratio is sometimes still used as the measure of the cost of equity capital. However, this is clearly incorrect since k, the cost of equity capital, in the constant growth model is:

$$k = E / P + g \tag{21.4a}$$

In Equation (21.4) g cannot be greater than k. Nor can the growth rate for an individual firm or group of firms exceed the growth rate of the economy to perpetuity. Hence some assume g to be the same as the growth rate in the economy. But individual firms are likely to have time patterns of varying levels of growth.

The correct way to deal with the above problems in estimating the cost of equity is to solve for k in Equation (21.2) as set forth by Malkiel (1979), taking differences of risk into account. The theoretically correct procedure would require much more effort than previous studies. Some past estimates of comparative capital costs find that US firms have a positive FDCA, others negative; some find small positive or negative FDCAs, some large.[2] The diverse results suggest that measurement errors may account for apparent differences and that actual FDCA differences are not known.

Alternative Approaches to FDCA Measurement

In contrast to the DCF/WACC studies, others focus on US macroeconomics policies in comparison to those of other countries said to produce a negative FDCA for US firms. But the link between the theory and evidence has not been established. Writers differ on the national economic policies to be changed, which is to be expected since many macroeconomic factors can affect FDCA as shown in Table 21.2.

Because many factors could produce FDCAs, positive or negative, it is not enough to assert: (1) Government policies XYZ can affect FDCA. (2) Some data show FDCA. (3) Ergo, FDCA exists and is produced by policies XYZ. The logic is weak at each step. Even if FDCA existed, economic analysis would have to relate it back to specific national policies, *excluding* other possible explanations. What may really be involved is differences in macroeconomic philosophies among the writers. Further, if FDCA does not exist, the syllogism collapses.

These difficulties stimulate consideration of an approach stemming from developments in the modern theory of financial economics. This research tests for the possibility of FDCA without directly measuring it.

Capital Market Integration

The Nobel prize in economics in 1990 was awarded to three financial economists for their work in developing the theory of capital market asset pricing.[3] One result of the Markowitz-Miller-Sharpe contributions was the Capital Asset Pricing Model (CAPM), which measures the required return to assets and securities by a risk-free rate plus a risk premium calculated by the product of the market price of

Table 21.2 Policies and variables affecting FDCA

- I. Macroeconomic Policies
  - A. Budget surplus or deficit
  - B. Tight or easy money policy
  - C. Social security policy
  - D. Tax policies
    1. ITC
    2. Accelerated depreciation
    3. Reserves against losses
    4. Administrative policies
  - E. Spending policies and patterns
    1. Defense
    2. Welfare
    3. Productive
    4. Unproductive
  - F. Industrial policy
    1. Direct and indirect research subsidies
    2. Direct and indirect effects of tax policies on individual industries
    3. Executive or legislative pressures
  - G. Governmental and institutional environments
  - H. Wage policy
    1. Gain sharing
    2. Wage changes in relation to CPI and productivity changes
    3. Management of human resources
    4. Capital/labor ratios
- II. Macroeconomic Variables
  - A. Savings rates
  - B. Investment rates
  - C. Price behavior
  - D. Rates of productivity change
  - E. Quality of the educational system
    1. Primary
    2. Secondary
    3. Graduate
    4. Relations between education, business, and government
  - F. Investment opportunities
  - G. Growth rates of the economies and individual segments
  - H. Rates of innovation in the economy
  - I. Land prices
  - J. Exchange rates
  - K. Instability of economic, political, and social environments
    1. Instability of GNP levels
    2. Instability of interest rates
    3. Instability of foreign exchange rates
    4. Instability of government regimes
    5. Ability of government to make decisions
    6. Leadership qualities of top level government policy makers

risk times a measure of the non-diversifiable risk of the returns to the individual asset or security. Empirical tests used groups of portfolios to calculate risk-adjusted costs of capital. A subsequent more general development is the Arbitrage Pricing Theory (APT) (Ross, 1976; Roll and Ross, 1980). APT holds that the returns to assets or securities are determined by multiple factors, such as (1) market returns, (2) unanticipated inflation, (3) unanticipated changes in risk premia or in (4) twists in the yield curve. An illustration of the APT is Equation (21.5).

$$k = r_f + \lambda_1\beta_1 + \lambda_2\beta_2 + \lambda_3\beta_3 + \lambda_4\beta_4 \qquad (21.5)$$

where k is the expected return for the security; r_f is the riskfree rate; β_1 through β_4 are the assets' covariation (firm specific risks or sensitivities) with the factors; and λ_1 through λ_4 are the "prices" of these risks or the market risk-premia rates. Some illustrative numbers with the λs in parens:

$$k = .07 + (.05).4 + (.02).5 + (.04).1 + (.03).2 = 11\% \qquad (21.5a)$$

To facilitate graphical exposition, we postulate that the several APT sensitivity factors are encompassed by a composite risk factor designated beta (β) measured along the horizontal axis of Figure 21.1, which portrays an asset pricing line in which dollars are the numeraire currency.

An issue is whether the dollar risk-free and riskpremia rates (jointly) are equal for the (u) securities of the United States. as compared with other countries indicated by the letter j in Figure 21.1. One possibility provides a perspective on the DCF/WACC studies. Figure 21.1 illustrates a different required return for the u country securities as compared with the j country securities. There is only one asset pricing line, capital market integration obtains between the countries, but firms in the j country have a lower required cost of capital. The reason is that they have less risk. In any given country, different firms face different risks and would therefore have different required rates of return or costs of capital. But this is not FDCA.

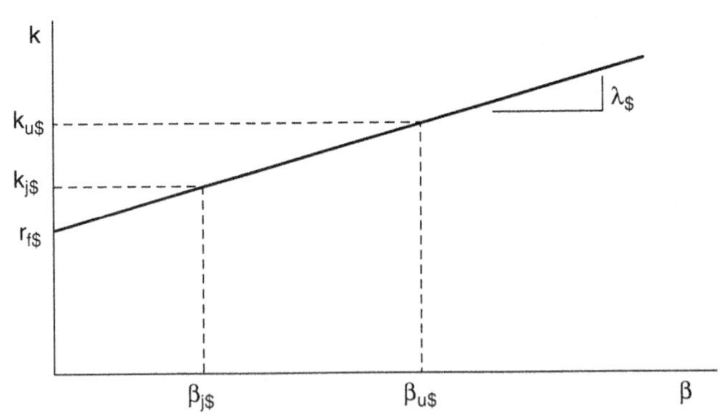

Figure 21.1 An asset pricing line in dollars.

Two recent studies have tested for capital market integration using APT. In addition to local risk-free securities, Cho et al. (1986) used monthly return observations (using dollars as the numeraire currency) for 60 US securities and 55 Japanese securities during the 11-year period 1973–1983. Risk-free and risk-premia rates for five risk factors were derived from these data, *separately* for the United States and Japanese securities. A statistical test that the dollar risk-free and risk-premia rates (jointly) were equal for securities of the different countries was rejected, indicating a lack of capital market integration and the possibility of FDCA during this period. Gultekin et al. (1989) tested the equality of risk-free and risk-premia rates during two separate four-year sample periods, 1977–1980 and 1981–1984. The distinction between periods was intended to isolate any effects of the Japanese capital market liberalization reforms of late 1980. The Gultekin et al. observations were weekly security returns, again calculated using dollars as the numeraire currency, of 110 US and 110 Japanese firms along with the local risk-free rates. While they found statistically significant differences for risk-free and risk-premia rates during the earlier period, no such differences were evident during the later 1981–1984 period, implying no FDCA after 1980.

Economic Integration

Solnik (1983) has shown that it is not enough that portfolios of US and other country securities have the same r_f and λs when calculated in one numeraire currency. A further requirement for no FDCA is that when the other currency is used as the numeraire, the same real r_f and λs are obtained. When these equalities hold so that dollar and yen (e.g.) pricing equations are identical on a real basis, *economic integration* holds. When the interest rate parity (IRP) and purchasing power parity (PPP) conditions hold (approximately), the real risk-free rates among countries are equal. For economic integration, the λs must also be equal.

Empirical work to date has not performed the further test of using the foreign currency as a numeraire as well as the domestic, but some inferential evidence is available. Using long-term government bond yields, Bernheim and Shoven (1986) estimated the 1971–1982 real interest-rate differential to be between 0.23 and 0.93 percent, depending on the method by which the inflation rate was measured. They also noted an increase of this differential to about 2 percent (average) during the 1983–1985 period. Using similar long-term bond data from the first quarters of 1986–1988, French and Poterba (1989) estimated the differential at just 0.58 percent. Some tentative, indirect evidence from Hamao (1988) suggests that the risk premia differences across countries are negligible. These results are consistent with economic integration and no FDCA. Studies which use inflation-adjusted interest rate differences between the United States and other countries as evidence of FDCA fail to recognize the implications of (approximate) parity conditions.

Conclusions

There are potentially serious biases in studies using the DCF/WACC methodology to discern a financially derived competitive advantage (FDCA) between United

States and other firms. The principal sources of this bias are a neglect of differences in the time-growth profiles of equity cash flow streams and their riskiness.

While not conclusive, the available empirical evidence suggests the following: US and other capital markets have been integrated since 1981. If there are no significant tax or subsidy differences among countries, studies that appear to show differences in cost of capital between United States and other countries may be reflecting measurement errors or failure to recognize the implications of economic integration.

Acknowledgment

The author thanks Clement G. Krouse for considerable guidance in preparation of this chapter.

Notes

Originally published in *Business Economics*, Vol. 26, No. 2 (April 1991), pp. 33–37.

1. For a more complete treatment of the topics in this chapter see, C. G. Krouse and J. F. Weston, "Financially Derived Competitive Advantage: An Overview of Key Issues," ms., 1/31/91.
2. A. Ando and A. Auerbach, 1985, 1988a, 1988b, 1990; D. Bernheim and J. Shoven, 1986; G. Hatsopoulis and S. Brooks, 1986; K. French and J. Poterba, April 1989; R. McCauley and S. Zimmer, Summer 1989; J. Frankel, 1990.
3. H. M. Markowitz, *Portfolio Selection: Efficient Diversification of Investments,* New York: John Wiley and Sons, 1959; M. H. Miller, "Debt and Taxes," *Journal of Finance,* 32, May 1977, pp. 261–275; W. F. Sharpe, "Capital Asset Prices: A Theory of Market Equilibrium Under Conditions of Risk," *Journal of Finance,* September 1964.

References

Ando, A., and A. Auerbach, "The Corporate Cost of Capital in the U.S. and Japan: A Comparison," in J. Shoven, ed., *Government Policy towards Industry in the United States and Japan,* Cambridge: Cambridge University Press, 1985, pp. 21–49.

———, "The Corporate Cost of Capital in Japan and the United States: A Comparison," in J. Shoven, ed., *Government Policy towards Industry in the United States and Japan,* Cambridge University Press, 1988a.

———, "The Cost of Capital in the United States and Japan: A Comparison," *Journal of the Japanese and International Economics,* 2, 1988b, pp. 134–158.

———, "The Cost of Capital in Japan: Recent Evidence and Further Results," NBER Working Paper No. 3371, 1990.

Bernheim, D., and J. Shoven, "Taxation and the Cost of Capital," unpublished manuscript, Stanford University, 1986.

Cho, D., C. Eun; and L. Senbet, "International Arbitrage Pricing Theory: An Empirical Investigation," *Journal of Finance,* 41, 1986, pp. 313–329.

Frankel, Jeffrey A., "Japanese Finance: A Survey," NBER Working Paper No. 3156, 1990.

French, K. and J. Poterba, "Are Japanese Stock Prices Too High?" CRSP Seminar on the Analysis of Prices, University of Chicago, April 1989.

Gultekin, M., N. Gultekin; and A. Penati, "Capital Controls and International Capital Market Segmentation: The Evidence from the Japanese and American Stock Markets," *Journal of Finance,* 44, 1989, pp. 849–869.

Hamao, Y., "An Empirical Examination of the Arbitrage Pricing Theory Using Japanese Data," Working Paper, University of California, San Diego, 1988.

Hatsopoulis, George N. and Stephen H. Brooks, "The Gap in the Cost of Capital: Causes, Effects, and Remedies," in R. Landau and Dale Jorgensen, eds., *Technology and Economic Policy,* Cambridge: Ballinger, 1986, Chapter 12, pp. 221–280.

Malkiel, Burton G., "The Capital Formation Problem in the United States," *The Journal of Finance,* 34, May 1979, pp. 291–306.

McCauley, R., and S. Zimmer, "Explaining International Differences in the Cost of Capital," *FRBNY Quarterly Review,* Summer 1989, pp. 7–28.

Roll, R.W. and S.A. Ross, "An Empirical Investigation of the Arbitrage Pricing Theory," *The Journal of Finance,* 35, December 1980, pp. 1073–1103.

Ross, S. A., "The Arbitrage Theory of Capital Asset Pricing," *Journal of Economic Theory,* 13, December 1976, pp. 341–360.

Solnik, B., "International Arbitrage Pricing Theory," *Journal of Finance,* 38, 1983, pp. 449–457.

CHAPTER 22

1993

HEALTH INSURANCE DERIVATIVES: THE NEWEST APPLICATION OF MODERN FINANCIAL RISK MANAGEMENT

James A. Hayes, James A. Hayes & Associates, Inc.

Joseph B. Cole, Kiddler, Peabody & Co.

David I. Meiselman, Virginia Polytechnic Institute & State University

We are in the midst of a giant economic, business and financial revolution, particularly with respect to understanding and managing risk and uncertainty. The revolution is worldwide and is an important factor in globalizing markets. This revolution has significantly changed the way businesses and financial firms are managed, the way markets, products, and services are structured and analyzed, and the way economists and financial experts perform their analytical and operating tasks.

According to estimates of the Futures Industry Association, the 1990 volume of exchange-traded financial derivatives was double that of 1985 and almost seven times the 1983 volume. Derivative exchanges spread to the world's major financial centers, such as London, Paris, Tokyo, and Singapore, and in the United States from Chicago to New York and Philadelphia. The growth of the over-the-counter (OTC) financial derivatives has been extraordinary. Prior to the 1980s, the primary OTC market was the interbank foreign exchange market, involving forward currency contracts. In the 1980s, the growth in the OTC market was based on innovative financial engineering, resulting in a host of new instruments such as swaps, caps, floors, collars, and swaptions. The International Swap Dealers Association (ISDA) estimates that in 1987 outstanding currency and interest rates swaps totaled almost $1 trillion. By 1990, only three years later, these swaps tripled to close to $3 trillion.

What accounts for this phenomenal growth, and what are some of its effects? First and foremost, the markets in derivatives have grown because these markets present a better and a cheaper way to manage risk and to design useful, innovative products. The main elements of how price risks in agricultural markets could be managed or hedged were well-known many years ago, as was the related price discovery function of futures markets, that is, as a byproduct of markets for future delivery, prices in those markets could be seen by all. People therefore could easily "discover" the market's judgments about future price as well as the prices at which transactions for deferred delivery could be executed today. The ability to do these trades was made accessible to a wide range of people; the market determined the price of the contract, which was the same to all.

The wave of innovation really began once it was recognized that essentially the same analysis and risk management techniques applicable in commodities futures markets were appropriate to financial markets as well. David Meiselman's research more than 30 years ago was path-breaking and was published in his *The Term Structure of Interest Rates* (Prentice-Hall, 1962).

Risk reduction and management opportunities afforded by derivatives reduce the cost of achieving a desired or optimal level of risk. Risk became something to be managed and controlled and a central matter for sophisticated, responsible management. Price discovery gives ultimate transactors and wealth holders the ability to dispose of some or all of the risk by appropriate buying or selling. In addition, risk can be shifted to those who prefer to carry these risks or who are effectively paid to do so. The result is a more efficient allocation of risk, with resulting overall wealth and income gains that more than compensate for added transactions costs.

These results came in three major phases:

1. In the first phase of the growth of derivative instruments and markets, especially exchange-traded futures, the number and use of these instruments and markets increased enormously, including Treasury bonds of various maturities, foreign exchange, short-term money market instruments such as Eurodollars and now even the federal funds rate. During this time, there was a parallel development of options markets, first on individual stocks, then options on futures and currencies, and then options on various indexes. The put-call parity conditions tied together the options, spot and futures markets.
2. The second major phase began once people learned how to manage and control risk. The next step moved from relatively simple contracts that required decomposition of complex bundles of composite products and balance sheets to more precise customizing of individual products for specific purposes, often by combining components from different derivative markets. These new products include leaps, bounds, mitts, lyons, and lynx.
3. The new, third phase of the derivatives revolution is the movement of cash through the clearing system, not the delivery of the underlying product. Transactions costs are reduced by avoiding the costs of holding or dealing

> in the underlying product, whether wheat or bonds or stocks. In derivatives markets there are essentially side bets on prices of the underlying contracts, with cash settlement of the change in the price. There need be no delivery, and even in markets where delivery takes place, there is relatively little of it.

Because of the enormous importance of health care expenditures, now exceeding 13 percent of GNP, and the impact of volatility and uncertainty of health care costs on buyers and sellers of health care and health care insurance, a natural market exists for still another significant derivative product to manage the risk of changes in health care costs. The product, as with other derivatives, will facilitate price discovery, risk transfer, and risk management.

Health Insurance Futures Contacts

Insurance futures were discussed in the early 1970s in Robert Goshay and Richard Sandor's paper "An Inquiry into the Feasibility of a Reinsurance Futures Market" (*Journal of Business Finance*, Vol. 5, No. 2, 1973). Nearly 20 years later, James Hayes published probably the first paper specifically on health insurance futures in "Hedging Opportunities in Health Care" (*Health Care Strategic Management,* March 1990).

The National Association of Business Economists (NABE) took an early and aggressive lead in providing information on the development of health insurance futures to its members. The Chairman of the NABE Health Roundtable, Gerald Musgrave, invited Hayes to give the first public presentation on health insurance futures at its San Francisco meeting in 1989. Since then, Hayes made presentations on health insurance futures at NABE Health Roundtables in 1991 and 1992.

Meanwhile, the Chicago Board of Trade (CBOT) began new product development of insurance futures, specifically including health and automobile. A formal, public announcement was made by the CBOT in mid-1990 of its undertaking. Since then, new product development work commenced on homeowners and catastrophic insurance futures and options as well.

Leslie Rosenthal, former CBOT Board of Directors Chairman and currently Chairman of the Insurance Subcommittee at the CBOT, among others, advocated the development of insurance futures at the exchange and is responsible for completing the design of these contracts with the support of the CBOT Economic Analysis and Planning Department staff. Several contracts, including health insurance futures contract, have been approved by the Commodities Futures Trading Commission (CFTC).

The CBOT began trading catastrophic insurance futures and options contracts on December 11, 1992. It also plans to list homeowners and health insurance futures and options contracts in the first half of 1993. The introduction of trading on insurance futures and options at the CBOT offers insurers, reinsurers, and, in the case of health insurance, health care providers and hospital managers, low-cost hedging alternatives. Additionally, these new instruments provide opportunities for the development of new insurance products.

These new insurance products will apply to insurers, including managed care firms, indemnity companies, and self-insured employers. Providers will also be able to hedge and design new insurance products, such as multiyear fixed-price purchase agreements with insurers.

How Health Insurance Futures Work

The health insurance futures contract prices claims in the small group market, details of which are provided below. If claims go unexpectedly up, the futures price rises. If claims go unexpectedly down, the futures price falls. Because insurers of all kinds suffer when claims rise, given that they quoted a fixed premium for the benefit period, they are natural buyers or longs of this contract to protect themselves. Since providers of health care have to plan and budget, any decline in their expected cash flow from claims payments affects them adversely. Therefore, providers are the natural sellers or shorts in this market.

The main purpose of hedging with the proposed health insurance futures is the management of the risk in changes in claims costs arising from unexpected volatility in the trend of these costs. Although the CBOT health insurance futures contracts have been designed for the hedging use of insurers and reinsurers, it is important to note that these new futures contracts do not provide insurance coverage. In fact, the key element of insurance, "insurable interest," is not present because no insurance liability is being contracted or issued. Health insurance futures are not alternative forms of insurance or reinsurance policies.

There are several other distinctions between insurance policy coverage and the CBOT health insurance futures contract:

1. A futures contract is a standardized agreement to buy or sell a commodity or financial instrument at some time in the future at a price agreed upon today on an organized futures exchange. The underlying commodity or financial instrument of the health insurance futures contract is actually an index that tracks the insurance losses of a minimum of ten health insurance carriers, including Blue Cross and Blue Shield plans and commercial insurance companies, that report to a pool calculation manager.
2. Insurance policies that are ceded to reinsurers are generally implemented via bilateral contracts negotiated on either a treaty or facultative basis. In contrast, CBOT insurance futures are standardized contracts that may only be traded through Futures Commission Merchants (FCMs) on the floor of the exchange and are regulated by the CFTC.
3. Users of health insurance futures contracts must post an initial margin, which acts like a performance bond. Users are also responsible for a daily variation margin representing the daily change in value of the futures position. This updating of accounts is referred to as the daily mark-to-market procedure. These margins enhance creditworthiness by greatly reducing the risk of default by the counterparties. Furthermore, the clearinghouse corporation acts as the ultimate guarantor of all trades.

These features of the health insurance futures contract—a standardized contract, traded on an organized and regulated market with superior creditworthiness—will permit insurers and reinsurers to hedge the systematic risk component of their insurance liabilities as related to the underlying index of health insurance policies. Properly utilized, the health insurance futures contract will have gain and loss characteristics of proportional, or pro rata, reinsurance. In addition, call options on the health insurance futures may be employed to provide payouts similar to non-proportional or excess-of-loss reinsurance.

Before providing a description of the health insurance futures contract, an examination of the timing of the introduction of this new contract may provide insight into its probability of use and success as a hedging instrument. Generally speaking, there are six necessary conditions for a successful futures contract: price variability; competitive determination of prices; homogeneity; viable cash market; insufficient hedging alternatives; and contract design.[1]

The underlying commodity should be fairly homogeneous in nature and be characterized by a volatile and competitively determined price. In addition, the cash or spot market for the commodity on which a successful futures contract exists is usually viable and dynamic but lacks sufficient hedging alternatives for risk management. Finally, the design of the futures contract must appropriately balance the factors of standardization, liquidity, arbitrage, and dealer acceptance, among others, to be successful.

Two key considerations for the introduction of a health insurance futures contract in today's market are the existence of insufficient hedging alternatives and price variability. For example, using figures reported by the Health Insurance Association of America (HIAA), the most recent annual *increase* in health care costs per employee is greater than the *level* just over a decade ago. For the automobile industry in the United States, the dollar amount per employee of health care cost is now $1100 for Chrysler, $900 for General Motors and $525 for Ford. These numbers are greater than the cost of steel per vehicle and are difficult to manage or hedge.

The lack of insufficient hedging mechanisms may be illustrated by contrasting the health care component of the consumer price index (CPI) with the CPI itself. The CPI and its medical care component both increased substantially over the past two decades. But a correlation between the two implies an R-squared of around 5 percent, which means 95 percent of a hedge between these indexes would be due to unexplained phenomena. Thus, existing financial instruments or other commodities that are highly correlated with the CPI provided a poor cross-hedge for health insurance costs.

The objective of the contract design of the CBOT health insurance futures contract is to create an index that reflects value for the industry. The underlying index of health insurance losses for the futures contract will be based on a large sample of reported incurred losses for a pool of health insurance policies. The pool will consist of a minimum of ten carriers with no single issuer representing more than 15 percent of the pool. Minimum expected pool size is $100 million of annual premium or 1,000 policies at inception.

The pool will be balanced in terms of group size, demographics, and cost area. Losses that occur during a particular quarter and are reported during the quarter, or up to three months thereafter, will be included in the calculation. Eligible health policies that go into the pool will provide fully insured health indemnity benefits, and will cover 25 to 500 group members by a single employer. In addition, the policies will have a one-year term with a stable premium, take effect at the beginning of the pool formation month, provide rich, but not unusual benefits, and have a maximum deductible of $500 and maximum coinsurance of 20 percent.

The CBOT plans to form two pools of acceptable small group health insurance pools per year. The criteria for policies in the pool are described in materials prepared by Coopers & Lybrand, the pool manager. One pool will be comprised of policies that start or renew on or about January 1st. The second pool will be comprised of policies that start or renew on or about July 1st. Each pool will last 12 consecutive months plus a run-off.

There will be four contracts per pool per year. The months traded will correspond to the dates of these four contracts. The pool manager will calculate and report the quarterly premium for the health insurance index pool of policies for each contract. The names of the reporting companies and the estimated quarterly premium will be publicly announced by the CBOT prior to the start of trading for any health insurance futures contract.

The health insurance futures index may be calculated by standardizing the paid claims in the pool by dividing the claims by the pool premium. The resulting loss ratio for the industry pool is then multiplied by the contract size of $100,000:

$$\text{Index Value} = (\$100{,}000) \times \frac{\text{Paid Claims}}{\text{Premiums}}$$

To understand the contract better, consider the following hedging example provided by the Chicago Board of Trade. An insurance company expects to incur claims of about $8 million during the April through June period and earn associated quarterly premiums of $10 million. The company expects that by the end of September they will have paid 90 percent of their claims, giving them a loss ratio of 90 percent times the incurred claims paid out, or 72 percent.

Similarly, the loss ratio for the industry pool for the futures contract is expected to be 63 percent during the same period, where the difference is attributable to the composition of the workforce by age, by region, or by income. (See Table 22.1)

Thus the expected index value at the end of September for the September futures contract is 0.63 times $100,000 or $63,000. In order to hedge against unexpected increases in claim costs, the company would buy, or go long, health insurance futures

Table 22.1 Actuarial forecasts

Variable	*Company*	*Pool*
Incurred Claims	$ 8,000,000	$ 70,000,000
Premiums	$10,000,000	$100,000,000
Claims paid as % of incurred claims by end September	90%	90%
Loss Ratio (Sept.)	72%	63%

Table 22.2 Number of contracts to buy

$$\frac{\text{Premium Written}}{\text{Contract Size}} \times \frac{\text{Hedged Claims}}{\text{\% Complete}} = \frac{\$10,000,000}{\$100,000} \times \frac{1.00}{0.90} = 111$$

contracts. The appropriate number of contracts to buy may be found by dividing $10 million in premium by the $100,000 contract size times the ratio of hedge claims to claims completed in the period. Employing this calculation, shown in Table 22.2, the company would hedge by purchasing approximately 111 contracts.

Now assume that the final index value turns out to have a loss ratio of 0.675 instead of 0.63. This loss ratio was higher than anticipated and causes the original $63,000 contract value to increase to a final settlement value of $67,500. The futures change turned out to be the difference between $67,500 versus $63,000, or $4,500 per contract; when multiplied by 111 contracts a futures gain of $499,500 is achieved. Suppose the company experiences actual incurred claims of $8.5 million instead of the expected incurred claims of $8 million, for an unexpected loss of $500,000. Utilizing the hedging gains of $499,500, most but not all of the unexpected losses may be offset. The difference between the future gain and unexpected claims losses is referred to as a basis risk.

Basis gains and losses may be attributed to a variety of factors. One, for example, is the region that the work force is located in. Employing data from the HIAA, standard operating procedures by different hospitals may vary considerably in cost. Growth rates for operation costs are also different in these areas. These cost-area factors, as well as workforce education and age, will influence a hedger's claim cost relationship relative to the national average or industry pool comprising the health insurance index.

Conclusions

The derivatives revolution is now entering the insurance markets, particularly health insurance. This chapter summarizes key trends in this revolution, recounts steps in the development of health insurance futures, and provides a hypothetical hedging example for a health insurer. The GNMA CDR futures contract led the way to the Treasury bond contract and other financial futures to hedge the yield curve. The heating oil futures contract led the way to crude oil futures and other energy futures to hedge energy costs. This health insurance futures contract will lead the way to health care futures contracts to hedge rising health care costs.

Notes

Originally published in *Business Economics*, Vol. 28, No. 2 (April 1993), pp. 36–40.

1. For additional discussion of conditions for a successful futures contract, see Richard Sandor, "Financial Futures Markets," *Proceedings from Conference Honoring Dewey Daane*, April 13, 1989; Vanderbilt University.

PART IV

1995–2004

CHAPTER 23

1996

THE ADAM SMITH ADDRESS
AN AMBITIOUS AGENDA FOR ECONOMIC GROWTH

Murray Weidenbaum, Washington University in St. Louis

In this presidential election year, it has become fashionable to advocate faster economic growth as the elixir to cure all that ails the American society. Surely an average annual growth rate in the neighborhood of 2 percent is anemic, whether we view it in historical terms or by the current standards of the economies of China and Southeast Asia. Faster growth produces all sorts of good things, such as lower budget deficits, more new jobs, higher incomes, and rising living standards. Thus, who can object to the general idea of achieving larger economic output?

Economists are destined to bring the wet blanket to the party. We have to raise the question ignored in this campaign: How can we not just achieve but maintain a more rapid and more durable pace of economic expansion? The two most popular ways of attaining faster growth fall short of providing a satisfying response. The first simple growth policy is to order the Federal Reserve System (Fed) to put its collective foot down harder on the monetary gas pedal—or, at the least, to take the other foot off the monetary brake.

The second approach requires Congress just to cut taxes, providing a one-shot fiscal stimulus for a sluggish economy. Both responses are clear, simple—and in today's circumstances—inadequate or inappropriate. Both are kissing cousins, quick-fix variants of the age-old desire to pump up the economy or—to continue the automotive metaphor—to put air in a flat tire without patching up the holes.

In recent decades, we have learned that a rapid and sustained expansion of the money supply unaccompanied by substantial change in policy toward the real economy will mainly generate escalating inflation. Rising inflation, later if not sooner, will cause the Fed to shift gears and to pursue a policy of slowing the growth of or even cutting the money supply. In the process, interest rates will rise. More often than not, that sequence of actions will end the economic expansion and precipitate the next recession. So much for a faster growth track via monetary policy.

The currently popular fiscal alternative, just cutting tax rates, is likely to result in a similarly undesirable sequence of events. However, the process will probably be a bit more indirect. As an old budget hand—I cut my eyeteeth in Harry Truman's Budget Bureau—I always worry that proposed tax cuts will not be offset by new expenditure cuts. Merely meeting the requirements of balancing the budget under the existing tax structure is likely to exhaust all reasonable opportunities for reducing federal outlays.

Surely, cutting income taxes alone is not going to energize the economy sufficiently to prevent a rise in the budget deficit. On the basis of experience—I also bear the scars of the 1981–1982 cycle—those deficits can lead to a variety of negative effects. These range from a diminution of investment capital available for private business expansion to scaring the Fed into tightening the flow of money and credit.

A Nonpolitician's Approach

But mine is not a counsel of despair. There is a third way of responding to the poor performance of the US economy. It, too, is a supply-side approach but it is more subtle—and avowedly more difficult—than just cutting taxes. We must deal with the structural defects in the American economy that depress productive capacity and productivity. Many of these defects arise from the operation of government policies and programs. The fact that, in the main, these adverse effects on the economy are unintentional provides an especial opportunity for reform. An example of these structural and institutional shortcomings will provide an inkling of the type of economic cure that I have in mind. Although the initial example is regulatory, my analysis will cover the gamut of government operations, especially expenditure programs and the tax system.

Dale Jorgensen of Harvard has estimated that, by the year 2005, when the new Clean Air Act is fully in effect, the compliance with that statute and other environmental laws will reduce the nation's capital stock by over 4 percent. It will increase the cost of capital by more than 5 percent, and reduce the economy's growth rate by more than 3 percent a year.

Nevertheless, there is no responsible pressure to dismantle these environmental programs. The Manufacturing Institute, for example, suggests that reasonable regulatory and tax reforms can yield technological advances and greater capital investment that could raise the growth rate by a half percentage point. If that number seems small, please remember that compounding it over a decade generates a large cumulative increase in production, income, employment, and living standards.

To clear the air (I mean that in more than one sense), this is not a plea to swing the public policy pendulum from the present polar alternative of increasingly tough environmental regulation, regardless of the economic consequences, to the equally undesirable extreme of trying to maximize economic growth while ignoring environment, safety, and other social concerns. Rather, we need to rethink the whole gamut of government regulation of business as part of a comprehensive economic reform strategy.

Similarly, while I can restrain my inherent enthusiasm for simply cutting tax rates, I believe that simultaneously altering the fundamental structure of the government's revenue system can contribute in highly desirable ways to strengthening the overall economy. Likewise, substantially shifting the composition of government expenditures to favor investment over consumption can help quicken the economic growth rate in a sustainable fashion.

I readily agree that the approach I am presenting will not be an easy strategy to achieve. However, accomplishments along these lines of structural reform will be far more lasting than merely tinkering with the conventional dials of macroeconomic policy.

Shifting the Composition of Government Spending

Let us start with the opportunities for reforming government spending. Voting to approve the general idea of a balanced budget is only a start on the path of fiscal sensibility. The really tough job is to make the specific spending cuts. Few objective criteria have been developed to guide that effort. My suggested guide is to concentrate on reducing or eliminating expenditures that hurt the economy. Inefficient public sector programs represent a deadweight loss to the economy. They produce lower benefits than if the same funds were invested in private activities that meet the test of the marketplace.

Let us assume that we have the duty of preparing guidelines to assist the Congress in this arduous assignment. The most popular formula—eliminating waste, fraud, and abuse—is not adequate to the task. Of course, there are numerous individual examples of fraud, waste, and abuse, however we define those terms. The reports of prisoners who illegally receive social security checks are surely upsetting. So are the stories of companies trying to sell the government shoddy products. These situations should be dealt with severely, but that is just a small start.

Here are five fundamental guidelines for serious budget cutting:

1. *Focus reductions on the large consumption part of the federal budget rather than the small investment component.* Such a change would curb the tendency for deficit financing to be a powerful mechanism for converting private saving into public consumption. On occasion, the federal government actually does make worthwhile investments. Some outlays for education help the recipients achieve careers in which their added incomes generate added tax payments that more than repay the government's original investment.

Alas, such examples of effective federal investments are rare. Virtually the entire increase in federal outlays since 1980 has been in the form of consumption-type spending—aside from interest on the national debt. As a result, consumption outlays dominate the budget. In 1992, federal civilian investment outlays (education and training, research and development, and infrastructure) were only $83 billion, or 6 percent, out of a total budget of $1.4 trillion. Under these circumstances, large reductions in federal spending would be economically beneficial, because they would almost invariably fall on consumption.

By far, the dominant segment of federal consumption outlays consists of transfer payments or, to use the prevailing euphemism, entitlements. Unfortunately, in the largest such program, social security, the recipients have been led (or rather misled) to believe that they have earned the money they receive.

The typical beneficiary has contributed only a portion of the monthly check issued to him or her. A key fact overlooked by most senior citizen groups is that the total of such contributions plus matching employer payments plus interest does not begin to cover the monthly benefit payments. The balance is a gift from the working population. While I was still in the White House, I had the audacity to label that gift the economic equivalent of welfare. There were immediately calls in Congress for my impeachment. Ronald Reagan, bless him, ignored such ill-considered responses to telling the truth.

As a private citizen, I feel obliged to repeat that accurate point: there is a large but hidden welfare component in the major middle class entitlements. In the long run, privatization may be the most effective response. Meanwhile, reformers need to face the hard fact that recipients have not earned the annual cost-of-living increase (COLAs) that they now expect as a matter of right. The COLAs violate the insurance principle that, on average, you get what you pay for, and they arbitrarily tilt the federal budget even more to consumption expenditures.

If it is not possible to eliminate the annual COLA payments, a "diet COLA" could be limited to the annual inflation in excess of 2 percent. After all, the average working person is not protected completely from the effect of inflation.

2. *Target the many subsidy programs that provide special benefits to limited parts of the population at the expense of the national taxpayer.* Such subsidies inherently divert resources away from their most productive uses.

Contrary to widespread belief, especially in the business community, the word "farm" does not always precede the term "subsidy." Subsidies to agriculture are the largest component of the subsidy category. Nevertheless, generous subsidies are also provided to business and labor.

Here, I suggest teaming up with an important interest group often at loggerheads with economists—environmentalists. Many government programs are both economically wasteful and environmentally undesirable. For example, we continue mining for many metals and minerals at a time that the federal government maintains over $6 billion of these same items in a military stockpile that the Department of Defense now admits is not needed. That surplus should be sold on the open market. Those sales would reduce the need for some mining activity that, even when commercially necessary, is environmentally invasive.

Other economically wasteful activities of the federal government that are also environmentally unsound include selling governmentally produced electricity—as well as water, timber, and grazing rights—at below-market prices. Eliminating these subsidies would simultaneously enhance the efficiency of the economy and reduce environmental pollution.

3. *Avoid funding expenditure programs designed to offset problems created by regulation.* A more cost-effective way of dealing with the problem is to change the original regulation that created the problem. To maintain the status quo is to ensure fiscal perpetual motion.

A major example of this shortcoming is regulation of the workplace. For years, economists have written about discouraged workers who drop out of the work force because they do not believe suitable jobs are available for them. Government has created a new category—the discouraged employer, discouraged by the host of government impediments to hiring people.

Regulatory and mandated burdens on the employment process are rarely considered in relationship to the expensive array of government programs that offset their adverse affects by trying to increase the supply of workers. Yet the record of these offsetting programs, such as job training, is not heartening. The society would be far better off with a combination of regulatory reform and expenditure reductions. Such a combined effort would reduce the gap between federal income and outlay and eliminate serious inefficiencies in the American workplace.

4. *Privatize activities that are properly the responsibility of the private sector.* We need to go beyond the useful notion of having the private sector produce items under government contract. Although an improvement over relying on government arsenals, this approach to privatization still leaves to the public sector the determination of how much of the nation's resources should be funneled to the designated activity. Many goods and services should no longer be paid for by the taxpayer, no matter who produces them. The extent to which those items are produced should depend on the interaction of market forces.

This is not a simple recipe for cutting services to the public. For example, privatizing the air traffic controller functions of the Federal Aviation Administration would enhance the efficiency of air transportation. The airlines are willing to pay higher fees for a more efficient system than the government now provides. The resultant reductions in congestion and waiting times would more than pay for the private expansion of the air traffic control system.

5. *Use economic efficiency considerations throughout the budget process.* The key to success is to enforce this guideline. Benefit-cost analysis has often served to sanctify the pork barrel by overestimating benefits and underestimating costs. The use of basic economic efficiency tests would surely improve the overall effectiveness of government spending and likely lower the aggregate level while contributing to more efficient use of the nation's resources. Here are two examples of what is possible:

1. Charge competitive, market interest rates for all federally provided credit. That one change will quickly reduce the many demands for federally subsidized lending. Under the status quo, numerous borrowers who could obtain credit on their own are given an incentive to seek aid simply because the government charges a lower interest rate than commercial banks and other private lenders. Moreover, the current arrangement encourages the extension of credit to borrowers who do not meet the objective tests of the marketplace.
2. Use the comparable market rates of interest when evaluating proposed federal investment projects. Unrealistically low interest rates result in pulling investment funds from the private sector to lower-yield public projects. By definition, such spending is inefficient and a poor use of the taxpayers' money. Traditionally, these programs are referred to as the "pork barrel," and are an appropriate candidate for a federal diet.

Tax Reform

After more than a year of public debate, it is fair to say that there is no universal agreement on how to reform the tax system. Do we streamline the income tax by shifting to a flat tax? Do we adopt a saver-friendly reform known as the USA Tax? Or do we replace the income tax with a national sales tax? It will take much more discussion and analysis before a specific tax reform emerges with enough support to be enacted. Nevertheless, progress has been made on a broad consensus on the direction of change.

The most widely held conclusion is the notion that the tax system is unfair and too complicated. And, when we step back from the mass of specific provisions, it can be seen that the Internal Revenue Code, with its heavy dependence on income taxation, depresses the economy.

There are several key arguments that economists offer for shifting the base of taxation from income to consumption. Consumption-based taxes put the fiscal burden on what people take from society—the goods and services they consume—rather than on what they contribute by working and saving, as do income taxes. Thus, under a consumption-based tax system, saving—and investment—is encouraged at the expense of current consumption. Over a period of time, the society is likely to achieve higher levels of saving and consumption, because the added investment, by generating a faster growing economy, will lead to a bigger income "pie" to be divided among the various participants in economic activity.

A constant theme voiced by tax reformers is the need for increased incentives for saving, capital formation, and economic growth. Under a consumption-based tax, the incentives would be very favorable: the basic way to cut tax payments—legally—would be for individuals and families to save more and for companies to invest more. By increasing the amount that we save and invest, a shift to consumption taxation would augment the forces that create the formation of capital and make possible a more rapidly growing economy.

Combining general tax cuts with comprehensive reform would have special charm. Any reform, no matter how carefully drafted, is bound to generate losers as well as winners, thus reducing the chances of enactment. In contrast, combining reform and rate reductions, for example, will result in more winners and fewer losers, brightening the prospects for the reform being carried out.

The various plans for tax reform are not interchangeable. Each comes with its own set of advantages and disadvantages, but I will spare you a recital of that sleep-inducing detail. Nevertheless, compared to the existing tax structure, any of the three alternatives is simpler, and all of them would encourage saving and investment and result in a faster rate of economic growth. All are variants of consumption taxes, and several would provide immediate expensing of investment. Just as there may be more than one path to salvation, there is more than one approach to tax reform that can achieve the public's expectations.

Reforming Government Regulation

Although no regulatory agency has been given the express mission to depress the economy, many of their actions have that undesirable effect. The popular view of regulation is wrong. It is not a contest between the "good guys" (government and the consumer) and the "bad guys" (business). The reality is that the consumer is at the receiving end of the benefits as well as the costs generated by government regulation. Business is the middleman (or woman).

The pervasiveness of regulation becomes apparent when we look at the impact on the typical company. Each box on its organizational chart has several government agencies that are counterparts: Environmental Protection Agency (EPA) and construction of new facilities, Occupational Safety and Health Administration (OSHA) and the workplace, Equal Employment Opportunity Commission (EEOC) and human resource policies, etc. Each of those regulators is heavily involved in the company's internal decision-making. So are CFTC, CPSC, DOC, DOD, DOL, FAA, FCC, FERC, FMC, FTC, ITC, NHTSA, NLRB, NRC, OFCC, PBGC, SEC, and USDA.

The impact of governmental rulemakers is in one predictable direction: to increase the firm's costs and reduce the resources available to produce goods and services for the customer. Consider what it takes to locate a new factory. A company must obtain approval from dozens of agencies at three or more levels of government. A single "no" anywhere along the line can halt years of planning and investment.

The Shoreham nuclear powerplant on Long Island is a good—or really terrible—example of the economic waste that results. The multimillion-dollar plant was built after obtaining all the required approvals for construction. But the company could not operate the facility because the state governor refused to give the final approval—citing reasons that were well known before construction ever started. The victims extend far beyond the nuclear industry. The companies and residents of New York State now suffer extremely high costs of electricity.

Even when the regulators say "yes," the paperwork burden alone is staggering. It takes approximately 55 million hours each year just to work up the reports required by federal environmental statutes—at an estimated annual cost of $2.9 billion. To get a feel of the "opportunity cost" of these clerical chores, that sum is more than the annual budget of the National Science Foundation.

Regulation also reduces the flow of innovation because so many government regulatory agencies have the power to decide whether or not a new product will go on the market. For example, the major obstacles to the development of a new biotechnology industry are not financial or technological, but regulatory.

Higher regulatory costs also erode the competitiveness of American companies struggling in an increasingly global marketplace. Compare the cost of cleaning up a hazardous waste site in the United States and Western Europe. Our average of $30 million per site compares to $1 million in the Netherlands and $1 million to $5 million in the United Kingdom.

The benefits of regulation should not be overlooked. But it is too generous to assume that every regulation is effective. We must ask ourselves three serious questions: What benefits does the regulation produce? Are the benefits worth the costs? Is there a better way?

Regulators tend to forget that usually competition is the most effective way of protecting the consumer. Deregulation of interstate trucking, for example, has resulted in 30,000 new businesses entering the trucking industry. The heightened degree of competition has forced sizable reductions in the cost of trucking, which ultimately shows up in lower prices of the items that move by truck.

When government does regulate (as in the case of environmental pollution), it should make the maximum use of economic incentives. To an economist, the environmental pollution problem is not the negative task of punishing wrongdoers. Rather, the challenge is the positive one of changing people's incentives so that they voluntarily modify their behavior. People do not pollute because they enjoy messing up the environment, but because it often is cheaper or easier than not polluting.

What about the existing array of command-and-control regulation? Benefit/cost analysis can help to make sure that any given regulation does more good than harm. Of course, many federal agencies already prepare that type of economic analysis before issuing a new regulation.

However, the entire process of executive branch review of proposed regulations is reminiscent of locking the stable after the horse has departed the premises. Frequently, the agency is stuck with trying to come up with the most cost-effective way of writing a regulation that should not be issued in the first place. Each congressional committee should do a benefit-cost analysis before it takes action on a proposed regulatory statute. Regulatory barriers to innovation should be prime candidates for reform and modernization. Candidates for such judicious pruning—I do not advocate using the meat axe—include the EPA, the FDA, and a host of agricultural agencies.

Regulation is properly viewed as a hidden tax on production of goods and services in the United States. Given the current estimate of compliance cost of $600 billion a year, if sensible reforms could reduce those outlays by 10 percent, we would have the benefits of a $60 billion tax cut!

Conclusion

Experience teaches us to beware of simple answers to complex questions. There is no quick cure to the slow growth of the American economy. Nevertheless, an extensive array of expenditure, tax, and regulatory reforms could shift the American economy to a sustainable higher growth path. Yet, as we have learned from experience, carrying out needed economic changes requires more than developing attractive new programs. It also means making a continuous stream of hard choices. Aye, there's the rub.

Note

Originally published in *Business Economics*, Vol. 32, No. 1 (January 1997), pp. 7–11.

CHAPTER 24

1998

THE ADAM SMITH ADDRESS
CAPITALISM AND ITS DISCONTENTS

Michael J. Boskin, Stanford University

I am grateful to the National Association for *Business Economics* for presenting me the 1998 Adam Smith Award. I accept the honor humbly, given the impressive roster of former recipients, the importance of the organization awarding it, and, especially, the greatest of all economists for whom it is named.

I had thought of speaking on a subject of particular relevance to my own research or policy experience: difficulties in measurement in a rapidly evolving economy and their implications both for understanding economic progress and for making economic policy; the impact of changing demography on consumption and saving; new ways of thinking about comparing economic performance across countries or of understanding economic growth; or budget, social security and/or tax reform. But recent events, and my remembrance of the broad sweep of Adam Smith's penetrating insights and analysis of the evolution and comparison of economies, plus his emphasis on the performance of alternative economic systems, have led me to choose a broader and perhaps more fundamental topic: capitalism and its discontents.

Role of Government in the Economy

Adam Smith, regarded by many as the intellectual godfather of modern economics and the case for a decentralized competitive market economy, focused his heaviest guns on mercantilism, a topic, by the way, not without relevance today. In the almost two and a quarter centuries since Smith wrote *The Wealth of Nations,* economic systems have developed in various forms in different places. Serious scholars as well as a much larger number of pundits have debated their relative economic success and moral underpinnings. Within our own profession, the center of gravity has waxed and waned among different schools of thought and political and economic persuasions. It was not all that long ago that Hayek and then Friedman were relatively lonely voices calling for restraining, indeed reducing, the role of government in the economy.[1]

What I would like to do briefly is review a few such episodes in economic and intellectual history, to shine some light on the recent calls for abandoning the capitalist model (or, more accurately, usually some highly distorted caricature of the capitalist model) in favor of some alternative. These episodes include: during the Great Depression, communism; in the post-World War II period, market socialism; as recently as the 1980s, the convergence of all economic systems to heavily managed gigantic welfare states; in the 1990s, calls for a "third way," based on some other system of values; and the almost hysterical recent calls from hedge fund managers, prime ministers, pundits and even economists who should know better, to "do something" about "global capitalism." Commentaries with titles such as *The Crisis in Global Capitalism, Global Capitalism RIP, Collapse of Capitalism, Who Lost Capitalism?* and *The Free Market's Crisis of Faith* deserve a response, for their prescriptions of capital controls and even larger government almost certainly will cause great harm to those the authors claim to want to protect.

My own strongly held belief is that a limited government-based capitalist economic system not only is the system most likely to deliver the greatest economic progress but is the model most consistent with substantial personal economic and political freedom. However, I want to focus primarily on results, to play the role of positive scientist, not moral philosopher, in spite of the temptation to do so given that Adam Smith himself was a Professor of Moral Philosophy. Let me emphasize that I am discussing large differences in the economic role of government. Criteria for determining the appropriate role of government are discussed below.

The Great Depression

Many of us are too young to have known from personal experience, but recall from what we were taught and what we read, that in the Great Depression of the 1930s, a large number of intellectuals and others in Western Europe and North America turned to communism, or at least turned a sympathetic ear to it, given the horrible destitution of that period. (In the United States, real GDP fell by one-third from 1929 to 1933, and the unemployment rate reached almost 25 percent.)

Many writers had emphasized booms and busts in economic systems or economic history. These were not, of course, confined to the post-industrial revolution capitalist market economies. In earlier times, of course, a bad agricultural harvest could devastate a country operating under a monarchy or feudal system. But Marx, and others, had preached the collapse of capitalism and its tendency to exacerbate booms and busts. Whether it is the case that an economic system that leads to more substantial economic progress is more subject to episodic downturns is an open question, but I know of no convincing study that suggests this is more likely in a modern mixed-capitalist economy than in other economic systems.

But the long-run improvement in the standards of living of large segments of the world's population has been greatest in the capitalist era, as has the correlated evolution of personal freedom. There has never been a period in human history that even remotely compares to the tremendous growth in material wealth and personal freedom in the period since Smith wrote *The Wealth of Nations.* (See D. Landes, 1998.)

To be sure, large segments of mankind were left behind, both economically and politically. As a gross historical generalization, they were in societies that lacked both economic and political freedoms and competition. While the capitalist economies have wide dispersions in the distribution of consumption, the average poor family in the United States has a standard of living well beyond that of the average Russian, for example, and above that of the average American of a couple of generations ago.[2] And the most entrenched poverty in the American economy occurs in pockets of a quasi-socialist economy, with little competition, private capital or private incentives, such as inner city public housing and schools.

Returning to the great depression, the most famous economic treatise of the time, Keynes' *General Theory of Employment, Interest and Money,* was viewed by Keynes himself as an attempt to salvage capitalism itself from the onslaught of communism. While parts of the *General Theory* have subsequently been questioned, revised, reinterpreted or rejected, what Keynes saw himself trying to do was much more than an intellectual exercise to explain how an economy could wind up in a low level equilibrium with massive unemployment for extended periods of time, something that could not be readily explained in the classical model, because wage rates would have fallen or some other mechanism would allow the economy to get back quickly to full employment. He viewed himself as proposing policies by which modern capitalist economies could mitigate some of the excesses of business cycles (although there is nothing so regular to the periodicity and amplitude of fluctuations to warrant the term "cycle"), and thereby preserve much of the basic microeconomic structure and individual decisionmaking and personal freedoms of market economies. Keynesian economics, of course, became an important part of the intellectual justification for the growth of government in the post-World War II era.

Postwar Growth of Government

The post-World War II era has been one of expansion of the absolute and relative size of governments in most market economies and democracies. In the United States, for example, in the mid-1950s during the Eisenhower administration, federal government spending was only \$70 billion; today it is more than five times as large in constant dollars and a larger share of GDP. Also, during the Eisenhower administration one out of every seven dollars of the then absolutely and relatively much smaller government spending was on transfer payments, whereas six out of every seven dollars was on purchases of goods and services, from defense procurement to the interstate highway system. Today, the majority of the much larger absolute and relative size of federal spending, net of interest on the debt, is on transfer payments to people. Thus, it is not only the size, but the role of government that has changed.

Of course, in Western Europe, government had become larger earlier. Taxes and spending accounted for over half of GDP, massive transfers were undertaken, and substantial regulation, nationalization of key industries and restrictive labor market rules were implemented or followed. Sweden, often the darling of Western intellectuals based on its economic performance in the early postwar period, at one time had almost 9 percent of GDP devoted to industrial subsidies! At the same time, we had a communist, authoritarian, centralized, bureaucratic, command and control model, most often associated with the Soviet Union and other economies in Eastern Europe, but also with important less-developed economies such as China. It was not just Hayek and Friedman who thought that these economies would collapse of the weight of all this government taxing, spending and regulation, which would not only mean a smaller private sector, but substantial stifling of private initiative, to work, save, invest and innovate.

The other alleged "intermediate" model was the market-socialism of then Yugoslavia. A popular prediction of politicians, economists, and pundits was that the world's economic systems would somehow converge somewhere in the region between the Swedish and Yugoslav economies. The capitalist economies would grow larger welfare states, and the communist countries would round off some of their rough edges, and we would all happily converge in the "middle." This of course was ridiculous, and not just in hindsight.

Meanwhile, the United States did experience an explosive growth of government in the 1960s and 1970s, accompanied by high and rising inflation (as the then unindexed tax system dragged a large fraction of the population into higher tax brackets); more regulation (both of traditionally regulated industries and for social purposes, often of a command and control structure); and huge growth and centralization of the government. Still, the total size of government in the US economy relative to Western Europe was modest, about two-thirds as large as measured by the government spending and tax shares of GNP. The same could be said of Japan, the other major industrial economy.

The Case of Japan

The rapid growth of Japan led to the next nonsensical attack on the limited government capitalist model. The Japanese economy grew rapidly in the postwar period and the Japanese did many things that any economist would applaud. They had high rates of saving and investment, worked hard and long hours. The relative success of the Japanese economy and to a lesser extent the German economy led in the 1980s to calls for the United States to emulate these economies. How quaint these calls seem now, given the immense problems of the German and Japanese economies in the 1990s. The calls were for a larger role for government, worker/business/government councils, government direction of private pension funds into "needed infrastructure," (a proposal both in President Carter's 1980 reelection campaign and in Clinton's 1992 campaign), managed trade and an industrial policy of the government picking winners and losers for subsidies and protection (see L. Tyson, 1993 and R. Reich and I. Magaziner, 1982). Indeed, I recall in 1989 when I was first sworn into office, the very first thing I did was put my personal standing and credibility on the line with President Bush to help stop a multibillion dollar "Let's catch-up with the Japanese in HDTV" (analog high definition TV). The Japanese were ahead of us, the fear of the Japanese in the late 1980s was incredibly palpable. They were growing rapidly, we were growing slowly; there was large Japanese investment in the United States (although, hardly mentioned were the larger British and Dutch foreign investment in the United States); many predicted they would overtake or outcompete us (see L. Thurow, 1992). Some panicked pundits and political figures, joined by some powerful business interests and some economists and would-be economists, clamored for the government "to do something."

Clearly, the Japanese markets were not nearly as open as ours, or as they should be as a rich industrial country benefiting from the global trading system. But the notion that we should spend billions of dollars to catch up with them in a policy chosen by government bureaucrats and congressional staff seemed pretty ridiculous to me. Knowing I would be accused of being an ivory tower academic, I called the CEOs of the firms that would likely be involved and asked to speak with their top scientific people. Every single one of them told me that we would never catch-up, but, even more importantly, that analog would soon be surpassed by digital, probably within ten years.

Of course the digital age came sooner, analog HDTV became obsolete. Led by then Senator Gore and House Majority Leader Gephardt, the calls for an American industrial policy were intense. The Congress demanded the Administration list all critical technologies, presumably as a prelude to government subsidies replacing market decisions. Fortunately, President Bush said "No" to the HDTV subsidies, and we did not waste billions of dollars trying to emulate some other economic system.[3]

Much more fundamental, whatever the merits of a particular case, was the misreading, or perhaps misappropriation for political purposes, of Japanese economic history. Japan's success had little or nothing to do with the government's micromanagement of the Japanese economy. And we have seen in the 1990s how that micro-management has caused severe problems and has made it immensely difficult to unwind foolish economic policies. In fact, the notion that the Japanese government was heavily subsidizing "sunrise" industries while we were foolishly ignoring them flies in the face of facts. In Japan, heavy subsidies in terms of protection, direct subsidies, tax breaks, and the like, went to industries such as textiles, mining and agriculture (Beason and Weinstein, 1994), which is perhaps not surprising to anybody who studies politics, because they were entrenched industries with strong political constituencies and large employment. The same "We know better than the market" Japanese bureaucracies tried to get the Japanese auto companies in the 1950s to produce a Japanese version of the Volkswagen Beetle; instead they went their own way and were highly successful. They tried to prevent Sony from getting into the consumer electronics business. And their 5th Generation computing project as well as the analog HDTV effort have been colossal failures. The Japanese government tried to end the subsidies to the electronics firms a few years ago but had to back down under intense political pressure. Well, does anyone still believe most Americans would benefit much from emulating the German or Japanese models?

More vs. Less Government Intervention

The American economy, which has been, even during our most difficult episodes, the largest and most productive economy with the highest standard of living among the industrial economies, appeared triumphal in the 1990s as we came out of the nationally brief, mild 1990–1991 recession (although it was regionally severe, lasting longer and reaching deeper in the northeast and California than in the rest of the country). First, the fall of the Berlin Wall and the collapse of the communist countries, together with the much more open access to the then Soviet Union demonstrated beyond doubt to all how pathetically poor the communist economies were. Combined with the stagnation of Western Europe and the collapse of the Japanese economy, events temporarily short-circuited this attack on the greater reliance on markets and individual initiative, less reliance on government approach. Governments all over the world were trying to emulate economic systems they saw as more successful, as their citizens called out for more personal freedom and greater economic progress.

The practical lesson learned from comparing economic performance in the United States and Western Europe during the past three decades on the damage done by excessive government is compelling. While worker compensation has been growing more slowly for the past 20 years than in the previous two decades, the American economy has been flexible and dynamic enough to provide employment to virtually all those who seek it. Compare that performance with the sorry state of Western Europe, where the unemployment rate is now 11 percent, more than double that in the United States.

There were 30 million more working-age people in Western Europe in 1994 than in 1970. The labor force however, grew by only 19 million, and unemployment and government employment swelled. And, there were 1 million fewer private sector employees in Western Europe at the beginning of 1994 than at the beginning of 1970! What a stark indictment of an inflexible, protectionist, highly regulated and overtaxed economic system. By comparison, there were 40 million more working-age people in the United States, the labor force grew even more, and, in spite of a small increase in unemployment and government employment, the overwhelming bulk of the workers found productive private sector employment. The problems of Western Europe offers us a window on our own future if we allow a marked expansion in government's role.

On the relative merits of capitalism and socialism, as we hear today calls from economies in transition to return to central planning, let me share with you a personal experience perhaps only fellow economists can fully appreciate.

I was an economics major in college some years after Soviet Premier Nikita Khrushchev shouted to an American president, "We will bury you!" Khrushchev was not talking about military might. He was projecting the growth of the Soviet economy relative to the slower growth of the American economy. Khrushchev proclaimed that the Soviet economic system with its central planning, bureaucracy, controls and state enterprises was a superior economic engine. After all, industrial production grew more rapidly in the USSR than in the United States, and they had no unemployment and no inflation. Of course, while prices did not rise, goods were not available on the shelf at these unchanged prices; while everyone nominally had a job, there was unemployment and massive underemployment; and some of that extra steel production went to increase ball bearing production that was not needed and hence was melted back down for future steel production.

Little did I know as an economics undergraduate that a couple of decades later President Bush would dispatch me to Moscow to help Gorbachev with Soviet economic reform. When I arrived in Moscow in 1989, in addition to Gorbachev, who knew very little economics, I met with the head of the state planning agency, (Gosplan), the Finance Minister, and the head of the Central Bank.

The head of Gosplan was supposed to preside over price reform in the Soviet Union. Instead of administered prices, there was supposed to be a move to a free market. At our first meeting he inquired of me, "Who sets the prices in your economy?" Flabbergasted at this remark, I explained that, while we had a few industries that were regulated by government, for the overwhelming bulk of products the interaction of numerous producers and still more numerous consumers determine prices in our economy. Furthermore, repeating Adam Smith's famous dictum, this invisible hand of the market produced the greatest good for the greatest number. The head of Gosplan repeated, "So who sets the prices in your economy?" Thinking that there might have been something wrong with the translation, we went back and forth several times. It was clear he could not think of an economy in which somebody in the government did not set the prices. He pulled out a 1960s-style giant computer printout that was the price list for virtually every product in the Soviet Union. America had a market economy, I was the American President's economic advisor, he had been told by Gorbachev that I would help, so who, he thought, was better able to determine what the new prices should be?

I next went to the Finance Ministry, where I discussed making the ruble convertible with Finance Minister Pavlov, who subsequently became prime minister and was involved in the coup against Gorbachev. After a similar to-ing and fro-ing, trying to explain concepts, Pavlov motioned for me to wait in his office in the Kremlin and disappeared through a secret door behind his desk. Remember, this was when there was still a Soviet Union, a Warsaw Pact and a Communist Party. A few minutes went by, and I started feeling a bit like a character in a Robert Ludlum novel, worrying that no one at the Embassy knew exactly where I was. Eventually, Finance Minister Pavlov returned and handed me a little case and motioned for me to open it. Inside was a coin. And there was the first Soviet version of the convertible ruble. A coin that said on one side 1 ruble and on the other side 1 dollar. Well, I've won teaching awards in my day, but I knew I had a long way to go.

Needless to say, when I returned to Washington and debriefed the President, the Treasury Secretary, the Federal Reserve Board Chairman, the National Security Advisor and the CIA Director, I was pretty pessimistic about Gorbachev's chances of pulling this off and about Soviet economic reform. I told them it's going to be a rough road, think in decades, not years, and this group can't possibly pull it off. Either they'll be gone, or there will be a political backlash that stops the reforms.

Convergence of Economic Systems

My personal journey is echoed in the intellectual and historical experience of the past quarter century. As mentioned above, back in the 1960s, 1970s and 1980s—and I am told occasionally still on some college campuses—a prevailing view was that the world's social and economic systems would somehow converge toward a central tendency, somewhere, say, to the left of where Sweden was in the 1970s. The communist economies, it was said, would round off some of the rough edges by allowing a littler freer reign to private incentives, whereas the advanced capitalist economies would evolve into ever larger welfare states with more government planning, intervention and control in their economies. We would all happily converge roughly on the same system, with roughly the same results.

Well, history has performed that experiment. Compare the former East and West Germany. Both were shattered by World War II. Both had similar problems and opportunities. One was dosed with communism—the heavy hand of state planning, controls and government intervention, regulation and state ownership of virtually everything. Once the Erhard reforms created a currency in which people had confidence and freed up prices from postwar controls, West Germany was dosed with capitalism. The West grew into an economic superpower—struggling now under the burden of economic integration with the East—while the East stagnated. When the two Germanys were reunited, the standard of living in the West was five times that in the East, which had a spoiled environment, decrepit capital stock and demoralized labor force. Indeed the saying among East German workers was, "They pretend to pay us and we pretend to work." That is about as close as we get to a natural experiment in economics. And the answer is unambiguous. There is no longer any doubt about whether there are two alternative paths to economic prosperity. Socialism and central planning do not work. Only some form of capitalism and free markets, in spite of their problems, do work over the long haul.

Criteria for Determining Size and Role of Government

I am focusing here on major differences in the role of government in the economy and society across a broad spectrum, not disagreements over this or that program or the relative size of the government within a modest range around where it is now in the United States. What I believe is abundantly clear is that the greatly expanded role of government that some have called for would be a tragic economic mistake. I also believe that arguments over specific programs that might lead to a minor decrease or increase in the relative size of government will almost certainly wind up reflecting politics as well as the well-articulated and economically well-understood criteria for evaluating such programs: rigorously enforced cost-benefit analyses, the conceptual criteria of government financing of activity being potentially desirable if the expected benefits are likely to exceed the expected costs *and* the activities cannot be undertaken by the private sector (perhaps because the benefits cannot be appropriated by the private firms), and our usual notions of balancing marginal social benefits and costs to deal with externalities and public goods. National defense and basic research are classic examples of decisions that are amenable to application of such rigorous criteria. Of course, in the real world, they are conducted by people with various political as well as other pressures on them.

Analogous criteria have been developed for optimal tax systems, transfer programs, and government regulation. My own reading of the evidence, to the extent I can divorce it from my own philosophical predilections, is that we could do better with a somewhat smaller government on virtually all these accounts: lower tax rates, less and more flexible regulation, more market incentives in regulation, education and job training; slower spending growth; tax, budget and social insurance reforms; etc. All of these are likely to lead to a better performing economy and, at least after temporary transitions, improve the well-being of the vast majority of our citizens and the functioning of the programs. But that is another story for another time. My purpose here is to talk about big issues of major differences in the relative size of government, in spite of the deservedly intense political debate about modest changes in the size and role of government. That debate is important not only for ideological and economic reasons, but because development of new programs, or the relentless expansion of existing programs, can over time lead to that sizable expansion of government with which I am primarily concerned here.

Imperfect Markets vs. Imperfect Government Solutions

We all know that markets sometimes fail. Imperfect markets however, must be compared to imperfect government solutions implemented by fallible people. Thus, when we try to correct perceived externalities, we must really insist on strong, sound science and flexible market mechanisms, not on scare tactics and on command and control. When competition is stifled, naturally or otherwise, we need sensible rules, antitrust laws, and/or regulation enforced in a sensible manner. We need the foundation of serious protection of private property through contract and bankruptcy law; consistent accounting standards and supervision of financial markets that maximize openness and transparency. These are important foundations of well-functioning, market-based economies. In my view, the risk is that problems we face in the American economy will lead to too much, not to not enough, intrusion of the government in the marketplace.

The current hysteria over hedge funds is one simple example. The problem wasn't the financial instruments themselves. Futures, options and other derivatives generate sizable net benefits when properly used in hedging various risks. Of course, there are also potential costs in their misuse or abuse. When ridiculous amounts of leverage provided by banks and brokerages with little or no knowledge of the positions of the funds to whom they lend combined with positions that were not market neutral, potential bankruptcy loomed. This is no different conceptually from highly leveraged borrowing short and lending long betting on interest rate stability, the saga of the S&L industry in the United States; nor is it very different from Asian banks or industrial companies borrowing in dollars and lending in baht or rupiah, pocketing the spread, betting on currency pegs to continue indefinitely, unhedged; nor is it conceptually very different from Western banks' Russian investments, hedging with Russian banks. None of this has much to do with capitalism *per se.* It is has a lot to do with foolish financial decisions pressing at the limits, moral hazard and mispriced risk.

The answer is *not* to curtail the flow of global capital. The problems of the Asian and Russian economies are not primarily due to "global capitalism," a phrase now sometimes mentioned as if some communicable disease were encompassing all of mankind. The fundamental problems that led to the original crisis were severe imbalances in the Asian economies that were growing at an unsustainable pace, heavily leveraged risks with poorly supervised financial institutions, domestic economic policies that could not support the exchange rates at which they had pegged, given the declining inflation in the United States and their higher inflation rates. This is not just conjecture or opinion; it is straightforward Economics 101 that has been taught for decades: a country cannot maintain price stability (or, more generally, a particular stable inflation rate) and fixed exchange rates if prices are not stable (or inflation rates differ) elsewhere. Fixed exchange rates mean domestic monetary policy cannot be independent, and vice versa. The *only* way to reconcile the dilemma is a far worse course, controlling the free flow of capital. It is not theoretically, let alone practically, possible to reconcile fixed exchange rates, independent domestic monetary policy and free flows of investment capital; something must give. This was the core problem facing countries such as Thailand, Indonesia and South Korea and the primary cause of their financial crises. Unfortunately, some countries are retreating into capital controls; surely their need for foreign capital both to supply funds and the market discipline that properly priced foreign risk capital brings will be decisive to their long-run prospects.

Clearly, we need a serious reexamination of our international financial institutions. A combination of changing world economic conditions, mission creep, a mixed record of success including tragic recent failures, suggests that a serious rethinking of the purposes, procedures, resources and operations of these institutions is an urgent priority. The IMF should be playing the role of convenor of private lenders, lest lender runs on countries analogous to depositor runs on banks occur unnecessarily. The role of global lender of last resort requires a rapid determination of the difference between illiquidity and insolvency, something not easily done in a political context.

But let us not confuse traditional economic mistakes with fundamental problems of economic systems. For these economies to retreat back towards protectionism, capital controls, an even greater centralization of decisionmaking in government would be a disaster for the mass of mankind. Sensible improvements in the supervision of their financial institutions and better central bank policies are the place to start. For example, higher reserve requirements for short-term deposits and sensible risk-based capital requirements for financial institutions, if necessary, make a lot more sense than capital controls or taxes.

Conclusion

My conclusion is simple. In addition to its strong moral base in personal freedom, capitalism and competitive markets work to deliver substantial economic progress; communism, socialism, even large bureaucratic welfare state "third ways" do not work. They sap individual incentive, initiative and creativity and ultimately cannot deliver sufficiently rising standards of living to meet the expectations of their citizens for better material lives for themselves and their progeny. Episodic economic downturns or other perceived market failures create great opportunity for misplaced *permanent* expansion of government's role in the economy.

Clearly, we have learned government has a number of important roles to play in our economy and that we must remain vigilant to make sure that it plays *only* those necessary roles and does so in the least intrusive manner possible. A consistent rules-based monetary policy; the lowest possible level and rates of taxation; less command and control in favor of more flexible market-oriented incentive regulation; slower growth of government spending, including entitlement reform; expanded open rules-based trade; these are surely the lesson of economic history and would surely be Adam Smith's wise prescription today.

The theme of this year's NABE conference is "Winners and Losers of the 21st Century." Surely a large part of the answer to that implicit question is, "Those who can stay closest to the limited government capitalist model in the face not only of the natural tendency of the government's role in the economy to grow, but also the incredible impending demographic pressures that will greatly reinforce this tendency."

The calls for capital controls; greatly expanded taxes and spending; vast new regulation; extensive industrial policy; dangerous protectionism; all threaten our economic progress and personal liberty. Such calls are frequent and occasionally frenetic by pundits and decriers of capitalism, both inside and outside the economics profession. Of course, as economies evolve and conditions change, for example, due to changing demography, the role of government based on the sound market principles enunciated above may reasonably ebb and flow. But capitalism once again needs its defenders, teachers, exemplars, and champions. The alternative models have proven historically, intellectually and practically bankrupt. I have no doubt we would all be better off if the decriers of capitalism remained permanently discontent.

Notes

Originally published in *Business Economics*, Vol. 34, No. 1 (January 1999), pp. 7–13.

1. See Hayek (1944) and Friedman (1962), who have greatly influenced my thinking since my first undergraduate economics course.
2. See, for example, the discussion in Boskin, et al. 1998.
3. By the way, this episode appears to be the origin of the statement that I said it did not matter whether we produced computer chips or potato chips; not only did I not say so, I had never heard this quip until I read the now famous "unnamed source" claiming I did!

References

Beason, R. and D. Weinstein, "Growth, Economies of Scale and Targeting in Japan," 1955–1990, Harvard Institute of Economic Research, Discussion of Paper No. 1644, 1994.

Boskin, Michael J., Ellen R. Dulberger, Robert J. Gordon, Zvi Griliches, and Dale W. Jorgenson, "Consumer Prices, the Consumer Price Index, and the Cost of Living," *Journal of Economic Perspectives,* Vol. 12, Number 1, Winter, 1998, pp. 3–26.

Friedman, M. with the assistance of R. Friedman, *Capitalism and Freedom,* Chicago: University of Chicago Press, 1962.

Hayek, F., *The Road to Serfdom,* London: G. Routledge & Sons, 1944.

Reich, R., and I. Magaziner, *Minding America's Business: the Decline and Rise of the American Economy,* New York: Harcourt Brace Jovanovich, 1982.

Thurow, L., *Head to Head: The Coming Economic Battle Among Japan, Europe and America,* New York: Morrow, 1992.

Tyson, L., *Who's Bashing Whom? Trade Conflicts in High Technology Industries,* Washington, DC: Institute for International Economics, 1993.

CHAPTER 25

1999

PROTECTING AGAINST THE NEXT FINANCIAL CRISIS: THE NEED TO REFORM GLOBAL FINANCIAL OVERSIGHT, THE IMF, AND MONETARY POLICY GOALS

Henry Kaufman, Henry Kaufman & Company, Inc.

For many years I have been speaking, writing, and testifying to Congress on the inadequacies of the present outmoded system for supervising and regulating financial institutions and markets on a global basis. I have long believed that those inadequacies would have bad consequences—indeed that they posed real dangers to our financial system and to the global economy. A flawed supervisory and regulatory system increases the likelihood of repeated instances of financial excesses. In turn, those financial excesses are capable of causing a great deal of damage. They heighten volatility in the financial markets. They threaten the safety and soundness of individual financial institutions. And they bring about economic dislocations that are extraordinarily harmful, especially to those least able to protect themselves.

A little over a year has passed since the Secretary of the Treasury, responding to the Asian financial crisis that was just then reaching a critical phase, challenged all of us to give serious thought to the matter of improving the global financial architecture. Like a number of other interested market participants and scholars, I was eager to take up that challenge. The intervening events have demonstrated anew that all is not well with the current system and that the need for fundamental change has an even greater urgency today.

Challenges Caused by Financial Distress

The economic costs of financial distress have, if anything, been even worse than we might have feared. Debt-troubled Asian countries have endured a devastating recession. Even now, there are only tentative signs that the economic, financial, and social costs are lessening.

Moreover, financial contagion was not quelled but has spread to new territory. The first casualty was Russia, a country that has blundered badly in trying to make the transition from a communist to a free enterprise society. Unable to achieve financial and budgetary stability, the Russian Government responded in the worst possible way by unilaterally defaulting on a significant portion of its public indebtedness. In so doing, Russia breached every norm of responsible financial behavior so painstakingly developed since the awful debt crisis of the 1980s. Even now, the modalities of dealing with the rest of Russia's outstanding debt have not been resolved satisfactorily.

Shortly after came Brazil. This is a country that had made exemplary progress toward restoring a semblance of price stability and financial normality after decades of out-of-control inflation and recurrent debt difficulties. Its reelected government had realistic plans for coming to grips with a swollen budgetary deficit. But in the absence of a domestic political compromise on how to do that, not even a huge IMF preemptive bail-out could avert a run out of the Brazilian currency and out of its financial obligations. The situation remains tenuous. No one can be certain that Brazil will be able to meet all of its debt servicing obligations on time. Though improbable, there is always a danger of a reversion to the failed policies and hyperinflation of the past.

Right in the middle of this turmoil came one of the most vivid examples of the dangers of the kind of highoctane, highly leveraged, and performance-driven portfolio strategies that has long concerned me. The institution in question is Long-Term Capital Management (LTCM). Its near collapse raised the specter of a serious shock to global financial markets. Indeed, the risk of some kind of meltdown appeared to the Federal Reserve to be so high as to induce our central bank to get involved. It took the extraordinary step of convening LTCM's large creditors and encouraging them to reach an agreement to bail out the hedge fund. No one knows whether the Fed was actually prepared to inject any public money had a satisfactory resolution not been reached. But getting involved in the way the Fed did inevitably raised the question, at least to several experienced market observers, of whether the official safety net was being extended to an institution that was certainly not a bank.

There are those who claim that, because the crisis atmosphere has lifted to some extent in the past couple of months, it shows that the present system has weathered the storm and can be shored up with modest tinkering here and there. I disagree entirely. Settling for something less than a complete overhaul of the system will simply put off the hard decisions until the next big crisis, when perhaps even more startling events will compel far-reaching changes under less than ideal circumstances for making wise choices. It is far better to act now, while there is time for a careful analysis of alternative proposals and for a thoughtful debate on their merits.

Now, I would be first to argue that, in a deregulated, entrepreneurially based financial system, nobody can ever get rid of financial excesses entirely. Nor should we ever want that kind of world, because it would be one in which market participants would be so leery of taking on any risks that legitimate credit needs of the economy would not be met. History proves that too little credit creation is as harmful as too much. But in many respects the system that has been evolving during the past couple of decades may represent the worst of all possible worlds, in which credit availability and leveraging lurch from one extreme to another, whipsawing borrowers and lenders alike.

The Challenges

In actuality, the system faces three different but interrelated challenges. The first is how we can establish a structure of official supervision of financial institutions and markets that can temper the sometimes violent swings between market optimism and pessimism. What is needed is a mechanism for limiting excesses and keeping them within reasonable bounds. Internationally, it would be healthier if we could smooth out the flows of capital in and out of countries, many of which cannot manage the massive inflows that come in the heady days—and certainly not the massive outflows that occur when confidence abruptly collapses.

Second is the associated problem of how to improve the management of balance-of-payments crises, because even the most astute supervisory process will not eliminate financial mishaps entirely. This means redesigning the functions and responsibilities of the IMF.

The third dimension may turn out to be the most difficult. It is how to incorporate into monetary policy decisionmaking, not least in our own country, fluctuations in the value of financial assets. There is a great danger that current attitudes toward changes in financial asset values are highly asymmetric. By that I mean monetary policy tends to tolerate potentially excessive increases in the value of financial assets, thereby allowing the financial markets to bubble away, but reacts quite quickly to falls in financial asset values. It is questionable whether such an asymmetric approach is wise, because it can inadvertently create an especially pernicious form of moral hazard. Let me briefly discuss each of these challenges.

Role of Supervision in Deregulated Financial Markets

To begin with, the fundamental flaw with the current system of official supervision and regulation of financial institutions and markets is that they are out of synch with profound structural changes in the marketplace. We have an increasingly deregulated financial system in which traditionally managed financial institutions and conventional financial instruments play a progressively less central role. To my mind, the more financial institutions are freed from formal regulations, the more important it is to have effective, informal, and high-level supervision of the behavior of financial institutions, the business activities they are pursuing, and the risks to which they expose themselves. Similarly, the more deregulated financial markets become, the more important it is to have intelligent oversight of the functioning of those markets. The objective of this stepped-up supervisory approach is to gain an understanding of the collective risks that are being created through the activities of the various market participants, especially the largest participants.

This view used to be at odds with those who assumed that more deregulation entailed less supervision and oversight as well. But judging from the number of projects that have been launched by the G-7, the IMF, the OECD, the BIS, and others since the onset of the Asian financial crisis, I think it is fair to say that the distinction is better appreciated.

What would a more effective program of supervision of major financial institutions and markets have to contend with? I would select six developments as critically altering the demands on effective supervision.

The Backdrop of Structural Changes in Financial Markets

One is *securitization.* It is possibly the central feature of modern financial markets and has fundamentally changed the nature of financial assets. It permits the transformation of credit from a set of loans lodged on the books of a traditional financial institution, such as a bank, a thrift, or an insurance company, into an obligation that can be sold in the open credit market, where in normal times it can be traded and priced continuously.

This shift to marketable from nonmarketable assets has stretched credit creation. It tends to sustain borrowers longer in economic expansions and probably to expose them more in contractions. It also has had the important side effect of removing the illusion of price stability for nonmarketable assets. As a result, inhibitions against selling securities that have gone down in price fall away. Thus, securitization has opened up literally trillions of dollars worth of assets to the harsh glare of changing market circumstances, and therefore to market risks unimaginable just 20 years ago.

Two, *the globalization of financial markets* has broad significance. Foreign investors especially are opportunists. They plow funds into a country and, if risk perceptions change, they attempt to leave quickly, as we have seen recently in Asia, in Russian and in Brazil. More and more they represent large multinational institutions or immense pools of entrepreneurially managed money. They have a presence in all markets. They respond to the drumbeat of a more homogenized outpouring of financial analyses, views and forecasts. They all have access to the same information technology, which lets decisionmakers be located virtually anywhere and still be up to the second on new developments. The contagion of the past 18 months is one consequence.

Three, alongside these changes in the nature of assets and globally-interconnected markets, *the composition of financial institutions* themselves is undergoing significant change. As the relative weight of institutions managed in the traditional way has diminished, a new breed of institutional participants has come to the fore. They emphasize short-term investment performance, the heavy use of leverage, and the ability to move in and out of markets, whether equities, bonds, currencies, or commodities, wherever the prospective returns are thought to be the highest. Included in their number are not only the often highly publicized hedge funds, but also the largest commercial banks, securities firms, and insurance companies, all of which maintain hedge-fund-like departments. Moreover, a number of nonfinancial corporations have set up units specifically to participate in high-risk financial investment activities.

Performance-driven investors typically deploy considerable leverage in their activities. Leverage greatly magnifies the profitability of successful investments, but naturally also magnifies losses. Greater use of leverage usually has the side effect of generating a sharp increase in the volume of transactions in the marketplace. More often than not, a heavy volume of transactions is associated with greater volatility of financial asset prices.

Four, the growing use of *financial derivatives* creates new opportunities but also new risks that a modernized system of financial supervision will have to contend with. All agree that financial derivatives—whether in the form of futures, forwards, swaps, options or securities embodying derivatives—are only one part of the far-reaching structural changes in our financial markets that I have been describing. It is the interaction of all of these component elements that tends to nurture the various financial risks that investors, companies, and financial institutions seek either to profit from or to hedge against.

Not long ago advocates of financial derivatives maintained that they were primarily "risk management" products. The usually unspoken assumption was that derivatives were essentially risk-reducing in their overall effect on the financial positions of end-users, that is, tools for hedging risks that already existed. However, in the aftermath of what by now has become a long string of large and highly publicized financial debacles, this rather simplistic view is no longer tenable.

Five, in a world of securitized financial markets, market participants are often mesmerized by what I have referred to as the *"illusion of liquidity."* It is the assumption that anything can be bought and sold at any moment in time, and that open credit markets will always be open. But the functioning of secondary markets in existing debt instruments and access to fresh amounts of credit have always been and always will be discontinuous. When the credit quality of companies or governments is strong, modern financial markets are ready, willing, and eager to provide financing. Secondary markets are prepared to handle even sizable trades with relatively modest impact on the going price of the security. But what is commonly overlooked—or at least it was overlooked until the dramatic events of last fall, when the Russian debacle terrified investors and market makers alike—is how precarious this blissful market state really is. When companies or governments run into financial difficulty and their credit standing is open to question, there is likely to be a sharp discontinuity in the functioning of markets. Almost instantaneously bid-offer spreads widen out, dealers cut back the amounts they are willing to buy or sell, and security prices undergo abrupt and sharp movements. Credit availability evaporates. Borrowers are flung back into an uncomfortably old-fashioned world in which they are totally dependent on their bankers for support—and may or may not get it.

Six, *mathematics* and the computer technology that permits financial market participants to exploit its power has a dark side. Until the events of last year, a strongly held belief existed that financial risks are knowable, can be calculated with mathematical precision by massaging historical data, and can be diversified. These were always fallacies, but it took the near-collapse of LTCM, perhaps the most storied user of mathematical model-based investing, to prove the point. What we all know now is that historical trading patterns are a useful starting point for assessing risk but only a starting point. Most instances of sudden deterioration in the credit standing of a corporate or government borrower are not predictable. They reflect submerged weaknesses in underlying economic or financial structures that are not captured by the available data. And there is a high likelihood of contagion, as we have dramatically seen in the past two years.

In sum, the structural changes in the marketplace have fundamentally transformed the ways in which credit is created, assets are sold, traded, and priced, portfolios are managed, and risks are taken. Regrettably, the supervisory and regulatory system has lagged behind each of these changes, and that must be rectified.

While financial excesses and their hurtful economic consequences can never be fully eliminated, I do believe they can be mitigated by improved supervision of financial institutions and markets. The modern, globalized financial structure is based on innovation and risk-taking. Formal regulations and barriers to financial activities have been lowered, and over time they will probably come down further. However, a more deregulated, free-wheeling financial environment increases the need for better informal supervision of the financial institutions and markets by competent official bodies. Equally important there has to be more intensive and more informed market discipline of risk exposures, and that requires more information about what those exposures are. Oversight, whether by official institutions or by the market itself, has been uneven at best and usually tardy, with far too little information-sharing among official organizations and far too little dialogue with private lenders and investors.

A New Supervisory Institution Needed

The essential ingredient in an improved global financial architecture is to establish a new institution, alongside a reorganized IMF and World Bank, to overcome the inadequacies of current national and international structures for supervising and regulating financial institutions and markets. To deal with the growing potential for market excesses, I started to call attention to these changes in the structure of modern finance back in the early 1980s. Many times since then, I have recommended establishment of a Board of Overseers of Major Institutions and Markets to put teeth into the supervisory system. This Board would have the following mandate:

1. It would set forth a code of conduct for market participants to encourage reasonable financial behavior.
2. It would supervise risk-taking not only by banks and other financial institutions that have always been regulated and supervised, but also by new participants in the global markets.
3. It would be empowered by member governments to harmonize minimum capital requirements, to establish uniform trading, reporting, and disclosure standards, and to monitor the performance of institutions and markets under its purview.

Eventually, this new international supervisory body would rate the credit quality of market participants under its authority. Institutions that failed to abide by the standards would be sanctioned. Lending to banks in countries that choose to remain outside the new system would be subject to higher capital requirements and limitations on maturities. Also, nonmember countries would be limited in their ability to sell new securities in the equity, bond, and money markets of members. The new board would not enact specific regulations to truncate flows of capital internationally, but it would visibly raise the bar to take advantage of the benefits of open capital markets. That will dramatically reduce risks in the system, although it will not eliminate them entirely.

IMF Reform

At the same time this new global financial supervisory institution is established, the IMF needs to be reorganized in order to perform competently a more targeted set of core functions. The events of the past two years or so have highlighted the inherent flaw in the IMF's traditional organization and mandate. Simply put, the IMF has too many assignments that conflict. It has the responsibility for reviewing the economic policies of its members but has no formal authority for demanding policy changes in situations that it believes are unsustainable. Worse, it understandably does not want to be put into a position of precipitating a payments crisis even for a country that ignores its policy advice. Essentially, the IMF's only policy has been to throw money at payments problems once they break out into the open. But that only serves to highlight just how inadequate IMF resources are to play the function of a lender of last resort, which requires basically unlimited resources. Because of the huge scope for flows of funds to move across the capital markets these days, this perceived gap will only grow in the future. So the IMF has a recurrent tendency to soft-pedal criticisms and to downplay statistical data that would justify a sterner response.

Moreover, the bulk of IMF's staff expertise is in the area of macroeconomics. Yet, virtually every crisis in recent years in which it has had to provide credit assistance has involved a domestic banking crisis. Even the IMF's most faithful supporters concede that in this highly technical field it was ill-prepared for containing the contagion once it hit.

What needs to be done goes along the following lines: A reformed IMF, like today's IMF, would be responsible for organizing and partially funding emergency lending operations to protect the safety and soundness of the global system when member governments face intense balance-of-payment problems and are shut off from normal sources of external financing. It would continue to have the responsibility for setting policy conditions that borrowers must follow to qualify for emergency loans. Redesigning conditionality in order to avoid the kind of wrenching business recessions that have become almost routine deserves a high priority.

In contrast to present practices, however, the new IMF should have the responsibility to anticipate problems and press member governments to take timely preventative actions. It would be responsible for judging the economic and financial strength of its members. It would evaluate their monetary and fiscal policies as well as the structures of their economies. Where it detected deficiencies that could lead to excessive dependence on inflows of short-term capital from abroad or could compromise the health of the domestic banking system, it would demand early remedial actions. If the member governments refused to act, the reorganized IMF would make the reduced credit rating public. Because that would, of course, have the effect of dramatically shrinking the recalcitrant country's access to the open credit markets, it would represent a powerful incentive for the member to cooperate.

Rating the credit worthiness of sovereigns is a tough job, but the IMF, with its official international standing, would have a far better chance of doing the job effectively than the private credit rating agencies, which are handicapped by a lack of the kind of the detailed and timely information that the IMF would be able to get.

Monetary Policy Implications

Finally, the changes in the structure of the financial markets will continue to have a profound influence on the way the economy interacts with the financial system and therefore pose some tricky problems for the conduct of monetary policy. The first problem is that a more open, deregulated, securitized, and global financial system tends to keep debtors in the game longer than in times past. Securitization is a force for liberality in granting credit.

Moreover, the rapid development of financial derivatives also perpetuates a more relaxed attitude toward granting credit. Higher-rated corporations can arbitrage their credit standing to lower their cost of funds by issuing long-term fixed rate debt and then swapping the proceeds against the obligation to pay at a floating rate. Lower-rated corporations that would ordinarily be squeezed out of the bond market as the credit cycle matures are able to lock in long-term yields by borrowing short and swapping into long-term maturity obligations. The bankers in the middle view their role as relatively risk-free.

The upshot is that it will tend to take relatively steep increases in the level of interest rates for the central bank to engineer an end to a period of possibly excessive economic expansion that may put upward pressure on the rate of inflation. This is exactly the position in which the Bank of England found itself last year. It imposed the highest short-term interest rates of any advanced industrial country, yet for some time the UK economy still managed to chug along at a brisk pace. At some point the Federal Reserve may face a similar dilemma as the possibly transitory factors holding down the US rate of inflation—a high value of the US dollar in the foreign currency markets, weak economic activity in Asia that keeps many product markets highly competitive, and low commodity prices—begin to reverse.

A second problem for monetary policy is that the structural changes in the financial markets make conventional methods for anchoring monetary policy obsolete. Monetary targeting has been the initial casualty. For example, the Federal Reserve continues to set target ranges for the rate of growth of several definitions of the money supply, but it goes to great lengths to assert that it doesn't take the targets very seriously, because old relationships between money and the rest of the economy have become unreliable. That is true also for measures of credit. Securitization is associated with a diminished role of depository institutions in the intermediation of credit flows, and so debt aggregates are just as unreliable as monetary aggregates. Paradoxically, while private sector institutions are increasingly relying on mathematical models in the quantification of risk, the central bank is shying away from a quantitative approach to conducting monetary policy.

What are the alternatives? There are not many. A central bank can do as the Bank of England has done and condition policy on meeting an intermediate-term inflation target. Or a central bank can set an inflation target and to try to attain it by pursuing a formal monetary conditions rule, along the lines of how the Bank of Canada is operating. Or it can do as the Federal Reserve has been doing, setting the loose and unquantified objective of "reasonable price stability" and using discretionary policy changes in pursuit of that goal.

Controlling Asset Price Fluctuations

But in each case the objective is cast solely in terms of the price indexes for goods and services. It explicitly leaves out any room for taking account of inflation (or deflation) of asset prices. But financial well-being depends on much more than merely attaining a low and stable rate of inflation. The proof of that is the case of the United States in the 1920s and that of Japan in the 1980s and 1990s. Both would meet any reasonable definition of price stability, but both suffered horrendous economic consequences from excessive asset price inflation followed by asset price collapses. Surely monetary policy should be not indifferent to such potentialities.

The dilemma for monetary policy is to what extent the central bank should take into account inflation (or deflation) in asset prices and how to weigh that consideration against more traditional variables. Naturally, inflation in asset prices is normally going to be highly popular, whereas inflation in the prices of goods and services usually hurts the average individual or family.

However, excessive inflation in financial asset prices sets in motion a series of forces that over a period of time can undermine the foundations of a stable economy. For one thing, it stifles the incentives to save. This is most conspicuous in the United States, where the personal saving rate has essentially vanished in recent years, as a result of the prolong stock market rally. Also, excessive inflation in financial asset prices can breed excesses in business investment, whether in real estate or in plant and equipment spending. Asset price inflation can contribute to undue economic and financial concentration as mergers and acquisitions become rampant. And it can encourage questionable flows of funds into risky markets on the part of inexperienced investors.

From a US perspective, those who have looked closely at the question of how the Federal Reserve has reacted in the past to changes in financial asset values have seen a lack of symmetry. The record shows that when asset prices have suddenly fallen, most dramatically as in October 1987 but also in the fall of last year, the Federal Reserve has eased monetary policy with alacrity to take account of the need for the financial markets to have access to greater liquidity at a time of stress. But there is little evidence of a symmetrical response when asset prices have advanced strongly and financial wealth, and liquidity as well, have escalated.

Thus, there is an expectation by many in the market that faulty investments will be bailed out.

Political support for such an asymmetrical monetary policy approach to asset price movements is understandably hardening. Business never favors any policy action that may restrain its sales or profits. Politicians of all ideological stripes have an in-grown skepticism toward prudence in monetary policy except when inflation is a clear and present danger. But in addition, households have a newfound interest in the success of the stock market now that it is perceived as directly strengthening their net worth. They will tend to oppose monetary tightening to keep from enjoying those rewards. By contrast, not so long ago, when households put most of their savings in simple bank deposits, many risk-averse people, especially among the elderly, actually had a preference for higher rates.

A fundamental choice has to be made. If we want to have an economic and financial system that is truly founded on the free market, then we cannot have an asymmetrical policy toward financial asset prices by the central bank. The needed discipline is that sharp declines in financial asset prices would be checked by an easing of monetary policy only to the extent that sharp advances of asset prices were also resisted by monetary policy. If, however, we collectively decide that we live in a complex industrial, social, and internationally linked setting, an asymmetrical policy might be justified. But if so, the central bank would have to recognize and be sensitive to the inherent moral hazard in such an approach. Market participants will always tend to push risk-taking to the edge, on the assumption that they will be bailed out in the case of a generalized collapse of financial asset values. Credit excesses are more or less inevitable. Moreover, all this tends to lead to a system in which large institutions and large corporations will tend to prevail, protected by either the formal or an informal safety net, while all but the flawless small ones will disappear over time.

The state of play is that there is no mandate at the present time for any central bank to take into consideration financial asset prices explicitly in the formation of monetary policy. Nevertheless, the financial bubbling in the American financial market is an untenable situation. The way events are unfolding now, one of several contingencies could topple the exuberance. One is a more noticeable profit squeeze than is now beginning to emerge. Another would be the failure of a large financial institution here or abroad. With all financial institutions so closely linked globally, problems are bound to ricochet across the system. Still another problem will confront us if by the unlikely chance both Japan and Europe stage strong economic rebounds. This would end the surge of foreign funds to the United States, lead to a recovery in commodity prices, and reawaken now largely dormant fears of an upturn in global inflation.

From my perspective, it is not a question of whether it will happen, but when and from what level of the market. Thus today's euphoria in the stock market will be followed by a sharp stock market setback. In the immediate aftermath, the central bank will then try to counter the sharp declines in asset prices by easing monetary policy significantly. After that, I suspect a more definitive monetary strategy incorporating financial behavior is likely to be formulated.

I believe that it is essential to incorporate in monetary policy strategy and in official supervision and regulation the new dimensions of the financial world. The failure to do so has already caused serious economic travail around the world. The risks are rising that our economy will be damaged before adequate official remedial actions are undertaken.

Note

Originally published in *Business Economics*, Vol. 34, No. 3 (July 1999), pp. 56–64.

CHAPTER 26

1999

HOW THE ECONOMY CAME TO RESEMBLE THE MODEL

Alan S. Blinder, Princeton University the G7 Group

George Stigler (1976, p. 351) wrote that "economists exert a minor and scarcely detectable influence on the societies in which they live." I don't believe that is true any longer. In fact, I want to make—and then defend—an audacious claim that directly contradicts Stigler. Since he wrote those words, real-world economies, including ours, have changed in a number of ways that bring them into closer alignment with the pristine model envisioned by economic theory. In this curious sense, life has come to imitate art.

But this essay is not meant as a piece of boosterism for economic theory. The arguments of economists, persuasive as they may have been, were not necessarily the main reason for the changes in real economies. Nor were all these changes unambiguously for the better. Nor do I claim that every previous discrepancy between the real world and the model has been resolved in the model's favor. However, I *do* perceive a general pattern, and it is an ironic one. One might have assumed that economists would have to adjust their models to fit reality, rather than the other way around. That's certainly the way it works in the natural sciences. Germs did not change their behavior to accommodate Pasteur's theory, nor was Mercury's orbit perturbed so that Einstein wouldn't be. But economists appear to have bent reality (at least somewhat) to fit their models. That's quite a feat.

The Fall of Socialism

I begin with the most obvious, and certainly the most important, change that falls under this rubric: the replacement of socialism by capitalism in almost all the formerly socialist countries. No other victory of the model is nearly so fundamental. But, because it is so obvious, I will deal with it only briefly.

Received economic theory is, of course, a theory of *capitalism*. Our models envision owners of capital who hire workers, pay them a wage, and keep the residual (positive or negative) for themselves. Workers do not hire capital at a fixed rental rate. But other systems of organizing production are imaginable. Back in the 1930s, there was a lively intellectual debate on the possibility of "market socialism," examining (among other things) whether a socialist system could replicate or even surpass the virtues of the invisible hand, despite public ownership of capital.[1] I claim no great expertise on that debate. But I think a bowdlerized version of the outcome was that market socialism could indeed mimic the achievements of capitalism in the realm of static efficiency—at least at the level of pure theory, but that market socialism would find capital formation and allocation problematic, and would founder badly when it came to risk-taking and entrepreneurship.

The latter proved true, of course. Socialist economies found themselves noticeably short of "high rollers" and more or less incapable of coping with Schumpeterian "creative destruction." They were, instead, bureaucratic and ossified. In fact, the competition between capitalism and socialism proved to be even more lopsided *in practice* than it was *in principle*. Real-world versions of socialism in Eastern Europe and elsewhere fell vastly short of Lange's market socialist ideal and thus failed to come close to matching capitalism—even on the comparatively "easy" criterion of static efficiency. One main reason was that communist governments granted far too little freedom of choice to individuals and managers—this freedom of choice being just as central to Lange's arguments as it had been to Adam Smith's 160 years earlier.

In any event, the verdict of history is in. Leaving aside the extreme (and dysfunctional) regimes in North Korea and Cuba, there are now essentially no socialist countries left on Earth. Score one for the economic model. It would be presumptuous to claim that economic *theory* played much of a role in ending the Cold War, but economic *reality*—specifically, the abject failure of the Soviet economic system—certainly did. In any case, the world economy clearly took a giant step closer to the economists' model.

The Trend toward Privatization

In many ways, the choice between pure socialism and pure capitalism is much too stark. All real economies have always blended privately owned and publicly owned assets. The genuine public-private ownership issue is quantitative: Where shall society draw the line?

Standard economic theory tacitly views all assets except (I suppose) government buildings and genuine public goods—such as battleships[2]—as private property managed for the benefit of owners. This ownership arrangement is presumed to produce maximal efficiency. As Adam Smith (1976, p. 824) put it in *The Wealth of Nations*:

> In every great monarchy in Europe the sale of the crown lands would produce ... a much greater revenue than any which those lands have ever afforded to the crown.... When the crown lands had become private property, they would, in the course of a few years, become well improved and well cultivated.[3]

Look at the real world, however, and you will see governments owning transportation systems (subways, bus lines, railroads, even airlines), public utilities (water systems, electricity, telephone), and schools—to name just a few. But the line between public and private ownership has been moving perceptibly—especially outside the United States. The share of assets that is publicly owned is declining, as governments privatize their industrial facilities, airlines, telephone companies, and more. Forget about the transition economies, where changes have been dramatic, even the traditional Western European democracies now have smaller socialized sectors than they did a decade or two ago.

The United States has privatized fewer assets than many other countries for a simple reason: We had so few publicly-owned assets to begin with. While power generation, telecommunications, and transportation, for example, were typically public in most foreign countries (and in many cases have been privatized), they were always private in the United States Even here, however, recent years have witnessed considerable privatization in the health-care industry (e.g., the replacement of public or voluntary hospitals by for-profit hospitals) and a bit in education (e.g., the Edison Project). There is now even an intense debate over whether to privatize Social Security, which is not only the federal government's biggest tax-and-transfer program but also its main tool for income redistribution.

The Social Security debate makes an interesting case in point.[4] Standard economic theory offers little justification for a government program that not only compels saving for retirement but regulates both its volume and form.[5] Rational individuals should make such decisions for themselves; in dynamic optimization models, they do so all the time! So why is this seemingly-private function placed squarely in public hands? The main reasons, I believe, are "non-economic" in the sense that they are based on the belief that *homo sapiens* behave differently than *homo economicus.* In particular, real people are likely to be short-sighted and therefore to underprovide for their old age. Social Security forces them to do something (save for their retirement) that makes them better off. Read that sentence again: "Social Security forces them to do something that makes them better off." That is *not* the normal perspective of economics, whose image of man is a rational, self-interested calculating machine. Thus, if Social Security is privatized, that will mark one more step back toward the pure economic model.

Has the recent interest in privatizing Social Security been driven by economists' ideas? I think it is fair to answer: yes. But it has also benefited mightily from the support of vested interests who envision large fees from millions of new accounts to manage. Adam Smith would have understood that, too.

More Single-Minded Concentration on Profit Maximization

In the model, of course, a capitalist controls the decisions of the firm and does so to maximize profits. In a multi-period context with risk, this translates into maximizing the expected discounted present value of profits. If the stock market values future earnings streams properly, that in turn means maximizing the value of the company's stock. Hence, standard economic theory hypothesizes that businesses have only one goal: maximization of the company's stock market value.

But what about the goals of real business managers? My contention is that the stark assumption of value maximization comes much closer to the mark today than it did a decade or two ago.

In the United States these days, and increasingly in other countries, it is taken as axiomatic that management's job is to maximize "shareholder value"—to the near exclusion of all other objectives. It is hard to marshal hard evidence in support of this assertion, but Margaret Blair (1995, p. 206), a keen observer of such matters, asserts that "By the early 1990s, it had become quite unfashionable for corporate executives to talk about their jobs in any terms other than maximizing shareholder value."

It was not always thus. For decades, economists debated whether firms "really" maximized profits. For example, there was a spirited and well-known exchange in the 1946 *American Economic Review* between two Princeton economists of an earlier age: with Richard Lester (1946) using interview evidence to attack the assumption of profit maximization, and Fritz Machlup (1946) defending it. In the eyes of the jury of economists, Machlup had the better arguments, but realists long suspected that Lester was closer to the truth.[6]

Even when I began to study economics in the 1960s, considerable attention was still accorded to Baumol's (1959) sales maximization hypotheses, Simon's (1959) satisficing (rather than maximizing) hypothesis, and other alternative goals of the firm. Why? Because they were viewed as more realistic descriptions of firm behavior than strict profit maximization. There was even a branch of economics called the "behavioral theory of the firm," which sought to build models of business decisions as they really were made, rather than as economists pretended they were made.[7] In brief, efforts were underway to push the economic model closer to what was perceived as reality.

But then things began to change. Berle and Means' (1932) emphasis on the divorce of ownership (the shareholders) from control (the managers) was revived and given new intellectual form by Jensen and Meckling (1976) in their famous article on "agency costs." They observed that managers who own only a small share of the stock have an incentive to overindulge in perquisites at shareholders' expense, and they recommended heavily debt-laden capital structures to mitigate such agency costs. A decade later, Jensen (1986) highlighted "free cash flow"—cash flow in excess of (profitable) investment needs—as the feedstock of managerial slack and again advocated the heavy use of debt financing to limit managerial discretion. Coupled with the general shift toward economic fundamentalism in the 1970s and 1980s, these important intellectual developments shoved every alternative to profit maximization right off the stage. Students these days hear little, if anything, about sales maximization, satisficing, or any goal other than profit maximization.[8]

At about the same time, things were changing rapidly on Wall Street and in corporate boardrooms all over America. The rise of institutional investors and, especially, the emergence of an active (if not vicious) market for corporate control in the early 1980s, held managerial feet to the value-maximization fire as never before. These two devices for managerial discipline—debt financing and the threat of takeovers—were neatly combined in the leveraged-buyout craze that swept (and, I might say, terrorized) corporate America in the 1980s.

Not by coincidence, forms of managerial compensation changed dramatically in just the direction suggested by economic theory: To align the interests of owners and managers, executive compensation turned increasingly toward stock options. Jensen played a role in this development, too. An influential study with Kevin Murphy (1990) found that CEOs captured on average only about 0.003 percent of the increase in the value of the firm—which, to Jensen and Murphy (p. 138) meant that "corporate America pays its most important leaders like bureaucrats."

The remedy was simple and obvious: Managers could be relied upon to pursue value maximization more single-mindedly if their compensation was tied more tightly to the company's stock price. The resulting changes in compensation practices were revolutionary. In the mid 1980s, only about two percent of CEO pay came in the form of stock options (using the Black-Scholes formula to value these options); by 1998, this share was over 53 percent.[9] Part of this spectacular rise was, of course, a byproduct of the stunning bull market of the 1990s; but there is no doubt that the prototypical compensation package changed, too. Who today would say that managers are paid "like bureaucrats"?

An interesting question is, once again: To what extent did intellectual developments drive, or at least heavily influence, these changes in real-world management attitudes and/or in the market for corporate control? Metaphorically, did Michael Jensen create Michael Milken? We may never know, but I am inclined to give considerable credit or blame to economic theory for influencing economic reality. The arguments of Jensen and others were persuasive. But self-interest didn't hurt, either.

Did these changes improve corporate performance? That is far from obvious. For example, aggregate productivity growth remained weak until the late 1990s.[10] The reasons for America's sluggish productivity performance are many, varied, and controversial. So, rather than trying to adjudicate that debate, let me confine my remarks to some possible reasons why the revolution in executive compensation may have failed to deliver on the promise held out by economic theory.[11]

Briefly, I think economic theorists underestimated three interrelated phenomena. First, movements in a particular company's share price can be dominated by general market trends, for which the CEO bears no responsibility, rather than by idiosyncratic factors that may be under his control.[12] Second, compensation committees, which are dominated by other CEOs, have typically not tied rewards directly to performance by, for example, benchmarking—which would be axiomatic in the economic model.[13] The consequence has been that even CEOs who underperform the overall market or their industry average have been richly rewarded by the unprecedented bull market. Third, some CEOs have displayed a remarkable ability to game the system for their own advantage. Some examples include: Options on underperforming stocks are frequently repriced; many corporations have boosted their share prices by buying back equity despite the extraordinarily low cost of equity capital offered by the bull market; and a number of companies have been accused of practicing what has come to be called "earnings management"—a euphemism for rigging the books to manipulate reported earnings.

Viewing Labor as "Just a Commodity"

In the academy, we have a special subdiscipline of economics called "labor economics." But there are no subjects called "equipment economics" or "ball-bearing economics." Why not?

A major reason, I believe, is that many economists of earlier generations refused to accept the idea that the market for labor should be treated just like any other input market—with an upward-sloping supply curve, a downward-sloping demand curve, and equilibrium where the two curves cross. Instead, there was a long and deep tradition of *institutional* labor economics—names like Lester, Sumner Slichter, Arthur Ross, and John Dunlop come to mind. These scholars thought it important to observe the operations and institutions of labor markets up close and in detail precisely because they believed that neither suppliers nor demanders treat labor as "just another commodity."

While not necessarily inconsistent with the main body of economic theory, their approach was certainly different. And I think many economists grudgingly accepted the view that labor had to be treated differently from other factor inputs. It did not sit there passively as it was bought and sold to maximize profits. It talked, it complained, it had feelings, it formed unions, it went on strike!

While marginal productivity theory insists that labor is always paid its marginal revenue product, astute observers of labor markets thought they saw something different—like slack and what we would now call rent-sharing; like long-term implicit contracts that granted workers something approaching (but not quite reaching) tenure; like unions and collective bargaining. None of these institutional features of labor markets were inconsistent with economic theory, but each of them required modifications that bent the model closer to perceived reality. Correspondingly, while the institutionalists are all but gone today, contemporary labor economics remains, I believe, closer to the earth than many other subdisciplines.

But look what's happening in labor markets now. Unions are on the decline—down from 36 percent of American workers in 1945 to just 14 percent today. Slack is being squeezed out as firms strive more single-mindedly to maximize profits.[14] Long-term relationships between firms and their employees are under siege.[15] Jobs are being outsourced both to reduce benefits and to rid firms of the burdens of long-term relationships. Temporary and contingent work, though still small shares of total US employment, are growing rapidly. In brief, labor is increasingly being treated as "just another commodity" to be bought and sold on a spot market. Thus the real world, though still far from the simple economic model, is again moving closer to it.

What is behind these changes? I do not believe the drive to turn labor into a commodity was rooted in intellectual arguments that real-world human resource practices were dysfunctional and ought to be replaced by more strictly economic, arm's-length, price-mediated transactions. In fact, a substantial empirical literature argues that what are sometimes called "advanced" or "high road" human-resource practices are highly productive.[16] And there is even a train of theory—emanating from Akerlof's famous (1982) paper on gift exchange—that supports these empirical findings. Rather, President Ronald Reagan helped break the back of the union movement when he smashed the PATCO strike in 1981. And the general political shift to the right probably emboldened management to oppose unions more vigorously and to claw back some of the rents it had previously shared with labor. Increased international competition may also have weakened labor's hand, although that view remains controversial.

Nonetheless, economists' ideas did play an indirect role, I believe. Specifically, the greater concentration on profit maximization that I have previously discussed carried a stark corollary for the labor market: Slack had to be squeezed out. Thus economic logic may have played a supporting role in creating the harsher climate that labor now faces.

Perfect Information and the "Law of One Price"

In the world envisioned by simple economic theory, all buyers and sellers are perfectly informed about the market price, and all units of the commodity that trade on a given market sell at that common price. Indeed, one of the most stunning intellectual claims made by the proponents of free markets is that the price system achieves a remarkable economy of information: Everything a market participant needs to know is embodied in the market price.

Of course, the ideas that information is imperfect and that price dispersion may exist within a given market are hardly foreign to economic theory. The entire body of search theory, for example, is built on these ideas. Furthermore, empirical researchers have long known that the "law of one price" is egregiously violated in practice.[17]

Here, it seems to me, an important technological development, not the spread of economic gospel, may be bringing the real world into closer alignment with the simple model. Specifically, the easy availability of price quotations on a wide variety of goods and services over the Internet may make the law of one price a closer approximation to reality in the future than it ever was in the past. But that is conjectural at this point.

Developments in Financial Markets

Aspects in which financial markets have changed to bring them closer to economists' idealized models may be the phenomena most familiar to this group. At some risk of describing a caricature rather than a model, let me just say that our canonical models envision markets that are efficient in the strong sense (all known information is embodied in the price), highly competitive, and pretty much "complete"—meaning that you can buy or sell futures on just about anything. In the rarefied heights of general equilibrium theory, a full menu of Arrow-Debreu securities—defined by date, place, and "state of nature"—is assumed to exist.

The real world is not quite like this, of course, but it seems to be moving rapidly in that direction.

The proliferation of futures contracts, options and other derivatives, and the "securitization" of seemingly everything have greatly broadened the available asset menu in recent years, bringing it closer to the full set of Arrow-Debreu securities.

It would be a gross exaggeration to say that investors can now buy "contingent commodities," but newly-created assets have greatly expanded the possibilities for both hedging and gambling. You can now buy bonds whose payments are tied to the occurrence of hurricanes or to the receipts of rock stars.

The basic theoretical insights into finance originally contributed by Markowitz's (1952) portfolio selection model, Sharpe's (1964) capital asset pricing model, and others have been so thoroughly incorporated into contemporary financial practice that they are now considered commonplace. Reports on stocks that you receive from investment advisers routinely include the company's "beta" and "Sharpe ratio."

Options pricing has gone even further and now accords extraordinarily well with the Black-Scholes (1973) theory, which is based on exactly the sort of no-arbitrage condition which is the mother's milk of economic theory. Once options traders acted on intuition and hunches; now they carry hand-held computers programmed with the Black-Scholes formula. When prices deviate from this theoretical benchmark, money moves quickly to arbitrage away any differences. Indeed, the theory is so universally accepted that, rather than using price data to test it, financial experts now routinely assume the validity of the Black-Scholes formula and use it to "back out" the market's implied estimates of volatility.

Some years ago, economists began to suggest that mutual funds should mechanically replicate broad stock indexes so that investors could ignore expensive but useless professional advice and simply buy "the market portfolio" with minimal transactions costs.[18] Now, of course, index funds like the Vanguard 500 are so large that some observers worry that the demand thereby generated for S&P 500 stocks has inflated their values.[19] Even longer ago, economists argued for indexed bonds tied to the price level,[20] which now also exist in several countries. The large equity premium pointed out by Mehra and Prescott (1985) has become not only a well-known fact but a perceived reason to invest in stocks rather than bonds for the long run.[21]

In brief, more and more investors seem to have been persuaded by expert opinion that stocks are better long-term investments than bonds despite the day-to-day volatility, that portfolio diversification pays, that dips in the market are buying opportunities, and that professional portfolio managers typically underperform the market, so it is better to invest in index funds.

Commensurate with these developments, the major financial markets have become much more technical places. Generalists with square jaws and firm handshakes, family connections, and country club memberships have had to make room for more technically-minded "rocket scientists" with fewer social graces but more advanced degrees in economics, mathematics, and physics. A whole new breed of investors called "macros" makes huge financial bets on interest rates and exchange rates based—I am *not* making this up—on the application of macroeconomic theory.[22]

Financial practice on the supply sides of the markets has also been transformed. A decade or more ago, economists wondered why corporations paid dividends when, for example, stock buybacks could hand over the same money to shareholders at more favorable capital-gains tax rates. Some fascinating theoretical literature was developed to explain this "strange" (to economists) practice. The question was: What were our simple theories missing?[23] But now the tables appear to have turned. Economists may never have explained corporate dividend payments satisfactorily, but corporations seem to have caught on to the message of economists! They now pay fewer dividends and engage in more stock buybacks. In just ten years, the dividend yield on the S&P 500 has fallen from 3.5 percent to 1.2 percent.[24] Repurchases of shares by corporations rose seven-fold between 1985 and 1996.[25]

The preceding list is not exhaustive. For better or for worse, the influence of economics on the financial markets has been pervasive. But does this influence derive from the power of ideas? In part, I think the answer is yes. But it certainly didn't hurt that many of these ideas were about new ways for financial market players to make money.

Greater Global Mobility of Goods and Capital

Although barriers to mobility have long been recognized in trade theory, I think it fair to say that *homo economicus* inhabits a world in which both goods and capital move freely around the globe in search of the most favorable terms. A few decades ago, that was a ludicrous description of reality. But of late the world is said to be "globalizing" at a prodigious rate. For example, world trade has grown much faster than GDP since World War II, and cross-border financial flows have grown vastly faster than trade in goods and services.[26] In many ways, these trends are simply a return to the situation that existed before two world wars and a worldwide depression effectively shut down international trade and capital flows, but with this significant twist: Many more countries participate in the global economy now than did in 1910.

Once again, can we attribute this development to the persuasiveness of economists' ideas? Partly. Comparative advantage, which is surely one of history's most powerful thoughts, lies at the intellectual heart of the successive rounds of trade liberalization since World War II. But world peace (comparatively speaking) and technological advances in transportation and telecommunications must have played much bigger roles.

Government Regulatory Policies

Finally, even the purest versions of economic theory recognize several roles for government. Two I have already mentioned in passing: the provision of public goods, and the redistribution of income. I want to focus now on how economists' ideas have changed the way the state carries out its regulatory functions.

Start with environmental policy. At least since Pigou (1912), economists have believed that environmental externalities create a *prima facie* case for government intervention, and that such interventions are best carried out by levying appropriate taxes and subsidies. Some decades later, a consensus of sorts emerged that a system of tradable permits might work better than effluent charges in practice.[27] But for years this sage advice, though accepted almost universally among economists, had essentially no impact on policy. Governments either ignored environmental externalities and let markets do their thing, or adopted clumsy command-and-control policies that reduced pollution at enormous cost. As late as 1987, when I included a chapter on this subject in my book *Hard Heads, Soft Hearts,* economists' arguments had made little headway in the policy arena.

But things are vastly different today. While we have a long way to go, the economist's approach—whether in the form of emissions taxes or tradable permits—is now central to the public debate on environmental policy. One stunning example is the market in sulphur dioxide permits that has been running now for nine years, including these days trading on the Chicago Board of Trade. The permits cost vastly less than early estimates had supposed, presumably reflecting sharply lower costs of reducing SO_2 emissions.[28] Tradable carbon emissions permits and variants thereon are also central elements in the US government's policy toward global climate change—though, unfortunately, they are not so central to the policy recommendations of many other nations.

The influence of economists' ideas is also apparent in court cases and regulatory policies designed to promote and protect competition—and I don't mean only the famed Chicago law-and-economics school. Many lawyers and even some judges have now studied enough economics so that concepts like marginal cost, oligopoly, and prisoner's dilemmas are now standard fare at regulatory hearings and trials. For example, the most widely accepted test of "predatory pricing" is whether price is below marginal cost. Criteria drawn from the economic literature have been used in the regulation of telecommunications, railroads, electric utilities, even garbage removal.

In both of these important examples—environmental policy and regulation—I think a strong case can be made that the power of ideas triumphed with relatively little help from the vested interests—which, in fact, often opposed the policy changes.

The Other Side of the Story

I could go on detailing areas in which economists have had a "detectable influence on the societies in which they live"—but I won't. Instead, let me quickly balance the scales by mentioning a few places where the ideas of economists have not traveled very far:

- As far as I can tell, the huge and intensely interesting scholarly literature on optimal taxation has had negligible influence on the design of actual tax systems—which sometimes appear to *maximize,* more than minimize, deadweight losses.
- Peak-load pricing, that old economists' favorite, has admittedly made some inroads; so perhaps it should have made my earlier list. But I remain struck by how rare it is, not how common.
- Our international trade policy, though liberal in the large, remains highly protectionist in the small. In particular, anti-dumping cases—which may be economists' least-favorite policy—are increasingly common both here and

abroad. (On the other hand, both tariffs and many nontariff barriers have come down.)

- The private sector, at least in the United States, has shown itself singularly uninterested in indexing, even though economic theory suggests that virtually all contracts should be partially or totally indexed.[29] I can't help thinking that money illusion lies behind the dearth of indexing clauses—but that's truly a noneconomic thought.
- Although behavioral economists and psychologists have documented many anomalies in consumer decision-making,[30] I am not aware of any evidence suggesting that people have reacted to this news by altering their behavior patterns to conform better to economic theory.
- Economists' basic theory of the term structure of interest rates—that long rates are the appropriate average of future expected short rates—badly fails statistical tests,[31] and the rapid evolution of financial markets does not appear to be making it work any better.
- Similarly, the interest-rate parity theory of exchange rates continues to do a very poor job of either predicting or explaining either cross-country interest-rate differentials or changes in exchange rates.
- Related to these last two points, but with broader applications, data from a wide variety of sources continue to show that expectations are not rational, despite economists' protestations that they must be. How could *homo economicus* do anything else?

Why Did It Happen?

In none of these cases, however, is there any strong reason to believe that the discrepancies between reality and the economic model have been widening over time. Thus I have now presented two lists. The first, more detailed list catalogued ways in which real economies have converged toward the model. The second, briefer, list offered respects in which the model and reality remain far apart, but with no indication of divergence. Hence my basic conclusion: On balance, life is coming to imitate art. The question is why.

There is no single answer, but let me begin by reminding you of one of Keynes' (1936, p. 383) most famous quotations. You have heard it before:

> [T]he ideas of economists and political philosophers...are more powerful than is commonly understood. Indeed the world is ruled by little else. Practical men, who believe themselves to be quite exempt from any intellectual influences, are usually the slaves of some defunct economist.

Ideas do have power. I believe economic ideas may have been among the predominant influences in such developments as the privatization of social security, the revolution in executive compensation, the myriad of changes in the financial system, and the gradual movement toward freer trade. This is the truest sense in which life has imitated art.

But notice that in most of these cases powerful vested interests buttressed and magnified the force of the underlying ideas. Stock brokers stand to earn huge fees if Social Security is privatized, mutual fund managers and others who controlled capital pushed corporations to maximize profits more vigorously, financial innovations offered money-making opportunities, and so on. Clearly, ideas make more headway when they can harness the power of the invisible hand. It is hardly surprising that strictly economic ideas often, but not always, favor the interests of the haves over the have-nots.

These two factors are generic. But I'd also like to call attention to three aspects of recent history that have, I believe, contributed mightily to the economic changes I have been discussing.

First, the worldwide shift of the political spectrum toward the right made many countries more receptive to neoclassical economic ideas than they once were. Economics is, after all, a rather "conservative" discipline, especially compared to the other social sciences. We economists emphasize efficiency over equity, glorify greed, and exalt the achievements of free markets, to name just a few. It is no accident that it is right wingers, not left wingers, who wear Adam Smith neckties.

Second, the failure of socialism and the ascendancy of the United States as the world's only superpower left many people around the world (including in the United States) thinking that the American way must be the right way. And the American way is arguably the closest thing to textbook capitalism that exists in any major country.

Finally, although this entire talk has been about *microeconomics,* I must close by pointing out the crucial role of *macroeconomic* success and failure in inducing life to imitate this particular form of art.

As the cliche goes, nothing succeeds like success. And that's just what the US economy has enjoyed ever since it began to recover from the depths of the 1981–1983 recession—and especially since 1992. By contrast, Japan, with a unique microeconomic system that comes much closer to Akerlof's gift exchange model than to a spot market in labor, has suffered an utter macroeconomic collapse in the 1990s. And continental Europe, with its many restrictions on markets and thick social safety nets, has languished with high unemployment for the better part of two decades. The natural inference, to which many have jumped, is that America's purer, more hard-edged brand of capitalism must work better than either Europe's softer version or the Japanese system, which has been characterized as "human-capitalism."[32]

Decades ago, Paul Samuelson wrote of a "neoclassical synthesis" in which proper application of macroeconomic stabilization policy would create the full-employment conditions necessary to validate neoclassical microeconomics. Well, to a first approximation, we have now achieved that neoclassical synthesis in the United States. Thus did the intellectual descendants of John Maynard Keynes pave the way for the worldwide comeback of Adam Smith.

Acknowledgment

I am grateful to Orley Ashenfelter, William Baumol, Douglas Bernheim, Margaret Blair, Patrick Bolton, John Campbell, Dennis Carlton, and Henry Farber for helpful suggestions, and to Celina Su for excellent research assistance.

Notes

Originally published in *Business Economics*, Vol. 35, No. 1 (January 2000), pp. 16–25.

1. Perhaps the most celebrated contribution to that debate was Lange (1936, 1937). In more recent decades, the unusual economic system in what was then Yugoslavia led to some scholarly literature on the worker-managed firm. See, for example, Prychitko and Vanek (1996).
2. There is some debate over whether a lighthouse, Adam Smith's favorite example, is really a public good.
3. I owe this quote to Sheshinski and Lopez-Calva (1999, p. 9.)
4. For a good, up-to-date summary of the debate, see Aaron and Shoven (1999).
5. This is not to say that it is impossible to provide an economic rationale for Social Security. See for example (Diamond (1977) and Blinder (1981).
6. A few years earlier, Hall and Hitch (1939), in the famous British survey that led to the kinked-demand curve theory, had concluded that firms did not follow marginal cost pricing.
7. See, for example, Cyert and March (1963).
8. They do, however, hear a great deal about agency costs and related incentive problems that may interfere with profit maximization.
9. *The Economist,* August 7, 1999, page 18.
10. It did, however, improve in manufacturing.
11. Some might argue, however, that the stock market boom is evidence that it has delivered.
12. Forthcoming research by John Campbell, Martin Lettau, Burton Malkiel, and Yexiao Xu finds that overall market movements accounted for about 20 to 30 percent of the variance of individual stock prices changes in the 1970s and 1980s, but much less in the 1990s.
13. One possible reason is a dysfunctional accounting rule in the United Sates. Stock options with an explicit performance benchmark are counted as business costs, but conventional stock options are not.
14. It has been argued, correctly I believe, that Japanese firms have been less interested in profit maximization than American firms. See for example, Blinder (1992).
15. This point is often exaggerated. While job tenure has declined a bit, the major change seems to be that white-collar workers are more exposed to the risk of job loss than they used to be—although still far less so than blue-collar workers. See, for example, Farber (1997).
16. See, for example, Ichniowski, Shaw, and Prennushi's (1997) careful study of steel mills; for a number of older articles and many references, see Blinder (1990).
17. For some examples, see Pratt, Wise, and Zeckhauser (1979), or Carlton and Perloff (1994).
18. I attribute this idea to the first edition of Burton Malkiel's classic, *A Random Walk Down Wall Street,* which was published in 1973.
19. See Shleifer (1986).
20. The suggestion, I believe, goes back to Marshall (1925, p. 197).
21. See Siegel (1994).
22. George Soros is only the most famous of this breed.
23. One suggestion: The ability to pay dividends signals a firm's profitability to investors. See Bernheim (1991).
24. But the ratio of dividends to corporate profits (which is volatile from year to year) was about the same in 1988 and 1998. Profits as a share of GDP have increased substantially.

25. According to *Barron's*; see Lazo (1999).
26. For example, foreign exchange turnover has increased nearly 100-fold since 1973, and cross-border purchases and sales of bonds and equities by Americans jumped from 9 percent of GDP in 1980 to 164 percent in 1996. See *The Economist* (1997).
27. See Baumol and Oates (1979).
28. See Schmalensee et al. (1998), esp. pp. 61–63.
29. See Gray (1976) or Blinder (1977).
30. See, for example, Thaler (1992).
31. See, for example, Campbell (1995).
32. Itami (1994).

References

Aaron, Henry and John Shoven. *Should the United States Privatize Social Security?* Cambridge, MA: MIT Press, 1999.

Akerlof, George A. "Labor Contracts as Partial Gift Exchange," *Quarterly Journal of Economics*, Vol. 97, No. 4, November 1982, pp. 543–569.

Baumol, William J. *Business Behavior, Value and Growth*, London: Macmillan and Co., 1959.

Baumol, William J. and Wallace Oates. *Economics, Environmental Policy, and the Quality of Life*, New York: Prentice-Hall, 1979.

Berle, Adolf and Gardiner Means. *The Modern Corporation and Private Property*, Chicago, IL: Commerce Clearing House, Corporation Trust Charge, 1932.

Bernheim, B. Douglas. "Tax Policy and the Dividend Puzzle," *Rand Journal of Economics*, Volume:Vol. 22, No. 4, Winter 1991, pp. 455–476.

Black, Fischer and Myron S. Scholes. "The Pricing of Options and Corporate Liabilities" *Journal of Political Economy*; Vol. 81, No. 3, May/June 1973, pp. 637–654.

Blair, Margaret M. *Ownership and Control: Rethinking Corporate Governance for the Twenty-First Century*, Washington, DC: The Brookings Institution, 1995.

Blinder, Alan S. "Indexing the Economy Through Financial Intermediation," in K. Brunner and A. H. Meltzer (eds.), *Stabilization of the Domestic and International Economy*, Carnegie-Rochester Conference Series (a supplement to the *Journal of Monetary Economics*), Vol. 5, 1977, pp. 69–105.

——— *Private Pensions and Public Pensions: Theory and Fact*, W.S. Woytinsky Lecture No. 5, University of Michigan, December 1981.

——— *Hard Heads Soft Hearts*, Boston, MA: Addison-Wesley, 1987.

——— ed., *Paying for Productivity: A Look at the Evidence*, Washington, DC: Brookings Institution, 1990.

——— "International Perspective: Trading With Japan: Why the U.S. Loses—Even on a Playing Field," *Business Economics*, January 1992.

Campbell, John Y. "Some Lessons from the Yield Curve," *Journal of Economic Perspectives*, Summer 1995, pp. 129–152.

Carlton, Dennis and Jeffrey Perloff. *Modern Industrial Organization*, Boston, MA: Addison-Wesley, 1994.

Cyert, Richard and James March. *Behavioral Theory of the Firm*, Englewood Cliffs, NJ: Prentice-Hall, 1963.

Diamond, Peter A. "A Framework for Social Security Analysis," *Journal of Public Economics*, Vol. 8, No. 3, December 1977, pp. 275–298.

Farber, Henry S. "The Changing Face of Job Loss in the United States, 1981–1995," *Brookings Papers on Economic Activity: Microeconomics*, 1997, pp. 55–142.

Gray, Jo Anna. "Wage Indexation: A Macroeconomic Approach," *Journal of Monetary Economics,* April 1976, pp. 221–235.

Hall, R. L. and C. J. Hitch. "Price Theory and Business Behavior," *Oxford Economic Papers,* May 1939, pp. 12–35.

Ichniowski, Casey, Kathryn Shaw, and Giovanna Prennushi. "The Effects of Human Resource Management Practices on Productivity," *American Economic Review,* June 1997, pp. 291–313.

Itami, Hiroyuki. "The 'Human-Capital-ism' of the Japanese Firm as an Integrated System" in Kenichi Imai and Ryutaro Komiya (eds.), *Business Enterprise in Japan: Views of Leading Japanese Economists,* Cambridge and London: MIT Press, 1994, pp. 73–88.

Jensen, Michael. "Agency Costs of Free Cash Flow, Corporate Finance, and Takeovers," *American Economic Review,* May 1986, pp. 323–329.

Jensen, Michael and William Meckling. "The Theory of the Firm: Managerial Behavior, Agency Costs, and Ownership Structure," *Journal of Financial Economics,* October 1976, pp. 305–360.

Jensen, Michael C. and Kevin J. Murphy. "CEO Incentives—It's Not How Much You Pay, but How," *Harvard Business Review,* May/June 1990, pp. 138–150.

Keynes, John Maynard. *The General Theory of Employment, Interest and Money,* New York: Macmillan and Co., 1936.

Lange, Oscar. "On the Economic Theory of Socialism," *Review of Economic Studies,* October 1936/February 1937.

Lazo, Shirley A. "Speaking of Dividends: Dividends vs. Buybacks," *Barron's,* September 6, 1999, p 39.

Lester, Richard A. "Shortcomings of Marginal Analysis for Wage-Employment Problems," *American Economic Review,* Vol. 36, No. 1. March 1946, pp. 63–82.

Machlup, Fritz. "Marginal Analysis and Empirical Research," *American Economic Review,* Vol. 36, No. 4, September 1946, pp. 519–554.

Malkiel, Burton. *A Random Walk Down Wall Street,* New York: W.W. Norton & Co., 1973.

Markowitz, Harry. "Portfolio Selection," *Journal of Finance,* Vol. 7, No. 1, March 1952, pp. 77–91.

Marshall, Alfred. Memorials of Alfred Marshall, *Remedies of Fluctuations of General Prices,* New York: Macmillan & Co., 1925.

Mehra, Rajnish and Edward Prescott. "The Equity Risk Premium: A Puzzle," *Journal of Monetary Economics,* March 1985, pp. 145–161.

"One world?" *The Economist,* October 18, 1997, pp. 79–80.

Pigou, Arthur C. *Wealth and Welfare,* London: Macmillan and Co., 1912.

Pratt, John W, David A. Wise, and Richard Zeckhauser. "Price Differences in Almost Competitive Markets," *The Quarterly Journal of Economics,* Vol. 93, No. 2, May 1979), pp. 189–211.

Prychitko, David L. and Jaroslav Vanek. *Producer Cooperatives and Labor-Managed Systems,* Cheltenham, UK: Elgar, 1996.

Schmalensee, Richard, et al, "An Interim Evaluation of Sulfur Dioxide Emissions Trading," *Journal of Economic Perspectives,* Vol. 12, No. 3, Summer 1998, pp. 53–68.

"Share Options." *The Economist,* August 7, 1999, pp. 18–20.

Sharpe, William. "Capital Asset Prices: A Theory of market equilibrium under conditions of risk," *Journal of Finance,* Vol. 19, No. 3, September 1964, pp. 425–442.

Sheshinski, Eytan and Luis Felipe Lopez-Calva. "Privatization and Its Benefits: Theory and Evidence," mimeo, Harvard Institute for International Development, January 1999.

Shleifer, Andrei. "Do Demand Curves for Stocks Slope Down?," *Journal of Finance,* Vol. 41, No. 3, July 1986, pp. 579–590.

Siegel, Jeremy J. *Stocks for the Long Run: The Definitive Guide to Financial Market Returns and Long-Term Investment Strategies,* Burr Ridge, Ill.: Irwin Professional, 1994.

Simon, Herbert A. "Theories of Decision-Making in Economics and Behavioral Science," *American Economic Review,* June 1959, pp. 253–283.

Smith, Adam. *The Wealth of Nations,* Oxford: Clarendon Press, Oxford University Press, 1976.

Stigler, George. "Do Economists Matter?," *Southern Economic Journal,* January 1976, page 351.

Thaler, Richard H. *The Winner's Curse: Paradoxes and Anomalies of Economic Life,* Princeton, NJ: Princeton University Press, 1992.

CHAPTER 27

2000

THE ADAM SMITH ADDRESS

WHAT WOULD ADAM SMITH SAY NOW?

Henry Kaufman, Henry Kaufman & Company, Inc.

I greatly appreciate receiving from you the Adam Smith Award. It is a recognition that I will always cherish. To be recognized by you, the leading organization of business economists, is a great honor, indeed. While in my own career I have occasionally had responsibilities involving a number of activities in banking, I have always taken great satisfaction and pride in my role as an economist. To be identified through this award with Adam Smith was far beyond my aspirations when I graduated college and started in my first job as a credit analyst in an industrial bank over 50 years ago.

Who Was Adam Smith?

Adam Smith was a remarkable individual. He left an indelible imprint on economic thought. He differed in many ways from the modern-day economist. As measured by our contemporary standards, Adam Smith was not a trained economist. He did not have a PhD in economics. None was actually available at the time. Instead, he studied mathematics, the natural sciences, philosophy, and classical writings. These groundings probably contributed to the comprehensiveness of his economic thought.

He became professor of moral philosophy at the age of 27 at Glasgow University, where he delved into questions raised by moral philosophy and political economy. He became a very popular teacher. As one historian noted, "a multitude of students from a great distance resorted to the University merely upon his account." Today, the emphasis by many academicians is first on research and then on their interplay with students. Of course, research is important to advance economic knowledge. Nevertheless, greater weight should be given today to the teaching merits of a professor. When we think back to our college days, most often we remember outstanding lectures, the extraordinary capacity of a professor to simplify complex matters, and the professor who spent time with us individually.

Publish or perish still seems to be in the forefront of academic life. This is a market-driven phenomenon, which Adam Smith would readily acknowledge. Publications help to establish a national identity while teaching reaches only a local student audience, but Adam Smith actually published only two works. The first was *The Theory of Moral Sentiment* when he was 36 years old and then *The Wealth of Nations* when he was 53. The first brought him considerable renown. But, what did he write about? In *The Theory of Moral Sentiment,* he expounded on such matters as the propriety of action, the objects of reward and punishment, on the character of virtue, and on the system of philosophy. These are hardly the subjects economists would delve into today. Nevertheless, his views on these subjects provided the foundation for the thoughts he expressed in his landmark book, *The Wealth of Nations*—a book full of great insights written in a grand style without the mathematical equations that we tend to insert in our learned journals.

Among other things, Adam Smith believed that it was part of human nature to strive for economic growth and that this could best be achieved through unfettered competition, the division of labor, and free trade. As we all know, Adam Smith had a circumscribed role for government. He limited it to protecting society from violence and invasions, to protecting every member of society from injustice or oppression, and to providing certain public works and institutions. At the same time, he warned that "No society can surely be flourishing and happy of which the far greater part of the members are poor and miserable." Incidentally, Adam Smith did not favor a flat tax. He was very specific in this matter, "The subjects of every state ought to contribute toward the support of government, as nearly as possible in proportion to their respective abilities."

What Adam Smith Would Applaud

What would Adam Smith say about economic and financial developments since his death in 1796? He would certainly applaud the rise in living standards and the rapid industrialization in many parts of the world that has been driven by innovations and a division of labor far beyond anyone's vision two hundred years ago. Even just a century ago, US industrial workers toiled ten hours a day, six days a week and earned an average of $375 a year. At that time, working conditions were typically unsanitary, unsafe, and often fatal, and there were few protections. Among American males of all occupations one hundred years ago, whites lived an average of only 47 years; and blacks a mere 33. Jefferson and Adams crossed the Atlantic at the time of Adam Smith in six weeks. We now do it in seven hours, and if you fly the Concorde the time is cut in half. Adam Smith would also marvel at the advent of the Internet and the Web, at biotechnology from high-tech pharmaceuticals to genetic engineering, at electronics and the miniaturization that has progressed within this field within a short time.

Adam Smith would have welcomed the expansion of free trade among nations during the past two centuries. He believed that the bigger the market, the greater division of labor within countries, and the greater the economic benefit for all involved. He believed that tariffs and subsidies divert capital investment away from the most productive sectors of the economy and toward the most inefficient ones.

Where Adam Smith Would Be Encouraged but See Unfinished Business

How far have we really come along Adam Smith's economic path? The defeat of Communism as symbolized by the collapse of the Soviet Union was a victory for capitalism. Karl Marx was proven wrong. A system in which most property and the means of production were owned by the state, in which most economic activities were centrally planned by government officials and in which goods and services are produced by the citizens of the state and are distributed among the citizens by the government just did not work. While Adam Smith would have greeted the defeat of Communism with great delight and a vindication of his economic philosophy, he would nevertheless quickly note, as he did in his writings, that the potential excesses of capitalism could be very dangerous.

Remember, he believed in a system that encourages individuals to pursue their self-interest and that society will benefit as long as self-interest is restrained by competition. He warned that competition could be compromised by collusion, monopolistic practices, and limitations on international trade.

The United States comes closest to the economic society envisioned by Adam Smith, although we are far from what he prescribed. We tend to aspire to live in what I call an economic democracy in which equal opportunity and not equality of outcome takes precedence. The idealistic American view looks to market forces to determine economic outcomes and accepts the fact that great economic disparities between winners and losers are a normal consequence of the free market system. In contrast, in the social democracies around the world, legislatures, elected officials, and elite bureaucrats play important roles in the economic decision-making process. In Europe, the political emphasis is on social justice, fair trade, and on an economic system that produces a kinder and gentler outcome than is suggested, at first glance, by a highly competitive society. In Japan, an economic system run through a consensus approach still has a powerful appeal. Even after a decade of virtually no economic growth, many Japanese still believe that their society and culture are based on a foundation of harmony. In Japan and in Europe, the tight interplay between big government, big business and big labor all combine to limit the freedom of decision-making, the mobility of labor, and the determination of business to excel. These features induce a rigidity that Adam Smith would abhor.

Globalization of business activity, in which the United States has been a leader in the post World War II years, is also a development that would have been highly favored by Adam Smith. This is because the underlying premise of globalization is that it maximizes comparative advantages and therefore produces goods and services at the lowest cost. For quite a while, the main thrust of globalization was for Americans, Europeans, and Japanese to establish or to acquire facilities outside their own country with the intent to take advantage of lower costs of labor, of the nearness of raw materials, or of the nearness to customers.

In the last few decades, another development has enhanced globalization—namely the increase in the mobility of labor. Political freedom spread into Eastern Europe and Russia. China has become more politically open-minded. Transportation and communication have improved vastly. All of these developments are encouraging individuals to seek an improved return for their labor. While the United States has always been more favorably inclined toward immigration, Europe and Japan have not. To be sure, the US limits immigration, but the integration of immigrants into the mainstream of society is one of its distinguishing features. That cannot be said of Europe generally and of Japan particularly. Immigrants in those countries are tolerated, but it is difficult for them to acquire new citizenship. And their presence invites outbursts of nationalism and social unrest, especially during business slowdowns. I suspect that Adam Smith would ask, "How can there be efficient globalized markets when capital is free to move and labor mobility is restrained?"

Thus, it would seem that if globalization of business and financial activity were pursued along the philosophical views of Adam Smith much good ought to come of it. It would create a strong dynamic for change and efficiency. It would tend to promote a better allocation of resources at the company, global, and national level. It would foster innovations and competitiveness. It would improve decision-making capabilities because investors would receive full information from companies and punish issuers of securities that try to subvert the company. It would broaden risk taking across society and breed a healthy awareness of profits.

We are, however, nowhere near that ideal economic system. Today, there is a wide range of checks and balances on the behavior of business and financial enterprises that we have incorporated into our system. Even after a generation of deregulation, our system is honeycombed with regulations through our tax codes, social safety nets for citizens, and industries that are deemed to have special needs. At the local, state, and federal levels, government plays an active role in economic affairs, sometimes helping to improve economic efficiency; but very often its interference is detrimental.

Nor does our system tolerate well the harshest of competitive outcomes—business failure—especially when it comes to the largest corporations, banks, and other enterprises. In America's imperfect economic democracy, these entities are, in effect, "too big to fail." Historically, when they have fallen into serious trouble, the government—weighing the immediate social and economic costs—has shown a propensity to step in to shore up the faltering giants with loan guarantees, tax breaks, and other subsidies. Under the strict rules of market capitalism, such firms would be left on their own to endure the rigors of market discipline; indeed, Adam Smith would argue that faltering firms are, by definition, weaker firms, and that their failure is good for the economy. Moreover, free trade globally does not prevail. Anytime there is a significant economic slowdown, the proponents of "managed" and "fair" trade come to the fore.

Where Adam Smith Would Be Deeply Troubled

There is one powerful development in place today that, in the long run, will drastically reduce competition and turn us completely away from any tendencies toward an economic democracy. This is the massive consolidation that is taking place in business and finance. Of course, Adam Smith's opposition to monopolies and their practices was unequivocal. In the last few decades, mergers and consolidations have accelerated. They have taken on huge proportions and have encompassed industries such as airlines, autos, chemicals, communications, oil and natural gas, and health care in the non-financial sector. They have not just taken place within national borders but many have global dimensions.

We often hear that driving these consolidations are the very large capital requirements that are necessary for corporate survival. That may be valid for some businesses, especially in view of the rapidity of technological changes. However, two other driving forces are more likely. First, consolidation provides an opportunity to reduce costs, increase profits, and may perhaps improve customer services. That is the first stage, which seems highly desirable. Second, it permits the surviving business to have improved control over the prices charged to customers and over the entire innovative process. As a result, competition is reduced and economic democracy is seriously impaired.

I am especially concerned about the many adverse consequences that will ensue over the next few decades as the rapid consolidation continues in the financial sector. Here are just a few examples of what has already happened. The top ten US banks held 19 percent of insured deposits of commercial banks in the early 1980s. This percentage rose to over 40 percent last year. In the mutual funds industry, the 25 largest mutual fund organizations held over 70 percent of all mutual fund assets last year. These concentration ratios will probably rise rapidly in this decade. Huge financial conglomerates are emerging. They have within their conglomeration such activities as banking, insurance, leasing, investment banking, securities trading, financial asset management, consumer financing and credit card entities.

What are the challenges that these huge institutions pose? First, they are extremely difficult to manage. In the long run, this will decrease economic efficiency. The wide range of financial activities does not allow the senior management to have much direct involvement in the day-today activities of the business. The senior management becomes increasingly dependent on middle managers, many of whom are mathematically highly skilled in their specialty and tend to be biased to take increasing risks in order to achieve higher compensation for themselves. For many activities, the parameters of risk taking are mathematically quantified through techniques such as value-at-risk formulations. Heavily influenced by historical inputs, these techniques can never fully tell the totality of risk taking, but they have a tendency to comfort senior managers. The 1998 financial crisis attested to the reliance and shortcomings of this heavy dependence of detailed risk quantifications. The pace and complexity of change makes certain rules of thumb obsolete. Replacing common sense with vigorous quantification is not the answer.

Second, financial conglomeration is full of conflicts of interest. They reduce the choices of borrowers and investors. For example, they offer one-stop financing not necessarily as a choice but as part of the deal. The institution will provide the borrower with a variety of loan facilities, underwritings, and asset management. As financial concentration continues, the customer will not only have fewer opportunities to shop for financing packages but will find few places in the market that will provide financing costs for each service.

This conflict of interest has now come to the fore in the research activities of financial conglomerates. It has become quite obvious that the research effort has often been compromised because of the pressure to support trading and underwriting activities. This problem will worsen as financial conglomeration continues.

Actually, economists and research analysts face this challenge of maintaining objectivity in other places. For example, the corporate economist tends to keep a negative view about his industry within the narrow confines of his corporation. At the governmental level, no high-level governmental economist such as the Chairman of the Council of Economic Advisers or any other high-level economic adviser to the President of the United States has ever forecast a business recession.

The third challenge that large financial conglomeration, and indeed our large business organizations, poses is that they are deemed too big to fail. There have been quite a few instances of governmentally assisted bailouts because the institution involved posed a systemic risk or the debtor involved was important to our national interest. No matter how one examines this approach, the too-big-to-fail approach skews the economic system in favor of bigness and weakens the market's competitive process.

Increased financial concentration will have a profound effect on market activity itself. Eventually, the breadth and depth of the secondary markets will diminish. With fewer participants whom do you really trade with? How can you make effective markets when there are relatively few buyers or sellers? As a result, the accuracy of marking portfolios to market will become questionable. The contagion effect as it is talked about today will move to a much higher level as huge institutions straddle the globe with generally uniform rather than diverse views influencing their decisions.

Unfortunately, there is little popular political or governmental opposition to consolidation that compares with the contentious antitrust movement of a century ago. Frequently, mergers are justified as a way of meeting international competition. Politicians tend to have little motivation to take on the "big interests," especially when there is little public support to do so. The public's attitude has shifted from a century ago, when large businesses were owned or controlled privately. Today, many households invest in stocks and reap immediate benefits from mergers. Moreover, the problem I am describing does not get full attention because what I am describing is a drift away from an economic democracy rather than an abrupt change. It will gradually envelop us. So, let someone else tackle the problem.

It is also unfortunate that central bankers do not meet the too-big-to-fail problem head-on. They do not want to recognize the subtle way through which financial competition is diminishing. Conflicts of interest do not receive high priority in their decisions. Periods of monetary restraint frequently result in the disappearance of smaller and medium-sized financial institutions and of only a few large ones. Central bankers are not sufficiently concerned about the moral hazard underlying the too-big-to fail approach. They claim that when a large financial institution gets into trouble, the stockholders and lenders are forced to accept losses and the senior management may also be removed. This is hardly a satisfactory rationale.

Too-big-to-fail institutions can contribute to massive excessive debt creation and to a serious weakening of the credit structure before the central bank intervenes to stop their malpractices.

Eventually, large institutional concentrations will transform the global landscape. In Japan, for example, where the number of financial institutions is contracting sharply, will the few surviving institutions be more independent, or will they be beholden to the Japanese government? I believe it is the latter.

The very complexity in the structure of large financial institutions, together with the comfort provided by too-big-to-fail, invites aggressive risk taking. The leveraging incentives will always tend to overwhelm prudent judgments. Central bankers become the heroes of the bailout, but their competence should be judged on how well they have managed to contain financial excesses.

Adam Smith's writing on this issue over 200 years ago, when financial markets were not as developed as they are today, was quite visionary. He said, "The state should give monopolies to no one, but should encourage the creation of as many as possible. In this way, the bad consequences of the errors of speculation of a few banks, resulting in their ruin, would be dispersed throughout the system so that no serious damage could result."

There is no clarion call today warning us of the threats to our imperfect democracy and to some of the principles incorporated in our American way of life that were an essential part of Adam Smith's view of economic life. The drift is toward global business and financial consolidation. As this takes hold over the next few decades, a new powerful alignment will take place between big business, big government, and a newly shaped labor force. Over time, economic and financial freedom will be constrained. Large private institutions will look more like public utilities than the independent organizations they view themselves as presently. Politically, we need an up-to-date Teddy Roosevelt, who will stand up to all the vested interests and arrest this dangerous drift. Unfortunately, the center of attention for economists is largely concentrated today on near-term market and economic developments. Let us, however, think beyond and begin to confront the challenges posed by concentration, if we aspire to preserve the benefits of economic and financial freedom.

Note

Originally published in *Business Economics*, Vol. 36, No. 4 (October 2001), pp. 7–12.

CHAPTER 28

2001

INFORMATION TECHNOLOGY AND THE U.S. PRODUCTIVITY REVIVAL: A REVIEW OF THE EVIDENCE

Kevin J. Stiroh, Federal Reserve Bank of New York

The US productivity revival is by now well known, and because US firms have invested trillions of dollars in information technology (IT), there is considerable interest among the business community, policy-makers, and academics in the role of IT. However, it is quite difficult simply to measure IT accurately; and quantifying the impact on productivity is even more difficult. Nonetheless, a substantial body of evidence is accumulating that suggests IT has played an important role in the US productivity revival.

Beginning at the aggregate level, the key insight in understanding the link between productivity and IT is to recognize that IT is both an output and an input for the US economy. Fundamental technological progress in IT-producing industries—the ability to produce ever more powerful computers—generates dramatic gains in the performance/price ratio of IT goods. This progress is measured as rapid total factor productivity (TFP) and average labor productivity (ALP) growth in IT-producing industries.[1] The rest of the economy responds to the dramatic declines in relative prices by investing heavily in IT. This IT-related "capital deepening" contributes to ALP growth in those industries and firms that use IT most intensively. Aggregate data show both channels have made important contributions to economy-wide productivity growth in the late 1990s.

One can also examine the relationship between IT and productivity using more disaggregated data for individual industries or firms. Here, too, the evidence shows a link between IT and productivity gains. Industries that made the largest IT investments in the 1980s and early 1990s, for example, showed larger gains in productivity in the post-1995 period. Similarly, firm-level evidence shows large returns to IT, although IT alone is not enough to drive productivity gains. That is, firms must make complementary investments in human capital and firm restructuring to maximize the benefits of IT. Finally, there are compelling case studies of specific business applications that show IT is a critical driver of improved performance.

The chapter is organized as follows. The next section discusses the links behind IT and productivity growth as technological gains in the IT-producing industries induce capital deepening in IT-using industries. I then present a framework for measuring these contributions with aggregate data and summarize estimates from several recent studies. The chapter then moves beneath the aggregate data to examine the evidence from industries and firms that links IT with productivity gains.

Information Technology and Productivity

The interest in IT and productivity growth reflects the recent success of the US economy, and two pieces of data are driving this research agenda. As shown in Figure 28.1, annual productivity growth for the US non-farm business sector jumped from 1.3 percent per year for 1973–1995 to 2.5 for 1995–2000.[2] The sudden end to the slowdown in US productivity growth coincided with accelerating investment in IT (computer hardware, software, and telecommunications equipment) and the rapid diffusion of new applications and uses. For example, real IT investment grew 22 percent per for 1995–2000, compared to 14.9 percent per year for 1973–1995, and IT investment reached $562 billion (in chain-weighted dollars) in 2000, and 31.6 percent (in current dollars) of private fixed nonresidential investment.[3]

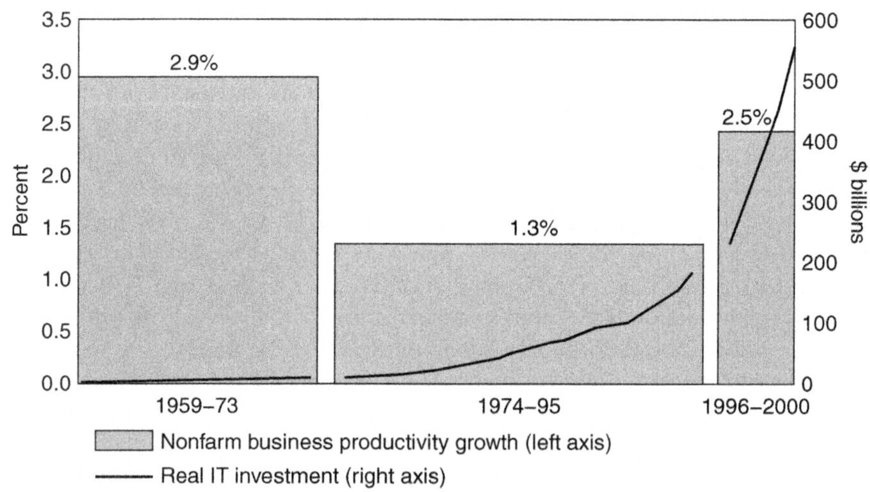

Figure 28.1 Surging IT investment and accelerating productivity.

Notes: Productivity is average annual growth for the three sub-periods. IT investment is for computer hardware, software, and telecommunications equipment, in chain-weighted dollars. Productivity data from BLS (2001b). Investment data from BEA, August 2001.

The productivity effects of IT begin with the small part of the economy that produces computer hardware, software, semiconductors, and telecommunications gear. The firms and industries that produce these IT assets have expended considerable resources and benefited from the extraordinary technological progress that enabled them to dramatically improve the design and performance of IT goods. Fundamental technological progress epitomized by Moore's Law, the doubling of computer chip power every 18 months, is the catalyst behind the IT revolution.[4]

From an economic perspective, these dramatic improvements in the speed, power, and performance of IT assets are measured as rapid total-factor productivity (TFP) growth in the IT-producing industries. The electric and other electronics good industry (SIC 36), which includes production of semiconductors and telecomm equipment, enjoyed TFP growth of 8.1 percent per year for 1995–1999; and the commercial and industrial machinery industry (SIC 35), which includes production of computer hardware, posted annual TFP growth of 6.9 percent.[5] These growth rates far exceed the 1.1 percent annual TFP growth for the non-farm business sector and the 2.5 percent annual TFP growth for manufacturing as a whole and show the amazing pace of technological progress in the sectors that produce high-tech capital assets.

These large technological gains yield dramatic improvements in the performance/ price ratio of IT goods. The US national accounts use a variety of methodologies to account for the quality change of high-tech assets and translate these improvements into declining prices. That is, hedonic techniques, matched. model approaches, and other methodologies translate *better* IT goods into more quality-adjusted units with falling prices. To show how dramatic these changes are, Figure 28.2 plots the US GDP deflator versus the price index for computer

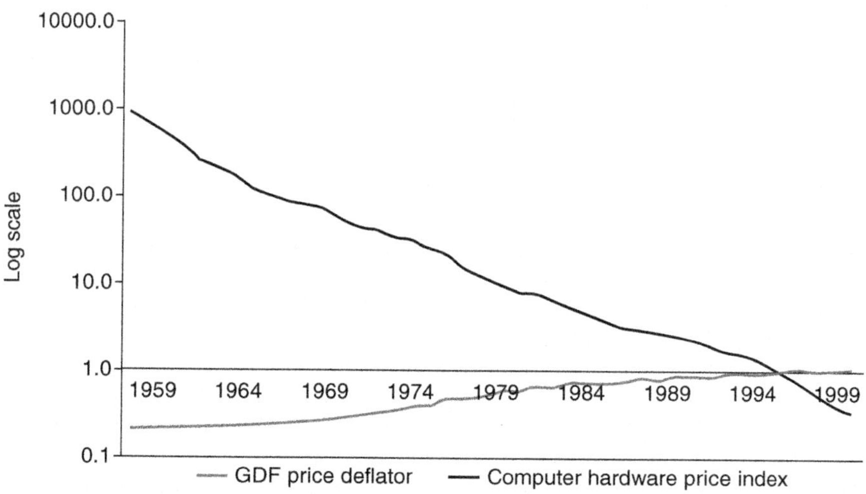

Figure 28.2 Large price declines for computers index (1996=1.0).

Source: BEA, August 2001.

hardware investment. From 1959 to 2000, the GDP price deflator rose 3.9 percent per year, while computer prices fell 19.3 percent per year.

The large declines in the computer price index obviously reflect the underlying deflation methodologies, but the improved performance/price ratio of IT assets is a real phenomenon that provides a strong incentive for firms to substitute between production inputs and invest in the relatively cheap IT assets.[6] This input substitution can be seen in the extraordinary growth rate of IT equipment in the 1990s, which is much more rapid than for other forms of fixed investment or labor inputs. For example, while IT investment grew 22 percent per year from 1995–2000, private fixed investment as a whole grew only nine percent per year.

As US firms accumulate IT goods through massive investment, this "capital deepening" enhances ALP in the firms and industries that provide their workers with more and better physical capital. These potential productivity gains reflect a number of complementary channels: improved information flows within firms that allow more efficient organization; better inventory management that reduces factory downtime and increases product availability to consumers; substitution of low-priced IT for high-skilled labor (e.g., automated payrolls or account management systems).[7] All of these changes are linked to IT and raise the productivity of those firms best able to restructure their activities to implement IT.

Skeptics, however, have argued that these effects are not likely to be large. For example, IT may be primarily used to reallocate market share between competing firms (think about an online book seller competing against a traditional bookstore), replicate existing activities (a retailer offering both Internet and catalog shopping), increase on-the-job-consumption, (workers playing video games or day-trading), or may be associated with large adjustment costs (the training, learning, and support costs that often accompany IT investment). If these forces are large enough, one might see little link between IT investment and productivity gains.[8]

Measured productivity has in fact accelerated since 1995, however, so the pessimistic view is bolstered by the observation that productivity is pro-cyclical due to resource utilization changes, productivity shocks, increasing returns, and reallocation effects. Therefore, it is likely that part of the US productivity resurgence reflects the particularly strong output growth during the late 1990s. Disagreement remains, however, about how much of the recent productivity surge reflects improvements in the underlying trend and how much should be attributed to cyclical forces.

Aggregate Evidence

An appropriate starting point for a discussion of the aggregate impact of IT is the familiar aggregate production function, which relates the amount of output an economy produces to the amount of inputs used in production and the level of technology. This approach has a long history in macroeconomics and has been an integral part of the IT debate. Early studies by Oliner and Sichel (1994) and Jorgenson and Stiroh (1995), for example, employed an extended aggregate production function and found relatively little impact from IT. More recently, BLS (2001a), CEA (2001), Jorgenson and Stiroh (2000), Jorgenson (2001), Jorgenson, Ho, and Stiroh (2002), Oliner and Sichel (2000, 2002), Sichel (1999), and Whelan

(2000) have employed variations of this approach and found a considerable productivity impact from IT in the aggregate US data.

The standard framework can be extended to account for the two channels for IT mentioned above. First, IT investment is an output, so output (Y) is decomposed into an IT investment portion (I_{IT}) and a non-IT portion (Y_N). Second, IT investment creates a capital input, so the service flow from the installed capital stock is broken into an IT portion (K_{IT}) and a non-IT portion (K_N). One can write an extended production function to highlight the role of IT as:

$$Y = Y\left(I_{IT}, Y_N\right) = A \cdot f\left(K_{IT}, K_N, L\right) \tag{28.1}$$

where L is a measure of labor input that represents both the quality of the labor force and the number of hours worked. A is TFP, which measures how effectively inputs are transformed into outputs.

Under standard economic assumptions about labor, capital, and output markets, theory suggests that Equation (28.1) can be mechanically transformed to yield the following relationship for ALP growth:

$$\begin{aligned} d\ln\left(\frac{Y}{H}\right) = {} & v_{K_{IT}} \cdot d\ln\left(\frac{K_{IT}}{H}\right) + v_{K_N} \cdot d\ln\left(\frac{K_N}{H}\right) \\ & + v_L \cdot d\ln\left(\frac{-L}{H}\right) + d\ln A \end{aligned} \tag{28.2}$$

where H is hours worked, v represents the share of the subscripted input in total income, and $v_{K_{IT}} + v_{K_N} + v_L = 1.0$.

Equation (28.2) breaks down labor productivity growth into several factors. The first two terms reflect capital deepening; workers are more productive when they have more or better physical capital with which to work, and this capital deepening is decomposed into an IT and non-IT portion. Next is a labor quality effect that measures productivity gains as firms substitute toward workers with more skills and higher marginal products; again, labor productivity grows in proportion to the growth in labor quality, which is defined as the growth in labor input per hour worked. The final factor is TFP, a catch-all term that captures the impact of technological change, as well as increasing returns to scale, omitted variables, reallocations from low to high productivity activities, and any remaining measurement error. This TFP residual can then be further decomposed into a portion associated with IT-production and all other TFP gains.

Table 28.1 presents alternative estimates of the US labor productivity revival using this framework and shows that the two IT-related forces were driving the acceleration in productivity in the late 1990s.[9] First, TFP gains in the production of IT made a substantial contribution to aggregate ALP growth, for example, about 0.2 to 0.3 percent in all studies. Second, IT-related capital deepening made a substantial contribution, ranging from 0.62 percentage point in CEA (2001) to 0.44 percentage point in Jorgenson, Ho, and Stiroh (2002). Based on a different model of obsolescence, Whelan (2000) reports an even larger contribution from computer capital. Despite conceptual and methodological differences, the common

Table 28.1 Alternative explanations of the US Productivity revival

	BLS	*CEA*	*Gordon*	*Jorgenson, Ho, & Stiroh*	*Oliner & Sichel*
ALP Revival Period, 1995–1999	2.40	3.01	2.75	2.36	2.57
ALP Early Period, 1973–1995	1.39	1.39	1.42	1.44	1.41
Acceleration	1.01	1.62	1.33	0.92	1.16
Capital Deepening	0.30	0.38	0.33	0.52	0.33
IT-Related	0.48	0.62	-na-	0.44	0.50
Other	−0.21	−0.23	-na-	−0.08	−0.17
Labor Quality	0.06	0.00	0.05	0.11	0.04
TFP	0.70	1.19	0.31	0.51	0.80
IT-Related		0.18	0.29	0.24	0.31
Other		1.00	0.02	0.24	0.49
Cyclical Effect		0.04	0.50		
Price Measurement			0.14		

Notes: Revival period is 1995–2000 for CEA and 1995–1998 for Jorgenson and Stiroh. BLS, CEA, Oliner and Sichel, and Gordon examine nonfarm business sector; Jorgenson and Stiroh include business sector plus private households. Gordon compares the revival period to trend productivity growth for the early period. IT-related capital deepening refers to information processing equipment and software for BLS and CEA, and computer hardware, software and telecommunications equipment for Jorgenson and Stiroh and Oliner and Sichel. IT-related TFP is from computer and communications production for CEA, from computer plus computer-related semiconductors for Gordon and Oliner and Sichel, and from computer harder, software, and telecommunications for Jorgenson and Stiroh. Numbers may not add up due to rounding.

Source: BLS (2001a), CEA (2001), Gordon (2000), Jorgenson, Ho, and Stiroh (2002), Oliner and Sichel (2000).

conclusion is that both the production and the use of IT have made important contributions to the US labor productivity revival.[10]

These aggregate studies are driving the emerging consensus on the impact of IT, but there are some limitations. For example, these studies typically assume constant returns to scale and competitive markets, and factor shares are often used as proxies for output elasticities. This essentially assumes that there is a productive impact of IT investment, so it is critical to also econometrically test for a link between IT-use and productivity gains. In addition, aggregate studies may miss important variation among industries. For example, Figure 28.3 plots the distribution of the share of IT capital in total capital and shows enormous variations, with IT capital shares ranging from essentially zero (0.4 percent in farms) to sizable shares (38.6 percent in telephone and telegraph). Clearly, this enormous heterogeneity in IT-intensity plays an important role in understanding the productive impact of IT and is addressed next.

Industry and Firm Evidence

There is a large body of industry and firm level evidence that searches for a productive and economic impact of IT. Brynjolfsson and Hitt (2000) survey this literature

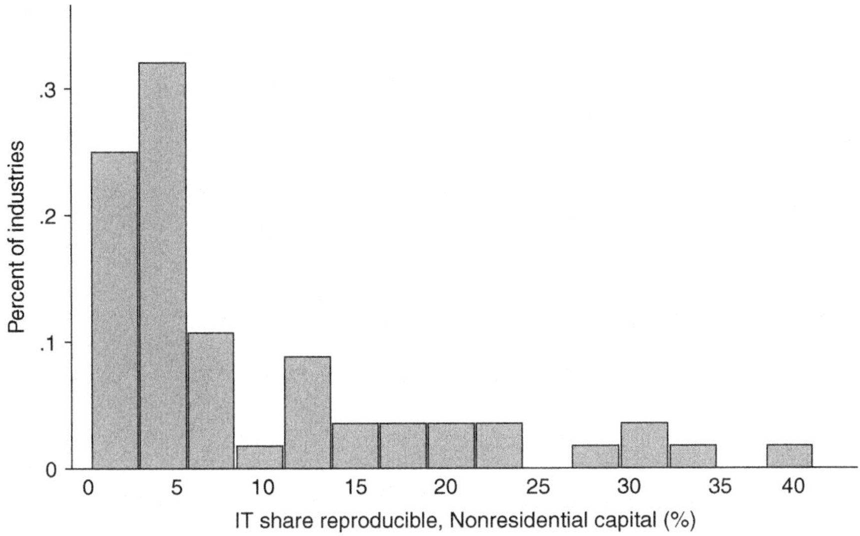

Figure 28.3 Wide distribution of IT-intensity in 1999.
Source: Stiroh (2001).

and conclude, "Taken collectively, these studies suggest that information technology is associated with substantial increases in output and productivity" (p. 32). This section summarizes more recent work done using industry level productivity data in Stiroh (2001, 2002) for the late 1990s,[11] and discusses several interesting case studies about how IT changes business outcomes.

One simple approach compares the productivity performance of different parts of the US economy, where the economy is broken into IT-producing, IT-using, and other industries.[12] If the IT-producing and IT-using industries show larger productivity acceleration than other industries, this is consistent with the idea that IT has contributed to the US productivity revival. If there is little difference between IT-related and other industries, however, one might conclude that there is little benefit from IT, and the productivity revival could be attributed to other forces like normal cyclical productivity gains that affect all industries.

Table 28.2 reports average ALP growth rates for 1987–1995 to 1995–1999 for three sets of industries—IT-producing industries, IT-using industries, and other industries. The two IT-producing industries show a mean productivity acceleration of 3.7 percentage points, while the 26 IT-intensive industries posted an increase of 2.0 percentage points. Both of these are quite strong by historical standards, and much bigger than the about 1.0 percentage point increase for the US economy as a whole. In sharp contrast, productivity gains for the other 29 industries averaged only 0.4 percentage points. These differences are quite striking and support the idea that IT has real productivity benefits.

Table 28.2 IT-related industries show the largest acceleration in productivity

	Number of Industries	Average Annual Productivity Growth 1987–1995	1995–1999	Change
IT-Producing Industries	2	8.53	12.22	3.69
IT-Intensive Industries	26	1.18	3.16	1.99
Other Industries	29	1.87	2.30	0.43

Notes: Estimates for each group of industries are means of the average annual productivity growth rates for each period. IT-intensive industries have a 1995 IT capital share above the 1995 median, except for SIC #35 and #36, which are the IT-producing industries.

Source: Stiroh (2001).

More sophisticated econometric tests that compare the change in ALP growth rates after 1995 with 1995 IT-intensity also suggest that IT is a determinant of productivity gains. A difference-in-difference analysis, for example, shows that the productivity acceleration from 1987–1995 to 1995–1999 is significantly related to the level of IT-intensity in 1995.[13] This holds true even when the IT-producing industries are excluded from the analysis and again supports the idea that IT-use has real productivity benefits.

It is important to remember, however, that complementary innovations like organizational restructuring, skill changes, and research and development efforts are key parts of the complex process that business must undergo to reap the rewards of their IT investment. Thus, it is quite difficult to identify the precise effects of IT capital alone, and these IT capital shares should be thought of as indicators of participation in the broadly defined IT revolution.[14] With this caveat in mind, one can then ask whether the IT-related variation in industry productivity matters at the aggregate level. That is, are these differences large enough to drive the US productivity revival?

Using a similar breakdown of industries as in Table 28.2, one can calculate the size of the industries and their net contribution to the aggregate productivity revival.[15] The IT-producing industries produced about four percent of US output in the late 1990s, while the IT-using industries produced 51 percent, and the other industries produced the remaining 44 percent. In terms of the contribution to the US labor productivity revival, the IT-producing industries contributed 0.22 percentage point, the IT-using industries contributed 1.16 percentage points, and the other industries made a *negative* contribution of 0.21 percentage point. Thus, all of the labor productivity revival that can be attributed to individual industries came from either those industries that produce IT or those that use IT most intensively, which implies IT has played a critical role in the US productivity revival.[16]

These industry level results suggest that IT use has indeed contributed to US productivity gains, although two caveats deserve mention. First, while IT-intensity is defined in 1995 prior to the productivity revival, there is still the possibility of a reverse-causality explanation, that is, only high productivity industries invested in

IT. Because a portion of the recent productivity acceleration is undoubtedly a result of the strong output growth in recent years, this is a legitimate concern. Given the wide variation in productivity growth rates that appear linked with lagged IT-intensity, however, it is unlikely that this is the whole story.

Second, IT-intensity is defined by investment or capital shares for computer hardware, computer software, and telecommunications equipment, although there is much more to the IT revolution. Semiconductors, for example, are now routinely embedded in other types of goods, ranging from numerically controlled machine tools to modern farm tractors; so these estimates may be understating the true economic impact of the IT revolution.

As a final line of evidence, it is interesting to look at detailed case studies that show how IT actually affects business performance. Brynjolfsson and Hitt (2000) provide specific examples, and this section concludes with two interesting additions. Hubbard (2001), for example, shows how on-board computers have dramatically improved capacity utilization in the US trucking industry. In particular, the adoption of electronic vehicle management systems (EVMS) allows dispatchers to monitor their trucks in real-time, decrease truck downtime, and improve resource allocation and truck loads, all of which increases productivity and efficiency. Similarly, Athey and Stern (2000) find that information technology incorporated in "enhanced 911" systems substantially improves survival rates and reduces the costs of emergency patients. While these results apply only to specific industries and may not even be measured in the official productivity statistics, they give concrete examples about how information technology improves productivity and business performance.

Conclusions

The revival in US productivity growth in the late 1990s is a critical development for the US economy because faster productivity growth contributes to rising living standards, helps keep inflationary pressures under control, and supports business profitability. Understanding the sources of productivity growth and why it fluctuates, however, is a difficult task and many factors contribute to its rise and fall.

This chapter focuses on one specific factor—information technology—and reviews the evidence on whether IT has contributed to the recent period of strong productivity growth. While some discussion remains, there is a growing consensus that IT has played a critical role. At its heart, this is a story of profound technological progress in the production of IT assets like computer hardware, software, and telecommunications equipment. This generates large productivity gains in the industries that produce IT assets and provides powerful incentives for other firms to invest in the latest IT assets. The accumulation of evidence from aggregate, industry, and firm level studies suggests that these effects are economically large and have contributed substantially to the US productivity revival.

Notes

Originally published in *Business Economics*, Vol. 37, No. 1 (January 2002), pp. 30–37.

1. TFP growth is defined as output per all inputs, and ALP growth is output per hour worked. See the discussion of productivity in the July 2001 issue of *Business Economics* for details.
2. Throughout this article, the productivity revival is assumed to begin at the end of 1995. More recently, productivity growth has slowed with the economy, posting an annual growth rate of 1.7 percent in the first three quarters of 2001 (BLS, 2001b).
3. Some of the IT investment in the late 1990s was likely related to Y2K replacement investment and other temporary factors. The rate of growth of IT investment slowed in 2001, but the level remains quite high and the long-term trend is clearly upward.
4. See Ceruzzi (2000) for details on the developments in the U.S. computing industry.
5. BLS (2001a).
6. See Jorgenson and Stiroh (2000) for a detailed description of IT deflation and methodologies in the U.S. national accounts.
7. See Brynjolfsson and Hitt (2000) for several case study examples of IT benefits. Section IV discusses two specific cases of successful IT applications.
8. See Baily and Gordon (1988), Kiley (1999, 2000) and Gordon (1999, 2000) for details.
9. The estimates differ due to how they define the economy, what periods are examined, and how IT is defined and measured. Note that all of of these studies were done prior to the August 27, 2001 revision to GDP and the subsequent restatement of productivity estimates.
10. Note that Gordon (2000) attributes 0.50 percentage point to cyclical forces and 0.14 to measurement effects, so that he estimates a much smaller acceleration in trend TFP growth.
11. Nordhaus (2000) and CEA (2001) report similar results.
12. These definitions and estimates are from Stiroh (2001), which calculated labor productivity growth for fifty-seven industries from 1987 to 1999 using gross output data from the BEA. As discussed earlier, the two industries that produce IT hardware (SIC 35 and 36) have enjoyed fundamental technological progress and strong productivity growth, so it is useful to examine those industries individually. The IT-using industries are then defined as twenty-six industries with an IT capital stock share above the 1995; other industries include the twenty-nine remaining industries. Note that IT-intensity is defined in 1995, prior to the productivity revival, which helps to reduce endogeneity concerns.
13. See Stiroh (2002) for details.
14. See Black and Lynch (2001) and Brynjolfsson and Hitt (2000) for more on complementary firm practices that contribute to productivity gains along with IT.
15. Each industry's contribution to aggregate productivity growth is measured as the value-added share weighted growth rate of industry value-added ALP. These estimates are from Stiroh (2002).
16. The McKinsey Global Institute (MGI, 2001) presents an alternative decomposition and concludes that just six industries accounted for the entire U.S. productivity revival. The MGI decomposition, however, relied on an *ex post* identification of important industries that simply chose the industries that made the largest contribution. In contrast, the decomposition in Stiroh (2002) identified industries *ex ante* as computer-producing, computer-using, and other industries, which helps to identify IT as part of the story.

References

Athey, Susan and Scott Stern. 2000. "The Impact of Information Technology on Emergency Health Care Outcomes." NBER Working Paper 7887. September.

Baily, Martin Neil and Robert J. Gordon. 1988. "The Productivity Slowdown, Measurement Issues, and the Explosion of Computer Power." *Brookings Papers on Economic Activity.* 2. pp. 347–420.

Black, Sandra E. and Lisa M. Lynch. 2001. "What's Driving the New Economy: The Benefits of Workplace Innovation." Federal Reserve Bank of New York Staff Report #118. March.

Bureau of Labor Statistics. 2001a. "Multifactor Productivity Trends, 1999." USDL 01–125. May 3.

Bureau of Labor Statistics. 2001b. "Productivity and Costs, Third Quarter 2001." USDL 01–402. November 7.

Ceruzzi, Paul E. A History of Modern Computing. 2000. Cambridge, MA: The MIT Press.

Council of Economic Advisors. 2001. "Annual Report of the Council of Economic Advisors." In the *Economic Report of the President.* January.

Brynjolfsson, Erik and Lorin Hitt. 2000. "Beyond Computation: Information Technology, Organizational Transformation and Business Practices." *Journal of Economic Perspectives.* 14(4). Fall. pp. 23–48.

Gordon, Robert J. 1999. "Has the 'New Economy' Rendered the Productivity Slowdown Obsolete?" Manuscript. Northwestern University. June 12.

——— 2000. "Does the 'New Economy' Measure Up to the Great Inventions of the Past?" *Journal of Economic Perspectives.* 14(4). Fall. pp. 49–74.

Hubbard, Thomas N. 2001. "Information, Decisions, and Productivity: On-Board Computers and Capacity Utilization in Trucking." Mimeo, University of Chicago Graduate School of Business. September 17.

Jorgenson, Dale W. 2000. "Information Technology and the U.S. Economy." *American Economic Review.* 91(1). March. pp. 1–32.

Jorgenson, Dale W, Mun Ho, and Kevin J. Stiroh. 2002. "Projecting Productivity Growth: Lessons from the U.S. Growth Resurgence." *Economic Review.* Federal Reserve Bank of Atlanta. Forthcoming.

Jorgenson, Dale W. and Kevin J. Stiroh. 1995. "Computers and Growth." *Economics of Innovation and New Technology.* Vol. 3. No. 3–4. pp. 295–316.

——— 2000. "Raising the Speed Limit: U.S. Economic Growth in the Information Age." *Brookings Papers on Economic Activity.* (1). pp. 125–211.

Kiley, Michael T. 1999. "Computers and Growth with Costs of Adjustment: Will the Future Look Like the Past?" Federal Reserve Board. Finance and Economics Discussion Series Paper. 1996–1936. July.

——— 2000. "Computers and Growth with Frictions: Aggregate and Disaggregate Evidence." Federal Reserve Board. Mimeo. October.

McKinsey Global Institute. 2001. "US Productivity Growth 1995–2000: Understanding the Contribution of Information Technology Relative to Other Factors." Washington DC. October.

Nordhaus, William D. 2000. "Productivity Growth and the New Economy." Yale University. Mimeo. November 20.

Oliner, Stephen D. and Daniel E. Sichel. 1994. "Computers and Output Growth Revisited: How Big Is the Puzzle?" *Brookings Papers on Economic Activity 2.* pp. 273–334.

——— 2000. "The Resurgence of Growth in the Late 1990s: Is Information Technology the Story?" *Journal of Economic Perspectives.* 14(4). Fall. pp. 3–22.

Oliner, Stephen D. and Daniel E. Sichel. 2002. "Information Technology and Productivity: Where are We Going Now and Where are We Going?" *Economic Review.* Federal Reserve Bank of Atlanta. Forthcoming.

Sichel, Daniel E. 1999. "Computers and Aggregate Economic Growth." *Business Economics.* Vol. XXXIV. No. 2. April. pp. 18–24.

Stiroh, Kevin J. 2001. "Investing in Information Technology: Productivity Payoffs for U.S. Industries." Current Issues in Economics and Finance. Federal Reserve Bank of New York. 7(6). June.

——— 2002. "Information Technology and the U.S. Productivity Revival: What Do the Industry Data Say?" *American Economic Review.* Forthcoming.

Whelan, Karl. 2000. "Computers, Obsolescence, and Productivity." Federal Reserve Board. Finance and Economics Discussion Series, 2000–2006. January.

CHAPTER 29

2002

PRESIDENTIAL ADDRESS

UNDERSTANDING INFLATION: LESSONS FROM MY CENTRAL BANKING CAREER

Harvey Rosenblum, Federal Reserve Bank of Dallas

The theme of NABE's 2002 annual meeting was "Understanding Cycles and Shocks." In light of what's happened to the economy, to NABE, and to its membership since our 2001 annual meeting at the World Trade Center in New York ended prematurely last September 11, I can think of no better theme for the annual meeting.

Economic policymakers responded quickly to the September 11 terrorist attacks. The Federal Reserve remained open for business and provided massive liquidity to the financial system to keep it running. Monetary stimulus was boosted through four additional reductions in the Federal funds rate target, bringing it to 1.75 percent on December 11, 2001, the lowest rate in four decades. As spending on the military and homeland security were added to other federal government spending, deficits ballooned and fiscal policy turned quite expansionary as well. Both monetary and fiscal policy rolled into high gear simultaneously, for the first time since the 1970s. We know how badly the 1970s policy mix worked out for the economy. As I speak, many of my colleagues in the economics profession are forecasting rising inflation. Others believe, however, that easy monetary and fiscal policies are barely offsetting the shortfall in demand.

What will happen to inflation? NABE surveys conducted throughout 2001 and 2002 suggest inflation will remain quiescent during 2003. Beyond that time frame, the outcome is a matter of open debate. In spite of the fact that inflation is such an important macroeconomic variable, I have come to the conclusion that economists don't fully understand the subject and have tried to oversimplify what turns out to be an extremely complex phenomenon.

My career as an economist began in August 1970 when I joined the Chicago Fed. Let me summarize what I've learned since 1970 about inflation and the processes that generate it.

- The Phillips Curve is not a reliable relationship. As soon as you (re)gain faith in it, the curve will shift and break your heart.
- Strict monetarist ideology no longer works in the modern-day financial system. Money is difficult to define, its growth even harder to control, and its relationship to economic activity often uncertain.
- Inflation is an evolving and very complex phenomenon that embodies a combination of macro and microeconomic forces. The economics profession has not fully appreciated the microeconomic factors.
- When the anecdotes and economic data do not corroborate one another, one of them is wrong. More often than not, it's the data. When the anecdotes and the data are in concordance, but the economic models suggest a different outcome, it's time for a new model. When the Fed's Beige Book respondents say they have no pricing power and the inflation statistics are drifting lower, we should seek to find the missing variables in models that forecast rising inflation.
- Macroeconomic models do not deal well with a changing economic structure, let alone paradigm shifts. Policymakers must make decisions in real time and cannot wait for the parameters in their economic models to catch up and stabilize. When in doubt, policymakers should pay greater attention to the anecdotes, especially large volumes of systematically gathered anecdotes like the ones the Fed analyzes regularly from the Beige Book.
- Last, the inflation experience of the 1970s is an aberration. It was a combination of bad policy and bad shocks played out against a backdrop of bad institutions—monopoly pricing power for business and labor, increasing regulations, and complacency.

Confessions of a Monetarist

I was hired by the Chicago Fed in 1970 to work on micro-banking issues. I was happy to take the job because I thought I would be able to put my other expertise, monetary economics, to good use at the Fed. Armed with the monetarist teachings of Professor Robert E. Weintraub, I sought to educate my colleagues on a few simple principles. Namely, the Fed could expand or contract its balance sheet as needed to control the monetary base and in the process, exercise effective control over the money stock. By smoothing and slowing down the growth of money, the Fed would be able to reduce the rate of inflation, which had been trending up the prior few years. My ideas were not appreciated and were ignored. The St. Louis Fed had advocated a similar plan for several years, but the Federal Reserve System stuck to its operating plan, which sought to smooth fluctuations in short-term interest rates at the expense of influencing the rate of monetary growth. Inflation drifted up throughout the 1970s.

Ironically, the ideas I espoused were not new and had a long and distinguished pedigree. Indeed, these ideas had been enunciated very clearly just a few years earlier in Milton Friedman's Presidential Address to the American Economic Association. Friedman (1968) was succinct: "Inflation is always and everywhere a monetary phenomenon."

It was adherence to this belief that induced then Federal Reserve Chairman Paul A. Volcker and the Federal Open Market Committee (FOMC) on October 6, 1979, to abandon conducting monetary policy by setting the federal funds rate and to instead focus more directly on controlling the growth rate of money. In part because extreme volatility of interest rates accompanied monetary targeting, and in part because inflation had become more muted, the FOMC's experiment with rigid monetary control ended three years after it began.

Although the inflation rate dropped from double-digit levels in the late 1970s and early 1980s, it rarely fell below the three percent to four percent range. The Fed finally abandoned monetary targeting altogether in mid-1993. The FOMC announced its downgrading of M2 and Ml as intermediate targets because it recognized, in the words of Fed Chairman Alan Greenspan, "that the relationship between spending and money holdings was departing markedly from historical norms. . . . The FOMC would continue to monitor the behavior of money-supply measures, but it would base its policy actions on a wide variety of economic indicators." In other words, the Fed was abandoning the monetary aggregates because their behavior, at least in the short run, had abandoned us.

In spite of these problems, inflation was well-contained. The inflation experience of the 1990s can be seen in Figure 29.1. The latest research findings suggest not that money growth doesn't matter, but that it matters over much longer horizons. Work by the Cleveland Fed concludes that "a relatively close relationship between money growth and inflation may exist over eight-year time horizons, at least for the broader monetary aggregates." In other words, money growth is not

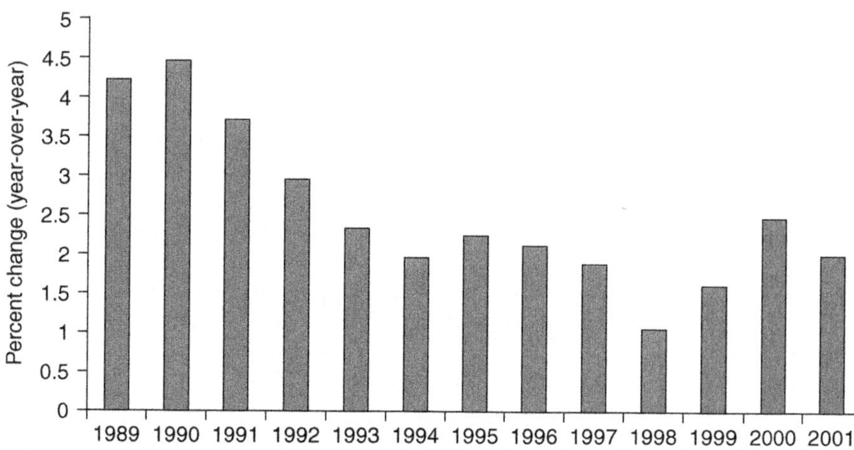

Figure 29.1 1990s core inflation drifts downward.

a particularly useful guide for short-term monetary policy decisions, but long-run inflation trends are significantly influenced by the long-run growth rate of the money supply. However, recent studies convince me that the definition of "the long run" keeps getting longer, and longer.

The Phillips Curve and Related Concepts

Economists are well known for airing and discussing their differences in public. This has given the economics profession a reputation for never agreeing on much of anything. Nothing could be further from the truth. Economists agree on a great deal and their points of agreement fill the best-selling textbooks in principles of economics, most of which have expanded by a couple of hundred pages over the last decade or so. Can we infer that economists agree on more than they used to? Probably not!

It is a rare text that doesn't spend a dozen or more pages on the Phillips Curve and its cousins, the NAIRU (the non-accelerating inflation rate of unemployment) and the natural rate of unemployment (for short, the natural rate). Until about 1995, the Phillips Curve, which depicted a negative association or tradeoff between inflation and unemployment, generally looked as it was supposed to, though it did tend to shift roughly once a decade. This can be seen in Figure 29.2. A line fitting the points labeled "1961–1970" is the Phillips Curve that prevailed when I studied undergraduate and graduate economics in the 1960s. Following President Nixon's experiment with price and wage controls in 1971–1973, the Phillips Curve relationship shifted in 1974; and over the next decade, US policymakers were confronted with a Phillips Curve array that offered choices that by today's standards would be labeled "bad" and "worse."

Once the Paul Volcker Fed succeeded in reducing the inflation expectations of labor and business management, the Phillips Curve shifted once again around 1984. This relationship remained in place through 1992. The relationship began

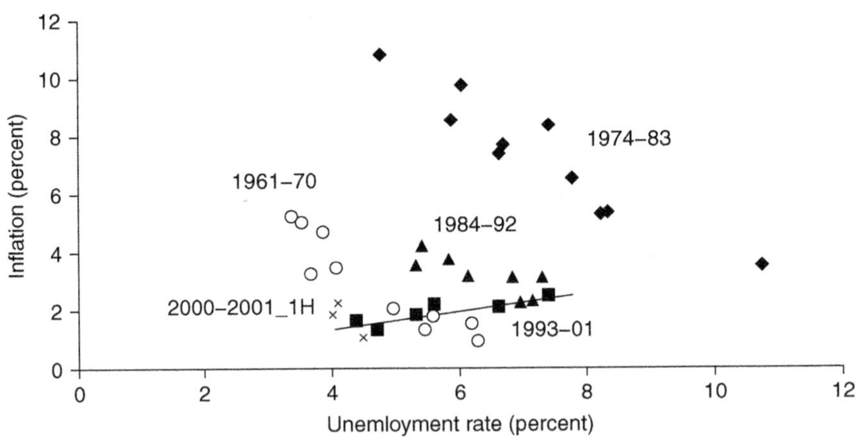

Figure 29.2 The Phillips Curve slopes up in the 1990s.

to change in 1994, but this was not apparent until 1995 or 1996. My point is simply that at any given time, it is difficult to know whether the economy is on what is thought to be the then-prevailing Phillips Curve or whether the curve was in the process of shifting to a new location. You just can't be sure.

By 1996 it was becoming apparent that the rate of inflation associated with any given state of macroeconomic performance had shifted, and by the end of 1997, it was beginning to appear as though the tradeoff, if it ever really existed, was becoming quite favorable. Indeed, some economists began to wonder whether the US economy had entered a world where less inflation could be accompanied by *lower* unemployment!

Shifts in the Phillips Curve had happened previously, but a positively sloped Phillips Curve was unprecedented. (As I discuss later, this very different Phillips Curve gave rise to discussion of a "new" economy.) Many economists still believe the Phillips Curve relationship is immutable and that one-time forces occasionally disrupt the relationship in the short run. Examples abound.

Several studies have been published in the last few years that augment the Phillips Curve relationship by including a number of special factors that have suppressed inflation in the 1990s. To name a few: energy prices, import prices, fringe benefit costs, markup of prices over unit labor costs, maturing of the workforce, and the growth of international trade.

I offer two critical comments. First, the fact that many different combinations of supply shocks can be used to set the Phillips Curve relationship back together is somewhat disturbing. Second, how many years must elapse before it becomes apparent that the Phillips Curve must be augmented by some combination of supply-side forces if it is to have any validity? This underscores my earlier point that the Phillips Curve relationship has ceased to be useful for making monetary policy choices *in real time*.

The dominance of disinflationary forces on changing the nature of the Phillips Curve during the period 1993–1999 can be seen in the *upward-sloping* Phillips Curve shown in Figure 29.2. Let me add, however, that it is not clear whether the period for the upward-sloping Phillips Curve extends beyond 1999. Observations for 2000, 2001, and the first half of 2002 could be interpreted as still another shift and rotation in the Phillips Curve.

Other Inflation Indicators

What about other inflation indicators? A recent Chicago Fed study by Fisher, Liu and Zhou (2002) finds that Phillips Curve models sometimes improve upon naive inflation forecasts in that they help forecast the direction of inflation changes, but not the magnitude, particularly when there has been no change in the monetary policy regime. The authors characterize the period 1977–1984 as a shifting monetary regime. During this period the Fed had three different chairmen: Arthur F. Burns, G. William Miller, and Paul A. Volcker. Volcker's extreme methods of confronting inflation certainly did differ from his two predecessors. But monetary policy was not the only regime shift occurring at that time. Deregulation of several industries—including airlines and natural gas

(1978), trucking (1980), railroads (late 1970s), telephones (1982), and banking (1980, 1982)—began in the late 1970s. President Ronald Reagan provided overt support to the Fed's inflation-fighting efforts during the presidential election campaign in 1980 and when he took office in 1981. And President Reagan's willingness to fire the air traffic controllers, thereby breaking the union, and imposing downward wage flexibility was another regime shift. The bankruptcy of Chrysler and the wage and work rules concessions made by the auto workers in order to keep the company and their jobs alive, was another regime shift. The need for companies and unions to react to a changing competitive landscape by reducing their pricing power may have been just as important to inflation developments in the 1980s as was the Fed's effort to match its monetary policy to its stated goal of price stability.

That increased product market competition has impacted labor markets and inflation trends is shown in a couple of papers by my Dallas Fed colleague John Duca (1998, 2000). He presents evidence that increased competition has been associated with a declining rate of unionization, a falling incidence of CPI indexation clauses in union contracts, and increased use of profit sharing arrangements. These three trends are most evident in sectors that have experienced either deregulation or increased foreign competition since the 1970s. Duca's more recent work demonstrates that the increased flexibility in US labor markets stemming from greater competition has restrained US inflation and reduced the NAIRU in the 1990s. Or to put it another way, the increased competitive pressures faced by many US businesses has, during the 1990s, lowered the amount of inflation associated with any given set of macroeconomic conditions.

Is the reduced inflation associated with past deregulation and a tougher competitive environment sustainable? Have the inflation benefits run their course? I can only hazard a guess. Most economists argue that if deregulation affects inflation, it is a one-off phenomenon that results in a one-time change in the price level, not a sustained impact on the rate of inflation. That position may be correct, but it misses the underlying industry dynamics. Next year will mark the 25th anniversary of airline deregulation. The airline industry is still adjusting. So too are its competitors, customers, and suppliers. Moreover, its railroad and trucking competitors are still adjusting to their own deregulation.

The impact of telephone and telecommunications deregulation will not be complete for years to come. The greater prevalence of market forces in several key sectors of the economy allows the forces of creative destruction to work more quickly and completely throughout the economy. The era of lower inflation for any given monetary/fiscal policy regime and set of macroeconomic conditions could last for many more years. Further efforts to deregulate and privatize would help; but increased regulation and government ownership of productive resources could undermine, and even reverse, the disinflationary process. The trend toward increased regulation, government intervention, and the socialization of airport security in the aftermath of September 11 may already be adversely impacting pricing decisions.

A Confession Digression

It is time for a confession. I am not a macro-economist. My doctoral dissertation and the bulk of my research over my career has been in industrial organization, with special emphasis on banking and financial markets. My focus is microeconomics. Within the Fed, I'm a micro guy in a macro world! I don't fit in, nor do I belong. I have been trained to believe that:

- Pricing decisions are made by private sector businesses and that competition, innovation, and flexibility are paramount factors affecting these pricing decisions.
- The price level is determined by the intersection of aggregate supply and aggregate demand.
- The rate of inflation depends upon how fast aggregate demand grows relative to aggregate supply.
- The disinflation of the 1990s is a result of millions of businesses being forced to compete and innovate and having access to a wider source of labor resources and other inputs than was true in the two prior decades.
- In the 1990s, most of the millions of businesses, whose individual supply of goods and services add up to US aggregate supply, became more elastic in their supply function than previously, implying that any increase in aggregate demand could be accompanied by a smaller increase in the price level.

In this world, increased growth of the economy can be consistent with falling inflation, and even deflation. It's not that businesses seek this outcome, it's just that more contestable markets give them *no other choice.*

An expanded market for sourcing inputs of labor, financial capital, and materials will shift out the aggregate supply curve, at least for awhile. The passage of the North American Free Trade Agreement (NAFTA) in 1993 allowed and encouraged the North American automobile industry to reorganize itself so it could optimize the production of autos and light trucks utilizing labor and materials from Canada, Mexico, and the United States. This increased the effective labor supply that was available and contributed to a reduction in cost. It may be a coincidence, but the fact that the CPI for automobiles has been falling over the last several years likely has something to do with NAFTA (Figure 29.3).

The benefits of freer trade in general, and NAFTA in particular, have not been limited to the automobile industry. One of the best-kept secrets in Washington, D.C., is that NAFTA is a success. Mexico has become our second-largest trading partner, with exports to Mexico currently exceeding $100 billion annually. Because US companies are sharing production among their US, Canadian and Mexican plants, the epicenter of US manufacturing has shifted from the Northeast and Midwestern states to the Southwest, as shown in Table 29.1. If maquiladora manufacturing is thought of as a physical extension of Texas and California production, the locus of manufacturing employment has clearly shifted during the past 15 years. Moving production to its lowest cost location allows US firms to

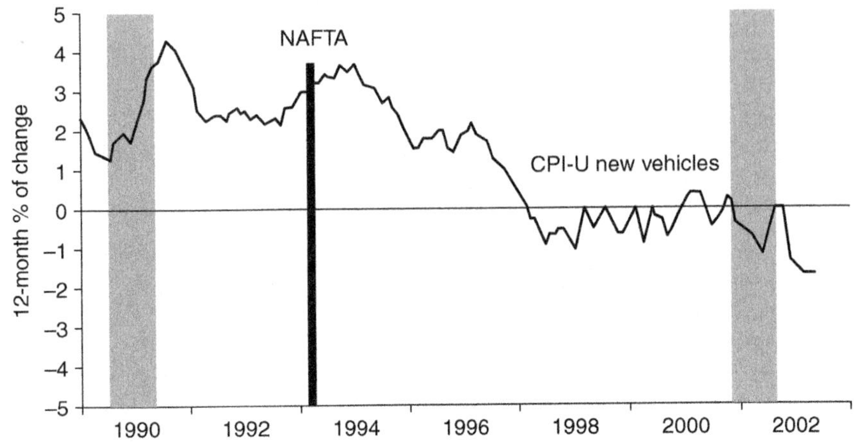

Figure 29.3 NAFTA impacts new vehicle prices?

Table 29.1 Locus of manufacturing shifts to the southwest

1985		*1999*		*2002*	
Rank	*State*	*Rank*	*State*	*Rank*	*State*
1	California	1	California	1	California
2	New York	2	Maquiladoras	2	Maquiladoras
3	Ohio	3	Texas	3	Texas
4	Pennsylvania	4	Ohio	4	Ohio
5	Texas	5	Illinois	5	Michigan
10	Maquiladoras				

Source: Bureau of Labor Statistics, Institute Nacional de Estadistica, Geographica e Informatica.

compete more effectively with foreign companies. This has permitted output to grow while both unemployment and inflation fall.

The economy has been undergoing a number of structural changes in recent years, most, but not all of which have fostered lower inflation. One recent structural shift, the transition from a peace-time to a war-time economy that has occurred following the terrorist attacks on September 11, is working in the opposite direction. War is notorious as a period when demand outstrips supply, when governments run large deficits often financed by printing money and taxing through increased inflation, and where borders tend to be more closed, thereby restricting the input of foreign goods and labor.

Demographics and Immigration

Let's turn now to the subject of demographics, with special emphasis on immigration. Demographers are fond of the saying: "Demographics is destiny." The

United States is a nation of immigrants; as such, the United States redefines its demographic destiny whenever it changes its immigration laws, their enforcement, or lack thereof. Over the last two decades, there has been a sharp increase in legal (i.e., measured) immigration, not to mention a sizeable increase in unmeasured immigration because of benign neglect in enforcement. Consequently, I have often said that the term "immigration statistics" is an oxymoron.

Over the 1990s decade, and to a lesser extent during the 1980s as well, structural demographic forces acted to lower the NAIRU and the inflationary pressures that otherwise might have prevailed. The entry of the baby boom generation into the labor force during the 1970s raised the NAIRU by about 0.75 percentage points, but the subsequent aging and increased experience of the boomers over the 1980s and 1990s lowered the NAIRU by a roughly equivalent amount. Future reductions in the NAIRU from a changing composition of the labor force are expected to be moderate.

A substantial rise in incarceration rates has occurred over the last decade. The removal of this high unemployment group from the labor force has reduced the NAIRU by about 0.2 percentage points. The combined effect of age composition shifts together with better law enforcement and prosecution, has contributed to a decline in the NAIRU of about one full percentage point, thereby reducing the inflationary pressures that might otherwise have been expected as the unemployment rate fell by more than three percentage points during the 1990s expansion. The equilibrium unemployment rate has also been lowered by improvements in job matching efficiency, for example, the rise of private-sector-employment intermediaries, temporary-help firms that deliver just-in-time labor, and such private-sector Internet sites as Monster.com. The improved technology that matches employers with jobseekers has lowered the equilibrium unemployment rate by as much as 0.4 percentage points.

Immigration. Immigration increases the supply of labor and reduces shortages of workers in a wide range of skill groups. The 1990s was a period of surging immigration unmatched since the first decade of the twentieth century. During the 1990s, 43 percent of US population growth came from immigration; during the 1980s, 32 percent of population growth was from immigration. Legal immigrants appear to have supplied roughly 40 percent of the growth of the US labor force in the mid-1990s.

How has immigration affected inflation? To the extent that immigration has restrained wage growth while allowing output to increase to keep up with demand, inflation is probably lower than it would have been with the slow-growth labor force we would have had without immigration. Immigrants filled about five million new jobs in the 1990s. Without immigration, the unemployment rate would have been well below four percent, possibly reaching three percent or lower. The eased pressure on wages certainly was a factor in restraining inflation—and still is.

When businesses have been unable to bring workers to the job location, they have sometimes managed to take the job to the workers. Such "virtual immigration" is made possible by the Internet and other low-cost communications technologies that have allowed information-processing jobs—such as writing software or processing credit card and hospital bills—to be shipped to other countries, including Ireland, India, and Mexico. This has increased the pool of available labor beyond the conventional measures of the domestic labor force.

Will demographic forces in combination with immigration continue to maintain downward pressure on inflationary forces in the future? In the environment post September 11, 2001, the answer is not encouraging. The barriers to immigration are on the rise, thereby reducing labor force growth.

The Role of Economic Policy

I turn next to the role of economic policy on reducing inflation. Monetary policy became more focused on reducing inflation, at least since Paul Volcker became Fed Chairman in 1979 followed by Alan Greenspan in 1987.

The Fed has been a catalyst in fostering an environment where the concept of price stability became an underlying reality, and where private sector behavior changed to fit that emerging reality. This is no small accomplishment. This position is supported by the academic literature on this subject.

John Taylor (1998) argues that the change in the Fed's post-1979 reaction function to rising inflation "has been the key to keeping the real economy stable." In particular, he finds that the Fed roughly doubled its sensitivity to rising inflation between the 1965–1979 period and the period from 1980–1998. Since October 1979, the Fed generally raises the federal funds rate by 150 basis points for every percentage point increase in inflation, thereby raising the short-term real interest rate. Taylor dismisses or relegates to minor importance a range of other factors that are believed by others to have contributed to the increased stability of the US economy over the last two decades. These include discretionary fiscal policy, a more service-oriented economy, improved inventory control, and fewer and/or smaller shocks. Taylor believes that, "Focusing on keeping the inflation rate low and stable and responding aggressively with interest rates is the most important thing the Fed can do to keep the economy stable."

More recent work by Christina and David Romer underscores and reinforces Taylor's findings. A key empirical finding of Romer and Romer (2002) is "that had Paul Volcker or Alan Greenspan been confronted with the inflation of the 1960s and 1970s, they would have set the real federal funds rate nearly three percentage points higher than did Arthur Burns and G. William Miller."

The Volcker FOMC believed that aggregate demand policy not only could, but must, be used to combat inflation. They subsequently raised the real federal funds rate by nearly seven percentage points from 1979:Q3 to 1981:Q3, and it remained high through the 1980s. Equally important was the support the Fed received from fiscal policymakers. This point is made eloquently by Robert Samuelson (2002): "If the great boom of the 1990s had godfathers, they were Paul Volcker... and Ronald Reagan: Volcker for controlling inflation and Reagan for supporting him." Romer and Romer credit the Greenspan Fed for not raising rates despite very low rates of unemployment in the late 1990s. Because monetary policy in the 1990s maintained the same strong aversion to inflation that characterized the 1980s, the Greenspan Fed deserves at least some of the credit for the 1990s disinflation experience of falling inflation accompanied by strong economic growth, together with very low unemployment rates.

A New Economy?

To a Shumpeterian economist like myself, who believes in the renewal powers of creative destruction, the idea of a "new economy" seems like a truism. As noted by Robert Samuelson (2002), "the economy is constantly recreating itself. It is always 'new,' if 'new' means different from the past." Yet, around 1997 I was talking publicly about the economy being "new and different," not just different.

Let me add some context. As I've mentioned, I have spent a long career with the Fed and the central theme of my career has been understanding inflation, taming inflation, and helping to bring in and maintain an era of price stability before I retire. Something happened during the 1990s to inflation that was not just different from the prior 25 years; it was markedly different. A confluence of inflation-depressing forces, each with a half life of five-to-seven years, and perhaps longer, converged on the US economy in the 1990s. Inflation subsided when our economic models said it should have risen. To a central banker whose focus had been on inflation the prior 25 years, this was a sufficiently different and potentially long-lived experience to be labeled "new." This had the potential to accelerate my retirement, not because my investments were doing well, but because my inflation goals were being met ahead of schedule and my leadership legacy could be in place faster than anticipated.

When I studied economics in school, I read about cost-push inflation. In my speeches now, I routinely use the term "cost-compression disinflation." I studied about a wage-price spiral and prices and wages moving in only one direction, up, never down. We have two-way price and wage flexibility today: in my lifetime this is "new."

Earlier, I mentioned that I'm a micro guy in a macro world. Consequently, my views on the new economy focus on the environment in which microeconomic decisions are made. To me, the essence of the "new economy" is that when businesses are confronted with rising costs, their impulse is to boost productivity, not prices. Unlike the 1960s and 1970s, there is an economic imperative to boost productivity: raising prices is a last resort. This is fundamentally different. The competitive climate makes raising prices considerably more difficult today than it was three decades ago. These conditions won't last forever, and I have already alluded to ways in which the economic climate is changing since September 11, 2001.

I am not alone in my beliefs about a new economy and the prospect that it will be with us for several years. Former CEA Chairman Martin Baily (2002), who has addressed NABE several times in recent years, defines the driving force behind the new, or different, economy of the 1990s much as I have done. His findings suggest that the main driver of productivity acceleration was increased competitive pressures that forced improvements in business operations. He adds that the 1990s economy "experienced heightened competition in an increasingly deregulated economy with strong international competition." Firms across a wide range of industries sought out new technologies, not because they wanted to, but to repeat a term I used earlier, because they had no other choice. Baily projects that these competitive driving forces will be around for several years.

While Martin Baily and I put a changed competitive environment at the center of the "new economy," DeLong and Summers (2001) ascribe the essence of the new economy to the "four-billion-fold increase in the world's raw automated computational power in 40 years, an average annual growth rate of 56 percent per year." Given that Moore's Law is expected to hold up for at least a decade, DeLong and Summers view the "new economy" as having a sustainable life. They conclude "that the principal effects of the 'new economy' are more likely to be 'microeconomic' than 'macroeconomic'."

Policy Implications

Had it not been for the events of September 11, 2001, which ended NABE's 2001 annual meeting and altered the course of US economic history, I would have forecast that the US economy would have entered a period of sustainable price stability somewhere in the 2004–2007 time frame. As shown in Table 29.2, the disinflationary forces that characterized the 1990s—in particular, an aggressive and generally tight monetary policy operating against a backdrop of microeconomic forces that suppressed the economy's old inflationary tendencies of the 1970s and '80s—were reinforcing one another and bringing the rate of inflation toward the low one percent range, a level that many economists would agree was the operational equivalent of price stability.

While it is possible that the disinflation momentum could have overshot the price stability region and produced an era of deflation, it is the job of monetary policy to make sure this does not happen. Throughout the 1980s and 1990s, the Fed's job has been to cap the rate of inflation from above. Put differently, the Fed attempted to and succeeded in putting an ever-lower ceiling on the inflation rate. As the economy approaches price stability, the Fed's job has shifted

Table 29.2 Today's inflation tug of war

1990s Disinflation Forces	*Post September 11 Inflation Forces*
• Monetary policy	• Homeland security
• Microeconomic forces	• Federal deficits
• Globalization	• War on two fronts
• NAFTA	• Nationalization (e.g., airport security)
• Deregulation	• Reregulation (Patriot Act)
• Immigration	• Protectionism (e.g., steel, lumber, agriculture)
• Technology	• Immigration barriers
• Competition	
• Productivity	

to one of maintaining a floor under the rate of inflation, probably at some very low, but positive inflation rate, on average. Staving off, or fighting deflation, requires a very different monetary policy from the inflation fighting policies of the 1979–2002 era. The Fed's leadership understands this, but, in reality, has no experience with deflation—something not experienced in the United States, in any serious way, since the 1930s. (See Bernanke, 2002)

As alluded to throughout this chapter and as shown in Table 29.2, several inflationary forces have impinged upon the US economy, especially since September 11, 2001. These inflationary forces will likely postpone the start of an era of price stability and render moot the discussion of deflation in the years immediately ahead.

Summing Up

In my discussion of inflation, and what I have learned about it in more than 40 years of studying the topic, I have said nothing that is "new" to this audience. I have merely elaborated upon the footnotes and qualifying assumptions that appear in most standard economic textbooks. The concept of a natural rate of unemployment assumes that economic and political institutions remain constant. From quarter-to-quarter and year-to-year, this is a reasonably valid assumption. Over a time frame that spans decades, it is not. Monetarist ideas were clearly appropriate when the media of exchange were monopolized by currency issued by central banks and deposits issued by a highly regulated commercial banking system. In 2002, my children can sit in an outdoor café in Paris and rearrange their portfolio of bank deposits, stocks and bonds on their Palm Pilot or Blackberry. Dick Tracy's wrist radio, once the subject of science fiction, has been superceded by telecommunications equipment available to the masses. Is money these days a stock or a flow, and how do you define it and measure it, let alone control it?

The one constant over the last 40 years is that most prices in our economy are determined by market forces that rule over the interactions between businesses, households and governments. Buyers have alternative sources: competition, entrepreneurship, and innovation have not gone away If anything, they are at least as important as in the past, maybe more important.

I have argued that changes in inflation over time are affected by a wide range of forces, only a few of which have made their way into macroeconomic models. The purpose of models is to simplify the world, not to add complexity. Macro models are further constrained by the availability of a limited number of time series and by the fact that data are collected in discrete units of time such as weeks, months, quarters, and years. Supposedly one-off events like NAFTA or deregulation of airlines can be represented by dummy variables, but not very well, especially when many of these events come in rapid-fire sequence and have mutually-reinforcing impacts on the inflation process, all of which is distributed and propagated over a decade or more.

My conclusion is very simple. Economists have a pretty good understanding about the role of money growth in causing inflation. Over my career, central banks have not only gained this understanding, but they now practice it everyday. Better monetary policy has contributed to overall economic stability.

While the economics profession and central bankers understand that part of inflation that comes from the production of too much money, we don't fully appreciate that part of inflation that derives from the dozens—indeed hundreds—of one-off things like Monster.com or China's accession to the WTO that occur with varying frequencies and that impact with long, mostly unknown, overlapping and variable lags.

To paraphrase Brad DeLong (2000), if economists are to be of any use, they need to come up with a better—and more sophisticated—approach to understanding why inflation rises and falls. Much work remains to be done.

Note

Originally published in *Business Economics*, Vol. 38, No. 1 (January 2003), pp. 7–16.

References

Baily, Martin Neil. 2002. "The New Economy: Post Mortem or Second Wind?" Paper prepared for the Distinguished Lecture on Economics in Government, ASSA Meeting, Atlanta. January.

Bernanke, Ben S. 2002. "Deflation: Making Sure 'It' Doesn't Happen Here." Speech before the National Economists Club, Washington, DC November 21.

DeLong, J. Bradford. 2000. "What Happened to the Phillips Curve?" *New York Times*. March 9.

DeLong, J. Bradford, and Lawrence H. Summers. 2001. "The 'New Economy': Background, Historical Perspective, Questions, and Speculations." Federal Reserve Bank Kansas City Symposium: *Economic Policy for the Information Economy.*

Duca, John. 1998. "How Increased Product Market Competition May be Reshaping America's Labor Markets." Federal Reserve Bank *Dallas Economic Review*. 4th Quarter.

Duca, John and David D. Van Hoose. 2000. "Has Greater Competition Restrained U.S. Inflation?" *Southern Economic Journal*. January.

Fisher, Jonas D. M., Chin Te Liu, and Ruilin Zhou. 2002. "When Can We Forecast Inflation?" Federal Reserve Bank. *Chicago Economic Perspectives*. First Quarter.

Friedman, Milton. 1968. "The Role of Monetary Policy." *The American Economic Review*. Vol. LVIII(1). March.

Romer, Christina D. and David H. Romer. 2002. "The Evolution of Economic Understanding And Postwar Stabilization Policy." Prepared for Federal Reserve Bank of Kansas City Symposium: *Rethinking Stabilization Policy*. August.

Samuelson, Robert J. 2002. "The Age of Inflation." *The New Republic*. May 13.

Taylor, John B. 1998. "Monetary Policy and the Long Boom." Federal Reserve Bank. *St. Louis Review*. November/December.

CHAPTER 30

2004

MANAGING EXCHANGE RATES: ACHIEVEMENT OF GLOBAL RE-BALANCING OR EVIDENCE OF GLOBAL CO-DEPENDENCY?

Catherine L. Mann, Peterson Institute for International Economics

How are exchange rates related to the US external accounts and macro policy management? There is no doubt that further depreciation of the dollar will be part of the package of policy moves and economic responses that will yield "global re-balancing."[1] This term implies the complementary narrowing of two imbalances around the world. One is the yawning US current account deficit, and the other is the widely geographically disbursed but nevertheless persistent dependence of the rest of the world on net exports to the United States. Underlying these external imbalances are internal imbalances in both countries and regions with respect to savings and investment and to domestic demand and production.

Is the dollar depreciation to date moving the imbalances along a path of adjustment? Moreover, can any realistic magnitude of change in the value of the dollar do the job of global re-balancing? Relying on exchange rate adjustment is likely to be more difficult than it appears, for evidence suggests a global co-dependency of policy choices and structural characteristics in both the United States and other countries. US structural characteristics and policy choices are revealed in domestic and external behaviors that stand in the way of the dollar 'doing its job' to rectify the US side of the global imbalance. By the same token, policymakers in the rest of the global system, for their own structural reasons, are actively inhibiting the dollar's move toward broad-based depreciation. Taken individually, the US path and the rest-of-world path are not sustainable, but together they may well be sustained for an extended period—thus the term global co-dependency.

Hence, in the near-to-medium time period, despite much theory and empirical suggestion that the dollar *should* depreciate a lot, it likely will not; and global imbalances are likely to widen further. Global co-dependency, which keeps the dollar from steady and significant depreciation and keeps the current configuration of global imbalances in place, could have a very long duration. But, with cumulative imbalances weighing ever more heavily on the individual countries and the global system, it will become increasingly difficult to untangle the global co-dependency without precipitating a crisis in currencies, international exchange of goods and financial assets, and domestic and global growth.

The Dollar and Global Re-Balancing in Historical Perspective

The dollar has played a role in global re-balancing in the past. Figure 30.1 shows the historical record of the current account, trade balance, and the Federal Reserve's broad real effective exchange rate (REER) index for the dollar. The current account is driven predominantly by trade in goods and services, which in turn is largely determined by US and foreign income growth, along with relative prices, for which the exchange value of the dollar is a good proxy.

With respect to growth differentials, movements in the US trade balance are in part influenced by the degree to which the US and foreign economic cycles are out of sync (Ch. 8 in Mann, 1999 and Mann, 2002). In the early 1980s, and again in the early 1990s, the US economy slipped into recession and imports slowed. During those cycles, world growth remained relatively robust, so US exports rose. The trade deficit narrowed from both sides. But, during the late 1990s as well as the last few years, anemic growth in Japan, Europe, and other markets around the world has dampened demand for US exports. US growth has rebounded far more quickly than expected. Consequently, both the current account and trade deficit have widened into unprecedented territory, both in dollar terms and as a share of GDP. (The current account was at $580 billion and 5.1 percent of GDP by first quarter 2004, annual rate).

Until recently, not only income differentials, but also relative prices (as proxied by the real exchange value of the dollar) have tended to augment the US trade and current account deficits. In fact, consistent with models where asset-prices overshoot, the movement of the dollar has often tended to exacerbate growth differentials and further widen the external deficits. In the early 1980s, the considerable appreciation of the dollar bolstered import growth and held back export growth. Similarly, in the late 1990s and through 2001, the exchange value of the dollar continued to appreciate even after growth differentials in favor of the United States waned. In contrast, when both dollar and growth differentials worked together, the current account and trade deficit narrowed (late 1980s to mid 1990s). During this period, Figure 30.1 shows that the Federal Reserve real broad exchange rate index exhibited relative stability at about index value 85, an observation to which we will return.

Now that the current account is beyond all historical precedent, and in light of other findings that determine that the supply of US assets being offered into the global financial markets is large with respect to the growth in home-bias adjusted

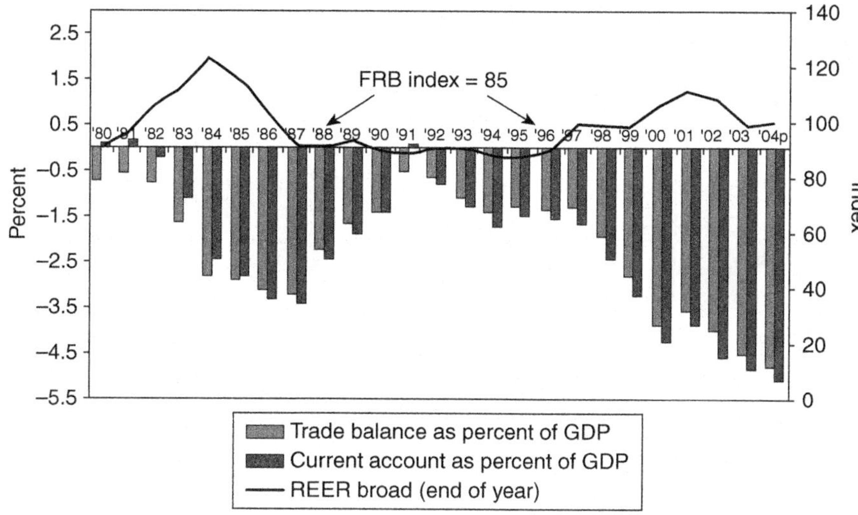

Figure 30.1 The US current account, trade balance, and exchange rate 1980–2004.
Source: Bureau of Economic Analysis. US Transactions Data: Federal Reserve.

wealth, the dollar should be under significant depreciation pressure (Mann, 2003a). However, structural factors and current policy stances in the United States and the rest of the world will influence the manner in which global imbalances will, or will not, be re-balanced.

Global Imbalance: The US Side

For the international trade economist, there is an empirical regularity in the data on how income affects US trade: US imports grow relatively faster when US income grows as compared to how much US exports grow when foreign income grows. This empirical finding (the so-called Houthakker-Magee asymmetry) goes back to the early post-war period and has remained a fixture of US trade data since then. When looking at disaggregated data, the Houthakker-Magee effect is particularly serious. Moreover, disaggregation highlights key regularities both in domestic and international data.

With respect to the domestic data, Figure 30.2 shows a decomposition of the national income and product accounts into the savings-investment balance. A downward trend in net household savings is clear. During the 1990s, the narrowing of the fiscal budget, ultimately into surplus, helped finance the increase in investment of that period. The complex relationship between the fiscal position and other economic factors further supported consumption (and diminished household saving) through higher wealth—both stock market and housing assets. In the last several years, with a changed economic environment, household savings has rebounded a bit; but the fiscal position has returned to deficit, in part due to significant tax cuts to individuals. Overall, private consumption has been robust through both fiscal

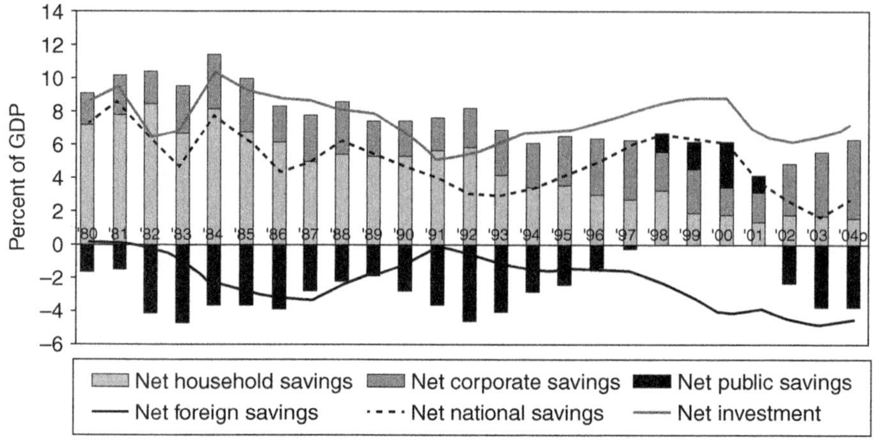

Figure 30.2 US investment and savings by sector, 1980–2003.

Source: Bureau of Economic Analysis. NIPA Table 1.1.5.

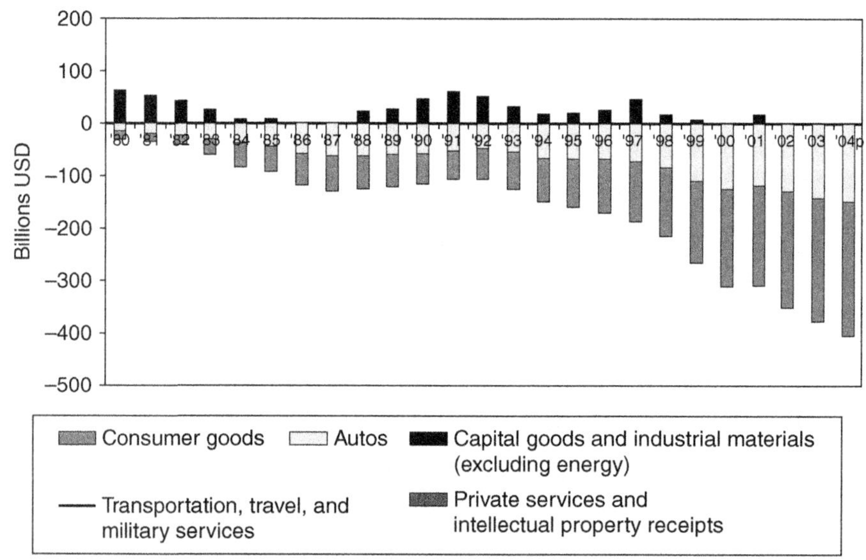

Figure 30.3 US trade balance: major components.

Source: Bureau of Economic Analysis. US International Transactions Data.

surplus and fiscal deficit, and net household savings continued to trend downward throughout the period.

The pattern of robust and structurally supported consumption shows up in a disaggregated presentation of the trade balance (Figure 30.3). Examining the trade deficit using the Bureau of Economic Analysis 'end-use' categories reveals that the biggest component of the overall trade deficit is in consumer goods and autos—reflecting the downward trend of household savings. Indeed, nearly the whole of the deficit can be accounted for by these two categories! Only outright recession (in 1991 and 2001) has stemmed the widening in these components of net trade. Moreover, services, such as transportation tied to the US import boom (and, more recently, government service outlays related to terrorism and the war in Iraq), have added to the trade and current account deficits. While it may be the case that the United States has a comparative disadvantage in consumer goods and autos, the trend widening of these components of the trade deficit and their relationship to trend net household savings point to the difficulty of turning the trade deficit and current account around, particularly in light of current fiscal policies that favor additional tax cuts to individuals.

On the other hand, US services continue to reveal international competitiveness. The balance of trade in "other private services" such as education, finance, and business and professional services is persistently positive and has continued to rise despite slow growth abroad. This is particularly impressive given that the asymmetry in trade with respect to growth in income, discussed above in the context of trade overall, is nearly absent or is reversed for this category of trade in services, so that slow growth abroad disproportionately tends to hold down exports of these services (Mann, 2004). (It is unclear whether offshore outsourcing, as enabled by information technology, will alter these trends and the trade balance in other private services. But that phenomenon is too recent to be addressed by this analysis.[2])

An important puzzle is the balance of trade in capital goods and industrial supplies and materials, excluding oil. Up until 1997, this balance cycled through larger and smaller surpluses depending in large part on the US and global business cycles. Since about that time, however, the trade balance in this category fell from a surplus of about $50 billion to about zero. Moreover, both exports and imports abruptly changed their time-series properties around 1997, when growth slowed, then speeded up to a peak in 2000, and then dropped again with no recovery to date. Is this evidence of the appreciation of the dollar and slow growth abroad weighing more heavily on this category of goods than on US trade overall, or of a changing international supply chain for production of capital goods. Or, is it related to lasting fallout from the Asian financial crises?

In sum, the US structural tendency toward consumption and a savings-investment imbalance is reflected in a trending downward in household savings and a structural predilection toward imported consumer goods and autos. At this point in time, net national savings and net household savings rates are near or at historical lows, and consumer-good and auto net trade are in unprecedented deficit. This implies tough initial conditions of structural imbalance in which global rebalancing will have to take place.

Global Imbalance: The Rest of the World

Structural imbalances of two types also exist in the rest of the world (as measured by the global current accounts of other countries), and vis-à-vis the United States (as measured by bilateral trade with the United States). Increasingly, these rest-of-world imbalances fit as a mirror image to the US external deficit. That these imbalances are widespread across international trading partners should not imply that they are any less difficult to re-balance. On the contrary, the combination of these rest-of-world imbalances may point to structural difficulties that will impair the adjustment in the dollar necessary to ameliorate the situation.

Around the world, certain regions and countries tend toward persistent current account surplus—Japan for example. (See Figures 30.4a and 30.4b.) On balance, though, over all countries and the whole of the 25-year period being considered in this exercise, there is no dramatic trend toward rest-of-world imbalance between savings and investment when trade among all countries is considered. Looking just since 1990, a modest trend toward current account surplus is observed for some countries (China and Canada, for example). For Asia/Pacific, the impact of the financial crises continues to reverberate in the data, with increasing surpluses registered as a share of GDP for these countries. For these countries, their experiment with growth led by domestic demand during the 1990s (when they ran balanced global current accounts) ended in a financial distress and a return to the more familiar export-led growth strategy.

When countries' global current accounts are examined more narrowly through the lens of bilateral trade with the United States, the mirror to the US trade deficit is dramatic—over all countries and regions there are wide trade surpluses vis-à-vis the US. (Figure 30.5). The widening US trade imbalance is not just about imports from China or Japan, but is broad-based across all trading partners. Indeed, the worsening of the bilateral US trade balance vis-à-vis Europe is about the same dollar magnitude as with China. Thus, any re-balancing of the US trade deficit implies a narrowing, to a greater or lesser degree, in these bilateral surpluses, and hence the

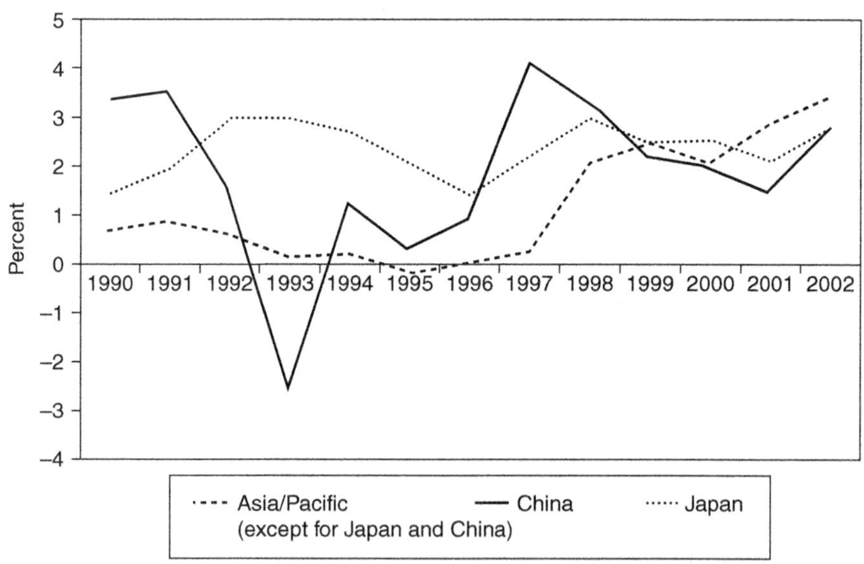

Figure 30.4a Current account balances of rest of the world (Percent of GDP).

Source: The World Bank, World Development Indicators, June 2004.

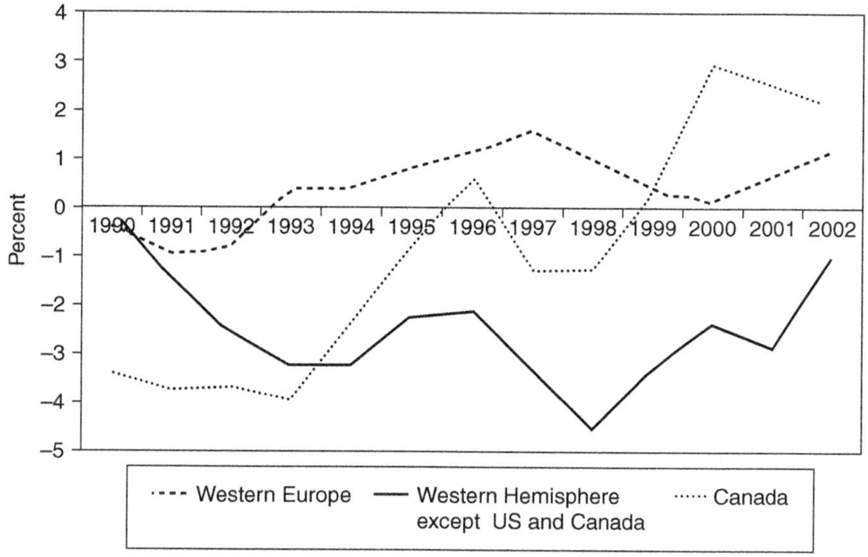

Figure 30.4b Current account balances of rest of the world (Percent of GDP).
Source: The World Bank, World Development Indicators, June 2004.

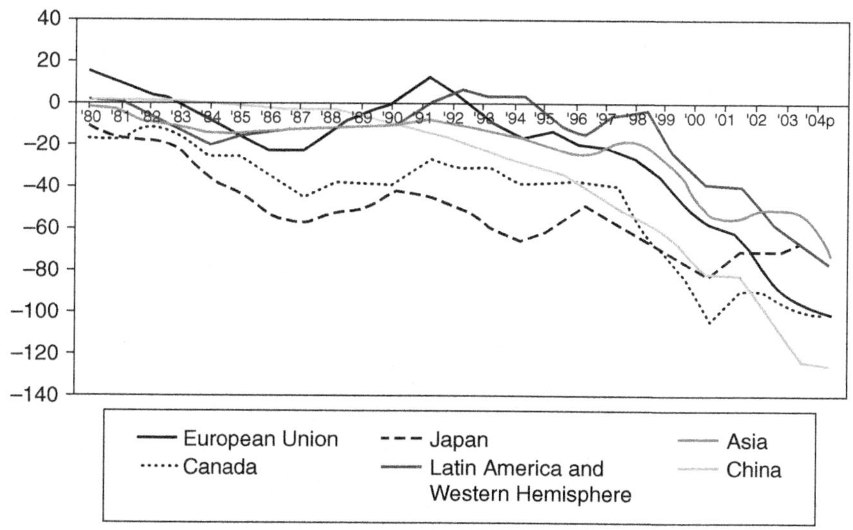

Figure 30.5 US goods balances with selected trading partners (Billions of USD).
Source: Bureau of Economic Analysis. US International Transactions Accounts Data.

behavior of many countries. When juxtaposed against these economies' current account positions with the whole world, what does this rebalancing vis-à-vis the United States imply for countries that are persistently in current account surplus with the rest of the world (Asia) versus for those countries that are more balanced on a global current account basis (Europe, Western Hemisphere)?

In sum, when the global current account data are combined with the bilateral US trade data, a true rest-of-world global imbalance appears. To an inordinate degree, all countries and regions in the rest of the world have depended on net exports to the United States—both directly and indirectly—for economic growth. Domestic demand as a source of growth has lagged. This is the global imbalance that is both widespread and will be hard to re-balance. But, it is in Asia that the combined domestic imbalances of aggregate demand relative to production and external imbalance in dependence on net exports to the United States are particularly apparent.

Global Co-dependency

It is a reality that countries have a vested interest in a large and chronic US trade deficit. Their dependency on US demand as a source of growth matches the US dependency on foreign savings to finance domestic investment. What is the evidence, and how does it impact the ability of the dollar to act as the re-balancing mechanism?

Foreign official purchases of US financial assets during times of dollar depreciation are not new (Figure 30.6). Important foreign official purchases appear in 1986–1989 and again in the mid 1990s, both periods of time when the dollar was experiencing depreciation pressures. However, official purchases have accelerated in recent quarters and are unprecedented both in terms of dollar value and as a share of total financial inflow. ($500 billion and 28 percent of foreign purchases of US assets as of first quarter 2004, annualized).

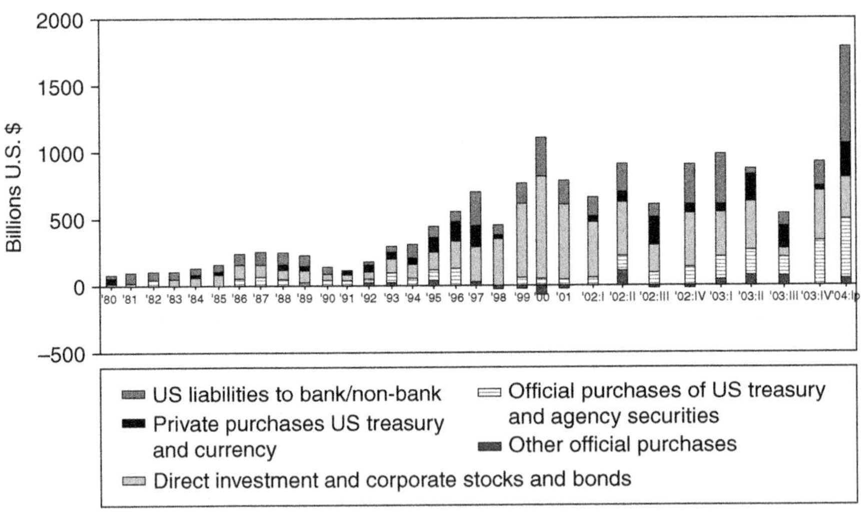

Figure 30.6 Foreign purchases of US assets by asset type and purchaser.

Source: Bureau of Economic Analysis. US International Transactions Accounts Data.

Foreign official purchases are reflected in different rates of appreciation of individual currencies against the dollar. This is shown for US major trading partners in Figure 30.7. Currencies that are traded through liquid private markets—such as the Canadian dollar, British pound, Swiss franc (not shown), Australian dollar, and euro—have appreciated some 15 percent (Canada) to 27 percent (euro) against the dollar since the beginning of 2002 (when the dollar started a generalized depreciation).[3] For currencies that are not traded widely or are in illiquid markets, official intervention can play an important role in affecting currency price. Prominent examples are the Korean won, Indian rupee, Thai baht (not shown), the Taiwan dollar, and the Chinese renminbi (not shown because its value has been held constant relative to the dollar for almost two years). For these currencies, the appreciation has been relatively little or nil. Asian policymakers are amassing large stocks of US official assets and working hard to inhibit dollar depreciation and global re-balancing. Why, and at what potential future cost?

With the financial crises still fresh, some are buying assets to give themselves a larger stock of dollar ammunition should private markets turn against them again. At the same time, for some of these countries, the financial crises proved the "folly" of a domestic-led growth strategy and renewed their preference for the more dependable, export-oriented growth strategy. With this renewed attention to net exports (particularly to the United States), competition with China for market share is intense. Thus, purchases of US assets are key to keeping their currencies and products competitively priced for the US consumer.

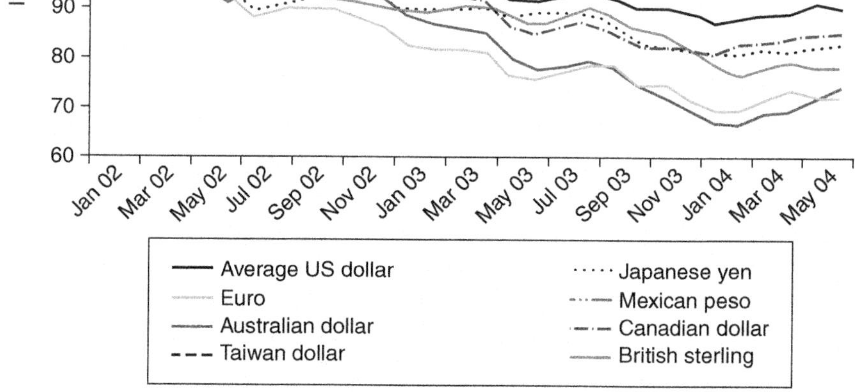

Figure 30.7 Nominal average dollar and bilateral rates January 2002 =100 selected major trading partners.

Source: Bureau of Economic Analysis. US International Transactions Accounts Data.

However, this strategy constitutes a bargain with the devil in the sense that when their own currencies eventually do appreciate, not only will their exports fall, but so, too, will the value of the US assets in their portfolios. Thus, these policymakers are trading off the positive certain benefits of export-led growth today against the negative certain capital loss on their holdings of US assets tomorrow. With a high enough rate of time preference, the cost of that negative certainty is small in today's terms, making sense of their side of the global co-dependency.

It is not just official purchase of US assets, however, that has moved the dollar. Even amongst the market-traded currencies, the tendency toward dollar depreciation has attenuated in recent months. For private traders, it is somewhat more of a puzzle as to why they continue to purchase US assets. After all, it made sense to increase US holdings when the United States was clearly outperforming other markets during the latter half of the 1990s. But now? To some degree, the markets no doubt have overshot in terms of reallocating portfolios away from US assets toward assets of other markets. Going forward, it remains to be seen whether private markets' assessment of US relative to foreign rates of return will be actualized and what might happen when those expectations are dashed.

From the standpoint of the US side of the global codependency, the official purchases along with private market purchases have tended to hamper dollar depreciation at a time when it is increasingly important for US export growth. At the same time, low interest rates and the expansion of buying power coming from individual tax cuts in the United States keeps US import growth robust—particularly in consumer goods and autos. Hence the trade and current account deficits will continue to widen.

Is the accumulating negative net international investment position for the United States also a devil's bargain? The magnitude of internal and external debt will lead to a day of reckoning. But, a unique feature of US international borrowing—mostly in dollar denominated assets—is that a depreciation of the dollar in fact reduces the burden of debt. Thus, the certain future loss in purchasing power that comes with a dollar depreciation is offset to some degree by the certain future write-down in what the United States has to repay. There is some sense to the US side of the global co-dependency.

How long can this global co-dependency go on, and what are broader global ramifications of the US current account imbalance? Global co-dependency creates significant currency management issues for third parties. In particular, Europe, which has not leaned against dollar depreciation, has borne the brunt of currency adjustment so far. But Europe has also depended on the United States for its growth. The pressure of euro appreciation on firms and workers dependent on exports has been real, and offsetting macroeconomic stimulus by policy authorities there has been modest. The potential for Europe to grow more robustly and offer attractive returns to their investments (and thus validate the appreciation of the euro) may well be running out of steam. In Japan, although the official purchase of US assets has reached gargantuan levels, Japan appears to be shifting its dependence to someone else—China.

In sum, the US predilection to consume finds its mirror in the dependence of other countries on net exports to the United States, and in some to a predilection towards savings. In the near-to-medium term, despite much theory and empirical suggestion that the dollar *should* depreciate a lot, global co-dependency works to inhibit the process while at the same time increasing cumulative imbalances.

Global Rebalancing Via the Dollar?

Suppose the global co-dependency that has inhibited dollar depreciation breaks down. What might happen to the dollar and to the US current account and trade deficit? Figure 30.8 shows three scenarios.[4] Recall that the lowest sustained index value for the Federal Reserve REER is an index value of about 85 (to which the dollar has not yet returned). The assumptions that underlie this analysis are shown in Table 30.1.

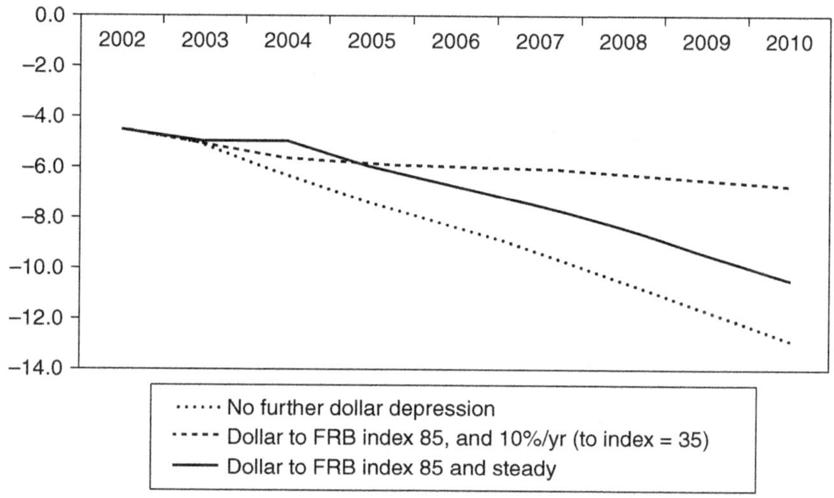

Figure 30.8 Scenarios for the US current account: current account/GDP (%).

Source: Bureau of Economic Analysis. US International Transactions Accounts Data.

Table 30.1 Assumptions for US current account scenarios

	2003	*2004*	*2005*	*2006*	*2007*	*2008*	*2009*	*2010*
US real GDP[a]	3.1	4.7	4.1	3.7	3.0	2.8	2.7	2.7
World GDP[b]	2.1	3.4	3.3	3.3	3.1	2.8	2.8	2.8
Interest rate	4.0	4.6	5.5	5.8	5.39	6.0	6.0	6.0

Export income elasticity of 1.0. Import income elasticity of 1.7.

[a]2003–2005 from April 2004 forecast; 2006–2010 from Dec. 9, 2003 long-term forecast.

[b]Multilateral trade-weighted real activity. 2003–2005 from April 2004 forecast, 2006–2010 from Dec. 9, 2003 long-term forecast.

Source: Macroeconomic Advisors LLC.

The first scenario is one where the dollar does not depreciate, resulting in a current account deficit of about 13 percent of GDP by 2010. It seems likely that the codependency will break down long before this.

The second scenario assumes that the dollar depreciates to index value 85 and stays there for a sustained period. Relatively little improvement in the current account results because the asymmetry in income elasticities are exacerbated by the initial conditions of the very large deficit. To narrow the current account, export growth (and implied foreign growth) would have to be dramatic, well outside the bounds of historical experience on a sustained basis, and import growth would have to fall to recession rates for this dollar to yield an narrower current account.

So, what dollar depreciation 'does the job' of narrowing the current account deficit? The third scenario shows that a steadily depreciating real dollar, at about ten percent per year, keeps the current account from widening as a share of GDP.[5] This experiment is wholly partial equilibrium, in that the feedback effect of such dollar depreciation on the growth of other countries is not accounted for.

These exercises serve to emphasize how large the global imbalances are, and how difficult re-balancing is. Perhaps not surprisingly, when the path to adjustment is so difficult, global co-dependency is just the easier course to take. Going forward, how will the global imbalances be re-balanced? Only a combination of structural change in the United States and abroad along with dollar depreciation appears to re-balance the global economies. Whether these changes can be accomplished before a global economic crisis forces them is an open question.

Acknowledgment

Many thanks to Katharina Plück for preparing the charts that accompanied the original presentation and this text.

Notes

Originally published in *Business Economics*, Vol. 39, No. 3 (July 2004), pp. 20–29.

1. Global rebalancing is a phrase first used by Steven Roach, chief economist of Morgan Stanley.
2. For a discussion of related issues, see Mann, 2003.
3. For a discussion of reasons why the dollar started to depreciate at the beginning of 2002, see Mann (2003a).
4. The simple spread-sheet model on which this analysis is based is outlined in Mann (1999, Chapter 10).
5. Not surprisingly, this is about the same story that Jeffrey Frankel (1985) told before the dollar started to depreciate and Paul Krugman and Richard Baldwin (1987) told after the dollar depreciated. The big difference between then and now? A ten percent depreciation of the dollar stabilizes the current account deficit at six percent of GDP instead of two percent!

References

Frankel, Jeffrey. 1985. "The Dazzling Dollar." *Brookings Papers on Economic Activity .1* 199–217.

Krugman, Paul and Richard Baldwin. 1987. "The Persistence of the U.S. Trade Deficit." *Brookings Papers on Economic Activity 1.* 1–43.

Mann, Catherine L. 2003. "Globalization of IT Services and White-Collar Jobs: The Next Wave of Productivity Growth." IIE Policy Brief No. PB03–11. Institute for International Economics. December.

———2003a. "How Long the Strong Dollar?" In John Williamson and C. Fred Bergsten, eds., *Dollar Overvaluation and the World Economy.* Institute for International Economics. 2003.

———1999. *Is the U.S. Trade Deficit Sustainable?* Institute for International Economics.

———2002. "Perspectives on U.S. Current Account Deficit and Sustainability." *Journal of Economic Perspectives 16* (Summer): 131–152.

———2004. "The US Current Account, New Economy Services, and Implications for Sustainability." *Review of International Economics 1.*

PART V

2005–2015

CHAPTER 31

2007

THE ADAM SMITH ADDRESS

THE EXPLANATORY POWER OF MONETARY POLICY RULES

John B. Taylor, Stanford University

It is an honor to be here today to receive the Adam Smith Award, and it is a pleasure to give the Adam Smith Lecture. Everything I have read about Adam Smith tells me that he was passionate about his research and that his passion spilled over into his lectures. Many years ago, Woodrow Wilson wrote about Smith's lecture style in his essay, *The Old Master.* As then Professor Wilson put it, "[Smith] constantly refreshed and rewarded his hearers...by bringing them to those clear streams of practical wisdom and happy illustration which everywhere irrigate his expositions." You may have heard that Adam Smith would visit my introductory economics lectures at Stanford from time to time, interrupting me and speaking enthusiastically from the heavens. Well, it wasn't really Adam Smith. It was my own recording of his voice piped through the lecture hall PA system. "Professor Taylor, Professor Taylor" the voice would say in an exasperated tone. "You told your students about economies of scale, and you didn't even mention my famous story of the pin factory. Well let me tell them about it." And then the students would listen to him reading out loud his famous, clear, practical story from the *Wealth of Nations.*

In this lecture I would like to discuss a long-time—40 years actually—research interest of mine: monetary policy rules. And I hope you will excuse me if I have trouble containing my own passion for this subject. I want to take the opportunity to step back and look at how a vast amount of recent theoretical and practical work on monetary policy rules by economists in academia, government, and business has influenced the broader "scientific" landscape of monetary and financial economics. Several years ago, the *Wall Street Journal* published a story by David Wessel on monetary policy rules. To be specific, it was about what they called the Taylor rule. It was headlined, "Could One Little Rule Explain All of Economics?" Today I will argue that, while monetary policy rules cannot, of course, explain all of economics, they can explain a great deal.

Origin and Use of Monetary Policy Rules

What is a monetary policy rule? At its most basic level, it is a contingency plan that lays out how monetary policy decisions are, or should be, made. Let me start with the example of the Taylor rule. It says that the short-term interest rate equals one-and-a-half times the inflation rate plus one-half times the real GDP utilization rate plus one. So, in 1989, for example, when the federal funds rate was about ten percent in the United States you could say that the ten percent was equal to 1.5 times the inflation rate of five percent (or 7.5) plus .5 times the GDP gap of about three percent (or 1.5, which takes you to nine) plus one, which gives you ten. Now, this is a very specific rule, and it can be written down mathematically as shown in equation 31.1. It can also be expressed by equation 31.2, which is the way the rule was written when first presented in 1992.

$$r = 1.5p + 0.5y + 1, \text{ or} \tag{31.1}$$

$$r = p + 0.5y + 0.5(p - 2) + 2, \tag{31.2}$$

where r is the federal funds rate, p is the inflation rate, y is the real GDP gap.

Of course, I did not name it the Taylor rule. Others did that later. Originally, the rule was meant to be normative: a recommendation of what the Fed should do. It was derived from monetary theory, or more precisely from optimization exercises using new dynamic stochastic monetary models with rational expectations and price rigidities. Like most rules or laws in economics, it is not as precise as most physical laws, though that does not mean it is less useful. It was certainly not meant to be used mechanically, though it now appears that monetary policy might operate even better if it stayed closer to the rule. Figure 31.1 shows how the inflation rate and GDP fed into the policy rule using the same illustrations and data I used in 1992. They described actual monetary policy very well during the brief 1987–1991 period, but that in itself was not as surprising as what came later.

Now, there are many other monetary policy rules. Milton Friedman's constant growth rate rule said to hold money growth constant and let the interest rate go where it might. But the kind of rule I am discussing here and which has become so ubiquitous in recent years has the interest rate on the left hand side, and that is a big difference. There are also other monetary policy rules for setting the interest rate. Some look at forecasts of inflation and real GDP rather than their current values. Others gradually adjust the federal funds rate. Still others react to the price level rather than to the inflation rate. But they are all very similar in that they describe the settings for the interest rate.

There has been a great debate over the years about the use of monetary policy rules; they were not always so pervasive, and there was a great deal of

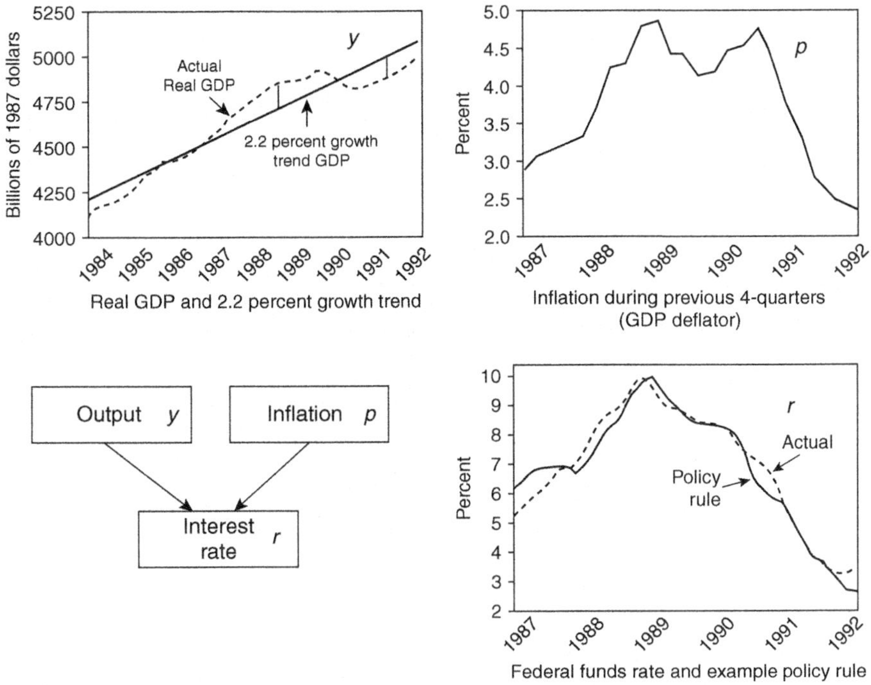

Figure 31.1 Taylor rule: Reproduction of original 1992 diagrams.

resistance to them at central banks. When I was in graduate school in the early 1970s, the textbook in monetary theory was Don Patinkin's *Money, Interest, and Prices*. If you flip through that book you will not find any references to monetary policy rules, except token mention of the Friedman rule. Certainly there were no references to interest rate rules. In contrast, consider the modern day equivalent, Michael Woodford's *Interest and Prices*. It is about nothing but monetary policy rules. Literally thousands of articles and papers have been written on monetary policy rules. The staffs of the Fed and other central banks use policy rules. Even if they do not like to talk about the use of policy rules in their own decision-making, central bankers assume that other central banks follow such policy rules when they make forecasts and assess trends. Just last week, at the annual Jackson Hole conference, Federal Reserve Governor Mishkin discussed policy rules and how they could be improved. It is hard to find a research paper on monetary policy that does not use a monetary policy rule in some form.

The breakthrough in the resistance to the practical use of policy rules appears to have occurred during the period between the late 1980s and the early 1990s. Historians of monetary thought can analyze why the change occurred. Academic work on the Lucas critique and time inconsistency may have been factors, but those ideas were over a decade old by the late 1980s. An important reason for the breakthrough, in my view, was that, following the Fed's aggressive disinflation effort under Paul Volker's leadership, there was a need for a practical framework—a practical rule—for setting interest rates in order to keep inflation low.

But whatever the reasons, let us examine some of the consequences of this development for our understanding of monetary and financial phenomena.

Surprising Predictions, Good and Bad

The first thing to observe is that policy rules turned out to be pretty accurate at predicting future interest rates. I illustrate the surprising aspects of this in Figure 31.2, where I reproduce a very interesting chart originally published in March 1995 by John Judd and Bharat Trehan at the research department at the Fed here in San Francisco. This was published 2–1/2 years after I first presented the Taylor rule in November 1992. I had nothing to do with this chart. I can't remember when I first saw it, but I went back and found it because I thought it would be a good way to illustrate my point. It includes data for the period I looked at in 1992, which I enclose with the oval shaded, but also for the period back to the early sixties and then up to the present (1995).

As Judd and Trehan report in their paper, "Taylor had already shown that his rule closely fit the actual path of the funds rate from 1987 (when Alan Greenspan became Fed Chairman) to 1992 (when I did my original study). Figure 31.2 shows that the same close relationship continued to hold over 1993 and 1994 as well." I show this by the small oval around 1993 and 1994. This was probably the most

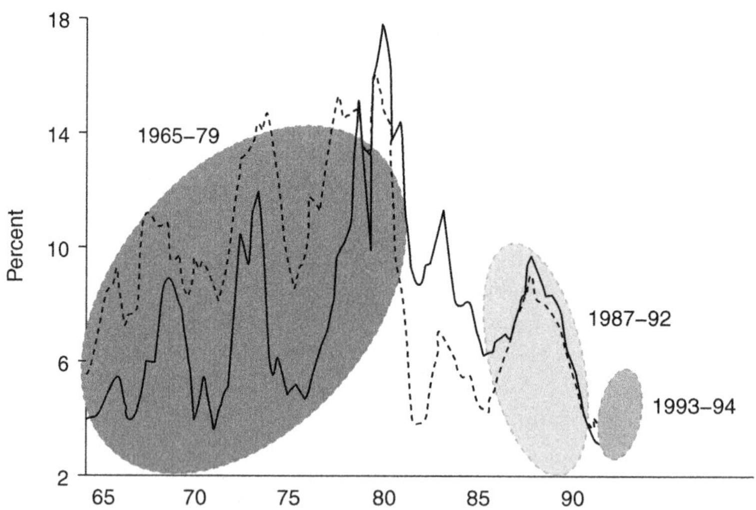

Figure 31.2 Federal funds rate: Actual vs. Rule's prescription for fed behavior.

Source: "Has the Fed Gotten Tougher on Inflation?" The FRBSF Weekly Letter, March 31, 1995 by John P. Judd and Bharat Trehan of the San Francisco Fed.

amazing thing to observers at the time because obviously, nobody had any idea that this was going to happen back in 1992. If they try, economists can always fit equations very well to past data—during the "sample period," but rarely do things come out so well in the future, after the work is done. So it was a scientific validation of the approach.

Moreover, you seemed to be getting more out of policy rules than you were putting in, which is a sign that you had something. Recall that policy rules were derived from monetary theories which suggested that they would lead to good macroeconomic results: low inflation and output variability. The rules were not designed to be useful for forecasting. They were meant to be normative, not positive, yet now they were mysteriously shown to be both. Figure 31.3, which is drawn from a paper published by Bill Poole, President of the Federal Reserve Bank of St. Louis, shows that this general ability to track continued over the years, though not as well as Judd and Trehan had found in 1993–1994. Note also that there are some particularly interesting periods where the actual policy deviates from the rule, especially in 2003–2005, an issue which I will return to.

In any case, this predictive value obviously interested business economists and policy makers, especially those working in the financial markets. John Lipsky, then at Salomon Brothers, wrote newsletters as early as 1993 that used monetary rules to forecast and analyze Fed decisions. Gavyn Davies at Goldman Sachs soon applied them to other countries. Janet Yellen, then a member of the Board of Governors of

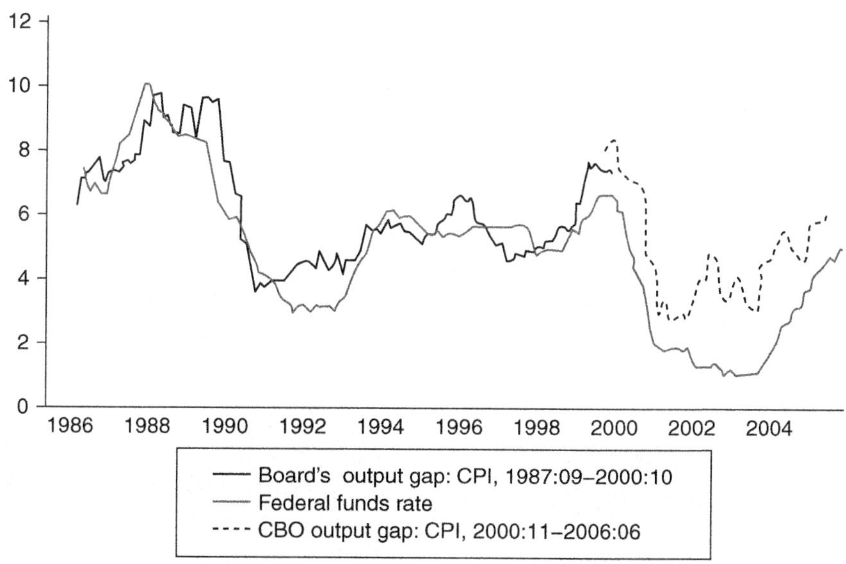

Figure 31.3 Greenspan years: Federal funds rate and Taylor rule. (CPI $p^* = 2.0$, $r^* = 2.0$) $a = 1.5$, $b = 0.5$

Source: From William Poole. "Understanding the Fed" St. Louis *Review*, Jan/Feb 2007.

the Fereal Reserve, discussed policy rules at the Federal Open Market Committee in 1995 and referred to monetary policy rules in a speech at NABE in March 1996, mentioning their predictive power.

Another surprising feature of the predictions was discovered by Judd and Trehan by looking back at the 1960s and 1970s, which I show by the big oval in Figure 31.2. During this period the rule does not fit very well. In fact it is a terrible fit. It would have predicted very poorly during this period. Generally speaking, the actual interest rate is way too low compared to what the rule says it should be. But this finding was interesting, because it was during this early period that monetary policy was delivering pretty lousy results: inflation was high and volatile, and there were many business cycles.

Figure 31.2 shows that monetary policy decisions were quite different in the period before the early 1980s. But is it possible to determine more precisely what exactly was different about policy? Was it too responsive to changes in the economy or not responsive enough? And did the size of the response differ for inflation versus real GDP? The mathematical form of monetary policy rules enables one to answer such questions. By regressing the short-term interest rate on inflation and output one finds that the response coefficients on both inflation and real GDP were much smaller in the earlier period. Figure 31.4 illustrates that the coefficients nearly doubled, though the precise size of the increase varies from study to study. Thus, policy became much more responsive regarding inflation and real GDP. Figure 31.5 shows an example of this increased responsiveness. In the late 1960s when inflation was rising above four percent, the federal funds rate was still under five percent. In the late 1980s when inflation rose to that same level, the interest rate rose to nearly ten percent. Thus, policy moved toward the policy rule by increasing both the response coefficients on inflation and GDP. They started out too small and grew, rather than starting out too big and shrunk.

Explaining the Great Moderation

Having looked at the predictive power of monetary policy rules let me now consider their capability of explaining economic phenomenon that would otherwise be difficult to explain. Perhaps the most important macroeconomic event

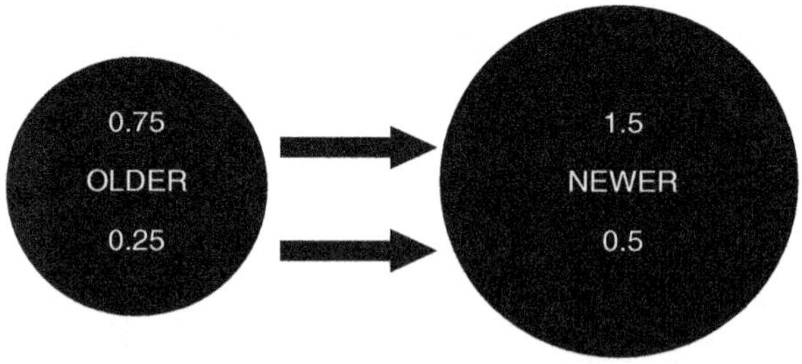

Figure 31.4 Growth of response coefficients to both inflation and output.

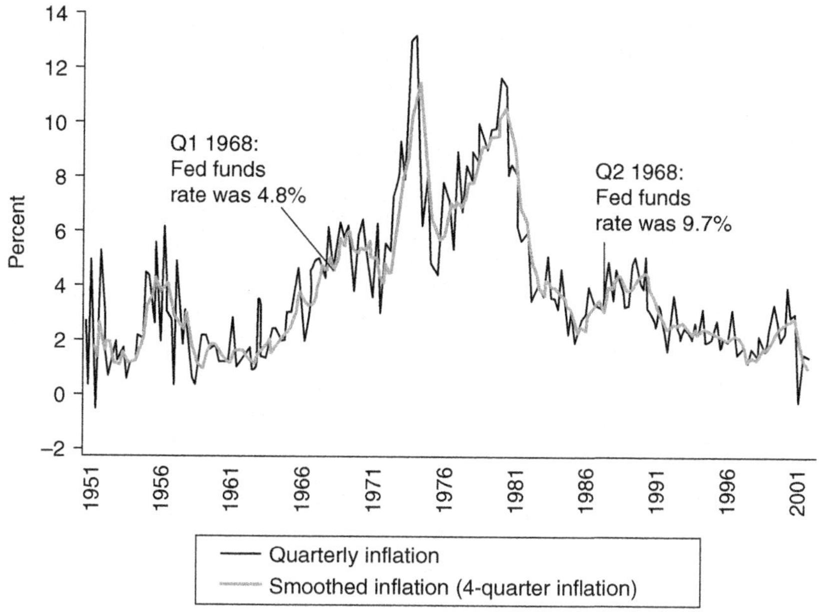

Figure 31.5 Inflation in the United States and the federal funds rate: Two eras.
Source: Federal Reserve Board.

in the last half century has been the remarkable decline in the volatility of inflation and real GDP. Economists call this the Great Moderation or the Long Boom. Econometricians have determined that the change occurred in the early 1980s, which is what one observes clearly in Figure 31.6. There were recessions every three a four years in the earlier period, a remarkably poor performance compared to what has happened since. The theory of policy rules has provided a good explanation of this phenomenon, as discussed recently by Ben Bernanke (2004).

The elements of the explanation are based on the observed changes in the policy rule coefficients, illustrated in Figures 31.4 and 31.5. During the period of the Great Moderation the monetary policy response of the interest rate to increases in inflation and to real GDP was much larger than in the period of poor economic performance. So there is a clear difference between the policies in the two periods. And the change in policy occurs at the time the economic performance changed. So the timing is right. To complete the explanation, one notes that according to monetary theory the greater responsiveness leads to more stable inflation and more stable real GDP. In fact, that the response was greater than one in the later period has become an important principle of good monetary policy.

To be sure, there are rival explanations for this phenomenon (globalization, increased service production), but none fit the facts so closely.

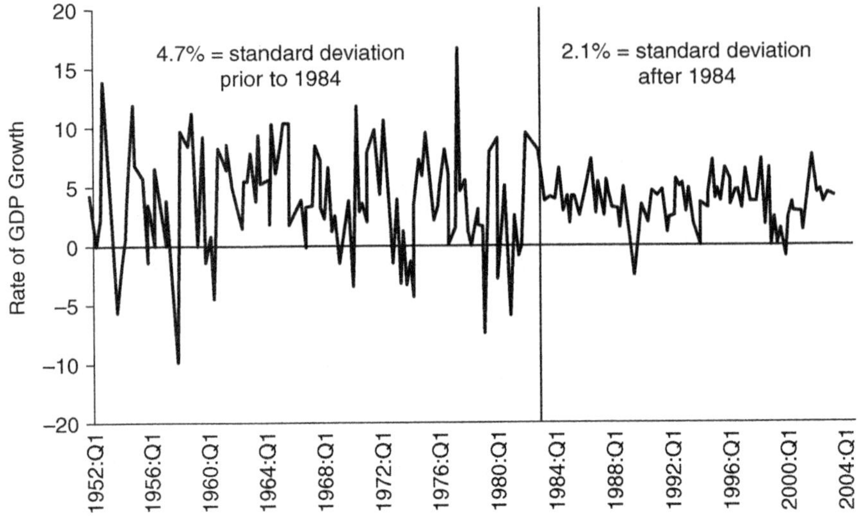

Figure 31.6 The great moderation or the long boom.

Source: Federal Reserve Board.

And the Great Moderation of Housing Volatility

Figure 31.7 shows that there has also been a great reduction in housing volatility. Before the early 1980s the standard deviation of residential investment relative to trend was around 13 percent; in the later period it was only five percent, and this includes the most recent fluctuation, which is quite large. In fact, housing volatility came down more than the volatility of GDP and, thereby, more than the other components of spending. The theory of policy rules explains this too.

The explanation starts with the explanation for the Great Moderation. By reacting more aggressively to increases in inflation the Fed has prevented inflation from rising as much as in the past, and this has reduced the ultimate size of the interest rate swings. Again using the Taylor rule, the response coefficient to inflation has increased from less than one to greater than one, and the response coefficient to real output has also increased. These larger responses have thus reduced the boom-bust cycle and the large fluctuations in interest rates that had caused the large volatility of housing. The reduction is larger than for the other components of spending because housing is more sensitive to interest rates. Another possible explanation is that housing became less impacted by a given change in the federal funds rate due to securitization and deregulation of deposit rates. But that alternative does not stand up because the effect of changes in the federal funds rate on housing show no evidence of a shift between these two periods. Moreover, no other explanation I am aware of has the timing so precise.

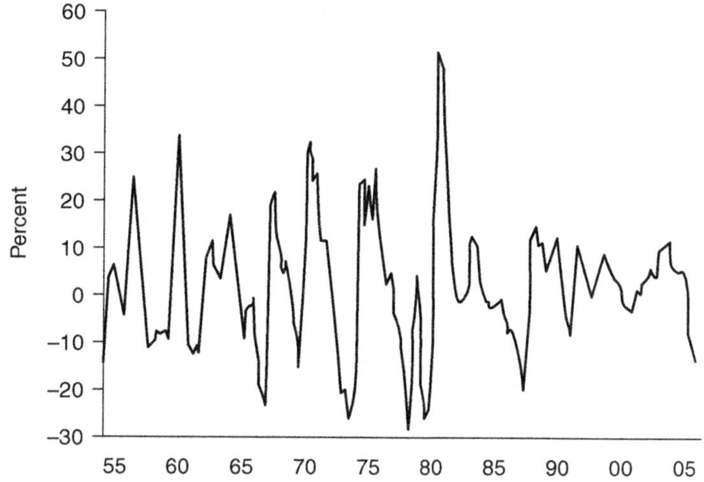

Figure 31.7 Percentage change in residential investment (over previous four quarters).

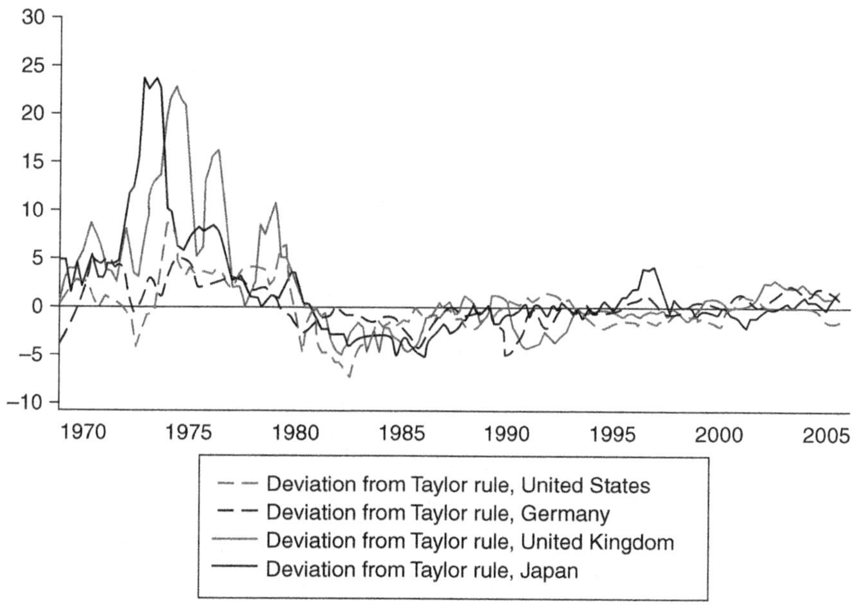

Figure 31.8 International comparisons of the Taylor rule.

Source: Cecchetti, Hooper, Kasman, Shoenholtz, Watson (2007).

It Works in Other Countries Too

Another striking finding is that the theory of policy rules seemed to work in other countries too. I don't think anybody anticipated that 15 years ago. Figure 31.8 is a nice illustration, drawn from a paper published earlier this year by a group that includes both business economists and academics. It shows the deviations from the Taylor rule in the United States, Germany, United Kingdom, and Japan. It shows how off they were up until around 1980 and then how much closer they have been since then. It shows that the same type of chart used by Judd and Trehan (Figure 31.2) in 1995 would describe events in these other countries. Moreover, these countries also experienced a great moderation, with timing different from country to country.

While the results in these figures pertain to developed countries, the policy rule concept has also been useful for understanding monetary policy developments in emerging market countries for which they were clearly not designed explicitly. In these countries, monetary policy rules have been especially useful for implementing inflation targeting. There are very few countries around the world where someone has not tried to see if monetary policy rules work there.

Explaining Exchange Rates Puzzles

What else can we understand with monetary policy rules? When the US inflation rate rises by more than people in the markets anticipate, you usually see the dollar appreciate. At least that's been the case since the early 1980s, when monetary policy rules have described Fed behavior. What has puzzled economists about this correlation is that, according to purchasing power parity theory, a higher price level should mean a depreciation of the currency. But if you bring a policy rule into play you get a nice, simple explanation of what is going on. You see that as the inflation rate rises, the Fed will increase interest rates (according to the policy rule), and that will tend to make the dollar more attractive, so it appreciates. Engel and West (2006), Engle, Mark, and West (2007), and Clarida and Waldman (2007) have been showing in detail how this and other related exchange rate phenomenon can be explained by policy rules.

Explaining Term-Structure Puzzles

Policy rules also help explain certain puzzling features of the term structure of interest rates, as shown by Fuhrer (1996) and Ang, Dong, and Piazzesi (2005). For example, Smith and Taylor (2007) empirically document a large secular shift in the estimated response of the entire term structure of interest rates to inflation and output in the United States. As shown in Figure 31.9, the impact of inflation and real GDP on long term interest rates of all maturities increased significantly. The shift occurred in the early 1980s and apparently had no previous explanation. However, there is a direct link between these coefficients of the central bank's monetary policy rule for the short-term interest rate.

There are two countervailing forces: the larger response of interest rates to these two macro variables and their reduced persistence due to the larger response. Using the link, one can see that the former dominates, thereby showing that the shift in the policy rule for the short-term interest rate in the early 1980s, which I

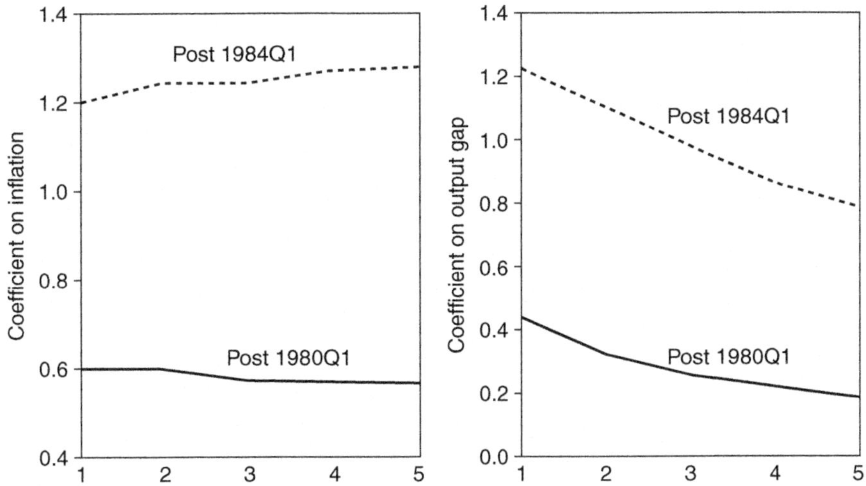

Figure 31.9 The Taylor rule and term structure of interest rates.

Source: Smith and Taylor (2007).

mentioned earlier, provides an explanation for the puzzling shift in the long-term responses.

This approach also explains the "conundrum" in which policy rate increases in the 2004–2005 period had little effect on long term rates. In this case, a model of shifts in policy rules is needed for a complete explanation (Davig and Leeper, 2007).

Explaining and Assessing Deviations from Policy Rules: 1998 and 2003–2005

The increased focus on monetary policy rules has led monetary economists to focus more on deviations from rules. I believe this is because there is less debate about the periods when the central banks are on the policy rules, which must be interpreted as a real success for the policy rule approach.

In their review of the Greenspan period, Blinder and Reis (2006), for example, focus mainly on the deviations from a Taylor rule in assessing the Greenspan era. In commenting on that paper at the Jackson Hole conference where it was delivered, I argued that following the principles imbedded in such a rule is why the Greenspan policy was so successful.

In any case, as mentioned at the start of this lecture, there are a few periods where there have been sizable deviations from the typical policy rule. By far the largest in the United States was during the period from 2003 to 2005, when the federal funds rate was well below what the experience of the Great Moderation would have predicted. This deviation is quite evident in Figure 31.3, which was the biggest deviation shown, comparable to the turbulent 1970s in Figure 31.2.

The rationale for this period of prolonged low interest rates was that it was needed to ward off deflation, but the low rates were also a factor in the eventual housing boom and bust. Similarly, there was a deviation in 1998 and 1999, which may have been a factor in the boom and bust in asset prices in 1999 and 2000. In any case, it is now possible to go back and assess such deviations and learn lessons for the future about their advisability. As such episodes are being reviewed, I see the disadvantages becoming more apparent compared to the advantages perceived at the time. If this trend continues, then the rationale for large deviations from monetary policy rules will diminish. This will increase the likelihood of staying with systematic, predictable, rules-based policy that has worked well for most of the Great Moderation period. The short-term interest rate would then adjust mainly according to the major developments in the macro economy: inflation and real GDP.

Staying close to policy guidelines will also avoid moral hazard and show that there is no "put" in which the central bank bails out individual investors. If investors understand and believe that policy responds mainly to macroeconomic variables, then they will know that the central bank will not help them out if their risky investments fail.

Conclusion

In this lecture, I have focused mainly on the "scientific," as distinct from the "policy," contributions of monetary policy rules. In other words, I have tried to look for predictions, explanations, or better understandings of macroeconomic and financial phenomenon that monetary policy rules have brought. And I think I have found quite a few. The scientific contribution of an idea is measured by how much it helps us understand areas beyond the original idea. The more you get out of an idea compared to what you put into it, the bigger is the contribution. Of course, we live in a fluid economic world, and we do not know how long these explanations or predictions will last. I have no doubt that in the future—and maybe the not so distant future—a bright economist—maybe one right in this room—will show that some of the explanations discussed here are misleading, or simply wrong. But in the meantime, this is really a lot of fun.

Note

Originally published in *Business Economics*, Vol. 42, No. 4 (October 2007), pp. 8–15.

References

Ang, Andrew, Sen Dong, and Monika Piazzesi. 2005. "No Arbitrage Taylor Rules." Chicago Business School.

Bernanke, Ben. 2004. "The Great Moderation." Board of Governors of the Federal Reserve System.

Blinder, Alan and Ricardo Reis. 2006. "Understanding the Greenspan Standard." Jackson Hole Conference, Federal Reserve Bank of Kansas City.

Clarida, Richard and Daniel Waldman. 2007. "Is Bad News About Inflation Good News For the Exchange Rate?" Columbia University.

Davig, Troy and Eric M. Leeper. 2007. "Generalizing the Taylor Principle." *American Economic Review*, 97(3): 607–635.

Engel, Charles and Kenneth West. 2006. "Taylor Rules and the Deutsche-Dollar Real Exchange Rate." *Journal of Money Credit and Banking*, 38: 1175–1194.

Engel, Charles, Nelson Mark, and Kenneth West. 2007. "Exchange Rate Models are not as Bad as You Think." *NBER Macroeconomics Annual* 2007.

Fuhrer, Jeffrey. 1996. "Monetary Policy Shifts and Long-Term Interest Rates." *Quarterly Journal of Economics*, 111(4): 1183–1209.

Judd, John and Bharat Trehan. 1995. "Has the Fed Gotten Tougher on Inflation?" The FRBSF Weekly Letter, March 31, Federal Reserve Bank of San Francisco.

Patinkin, Don. 1965. *Money, Interest and Prices.* New York: Harper and Row.

Smith, Josephine M. and John B. Taylor. 2007. "The Link between the Long End and the Short End of Policy Rules." Stanford University.

Woodford, Michael. 2004. *Interest and Prices.* Princeton, NJ: Princeton University Press.

CHAPTER 32

2008

THE ADAM SMITH ADDRESS

ADAM SMITH AND THE POLITICAL ECONOMY OF A MODERN FINANCIAL CRISIS

Michael Mussa, Peterson Institute for International Economics

The United States is now in the midst of a major financial crisis that has spread to affect credit and equity markets and financial institutions all around the world. Many have characterized the present crisis as the worst since the Great Depression—a description that is becoming more apt with each passing day. Whatever the ultimate scale of the present crisis, it is not the only important financial crisis to beset the United States in the past 50 years; by my count there have been at least seven: 1971, 1974–1975, 1980–1982, 1987, 1991, 2000–2002, and 2007–?. Looking further back through the 19th and 20th centuries, the average frequency of crises has been roughly constant at about one per decade. Most other countries, both economically advanced and developing, also have histories of not infrequent financial crises.[1]

During my career as an economist, I have had a good deal of experience with financial crises, perhaps most dramatically as the macroeconomic member of President Reagan's Council of Economic Advisers during the stock market crash of October 1987. During the 10 years that I served as the chief economist of the International Monetary Fund, I witnessed about 40 cases of countries involved in financial crises, sometimes in isolation but often in combination. Once during this period a journalist asked, "What does the IMF do in financial crises?" "Well," I replied, "we help to manage them." "And, how are you doing at this job?" was the next question. "Well," I replied, "recently we have managed to have quite a lot of crises."

Because financial crises have been important and relatively frequent occurrences going back hundreds of years, it is not surprising that the greatest economist of all time, Adam Smith, has something relevant to say on the subject in his great book, *An Enquiry into the Nature and Causes of the Wealth of Nations.*[2] Because this lecture is presented in connection with the annual Adam Smith award by the National Association for Business Economics, it is appropriate to reflect here on what that great economist can still teach us about the causes and consequences of such crises and about what both private behavior and public policy might do to help avoid them or ameliorate their consequences.

I shall not argue that everything important that we might hope to learn about the political economy of financial crises is in Smith. Indeed, Smith's greatness as an economist derives from immense and detailed knowledge of operation of the economies of his day and earlier times, combined with ability to abstract (making use of the ideas of other thinkers) general theories that explained these operations.[3] Our economies and our monetary and financial systems are quite different and in most respects far more developed and complex than they were in Smith's day. Accordingly, it would be unreasonable to expect that any empirically grounded economist, even one with the intellectual caliber of Adam Smith, could have foreseen and understood all of the important issues that arise in modern financial crises. Nevertheless, Smith's analysis provides key insights that are useful both in understanding the present financial crisis and in assessing how the risk of such crises might be reduced in the future.

This central theme is developed first by reviewing some of the key ideas in Smith's discussion "Of Money Considered as a Particular Branch of the General Stock of the Society, or of the Expense of Maintaining the National Capital," which is the subject of Chapter II of Book II of *The Wealth of Nations.* Next, these ideas will be applied to an analysis and explanation of important developments in the present financial crisis. Finally, inspired by Adam Smith but based mainly on my own ideas, some comments are offered on how the present crisis is being handled, on how we might better have avoided or ameliorated the present crisis, and on how we might do somewhat better at this in the future.

Smith's Theory of Money and Credit

Adam Smith recognized that stock of money was an essential part of the economy's total stock of useful capital. However, unlike other forms of capital, money was not directly useful either in consumption or in production. Rather, money played the essential role of the "great wheel of circulation" that made possible the distribution of labor and material inputs to their various productive uses and the means by which "every individual in the society has his subsistence, conveniences, and amusements distributed to him in their proper proportion." More specifically, Smith argued, "The great wheel of circulation is altogether different from the goods which are circulated by it. The revenue of society [gross or net national product in today's terminology] consists altogether in those goods, and not in the wheel that circulates them." Nevertheless, Smith maintained that "...the stock of money which circulates in any country must require a certain expense, first to collect it, and afterward to support it, both [of] which...are...deductions from the neat [or net] revenue of society. A certain quantity of gold and silver and of very curious labor [i.e., bankers]...is employed in supporting that great but expensive instrument of commerce..." instead of in directly productive activities.

The stock of "money" to which Smith refers in this discussion is comprised of gold, silver, and lesser coins and "...several sorts of paper money, [most importantly] the circulating notes of banks and bankers." The key characteristic of circulating bank notes that makes them useful as money is their ready acceptability as payment in a wide range of transactions on an essentially equal footing with gold or silver money. "When the people of any particular country have such confidence in the fortune, probity, and prudence of a particular banker, as to believe that he is always ready to pay upon demand such of his promissory notes as are likely to be at any time presented to him; these notes come to have the same currency as gold and silver money, from the confidence that such money can at any time be had for them."

The Private and Social Virtues of Paper Money

Smith repeatedly emphasizes the virtues of paper money both to the banks that create it and to society as a whole. This virtue, in both cases, fundamentally reflects a violation of the principle that *there is no such thing as a free lunch*. By creating paper money at very little cost that may be used with essentially equal convenience in place of metallic money (gold or silver) that can only be obtained at considerable expense, the banker creates essentially out of nothing something that has considerable value for himself and for society. Smith explains this remarkable phenomenon as follows:

> The banker who advances to the merchant whose bill he discounts, not gold or silver, but his own promissory notes, has the advantage of being able to discount the greater amount of the whole value of his promissory notes, which he finds by experience, are commonly in circulation. He is thereby enabled to make his clear gain of interest on so much a larger sum.
>
> It is not by augmenting the capital of the country, but by rendering a greater part of that capital active and productive than would otherwise be so, that the most judicious operations of banking can increase the industry of the country...The gold and silver money which circulates in any country, and by means of which the produce of its land and labour is annually circulated and distributed to proper consumers, is...all dead stock...The judicious operations of banking, by substituting paper in the room of a great part of this gold or silver, enables the country to convert the great part of this dead stock into active and productive stock.

Limits on Paper Money and Bank Credit

Smith also emphasized that there were limits to the amount of paper money that could prudently be created by an individual bank and within a country, and that serious dangers ensued if too much paper money was created. In Smith's view, the effective limit on the amount of paper money was an amount somewhat less than the amount of metallic money that would be held if no paper money were available. This was based on Smith's analysis that sound paper money could efficiently be used in domestic commerce in substitution of most metallic money. Individual bankers, however would need to hold some fractional reserve of gold and silver to maintain their commitments to convert their paper money into metallic money on demand. And for the country as a whole, metallic money would also be needed in transactions with foreigners who ordinarily would not accept domestic paper money.

If an individual bank expands its issue of paper money too much, it could face a run in which holders of its money demand immediate conversion into gold and silver. If the bank could not meet the run out of its own reserves or with metallic money obtained by rediscounting some of the bills it holds (against which it had advanced its own money), the bank will fail. The customers of the bank will be hurt by such a failure, in addition to the loss incurred by the bank. If the general supply of paper money becomes too large, then many banks may face runs in a general panic. Unless additional gold and silver (or freely convertible notes of a central bank like the Bank of England) can be obtained to stem the panic, the financial crisis will create general economic distress—a phenomenon that had been observed on many occasions.

Smith proposed several solutions to the problem of excessive creation of paper money, but his analysis here is somewhat confusing and contradictory. At the end of his chapter on "Money...," Smith embraces, with two provisos, the solution dear to the hearts of today's ardent deregulators—freely competitive banking. "If bankers are restrained from issuing any circulating bank notes or notes payable to the bearer, for less than a certain sum; and if they are subjected to the obligation of an immediate and unconditional payment of such banknotes as soon as presented, their trade may, with safety to the public, be rendered in all other respects perfectly free." However, Smith's discussion earlier in the chapter makes clear that the actual experience with banking and paper money in Scotland, England, and the American colonies raised substantial doubts about whether the private incentives for prudent banking under the discipline of competition would provide adequate safeguards against the dangers of excessive money creation.

Indeed, Smith embraces constraints on banks' creation of paper money and extension of credit that would be anathema to modern advocates of financial deregulation. In particular, Smith's explicit proviso that paper money issued by banks should not be "for less than a certain sum" is far from innocuous. The "certain sum" that Smith recommended was five pounds sterling. Although today, five pounds sterling is worth about eight US dollars and will pay for no more than a short taxi ride in London, in the late 18th century, five pounds sterling was the monthly wage of a skilled craftsman, equivalent in today's money to about $5,000. As Smith made clear, paper money issued by banks was for use in business transactions, among dealers and merchants who were presumably sophisticated about the ways of business and finance. Paper money was not supposed to be a substitute for the coinage used in everyday retail transactions.

More generally, Smith argued forcefully that the total issuance of paper money within a country should be constrained by what later came to be known as "the real bills doctrine." Specifically, paper money should be paid out only on bank credit extended in the discounting of "real bills" that corresponded to actual trade among merchants. Smith argued that such lending was fundamentally safe and would not involve an undue expansion of paper money. But that any other bank lending should only be to such customers where the bank can "...observe with great attention, whether in the course of a short period...the sum of repayments it receives from them, is...fully equal to that of the advances which it [the bank] commonly makes to them."

Another constraint on bank issuance of paper money and creation of credit that Smith recommended was an 18th century version of the Glass-Steagall Act. Banks should limit their extensions of credit and associated issuance of paper money to short-term lending primarily related to the discounting of real bills. All forms of longer-term lending [generally secured by bonds or mortgages] should be the domain of "...such private people as propose to live upon the interest of their money...and who upon that account [are] willing to lend...to such people of good credit as are likely to keep it for several years."

Closely related to Smith's advocacy of the real bills doctrine and the preclusion of banks from longer-term lending is Smith's abhorrence of what I would term "money-credit merry-go-rounds." Smith describes the abhorrent phenomenon as follows:

> Trader A in Edinburgh...draws a bill upon B in London, payable two months after date. In reality B in London owes nothing to A in Edinburgh; but he agrees to accept of A's bill, upon condition that before the term of payment he shall redraw on upon A in Edinburgh for the same sum, together with the interest and commission, another bill payable likewise two months after date...A in Edinburgh...before the expiration of the second two months, draws a second bill upon B in London, payable likewise two months after date; and before the expiration of the third two months, B in London redraws on A in Edinburgh another bill, payable also two months after date. This practice has sometimes gone on, not only for several months, but for several years, the bill always returning upon A in Edinburgh, with the accumulated interest and commission or all former bills...Though the bills upon which this paper had been advanced, were all of them repaid in their turn as soon as they became due; yet the value which had been really advanced upon the first bill, was never really returned to the banks which advanced it...The paper which was advanced upon those circulating bills of exchange, amounted on many occasions, to the whole fund destined for carrying out some vast and extensive project of agriculture, commerce, or manufactures...The greater part of this paper was, consequently, over and above...what the circulation of the country could easily absorb and employ...

Smith emphasizes that this merry-go-round of money and credit becomes even more dangerous when it becomes opaque through the involvement of many different banks. "When two people, who are continually drawing and re-drawing upon one and other...with the same banker, he must immediately see what they are about...But this discovery is not altogether so easy when they discount their bills sometimes with one banker and sometimes with another, and when the same two persons do not constantly draw and redraw upon one another, but occasionally run the round of a great circle of projectors, who find it in their interest to assist one another in this method of raising money...[Even] when a banker has made this discovery, he might sometimes make it too late, and might find that he had already discounted the bills of those projectors to so great an extent, that, by refusing to discount even more, he would necessarily make them all bankrupts, and thus, by ruining them, might perhaps ruin himself."

Smith concludes his argument for prudent limits on money creation by describing what happened in Scotland when the issue of paper money and credit became unsustainably large and prudent banks began to cut back. Protests by those who desired even further extensions of money and credit led the establishment of a new bank "...for the express purpose of relieving the distress of the country...This bank was more liberal than any other had previously been, both in granting cash accounts and in discounting bills of exchange...This bank, no doubt, gave some temporary relief to those projectors [who favored and supported its establishment], and enabled them to carry on their projects for about two years longer than they could otherwise have done. But it thereby only enabled them to get so much deeper into debt, so that when ruin came, it fell so much the heavier upon both them and their creditors."

Applying Smith's Analysis in the Present Financial Crisis

In applying Smith's analysis of money, credit, and banking to the present day, it is important to keep in mind some key differences between monetary and financial arrangements in Smith's time and their modern equivalents. The paper money to which Smith refers is not analogous either to the currency that we carry around in our wallets or to the measure of the "money supply" that consists of transaction balances of households and businesses (reported as M1). In Smith's time, payments in business transactions were normally made by physical transfer of gold and silver coins or paper bank notes (including both notes issued by private banks and by the quasi-official Bank of England). It was also common for payment in business transactions to be made with private credit instruments in the form of private bills of exchange, especially bills that had been accepted for potential conversion into paper money or specie by a bank.

Since the creation of the Federal Reserve, US commercial banks have ceased issuing paper currency. Today, finality of payment in most business transactions is through transfers between accounts at banks that participate in the interbank payments system. Paper checks are still used in some of these payments, but electronic transfers now account for the bulk of transactions. The total volume of transactions is enormous. In 1996, the annual ratio of debits to demand deposits at US commercial banks reached almost one thousand or about one hundred times annual gross domestic product (GDP). These ratios have probably at least doubled over the past 12 years.

In Smith's analysis, the issuance of paper money as a circulating liability of banks is intimately tied up with the operations of banks on the asset side of their balance sheets, primarily making loans through the discounting of bills of exchange and other similar paper. Today, the operations of banks and other financial institutions with bank-like activities involves a much wider set of highly liquid short-term assets—well beyond the balances held in accounts that are directly linked to the interbank payments system. The reason for this is clear. With an enormous daily volume of payments and receipts, banks need to be concerned about payments imbalances that might drain away their reserves. Hence, they maintain secondary reserves in the form of assets that can be sold easily and quickly without significant loss of value or that will be readily acceptable as collateral on short-term loans of reserves from other banks or the central bank. For the same reason, businesses with high volumes of payments and receipts typically hold secondary reserves (beyond their transaction account balances) in the form of highly liquid short-term assets or lines of credit that may be rapidly drawn to restore depleted transaction account balances. Thus, in the modern world, the "great wheel of circulation" that keeps business running depends on a banking and financial system that provides and utilizes a wide range of liquid assets and liabilities that support the efficient and reliable operation of the payments system. If any significant part of this complex system is seriously disrupted, the operation of the whole system can be significantly impaired, with important adverse consequences for economic activity.

In Smith's analysis the main danger of financial disruption came from excessive expansion and subsequent collapse of money and credit created by banks. This danger arose from the ability of banks to endow the paper money they created with the magical property of liquidity and from the private incentives to do so to excess. Accordingly, as a safeguard against this danger, Smith focused on limiting the supply of paper money to a proper fraction of the gold and silver money that would otherwise circulate in a country. In the modern world, banks no longer issue paper money, but banks and other financial institutions still engage in the magic of creating "liquidity."

Banks and similar financial institutions issue a wide variety of claims against the value of the assets that they hold in their portfolios. From the perspective of the holders of these claims, they possess "liquidity" to the extent that they can be converted into transactions balances with high speed, limited cost, and reasonable certainty of value.[4] The effort of banks and similar financial institutions is to create value by endowing the claims they issue with greater liquidity than the assets they hold. This principle applies to Smith's paradigmatic case of a bank that issues paper money (which it agrees to redeem for specie on demand) against a small reserve of specie and a substantial volume of earning assets. It also applies much more generally when a financial institution uses a variety of means to persuade holders of claims upon its assets that they are more liquid than those assets. The incentive to do this is great because success enables the institution to capture much of the surplus value from the liquidity it has created. The danger is that too much liquidity will be created if it somehow turns out that financial institutions cannot fulfill the expectations of holders of their claims concerning the speed, cost, and certainty of value with which these claims can be converted into the means of payment.

Underlying Causes of the Current Crisis

The present crisis in United States and global financial markets has a complexity of causes—some but not all of which are related to the analysis of Adam Smith in *The Wealth of Nations*. The origins of the crisis trace back to the unsustainable upsurge in homebuilding and house prices in the United States in 2004 through 2006, the associated buildup in mortgage credit and the rapid expansion of lower quality subprime and alt-A mortgages, the development and worldwide marketing of complex and opaque financial instruments that were based on mortgages and other forms of debt, and the explosion of over-the-counter derivatives (including credit default swaps) that further clouded who would bear what risks—especially in situations of market stress. These developments came in the general context of a remarkable global economic expansion that ultimately became unsustainable in the face of a worldwide upsurge in commodity prices and uncomfortable increases in general price inflation. As these excesses began to unwind, starting in the summer of 2007, stresses began to emerge in key financial markets, leading ultimately to the freezing up of essential short-term credit markets, sharp falls in global equity prices, and the collapse of many commodity prices by the early autumn of 2008. Economic growth, which had already weakened significantly in many countries, turned into steep decline.

The main actors in this drama of unsustainable boom followed by spectacular collapse are surely developments in the private sector of the economy and in private financial institutions and markets. Policy mistakes and misjudgments played a supporting role. In particular, low short-term interest maintained by the Federal Reserve and low longer-term interest rates that were partly the result of surging capital inflows (reflecting reserve accumulation by foreign governments and central banks) undoubtedly gave some boost to house prices and to mortgage lending in the United States. Weak regulation of mortgage lending practices in the United States added something to these problems. However, no government policy compelled people to buy homes at unsustainably inflated prices or to borrow beyond their means in the expectation that already absurdly high home prices would continue to go even higher. Similarly, while regulators should have cracked down harder on unsound and abusive mortgage lending practices, no government agency insisted that people should take up such mortgages, or that dealers should purchase and repackage these mortgages, or that investors in mortgage-related instruments should fail to exercise due diligence in assessing the risks in what they were buying.

Concerning the large role that private sector mistakes and misjudgments played in the origins of the present crisis, Adam Smith's analysis provides key insight into at least an important part of the explanation. Financial institutions used their power to enhance the apparent liquidity of a wide array of mortgage-related and other asset-backed financial instruments and thereby raised the value of these instruments to investors (often including themselves) above the cost of the underlying assets that backed the instruments—utilizing the same basic principle that Adam Smith recognized as responsible for the economic gain from banks' creation of paper money. As a result of these activities, the financial institutions that engaged in them reported high profits and paid big salaries and huge bonuses to their top management and staff. Investors, too, were happy with the arrangement—at least until the crisis came—because they earned reasonably attractive returns on instruments that were perceived to have the additional advantage of relatively easy and quick convertibility into cash without much loss or value.

What was going on here was basically a vastly elaborated version of Adam Smith's "money-credit merry-go-round"—a virtual Disneyland of complex and opaque financial instruments where no one really understood exactly what the risks were and who was bearing them. For a while, as the system continued to expand, everyone was happy. The holders of supposedly liquid assets found that they were generally able to convert them with high speed and low cost into well-assured values in terms of cash. Thus, the value of these claims was sustained by their demonstrated liquidity and by the moderate yield advantage that they enjoyed over truly liquid instruments.

Trouble began when some of the assets underlying these financial instruments started to go bad at rates significantly greater than earlier anticipated. This was not due to actions of the financial institutions that created these instruments and sought to enhance their liquidity; it was the result of the downturn in the housing market or in the markets for other underlying assets. Nevertheless, holders of the instruments had to write down their values in light of declines in the values of the underlying assets. Fears of further declines in the values of underlying assets forced further writedowns. In addition, rising uncertainty about what the instruments were really worth drove down their values even further. In this process, the instruments lost most if not all of the value associated with their originally perceived liquidity; the special additional value that these instruments had acquired from ease and quickness of convertibility into cash at very close to a known price simply disappeared for instruments that no longer had these perceived characteristics.

Many financial institutions that had created and distributed such instruments to their customers felt obliged (due to fears of lost future business) to repurchase them at prices not too depressed from their original issue prices. These institutions then had to take losses on these repurchased instruments, as well as any similar instruments that they had decided to keep in their own portfolios. In this regard, the problem was not—as some have suggested—that the financial institutions that provided enhanced liquidity to a wide array of asset-backed instruments did not have enough "skin in the game." They had plenty of skin in the game—more than they really recognized—in their own portfolios and in instruments that they were compelled to repurchase from customers. Without this skin in the game, these institutions would not have faced such substantial losses in the present crisis.

The Case of Municipal Auction Rate Preferred Shares

There is a wide array of financial claims that exhibited the problems that have just been described, including collateralized mortgage obligations (CMOs), collateralized debt obligations (CDOs), collateralized loan obligations (CLOs), asset-backed commercial paper (ABCP), and more complex forms of claims that were based on these classes of financial instruments. I am not familiar with the details of most of these classes of instruments, but from work years ago on municipal bonds [Mussa and Kormendi 1979], I may be able to provide some further insight in the special case of auction rate preferred shares (ARPS) issued by closed-end municipal bond funds.

Interest on municipal bonds in the United States is generally exempt from federal income tax and often exempt from state and local income taxes in the state of issuance. As a result of this tax advantage, municipal bonds generally have yields that are below yields on taxable bonds thought to have similar risks of default. Indeed, most municipal bonds with investment grade ratings usually have yields that are below yields on US Treasury obligations of similar maturity. Investors in municipal bonds include individual in high tax brackets, who may hold bonds directly, in open-end or closed-end mutual funds, or in trust accounts. Businesses do not generally invest in municipal bonds because the arbitrage rules of the IRS prohibit businesses from receiving tax exempt interest income on municipal bonds while deducting interest expense on their own debt. (The arbitrage rule also generally applies to individuals with respect to interest deductions other than for home mortgages.) Commercial banks and fire and casualty insurance companies are generally not subject to the arbitrage rule, and both types of institutions have long been important holders of municipal bonds. Commercial banks have usually been dominant buyers of short-term municipals. Reflecting the 35 percent corporate tax rate, arbitrage by banks between high-grade short-term municipals and high-grade short-term loans or commercial paper has generally kept the interest rate on such municipals below the yield on three-month treasury bills, at about 65 percent of the yield on high-grade commercial paper. At longer maturities, yields on higher-grade municipals are generally below those on similarly rated corporate bonds by something less than the corporate tax rate, and yields on the highest grade municipals usually run about 80 percent of the yield on long-term Treasuries.

Closed-end municipal bond funds cannot increase the yields to their common shareholders by leveraging their holdings of (mainly longer-term) municipal bonds by issuing debt, as this would run afoul of the IRS arbitrage rule. However, with the aid of major commercial and investment banks, these funds innovated a way to obtain leverage by issuing some fraction of the funds' shares in the form of ARPS. This mechanism is supposed to work as follows. Suppose that a newly established closed-end fund buys $1.5 billion of longer-term municipals, financed by issuing $1 billion in initial value of common shares and $500 million in initial par value of ARPS. Ignoring management fees, the common shareholders are paid each month all of the interest earned on the fund's holdings of municipal bonds, less the interest paid on the ARPS. As is true with all preferred shares, the holders of the ARPS must be paid what they are owed before the common shareholders get anything.

What the holders of the ARPS are owed is determined as follows. On most business days, a major commercial or investment bank holds an auction for a substantial fraction of ARPS, rotating through the entire stock of $500 million once every week or two. In the auction, the price is set at par, and the bidding is on the dividend that will be paid over the period until the next auction for this fraction of the ARPS. Participants in the auction will usually include existing holders who want to roll over, new bidders who will jump in if the yield is attractive, and perhaps the market maker who may take up some slack when bidding is weak. If there are sufficient bids to acquire the amount up for auction at a yield below a cut-off level, then the auction succeeds. If the auction fails, then existing holders are stuck with their positions at least until the next scheduled auction, and they earn the cut-off yield until then.

The cut-off yield is set (usually by a formula) at a level that is intended to insure that auctions will fail very rarely, if at all. For example, setting the cut-off yield somewhat above the yield on three-month Treasuries would generally be expected to avoid auction failures. The reason is that, as preferred shares, the ARPS are extremely high grade and the yield on high-grade, truly short-term municipals is almost always below the yield on three-month Treasury bills. The ARPS, however, are not truly short-term municipals where the issuer is obligated to redeem them at par within a few days. Legally, the ARPS are preferred claims on a closed-end pool of long-term municipal bonds—fundamentally a very illiquid investment. However, provided that the regular auctions for the ARPS succeed and are expected to succeed, these ARPS have *de facto* characteristics that are essentially the same as true short-term municipals. Through this mechanism, the ARPS have magically been endowed with the virtues of liquidity. As a consequence, investors are willing to purchase ARPS at yields only slightly above true short-term municipals, which are generally well below the average yield on the closed-end fund's portfolio of long-term municipals. The holders of ordinary common shares in the fund benefit from this arrangement. When holders of the ARPS are willing to accept significantly less than the average yield on the portfolio of bonds held by the fund, holders of the common shares (who are not much concerned with liquidity) are able to enjoy yields above this average.

However, once ARPS auctions start to fail with even modest frequency, the perceived liquidity advantages of these instruments tend to disappear quite rapidly. When auctions fail, holders of ARPS are locked in at the cut-off yield until auctions can successfully resume. The fear of being locked-in induces many existing holders of ARPS to withdraw rather than re-bid at the next auction; and it discourages potential new bidders and market makers from participating in auctions. The result is like a panic in which the auction failure rate rapidly shoots up toward 100 percent. With the panic, the special liquidity value previously enjoyed by the ARPS suddenly disappears into nothingness.

This is what happened to many municipal ARPS in late 2007 and 2008. The initiating factors for difficulties in the municipal ARPS market probably included contagion effects from the markets for financial instruments with some similar characteristics, including other ARPS and ABCP. Special factors were also at work in the municipal market. Commercial banks are usually important demanders of shorter-term municipals, but only to the extent that they have profits to shelter from federal (and state and local) income tax. When bank profits declined sharply in the face of large losses related to mortgage-related and other assets, bank demand for municipals necessarily took a sizable hit. At least partly for this reason, yields on high-grade municipal bonds at all maturities rose meaningfully above yields on comparable maturity Treasuries. Yields on true short-term municipals breached the cut-off yields set for many ARPS auctions, making auction failures virtually inevitable. Thus, through a variety of mechanisms, the general dangers of excessive liquidity creation that were well understood by Adam Smith manifested themselves in the boom and subsequent collapse of the market for municipal ARPS in the United States.

Managing the Present Crisis and Reducing the Hazard of Future Crises

Management of financial crises by the policy authorities is an art and not a science; and among the arts of public policy, it has a decidedly darker shade. Some useful lessons may be drawn from our vast experience with past financial crises here and abroad, but there are no fixed rules about the right things to do in particular circumstances. Crises inevitably involve great uncertainties about the effects of policy actions in the short and longer run. In the midst of a crisis, it is often difficult to assess whether a particular policy will be helpful or harmful until its effects are apparent. Even afterward, it is sometimes difficult to know whether policy responses have been appropriate (and impossible to know if they have been optimal) because it is not possible to assess with confidence what would have happened on the roads not taken.

Adam Smith had little to say on the management of financial crises other than in his analysis of how to avoid excessive issuance of paper money and extension of bank credit. In Smith's day, the policy tools that we now use, well or badly, to help manage financial crises did not exist. In particular, during Smith's life the Bank of England was only beginning to develop its role as lender of last resort.

Stepping forward where the great man chose not to wander, I offer the following remarks on policy management by the US authorities in the present crisis.

Monetary Policy

Looking to the period from mid-2003 through mid-2006, it may be argued that it would have been better if the Federal Reserve had started to tighten monetary policy somewhat sooner and/or moved more rapidly to a tighter policy. The fact that economic growth strengthened dramatically in the summer of 2003 indicates that the last 25-basis-point step of monetary easing in June 2003 was not really needed. Tightening from an exceptionally easy policy could have begun by late 2003 rather than mid-2004, and the target federal funds rate could plausibly have been raised to five percent by the autumn of 2005 rather than the spring of 2006. The failure of long-term interest rates to rise as they normally do during a cycle of Federal Reserve tightening and the continuing boom in housing and in mortgage finance provided further reason to accelerate monetary tightening beyond the very moderate pace actually pursued. Although a more aggressive path of monetary tightening might not have done much to slow longer-term foreign capital inflows, it would surely have pushed up interest rates on adjustable rate mortgages (which are predominant among subprime and alt-A mortgages) and would have helped somewhat to limit the housing boom. Accordingly, the financial crisis we presently face would probably have been of somewhat smaller proportions.

The Federal Reserve began to ease monetary policy with a cut in the target federal funds rate from 5.25 to 4.75 percent at the FOMC meeting in mid-September

2007. Clear evidence of intensification of stress in financial markets (especially for mortgage-related instruments) as well as a decline in payroll employment for August 2007 (reported in early September) provided the context for the Federal Reserve's move. Although payroll employment for August was revised upward to show a modest gain, and other data showed that the economy continued to grow strongly through the third quarter and (as initially reported) into the fourth quarter, the Federal Reserve cut the target federal funds rate in two further 25-basis-point moves by mid-December.

This was prudent, forward-looking monetary policy. In the autumn of 2007, there was good reason to anticipate that the economy would weaken significantly even if the data did not yet show it. Moving the stance of monetary policy from moderate restraint to rough neutrality made perfect sense. The Federal Reserve was not, as some have argued, "behind the curve" in its monetary easing at this point, especially not in comparison with the usual pattern of monetary policy adjustment. In particular, in many earlier recessions, especially those where high inflation needed to be curbed, the Federal Reserve kept monetary policy fairly tight well into the recession. In the 2000 to 2003 episode of monetary easing, the Federal Reserve kept the target funds rate at 6.5 percent through the end of 2000 despite clear evidence that the economy had slowed significantly after mid-2000 (with negative real GDP growth now estimated for the third quarter of 2000). By end 2007, the Federal Reserve easing was well ahead of schedule of this and other earlier recessions.

The economic data weakened sharply beginning in late December 2007, and it was clear that further Federal Reserve easing was in order. The Federal Reserve undertook an emergency 75-basis-point cut in the target federal funds rate on January 22, followed at the end of the month by another 50-basis-point cut. Here, I think that the Federal Reserve became somewhat too aggressive. The apparent impetus for the January 22nd move was the sharp sell-off (of approximately 4%) in foreign equity markets that were triggered by reports of large losses at a French bank due to speculations by a rogue trader. Although sudden monetary easing is sometimes an appropriate response to combat a meltdown in equity markets—as it was on October 20, 1987—it is a tool best used only on occasions when it is really needed. In the January 22nd operation, the Federal Reserve used up a significant amount of ammunition on a relatively minor disturbance and cheapened the value of its remaining ammunition in dealing with future challenges. Moreover, a total cut of the target federal funds rate of 75 basis points (rather than 125 basis points) in January 2008 would have been better aligned with a responsible and predictable response of monetary policy to incoming economic data.

Further monetary easing in March and April could plausibly have been kept at 50 rather than 75 basis points in view of economic data suggesting that the economy was sluggish but not in recession. This would have left the target federal funds rate at 2.5 percent through September 2008. When extreme turmoil beset world credit markets beginning around mid-September, this would have allowed a further 50 basis points of room to ease US monetary policy to combat the rising threat.

The Federal Reserve's efforts to address the present crisis have expanded well beyond the normal confines of monetary policy by allowing a wide range of financial institutions and some categories of commercial and industrial firms to access credit directly from the central bank. This is an enormous departure from the Federal Reserve's practices of the past 70 years. Before the Federal Reserve began its new policy in March, loans to financial institutions were limited to member banks and constituted only about 0.05 percent of the Federal Reserve's total assets. At its postwar peak, during the Continental Illinois crisis in the mid-1980s, lending through the discount window was about four percent of Federal Reserve assets.

Following the Bear Stearns crisis in March, access to the Federal Reserve's discount window was broadened to include US major investment banks. In the immediate aftermath of the failure of Lehman Brothers in mid-September, the insurance company AIG was lent huge amounts (under tough conditions) to help avert a collapse of the credit derivatives market. In subsequent weeks, Federal Reserve lending has been further broadened to encompass purchases of high-grade commercial paper and massive (indirect) lending to foreign banks through swap lines from the Federal Reserve to foreign central banks. Money market funds have been offered insurance through the FDIC and benefit from the opportunity to sell commercial paper to the Federal Reserve.

To support the mortgage market, the Federal Reserve has purchased large quantities of securities issued by Fannie Mae and Freddy Mac. To provide funds for these operations, the Federal Reserve has reduced substantially its own holdings of Treasury obligations; and the Treasury has deposited at the Federal Reserve the proceeds from large issues of additional debt. These deposits, in turn, have been used to finance Federal Reserve lending and asset purchases. The result is that Federal Reserve credit provided to entities other than the US Treasury has risen from a few hundred million dollars in the summer of 2007 to over 1.5 trillion dollars in the autumn of 2008 and is still rising.

Although well warranted by the exigencies of combating the present crisis, these massive new initiatives by the Federal Reserve also raise serious concerns for the future. At some point, after the present financial crisis abates and the economy begins to recover, the massive easing of monetary and credit policy undertaken by the Federal Reserve will need to be unwound. The last time this happened (in 2003 to 2006), the issue concerned only the unwinding of an aggressive easing of traditional monetary policy; and doubts have already been expressed about how successfully this unwinding was carried out. This time, the unwinding will involve the additional and more complex issue of undoing the massive interventions of the central bank into particular financial markets and in support of a wide variety of financial institutions. There is little relevant experience to help guide this process, and common sense suggests that there are important dangers both from proceeding too quickly and from moving too slowly. Moreover, even if the Federal Reserve successfully withdraws from most of its present interventions, there remains the critical question of how the fact of these interventions in the present crisis will affect expectations about the Federal Reserve's likely behavior in future crises. This is part of the more general problem of "moral hazard."

Immoral Result and Moral Hazard

Official activities to deal with the financial crisis have raised intense concerns about the wisdom of "bailing out" financial institutions that face large losses and even bankruptcy primarily as a consequence of their own imprudence or mismanagement. These concerns are often expressed in terms of the "moral hazard" that is generated by government bailouts. Public outrage over these bailouts, however, is probably more directed at the "immoral result" from using public money to rescue particular institutions and individuals. Quite rightly, people are annoyed by the notion that they are being asked to pay for somebody else's excesses and mistakes—especially those of wealthy bankers and investment bankers. The "moral hazard" operating in the present crisis, however, comes not from present bailouts but rather from past bailouts. Earlier bailouts created expectations that those who undertake excessive risk through the creation or reliance on excessive liquidity can reasonably expect to see their losses ameliorated by government actions (including monetary easing) to help deal with a crisis. By the same principle, bailouts in the *present* crisis will inevitably generate *future* moral hazard, as people begin to appreciate the lesson that "immoral results" from today's bailouts suggest that imprudent risk takers in the future will benefit from future bailouts.[5]

Both "immoral result" and "moral hazard" are important features of the present crisis. Although it is not widely recognized, a key source of immoral result and moral hazard are the Federal Reserve's actions to cut to the target federal funds rate. The consequence of these interest rate cuts is to transfer hundreds of billions of dollars per year from the public's income on trillions of dollars of bank deposits and other money market instruments into the hands of those who make use of this cheap short-term credit. In comparison, the Federal Reserve's assumption of some risk on $29 billion of Bear Stearns assets in the rescue of that investment bank's creditors and preferred shareholders (and limited bailout of common equity holders) is a drop in the bucket. The massive use of the Federal Reserve's balance sheet to relieve stress in key credit markets may or may not have significant cost for the taxpayer and the general public. Because the cost of Treasury borrowing has fallen to exceptionally low levels, the cost of credit supplied by the Federal Reserve will, on this occasion, probably be well below the income earned on the loans made and securities purchased by the Federal Reserve. However, the precedent set on this occasion makes it more likely that the Federal Reserve (with the support of the Treasury) will be expected to, and will need to, intervene in a similar way in future crises. Experience in other countries suggests that in such circumstances, the prospects for massive borrowing by the Treasury at exceptionally low interest rates may not be as favorable as in the present episode.

The government's takeover of mortgage giants Fannie Mae and Freddy Mac—although unavoidable—involves meaningful risk of loss to the taxpayer. In effect, this is the bill coming due for decades of implicit subsidies to these two quasigovernment institutions and to the housing sector that they have supported. The $700 billion financial rescue package (the TARP) passed by the Congress in October 2008 implies risk to the taxpayer, while offering some possibility that the government might earn a profit. Indeed, the way in which most of the initial $350 billion of TARP resources have been deployed suggests a fairly high likelihood that the government (which can finance the TARP with very low cost borrowing) will ultimately earn a moderate profit. In contrast, government support provided through less transparent means, including exceptionally low interest rates set by the Federal Reserve and modifications of tax regulations by the Treasury, will have very substantial costs to the general public.

These government interventions and more that are probably yet to come will provide at least partial bailouts to some miscreants at the expense of the general public. Correspondingly, there will be considerable "immoral result" in the present and significant "moral hazard" will be generated for the future. These adverse consequences necessarily accompany virtually any meaningful effort to keep a major financial crisis such as that now underway from spinning out of control and doing substantial and unnecessary damage to the economy. Thus, government intervention to help deal with a major financial crisis is inevitably a balancing act. Bailouts that are too generous and too readily available generate too much immoral result and moral hazard and cost too much to the general public relative to the protection they provide to innocent bystanders. Interventions that are too weak to contain the crisis impose large costs on many (but not all) miscreants, but involve unacceptable collateral damage to the innocent.

In the present crisis, policy efforts are attempting to achieve the right balance. At least in some important respects, they may be better achieving this balance than in past crises. Broad application of mark-to-market accounting has forced many financial institutions to recognize large losses at a relatively early stage of the crisis—rather than disguising the situation with continued overvaluation of distressed assets. Financial institutions in the United States and Europe have been compelled to raise hundreds of billions of dollars of new capital, seriously diluting the position of existing shareholders. Some of those most responsible for the debacle have lost their jobs and seen their private wealth collapse. With respect to immoral result and moral hazard, these results compare favorably with what happened in the US Savings and Loan crisis of the 1980s or the Japanese banking crisis of the 1990s With substantial punishment already delivered to many of the guilty, as well as to many of the innocent, the most pressing issue now is containment of the real economic damage from the crisis. As the present crisis recedes, but before memory of it fades, it will be essential to reconsider how the risks of future crises can be diminished—especially in view of the intensification of future moral hazard problems arising from the extraordinary actions taken to help contain the present crisis.

Some have suggested that a useful way out of present difficulties is to suspend mark-to-market accounting and even to consider the re-introduction of accounting gimmicks like the "net worth certificates" that were useful in the 1980s in helping keep financial institutions artificially solvent. Indeed, it was fortunate in the early 1980s that applicable accounting practices did not force US depository institutions to promptly report large declines in the market value of their portfolios of loans, mortgages, and other debt securities. At that time, when monetary policy needed to focus on containment and reduction of inflation even as the economy was falling into deep recession, it would have been highly dangerous to reveal that the entire savings and loan industry was deeply insolvent and that many important commercial banks were at least moderately insolvent on a mark-to-market basis. At that time, allowing depository institutions to carry loans and securities at book values, rather than at deeply depressed mark-to-market values, was the well-established practice—derived from an era during which the behavior of depository institutions was tightly constrained by regulation and fluctuations in interest rates were generally modest. When this practice was not enough to disguise insolvency, net worth certificates—which I prefer to call the "absence of net worth certificates"—were created as a mechanism of regulatory forbearance that allowed institutions to maintain accounting measures of their capital above regulatory minimums. Commercial banks generally regained economic solvency by the mid- to late 1980s through the recovery of the economy, the decline in market interest rates, and the recovery in loan values. Consequently, the government was not stuck with large losses from the necessity to restore solvency to the commercial banking system (although some costs were incurred in restructuring individual banks). For savings and loan associations, the outcome was not so fortunate. The government was ultimately forced to absorb large losses in order to bail out depositors.

The key point, however, is not whether the government is ultimately forced to recognize large costs when it allows financial institutions to use deceptive accounting practices. Individual investors are entitled to believe that assets they hold are worth more than their current market values; indeed this is often the reason why investors hold particular assets. However, an individual investor, whatever his personal beliefs, is not allowed to overstate the probable market value of an asset he pledges as security for a loan—that is fraud. If the value of the asset drops after the loan is made, that is acceptable provided that the loan covenant does not provide for an increase in collateral in these circumstances. Once the loan reaches maturity, however, the value of assets pledged as collateral for a renewed loan must respect the market valuation of the assets at that time.

Similarly, financial institutions should be able to issue longer maturity claims with no promises about their value before maturity on the basis of assets of adequate initial market value.[6] Financial institutions, however, should not be allowed to issue purportedly liquid financial claims in excess of the current market value of the assets that back these claims. This goes well beyond the already somewhat dangerous practice of "banking" that seeks to endow financial claims with greater liquidity that the assets that back them. If the holders of the claims discover, or even suspect, that the value of the assets backing their supposedly liquid claims is less than the assumed value of these claims, a run is likely to ensue. The government may forestall such runs by providing explicit or implicit guarantees that will sometimes (but not always) result in open or disguised bailouts, but the consequence is that government policy is effectively facilitating financial fraud. The alternative and correct solution is to require that financial institutions that issue supposedly liquid claims to maintain sufficient capital to ensure that even when seemingly unreasonable declines occur in the market value of their assets, there will be sufficient backing for the claims that have been issued.

At present, mark-to-market accounting is already generally in place for most financial institutions. There are undoubtedly some difficulties about how this principle is applied, and some reforms are worthy of serious consideration. However, at this stage, going back to book value accounting in order to conceal losses in the values of assets held by financial institutions would simply be a lie—and not a very believable lie. Investors are unlikely to be fooled very much this time by accounting statements that they know are not fair representations of the economic health of financial institutions. The taxpaying public should not be deceived into taking on substantial additional risk by under-the-table actions of the regulatory authorities who seek to delay the recognition of losses in the hope that better times will wash these losses away. If public funds are needed to inject additional capital into weak financial institutions, the Congress and the general public should face up to the required legislation—and to the dangers of not enacting it. This is a vital safeguard against the danger that immoral result and moral hazard will get completely out of hand.

Finally, for the longer run, this crisis re-teaches an important lesson: When financial institutions generate substantial risks through the creation of liquidity, they need to understand these risks and to hold adequate reserves of capital to safeguard both themselves and the financial system. Unrealistic accounting and special gimmicks to conceal losses are not the answer. As Adam Smith recognized in *The Wealth of Nations,* the great wheel of circulation that keeps the economy running relies on the activities of financial institutions that perform the magic of creating liquidity. But great danger lies in allowing too much liquidity to be created without adequate reserves of capital.

Notes

Originally published in *Business Economics*, Vol. 44, No. 1 (January 2009), pp. 3–16.

1. Financial crises are, of course, a much studied topic in economics both in theoretical and in empirical research; see, for example, Flood and Garber [1994]. For me, the most interesting part of this literature are historical accounts of what has happened in various crises, in the United States and elsewhere; see, in particular, Friedman and Schwartz [1963], Hawtrey [1962], Kindleberger and Aliber [2005], Galbraith [1961], and Mayer [1997].
2. All of the quotations from Smith [1937].
3. Robert Heilbroner [1967] expresses his appreciation of Smith and his great work as follows: "For Smith's encyclopedic scope and knowledge there can be only admiration. It was only in the eighteenth century that so huge, all-embracing, secure, caustic, and profound a book (as *The Wealth of Nations*) could have been written...And perhaps no economist will ever again so encompass his age as Adam Smith."
4. Homage should be paid here to the work of James Tobin [1963] who emphasized that "money" was not uniquely important as a liquid asset and that commercial banks were not uniquely important as creators of "money." Rather, there is a wide array of assets from the perspective of their holders and liabilities from the perspective of their issuers with varying degrees of liquidity that are issued by a variety of financial institutions.
5. Smith was well aware of the general problem of "moral hazard" although he did not explicitly use this terminology. In Smith's day, however, the modern widespread practice of providing government guarantees and bailouts for financial institutions was not yet well developed. Accordingly, Smith does not comment on this issue.

6. This may be interpreted as a modified version of Smith's stricture that banks should not engage in any longer-term lending. Longer-term lending that is financed by issuing longer-term claims, with no explicit or implicit claim of shorter-term certainty of value, should be acceptable. But it is essential to guard against the ever-present danger that claims created in this way will be perceived to have greater liquidity than they are inherently capable of sustaining.

References

Flood, Robert P., and Peter M. Garber. 1994. *Speculative Bubbles, Speculative Attacks, and Policy Switching.* The MIT Press.

Friedman, Milton, and Anna J. Schwartz. 1963. *A Monetary History of the United States: 1867–1960.* Princeton University Press.

Galbraith, John Kenneth. 1961. *The Great Crash.* Houghton Mifflin Co.

Hawtrey, R. G. 1962. *The Art of Central Banking.* Frank Cass & Co.

Heilbroner, Robert L. 1967. *The Worldly Philosphers,* 3rd ed. Simon and Schuster.

Kindleberger, Charles P., and Robert Z. Aliber. 2005. *Manias, Panics, and Crashes,* 5th ed. John Wiley & Sons, Inc.

Mayer, Martin. 1997. *The Bankers: The Next Generation.* Truman Talley Books/Dutton.

Mussa, Michael, and Roger C. Kormendi. 1979. *The Taxation of Municipal Bonds.* American Enterprise Institute.

Smith, Adam. 1937. *The Wealth of Nations.* Modern Library (Random House).

Tobin, James. 1963. "Commercial Banks as Creators of 'Money'," in *Banking and Monetary Studies,* edited by Deane Carson. Richard D. Irwin; reprinted in James Tobin, 1971. *Essays in Economics: Volume I: Macroeconomics.* Markham Publishing Company.

CHAPTER 33

2009

UNDERWRITING, MORTGAGE LENDING, AND HOUSE PRICES: 1996–2008

James A. Wilcox, University of California, Berkeley

Underwriting standards for residential mortgages (henceforth: underwriting) are now generally regarded as having been unusually lax during the mid-2000s. Underwriting then tightened up again during the financial crisis that began in 2007. The laxity of underwriting and its ensuing tightness since the mid-1990s likely contributed considerably to the unprecedented rise and subsequent fall of mortgage volumes and house prices.

Conventional data do not satisfactorily measure aggregate underwriting over the past decade: Easing of underwriting, inside and especially outside of banks, was likely much more extensive than these data indicate. The Federal Reserve's survey data for banks' residential lending records, for example, that easing for 2004–2006 was about the same as the easing recorded for 1992–1994; the data also indicate the 2004–2006 easing was also about the same as the tightening recorded for 2001–2003. However, there is reason to believe that easing inside—and especially outside—of banks was likely much more extensive during 2004–2006. To the extent that underwriting eased more at nonbank lenders, the Federal Reserve [2009] and Office of the Comptroller of the Currency (OCC) [2008] survey data omit an important aspect of aggregate lending standards.

Although we have several indicators of underwriting, none seems sufficient alone. Therefore, in this paper we sought to summarize the information about underwriting that was contained in several variables that we judged to be related to underwriting during this period. We used the data from the Federal Reserve's questions to banks and from the OCC surveys that ask their examiners about banks' underwriting. We supplemented those data with other data that are related to underwriting: credit spreads, the market share of adjustable rate mortgages, and mortgage delinquency rates.

We argue that, for this time period, the method of principal components (PC) can usefully summarize the information in those variables about underwriting. We used the PC method to generate a single, new data series and show that the resulting indicator variable exhibits correlations with the input variables to the PC method that are consistent with its measurement of underwriting. In addition, the indicator variable suggested that underwriting eased considerably in the late 1990s and dramatically more in the mid-2000s. It also suggested that underwriting tightened in and after the recession of 2001 and tightened dramatically starting in 2007, as the financial crisis erupted. Thus, the derived indicator of tightness fits current understanding of past underwriting much better than conventional measures or the individual variables that were related to underwriting.

For the practicing economist, having a single variable that both summarizes multiple measures and more accurately measures a phenomenon, like underwriting, can be very valuable. Being able to present a single, summary variable, for example in a time series plot, is often very informative. A summary variable can be especially useful in practice when other candidate variables have well-known shortcomings. In the case at hand, for example, an audience might quickly understand that the Federal Reserve and OCC surveys only cover commercial banks, whose market shares of mortgages originated and held dwindled over the past decade and whose underwriting probably loosened much less than underwriting outside of regulated banks.

To assess the caliber of the derived underwriting variable, we used the variable in a vector auto-regression (VAR). In light of our current understanding of how underwriting evolved over this period, the estimated effects *on* the underwriting indicator variable provide information about the caliber of the indicator series itself. To the extent that the VAR estimates based on the underwriting indicator variable coincide with our understanding of housing and mortgage markets, our confidence in the PC method and in the underwriting indicator is strengthened.

Further, the estimated VAR suggests how, in turn, the other variables, such as house prices and the volume of and interest rates on mortgages, were affected *by* changes in underwriting. Again, to the extent that the estimated responses to underwriting laxity and tightening fit our understanding, they further raise our confidence in the indicator of underwriting that we derived. In fact, the VAR-based estimates suggest that our new indicator of underwriting helps account for the path of gross domestic product (GDP) and for the unprecedented movements of mortgage volumes and house prices during the mortgage and housing booms and busts.

Thus, we describe how PC helped in a specific instance with the challenges that economists generally face:

- How to summarize several, related, imperfect indicators of a particular phenomenon.
- How to convey the effects on, and the effects of, that phenomenon on other pertinent variables.

Events and Issues

Housing Markets since the Mid-1990s

Over the past decade, house prices and mortgages rose enormously, peaked, and then began their declines. Figure 33.1 plots two quarterly data series for 1996–2008: real house prices (RHP) and mortgage balances relative to potential nominal GDP (MORTPOT). Both series rose steeply, nearly doubling by 2006, before declining thereafter. (Appendix B describes the data series more precisely and provides their sources. All data series are national aggregates and seasonally adjusted as appropriate.)

Similarly, Figure 33.2 plots data for the four-quarter growth rate of nominal house prices (GNHP) and data for the percent difference between actual and potential real GDP.[1] Figure 33.2 shows that house prices not only rose considerably in the late 1990s, but that they accelerated thereafter, rising faster and faster through 2006, after which they decelerated and then, starting in 2007, the real and nominal levels of house prices declined. Figure 33.2 also shows that incomes (relative to potential GDP) also rose considerably during the late 1990s, but from 2001 onward, hovered just below potential GDP. Given the quite rapid advance of potential real GDP after 2000, actual incomes rose considerably too. But, Figure 33.2 also intimates that it would be difficult to attribute the strong and rising growth rate of house prices to accelerating income growth.

What Is Underwriting?

At various times, various analysts include different aspects of lending under the rubric of "underwriting." For concreteness here, we take underwriting standards

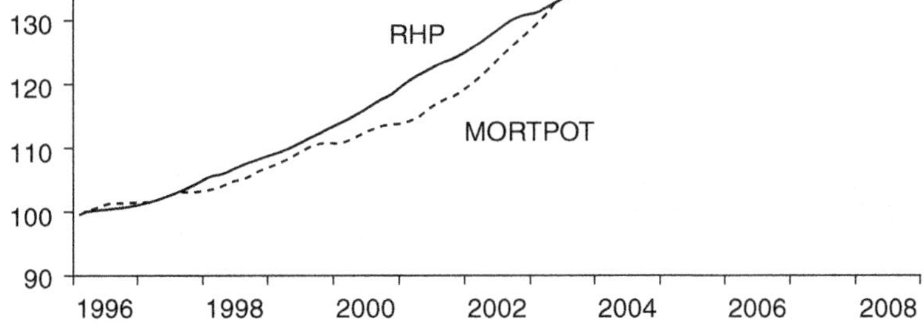

Figure 33.1 Real house price (RHP) and residential mortgage loans per potential gross domestic product (MORTPOT).

Indexed: 1996:1 = 100.

Source: Freddie Mac, Bureau of Economic Analysis. Federal Reserve, CBO quarterly data, 1996–2008.

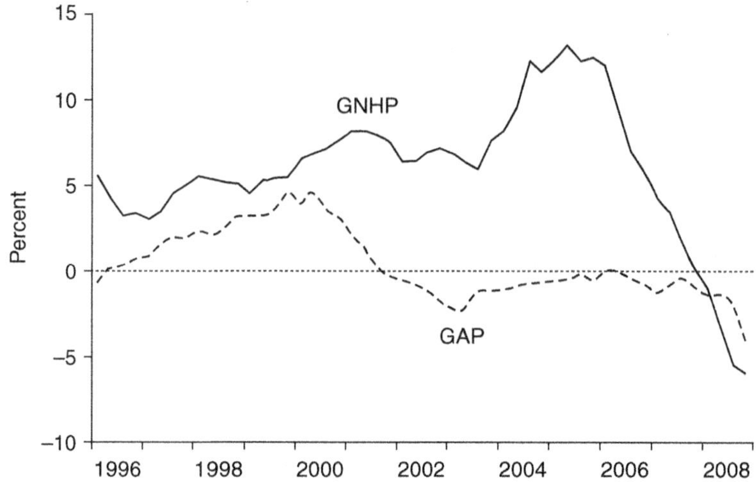

Figure 33.2 Growth in nominal house prices (GNHP) and output gap (GAP).
Source: Freddie Mac, Bureau of Economic Analysis, CBO percent, quarterly data, 1996–2008.

to consist of all noninterest-rate terms and conditions that affect decisions about mortgage applications. Thus, we consider, for example, a lender's choices about minimum Fair Issac Corporation (FICO) scores,[2] documentation requirements, the maximum loan-to-value (LTV) ratio, and applicants' debt-to-income (DTI) ratio. This is consonant with the Federal Reserve's survey question, which asks banks about their "credit standards for approving applications from individuals for mortgage loans to purchase homes..." (See Appendix A).

There are many ways that lenders can ease or tighten underwriting. Lenders might lower the minimum FICO score or down payment that they would consider. In addition to altering quantitative standards, lenders might also alter the nature of a standard. For example, during the housing boom of the mid-2000s, sellers (often builders) came to provide "gifts" of down payments to buyers to help them qualify for Federal Housing Administration (FHA) mortgages. From a very small share around 2000, by 2005–2006, the shares of FHA loans that included down payment gifts from nonprofits (which in effect were seller-funded) rose to nearly one-half of FHA mortgage originations.[3] Thus, there are myriad ways that lenders can ease or tighten underwriting.

Possible Indicators of Underwriting Tightness

Consider some of the better-known data series that we might use to better understand the time series of aggregate (residential mortgage) underwriting standards. Figures 33.3 and 33.4 plot average values of some variables for which lenders often have quantitative standards, say maximum LTV, based on data for LTV at the time that mortgages were originated. Figure 33.3a plots the average LTV based on data from the Federal Housing Finance Agency. The average LTV might have suggested

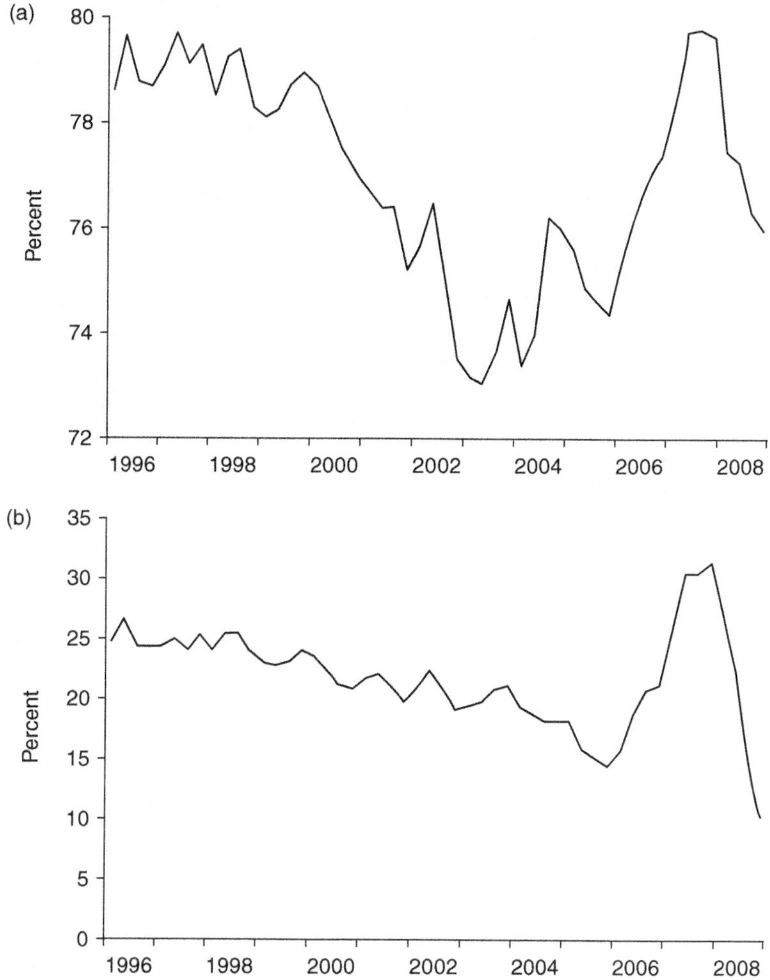

Figure 33.3 (a) Loan-to-value (LTV) ratio for all conventional single-family nonfarm mortgage loans; (b) Percent of conventional single-family nonfarm mortgage loans with loan-to-value (LTV) ratio greater or equal to 90 percent.

Source: Federal Housing Finance Agency, quarterly data, 1996–2008.

that underwriting had been tightening, as evidenced by LTVs falling (and therefore down payments rising), from the mid-1990s through the mid-2000s. Analogously, the higher LTVs in 2006–2008 might have been a signal of more lax underwriting then.

Figure 33.3b shows the share of all mortgage originations that had LTVs greater than 90 percent (or equivalently, had down payments of 10% or less). The data in Figure 33.3b could be seen as support for the pattern of underwriting tightening followed by laxity. The series shows a rather steady descent from the mid-1990s until 2006, when it had fallen to about half its average value recorded over the full decade of the 1990s (not shown). The share then leapt, rising during the financial crisis to about twice the low levels recorded in the mid-2000s. A priori, one might have thought that the share would have tracked overall underwriting tightening: if underwriting tightened, minimum down payments likely would rise, thereby reducing the share of borrowers who made down payments of 10 percent or less.

But, by virtually all accounts, the opposite was true: underwriting eased during the mid-2000s and then tightened sharply when the financial crisis struck beginning in 2007. How then did average LTVs move opposite to underwriting laxity? The answer, as we now understand it, is that, at least in part, second mortgages originated at closing (piggybacks) and other mechanisms allowed more borrowers to have first mortgages that had 80 percent or lower LTVs, thereby reducing the series in Figures 33.3a, b. To further upset the conventional correlation between underwriting and its indicators, Sherlund (2008) shows that, at least in the securitized portion of the subprime mortgage market, average FICO scores *rose* quite steadily over the 1997–2007 period.

However, some data series do conform more closely to underwriting having eased in the 2000s before tightening significantly during the financial crisis. For example, again based on securitized subprime mortgages, Sherlund (2008) shows that average ratios of DTI and of LTV rose, and the share of adjustable-rate mortgages (ARMs) rose. Figure 33.4, taken from Sherlund (2008), show that the combined first-plus-second mortgage-LTV (CLTV) rose and the share of originations that had full documentation declined throughout the 2000s, until the financial crisis began. And, the share of "low quality" mortgages, defined as those with low documentation and LTVs of at least 95 percent, rose markedly after 2002, before plummeting in 2007. Thus, the data in Figure 33.4 suggests evermore lax underwriting until 2007. Therefore, although some commonly used data series seemed to signal tightening of underwriting standards, other series were simultaneously signaling laxity during the mid-2000s and tightening thereafter. Thus, there is plenty of reason to suspect that the usual proxy variables for underwriting in the aggregate are unlikely to suffice for analyzing recent events in housing markets.

Survey Measures of Underwriting

Federal banking regulators regularly conduct surveys to ask more directly about banks' underwriting standards. The Federal Reserve asks banks themselves to report whether they have tightened underwriting; the OCC asks its own employees about whether the banks that they have directly examined have tightened underwriting standards.[4]

We use data series on the net percentage of banks each quarter that were reported to the Federal Reserve and by the OCC as having tightened underwriting.[5] Since we are more interested in the aggregate level of underwriting tightness than the number of banks that tightened each period, Figure 33.5 displays the cumulative sum of net tightening of underwriting since 1996:Q1 (when the series takes a starting value of zero). The two series have been highly correlated, but there were also some notable differences. The cumulated Federal Reserve series,

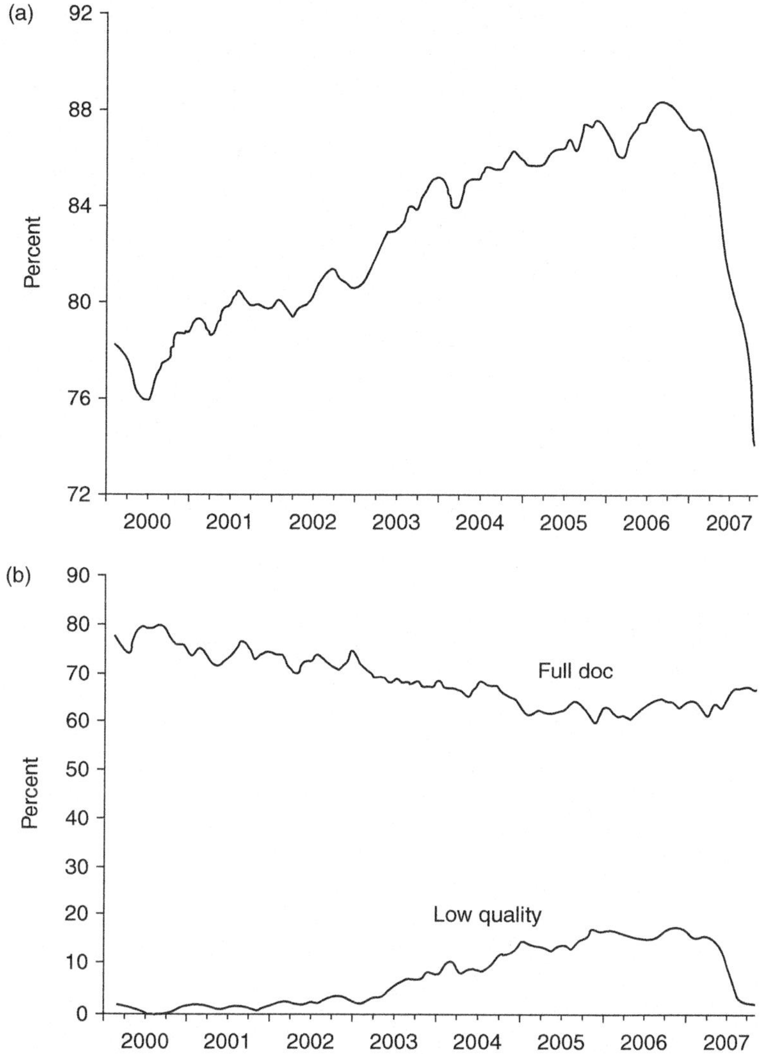

Figure 33.4 (a) Average combined loan-to-value at origination; (b) Loan documentation at origination.

Source: Sherlund (2008), monthly data, 2000–2007.

SUMUWFED, in Figure 33.5 implies *no net change* in underwriting during the late 1990s or even from 2002 through the end of 2006. By contrast, the cumulated OCC series, SUMUWOCC, implies that underwriting eased considerably before the 2001 recession. Especially notable, given the widespread sense that underwriting had broadly and significantly eased from 2004 onward, SUMUWOCC exhibits a large and steep decline until 2007. Thus, the OCC data paint a quite different picture of banks' underwriting standards. We cannot, of course, be sure which series more accurately portrays actual underwriting practices—presumably each series

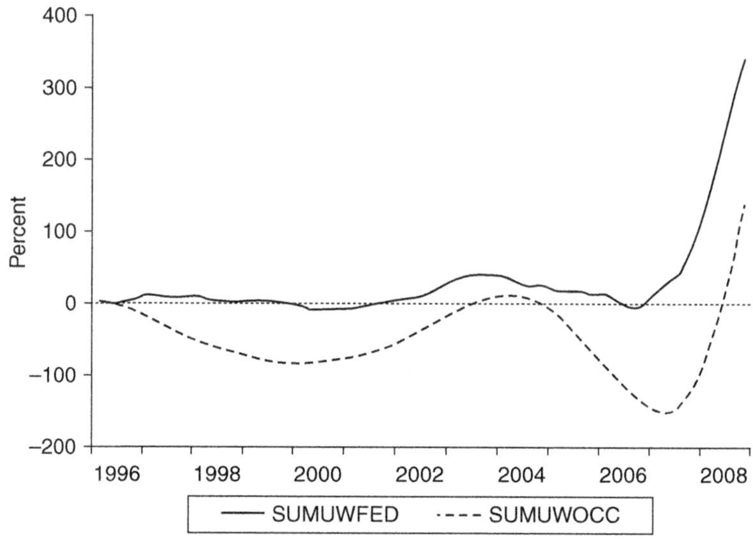

Figure 33.5 Cumulative net percentage tightening of residential mortgage underwriting standards.

Percentage of banks tightening minus percentage loosening, indexed 1996:1 = 0.

Source: Surveys of banks by the Federal Reserve (SUMUWFED) and the Office of the Comptroller of the Currency (SUMUWOCC), quarterly data, 1996–2008. OCC source data pertain to Q1; remaining quarters are linearly interpolated.

has some virtues. But, we can see that different series, even those that presumably are meant to measure quite similar phenomena in similar samples, can carry quite different information.

Other series are also likely to add information. They may cover different lenders or measure different aspects of underwriting. For example, the Federal Reserve and the OCC conducted surveys of commercial banks. Over this sample period, banks' share of mortgage originations and holdings fell significantly. That decline may be partly attributable to other lenders' having lower and lowered underwriting standards relative to those of the much more heavily regulated and examined commercial banks. Other variables might well allow for such developments. Thus, we seek a manageable list of other variables that might affect aggregate underwriting and/or might reflect changes in underwriting.

Other Indicators of Underwriting

One less direct, but potentially useful, indicator of underwriting might be based on (nonmortgage) interest rate spreads. The spread that we used as a proxy variable for spreads on risky bonds was the difference (in percentage points) between yields on high-yield corporate ("junk") bonds and US Treasury yields. This spread is one indicator of the amount of, and return per unit of credit risk.

Figure 33.6 plots SPREAD, the yield spread on high-yield corporate bonds. SPREAD declined until the Asian financial crisis of the late 1990s and then generally rose around the 2001 recession and thereafter. The spread then fell precipitously into 2005 and was at about record lows rose until the financial crisis that began in 2007. Thus, credit markets seemed to judge that there were relatively low default probabilities and or low rewards per unit of credit risk.

The results of Demyanyk and Van Hemert (forthcoming) can be used to estimate changes in underwriting for some of the years in the mid-2000s. Their estimates are based on a very large sample of mortgages that were originated in the 2000s by banks or by nonbanks. Their estimates control for the effects of a lengthy list of factors on delinquency rates: borrowers' FICO score, down payments, house price growth, and so on. Given the controls, we interpret the remaining changes in default rates as reflecting the tightness of prior underwriting standards: the higher the ensuing delinquency rates (importantly, given their long list of controls), the more lax were underwriting standards.[6] The mnemonic for this variable is XSDEL.

Finally, we used an indicator based on the relation between the prevalence of ARMs and the interest rates on adjustable- and on fixed-rate mortgages (ARMs and FRMs). Historically, and not surprisingly, the ARM share of mortgage originations has reliably risen as FRM rates rose relative to those on ARMs.

During this period, it appears that underwriting changes were perhaps concentrated among sub-prime and similar (e.g., Alt-A) borrowers. These borrowers disproportionately took on ARMs, which temporarily sometimes had fixed-rate-based

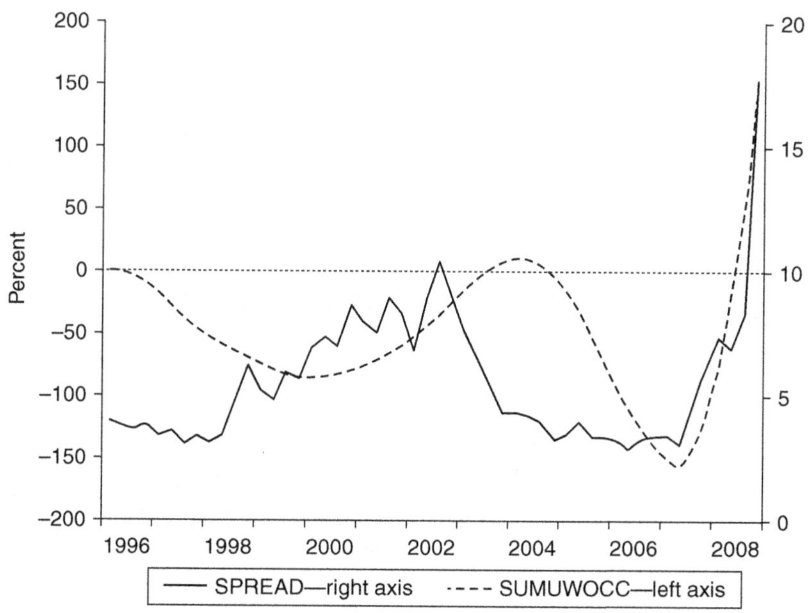

Figure 33.6 The yield spread between junk bonds and US Treasuries (SPREAD) and cumulative net tightening (SUMUWOCC).

Source: Economy.com. OCC quarterly data, 1996 2008.

payments and/or permitted negative amortization. Such "pay option ARMs" have become infamous. They also had become more numerous during the mid-2000s. Applications for these and other mortgages, as suggested by Figure 33.4b, were also subject to easing documentation requirements. Thus, through the mid-2000s, more and more borrowers were being approved for mortgages with essentially easier underwriting standards.

To allow for these developments, we constructed a data series, ARMRESID, which was the residual from a regression (over a longer, 1987–2008 sample period) of the market share of ARMs on a constant term, the nominal interest rate on FRMs, and the nominal interest rate on ARMs. The residuals from that regression indicate the otherwise-unexplained ARM share. We interpret the large positive values for ARMRESID over the 2003–2006 period as indicative of generally eased underwriting standards. These market developments may well be peculiar to this sample period. Thus, one would not want to presume that this indicator would be valid for other situations. But, for this period, it may well have captured an important part of the underwriting conditions that prevailed.

Other series are likely to convey additional relevant information about underwriting. But, we deliberately chose to exclude many of them. For example, numbers and volumes of mortgages, housing starts, residential construction expenditures, and house prices are likely to be useful indicators of mortgage underwriting. But, because our goal is to construct an indicator that we can then use to help account for movements in those and other variables, we chose not to include them in the construction of our indicator of underwriting.

Variable Reduction via PC

We have argued that we have five variables that serve as indicators of various aspects of bank and nonbank underwriting standards. Each of the five variables had some strengths and some weaknesses as indicators of aggregate underwriting standards. (If any one variable had been plausibly regarded as a "sufficient variable," we would have just used that variable.)

Because they each are related to overall underwriting, they tend to be somewhat correlated; the average simple correlation coefficient between them was 0.55; the multicollinearity of this group of five variables was naturally considerably higher than that. Because each variable pertained to underwriting, using the five indicators separately would render interpretation somewhat problematic. For all of these reasons, we applied the method of PC to our five indicator variables to derive a single, composite indicator of underwriting.[7] The resulting first PC is the single data series that most closely tracks the five variables used in the PC analysis: the Federal Reserve and the OCC underwriting data, the risky bond yield spread, the Demyanyk and Van Hemert "excess" default rates, and the "excess" ARM share variable. In that way, the PC method assimilates some of the information from each of the five series into a single indicator variable.

Use of the PC method in economics has often been hindered by the inability to attach persuasive structural interpretations to the results. In the case at hand, however, using input variables that are reasonably connected to underwriting increases our confidence that the first PC is a satisfactory candidate as an indicator of aggregate underwriting.

The First PC as an Indicator of Underwriting Standards

Our confidence is buttressed by the resulting equation for the first PC of the five chosen indicator variables. To the first PC, we assigned the mnemonic "UWPC":

$$\begin{aligned} \text{UWPC} = {} & 6.40 \\ & + 13.9 \times \text{SPREAD} - 9.16 \times \text{XSDEL} \\ & - 2.11 \times \text{ARMRESID} \\ & + 0.457 \times \text{SUMUWFED} \\ & + 0.576 \times \text{SUMUWOCC} \end{aligned}$$

As we might expect from an indicator of underwriting tightness, UWPC rose both with the Federal Reserve and with the OCC measures of underwriting tightness. UWPC also rose with increases in the bond-yield credit spread, SPREAD. On the other hand, UWPC fell, and thus indicated underwriting easing, as "excess" Demyanyk and Van Hemert adjusted delinquency rates (XSDEL) rose and as the "excess" share of ARMs (ARMRESID) rose. Thus, UWPC seems consistently to rise and fall with underwriting tightness and laxity.

By construction, UWPC is not perfectly correlated with any of the individual series but rather tends to reflect the common part of the movements that is present in each of the series. Nonetheless, the correlation with each of the series was quite high; the average of the five correlations with UWPC was 0.65, ranging from about 0.4 with ARMRESID to about 0.8 with SPREAD. To illustrate the differences in the time paths of some of the variables used to construct UWPC, Figure 33.6 plots SPREAD and the OCC-based cumulative tightening variable, SUMUWOCC. In general, SPREAD suggested episodes of tightening and loosening considerably before SUMUWOCC did. They both, however, pointed toward underwriting tightening starting with the 2007 financial crisis, an episode that everyone recognized.

Figure 33.7 shows that UWPC hovered near its average value (zero) from 1996 until 2000. UWPC then rose modestly into 2002. UWPC then declined significantly and quite steadily until hitting its lowest value in early 2007. In that respect, UWPC suggests that underwriting eased significantly from 2002 through 2006. As a result, UWPC may contribute significantly to explaining the housing boom of the mid-2000s.

The onset of the financial crisis in 2007 then saw UWPC rise very sharply, by more than double the prior decline, indicating extreme underwriting tightness. Again, the size and speed of the rebound of UWPC should not be too surprising in light of the extent to which the credit markets shut down in late 2008, which was reflected in SPREAD and in the upward jolts to net increase percentages recorded

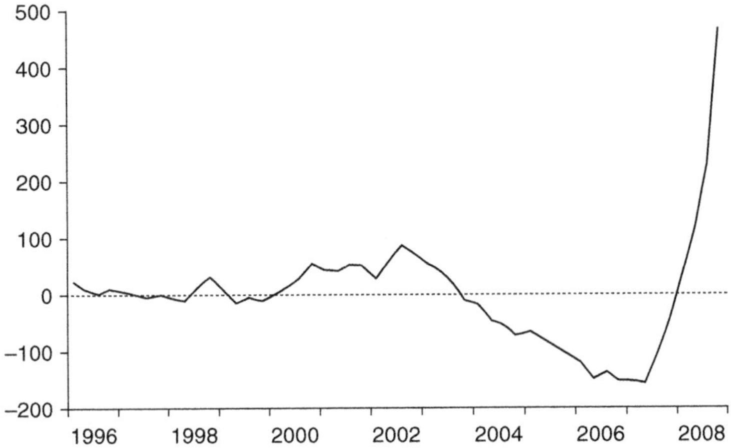

Figure 33.7 Underwriting standards estimated by first principal component (UWPC) of SPREAD, ARMRESID, SUMUWFED, SUMUWOCC, and XSDEL.

Source: Federal Housing Finance Agency, economy.com, Federal Reserve, OCC, Demyanyk and Van Hemert (Forthcoming) quarterly data, 1996–2008.

in the Federal Reserve and OCC surveys. In that regard, too, UWPC appears to have generally tracked the tightening of underwriting standards during the financial crisis.

Using Underwriting Measures

Estimating a VAR

One way to assess VAR results is to examine the estimated dynamic responses of each endogenous variable to "shocks" to other endogenous variables. These shocks, or innovations, are the movements in each variable that could not be explained by the past (and sometimes current) movements of the other variables included in the VAR. In the case at hand, the resulting impulse responses (IRs) functions can be used to help assess not only the dynamic structure of housing and mortgage markets, but also the caliber of the constructed underwriting variable, UWPC.

We used quarterly data from 1996:Q1–2008:Q4 to estimate a VAR. In addition to a constant term and a linear trend, the VAR included five endogenous variables in the following order: (As measured by GAP, GNHP, MORTPOT, UWPC, and IMORT. GAP measures the difference between actual and potential real GDP. GNHP is the growth rate of nominal house prices. MORTPOT is mortgage balances relative to potential GDP.) And, IMORT is the interest rate on FRMs. (Further descriptions and sources are given in Appendix B.) We chose these variables because we judged that they were important, aggregate variables that were likely to affect or be affected by underwriting, or both.[8]

Estimated Responses

Figures 33.8–33.12 display the IRs for the five variables in the VAR. Each figure shows the responses of the other four endogenous variables to a one-unit shock to an endogenous variable. (Not shown are the responses of each variable to a prior shock to itself.)

Overall, there were relatively few surprises or puzzling results. In general, the IR functions were consistent, with UWPC serving as an effective indicator of aggregate underwriting standards. Almost all of the IRs are consistent with that interpretation. Also, most of the other IRs are consistent with our prior understandings about the interactions of housing and mortgage markets.

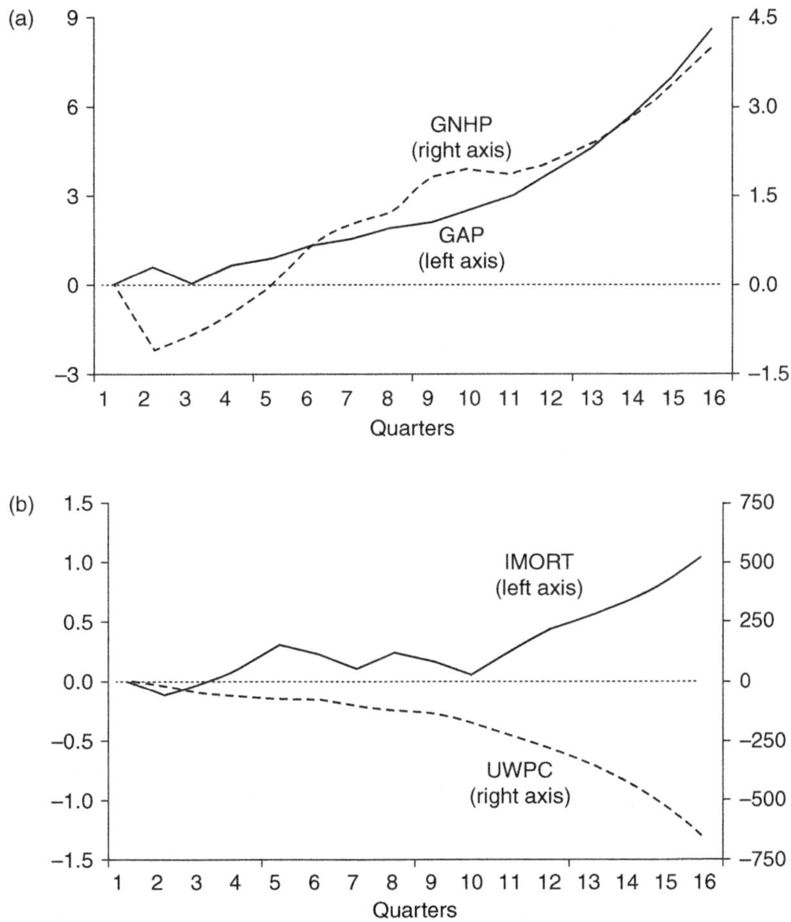

Figure 33.8 (a) Response of the output gap (GAP) and of growth in nominal house prices (GNHP) to a unit shock to mortgage balances (MORTPOT); (b) Response of mortgage interest rates (IMORT) and of underwriting standards (UWPC) to a unit shock to mortgage balances (MORTPOT).

Figure 33.8a shows that both incomes (GAP) and, on balance, house prices (GNHP) rose in response to an upward shock in the amount of mortgage balances. Those responses are consistent with the shock emanating either from the demand or supply sides of the mortgage market. Nor does Figure 33.8b sort out the source of the shock to mortgage balances. Figure 33.8b shows that the mortgage interest rate (IMORT) rose (consistent with responses to a demand shock) and the indicator of underwriting tightness (UWPC) declined (consistent with responses to a shock to mortgage supply) in response to a positive shock to mortgage balances.

Figure 33.9 displays the responses to an upward shock to GDP (as measured by GAP). Figure 33.9a shows, not surprisingly, that both house prices and mortgage balances rose following a shock to incomes. Figure 33.9b shows that a shock to GDP raised mortgage interest rates. On the other hand, it lowered UWPC. Again, that adds support for UWPC's serving as an indicator of underwriting tightness: as incomes rose, the likelihood of borrowers having payment problems receded; and as

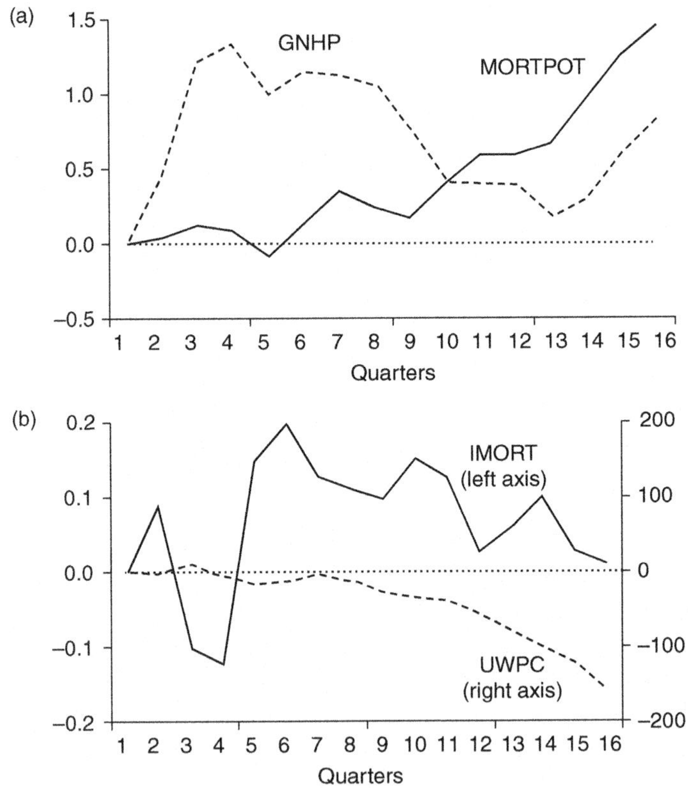

Figure 33.9a (a) Response of mortgage balances (MORTPOT) and of growth in nominal house prices (GNHP) to a unit shock to the output gap (GAP); (b) Response of mortgage interest rates (IMORT) and of underwriting standards (UWPC) to a unit shock to the output gap (GAP).

incomes also carried house prices upward, lenders may well have found it optimal to reduce their underwriting standards.

Figure 33.10 displays the responses to an increase in mortgage interest rates. Again, conforming to conventional wisdom, higher mortgage rates were estimated to reduce GDP lead to lower mortgage balances, and lower house prices. The estimated IR in Figure 33.10b suggests that higher mortgage interest rates were associated with lenders' tightening their underwriting standards. This suggests that the effect of mortgage interest rates might, in effect, operate not just through their impact on explicit borrowing costs, but also through tighter underwriting terms and conditions. That tightening of standards effectively adds to borrowing costs and reduces effective demand for mortgages and housing. To the extent that underwriting standards systematically rise with mortgage interest rates, the IR in Figure 33.10b further supports UWPC as a useful indicator of underwriting.

In Figure 33.11, the responses to a positive shock to house prices are shown. Figure 33.11a shows that an increase in house prices (controlling for all of the

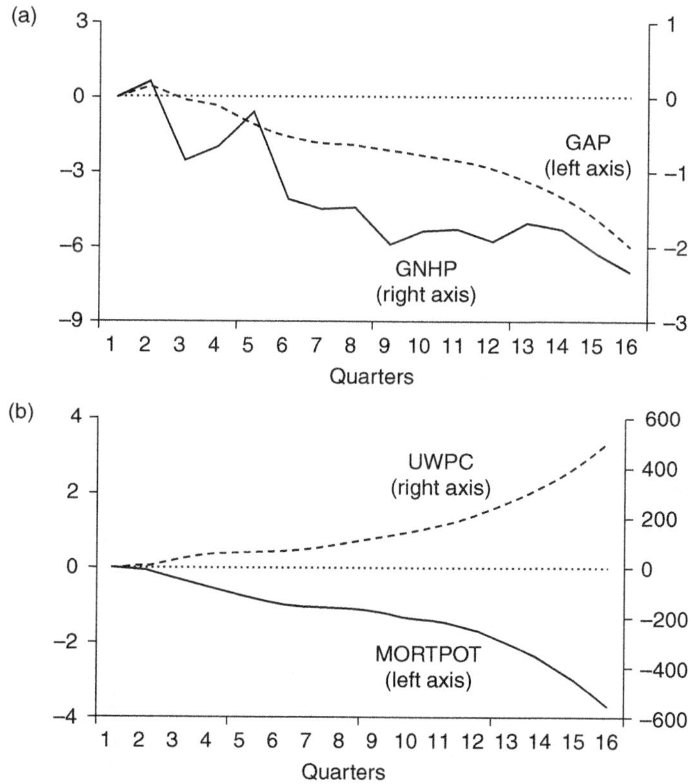

Figure 33.10 (a) Response of the output gap (GAP) and of growth in nominal house prices (GNHP) to a unit shock to mortgage interest rates (IMORT); (b) Response of mortgage balances (MORTPOT) and of underwriting standards (UWPC) to a unit shock to mortgage interest rates (IMORT).

effects that are embodied in the lags of all of the variables in the VAR), not surprisingly, tended to raise both mortgage balances and incomes (or, equivalently, aggregate output). More intriguingly, both UWPC and IMORT tended to fall (at least for the first two years) following an upward shock to house prices. Given the strong momentum observed in house prices, an upward shock reasonably presages even further increases in house prices. Sensibly forecasting that the prices of houses, which collateralize residential mortgages, were likely to continue to rise, it then seems entirely rational for lenders to ease their underwriting standards when house prices rise. And that is what the responses in Figure 33.11b point to: UWPC declines consistently in response to higher house prices.

For the same reason, lenders may have also been willing to reduce the spreads of their mortgage rates above a benchmark rate in response to higher house prices. Higher house prices reduce expected mortgage losses, thereby warranting lower mortgage interest rates. For the first two years following the shock to house prices,

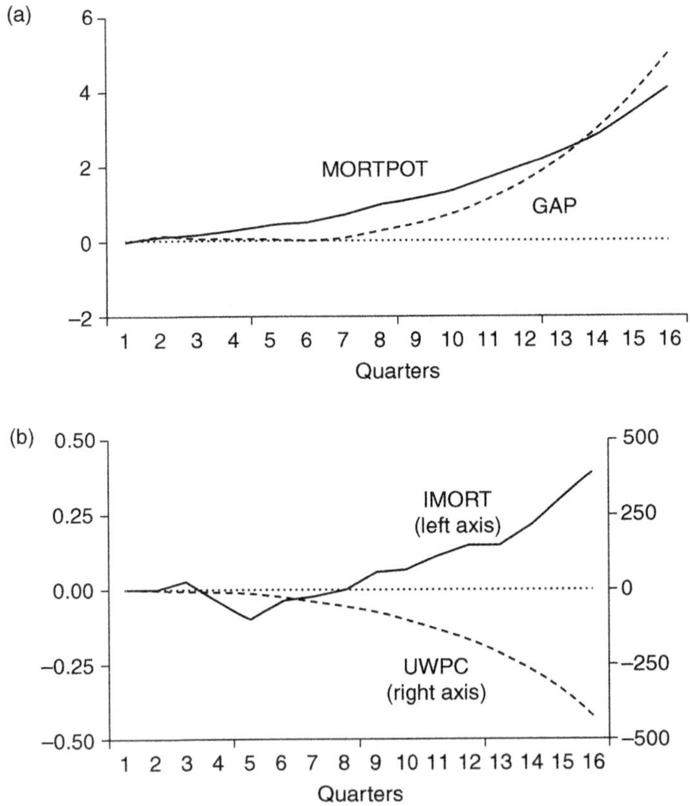

Figure 33.11 (a) Response of the output gap (GAP) and of mortgage balances (MORTPOT) to a unit shock to growth in nominal house prices (GNHP); (b) Response of mortgage interest rates (IMORT) and of underwriting standards (UWPC) to a unit shock to growth in nominal house prices (GNHP).

the responses of IMORT are consistent with lower rates. Over a longer horizon, higher GNHP raised mortgage rates.

Finally, Figure 33.12 displays the estimated responses to estimated shocks to (the estimated indicator of) underwriting, UWPC. In Figure 33.12a, an increase in UWPC, interpreted as a tightening of standards, led both to lower GDP (GAP) and to lower GNHP. Both responses are consistent with UWPC as an indicator of underwriting tightness. Figure 33.12b shows that tighter underwriting, in the form of an upward shock to UWPC, also tended to reduce total mortgage balances outstanding. The responses of mortgage interest rates to UWPC were mixed. It might well be that the positive effects result from lenders' business practices that tend to raise price and nonprice terms sympathetically. On the other hand, the negative effects might reflect that tighter underwriting would slow housing and mortgage markets and lead to lower rates. On balance, the effects on mortgage rates of UWPC did not come down as being consistently negative or positive.

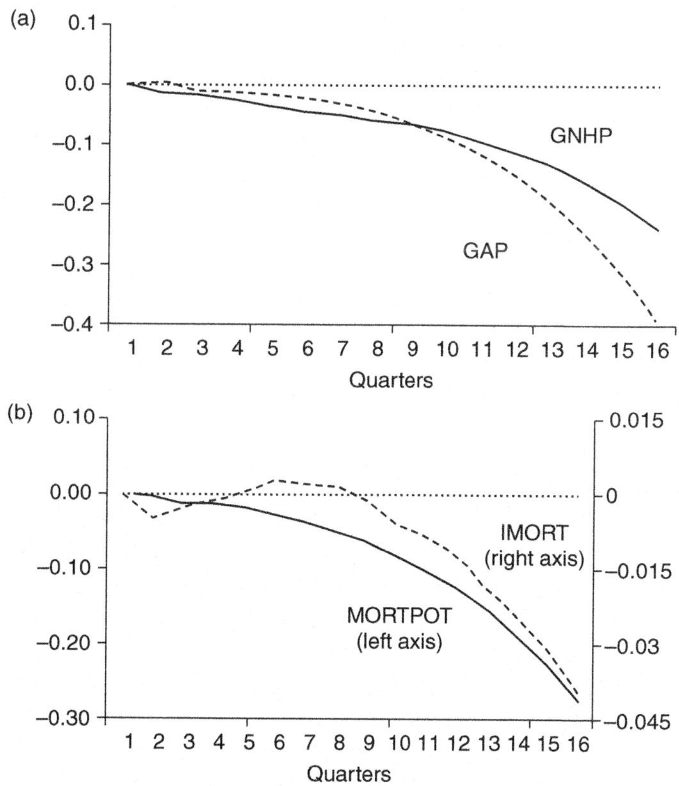

Figure 33.12 (a) Response of the output gap (GAP) and of growth in nominal house prices (GNHP) to a unit shock to underwriting standards (UWPC); (b) Response of mortgage interest rates (IMORT) and of mortgage balances (MORTPOT) to a unit shock to underwriting standards (UWPC).

Implications for Extrapolations

Summary

Underwriting standards may have contributed much to the unprecedented recent rise and subsequent fall of mortgage volumes and house prices since the mid-1990s. Conventional data do not satisfactorily track aggregate underwriting standards for this period. We used the method of PC to construct a superior indicator of underwriting standards. We briefly discuss how and why the method can be usefully applied more generally in economic analysis and presentations.

Unlike many conventional indicators, the underwriting indicator that we constructed. UWPC, tracks the increasingly lax underwriting in the mid-2000s, followed by the extreme tightening of effective underwriting standards during the financial crisis that began in 2007. Our analysis then showed how the indicator of underwriting affected, and was in turn affected by, house prices, mortgage balances. GDP, and mortgage interest rates. The underwriting indicator, as well as the mortgage and housing variables, generally responded in the directions that we expected. Taken together, then, the estimated responses to the indicator of underwriting provided considerable support for the interpretation that UWPC serves as a useful indicator of mortgage underwriting tightness. Thus, the method and its implementation here help us understand better some of the developments in mortgage and housing markets over the past decade.

Double Bubble Trouble?

That is not to say, however, that all of the patterns in these variables are explicable or even economically sensible. Estimating a single constant-coefficient VAR over this particular sample period is subject to at least two concerns. One is that the estimation period is short. The brevity of the sample resulted in part from the absence of data before 1996 for at least two of the five input variables that we used to construct the indicator of underwriting, UWPC. A consequence of the limited data is that sampling errors for the estimated responses loom unusually large.

Second, during part, but maybe not all, of the sample period, a mortgage and housing "bubble" may have taken place. It is standard to have various multiplier effects in the economy and in estimated models. But, bubble-like behavior may have imparted even stronger, extrapolative, or even temporarily explosive effects in mortgage and housing markets (and thus data) for some of the sample period. Such data movements may dominate much of the sample period here, which is partly what makes it so intriguing and worth analyzing. For example, the ever-increasing growth rates of house prices through the mid-2000s, as shown in Figure 33.2, hint at such extrapolative patterns in the data. To the extent that underwriting then responded to forecasted house price growth, as the estimates suggest, those extrapolations might then be transmitted to underwriting standards as well. Also, our indicator of underwriting standards trended downward significantly until the financial crisis struck in 2007.

When extrapolative behavior is long and strong enough, its resulting effects on data may show up in estimated responses. For example, in the estimated VAR, for both house prices and for the underwriting indicator, the estimated coefficients on their own lags summed to more than one. Those sums then can translate into estimated responses, like those in Figures 33.8–33.12, that do not dampen out soon, or maybe ever. Such estimates then may be accurate reflections of the operation of these markets in these years. But they are unlikely to be representative of the responses during more normal periods.

Thus, the estimates based on data from periods of mortgage and housing bubbles of the magnitude and character of those in the mid-2000s are not likely to be representative. Extrapolating them to other times or places entails atypically high risks. At the same time, such estimates are of independent interest, helping us to better understand recent tumultuous events in mortgage and housing markets.

APPENDIX A

The Federal Reserve and the OCC Surveys of Banks' Underwriting Standards

In their separate surveys, the Federal Reserve and the OCC ask about banks' mortgage underwriting standards.

The Federal Reserve conducts a "Senior Loan Officer Opinion Survey on Bank Lending Practices at Selected Large Banks in the United States." The sample of banks "is selected from among the largest banks in each Federal Reserve District. Large banks are defined as those with total domestic assets of $20 billion or more as of December 31, 2008. The combined assets of the 31 large banks totaled $6.2 trillion, compared with $6.5 trillion for the entire panel of 56 banks, and 10.7 trillion for all domestically chartered, federally insured commercial banks." (*Source*: April 2009 survey results report.)

In the April 2009 survey the Federal Reserve asked the following question:

"Over the past three months, how have your bank's credit standards for approving applications from individuals for mortgage loans to purchase homes changed?" In earlier periods, the questions typically did not distinguish between prime and other applicants.

The survey gives banks the following five choices for their responses: Tightened considerably, tightened somewhat, remained basically unchanged, eased somewhat, or eased considerably.

The Federal Reserve, and many other sources, commonly report an aggregate measure of net percentage tightening that is calculated as the sum of the shares of banks tightening considerably and tightening somewhat (each equally weighted) minus the sum of the shares of banks easing somewhat and easing considerably (each equally weighted).

The OCC conducts an annual "Survey of Credit Underwriting Standards." "The 2008 survey included examiner assessments of credit underwriting standards at the 62 largest national banks. This population covers loans totaling $3.7 trillion as of December 2007, approximately 83 percent of total loans in the national banking system." (*Source*: June 2008 survey.)

In 2008, the survey included assessments of the change in underwriting standards in residential real estate loan portfolios for the 55 banks engaged in this type of lending among the 62 in the survey. The survey gives examiners the following three choices for their responses: tightened, unchanged, and eased. We computed net percentage tightening as the share of banks tightening minus the share of banks easing.

APPENDIX B

Data Descriptions and Sources

GAP, the aggregate income variable, was calculated as the percentage difference between real GDP and real potential GDP. Real GDP was obtained from the Bureau of Economic Analysis (BEA) and real potential GDP from the Congressional Budget Office (CBO).

RHP was calculated adjusting nominal (ie., not adjusted for inflation) house prices using the GDP implicit deflator, which we obtained from the BEA. As data for aggregate house prices, we used the quarterly Freddie Mac conventional mortgage home price index.

GNHP, the variable used to measure the growth rate of nominal house prices, was calculated as the percentage change in house prices over the most recent four quarters.

IMORT, the mortgage interest rate, was measured as the quarterly, national-average, interest rate on 30-year, conventional, conforming FRMs as reported by Freddie Mac.

MORTPOT, our measure of mortgages outstanding, was calculated as the ratio (%) of total, nominal, mortgage balances to nominal potential GDP. Mortgage balances were obtained from the Federal Reserve.

UWPC, the indicator of aggregate underwriting standards, was the first PC from five data series. The five series and the method of PC are described more fully in the text.

Notes

Originally published in *Business Economics*, Vol. 44, No. 4 (October 2009), pp. 189–200..

1. Because the inflation rate was so steady relative to that of the percentage changes in nominal house prices over this period, the correlation between the percentage changes in nominal and real house price was over 0.99.
2. Risk-based scores that indicate the likelihood of borrower default.
3. A change in the law during 2008 attempted to outlaw the practice, presumably because the default rate on such mortgages was proving already to be much higher than on other FHA loans.
4. Appendix A lists the questions and answers for the Federal Reserve's and for the OCC's recent surveys about residential mortgage underwriting. Note that the Federal Reserve includes mortgage interest rates in its question about underwriting standards.
5. The OCC reports data for the first quarter of each year. To obtain the data for the other quarters, we linearly interpolated between the values reported for the first quarter. This almost guarantees that the OCC data here will be smoother and have more measurement error than the Federal Reserve data.

6. The Demyanyk and Hemert data cover 1997 through 2006:Q2. We set observations before 1997 equal to the 1997:Q1 value. For the quarterly values beginning with 2006:Q3. We added 0.75 to the prior quarter. Beginning with 2007:Q3, for each ensuing pair of quarters, we subtracted 1, then 2 and then 3 units.
7. The PC method is theoretically the optimal linear scheme, in terms of minimizing mean square errors, for generating a few (say, one) data series from many more (say, five) series. In that sense, it is a method to reduce the number of variables to be analyzed. The PC method is nonparametric and it requires no hypothesis about data probability distributions. By construction, the average value of the first PC here is zero.
8. The thrust of the results were not very sensitive to a number of alternative specifications. For example, the results were not much affected by substituting real for nominal house price growth.

References

Demyanyk, Yuliya, and Otto Van Hemert, Forthcoming. "Understanding the Subprime Mortgage Crisis," available at SSRN: http://ssrn.com/abstract = 1020396.

Federal Reserve May 2009. "The April 2009 Senior Loan Officer Opinion Survey on Bank Lending Practices," Washington, DC, www.federalreserve.gov/boarddocs/SnLoanSurvey/200905.

Office of the Comptroller of the Currency June 2008. "Survey of Credit Underwriting Practices 2008," Washington, DC, www.occ.treas.gov/cusurvey/2008Under writingSurvey.pdf.

Sherlund, Shane M. 2008. "The Past, Present, and Future of Subprime Mortgages," *Finance and Economics Discussion* Series No. 2008–63. Divisions of Research & Statistics and Monetary Affairs. Federal Reserve Board, Washington, DC.

CHAPTER 34

2010

THE IMPACT OF THE HOUSING MARKET BOOM AND BUST ON CONSUMPTION SPENDING

Jeremy A. Leonard, Manufacturers Alliance/MAPI Inc.

Consumers have always been the main pillar of aggregate economic activity in the United States, but never more so than in the most recent expansion. Consumption has hovered above 70 percent of GDP since 2002, culminating 20 years of slow but steady increases (Figure 34.1). Private consumption is also higher in relative terms compared with other large industrialized economies, where shares tend to range between 55 and 60 percent of GDP (Figure 34.2).

In 2008, the first year of the most recent recession, inflation-adjusted consumption growth slipped to a paltry 0.2 percent. This is only the fourth time since 1950 that consumption has grown at less than 1 percent annually: the other years were 1991, 1980, and 1974, all of them during recessions. The current recession is unusual relative to past post-World War II downturns, because it coincides with a real estate and financial crisis that has severely dented households' balance sheets: from their peaks, the net value of household real estate and financial assets fell by 40 and 20 percent, respectively. It is likely that this has put a brake on consumption as much or more than the fear or reality of job loss. It is well known among economists that the market value of personal wealth has an effect on consumption behavior, but much less clear is how households might react to the severe downdraft of the past several years. This paper examines trends in US consumption and provides updated estimates on the propensity to consume out of real estate and financial wealth.

Overview of Trends in US Consumption Spending

Of the major components of economic activity (consumption, investment, government spending, and imports and exports), consumption is one of the least volatile.

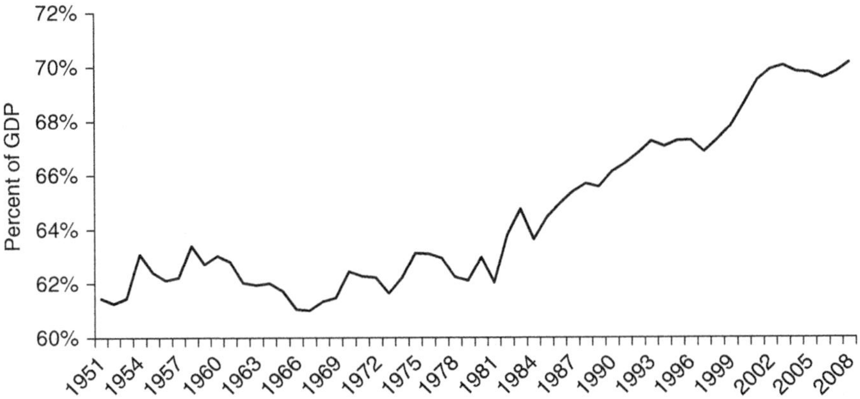

Figure 34.1 Total US personal consumption expenditures, 1951–2008.

Source: US Department of Commerce, Bureau of Economic Analysis.

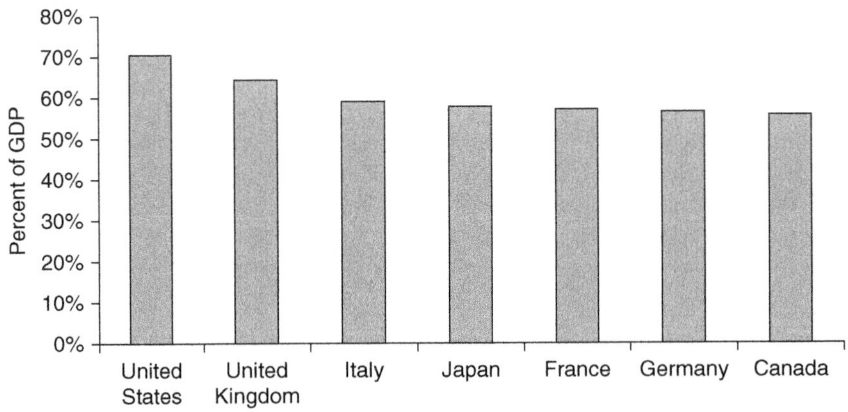

Figure 34.2 Personal consumption expenditures in G7 Nations, 2008.

Source: Organization for Economic Cooperation and Development.

Since 1950, inflation-adjusted consumption has grown by an average of 3.5 percent annually, with a standard deviation of about half of that average. At the other extreme, inflation-adjusted fixed investment has grown at a slightly faster annual rate on average—3.9 percent—but the standard deviation around that average is 7.5, almost twice the mean. This should not be surprising, because most households seek to avoid short-term fluctuations in their material standard of living to the extent they can, and thus use savings and borrowing to smooth consumption over time. In addition, certain policies (notably unemployment insurance and progressive income tax rates) act as "automatic stabilizers," mitigating aggregate income declines during recessions and restraining growth in booms.

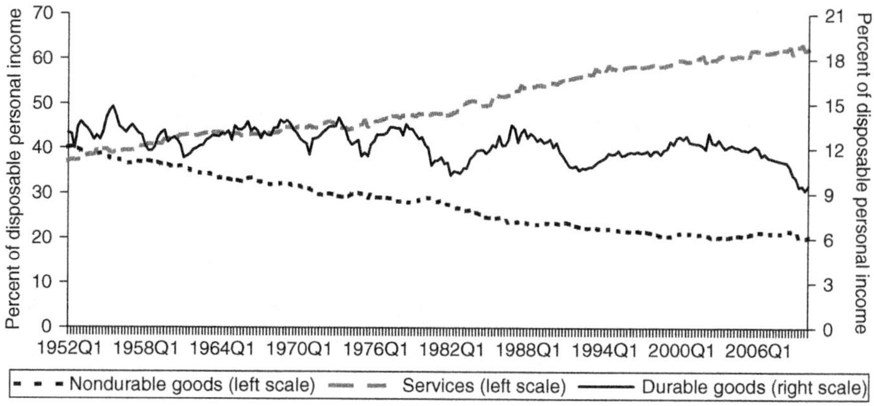

Figure 34.3 Personal consumption expenditures by broad type, 1952:Q1–2009:Q3.
Source: US Department of Commerce, Bureau of Economic Analysis.

Table 34.1 Trends in inflation-adjusted consumption around selected business cycle turning points by broad type

	Peak-to-Trough Percentage Change			*Percentage Change in 12 Months Following Trough*		
	Durables	*Nondurables*	*Services*	*Durables*	*Nondurables*	*Services*
1957–1958	−12.5	−1.7	3.2	16.1	4.7	5.1
1973–1975	−15.4	−3.5	2.7	14.0	3.7	3.8
1981–1982	−8.3	2.0	3.9	18.5	4.0	5.5

Source: U.S. Department of Commerce, Bureau of Economic Analysis and author's calculations.

Over the past 50 years, there has been a secular shift (in relative terms) in consumption toward services and away from manufactured goods (Figure 34.3). Consumption of services has risen from just over 30 percent of disposable income in 1952 to nearly 60 percent today. This has been mainly at the expense of nondurable goods (of which the largest subcategory by far is food and beverages, which accounts for nearly half of the total). Durable goods have not displayed the secular decline of nondurables, but are much more volatile than the other two broad subcomponents, particularly during cyclical downturns. During the 2008–2009 recession, consumption of durables has plummeted to a post-World War II low of 9.2 percent of disposable income.

A closer look at the major recessions of the past shows the degree to which they disproportionately affect durable goods consumption. Table 34.1 shows that consumption of services does not typically decline in recessions—its growth merely slows. At the other extreme, durable-goods consumption fell by an average in excess of 10 percent during the three deep post-World War II recessions. In the ensuing recoveries, however, these sharp declines were typically followed by much more rapid growth compared with other consumption classes.[1]

The Link between Wealth and Consumption

The theory of consumption is among the most well-developed and empirically tested in economics. In its simplest form, developed by John Maynard Keynes in the 1930s, households spend a given portion of their income based on their particular preferences for saving. In this formulation, consumption is taken to be a function of current-year income. However, a casual glance at the relevant data shows that this "propensity to consume" is not constant—it varies considerably depending on the phase of the business cycle. More importantly, the theory implies that households are myopic, because it implicitly posits that expectations about future income and wealth have no bearing on current consumption decisions. This limitation, clearly at odds with household behavior, led to alternative models that captured the fact that future expected income has some bearing on consumption decisions.

An early extension of the Keynesian model was developed by Duesenberry (1949), in which consumption and saving decisions are guided primarily by the desire to maintain a standard of living similar to or better than peer households ("keeping up with the Joneses") rather than being a direct function of income.

The permanent-income model of consumption developed by Friedman (1957) posits that households are more forward-looking and base consumption decisions on expected income over longer periods. The intuition is that transitory changes in income will have little effect on consumption, but permanent changes will affect behavior. This captures the fact that, during recessions, consumption generally falls by less than income, as households perceive income declines as temporary and dip into savings or increase borrowing to tide them over.

A closely related model is the life-cycle model developed by Ando and Modigliani (1963). The basic idea is that households try to consume a constant percentage of their best estimate of the present value of their lifetime income. In early life, consumption tends to exceed current income: students invest in education and training that will ultimately result in higher and growing incomes over their working life. During working life, in contrast, people tend to save for retirement (including mandatory contributions to Social Security, voluntary contributions to company pension funds and IRAs, other investments, and cash holdings). In retirement, individuals live off the income generated from financial wealth and draw down savings.

Both the permanent-income and life-cycle models also incorporate assets such as real estate and investment holdings explicitly into consumption decisions. Such wealth can affect consumption in two related ways. The first is the extent to which increases in wealth can substitute for current income, particularly with regard to retirement planning. If the expected return from financial investments increases, households will feel richer, and may increase the share of income devoted to consumption as a result. If necessary, they can offset any unanticipated future income declines by liquidating a portion of their faster-growing investment portfolio.

A second way is to use the appreciation in the value of one's home to finance consumption. The logic is the same as for investment assets, but until the mid-1980s

Table 34.2 Selected empirical studies of the wealth effect on consumption using US Data

Study	*Methodology*	*Wealth Data Used*	*Cents Per Additional Dollar of Wealth*	
			Housing	*Financial*
Bostic, Gabriel, and Painter (2009)	Five panels of more than 2,000 households, 1989–2001	Federal Reserve Board *Survey of Consumer Finances*	6	2
Carroll, Otsuka, and Slacalek (2006)	Quarterly time-series data for the United States, 1960–2004	Federal Reserve Board *Flow of Funds Accounts*	9	4
Case, Quigley, and Shiller (2005)	Quarterly time-series data for 50 states, 1982–1999	Federal Reserve Board *Flow of Funds Accounts* (financial assets); home price indices (real estate assets)	5–9	2
Benjamin, Chinloy, and Jud (2004)	Quarterly time-series data for the United States, 1952–2001	Federal Reserve Board *Flow of Funds Accounts*	8	2
Levin (1998)	Six panels of 11,000 households near retirement, 1969–1979	*Longitudinal Retirement Household Survey*	6	<2

Source: Author's compilation.

financial vehicles to tap home equity were not common, and the relative illiquidity of housing assets made it difficult to convert the value of one's house into cash. Now, however, the widespread availability of home equity loans has removed this obstacle; and, as will be shown later, rising home values have become a large factor in recent aggregate consumption trends.

There is a large body of empirical literature that confirms the positive relationship between increases in personal wealth and consumption, though relatively few studies disaggregate real estate and financial wealth. Those that do are unanimous in concluding that real estate wealth has a stronger effect than financial wealth (Table 34.2). This is not surprising, given the fact that, for most households, financial wealth is held in assets such as pension, retirement, and insurance accounts, which are essentially illiquid and are difficult to borrow against.[2]

The 2000–2001 collapse of the US stock market, during which the S&P 500 lost 30 percent of its value and the technology-heavy NASDAQ index declined by two-thirds, is broadly consistent with the notion that equity values have little effect on consumption: the recession that followed the tech bubble crash was short and shallow, and aggregate consumption spending slowed only modestly relative to medium-term underlying trends. Benjamin, Chinloy, and Jud (2004) conclude that the wealth effect from firm real estate values over the 2000–2001 period largely offset the already small negative effect of the stock market declines.

Recent Trends in Household Wealth

Over the past three years, the United States has seen the largest depreciation of household real estate assets in at least the past 60 years. Figure 34.4 tells the story succinctly: household real estate wealth growth (net of outstanding mortgages) turned negative on a year-over-year basis starting in the third-quarter of 2006 and that decline exceeded 20 percent through all of 2008. The only other period since consistent data collection began in 1952 during which net real estate wealth declined year over year was the 1990–1991 period, and the quarterly declines were negligible compared with current conditions. The recent declines come on the heels of nearly a decade of unusually large annual real estate appreciation—12.7 percent compared with the 1983–2006 average of 7.4 percent.

Figure 34.5 shows that household financial wealth has also declined sharply over the past 12 months, but recent circumstances are not entirely unprecedented. The dot-com bust in the early 2000s sent year-over-year growth in financial wealth negative for over two years, and households are much more accustomed to downside volatility in financial markets than they are to fluctuations in real estate asset values.

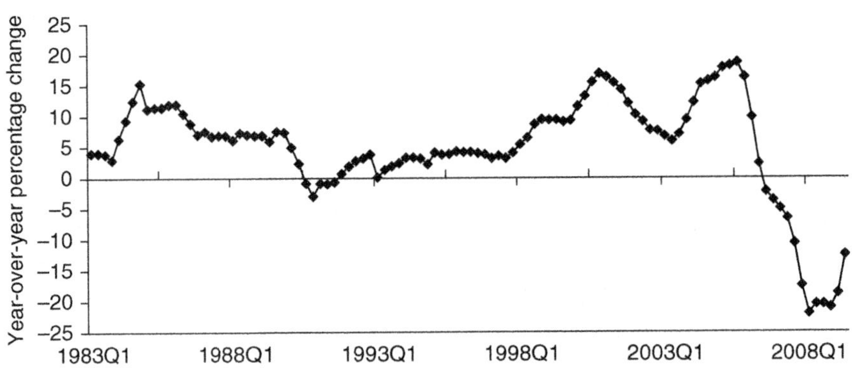

Figure 34.4 Market value of net household real estate assets, 1983:Q1–2009:Q2.

Source: US Federal Reserve Board.

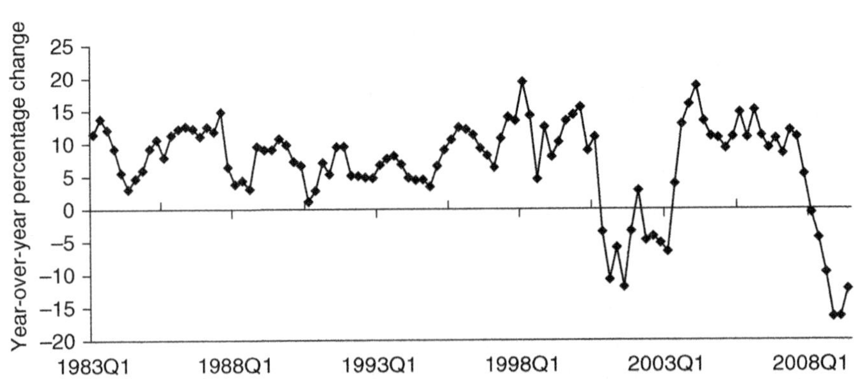

Figure 34.5 Market value of household financial assets, 1983:Q1–2009:Q2.

Source: US Federal Reserve Board.

In dollar terms, the recent losses are staggering. Total net household wealth peaked in mid-2007 at \$64 trillion, of which about 20 percent was held in real estate and the remainder in financial assets. As of the end of 2008, almost \$13 trillion of this market value had evaporated, nearly equivalent to a year's worth of gross domestic product.

Empirical Estimates of the Wealth Effect

Although the US econometric evidence has consistently shown that increases in real estate wealth induce additional consumption, it does not speak to the potential effect of a sustained and substantial *decrease* in real estate wealth. As noted earlier, the past two years are unique in that regard, and there has thus been no empirical evidence on which to base any conjecture of the aggregate size of the wealth effect in a down market. A microeconomic study by Engelhardt (1996) found that homeowners' consumption responses to fluctuations in the value of their own home are asymmetric, with a much stronger reaction to falling asset values. In other words, consumption declined proportionately more in response to a given decline in a home's value than it increased in response to an identical increase in value. This evidence is suggestive that the wealth effect is stronger going down than going up, though to date there have been no macroeconomic studies examining this question.

Basic Estimates

To examine this question, this analysis follows Benjamin, Chinloy, and Jud (2004) in implementing an empirical model based on the life-cycle theory of consumption developed by Ando and Modigliani (1963). As noted earlier, the model posits that the representative consumer seeks to consume a fixed proportion of the present value of his or her lifetime income (including that income derived from financial and real estate asset holdings). By algebraic manipulation (described in detail in the Appendix), the following empirical specification is derived:[3]

$$\Delta c_t = \alpha + \beta_1(\Delta g_t) + \beta_2(\Delta f_t) + \beta_3(\Delta h_t) + \varepsilon_t, \tag{34.1}$$

where variables (scaled to disposable personal income) are as follows: c = consumption; g = transfer payments from government; f = financial wealth; h = net housing wealth.

The base period of analysis is 1952:Q1 to 2005:Q4—essentially the period prior to the beginning of the recent unprecedented housing collapse. Ordinary least squares regression results for equation (34.1) appear in Table 34.3.

The results confirm those of previous analyses of financial and real estate wealth effects on consumption. The coefficients on the financial and housing wealth variables are positive and highly statistically significant. The point estimates imply that every dollar increase in financial wealth increases consumption by about two cents, and a dollar increase in housing wealth increases consumption

Table 34.3 Basic OLS regression results for life-cycle consumption function

	Current Results (1952–2005)			*Benjamin, Chinloy, and Jud (1952–2001)*		
Coefficient	*Estimate*	*T-statistic*	*Probability Coefficient = 0*	*Estimate*	*T-statistic*	*Probability Coefficient = 0*
α (constant)	−0.0002	−0.397	0.691	0.000	0.16	0.873
β_1 (transfers)	0.223	10.67	0.287	0.199	1.17	0.243
β_2 (financial wealth)	0.022	4.468	0.000	0.023	4.81	0.000
β_3 (housing wealth)	0.101	3.405	0.001	0.079	2.80	0.006
AR(1)	−0.294	−4.372	0.000	−0.223	—	—
Durbin-Watson	2.02	—	—	2.02	—	—
Adjusted R^2	0.232	—	—	0.20	—	—
Number of observations	213	—	—	197	—	—

Source: Author's calculations.

by 10 cents. The point estimate on housing wealth is considerably higher than that reported by Benjamin, Chinloy, and Jud, suggesting that the housing wealth effect strengthened in the 2001–2005 period, which was not included in their analysis. This may be due to the fact that the market value of housing wealth increased steadily, leading households to believe that such appreciation would continue over a long period.

The coefficient β_1 is a composite parameter that blends the propensity to consume out of government transfers (such as Social Security and unemployment benefits, food stamps, and other cash or cash-equivalent benefits) and all other income. It essentially measures whether households are more or less likely to spend transfers relative to other sources of income (see the Appendix for details). In the results shown in Table 34.3, the coefficient is not statistically different from zero, which implies that the marginal propensities to consume out of transfer payments and other sources of income are the same.

The adjusted R^2 (which is a commonly used measure of the "fit" of a model) seems small, but this reflects the fact that the model estimates *changes* in consumption rather than *levels* of consumption and hence abstracts from the strong influence of underlying trends over time.[4] Aggregate consumption levels based on the estimated coefficients reported in Table 34.3 are in fact remarkably close to actual observed values: for the entire sample period the mean absolute percentage error of the estimated values is just 0.6 percent. If we remove certain periods during which exogenous events affected consumer spending (such as the 9/11 terrorist attacks), that error falls to under 0.5 percent. Furthermore, the F-test of the joint significance of all regressors yields a test statistic of 17.0, implying a fairly tight model fit.

The results also confirm that the housing wealth effect is significantly larger (in a statistical sense) than that for financial assets. A Wald test of the hypothesis that

Table 34.4 OLS regression results for life-cycle consumption function, 1952–1982 and 1983–2005

	1952–1982			*1983–2005*		
Coefficient	*Estimate*	*T-statistic*	*Probability Coefficient=0*	*Estimate*	*T-statistic*	*Probability Coefficient=0*
α (constant)	−0.0002	−0.185	0.854	0.000	0.020	0.983
β_1 (transfers)	−0.268	−1.050	0.296	1.897	5.205	0.000
β_2 (financial wealth)	0.027	3.249	0.002	0.016	2.617	0.011
β_3 (housing wealth)	0.036	0.856	0.393	0.153	3.003	0.004
AR(1)	−0.270	−2.982	0.004	0.007	0.060	0.952
Durbin-Watson	1.98	—	—	1.99	—	—
Adjusted R^2	0.109	—	—	0.427	—	—
Number of observations	121	—	—	93	—	—

Source: Author's calculations.

the coefficients on housing and financial wealth variables are equal is rejected with 99 percent confidence.

The Rise of Home Equity Loans and the Wealth Effect

As noted earlier, prior to the mid-1980s it was relatively uncommon to tap the equity in one's home for cash to finance current consumption expenditures. Even though home equity loans (often called "second mortgages") have been in existence since the Great Depression, they did not come into wide use until federal laws were changed in the late 1970s and early 1980s to allow mainstream banks to offer them. The total amount of home equity loans was only $1 billion in 1982, compared with $1 trillion today.

These legislative changes suggest that the housing wealth effect for the period prior to 1983 may have been much smaller than it was in the post-1983 era. The hypothesis that the 1952–1982 and 1983–2005 periods (Table 34.4) have the same underlying structural consumption function can be tested using the Chow test of model stability. The exercise yields an F-statistic of 4.28, which permits rejection of this hypothesis with 99.9 percent confidence.

Estimating equation (34.1) for the two time periods illustrates the relevant contrasts. The most important difference is in the coefficient on housing wealth. It is not significantly different from zero in the 1952–1982 period (consistent with the difficulty in transforming owned real estate into cash), but jumps to 0.153 (or just over 15 cents per dollar) in the post-1982 period. This is significantly higher than for the total 1952–2005 period, and suggests that the growing popularity of home equity loans not only enabled the possibility of a housing wealth effect, but also that this effect is larger than previous empirical studies have concluded.

How Large Is the Housing Wealth Effect in a Down Market?

The more important question in the current context is whether or not the wealth effect that had helped buoy consumption until the end of 2005 would intensify in the opposite direction as aggregate housing wealth started to decline.

There are too few observations to independently estimate the housing wealth effect directly over the past three years of the period. However, another way to examine the question indirectly is to compare actual consumption from 2006 to the second quarter of 2009 with a forecast based on the regression estimates shown in Table 34.3. If forecast consumption exceeds actual consumption, this would suggest that the wealth effect is larger during wealth declines; conversely, if forecast consumption is less than actual consumption, the wealth effect is smaller on the downside.

The results of this exercise are shown in Figure 34.6. In the early part of the housing collapse through 2007, the forecast based on 1983–2005 historical relationships slightly underestimated consumption, such that by the fourth quarter of 2007, actual consumption was over $160 billion greater on an annualized basis (or 1.7% greater than forecast consumption) than past trends would have predicted. Assuming that the propensity to consume out of income had not changed appreciably over that time, this would mean that the wealth effect on consumption is smaller going down than going up.

However, the gap between forecast and actual consumption closed completely by the middle of 2008, which implies that consumers, perhaps because they came to

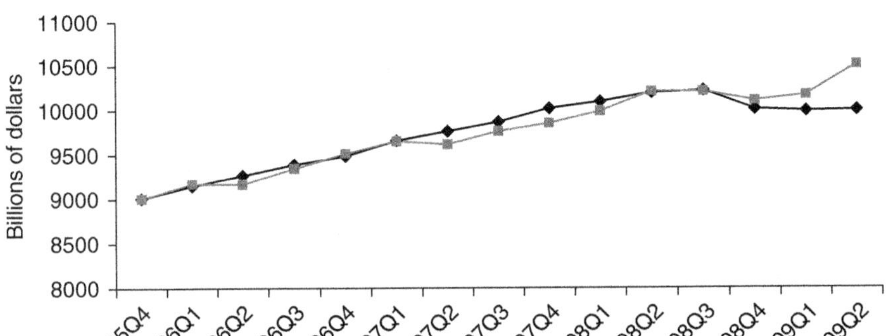

Figure 34.6 Actual and forecast personal consumption expenditures, 2005:Q4 2008:Q4.

Source: US Department of Commerce, Bureau of Economic Analysis and author's calculations.

Note: Actual data for the second and third quarter of 2008 have been smoothed to account for the one-time tax rebates, which shifted consumption between those two quarters.

believe that declining real estate asset values were likely to persist, began to retrench their consumption accordingly. The intensification of the recession in late 2008 and early 2009 caused a further pullback that was disproportionate to underlying trends in income and wealth, and by the second quarter of 2009, actual consumption was some $500 billion less than what the model would predict. This suggests that the wealth effect eventually becomes larger in a down market than an up market, as households believe that the losses they have suffered may be permanent enough to make more drastic spending adjustments.

The large swings in aggregate household real estate wealth, combined with a wealth effect that is stronger than that found in previous studies, imply that the housing boom and bust have had a significant macroeconomic impact. From the beginning of the 2000s expansion in late 2001, increases in real estate values added an estimated $644 billion to US consumption spending by the end of 2005, or over 35 percent of the total increase in consumption over that period. By the same token, falling real estate values accounted for about 40 percent of the $236 billion drop in consumption in the fourth quarter of 2008.

The Housing Wealth Effect by Type of Consumption

A final question of interest is what types of consumption are most sensitive to changes in housing wealth. A priori one might suppose that equity extracted from homes might be used to fund purchases of big-ticket durable goods, consistent with the notion that households would seek to use these borrowed funds for goods that provide benefits over a long period of time. In a recent paper detailing the disposition of cash extracted from home equity, Greenspan and Kennedy [2008] find that consumption is the single largest destination of home equity lines of credit, at 35% of the total (compared with 30 percent for home improvements and 20% for repayment of nonmortgage debt), but do not break out different types of consumption.

To examine differential wealth effects across broad classes of consumption, separate regression estimates based on equation (34.1) were estimated for consumption of durable goods, nondurable goods and services for the period 1983–2005. Those results are reported in Table 34.5.

Contrary to expectations, neither housing nor financial wealth has any discernible impact on durable-goods consumption. In fact, the overall fit of the model is much poorer than for other classes of consumption, none of the regressors is statistically significant, and the F-test for joint significance of the regressors is not nearly as strong as for the other specifications.

This suggests that other factors influence durable-goods consumption. It is important to recall that motor vehicles and home furnishings together account for 80 percent of durable goods consumption, and these are highly sensitive to factors other than income and wealth.

With regard to home furnishings, much of it is derived demand that results from construction and purchase of new homes, which over the longer term is fundamentally a function of the formation of new households. Simple demographics

Table 34.5 OLS regression results for life-cycle consumption function by type of consumption, 1983–2005

	Durable Goods		*Nondurable Goods*		*Services*	
Coefficient	*Estimate*	*Probability Coefficient = 0*	*Estimate*	*Probability Coefficient = 0*	*Estimate*	*Probability Coefficient = 0*
α (constant)	0.000	0.985	−0.001	0.002	0.001	0.086
β_1 (transfers)	0.201	0.226	0.365	0.003	1.273	0.000
β_2 (financial wealth)	0.003	0.329	0.004	0.058	0.009	0.008
β_3 (housing wealth)	0.021	0.301	0.049	0.004	0.089	0.005
AR(1)	−0.155	0.167	−0.003	0.975	0.087	0.451
Durbin-Watson	2.00	—	2.00	—	1.99	—
Adjusted R^2	0.068	—	0.261	—	0.468	—
Number of observations	93	—	93	—	93	—

Source: Author's calculations.

implies that over one million new households are formed each year in the United States, and it is very difficult for them to defer spending on the big-ticket purchases such as appliances and furniture required to make a new house or apartment habitable.[5]

In a similar vein, demand for motor vehicles is in part driven by demographic factors that are independent of changes in income and wealth. In addition, sustained large fluctuations in gasoline prices (which greatly affect the ongoing operating costs of vehicle ownership) may have as much influence on decisions to purchase a new vehicle as current income or wealth. That is consistent with trends in recent years. From 2004 to 2007 (before the onset of recession), average gasoline prices increased from $1.50 per gallon to $3.00 per gallon, and car and truck sales began declining in late 2005, well before the onset of recession and the worst of the housing collapse.

In short, durable-goods manufacturers have been hard hit by the sharp reduction in housing construction (which has drastically reduced consumption of complementary furnishings such as appliances, furniture, and fixtures), but they are largely insulated from the economic effects of gyrations in home values. This means that a turnaround in housing starts is likely to have an immediate salutary effect on these industries irrespective of the market value of housing in general.

In contrast, the housing wealth effect is clearly present in consumption of both nondurable goods and services, with an extra dollar of housing wealth inducing additional consumption of 4.9 and 8.9 cents, respectively. It would thus appear that increases in housing wealth have generally been used to increase day-to-day purchases rather than "splurge" on big-ticket items.

Conclusion

The sharp depreciation of financial and real estate wealth over the past several years, and concomitant negative effects on household balance sheets has raised concerns that American consumers will be unable to spearhead a strong and broad economic recovery or, worse, might be forced to pare back spending even further to offset wealth-driven consumption during the boom.

Empirical estimates of the housing and wealth effect find that, all else equal, an additional dollar of housing wealth generates about 15 cents of additional consumption, and an additional dollar of financial wealth generates about 2 cents of additional consumption. The estimate for housing wealth is substantially higher than found in other studies, which likely reflects the fact that use of home equity loans (and other methods to convert real estate assets to cash) has increased exponentially in the 2004–2005 period, which is not covered in previous analyses.

This paper confirms that the housing wealth effect that spurred so much of economic activity from 2002 to 2006 does work in reverse: declines in housing wealth were responsible for about 40 percent of the observed drop in consumption in the fourth quarter of 2008. However, wealth's impact on consumption is larger in persistent down markets than in up markets. Current consumption levels are substantially lower than those forecast under the assumption of a negative wealth effect of the same magnitude as the positive effect.

Durable-goods manufacturers can take some solace that demand for their consumer products is largely insensitive to changes in wealth. The housing wealth effect is roughly evenly distributed between consumption of nondurable goods and services. So, even though they are being buffeted by the effects of the deep recession, they will not depend on increasing asset values to get on the road to economic recovery.

APPENDIX

Description of the Empirical Model and Data

Following Benjamin, Chinloy, and Jud (2004), the basis of the empirical estimates of the aggregate US consumption function in this paper is the life-cycle model proposed by Ando and Modigliani (1963). The key implication of the theory is that, at any point in one's life, a utility-maximizing individual seeks to consume a proportion of his or her expected lifetime income.

Empirically, the aggregate resources available for lifetime consumption include cumulative total wages and salaries, government transfer payments (such as Social Security and unemployment benefits) and vouchers (such as food stamps), and potential income from housing and financial assets.

The aggregate stock of household real estate and financial assets is published by the Federal Reserve Board in the Flow of Funds Accounts. Net housing wealth is defined as the market value of household real estate less the value of outstanding household mortgage debt. Financial wealth is calculated as total household wealth less net real estate wealth.

To determine whether responses to changes in housing wealth are different from those due to changes in financial wealth, I posit a parameter that allows for differences in liquidity of housing and financial assets, and let the data provide an answer to that question.

The lifetime stock of wages and government transfers, by contrast, is not observable; only annual flows are published in the National Income and Product Accounts. But if we presume that unobservable scaling factors convert these observed flows into stocks, we can infer stocks of these sources of income.

With these definitions and assumptions, total wealth at time t can be written as

$$W_t = b_Y Y_t + b_G G_t + \lambda_F F_t + H_t, \tag{34A.1}$$

where b_Y = unobservable factor to convert Y from flow to expected lifetime stock; Y = disposable wage and salary income; b_G = unobservable factor to convert G from flow to expected lifetime stock; G = government transfer payments to individuals; λ_F = measure of liquidity of financial assets relative to housing assets; F = financial wealth; H = housing wealth.

Dividing equation (34A.1) by personal disposable income (defined as $Y + G$) and adding $(b_G G - b_Y G)$ to the right-hand side yields

$$w_t = b_Y + (b_G - b_Y) g_t + \lambda_F f_t + h_t, \tag{34A.2}$$

where lower case letters represent ratios of respective wealth types to personal disposable income. If we define μ as the marginal propensity to consume out of total wealth, then consumption can be written as

$$c_t = \mu\left[b_Y + (b_G - b_Y) g_t + \lambda_F f_t + h_t\right] \tag{34A.3}$$

or, using the notation in equation (34.1) of the paper,

$$c_t = \alpha + \beta_1 g_t + \beta_2 f_t + \beta_3 h_t, \tag{34A.4}$$

where

$$\alpha = \mu b_Y; \beta_1 = \mu(b_G - b_Y); \beta_2 = \mu\lambda_F; \beta_3 = \mu. \tag{34A.5}$$

Because of algebraic manipulation to simplify the estimating equation (most significantly by scaling the equation to disposable personal income), wage and salary income does not appear explicitly in equation (34A.4). What the equation focuses on is the propensity to consume out of changes in wealth that are NOT directly due to changes in disposable personal income.

Any differences in the propensity to consume out of labor income and transfer income are captured in β_1. Since μ is a nonzero positive number by presumption, if the coefficient β_1 is not statistically different from zero, then we can conclude that $b_G = b_Y$. If β_1 is positive, then $b_G > b_Y$, if β_1 is negative, then $b_G > b_Y$.

Note that equation (34A.4) is in levels, but the empirical implementation is in first-differences. With time series data, estimating equations based on levels is risky and can lead to erroneous statistical inferences, particularly if there are underlying trends over time (meaning that data series are not stationary and/or are cointegrated with one another). Benjamin, Chinloy, and Jud test for both unit roots and cointegration for the variables used in the empirical model over the period 1952–2001 and conclude that first differences must be taken to yield the stationary (that is, no upward or downward trend over time) variables required for accurate econometric estimation. This conclusion is confirmed by my own diagnostics over the period 1952–2008.

Notes

Originally published in *Business Economics*, Vol. 45, No. 2 (April 2010), pp. 83–93.

1. For further analysis of the dynamics of durable-goods consumption in business cycles, see Norman (2009).
2. According to the Federal Reserve *2007 Survey of Consumer Finances*, about 37 percent of household financial assets are held in life insurance and pension accounts, although this proportion is significantly higher for low- and middle-income households.
3. This reduced form equation does not explicitly contain income as a functional variable. However, as described in the Appendix, the propensity to consume out of income is embedded in the coefficient on Δg, reflecting the important role of current income in the life-cycle model.
4. When the variables in equation (34.1) were expressed as levels rather than as first differences, the adjusted R^2 was equal to 0.927. The use of levels rather than first differences, however, raises a separate set of econometric issues.
5. See Norman (2009) for additional discussion of these factors.

References

Ando, Albert, and Modigliani, Franco. 1963. "The 'Life-Cycle' Hypothesis of Savings: Aggregate Implications and Tests." *American Economic Review*, 53(1): 55–84.

Benjamin, John D., Chinloy, Peter, and Jud, G. Donald. 2004. "Real Estate Versus Financial Wealth in Consumption." *Journal of Real Estate and Financial Economics*, 29(3): 341–354.

Bostic, Raphael, Gabriel, Stuart, and Painter, Gary. 2009. "Housing Wealth, Financial Wealth, and Consumption: New Evidence from Micro Data." *Regional Science and Urban Economics*, 39: 79–89.

Carroll, Christopher D., Otsuka, Misuzu, and Slacalek, Jinka. 2006. "How Large Is the Housing Wealth Effect? A New Approach." NBER Working Paper No. 12476: National Bureau of Economic Research.

Case, Karl E., Quigley, John M., and Shiller, Robert J. 2005. "Comparing Wealth Effects: The Stock Market Versus the Housing Market." *Advances in Macroeconomics*, 5(1): 1–31.

Duesenberry, James S. 1949. *Income, Saving and the Theory of Consumer Behavior.* Harvard University Press, Cambridge, MA.

Engelhardt, Gary V. 1996. "House Prices and Home Owner Saving Behavior." *Regional Science and Urban Economics*, 26: 313–336.

Friedman, Milton. 1957. *A Theory of the Consumption Function*. National Bureau of Economic Research, Cambridge, MA.

Greenspan, Alan, and Kennedy, James. 2008. "Sources and Uses of Home Equity Extracted from Homes." *Oxford Review of Economic Policy*, 24(1): 120–144.

Levin, Laurence. 1998. "Are Assests Fungible? Testing the Behavioral Theory of Life-Cycle Savings." *Journal of Economic Behavior and Organization*, 36(1): 59–83.

Norman, Donald A. 2009. "A Silver Lining: The Pent-Up Demand for Consumer Durables," Issues in Brief No. E-514: Manufacturers Alliance/MAPI.

CHAPTER 35

2010

THE ADAM SMITH ADDRESS

MACROPRUDENTIAL SUPERVISION AND MONETARY POLICY IN THE POST-CRISIS WORLD

Janet L. Yellen, Board of Governors of the Federal Reserve System

When I look at the roster of previous recipients of the Adam Smith Award, it is very august company indeed. It's a tremendous honor to appear before you this year, and I am very grateful.

I should stress that my remarks represent my own views and not necessarily those of my Federal Reserve colleagues. Today I would like to cover a subject that is of surpassing importance for economic policy: the implications of financial market excesses for the supervision of the financial system, and beyond that, for the formulation of monetary policy.

Just two years ago, we lived through an almost unimaginable catastrophe—the near collapse of a global financial system that many economists had come to believe was impervious to the sort of panic that could bring on a worldwide recession. The prevailing view was that modern economic policymaking, and central banking in particular, had mastered the management of the business cycle, and that the application of modern risk-management tools had greatly increased the stability of the financial system. Financial markets were not held to be perfect, of course. But they were viewed as self-correcting systems that tended to return to a stable equilibrium before they could inflict widespread damage on the real economy.

That view lies in tatters today as we look at tens of millions of unemployed and the trillions of dollars of lost output and lost wealth around the world. These events should have convinced any doubters that our financial system is vulnerable to the kinds of catastrophic breakdowns that can wreck the overall economy. An inescapable conclusion is that a first-order priority must be to engineer a stronger, more robust system of financial regulation and supervision—one capable of identifying and managing excesses before they lead to crises. We must find a way to contain these threats without putting a straitjacket on financial innovation and risk taking. I don't claim this is an easy task, but it is an essential one.

Lessons from the Crisis

It is now clear that our system of regulation and supervision was fatally flawed. Despite volumes of research on financial market metrics and weighty position papers on financial stability, the fact is that we simply didn't understand some of the most dangerous systemic threats. Looking back, I believe the regulatory community was lulled into complacency by a combination of a Panglossian worldview and benign experience. The notion that financial markets should be as free as possible from regulatory fetters had evolved into the conviction that those markets could, to a very considerable extent, police themselves. Meanwhile, things went along so well for so long that the common belief came to be that nothing *could* go disastrously wrong. Over a period of decades, the financial system was tested repeatedly—the Latin American debt crisis, the savings and loan crisis, the Asian crisis, the failure of Long-Term Capital Management, and the stock market crashes of the late 1980s and early 2000s. With each crisis, policymakers rolled up their sleeves and beat back the systemic threat. The levees held. Despite these financial market ups and downs, economies in the United States and other parts of the world performed very well. We appeared to have entered a new era of stability. We even gave it a name: the Great Moderation. We were left with the mirage of a system that we thought was invulnerable to shock, a financial Maginot Line that we believed couldn't be breached. We now know that this sense of invincibility was mere hubris.

To understand what went wrong, I refer you to Hyman Minsky's (1992) pathbreaking work on speculative financial booms and busts. As Minsky showed, success can lead to excess, and excess to ruin. The Great Moderation saw a progressive growth of credit and extension of risk, which came to a head in the mortgage market. Credit flowed freely and cheaply, and households and financial institutions alike took on greater risk, borrowing to the hilt. House prices soared off the charts. Financial innovators found increasingly exotic ways of packaging loans for investors. Securities became so opaque that few understood their risks. Originators sold mortgages to investors whose due diligence consisted of glancing at ratings. The financial system became increasingly complex, interconnected, and hyperleveraged.

When housing prices plunged, the value of real-estate-related assets on the balance sheets of financial institutions, both in the traditional and shadow banking sectors, collapsed. Not only were many of those institutions highly leveraged, they had also relied heavily on short-term borrowing to acquire those assets. The combination of leverage and short maturity funding left them perilously vulnerable to runs. The result was panic and market breakdowns on an unimaginable scale, bringing us frighteningly close to a meltdown of the global financial system and a second Great Depression.

Thankfully, that depression never occurred. Governments and central banks around the world took extraordinary action to prevent complete collapse. But what we did get was bad enough—the deepest and most prolonged recession in generations. And the recovery has been agonizingly slow, held back, in part, by the ongoing efforts of over-leveraged households and financial institutions to repair their balance sheets. These events demonstrate both the natural tendency of the financial system to cycle through booms and busts and the potential, absent adequate supervision and regulation, for breakdowns in the financial system to threaten the global economy.

Financial market participants can be bipolar—prone to fads, manias, myopia, panics, and depression; driven by short-term gain; and easily caught up in the madness of crowds. One's belief about the beliefs of others is critical, like Keynes's example of a beauty contest (Allen and others 2006). In addition, the structure of compensation and incentives in the financial sector created strong motives for excessive risk taking, especially during boom years. Methods of modern risk management may have intensified the cycle because of their reliance on metrics such as value at risk that are highly sensitive to recent performance, especially volatility. In good times, volatility declined, and value at risk along with it. This pattern generated a procyclical willingness to take on risk and leverage, amplifying and propagating the boom and bust cycle. The vicious cycle of a collapse of confidence, asset fire sales, evaporation of liquidity, and a deleveraging free fall was the mirror image of the manic mortgage market that preceded it.

To avoid a repeat of these events, it is essential that we change the landscape of supervision and regulation. The landmark legislation recently passed by the Congress, the Dodd-Frank Wall Street Reform and Consumer Protection Act (Dodd-Frank Act), is designed to do just that. It requires regulators to contain risks to the financial system before they erupt into crises. And it creates a structure to collect data, identify emerging threats to financial stability, and formulate policies to contain these risks.

Within this structure, the Federal Reserve will play an important role. We will supervise all systemically important institutions and, jointly with other regulators in the new Financial Stability Oversight Council, establish stricter prudential standards for such firms. We will help ensure the safety of financial market utilities that are critical to our payment, clearing, and settlement systems. And we will actively support the council's mission to identify and address emerging risks to financial stability. At the same time, though, we must take care to preserve incentives for innovation and reasonable risk taking. We must remain prudent, while avoiding an overly strict approach that unduly impedes financial intermediation and stifles capital formation.

Vigilance to threats of systemic financial risk must also inform the conduct of monetary policy. We have seen that the eruption of a financial crisis can have severe economic consequences, compromising the ability of a central bank to attain its primary macroeconomic objectives. Monetary policymakers should also be aware that the decisions they make in pursuit of price stability and full employment could, in some circumstances, affect the development of systemic risk. For example, if compensation incentives in the financial sector are misaligned, low interest rates might heighten the ability and desire of financial market participants to reach for yield and take on risk.

Our goal should be to deploy an enhanced arsenal of regulatory tools to address systemic risk, making the financial system far more robust. That way, monetary policy can concentrate on its long-standing goals of price stability and maximum employment. Supervision and regulation *must* serve as the first and main line of defense in addressing systemic risk. We have at our disposal a tool kit of regulatory instruments that are well adapted for this purpose. Monetary policy cannot be a primary instrument for systemic risk management. First, it has its own macroeconomic goals on which it must maintain a sharp focus. Second, it is too blunt an instrument for dealing with systemic risk. All the same, I cannot unequivocally rule out the possibility that situations could emerge in which monetary policy should play some role in reining in risk taking behavior. I will return to this point later.

In the remainder of my remarks, I will discuss key issues that must be resolved before an effective policy regime for the containment of systemic risk can be established. First, we must understand the sources of systemic risk and design surveillance practices that enable us to detect threats to financial stability early on. Second, we must develop a tool kit of supervisory policy instruments—so-called macroprudential policies—and guidelines on how and when to deploy them. And third, we must strive to avoid situations in which macroprudential and monetary policies are working at cross-purposes, given that macroprudential policies affect macroeconomic performance and that monetary policy may affect risk taking incentives.

All of these issues raise complex questions of design and implementation. Interesting parallels may be drawn, however, between the design issues we face in macroprudential policy and those we have grappled with in conducting monetary policy. These parallels include the appropriate roles of rules vs. discretion, the need for policies that are robust in addressing uncertainty, and the assignment problem, all of which I will discuss later. The fertile field of monetary policy research may therefore offer lessons that can fruitfully be applied to managing systemic risk.

Systemic Risk: Sources and Surveillance

At its most basic level, systemic risk stems from the possibility that some event or sequence of events could result in severe impairment of the financial sector's ability to provide credit in the economy. At their most extreme, such events can trigger panicky attempts to withdraw credit, creating runs that lead to failures of important financial institutions and, ultimately, systemic collapse.

If policymakers are to detect emerging threats to the financial system, we must understand the determinants of systemic risk and develop appropriate metrics for measuring it. Economists have long studied these issues, and the recent crisis has intensified research on the subject. This work points to several key elements in the build-up of risks in the financial system. Let me mention three factors that current research suggests are critical.

One factor is the accumulation in the financial sector of very high levels of risk and leverage, along with excessive reliance on unstable short-term funding. The emergence of such behavior among the largest and most interconnected financial institutions is particularly dangerous, since these institutions are linchpins in our financial system, and their failure could cause significant damage to large numbers of counterparties and the system as a whole, as the examples of Lehman Brothers and American International Group demonstrate. However, a build-up of leverage and growing maturity mismatches are also worrisome when they occur more broadly in the financial system.

A second element is a high positive correlation of risk exposures across institutions. A wide array of commercial banks, investment banks, and other financial institutions held mortgages, mortgage-backed securities, or positions in mortgage-related derivatives. The result was the massive vulnerability of the financial system to a collapse of housing prices. What seemed like moderate risks taken by individual institutions ultimately led to an enormous risk to the system as a whole.

A third element is the extraordinary interconnectedness and complexity within the financial system. The intricate and opaque web of connections among financial players multiplies the dangers of contagion in the form of lost confidence, frozen liquidity, fire sales, and domino effects (Shin 2009). A key factor in this channel of systemic risk is the institutional arrangements in payment, clearing, and settlement systems. For example, weaknesses in the market infrastructure for repurchase agreements, or repos, and over-the-counter derivatives intensified the crisis (Duffie and others 2010; Payments Risk Committee 2010).

Systemic risk reflects the confluence of factors that may grow slowly over years. Therefore, surveillance must look at a variety of indicators and be forward looking, considering the paths of factors that influence such risk for years to come. To facilitate timely recognition of the emergence of systemic risk, we should design quantifiable indicators related to the three elements I just outlined: risk build-up at systemically important institutions and within the financial sector more broadly, positive correlations of risk among financial market participants, and interconnectedness among those participants.

Systemic risk surveillance will demand Herculean efforts by the regulatory agencies and the Office of Financial Research created by the new legislation. I see parallels between the way we take the pulse of the economy when considering monetary policy decisions and the way we should monitor and evaluate systemic risk when formulating macroprudential policies. In assessing the economy, we collect and analyze a myriad of data. In practice, though, we regard certain metrics as most critical, such as gross domestic product, employment and unemployment, and inflation. Similarly, in risk surveillance, we will gather an array of data on risk spreads, credit flows and volumes, asset prices, debt and leverage, markets, and institutions, including detailed, often proprietary, microdata on balance sheets, and data from such markets as those for over-the-counter derivatives and repos. Nonetheless, surveillance is likely to concentrate on key factors in the build-up of systemic risk such as the ones I identified: the accumulation of credit and funding risk on the balance sheets of systemically important institutions and throughout the financial system, the correlation of risk among financial market participants, and the extent of counterparty exposures.

Of course, we must also keep a close eye on broad credit and asset market conditions. One strand of surveillance will involve watching variations of risk and term spreads of bonds and other securities relative to historical norms. Narrow risk spreads and risk premiums may be a harbinger of excessive risk taking by investors. Another strand will focus more directly on measuring credit flows and exposures to credit risk. If overall credit growth is extraordinarily rapid, it may be a sign that financial institutions are taking greater risks onto their balance sheets. Because of financial system complexity, leverage is impossible to measure perfectly. Still, real-time indicators of the leverage of financial intermediaries would help identify where we are in a credit cycle. For example, we can look at the marginal leverage of new borrowing by examining data on collateral haircuts. We may also monitor data on repo market activity and haircuts to spot vulnerabilities relating to maturity mismatches. This information can be crosschecked against firm- and sector-level data on credit risk exposure.

One aspect of systemic risk surveillance that has garnered a great deal of attention is the identification of asset price bubbles. Bubbles present systemic danger when major financial institutions use leverage to finance investment in risky assets that they hold on their balance sheets. The systemic risk is multiplied when the asset bubble is accompanied by a credit bubble that fuels highly leveraged investment (Adrian and Shin 2008). So a top priority of systemic risk surveillance must be to assess whether asset price movements suggest the presence of a bubble and identify at an early stage those that might be particularly dangerous. In practice, of course, we will have highly uncertain notions of when excesses evolve into bubbles. Near the end of a bubble, it's pretty clear that something is amiss. But by then it's too late to do much about it.

We will also need to monitor the cross-sectional correlations of firms' risk exposures.[1] In addition, we need information on counterparty exposures through derivatives and other financial instruments. Finally, further development of financial sector stress testing, building on the tests carried out in the United States in 2009 and in Europe this year, will provide valuable information about the ability of the financial system to weather significant economic or financial shocks. We should refine the stress-testing methodology as we develop a more sophisticated understanding of institution-level systemic risk factors. These enhancements can be carried out by the quantitative surveillance unit that we have already established in our supervision of the largest financial institutions to better integrate macroprudential considerations with regular supervisory practice.

Qualitative information on credit will complement the quantitative evidence. The Federal Reserve recently introduced the Senior Credit Officer Opinion Survey on Dealer Financing Terms, adding to the information collected from the existing commercial bank Senior Loan Officer Opinion Survey on Bank Lending Practices, a survey on credit supply and demand.[2]

Systemic risk surveillance is both a science and an art: science in that we will analyze closely a wide range of data that research shows to be diagnostic, and art in that we will have to exercise judgment about when excesses become so dangerous that action is required. The Federal Reserve and other regulators in the United States and abroad have made important progress in developing systemic risk indicators. Still, we must recognize the inherent difficulty in forecasting crises and acknowledge the failure of past risk-monitoring efforts. Moreover, we must be mindful of the inadequacy of indicators that focus too specifically on the markets and channels that transmitted the crisis of 2007 and 2008. Like Tolstoy's unhappy families, every financial crisis is a crisis in its own way. For that reason, we need a flexible approach that combines science and art, and judgmentally weighs information from all indicators.

Macroprudential Policy Implementation

Refining our ability to identify systemic threats is well and good. But when we detect a threat, what will we do about it? This question brings me to the tools and implementation of macroprudential policies. The first tool is information to help focus attention in policy circles, and among investors and the public, on looming systemic risks. The detailed financial stability reports published by the International Monetary Fund and a number of central banks are intended to serve this purpose (Bank of England 2010; International Monetary Fund 2010). And the Financial Stability Oversight Council created under the Dodd-Frank Act is charged with preparing such a report once a year.

Admittedly, most such reports failed to identify the mechanisms behind the recent crisis. And even when vulnerabilities were identified and warning bells sounded, they were often greeted with yawns, as anyone who remembers the phrase "irrational exuberance" can testify. Those who sounded the alarms were seen as killjoys who refused to join the party. Words are important, but clearly they are not enough. We need strong policies to back them up. We need macroprudential policymakers ready to take away the punch bowl when the party is getting out of hand. We know that market participants won't take kindly when limits are set precisely in those markets that are most exuberant, the ones in which they are making big money. During the late stages of the housing boom, more than a few financial institution chief executive officers dismissed the warnings of their own risk managers with a wave of the hand.

So what should be the main tools of macro-prudential supervision? Many of them are similar to those of microprudential policy. They take the form of restrictions or incentives related to financial firms' balance sheets. Still, macroprudential policies differ from purely microprudential approaches in that they are intended to protect the financial system as a whole and, by extension, the broader economy. Macroprudential policies will be aimed at countering the procyclical nature of credit and leverage, leaning against the wind when systemic risk is accumulating. In addition, they will seek to stem risks related to interconnections and spillovers in the financial system.

The Basel Committee on Banking Supervision is playing a key role in designing this new regulatory regime as part of the Basel III initiative. And, under Federal Reserve leadership, initiatives to implement macroprudential supervision are well under way in the United States. Policymakers here and abroad agree that macroprudential policy must include requirements to hold more and higher-quality capital. And capital requirements must be reformulated to reduce the procyclicality of credit and leverage. Financial institutions may be required to build capital buffers in good times, which they can run down in bad times, thereby limiting credit growth during booms and mitigating credit contraction in downturns. Banks may also be required to have, in addition to their standard equity buffers, contingent capital in the form of debt that is convertible to equity if they experience significant losses. This additional capital would protect them from insolvency during busts while allowing them to benefit from debt finance in boom times. US regulators have also been charged with developing heightened prudential standards for systemically important institutions to constrain risk taking by those firms whose failures would pose the greatest systemic risk. One approach could involve imposing penalties or restrictions on financial firms based on factors such as the correlation of their strategies with those of other firms or by limiting risk exposure to individual counterparties.

Policies are on the drawing board to ensure that institutions avoid undue reliance on short-term debt and have adequate liquidity in market downturns. Such requirements would diminish the risk of the shortfalls and hoarding that could fuel a credit market meltdown. Policymakers might additionally put in place policies to discourage overreliance on short-term debt among investors more broadly through, for example, regulations on repo haircuts. To address unsustainable real estate price run-ups, some countries have chosen to cap maximum loan-to-value ratios on home loans. Such an approach deserves serious consideration. My expectation is that policies such as these will restrict dangerous procyclical movements in debt and leverage, diminish the extent of maturity mismatches and the potential for runs, and discourage unsustainable asset price appreciation. Importantly, the Federal Reserve and other US regulators have also taken steps to ensure that the financial institutions we supervise enforce compensation policies that control incentives for excessive procyclical risk taking.

Macroprudential supervision must be particularly attentive to risks that could impair the plumbing of the financial system—that is, the payments, clearing, and settlements systems—where breakdowns would relay and amplify systemic risk. Importantly, the Dodd-Frank Act significantly increases the trading of derivatives on exchanges and their clearing through central counterparties.[3] Because clearinghouses are themselves subject to risk from counterparties and are important linchpins in the financial system, they must be regulated to ensure that they operate safely.

Since the implementation of macroprudential supervision is a work in progress, I want to highlight several important design considerations. The first relates to the appropriate balance between fixed rules and discretion—a question familiar from monetary and fiscal policy. In both cases, we have learned that fixed rules offer distinct advantages. In fiscal policy, automatic stabilizers have proven helpful in mitigating the amplitude of cyclical fluctuations. They trigger fiscal support when needed in a timely and predictable way. In the realm of monetary policy, the Federal Reserve and other central banks commonly vary policy in a manner that researchers and market participants find predictable and systematic. Indeed, guidance from policy rules is increasingly used in actual decision-making since rule-based recommendations create a sensible starting point for deliberations. Rule-like behavior also aligns the expectations of markets and policymakers so that policy is transmitted quickly and effectively to the economy.

Nevertheless, neither fiscal nor monetary policymakers rely on fixed rules alone. Discretionary fiscal policy has been helpful, even essential, in some instances in responding to economic fluctuations resulting from large shocks. Similarly, in the realm of monetary policy, the Federal Reserve and other central banks certainly don't slavishly follow prescriptions from any rule. They retain discretion to deviate from such prescriptions when responding to severe shocks, unusually strong headwinds, or significant asymmetric risks.

In the implementation of macroprudential supervision, I believe it will be similarly advantageous to put in place a system of controls in which fixed rules play an important role while a place is preserved for the discretionary judgments of regulators. Fixed rules will diminish the need for policymakers to make the difficult decision to take away the punch bowl. Moreover, if discretionary macroprudential policy interventions are deferred until a boom is well under way, the macroeconomic spillovers could prove difficult for monetary policy to offset.

For these reasons, a stronger system of prudential controls designed to mitigate the build-up of systemic risk must be put into place, a system that will incorporate mechanisms to automatically counter procyclical behavior. All the same, discretionary interventions will inevitably play a part in macroprudential supervision. For one thing, it's important to keep in mind that financial institutions have been very adept at gaming rule-based systems. And, over time, there is always an incentive for risky financial activities to migrate outside the perimeter of supervision and regulation, even if that perimeter is moving. That's precisely what happened prior to the mortgage crisis, when leverage ballooned in the shadow banking system and investment banks and some nonbanks became principal participants in credit derivatives markets. Furthermore, the financial system will evolve in ways that preclude any wholly rule-based system from countering all emerging systemic threats. Discretionary macroprudential interventions are certain to be needed to address dangerous developments, and judgment must play a role.

A second consideration in macroprudential supervision relates to the need for robust policies. This concern derives from the observation that we still have a lot to learn about the behavior of financial institutions and their effects on systemic risk and the real economy. Our ability to model the channels by which disruptions in credit and finance affect the real economy and the ways these effects feed back into the banking and financial systems is getting more sophisticated.[4] But our understanding of the key channels, their quantitative importance, and the effects of our policies remain incomplete at best. It is therefore important that we implement policies that are likely to succeed in mitigating systemic risk in a future crisis regardless of the precise triggers and transmission channels. A rich monetary policy literature demonstrates that simple rules result in good, even excellent, performance when policymakers face uncertainty about the structure of the economy and the source of economic shocks (Taylor and Williams 2010). This conclusion may apply to macroprudential supervision as well.

A third consideration in the design of the macroprudential supervision relates to the need for extensive international cooperation. If the United States were to go it alone with tough policies, we could see our financial institutions flee in a race to the bottom. But I'm convinced that won't happen. We are working closely with our international counterparts to develop coherent and comprehensive approaches, aided by the Basel Committee on Banking Supervision, the Financial Stability Board, the International Monetary Fund, and other institutions (Lipsky 2010).

Finally, we must not forget that macroprudential policies will entail some costs as well as benefits. The magnitude of these costs remains a subject of debate. But, as with all forms of regulation, we must find the right balance between overly strict supervision and laissez faire. I don't know exactly where on the continuum that balance lies. But I do know that, before the crisis, we had veered disastrously too far in the direction of laissez faire, with consequences we know too well.

Interaction with Monetary Policy

One of the most challenging issues relating to systemic risk management is the appropriate interactions between macroprudential and monetary policy. To what extent, if at all, should monetary policy be used to mitigate systemic risk? And to what extent, if at all, should monetary policy be coordinated with macroprudential supervision? These issues are the subject of intense debate among policymakers across the globe. Of course, the question of whether monetary policy should lean against asset price bubbles is hardly new (Bernanke and Gertler 1999; Cecchetti and others 2000; Kohn 2006). What has changed is the sense of urgency surrounding this and related questions.

I noted previously—and it is now commonly accepted—that monetary policy can affect systemic risk through a number of channels (Yellen 2009; Bean and others 2010). First, monetary policy has a direct effect on asset prices for the obvious reason that interest rates represent the opportunity costs of holding assets. Indeed, an important element of the monetary transmission mechanism works through the asset price channel. In theory, an increase in asset prices induced by a decline in interest rates should not cause asset prices to keep escalating in bubble-like fashion. But if bubbles do develop, perhaps because of an onset of excessive optimism, and especially if the bubble is financed by debt, the result may be a build-up of systemic risk. Second, recent research has identified possible linkages between monetary policy and leverage among financial intermediaries (Adrian and Shin 2009). It is conceivable that accommodative monetary policy could provide tinder for a build-up of leverage and excessive risk taking in the financial system.

Macroprudential interventions may also have macroeconomic spillovers. For example, research suggests that rigorous enforcement of supervisory standards for capital following the real estate-related loan losses of the early 1990s may have slowed the economy's recovery from the recession. Today, we all understand the need for more stringent bank capital and liquidity requirements to stem systemic risk. But, with high unemployment in so many economies, the new Basel III agreement recognizes the desirability of a phase-in period for these standards. The implementation of tighter standards over a multiyear period should mitigate the concern that the macroprudential policies we are putting in place to control systemic risk will unduly restrict the availability of credit, thereby retarding economic recovery.

In this case, as it should, the implementation of macroprudential policy is taking account of spillovers that monetary policy, at least now, cannot easily offset.

Some would argue that the conduct of macroprudential and monetary policy should be closely coordinated, even integrated, because of the spillovers I described.[5] Indeed, the logic of this argument has led some observers to conclude that both macroprudential and monetary policy should be assigned to the central bank (French and others 2010). As I noted, the Dodd-Frank Act assigned the Federal Reserve an important role in the conduct of macroprudential supervision, and for good reasons. We have long experience in supervision, broad knowledge of financial markets, and an understanding of the linkages between financial markets and the economy. In addition, the insights derived from our supervisory role benefit the conduct of monetary policy. But the pursuit of macroprudential supervision under the new legislation involves other regulatory agencies beside the Federal Reserve, and the new Financial Stability Oversight Council will play an important role. And, of course, the Federal Reserve will keep sole responsibility for the conduct of monetary policy, retaining its independence. There are important reasons for this approach. One is that systemic risk surveillance will benefit from the perspectives of regulators with different windows on the financial system, all participating in the oversight council. Second, the principle of central bank independence in the conduct of monetary policy is widely accepted as vital to achieving maximum employment and price stability.

Fortunately, it is perfectly possible to attain good outcomes even if monetary policy and macroprudential policy are carried out separately and independently, and the goals of each are pursued using entirely separate tool kits. This conclusion is an application of the assignment problem made familiar by Robert Mundell (1962) and others who analyzed monetary and fiscal policy. A key insight from that literature is that satisfactory results can be attained without policy coordination, even though fully optimal policy generally calls for coordination when spillovers occur. Of course, it is necessary for monetary policy to take into account any macroeconomic effects resulting from macroprudential policy and vice versa.

This separate-assignments approach to formulating macroprudential and monetary policy has merit both in theory and practice. But I want to be careful not to push the argument for separation too far. I noted, for example, that situations may arise in which the Federal Reserve, in its conduct of monetary policy, might not be able to fully offset the macroeconomic effects of macroprudential interventions. This scenario could happen because of the zero bound on interest rates or monetary policy lags. In such circumstances, it makes sense for macroprudential policy to take macroeconomic effects into account. By the same token, I would not want to argue that it is *never* appropriate for monetary policy to take into account its potential effect on financial stability. Regulation is imperfect. Financial imbalances may emerge even if we strengthen macroprudential oversight and control. Some day in the future, it is possible that macroprudential regulators might let down their guard. In such situations, if emerging threats to financial stability become evident, monetary policy could be faced with difficult tradeoffs. My hope is that such situations will remain largely theoretical and, in practice, be exceedingly rare.

Overall, I am encouraged by the progress we are making in developing the new regulatory framework. Still, macroprudential supervision is a work in progress, and we must humbly recognize that we have a lot to learn.

Challenges

It's important to be realistic about the challenges that lie ahead. By its nature, policy designed to manage systemic risk fights dangers that may never lead to crises. We may sometimes be like the boy who cried, "Wolf!"—and the villagers may not be pleased about being rousted from their beds. Right now, we are still suffering from the shock of an epic financial disaster. The climate for macroprudential policymaking is relatively favorable. But memories will fade, as they always have before, and future policymakers may face harsh criticism. They will need to make difficult and potentially costly judgment calls, relying on imperfect real-time information. In this regard, it's worth recalling Paul Samuelson's quip that the stock market has predicted nine of the past five recessions. Will future regulators and monetary policymakers be accused of bursting ten of the past two asset bubbles?

These dangers are real. But the events we've recently lived through make it clear that we have no choice but to embark on this road. We've all been asked, "Didn't you see this mortgage disaster coming? Why didn't you do anything about it?" Our task now is to implement intelligent policies to contain future bubbles and credit binges, and to make sure that those that do occur inflict a lot less damage on the economy. Next time I hope we can say, "We did see it coming, and we did something about it."

Acknowledgments

I would like to thank John Williams and Sam Zuckerman, both of the Federal Reserve Bank of San Francisco, for assistance in preparing these remarks.

Notes

Originally published in *Business Economics*, Vol. 46, No. 1 (January 2011), pp. 3–12.

1. A number of promising measures of measuring systemic risk that take into account the correlations of firms' strategies have recently been developed. For example, the CoVaR approach aims to measure the marginal contribution of a financial institution to systemic risk, where systemic risk is measured by the value at risk of all firms together (Adrian and Brunnermeier 2009). See also the risk topography approach discussed in Brunnermeier and others (2010).
2. These surveys are available on the Federal Reserve Board's website: http://www.federalreserve.gov/econresdata/releases/surveysreports.htm.
3. See Duffie and others (2010) for a discussion of these issues.
4. For examples, see Brunnermeier and Sannikov (2010), Curdia and Woodford (2009), and Gertler and Karadi (2009), and the references therein.

5. See Bean and others (2010) for a discussion of the interaction of monetary and macroprudential policies.

References

Adrian, Tobias, and Hyun Song Shin. 2008. "Financial Intermediaries, Financial Stability, and Monetary Policy," paper presented at "Maintaining Stability in a Changing Financial System," a symposium sponsored by the Federal Reserve Bank of Kansas City, August 21–23. www.kansascityfed.org/publicat/sympos/2008/Shin.03.12.09.pdf.

Adrian, Tobias, and Hyun Song Shin. 2009. "Money, Liquidity, and Monetary Policy." *American Economic Review*, 99 (May): 600–605.

Adrian, Tobias, and Markus K. Brunnermeier. 2009. "CoVaR," Staff Report 348, New York: Federal Reserve Bank of New York, August. www.newyork fed.org/research/staff_reports/sr348.pdf.

Allen, Franklin, Stephen Morris, and Hyun Song Shin. 2006. "Beauty Contests and Iterated Expectations in Asset Markets." *Review of Financial Studies*, 19(3): 719–752.

Bank of England, 2010. *Financial Stability Report*, http://www.bankofengland.co.uk/publications/fsr/2010/fsr27.htm.

Bean, Charles, Matthias Paustian, Adrian Penalver, and Tim Taylor. 2010. "Monetary Policy after the Fall," paper presented at "Macroeconomic Challenges: The Decade Ahead," a symposium sponsored by the Federal Reserve Bank of Kansas City, August 26–28. www.kansascityfed.org/publicat/sympos/2010/bean-paper.pdf.

Bernanke, Ben S., and Mark Gertler. 1999. "Monetary Policy and Asset Price Volatility," paper presented at "New Challenges for Monetary Policy," a symposium sponsored by the Federal Reserve Bank of Kansas City, August 26–28. www.kansascityfed.org/publicat/sympos/1999/S99gert.pdf.

Brunnermeier, Markus K., Gary Gorton, and Arvind Krishnamurthy. 2010. "Risk Topography," unpublished paper, July. www.princeton.edu/~markus/research/papers/risk_topography.pdf.

Brunnermeier, Markus K., and Yuliy Sannikov. 2010. "A Macroeconomic Model with a Financial Sector," unpublished paper, May. www.princeton.edu/~markus/research/papers/macro_finance.pdf.

Cecchetti, Stephen G., Hans Genburg, John Lipsky, and Sushil B. Wadhwani. 2000. *Geneva Reports on the World Economy 2: Asset Prices and Central Bank Policy.* Centre for Economic Policy Research.

Curdia, Vasco, and Michael Woodford. 2009. "Credit Spreads and Monetary Policy," Staff Report 385: Federal Reserve Bank of New York, August. www.newyorkfed.org/research/staff_reports/sr385.html.

Duffie, Darrell, Ada Li, and Theo Lubke. 2010. "Policy Perspectives on OTC Derivatives Market Infrastructure," Staff Report 424, New York: Federal Reserve Bank of New York, January revised March. www.newyorkfed.org/research/staff_reports/sr424.html.

French, Keneth R., Martin N. Baily, John Y. Campbell, John H. Cochrane, Douglas W. Diamond, Darrell Duffie, Anil K. Kashyap, Frederic S. Mishkin, Raghuram G. Rajan, David S. Scharfstein, Robert J. Shiller, Hyun Song Shin, Matthew J. Slaughter, Jeremy C. Stein, and René M. Stulz. 2010. *The Squam Lake Report: Fixing the Financial System.* Princeton, NJ: Princeton University Press.

Gertler, Mark, and Peter Karadi. 2009. "A Model of Unconventional Monetary Policy," manuscript, New York University, April.

International Monetary Fund, 2010. *Global Financial Stability Report: Meeting New Challenges to Stability and Building a Safer System*, www.imf.org/external/pubs/ft/gfsr/2010/01/pdf/text.pdf.

Kohn, Donald L. 2006. "Monetary Policy and Asset Prices," speech delivered at "Monetary Policy: A Journey from Theory to Practice," a European Central Bank colloquium held in honor of Otmar Issing, March 16. www.federalreserve.gov/newsevents/speech/kohn20060316a.htm.

Lipsky, John. 2010. "Reconsidering the International Monetary System," panel presentation at the "Macroeconomic Challenges: The Decade Ahead," a symposium sponsored by the Federal Reserve Bank of Kansas City, August 26–28.

Minsky, Hyman P. 1992. "The Financial Instability Hypothesis," Working Paper 74, Jerome Levy Economics Institute of Bard College, May. www.levyinstitute.org/pubs/wp74.pdf.

Mundell, Robert A. 1962. "Appropriate Use of Monetary and Fiscal Policy for Internal and External Stability." *International Monetary Fund Staff Papers*, 9(1): 70–79.

Payments Risk Committee, 2010. *Task Force on Tri-Party Repo Infrastructure*, May. www.newyorkfed.org/prc/report_100517.pdf.

Shin, Hyun. 2009. "Financial Intermediation and the Post-Crisis Financial System," paper presented at the 8th BIS Annual Conference, June 25–26.

Taylor, John B., and John C. Williams. 2010. "Simple and Robust Rules for Monetary Policy," in *Handbook of Monetary Economics*, edited by Benjamin Friedman and Michael Woodford. North-Holland, Elsevier.

Yellen, Janet L. 2009. "Linkages between Monetary and Regulatory Policy: Lessons from the Crisis," presentation to the Institute of Regulation and Risk, North Asia. Held in Hong Kong, November 17.

CHAPTER 36

2011

THE ADAM SMITH ADDRESS

NIGHTMARE ON KAISERSTRASSE

Kenneth Rogoff, Harvard University

It is a great honor to receive the 2011 Adam Smith award from the National Association for Business Economics. It is an honor both because of the important group that awards it and because of the extraordinarily distinguished list of recipients that have come before me. In this chapter, I will begin by discussing why sovereign debt crises often follow after a wave of international financial crises. I will then turn to the ongoing crisis in Europe, which is at the epicenter of the current phase of the larger crisis. Finally, I will speculate on the long-term implications for the international monetary system of a significant break-up in the euro system.

The aftermath of the recent financial crisis, which Carmen Reinhart and I refer to as the "Second Great Contraction" (Reinhart and Rogoff 2009a), continues to spin off extraordinary events. The term "Great Contraction" was coined by Milton Friedman and Anna Schwartz in their follow-up book to their 1963 classic *A Monetary History of the United States*. Although the ongoing downturn is not as severe as the Great Depression, it is similar in the broad economy-wide contraction of credit, in addition to the contraction of employment and output. Reinhart and I argue that the overhang of debt (private and surging public) is perhaps the principal reason why recessions following financial crises are so deep and lasting. We chose the term "Great Contraction" in contrast to the current popular moniker, "Great Recession," to highlight the fact that the contours of the downturn are very different from those of a typical recession. The overhang of debt, and the subsequent slow recovery, makes it far more difficult for policymakers to simply temporize in dealing with debt problems, providing liquidity and then waiting for growth to ameliorate the problems. Unfortunately, that is exactly the strategy that has been adopted in Europe, and it is a very dangerous one.

Our book covers a wide range of financial crises, including banking, inflation, exchange rate, and domestic debt crises. But perhaps the oldest form of financial crisis that we treat is sovereign external debt crises, where a government defaults on debt to foreigners. Concerns over sovereign debt are at the heart of the ongoing Eurozone crisis, though of course sovereign debt and banking crisis risks are deeply interlinked. A key finding in our research is that after a wave of international financial and banking crises, there very often follows a wave of sovereign defaults.[1] Thus, in some respects, the trauma that is striking the Eurozone today is hardly unusual.

Banking Crises and Sovereign Debt Crises

Why do sovereign debt crises so often follow a wave of global banking crises? The reason is twofold. First, the aftermath of banking crises typically involves a large run-up in public debt (debt owed by the government). Reinhart and I find that for post-World War II deep financial crises, the average run-up in debt is 86 percent after three years, adjusted for inflation.[2] The run-up in debts follows from the deep and prolonged recessions that typically accompany banking crises (the main cause), but also from the cost of bank bailouts and, in some cases, fiscal stimulus. To save the economy, the government opens the deficit floodgates. But unfortunately, this sometimes involves extending itself beyond the county's sustainable borrowing capacity. A second important reason why sovereign defaults rise after a financial crisis is simply that the crisis shakes financial markets, typically leading to a loss of liquidity, a rise in risk premiums, and a generalized fall in asset values. Even in normal times, risky debtors are more likely to face problems when big shocks hit, even if they are not at the epicenter of the shocks. In many ways, the Eurozone crisis was an accident waiting to happen, but one that is more a result of the financial crisis than a primary initial cause of it.

I have stated that after a deep financial crisis, some countries end up finding themselves in unsustainable debt situations. Of course, the truth is that there is no bright red line above which a country suddenly cannot pay its debt. Neither economic theory nor empirics provide such a bright red line.

The theory of sovereign default, despite a large number of interesting and inventive papers, is still at a very early stage.[3] While theory lays out some useful general principles (countries that are very open to trade and with very highly integrated financial markets are less likely to default), most of our practical understanding of sovereign default still rests on empirical benchmarks. Reinhart and Rogoff (2009a, Chapter 2) argue that a country's default history is an important factor in determining how much debt it can handle without running into trouble. Emerging market economies with a history of problems may run into debt default difficulties at ratios of external debt to GDP as low as 30–40 percent, whereas the rare economies that have pristine or almost pristine records of repaying sovereign external debt can run up debt levels more than double that without running into trouble. (Even after many decades old defaults can affect a country's debt thresholds, with a long half-life.)

Indeed, benchmark debt levels are often a better guide to vulnerability than either interest rate risk premiums or ratings agency assessments. A number of studies find that interest rate risk premiums are very poor guides to assessing default risk, at least not very far in advance. Interest rates on sovereign debt typically rise significantly only within a month or two, or at most a year, of a default event. This reflects both the knife edge stability of confidence and expectation as well as the problem of "hidden debts," which often come jumping out of the woodwork in a crisis (Reinhart and Rogoff 2009a, Chapter 2; 2011). Ratings agencies, for many reasons, are under pressure to provide relatively smooth changes in assessments, which often in turn make ratings a lagging indicator of problems (and recovery).

The fact that relatively distant defaults are still correlated with a country's general financial fragility reflects a broader point about "graduation" to advanced economy status (again, a concept developed in my work with Reinhart). In general, it takes many decades, indeed often centuries, for a country to make the transition from emerging market to an advanced economy (Qian and others 2011). No class of economy has yet durably graduated from inflation crises, but advanced economies do not suffer nearly as much from defaults on their external debt. In some ways, the Eurozone experiment was an attempt to see if the process of "graduation" could be accelerated by integrating emerging markets such as Greece and Portugal into the euro system (not to mention Spain, Ireland, and Italy). Rather than accept the rule of thumb that emerging markets take generations to develop financially, economically and socially into advanced economies, European leaders pressed on with monetary unification as a leading edge of political unification. Skeptics, including it must be said many American economists, were told that they simply did not understand the conviction and commitment of Europeans to the single currency project (which by implication also meant the power and influence of the European elite, since polls typically showed a far more mixed view of the euro among the masses, particularly in Germany).

The result of the euro's introduction is now familiar enough. Thanks to their new status in international markets as advanced economies, the periphery European countries were able to reach external and public debt limits on the outer envelope of anything ever observed for emerging markets. Portugal's public debt of 90 percent of GDP may seem tame next to Greece at 140 percent, but both numbers are massive by emerging market standards. Of course, with Greece, Portugal, and Ireland combined representing only 6 percent of Eurozone GDP, it is possible that Europe will be able to cover its losses much the way West Germany carried East Germany after unification. But countries such as Italy and Belgium have massive debts over 100 percent of GDP, and Spain's debt might be as high when contingent claims from municipalities and the banking sector are accounted for, particularly if real estate prices continue to fall. Although European leaders have argued that the euro could never unravel—and they may yet prove right—it is interesting to at least think through the thought experiment of how it might happen, catastrophic as that might be.

What Could Happen If Greece Leaves the Eurozone?

Suppose, for argument's sake, that the Greek debt problem continues to founder, that European leaders ultimately realize that far deeper write-downs and debt forgiveness are required, far above 50 percent, and that Greece is pushed out of the euro. It should be noted that a Greek default does not necessarily imply an exit from the euro. States in the United States defaulted in the 1840s and the 1870s, with the latter defaults lasting in many cases until World War I. But the defaulting states (more than 10 in the 1870s) did not abandon the dollar. (Of course, during the US Civil War of the 1860s, the Confederate States did indeed abandon the dollar, but this is another story.) Greece, too, could remain a Eurozone country, but if it does so, it is hard to see how it will regain its competitiveness, which deteriorated massively in the decade after it joined the euro. In principle, it can have an "internal devaluation" by cutting wages and salaries, but deflations of this sort are exceptionally rare and painful, at least on the scale needed in Greece. Most countries after a financial crisis experience a massive currency depreciation, which boosts exports and tourism, helping lead to a large turnaround in the current account. If Greece stays in the Eurozone, any recovery could take a decade or more of slow growth or recession.

If Greece were to leave the euro, it could only accentuate the low-grade banking panics already taking place across the periphery countries, now including Italy. Just for argument's sake, suppose Portugal followed Greece out of the euro and suddenly Portuguese exports became hypercompetitive with Spanish exports. Assuming Germany chooses not to cast an ironclad safety net over the Spanish central government, it is easy to imagine the combination of banking panic and competitiveness problems forcing Spain out of the euro as well, putting Italy at a huge competitive disadvantage after Spain's new peseta in turn depreciates massively against the euro. Would France survive? Again, only with highly credible German backing. In the end, the euro could be reduced to just a few countries, including Germany, Austria, Luxembourg, and the Netherlands.

Can the Nightmare Be Prevented?

A collapse of this magnitude would surely be the ultimate nightmare on Kaiserstrasse, the street in Frankfurt where the European Central Bank is located. Can an unwinding of the euro be forestalled? Of course, the answer is yes, although as events move forward, the initial conditions are changing. Increasingly, the European strategy of trying to protect every country—no matter how weak its position—risks continually weakening credibility. Rather, Germany needs to cast its safety net at a credible boundary, guaranteeing central government debt in Spain and Italy and perhaps Ireland, but allowing Portugal and Greece to undergo needed restructuring.

The fate of the euro has huge implications for the global financial system. If the euro fractures and weakens, with a major chunk of countries breaking off, will it discourage other currency unions in the future? Until the past couple of years, there was a widespread belief in both academic and policy circles that a century or two from now, there would be far fewer currencies in the world than we see today, with a trend toward regional currencies in Asia and North America and perhaps South America as well. For all its flaws, the euro experiment was seen as a long-term trend as countries seek ways to achieve more productive and efficient globalization. Some scholars, such as Columbia's Robert Mundell, the intellectual father of the euro, believe that in an ideal world there would be a single global currency.

The growing pains of the euro are, of course, leading to a reassessment. The euro experiment has underscored gaps in the standard optimal currency framework that need to be filled before currency integration can be enthusiastically recommended to other regions. Much of the discussion about the Eurozone centers on having tighter borrowing restrictions for member states. I suspect any long-run solution will also have to address bias in financial systems toward nonindexed debt.

Of course, the euro may yet surprise skeptics like myself and survive intact, with the euro system proving more dynamic and politically flexible than we imagine it to be. If it does survive its current crisis, presumably after much constitutional reform, the euro may prove much the stronger for it. Then again, like all good horror movies, "Nightmare on Kaiserstrasse" might just spawn a sequel.

Notes

Originally published in *Business Economics*, Vol. 46, No. 4 (October 2011), pp. 191–194.

1. The point that waves of financial crises are often followed by waves of sovereign debt crises is highlighted in Reinhart and Rogoff (2009a), and explored in much greater detail in Reinhart and Rogoff (2011).
2. See Reinhart and Rogoff (2009a, Chapters 10 and 14) as well as Reinhart and Rogoff (2009b).
3. My own work on the theory of sovereign debt includes a series of joint papers with Jeremy Bulow. See "References" at the end of this chapter.

References

Bulow, Jeremy, and Kenneth Rogoff. 1988a. "The Buyback Boondoggle." *Brookings Papers on Economic Activity* 2: 675–698.

Bulow, Jeremy, and Kenneth Rogoff. 1988b. "Multilateral Negotiations for Rescheduling Developing Country Debt: A Bargaining-Theoretic Framework." *International Monetary Fund Staff Papers*, 35 (December): 644–657. *Reprinted* in Frenkel, Jacob A., Michael P. Dooley and Peter Wickham, eds. 1989. *Analytical Issues in Debt*. International Monetary Fund.

Bulow, Jeremy, and Kenneth Rogoff. 1989a. "Sovereign Debt: Is to Forgive to Forget?" *American Economic Review*, 79 (March): 43–50.

Bulow, Jeremy, and Kenneth Rogoff. 1989b. "A Constant Recontracting Model of Sovereign Debt." *The Journal of Political Economy*, 97 (February): 155–178.

Bulow, Jeremy, and Kenneth Rogoff. 1990. "'Introduction' to Symposium on New Institutions for Developing-Country Debt." *Journal of Economic Perspectives*, 4 (Winter): 3–6.

Bulow, Jeremy, and Kenneth Rogoff. 2009. "Cleaning Up Third-World Debt Without Getting Taken to the Cleaners." *Journal of Economic Perspectives*, 4 (Winter): 31–42.

Friedman, Milton, and Anna Jacobson Schwartz. 1963. *A Monetary History of the United States*. Princeton, NJ: Princeton University Press.

Qian, Rong, Carmen M. Reinhart, and Kenneth Rogoff. 2011. "On Graduation from Default, Inflation and Banking Crises: Elusive or Illusion," in *2010 NBER Macroeconomics Annual*, edited by Daron Acemoglu and Michael Woodford University of Chicago Press.

Reinhart, Carmen M., and Kenneth Rogoff. 2009a. *This Time Is Different: Eight Centuries of Financial Folly.* Princeton, NJ: Princeton University Press.

Reinhart, Carmen M., and Kenneth Rogoff. 2009b. "The Aftermath of Financial Crises." *American Economic Review*, 99 (May): 466–472.

Reinhart, Carmen M., and Kenneth Rogoff. 2011. "From Financial Crash to Debt Crisis." *American Economic Review*, 101 (August): 1676–1706.

CHAPTER 37

2013

THE ADAM SMITH ADDRESS

FINANCIAL SERVICES AND THE TRUST DEFICIT: WHY THE INDUSTRY SHOULD MAKE BETTER GOVERNANCE A TOP PRIORITY

Roger W. Ferguson Jr., TIAA-CREF

I want to begin by expressing my deep appreciation to NABE for recognizing me in this way. When I got the letter from Ken Simonson informing me about the Adam Smith Award, I was delighted. And when I saw the list of past recipients, I was both delighted and truly humbled to be among them. The Adam Smith Award is a great honor. Thank you for bestowing it on me. It is also an honor to have the opportunity to speak to the NABE membership again.

I spoke at last year's NABE Annual Meeting in New York City on bridging the gap between finance and the real economy. In my remarks then, I was able to point to some distinct glimmers of progress in what remained a challenging economic environment. Nearly a year on, it is good to be able to say those glimmers did not turn out to be a mirage. We have continued on a path of modest growth in the United States, and while we all would wish for more, it is a far better scenario than we might have imagined five years ago today. Indeed, to look back at some of the big headlines from September of 2008 is to be reminded of just how precarious and uncertain our situation was. That month alone:

- Freddie Mac and Fannie Mae were placed in government conservatorship.
- Bank of America announced its intention to buy Merrill Lynch.
- And, of course, Lehman Brothers filed for bankruptcy.

The memories of those days put the current economic situation in perspective. But the still-modest growth of today, 2.5 percent for the second quarter, also serves as a reminder that five years on from some of the darkest days of the financial crisis, we continue to deal with its lingering effects. We get a similar reminder from many of today's headlines:

- The unemployment rate remains stubbornly high and labor force participation low.
- The markets have been volatile in the face of concerns about the Fed's tapering plans.
- There is pain in emerging markets as investors decamp in droves.
- Rumors abound about the need for a third bailout in Greece.

All underscore that we're not yet free of the aftereffects of the worst economic downturn since the Great Depression.

Still, at this point in time, with growth on a seemingly solid—albeit slow—path and the worst dangers over, it would be wise to turn our collective energies to ensuring that we never have to endure a crisis like that again. Certainly, there's been a wave of activity in terms of regulation of the financial services industry, aimed at addressing the shortcomings that the crisis laid bare, and financial firms have undertaken a number of positive changes.

These are both good and necessary. But they are not enough. It is equally important to further improve corporate governance at financial firms. We need stronger and more effective corporate governance approaches, particularly at the institutions that have been deemed systemically important. This is absolutely critical to ensuring the continued stability of the financial system.

Today, I will focus my remarks on what more must be done by the financial services industry and its stakeholders. First, I will consider the landscape in which the industry is now operating, which is characterized by a widespread lack of trust. Second, I will argue that it is vital for the industry to turn this situation around. We need a strong and trusted financial services industry more than ever before to help Americans meet the demographic and economic challenges that have left millions uncertain about achieving lifelong financial security, even as they live longer and longer in retirement. And third, I will discuss why stronger corporate governance is so important to the health of our financial system and our continued economic progress, and I will highlight what the industry and its stakeholders must do to ensure stronger governance at all levels.

The Post-Crisis Landscape in Financial Services

To begin, let us look at the landscape in which the financial services industry is operating today. Americans have not forgiven the industry for its role at the center of the financial crisis. But that is perhaps not surprising given continued scandals around issues like LIBOR rate-fixing, insider trading, and multibillion-dollar losses from risky trades. Against this backdrop, the financial services industry has become one of the least-trusted industries in the world. This year, for the third consecutive year, banks and financial services firms placed dead last in the Edelman global ranking of trust in industries. Respondents cited both poor performance and the perception of unethical behavior as reasons for the lack of trust.

A Gallup poll conducted last year found equally grim results for the industry when it measured perceptions of honesty and ethics among different professions. Nurses came out on top in this survey, with 85 percent of respondents giving them high marks for honesty and ethics. Only 28 percent rated bankers as highly. Stockbrokers were viewed even worse, with just 11 percent of respondents giving them high ratings for honesty and ethics. They barely edged out members of Congress and car salespeople to escape landing at the bottom of that list too.

The Imperative of Rebuilding Trust

It is clear that the financial services industry has much work to do to rebuild trust. This brings to mind a great quote I read in an article about a speech given by Mark Carney, now the Governor of the Bank of England. As he so aptly put it: "Trust arrives on foot, but leaves in a Ferrari." As the financial services industry has figured out, neither does trust return in a Ferrari. It must be rebuilt painstakingly, and it won't happen overnight. But it is vital that Americans regain trust in the financial services industry, because the industry is simply too important to our economy and our global competitiveness to be looked on so warily by so many people.

The importance of financial services is not just the industry's contribution to GDP—which has steadily risen since the end of World War II and was 8.3 percent in 2011, higher than before the recession. Beyond purely economic calculations, finance has a larger social role. Robert Shiller argues that finance is one of the most powerful tools we have for solving common problems and increasing society's well-being.

In his book, Finance and the Good Society, Shiller (2012) says that finance is not about making money, per se, but that, "financing is really creating the architecture for reaching a goal. The goals served by finance originate with us." If you think about it in terms of the lives of average Americans, the financial services industry makes possible everything from college savings to 30-year-mortgages to life insurance to financially secure retirements.

The Retirement Challenge

Let us specifically consider that last one—retirement—for a moment, to illustrate why we need a strong, healthy, and trusted industry. Retirement has become a source of great angst in our nation. You may have seen the article in the *Washington Post* earlier this year saying that for the first time since the New Deal, a majority of Americans are headed to a retirement in which they will be financially worse off than their parents (Fletcher 2013). The reason is the huge deficit in retirement savings in our country. Last year, a Senate report calculated that deficit to be as much as $6.6 trillion, or about $57,000 for every household in America. Americans' confidence about having a comfortable retirement has hit record lows. More than a quarter of workers say they are "not at all confident" that they will have enough money for a comfortable retirement.

Certainly, the financial crisis and economic downturn have been big factors in creating this pessimism. But the bigger effect is from longer-term factors such as the shift away from traditional pensions to 401(k)s in the private sector, and with it, the shift in responsibility for funding retirement from employers to employees. Workers are being called on to make saving and investment decisions in a way that will generate enough income to fund years of life in retirement. The statistics are not encouraging. More than half of workers say they and their spouse have less than $25,000 in total savings and investments. Twenty-eight percent have less than $1,000. Only 57 percent of workers say they are currently saving for retirement. Even among people approaching retirement, the most recent national data show that median combined 401(k)/IRA balances were just $120,000 per household. That data are from 2010, so the balances are likely somewhat higher today, given the stock market's performance. But of course, many households in America do not even have a 401(k).

Meanwhile, the explosion in health-care costs threatens the long-term viability of even nest eggs that are well-funded. The public sector faces its own challenges, with unfunded liabilities for state and local pension systems estimated to be about $1 trillion. Across all sectors, future retirees worry—with good reason—that they will be unable to count on Social Security, Medicare, and Medicaid to the same degree that previous generations of retirees have. These programs are under great pressure due to the aging of the population—the result of both the rise in average life expectancy and the decline in the fertility rate.

One of our most pressing national challenges is making sure Americans can achieve lifelong financial security even as rising life expectancies mean they are living longer and longer in retirement. This is an especially important issue for women, who can end up with a retirement nest egg that is half that of a man of the same age and occupation. That is because on average, women still earn 77–81 cents for every dollar men earn—and they often spend an average of 10–12 years out of the workforce caring for children or elderly parents. Yet they also live longer than men. So they have to support themselves through a longer retirement with a smaller nest egg.

For both sexes, the bottom line remains: how do we ensure that people whose primary savings vehicle is the defined contribution plan save enough and then convert those savings into an adequate and secure income stream that lasts as long as they do? This is a challenge not just for those of us in the retirement industry, but for policymakers and researchers as well.

The issue of financial literacy is an important element of the challenge we face. People who are not financially literate will have a much tougher time preparing themselves for a secure retirement in this environment, in which the burden now falls primarily on their own shoulders. Yet the truth is that far too many Americans lack the financial literacy skills they need to make wise decisions about saving and investment.

Research has shown that financial literacy is important to achieving retirement security. People with a high degree of financial literacy are more likely to plan for retirement. And in turn, planning for retirement is a powerful predictor of wealth accumulation. People who plan for retirement have more than double the wealth of people who do not plan (Lusardi and Mitchell 2007). Conversely, people with a lower degree of financial literacy tend to borrow more, accumulate less wealth, and select mutual funds with higher fees. They are less likely to invest in stocks, more likely to experience difficulty with debt, and less likely to know the terms of their mortgages and other loans.

The lack of financial literacy among Americans is certainly a national issue. But when we view it through the prism of race, the effects are greatly magnified. Minorities have some of the lowest financial literacy rates in the nation. So, it is not surprising that when it comes to saving for retirement, studies have found serious gaps in the preparedness of African-American and Hispanic workers. This is the backdrop against which the financial services industry will be operating in the coming decades.

More than ever before, people will need help in achieving financial well-being throughout their lives and especially in retirement. They need sound advice—but advice that is given in the context of what is best for the customer, not what is best for the firm's bottom line.

Americans need a strong and trusted financial services industry that they can count on to step up and help them prepare for lifelong financial security. And the nation needs an industry that will tap its vast expertise to address the critical issue of improving financial literacy.

The Importance of Corporate Governance

What can the financial services industry do to regain the trust of the American people? Certainly, there's been an unprecedented process of regulatory reform to remedy the weaknesses that the crisis laid bare. And as I said earlier, that is important. But just as important is having stronger governance at financial firms.

Regulations and governance work hand-in-glove. Neither will be as effective as they can be without the other. I want to spend a moment talking about why corporate governance matters so much. The first thing to understand is that governance is more than just rules and processes. Rather, it involves the relationships between a company's management, board, shareholders, and other stakeholders—which in the case of the financial sector includes the regulators and supervisors charged with ensuring the system operates safely, soundly, ethically, and for the public good.

We know that weak governance played a key role in the financial crisis. One of the more influential reports on the crisis, issued in 2009 by the chair of the UK's Financial Services Authority (Turner 2009), identified seven proximate causes:

- Large global macroeconomic imbalances.
- An increase in commercial banks' involvement in risky trading activities.
- Growth in securitized credit.
- Increased leverage.
- Failure of banks to manage financial risks.

- Inadequate capital buffers.
- A misplaced reliance on complex math and credit ratings in assessing risk.

Weak governance was an underlying factor in each of these. There were shortcomings at all levels. Boards failed to grasp the risk that their institutions had taken on. Management failed to understand and control risks. Both management and boards, sometimes spurred on by shareholders, focused on performance to the detriment of prudence. Regulators and supervisors missed the potential systemic impact of entire classes of financial products, such as subprime mortgages, and they failed to spot the large systemic risks that had been growing during the previous two decades.

Since the crisis, some progress has been made in strengthening governance at financial firms, but no one should assume that the problems have been fixed. Much more must be done to translate the lessons of the crisis into sound governance practices.

Recommendations from the G30

I'd like to share some of the ideas for better governance recommended by the Group of 30, an international forum of public- and private-sector financial leaders of which I am a member. Our recommendations are based on an extensive survey we completed last year on governance at 36 of the world's largest, most complex financial firms, in 16 countries on 6 continents. We have outlined specific steps that boards, management, regulators and supervisors, and long-term shareholders should take to restore confidence and ensure the strength and stability of the financial system. A copy of our full report is available on the G30 website, but I will cover some of the highlights with you today.

First, we urge boards to take a long-term view that encourages long-term value creation in the interest of shareholders. Boards must ensure that firms are prudent in their decision making, without diminishing their capacity for innovation, and that short-term self-interest does not drive decision-making.

Second, we urge management to model the right kind of behavior and to support a culture that promotes long-term thinking, discipline, sound risk management, and accountability. Good governance requires a strong, well-functioning management team—one that creates a "no-surprises" environment where issues are elevated quickly, reasonable mistakes can be tolerated but malfeasance is punished, and organizational learning from those mistakes is promoted. Management must also proactively and continuously communicate up to the board, down through the organization, and to regulators, supervisors, and shareholders.

Third, we urge regulators and supervisors to take a broader view of their roles, one that includes understanding the overall business, strategy, people, and culture of the firms they oversee. They must recognize that it is not just about quantitative, rules-based regulatory requirements. The qualitative is equally important. And finally, we urge long-term shareholders to use their influence to keep companies honest about performance and focused on improving governance. While no one should depend on shareholders to steer firms away from a future financial crisis, we believe shareholders should recognize that they have a vital responsibility to press boards to implement stronger approaches to governance.

It is important that all of the key players remember that governance is not a fixed set of guidelines and rules but rather an ongoing process. In the end, what matters most are not the rules themselves—but how people actually behave. And behavior is driven largely by values and culture. Indeed, values and culture are the ultimate keystones of governance. They are what lead people to do the right thing, even when nobody is looking. That is why it is just as important for companies to focus on the so-called software of governance—culture, people, leadership, and values—as it is to focus on the hardware—structures and processes.

Leadership is an absolutely critical part of the equation. The tone is truly set at the top. It is vitally important for boards to champion an appropriate culture within the business—a culture of integrity, independence of thought, and respect—and for management to set high standards through their own example. Companies can have the most extensive processes and procedures, but if they have the wrong people as leaders—people who behave without transparency and integrity—then they won't have a culture that promotes doing the right thing.

The G30 has called on financial firms to spend the time and energy needed to ensure they have the right "software of governance" in place. We recognize that it is not easy to change culture and values. But it will happen given the right amount of encouragement and support from leadership. The truth is that we haven't seen enough progress on this front. It is imperative to change that now, with the lessons of the crisis still fresh and clear.

The four main participants in the governance system—boards, management, supervisors and regulators, and long-term shareholders—must act with urgency to strengthen governance. Only then can we fully restore confidence in our financial system and ensure its continued stability.

A New Paradigm for Regulators/Supervisors

The G30's work on this front continues. After we published our report last year, we heard from several supervisors as well as the Financial Stability Board, asking for additional insights into how they could strengthen governance. They were especially interested in how interactions between boards and supervisors could be enhanced and how firms' risk culture could be strengthened and assessed, particularly at systemically important financial institutions. So earlier this year we launched a new project, conducting interviews with the senior supervisors and board members of many of the largest, most complex global and domestic banks.

We have not yet released our report, but I can give you some highlights today. We believe it is time for a new paradigm in the relationship between boards and supervisors. There should be more proactive and regular interaction, both formal and informal—and not just in times of stress. The relationship should recognize the many shared interests of boards and supervisors and be based on trust and openness, grounded in two-way dialogue, and geared to ensuring the absence of surprises. Active interaction is particularly important in the supervisors' assessment of firms' strategies and risks, governance, and culture.

The goal is not a partnership. We recognize there will be inevitable tensions. But we think that both boards and supervisors will be more effective if they make the investment of time required to establish the kind of relationship we are suggesting.

Our report will talk about the specific ingredients required to make this happen, on the part of boards, supervisors, and national governments. It will also underscore the importance of recognizing that supervision is very different from regulation.

Supervision is not about rule-setting or assessing compliance with rules. Rather, it is about qualitative monitoring and assessment—of inherent risk, of appropriate corporate governance, of management capability, and of operational processes at the board and senior executive level designed to oversee, understand, measure, and manage risk. Supervision requires judgment and deep knowledge of the institution. It involves intervening early in areas where institutions are deficient, choosing appropriately from a variety of informal and formal tools, and avoiding unnecessary costs.

High-quality, timely supervision has the potential for big payoffs. It contributes to making institutions more resilient. It helps to reduce the likelihood and severity of material financial or operational problems. It enhances financial stability. I hope our new report will help both supervisors and boards as they strive to increase their effectiveness in support of safe, sound, and successful financial institutions.

Closing

I will close now by reiterating the main themes I've addressed today. First, five years on from some of the worst days of the financial crisis, there continues to be widespread mistrust of the financial services industry. Second, we need a strong and trusted financial services sector more than ever before, to help Americans meet the challenges they face in several areas, including ensuring their financial security in retirement and boosting the nation's levels of financial literacy. And third, improving corporate governance at financial firms is essential if the industry is to regain trust. Boards, management, regulators and supervisors, and long-term shareholders all have a role to play in making this happen—and in ensuring the continued stability of the financial system.

Note

Originally published in *Business Economics*, Vol. 48, No. 4 (October 2013), pp. 208–213.

References

Fletcher, Michael A. 2013. Fiscal Trouble Ahead for Most Future Retirees. *The Washington Post* (February 16).

Lusardi, Annamaria and Olivia S. Mitchell. 2007. "Baby Boomer Retirement Security: The Roles of Planning, Financial Literacy, and Housing Wealth." *Journal of Monetary Economics*, 54(1): 205–224.

Shiller, Robert J. 2012. *Finance and the Good Society*. Princeton, NJ: Princeton University Press.

Turner, Lord. 2009. "*The Turner Review: A Regulatory Response to the Global Banking Crisis*." Financial Services Authority, March.

CHAPTER 38

2014

US ECONOMIC PROSPECTS: SECULAR STAGNATION, HYSTERESIS, AND THE ZERO LOWER BOUND

Lawrence H. Summers, Harvard University

I would like to thank Michael Peterson very much for his generous words of introduction and for his thoughtful observations about the long-run economic challenges that our country faces. You do not, however, get to the long run except through the short run, and what happens in the short run has a profound impact on the long run. To reverse Keynes a bit, if you die in the short run, there is no long run. So my preoccupation this morning will be with a set of temporary but, I believe, ultimately long-term concerns.

Before I turn to those concerns, however, let me just say how grateful I am to be back with the National Association for Business Economics. It seems to me that the members of this organization make an enormous, ongoing contribution to evaluating, understanding, and responding to the flow of economic events. I have been coming to these meetings on and off now for more than 30 years, and I have always been struck by the sophistication and relevance of the analyses that are provided herein.

Indeed, I think it is fair to say that some of the themes that are today central to discussions of academic macroeconomists, but that had receded from the debate for many years, were always kept alive at the National Association for Business Economics. I think, for example, of the importance of the financial sector and the flow of credit. I also think of the issues surrounding confidence and uncertainty. These topics have long been staples of the discussions at NABE meetings.

Macroeconomics, just six or seven years ago, was a very different subject than it is today. Leaving aside the set of concerns associated with long-run growth, I think it is fair to say that six years ago, macroeconomics was primarily about the use of monetary policy to reduce the already small amplitude of fluctuations about a given trend, while maintaining price stability. That was the preoccupation. It was supported by historical analysis emphasizing that we were in a great moderation, by policy and theoretical analysis suggesting the importance of feedback rules, and by a vast empirical program directed at optimizing those feedback rules.

Today, we *wish* for the problem of minimizing fluctuations around a satisfactory trend. Indeed, I think it is fair to say that today, the amplitude of fluctuations appears large, not small. As I shall discuss, there is room for doubt about whether the cycle actually cycles. Today, it is increasingly clear that the trend in growth can be adversely affected over the longer term by what happens in the business cycle. And today, there are real questions about the efficacy of monetary policy, given the zero lower bound on interest rates.

In my remarks today, I want to take up these issues—secular stagnation, the idea that the economy re-equilibrates; hysteresis, the shadow cast forward on economic activity by adverse cyclical developments; and the significance of the zero lower bound for the relative efficacy of monetary and fiscal policies.

I shall argue three propositions. First, as the United States and other industrial economies are currently configured, simultaneous achievement of adequate growth, capacity utilization, and financial stability appears increasingly difficult. Second, this is likely to be related to a substantial decline in the equilibrium or natural real rate of interest. Third, addressing these challenges requires different policy approaches than are represented by the current conventional wisdom.

The Difficulty of Achieving Multiple Objectives

Let me turn, then, to the first of these propositions. It has now been nearly five years since the trough of the recession in the early summer of 2009. It is no small achievement of policy that the economy has grown consistently since then and that employment has increased on a sustained basis. Yet, it must be acknowledged that essentially all of the convergence between the economy's level of output and its potential has been achieved not through the economy's growth, but through downward revisions in its potential.

In round numbers, Figure 38.1 shows that the economy is now 10 percent below what in 2007 we thought its potential would be in 2014. Of that 10 percent gap, 5 percent has already been accommodated into a reduction in the estimate of its potential, and 5 percent remains as an estimate of its GDP gap. In other words, through this recovery, we have made no progress in restoring GDP to its potential.

Information on employment is similarly sobering. Figure 38.2 depicts the employment/population ratio in aggregate. Using this relatively crude measure, one observes almost no progress. It has been pointed out repeatedly and correctly that this chart is somewhat misleading because it neglects the impact of a range of demographic changes on the employment ratio that would have been expected to carry on even in the absence of a cyclical downturn.

But that is not the largest part of the story. Even if one looks at 25-to-54 year-old men, a group where there is perhaps the least ambiguity because there is the greatest societal expectation of work, Figure 38.3 shows that the employment/population

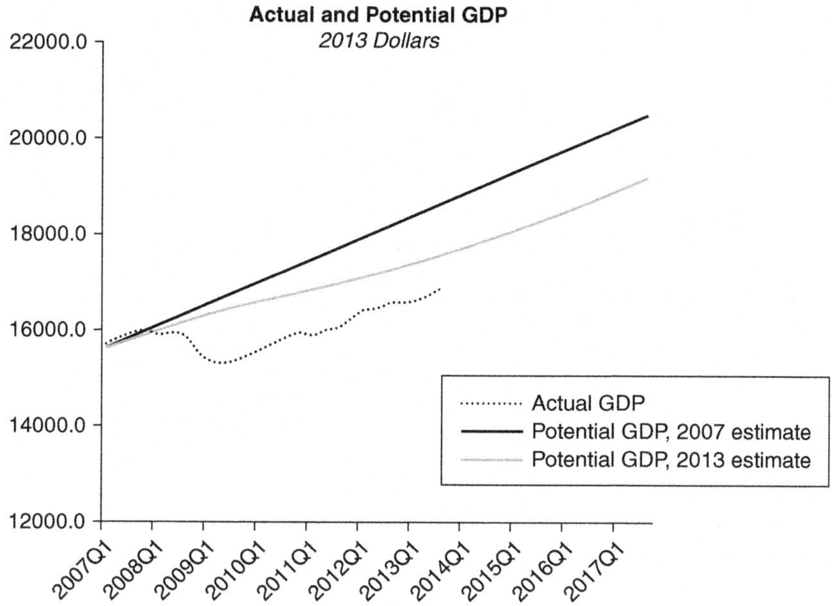

Figure 38.1 Downward revision in potential GDP, United States.

Source: CBO.

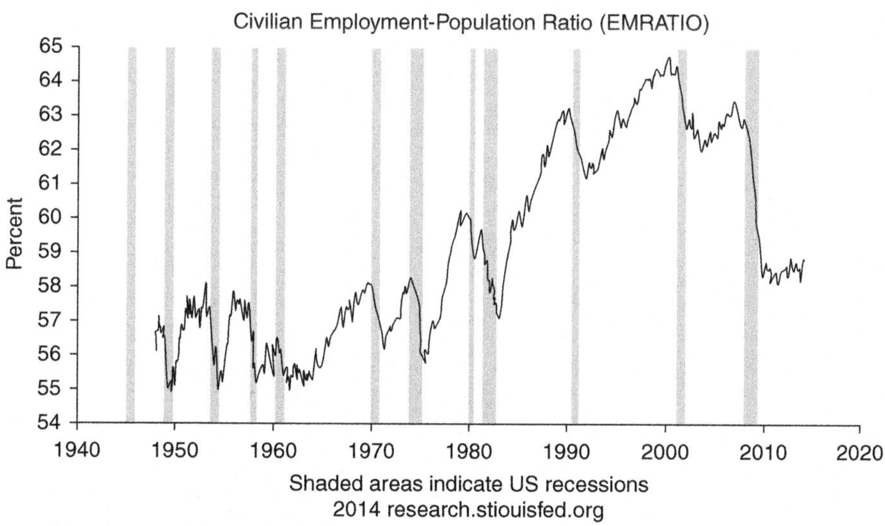

Figure 38.2 Employment/population ratio, aggregate.

Source: U.S. Department of Labor: Bureau of Labor Statistics.

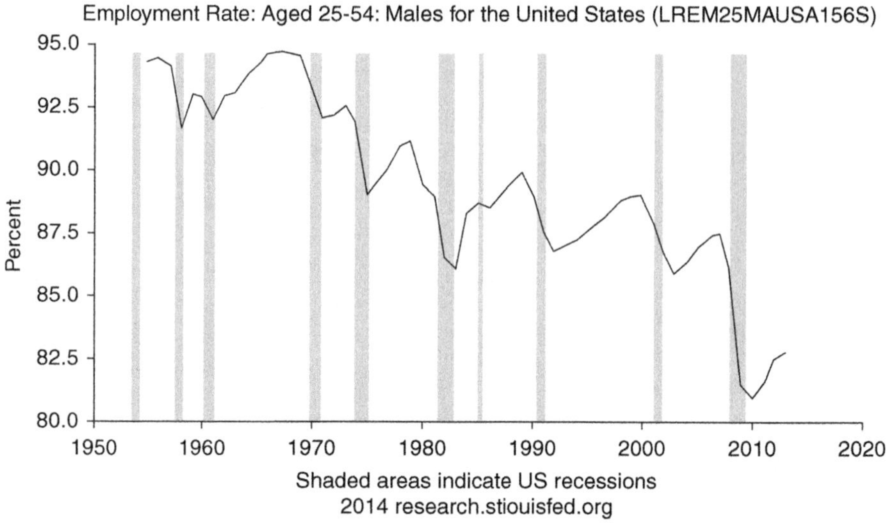

Figure 38.3 Employment/population ratio, Men 25–54.

Source: Organization for Economic Co-operation and Development.

- Potential GDP in 2014
  - 2013 estimate vs 2007 estimate: 10% decline
- Why did the estimate decline?

Component of Pot. GDP	Contribution to Decline in Estimate
Potential TFP	~10% (11%)
Capital	~50% (48%)
Potential hours worked	~40% (41%)

Figure 38.4 Why did potential GDP fall?

Source: CBO data. Author calculations.

ratio declined sharply during the downturn, and only a small portion of that decrease has been recovered since that time.

The recovery has not represented a return to potential; and, according to the best estimates we have, the downturn has cast a substantial shadow on the economy's future potential. Making the best calculations one can from the CBO's estimates of potential (and I believe quite similar results would come from other estimates of potential), one can see from Figure 38.4 that this is not about technological change. Slower total factor productivity than we would have expected in 2007 accounts for the smallest part of the downward trend in potential. The largest part is associated with reduced capital investment, followed closely by reduced labor input. Let me emphasize that this is not a calculation about why we have less output today. It is a calculation about why it is estimated that the potential of the economy has declined by 5 percent as a consequence of the downturn that we have suffered.

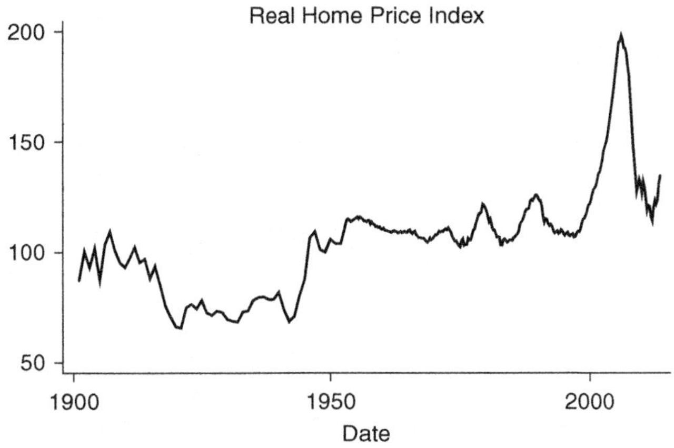

Figure 38.5 Home prices.

Source: Robert Shiller's website.

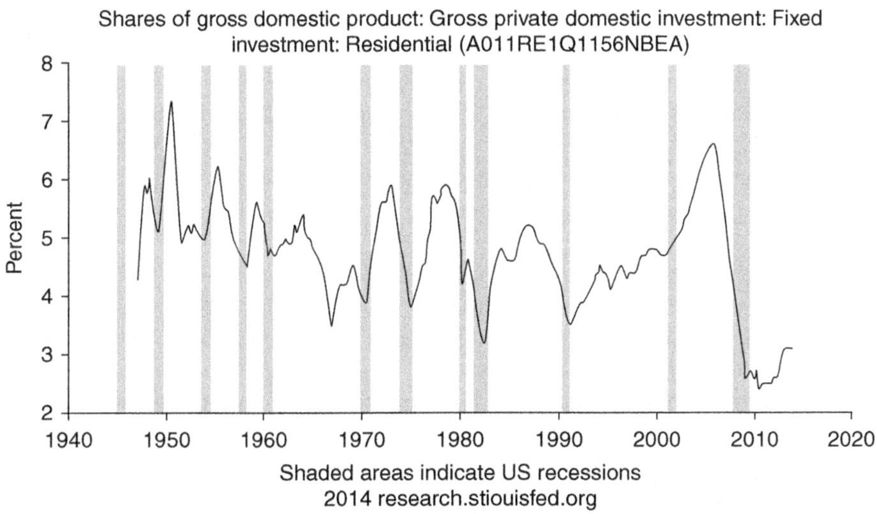

Figure 38.6 Housing share of GDP.

Source: US Department of Commerce: Bureau of Economic Analysis.

The record of growth for the last five years is disturbing, but I think that is not the whole of what should concern us. It is true that prior to the downturn in 2007, through the period from, say, 2002 until 2007, the economy grew at a satisfactory rate. Note that, there is no clear evidence of overheating. Inflation did not accelerate in any substantial way. But the economy did grow at a satisfactory rate, and did certainly achieve satisfactory levels of capacity utilization and employment.

Did it do so in a sustainable way? I would suggest not. It is now clear that the increase in house prices shown in Figure 38.5 (that can retrospectively be

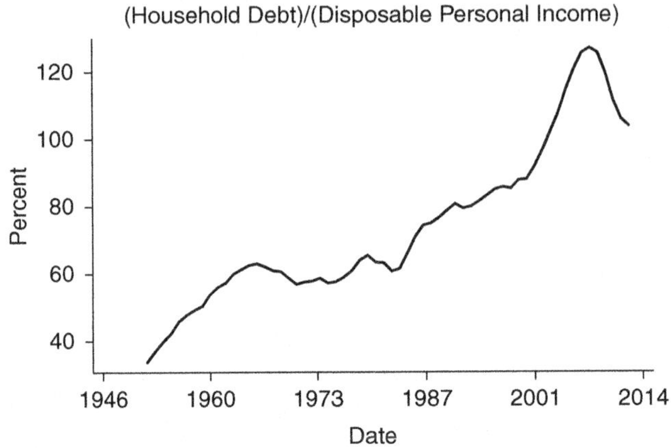

Figure 38.7 Debt/Income ratio for households.

Source: Federal Reserve (FRED).

convincingly labeled a bubble) was associated with an unsustainable upward movement in the share of GDP devoted to residential investment, as shown in Figure 38.6. And this made possible a substantial increase in the debt-to-income ratio for households, which has been reversed only to a limited extent, as shown in Figure 38.7.

It is fair to say that critiques of macroeconomic policy during this period, almost without exception, suggest that prudential policy was insufficiently prudent, that fiscal policy was excessively expansive, and that monetary policy was excessively loose. One is left to wonder how satisfactory would the recovery have been in terms of growth and in terms of achievement of the economy's potential with a different policy environment, in the absence of a housing bubble, and with the maintenance of strong credit standards.

As a reminder, prior to this period, the economy suffered the relatively small, but somewhat prolonged, downturn of 2001. Before that, there was very strong economic performance that in retrospect we now know was associated with the substantial stock market bubble of the late 1990s. The question arises, then, in the last 15 years: can we identify any sustained stretch during which the economy grew satisfactorily with conditions that were financially sustainable? Perhaps one can find some such period, but it is very much the minority, rather than the majority, of the historical experience.

What about the rest of the industrialized world? I remember well when the Clinton administration came into office in 1993. We carried out a careful review of the situation in the global economy. We consulted with all the relevant forecasting agencies about the long-term view for global economic growth.

At that time, there was some controversy as to whether a reasonable estimate of potential growth for Japan going forward was 3 percent or 4 percent. Since then, Japanese growth has been barely 1 percent. So, it is hard to make the case that over the last 20 years, Japan represents a substantial counterexample to the proposition that industrial countries are having difficulty achieving what we traditionally would have regarded as satisfactory growth with sustainable financial conditions.

What about Europe? Certainly, for some years after the introduction of the euro in 1999, Europe's economic performance appeared substantially stronger than many on this side of the Atlantic expected. Growth appeared satisfactory and impressive. Fears that were expressed about the potential risks associated with a common currency without common governance appeared to have been overblown.

In retrospect, matters look different. It is now clear that the strong performance of the euro in the first decade of this century was unsustainable and reliant on financial flows to the European periphery that in retrospect appear to have had the character of a bubble. For the last few years, and in prospect, European economic growth appears, if anything, less satisfactory than American economic growth.

In sum, I would suggest to you that the record of industrial countries over the last 15 years is profoundly discouraging as to the prospect of maintaining substantial growth with financial stability. Why is this the case? I would suggest that in understanding this phenomenon, it is useful at the outset to consider the possibility that changes in the structure of the economy have led to a significant shift in the natural balance between savings and investment, causing a decline in the equilibrium or normal real rate of interest that is associated with full employment.

The Decline in the Equilibrium Real Rate of Interest

Let us imagine, as a hypothesis, that this decline in the equilibrium real rate of interest has taken place. What would one expect to see? One would expect increasing difficulty, particularly in the down phase of the cycle, in achieving full employment and strong growth because of the constraints associated with the zero lower bound on interest rates. One would expect that, as a normal matter, real interest rates would be lower. With very low real interest rates and with low inflation, this also means very low nominal interest rates, so one would expect increasing risk-seeking by investors. As such, one would expect greater reliance on Ponzi finance and increased financial instability.

So, I think it is reasonable to suggest that if there had been a significant decline in equilibrium real interest rates, one might observe the kinds of disturbing signs that we have observed. Is it reasonable to suggest that equilibrium real interest rates have declined? I would suggest it is a reasonable hypothesis for at least six reasons, whose impact differs from moment to moment and probably is not readily amenable to precise quantification.

First, reductions in demand for debt-financed investment. In part, this is a reflection of the legacy of a period of excessive leverage. In part, it is a consequence of greater restriction on financial intermediation as a result of the experiences of recent years. Yet, probably to a greater extent, it is a reflection of the changing character of productive economic activity.

Ponder that the leading technological companies of this age—I think, for example, of Apple and Google—find themselves swimming in cash and facing the challenge of what to do with a very large cash hoard. Ponder the fact that WhatsApp has a greater market value than Sony, with next to no capital investment required to achieve it. Ponder the fact that it used to require tens of millions of dollars to start a significant new venture, and significant new ventures today are seeded with hundreds of thousands of dollars. All of this means reduced demand for investment, with consequences for equilibrium levels of interest rates.

Second, it is a well known, going back to Alvin Hansen and way before, that a declining rate of population growth, as shown in Figure 38.8, means a declining natural rate of interest. The US labor force will grow at a substantially lower rate over the next two decades than it has over the last two decades, a point that is reinforced if one uses the quality-adjusted labor force for education as one's measure. There is the possibility, on which I take no stand, that the rate of technological progress has slowed as well, functioning in a similar direction.

Third, changes in the distribution of income, both between labor income and capital income and between those with more wealth and those with less, have operated to raise the propensity to save, as have increases in corporate-retained earnings. These phenomena are shown in Figures 38.9 and 38.10. An increase in inequality and the capital income share operate to increase the level of savings. Reduced investment demand and increased propensity to save operate in the direction of a lower equilibrium real interest rate.

Related to the changes I described before, but I think separate, is a substantial shift in the relative price of capital goods. Figure 38.11 shows the evolution of the relative price of business equipment. Something similar, but less dramatic, is present in the data on consumer durables. To take just one example, during a period in which median wages have been stagnant over the last 30 years, median wages in terms of automobiles have almost doubled according to BLS data.

Cheaper capital goods mean that investment goods can be achieved with less borrowing and spending, reducing the propensity for investment.

Fifth, and I will not dwell on this point, there is a reasonable argument to be made that what matters in the economy is after-tax, rather than pre-tax, real interest

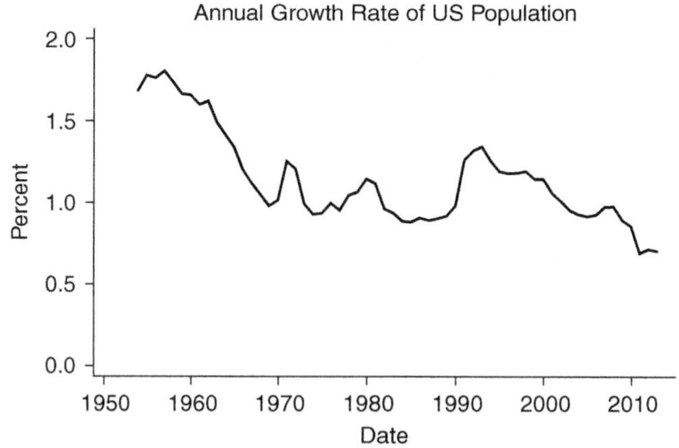

Figure 38.8 Population growth rate.

Source: Federal Reserve (FRED).

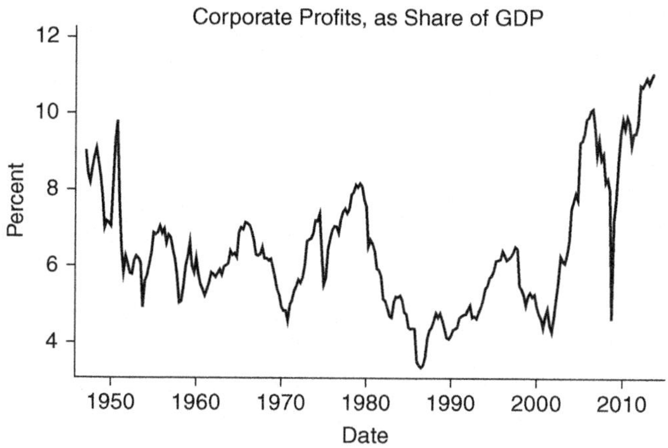

Figure 38.9 Corporate profits.

Source: Federal Reserve (FRED).

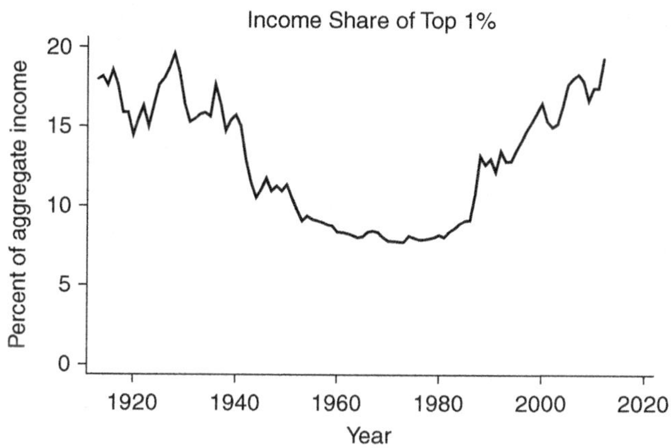

Figure 38.10 Top 1 percent.

Source: World Top Incomes Databases.

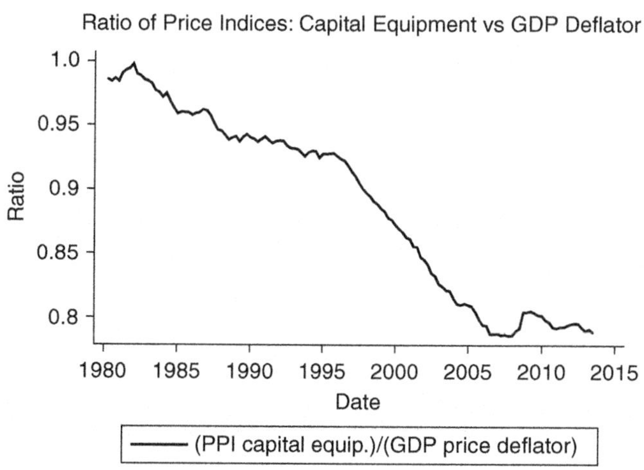

Figure 38.11 Price of capital equipment.

rates, and the consequence of disinflation is that for any given after-tax real interest rate, the pretax real interest rate now needs to be lower than it was before. Figure 38.12 demonstrates this relationship.

Finally, Figure 38.13 shows that there have been substantial global moves to accumulate central bank reserves, disproportionately in safe assets in general, and in US Treasuries in particular. Each of these factors has operated to reduce natural or equilibrium real interest rates.

What has the consequence been? Laubach and Williams (2003) from the Federal Reserve established a methodology for estimating the natural rate of interest.

- Consider investor in 40% tax bracket
- Pre-Tax Real Rate = $i - \pi$
- Post-Tax Real Rate = $(i)(1 - \tau) - \pi$

	Case 1 (inflation = 3%)	**Case 2 (inflation = 1%)**
Nominal rate	5%	1.67%
Pre-tax real rate	2%	0.67%
Post-tax real rate	0%	0%

Figure 38.12 Inflation, taxes, real interest rates.

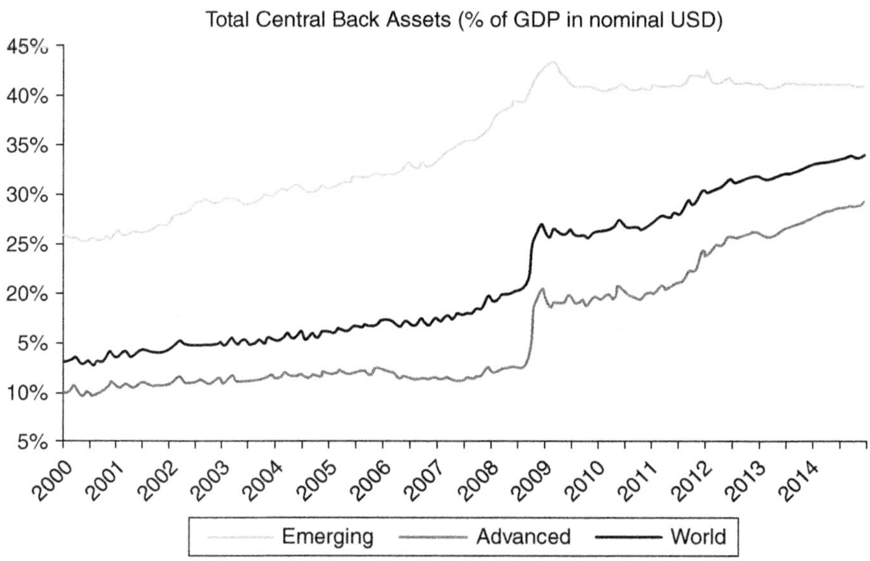

Figure 38.13 Central bank reserves.

Notes: Total assets in USD, ratio to nominal GDP in USD, Advanced economies: Australia, Canada, Denmark, the Euro Area, Japan, New Zealand, Norway, Sweden, Switzerland, the United Kingdom, and the United States. Emerging economies: Argentina, Brazil, Chile, China, Chinese Taipei, Colombia, the Czech Republic, Hong Kong SAR, Hungary, India, Indonesia, Korea, Malaysia, Mexico, Peru, the Philippines, Poland, Russia, Saudi Arabia, Singapore, South Africa, Thailand, and Turkey. Sources: IMF, National Data, Haver Analytics and Fulerum Asset Management.

Source: *Financial Times*.

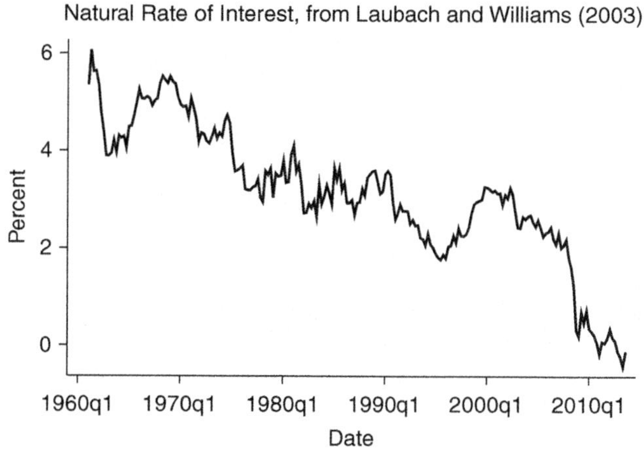

Figure 38.14 Natural rate of interest.

Source: Updated estimates from www.frbsf.org/economic-research/economists/john-williams/.

Essentially, they looked at the size of the output gap, and they looked at where the real interest rate was, and they calculated the real interest rate that went with no output gap over time. Their methodology has been extended to this point, as shown in Figure 38.14, and it demonstrates a very substantial and continuing decline in the real rate of interest.

One looks at a graph of the ten-year TIP and sees the same picture. Mervyn King, the former governor of the Bank of England, has recently constructed a time series on the long-term real interest rate on a global basis, which shows a similar broad pattern of continuing decline.

I would argue first that there is a continuing challenge of how to achieve growth with financial stability. Second, this might be what you would expect if there had been a substantial decline in natural real rates of interest. And third, addressing these challenges requires thoughtful consideration about what policy approaches should be followed.

Addressing Today's Macroeconomic Challenges

So, what is to be done if this view is accepted? As a matter of logic, there are three possible responses.

Stay Patient

The first possible response is patience. These things happen. Policy has limited impact. Perhaps one is confusing the long aftermath of an excessive debt buildup with a new era. So, there are limits to what can feasibly be done.

I would suggest that this is the strategy that Japan pursued for many years, and it has been the strategy that the US fiscal authorities have been pursuing for the last three or four years. We are seeing very powerfully a kind of inverse Say's Law. Say's

Law was the proposition that supply creates its own demand. Here, we are observing that lack of demand creates its own lack of supply.

To restate, the potential of the US economy has been revised downwards by 5 percent, largely due to reduced capital and labor inputs. This is not, according to those who make these estimates, a temporary decline, but is a sustained, long-term decline.

Reduce the Actual Real Rate of Interest

A second response as a matter of logic is, if the natural real rate of interest has declined, then it is appropriate to reduce the actual real rate of interest, so as to permit adequate economic growth. This is one interpretation of the Federal Reserve's policy in the last three to four years. Not in the immediate aftermath of the panic, when the policy was best thought of as responding to panic, but in recent years.

This is surely, in my judgment, better than no response. It does, however, raise a number of questions. Just how much extra economic activity can be stimulated by further actions once the federal funds rate is zero? What are the risks when interest rates are at zero, promised to remain at zero for a substantial interval, and then further interventions are undertaken to reduce risk premiums? Is there a possibility of creating financial bubbles?

At some point, however, growth in the balance sheet of the Federal Reserve raises profound questions of sustainability, and there are distributional concerns associated with policies that have their proximate impact on increasing the level of asset prices.

There's also the concern pointed out by Japanese observers that in a period of zero interest rates or very low interest rates, it is very easy to roll over loans; and therefore there is very little pressure to restructure inefficient or even zombie enterprises. So, the strategy of taking as a given lower equilibrium real rates and relying on monetary and financial policies to bring down rates is, as a broad strategy, preferable to doing nothing, but comes with significant costs.

Raise Demand

The preferable strategy, I would argue, is to raise the level of demand at any given rate of interest—raising the level of output consistent with an increased level of equilibrium rates and mitigating the various risks associated with low interest rates that I have described.

How might that be done? It seems to me there are a variety of plausible approaches, and economists will differ on their relative efficacy. Anything that stimulates demand will operate in a positive direction from this perspective. Fiscal austerity, from this perspective, is counterproductive unless it generates so much confidence that it is a net increaser of demand.

There is surely scope in today's United States for regulatory and tax reforms that would promote private investment. Although it should be clear from what I am saying that I do not regard a prompt reduction in the federal budget deficit as a high order priority for the nation, I would be the first to agree with Michael Peterson and his colleagues at the Peter G. Peterson Foundation that credible long-term commitments would be a contributor to confidence.

Second, policies that are successful in promoting exports, whether through trade agreements, relaxation of export controls, promotion of US exports, or resistance to the mercantilist practices of other nations when they are pursued, offer the prospect of increasing demand and are responses to the dilemmas that I have put forward.

Third, as I've emphasized in the past, public investments have a potentially substantial role to play. The colloquial way to put the point is to ask if anyone is proud of Kennedy Airport, and then to ask how it is possible that a moment when the long-term interest rate in a currency we print is below 3 percent and the construction unemployment rate approaches double digits is not the right moment to increase public investment in general—and perhaps to repair Kennedy Airport in particular.

But there is a more analytic case to make, as well. This will be my final set of observations. With the help of David Reifschneider, who bears responsibility for anything good you like in what I am about to say, but nothing that you do not like, we performed several simulations of the standard Federal Reserve macro-econometric model—including the version that he, Wascher, and Wilcox have studied—to address issues associated with hysteresis coming from the labor market. To be clear, this is the Federal Reserve model as it stands, not modified in any way to reflect any views that I have.

The simulations performed addressed a 1 percent increase in the budget deficit directed at government spending maintained for five years, tracking carefully the adverse effects on the impacts on investment and labor force withdrawal, which in turn affect the economy's subsequent potential. The simulations also recognize that until the economy approaches full employment, it is reasonable to expect that the zero interest rate will be maintained, and the standard Fed reaction function is used after that point.

The results of the simulations are shown in Figures 38.15 and 38.16 and reveal what you might expect them to show: that while the fiscal stimulus is in place, there is a substantial response, which is greater when allowance is made for labor force withdrawal effects than when no such allowance is made. What is perhaps more interesting is that you see some long-run impact of the stimulus on GDP after it has been withdrawn. That is why the potential multiplier can be quite large.

And my final point concerns the impact of this fiscal stimulus on the debt-to-GDP ratio, shown in Figure 38.17. You will note that with or without taking into account labor force withdrawal, this standard macroeconometric model indicates that a temporary increase in fiscal stimulus reduces, rather than increases, the long-run debt-to-GDP ratio.

Now, there are plenty of political economy issues about whether it is possible to achieve a temporary increase in government spending, and so forth. But I believe that the demonstration that, with a standard model, increases in demand actually reduce the long-run debt-to-GDP ratio should contribute to a reassessment of the policy issues facing the United States and push us toward placing substantial emphasis on increasing demand as a means of achieving adequate economic

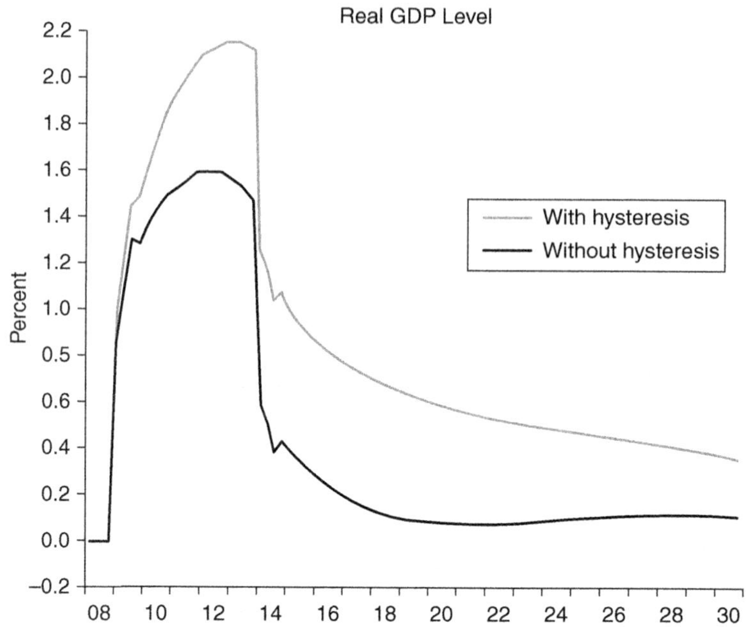

Figure 38.15 Simulation output: Real GDP.

Source: Summers and Reifschneider, ongoing analysis.

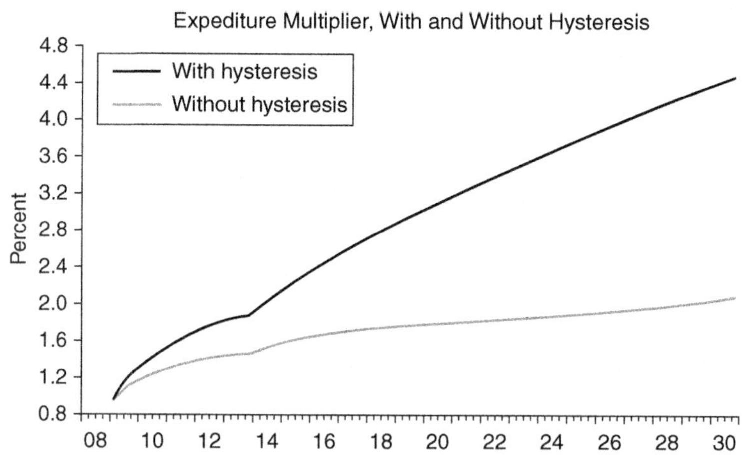

Figure 38.16 Simulation output: Expenditure multiplier.

Source: Summers and Reifschneider (2014), ongoing analysis.

growth. This should serve as a prelude to the day when we can return to the concerns that I think almost all of us would prefer to have as dominant: the achievement of adequate supply potential for the US economy.

Thank you very much.

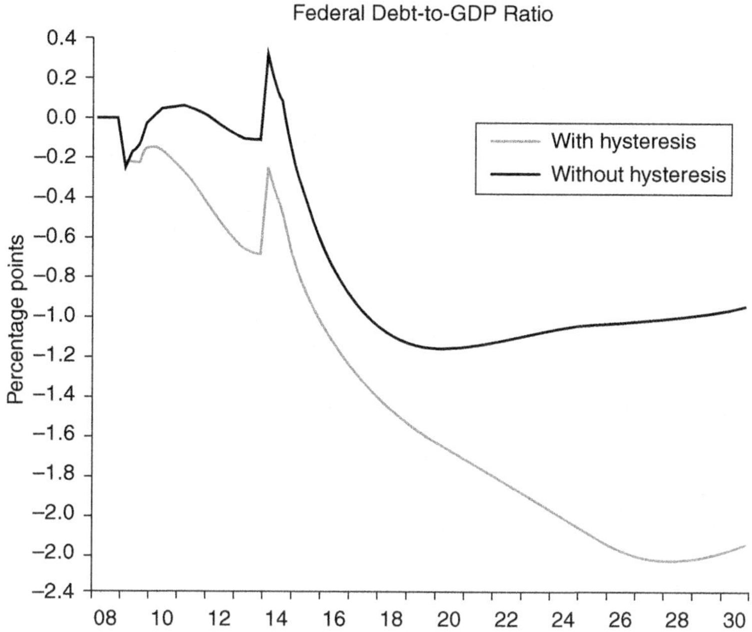

Figure 38.17 Simulation output: Debt/GDP ratio.

Source: Summers and Reifschneider (2014), ongoing analysis.

Note

Originally published in *Business Economics*, Vol. 49, No. 2 (April 2014), pp. 65–73.

Reference

Laubach, Thomas and John C. Williams. 2003. "Measuring the Natural Rate of Interest." *Review of Economics and Statistics*, 85(4): 1063–1070.

PART VI

FEATURE ARTICLES

Since 1985, *Business Economics* has included feature articles on recurring themes. Although these themes have varied somewhat over the years, the ones that have endured concern the statistics that business economists use, descriptions of particular industries and markets, and how applied economists go about their work. This volume includes one example of each of these types of feature articles.

CHAPTER 39

2011

FOCUS ON INDUSTRIES AND MARKETS

ELECTRIC POWER TRANSMISSION AND DISTRIBUTION EQUIPMENT

David A. Petina, The Freedonia Group

Michael Murphy, The Freedonia Group

Andrew C. Gross, Cleveland State University

The US electrical grid is in dire need of upgrading, but as is the case with infrastructure in general, the process is slow. Beyond the debate over energy sources for generating power, there is also a strong debate about the development of the next-generation electrical transmission and distribution (T&D) network.

In this chapter, we analyze the US market for electric T&D equipment. Electric energy in the current macro setting is discussed first, followed by a brief look at electricity supply and demand. Key regulations and technical developments that pose both restraints and opportunities are profiled. This is followed by a discussion of T&D equipment supply in terms of major product lines and T&D equipment demand by major end-use sectors. Then a specific sector, the commercial market, is highlighted. We conclude with an analysis of industry structure, marketing, collaboration, and merger activities.

Electric Power and the Macro Environment

Modern economies run on electricity; about one-third of the world energy is used for electric power. In the United States, electricity is integral and indispensable for homes, factories, and all types of commercial establishments. Any interruption in the steady supply of electric power is unwanted and can result in much economic loss. The nation's electric grid is a complex network of generation plants, transmission lines, and distribution systems. The North American grid consists of three major networks (Eastern, Western, and Texas) with 200,000 miles of high voltage transmission lines (110 kv to 765 kv) and million miles of distribution lines.

The federal government is currently pushing policies to upgrade the nation's aging electrical network. In mid-June 2011, Secretary of Energy Steven Chu called for a speed-up in the development of the next-generation electrical network (Vastag 2011). This so-called smart grid would deliver power more efficiently, coordinate traditional and renewable sources, reduce consumption, and alleviate the number and length of outages. T&D equipment should then be able to respond immediately to demand, yet maintain an instant response system to connectivity and other operating variables. At present, the nation's current electric grid is so creaky, according to Chu, that "Edison would feel at home with most of today's power system." Per US Department of Energy (DoE) figures, there were 349 blackouts in 2005–2009 vs. 149 in 2000–2004.

According to the chapter just cited, the new policies immediately drew skepticism, in part because the Electric Power Research Institute (EPRI), an independent institute funded by the electric utility industry, estimates the cost of implementation to be in the $338 to $476 billion range. Nonetheless, the federal government is determined to push the electric power companies to invest in new technologies, provide loans to upgrade the transmission lines in rural areas, and fund "smart grid" R&D activities from a DoE research hub. According to Dr. Chu, the technology underpinning the current US electrical grid lags behind that of other countries, including China and Ireland. Their systems have more efficient high-voltage transmission lines, up-to-date distribution equipment, and better integration of power generation from traditional and renewable sources.

If the administration's policies are implemented, they would provide a major boost to T&D investment. However, the fate of enabling legislation is highly uncertain.

The supply and demand situation for electric power T&D equipment is clearly affected by both cyclical and secular macroeconomic variables. The most notable influence was the recent recession and ongoing slow recovery, causing slower spending patterns by households, business, and governments. The overall weakening in the economy has forced business firms to shelve major expansion plans through 2013. A significant share of T&D equipment demand is related to fixed investment activity. Both electric utilities and other industrial-commercial users are slowing down their purchases of switchgear, transformers, and other types of equipment.

Electric Power (Electricity) Supply and Demand[1]

Before electric power is transmitted and distributed, it must be generated at conventional dedicated power plants, cogeneration facilities, or at such natural/renewable facilities as hydro dams, geothermal heat sources, solar farms, or wind turbines. The generation of electricity is forecast to climb at less than 1 percent per year to 4.3 trillion kilowatt-hours in 2013. This pace reflects the growing demand for electricity services being offset by efficiency gains from new appliance standards and investments in energy-efficient end-use equipment (US Energy Information Administration 2011). Increases in the efficiency of T&D equipment have also contributed to the slowing pace.

For much of the twentieth century, electricity came from regulated electric power utilities and specifically from their dedicated power plants that use coal, nuclear fission, and natural gas. Such utilities remain the largest generators of electricity at nearly half of the total output. Coal remains the dominant fuel at about half of utility generation. Still, the so-called independent power producers (IPPs) or non-utility generators (NUGs) have been more aggressive in constructing new generating capacity. These include cogeneration units that provide power and steam or other process heat for on-site use. Together IPPs are likely to provide almost half the nation's electricity by 2018. In Table 39.1, we show details on electric power generation by type of fuel and by type of industrial or generator facility. It is notable that while there is much publicity about renewable sources of electricity, these will provide only 14–17 percent of total output during 2013–2018.

Although the focus of this chapter (as well as the underlying 320-page report by The Freedonia Group on which it is based) is on T&D equipment, we should note that spending for power generating equipment is also significant. In 2008, a

Table 39.1 Electricity supply by type of fuel and type of facility, United States, 2003–2013 *(billion kilowatt-hours)*

				Annual Growth	
Item	*2003*	*2008*	*2013*	*08/03*	*13/08*
Electricity by Type of Fuel	3883	4105	4260	1.1%	0.7%
Coal	1974	1990	2070	0.1	0.8
Gas	666	890	720	6.0	4.3
Nuclear	764	805	820	2.2	0.4
Oil	119	45	50	−18.0	2.2
Renewable/Other	360	375	600	0.8	9.9
Electricity by Industrial Facility	3883	4105	4260	1.1%	0.7%
Dedicated electricity[a]	3525	3785	3915	1.4	0.7
Electric utilities	2462	2470	2360	0.1	−0.9
Indep. power producers	1063	1315	1555	4.3	3.4
Cogeneration[b]	358	320	345	−2.2	1.5
Electric power	196	175	185	−2.3	1.1
Other	162	145	160	−2.2	2.0

Source: The Freedonia Group (2009).

[a]"Dedicated electricity" means plants that strictly produce electric power, in contrast to combined heat and power facilities. Independent power producers are industrial firms and/or non-utility generators who came into existence after deregulation in the 1990s.

[b]Cogeneration is the simultaneous production of electric power and heat in industrial plants. They may generate it directly or as a byproduct (latter listed as "other" above). Such generation is usually for on-site use, however, in some cases it may be sold to outsiders.

total of $36 billion was spent on all types of electric power equipment; of this sum turbines and generators accounted for $12 billion, T&D equipment for $21 billion, and power wire/cable for $3 billion. The three categories combined—constituting two percent of nonresidential fixed investment in 2008—will rise to $42.5 billion in 2013 and to $50.7 billion by 2018. Within this total, turbines and generators are slated to rise at a 4.1 percent annual increase, compared with T&D equipment at a 2.6 percent annual pace and wires/cables at 5.1 percent per year during 2008–2013.

Demand for electricity increased more rapidly than GDP through 1960–1980 due to expanding production by end-users as well as new applications. The pace slowed slightly during 1980–2000, and then usage decreased and will continue to grow slowly in the present decade. The deceleration of demand is due largely to greater energy efficiency in end-use applications; price-induced and environment-related conservation by users; and specific legislation. Yet another factor is cogeneration in which industrial customers utilize heat from waste products rather than using electricity.

The use of electric power by major sectors of the US economy is shown in Table 39.2.

The so-called retail sales break into three categories: residential at 35, commercial also at 35, and industrial at 30 percent of the total in 2008. These proportions show little or no change during the coming years. The nonretail category, called direct use, shows a fast increase, albeit from a small base. This occurs where a facility generates electricity onsite and then uses that power directly or transfers it to a co-located facility. Such consumption, including cogeneration, is slated to rise 2.7 percent annually compared with only 0.6 percent for retail sales. In addition to increasing the efficiency of energy use in their production facilities, cogenerators may help to ensure a steady power supply to critical equipment, avoiding the threat of outages.

Table 39.2 Electricity demand by major end users, United States, 2003–2013 *(billion kilowatt-hours)*

				Annual Growth	
Item	*2003*	*2008*	*2013*	*08/03*	*13/08*
Electricity Generation	3883	4105	4260	1.1%	0.7%
Less net losses & exports	221	225	240	0.0	0.3
Electricity Demand by End Users	3662	3880	4020	1.1	0.7%
Retail sales	3494	3740	3860	1.4	0.6
Residential	1276	1390	1390	1.7	0.0
Industrial	1012	975	995	−2.8	0.4
Commercial	1206	1375	1475	2.3	1.4
Direct users[a]	168	140	160	−3.7	2.7

[a]Direct use includes commercial and industrial facility onsite generation; sales of transfers to adjacent/co-located facilities; and, barter transactions.

Source: The Freedonia Group (2009).

Regulations and Standards

Government regulations, industry standards, building codes, and a host of similar rulemaking procedures affect the generation, transmission, and distribution of electricity as well as its use and application. The most visible impact has been on the electric utility industry; the changing regulatory climate altered both the manner of power generation and how equipment suppliers position themselves. In brief, since the passing of the Public Utilities Regulatory Policies Act in 1978, electricity generation has shifted away from utilities and toward industrial firms and NUGs. Utilities have preferred equipment suitable for large, low-cost central stations, whereas NUGs tend to use equipment suitable for units with relatively low generating capacity. Competition encouraged by deregulation and cogeneration and renewable energy technologies derived from environmental concerns have increased. The result has been that generation has become much less centralized, making T&D more complex, contributing to emergence of the idea of the smart grid.

Producers of T&D equipment always had to comply with government regulations and industry standards. In the past, the focus of such rules and practices has been on safety and reliability. Now, other aspects have arisen as well: efficiency, environmental impact, access, compatibility, and connectivity. One key policy promulgated is that providers of electricity should vary their rates according to the costs that they incur, charging lower rates when relatively inexpensive base-load capacity is sufficient to meet demand and higher rates when expensive peak-load capacity must be brought on line. A related topic is to maintain system reliability even at times of high demand. Thus, it is not surprising that measurement is crucial and that meters are showing the fastest rate of growth in T&D equipment. This means that metering programs will be a key component to developing a smart grid with an emphasis on advanced monitoring. This trend is accelerated by "distributed generation," in which individual customers, say residences with roof-top photovoltaic generation, are enabled by regulation to sell power back to the grid.

The makers of T&D equipment have been negatively affected by the consolidation in the electric power utility industry that ensued after deregulation. Conversely, they benefited from the emergence of new, nonutility providers. At this time, the utilities are striving to enhance their relationships with large power users and allow them to purchase electricity in bulk. Such bulk purchases often require additional equipment, such as more switchgear and transformers. Other opportunities will come from the continuing penetration of renewable energy sources, the use of more circuit breakers for protection, and monitoring to improve connections, system stability, and reliability. Distributed generation and subsequent net metering programs require smart meters that can measure electricity flow both to and from the grid.

There are additional rules, standards, and practices that affect the installation and use of T&D equipment. These range from federal and foreign (non-US) rules to state and local regulations. The US Environmental Protection Agency has long singled out sulfur hexafluoride for strict scrutiny. This compound is used in circuit breakers, switchgear, and other T&D equipment for insulating, interrupting, and quenching capabilities, but it is also a potent greenhouse gas. Earlier, the European Union promulgated rules about use of various substances (lead, cadmium, and so on) used in T&D equipment. There has also been concern with old transmission lines being pushed beyond their design limits.

Technology—New Ideas, Innovative Products

The long lifespan of electric power T&D equipment has meant less pressure on providers to seek new ideas and products. The electric utility sector is in a mature stage, spending less than 0.5 percent of its revenue on R&D. Traditionally, it relied on the suppliers of T&D equipment, who have been spending between 2 and 3 percent of their sales on R&D. However, there are signs of change in an era that emphasizes deregulation and renewable, dispersed generating sources. These forces increase pressure to improve an aging network—to opt in new sources of power, reduce blackouts, conserve energy, improve connectivity, limit losses, and smooth out peaks and valleys of usage. The "smart grid" concept encompasses these goals by incorporating various devices such as meters, sensors, and other control devices. A system of variable pricing policies that allows prices to reflect costs by season and time of day will have to accompany the technical changes.

Various public and private bodies are hard at work on new protocols and products. At the federal level, two major agencies—the Federal Energy Regulatory Commission and the National Institute of Standards and Technology—joined with equipment vendors to lay the groundwork for interoperability of regional systems as well as intersystem communications. Operators will have a full or wide-area view of the system; coordinate generators, transmitters, and users; and maintain secure lines. At the local level, a pilot project is under way by Xcel Energy in Boulder, CO that offers efficiency and conservation options, starting with 15,000 smart meters and over 100 miles of cable for broadband communication over power lines. The smart grid idea offers many potential entry points for T&D product and service vendors. However, it is possible that more spending on sensors and controls could come at the expense of traditional T&D equipment, such as transformers and switchgear.

Beyond the smart grid, there are other specific technological advances. EPRI currently conducts programs on underground and overhead transmission, as well as on distribution, with the goal of improved reliability and security of both systems and equipment. One example is a robot that is designed to traverse and inspect 80 miles of transmission line for high-risk vegetation encroachment. The major equipment companies, such as General Electric, Eaton, Schneider Electric, and Siemens, are developing improved switchgear, such as arc-fault circuit interrupters. Hexaformer of Sweden is now producing transformers that offer different core shapes featuring less weight and smaller load losses. A public-private cooperative venture is looking at high temperature superconducting materials for use in advanced transformers.

T&D Equipment Supply—The Product Lines

T&D equipment is designed to assist both providers and users of electric power with smooth system operation, protection, and measurement. Such equipment is

Table 39.3 Electric power transmission & distribution (T&D) equipment, supply side (=product lines), United States, 2003–2013 *(million dollars except as noted)*

				Annual Growth	
Item	*2003*	*2008*	*2013*	*08/03*	*13/08*
Nonres. Fixed Investment (billion $)	1078	1553	1730	7.6%	2.2%
$ elec T&D eqp/000$invest.	13.4	13.4	13.6	—	—
Elec. Power T&D Eqp. Supply	14,472	20,750	23,550	7.5	2.6
Switchgear	8,169	10,550	11,950	5.2	2.5
Transformers	4,768	7,890	8,850	10.6	2.3
Pole & line hardware	795	1,200	1,350	8.6	2.4
Meters	740	1,110	1,400	8.4	4.8
Net Exports	(787)	(2,400)	(3,550)	—	—
Elec. Power T&D Eqp. Shipmts	13,685	18,350	20,000	6.0	1.7

Source: The Freedonia Group (2009).

the hardware that links generating plants and retail uses by farms, factories, offices, and households. Actual linkage occurs via high-voltage (138 kv and higher) transmission lines and low-voltage (under 50 kv) distribution lines. There are four categories of T&D equipment: switchgear, transformers, pole and line hardware, and meters. Supply of these four product categories is shown in Table 39.3. The first two groups are dominant in terms of revenues accounting for 51 and 38 percent of the total in 2008, and these shares are not expected to change in the current five-year span to 2013.

Switchgear

This term refers to a variety of circuit breakers, relays, fuses, and ducts designed to control and direct the flow of electric power to industrial, commercial, and residential users. Such control must assist uninterrupted power flow, but must also provide instant protection against disturbances such as abrupt changes in voltage, current, frequency, and so on. Detecting and isolating problems assure safety at user locations and for the network system as a whole. Switchgear can be found in outdoor locations, such as utility substations, and indoors in factory or office building control rooms. Switchgear is often coupled with other major devices such as transformers as well as with meters and communication equipment to achieve "intelligent control" of energy management.

Low voltage switchgear, rated at 600 volts or less, is often found in commercial and residential applications. It consists of switches, switchboards, panels, and circuit breakers. This subcategory accounted for about one-third of the total $10.5 billion shipped in 2008. Another third wastaken by metal-clad switchgear, metal-enclosed fuses, and molded case circuit breakers primarily used by utilities and industrial firms. The final subgroup consists of a mix of power circuit breakers, fuses, ducts, and relays. Low cost overseas producers compete intensely in many product lines.

Transformers

As the name implies, these units "transform power"—specifically, they provide a step-up or step-down for voltage. The key application is to increase voltage before transmitting electric power over long distances (up to 345 kv or even 765 kv) and then to decrease this high voltage for use in distribution at the retail or household level. Thus, generating plants can be located far away from population centers, and power can be transmitted using towers and wires/cables. During 2003–2008 transformer sales grew at an annual rate of 10.6 percent, reflecting in part the rapid increases in the prices of raw materials used, such as electrical steel, copper, and aluminum.

There are significant differences in the design and function between large power transformers and smaller, distribution transformers. The former are oil-cooled, equipped with monitors, and designed for long life; often they are custom-made for a specific application. The latter are compact, may be non-ventilated or air-cooled, and are mass-produced. Power transformers (500 kva-mva) accounted for 40 percent of the $7.9 billion total in 2008, distribution transformers at 28 percent, with specialty and other transformers plus parts taking 22 percent. These figures are not expected to shift much. Makers of large units experiment with new materials and core shapes, but buyers object to higher prices that can be 20 percent more. Further, new designs require testing for durability and regulatory compliance.

Pole and Line Hardware

This category consists of a wide variety of insulators, arresters, connectors, clamps, anchors, and fittings used for T&D between the generating plants and the final end users. Most of the hardware is used overhead but underground distribution is expanding in densely populated areas. Much of the hardware is made of steel, except for insulators. In the past, insulators have been formed from ceramics; now they combine a ceramic core for strength and polymer for reduced weight and improved electrical performance. The category as a whole is supported more by replacement requirements than new market opportunities. About 5 percent of the more than 80 million wooden and steel lattice utility pole structures is either replaced or have components upgraded annually, thereby generating demand for anchors and other line hardware.

Of the $1.2 billion worth of pole and line hardware shipped in 2008, just over one-half consisted of T&D and communication hardware, followed by insulators at 27 percent, with connectors, anchors, and other line hardware taking up the remaining 21 percent. While the sector may benefit from the building of new, major transmission lines, plus linkage with renewable sources of power, it will be adversely affected by growth in underground systems needing no pole hardware. The growth in more localized, distributed generation will also pose a risk to makers of pole and line hardware as small-scale production of power near end users makes the need far less for any further build-up or replacement of T&D facilities.

Electricity Meters

This category consists of various kinds of meters that record electric power usage by clients, measured in kilowatt-hours; such readings establish a billing cycle. But meters can also be used to record instantaneous demand (kilowatts) or maximum use over some interval; this can aid users and producers with energy savings. Sale of meters was traditionally driven by new construction and the replacement of old meters at regular intervals. But new housing and other new construction have slowed down, and the steady replacement rate is upset by growth in automated meter reading, net metering programs, and smart meters. As of 2010, all but six states had some form of net metering that allows customers to sell power that they generate in excess of their own needs to the grid. Smart meters offer advanced electronics, two-way communication, and pricing options for users.

The most widely used meter is the traditional alternating current (AC) watt-hour unit that has changed little since its invention by Otto Bathory in 1889; but it now comes as an analog or digital device. Of the $1.1 billion total meter shipments in 2008, AC watt-hour meters took 35 percent, followed by demand meters that measure watts at any given time at 26, other electric meters at 27, and parts and accessories at 12 percent. While meters constitute the smallest of the four major categories of T&D equipment, the group shows the fastest growth rate at almost 5 percent per annum between 2008 and 2013. Smart meters, while they often cost twice the traditional ones, will form an important part of the developing "smart grid" and allow providers of electricity net metering, time-of-day metering, and automated reading. Wind farms also use smart meters to measure generation.

T&D Equipment Demand—Markets or End-Users

The two largest markets for T&D equipment are electric utilities and industrial plants, followed by the commercial, residential, and government-institutional sectors. Details for all five are shown in Table 39.4. for the 2003–2013 period. In 2008, utilities accounted for 48 and the industrial sector for 33 percent; the remaining three sectors came in at 8, 7, and 4 percent, respectively. All five markets will experience much slower growth rates during 2008–2013 than they recorded for 2003–2008. Annual growth rates will be in the 2–4 percent range due to slow growth in the economy in general and nonresidential fixed investment in particular. In comparison, therefore, the future of T&D equipment sales in the five markets is seen as relatively bright.

Electric Utilities

The primary concern in this sector is facilitating electricity flow and protecting equipment all the way between generating plants and end users. Thus, utilities must purchase from all four product families; of the $9.9 billion spent in 2008, they

Table 39.4 Electric power transmission & distribution (T&D) equipment, demand side (=major markets), United States, 2003–2013 *(million dollars except as noted)*

Item	*2003*	*2008*	*2013*	*Annual Growth*	
				08/03	*13/08*
Nonres. Fixed Investment (billion $)	1,078	1,553	1,730	7.6%	2.2%
$ elec T&D eqp/000$invest.	13.4	13.4	13.6	—	—
Elec. Power T&D Eqp. Demand	14,472	20,750	23,550	7.5	2.6
Electric utilities	6,474	9,900	10,900	8.9	1.9
Ind'l & nonutil. gen.	4,757	6,870	8,050	7.6	3.2
Commercial market	1,396	1,735	1,945	4.4	2.3
Residential market	1,235	1,475	1,730	3.6	3.2
Gov'ts/Instit'ns	610	770	925	4.8	3.7
Net Exports	(787)	(2,400)	(3,550)	—	—
Elec. Power T&D Eqp. Shipmts	13,685	18,350	20,000	6.0	1.7

Source: The Freedonia Group (2009).

dispensed $4.4 billion for transformers and $3.7 billion for switchgear, with the remaining $1.8 billion for pole/line hardware and meters. Specifically, power and distribution transformers, circuit breakers and other switchgear were high on their shopping lists in the past, along with line hardware.

Responding, albeit slowly, to competition from NUGs and regulatory pressure, the utilities embarked on replacing aging equipment. They became more confident about their spending as state and federal rules eased and as cost-recovery schemes were approved. There have been some large mergers among utilities, and revenue streams have improved. On balance, emergence of renewable sources of energy and distributed generation are viewed as a plus for T&D sales in this sector. The equipment mix bought by utilities is slowly altering. Products with strong potential are electronic switches, metal-clad switchgear, and smart meters.

Industrial Users and NUGs

This is a dual market: in manufacturing plants, T&D equipment is used for operating, protecting, and monitoring expensive machinery; for NUGs purchase of T&D products assists with the production and distribution of electric power. In addition, deregulation of electric power generation spurred trends toward cogeneration and bulk power purchases by large industrial users; this enhanced the demand for T&D goods in the sector. In contrast to the electric utility sector, switchgear dominates transformers with the former at $4.0 billion and the latter at $2.6 billion in 2008, with line hardware plus meters at only $0.2 billion in sales. Advanced switchgear, specifically power circuit breakers, are favored by industrial users as they wish to protect their automated process lines from power surges, fluctuations, and outages.

Commercial Sector

Building owners, office managers, and store operators make wide use of computer systems, security arrangements, and inventory stockings, all of which must be protected against any abrupt—or even minor—changes in their power supplies. Air-conditioners and other indoor climate controls contribute also to the increasing use of electricity per square foot of office or retail space; our estimate is a rise from 28.2 to 32.6 kw-hr/sq.ft. from 2003 to 2013. Commercial space in the United States is increasing slightly, year after year, despite smaller cubicles and off-site work.

In Table 39.5, we show details for this sector by major product lines and by specific commercial end-users. Switchgear overshadows the purchase of transformers. Circuit breakers replaced fuses as they offer better protection and compatibility with advanced power distribution. Distribution transformers are still widely in use. Utilities are now shifting the purchase of meters to builders or building owners.

The three subgroups in this sector with the largest volume of T&D equipment purchases are mercantile, office, and warehouse entities. However, during the current span of 2008–2013, the fastest growing sectors will be lodging and food sales/service establishments, in short, the hospitality segment. Some of these operations will be using solar panels in the future and hence will opt for net metering programs.

Table 39.5 Demand in one specific sector: Commercial end-users' purchase of electric power transmission & distribution (T&D) equipment, United States, 2003–2013 *(million dollars except as noted)*

				Annual Growth	
Item	*2003*	*2008*	*2013*	*08/03*	*13/08*
Comm Mkt Elec Pwr Use (billion kwhr)	1206	1375	1475	2.7%	1.4%
$ elec T&D eqp/000kwhr	1.16	1.26	1.32	—	—
Commercial Market	1396	1735	1945	4.4	2.3
By product line					
Switchgear	1026	1200	1340	3.2	2.2
Transformers	338	465	515	6.6	2.0
Hardware & meters	32	70	90	16.9	5.1
By commercial sub-sector					
Mercantile & service	405	495	550	4.1	2.1
Office	399	490	540	4.2	2.0
Lodging	167	235	275	7.1	3.2
Food sales & service	95	120	140	4.8	2.0
Warehouse & other	330	395	440	3.6	2.2
Comm'l Market as % of Total Mkt	9.6%	8.4%	8.3%	—	—
Total Elec. Pwr. T&D Eqp. Mkt	14,472	20,750	23,550	7.5	2.6

Source: The Freedonia Group (2009).

Residential Sector

While the resident population and the number of households are rising in the United States, housing completions are projected to decline slightly from 1.8. million in 2003 to 1.7 million units in 2013. Residential floor space will show a small rise from 205 billion in 2003 to about 237 billion square feet in 2013. Sales of T&D equipment in this sector will continue to grow slightly above 3 percent per year. This growth is aided by the use of more electric and electronic devices (ranging from entertainment to security) in homes. Building codes are requiring higher levels of protection in new buildings, even to the specification of devices, such as the use of arcfault circuit interrupters. The use of solar panels or other power generation should benefit the market for smart meters and net metering programs.

Governments and Institutions

While this sector is the smallest, it is likely to grow the fastest in the current five-year span, though still under 4 percent per year. Factors affecting this sector is spending on infrastructure, both new construction and repair or upgrade of existing facilities. While some urban districts shut down old schools and other buildings, suburbs are seeing new units, such as recreation centers and neighborhood clinics. There will be more switchgear than transformer sales—in this sector, with hardware and meters accounting for less than 10 percent of the total. High-intensity discharge ballasts (a form of specialty transformer) are likely to record higher sales—in this as well as in the commercial and residential sectors—as they gain against fluorescent systems in lighting up dark spaces.

The World Market, Investment, and US Trade

The United States is the single largest market for T&D equipment, but its share is eroding as industrialization takes place around the globe. World demand for T&D equipment is estimated at about $68 billion in 2003 with projection to $142.5 billion for 2013. The US share should decline from 21 to 16.5 percent in that span. Both the North American and the West European market will grow below the world rate of 4.5 percent per annum. The fastest growth is slated for the Asia-Pacific region, led by China where sales of T&D units almost tripled between 2003 and 2008.

The electric power T&D equipment industry has become increasingly international in scope during the past two decades, with a rise in the volume of trade, the amount of direct foreign investment, and the number of collaborative ventures. In terms of product lines, advanced switchgear and high-voltage transformers are especially in demand in almost all regions. In terms of major end-use markets, the industrial and the commercial sectors show the strongest gains. Utilities are facing deregulation in several nations and are experiencing competition from the independent power providers and the NUGs.

Attracted by the large size of the US market, European firms established production facilities here. Among these entering were: ABB (Switzerland), Schneider

Electric, Areva, Carbone Lorraine (France), Siemens (Germany), and Philips (Netherlands). Hammond Power (Canada) and Mitsubishi Electric (Japan) also operate in United States. In turn, US firms have gone abroad, especially to Mexico, where Actuant, Basler Electric, Carling Technologies, Cooper Industries, and General Electric operate sole or joint venture facilities with Mexican partners (GE is linked to Prolec via Xignux). Of course, the US firms are investing well beyond Mexico and conduct much trade.

The US foreign trade situation in T&D equipment shows an ongoing deficit between 2003 and 2013. Exports as a percent of shipments are projected to move from 18.2 percent in 2003 to 20.7 percent in 2013. Imports as a percent of demand are seen as rising from 22.7 percent to about 32.7 percent during the same ten-year span. The result is a $2.4 billion deficit in 2008 (for details, see Table 39.3). Import growth is now driven by the commodity nature of low-end products such as fuses and molded case circuit breakers from low-cost manufacturers in Latin America and Asia-Pacific. However, Western nations are major markets for more sophisticated devices.

Of the $6.1 billion T&D equipment imported in 2008, Mexico contributed 39 percent. Next came Western Europe at 18 percent, China at 11 percent, and Canada at 10 percent. On the export front, US exports of T&D equipment recorded $3.7 billion worth of shipments to these destinations: Mexico at 22.5, percent Canada at 18.4 percent, Western Europe 12.3 percent, and Dominican Republic at 12.8 percent of the total in 2008.

Industry Structure, Conduct, and Performance

The T&D equipment field is a part of the larger electric power equipment industry. The latter includes a wide variety of equipment used at power plants such as a wide range of turbines and generators; also included in the broader category are poles, transmission towers, wire, and cable. But these are beyond the scope of this chapter and the far longer report on which it is based. For many of the leading firms in the broader arena, T&D equipment represents less than half their volume; the case for the smaller companies is just the opposite.

The T&D equipment sector is relatively mature and exhibits relatively low growth, plus limited potential for product innovation. Indeed, the conservative nature of the industry, and the long lifespan of many products delays the introduction of radical technologies. Still, many leading firms have increased their capital spending during 2005–2009. The cyclical nature of the industry favors those that can make substantial investment. At the same time, cooperative agreements have been forged, and the pace of mergers/acquisitions has risen in the past five years as firms plan to capture new ideas from partners, broaden their product lines, and expand into new foreign markets. Competition is usually on the basis of product differentiation for high-end goods and aggressive pricing for low-end, commodity-like devices.

Our estimate is that there are several hundred—possibly up to 500—companies active in the T&D industry in the United States, a good mix of domestic and foreign firms. Firms range from small ones operating in a given region only, say the Southwest, to large multinationals with diverse product lines across the United

States and abroad. There is some consolidation at the top, with six firms accounting for 40 percent of the total market in 2008. They are General Electric, Eaton, and Cooper Industries from the United States and ABB, Siemens, and Schneider Electric from Western Europe. There is a strong, second tier of firms with at least $200 million of sales: Howard Industries, Hubbell, Itron, Powell Industries, S&C Electric, and SPX from United States, Areva and Elster from Western Europe. Powerful Chinese companies may appear soon on this list.

Leading Firms and Brands

Many of the large companies in the industry operate through a division that was acquired earlier and has maintained its brand identity. Some small firms, due to longevity, are also able to emphasize their brands. In 2008, ABB acquired Kuhlman Electric, a privately held US maker of transformers and parts; it did sell some of the Kuhlman product line later to Power Partners. Siemens still uses the Osram brand for its high-intensity discharge ballasts and the related lighting products. GE Energy has a joint venture for transformer production with Xignux of Mexico; the operation is known as Prolec GE Internacional. Schneider Electric acquired Square D many years ago, a respected firm in United States. In a similar fashion, Eaton features the Cutler-Hammer and Heinemann brands, while Cooper Industries has the former Crouse-Hinds product line. Smaller firms with visibility include Buswell Energy, Hexaformer, and Preformed Line Products. The Waukesha Electric division of SPX is linked with Philips in development of superconducting transformers under the auspices of the US Department of Energy.

Marketing Activities

The marketing task for firms operating in this field is bound up with the specific category of product line and the markets served. For example, very large transformers are manufactured and then sold almost exclusively to large electric utilities. In contrast, millions of molded case circuit breakers are sold annually to a wide variety of users in all four major markets. The complex, high-value units are marketed by the elite sales forces of large firms and are often subject to high-level negotiations. In a similar fashion, the sales force would be involved in submitting bids on advertised contracts, usually to large, public entities that set their own product specifications and benchmarks. Reputation, experience, and word-of-mouth testimonials all come into play in such vendor-buyer relationships.

In the case of mass-produced, near-commodity products—such as fuses, simple circuit breakers, distribution transformers—large chain and/or small independent distributors are much more likely to be involved. Their inventory holdings will be relatively high and feature variants of the same product from several suppliers. As noted earlier, price plays an important role in the sale of such devices. At times, consulting engineering firms constitute yet another channel through which the commodity type products are marketed. This is the case when consultants take a role not just in design, but also the construction of a large project, integrating many components and subsystems. In some cases, specialized distribution channels arise, such as rural electric utilities have often formed cooperative ventures. Last but not least, the Internet/Web plays an increasingly significant role in marketing, as both large and small firms display product lines, technical information, manuals, and even prices and order forms on their websites. Consolidators have come into play too, such as btbplaza.com, which had more than 240 transformer factories in its database by 2009 and allowed potential customers to contact the vendors directly.

Collaboration and Merger/Acquisition

Several types of cooperative agreements have been put into place by large, medium and small firms in the T&D market. Examples are licensing, joint ventures, R&D/ technology, and marketing agreements. The rationale in such decisions can range from cost savings to sharing ideas, from expansion into foreign markets to sharing liability burden. A fundamental goal is to strengthen relationships with existing and potential customers. Examples are ABB's supply, distribution, and licensing arrangements with TVA, Power Partners, and Arteche Group; Eaton and Caterpillar forming Intelligent Switchgear, a joint venture; and General Electric forming Prolec with Xignux.

The T&D equipment industry has seen a definite restructuring and consolidation in the past decade, with several mergers and acquisitions taking place. Notable was Itron's acquisition of Actaris, combining two leading makers of meters on the two sides of the Atlantic. ABB acquired Kuhlman Electric from the Carlyle Group, thereby strengthening its position in the US market. Hammond Power of Canada purchased Delta Transformer; Littelfuse acquired Shock Block and Startco Engineering; and Thomas & Betts bought both Power Solutions and Joslyn Hi-Voltage from Danaher. In some cases, the acquisition is just for a specific product, such as Carbone Lorraine's Ferraz Shawmut purchasing the medium voltage fuse business of General Electric.

Notes

Originally published in *Business Economics*, Vol. 46, No. 4 (October 2011), pp. 249–259.

1. For methodology used in this study, see Deneen and Gross (2006), specifically p. 73: "Appendix: A Note on Methodology."

References

Deneen, Michael A., and Andrew C. Gross. 2006. "The Global Market for Power Tools." *Business Economics*, 41(3): 66–73.

The Freedonia Group. 2009. "Electric Power Transmission & Distribution Equipment," Industry Study #2503.

US Energy Information Administration. 2011. "Annual Energy Outlook 2011," Report Number: DOE/EIA-0383(2011).

Vastag, Brian. 2011. "White House Pushes Policies to Upgrade Nation's Aging Electrical Network." *Washington Post* (June 13).

CHAPTER 40

2014

FOCUS ON STATISTICS

INITIAL RESULTS OF THE 2012 ECONOMIC CENSUS

Robert P. Parker, Consultant on Federal Statistics

In March, the U.S. Census Bureau (Census) began the release of data from the 2012 Economic Census (EC) (US Bureau of the Census 2014b). The March release date is about six months after the originally scheduled date and largely reflects cuts by the Congress in the President's budget request. The House of Representatives actually wanted to eliminate the program in FY 2013, but through the efforts of NABE and many other organizations, funding was largely restored in the Senate (National Association for Business Economics 2012).

The EC, which is now conducted every five years, provides detailed industry and geographic data on establishments primarily engaged in industries covering almost 98 percent of private nonfarm industries. For the covered industries, data on employment, payroll, and output (sales, receipts, or shipments) will be presented by detailed industry—the six-digit North American Industry Classification System (NAICS)[1]—and detailed geographic areas, which for retail trade and service industries include the ZIP code level. For selected industries, data will be available on labor costs, output by type of product, operating expenses, purchased services, inventories, capital expenditures, and assets.[2] The 2012 EC also will include special reports on commodity flows by mode of transportation, franchising, Puerto Rico and the other island areas, and a new report on enterprises.

This chapter provides an overview of the 2012 EC, including differences with the 2007 EC because of changes to industry and geographic classification systems, and to data content. It also discusses differences with previously released 2012 Census Bureau data from its monthly, quarterly, and annual sample survey programs. Table 40.1 provides the latest Census Bureau release schedule for 2012 EC reports; all reports are scheduled for release by mid-2016.

Table 40.1 2012 Economic census release schedule

Publication Series	*Report Title*	*Release Dates*
Core Business Statistics	Advance Report	March 2014
Industry Series	Utilities and Finance	June 2014–February 2015
	Wholesale Trade	July 2014–February 2015
	Services	July 2014–February 2015
	Retail Trade	July 2014–January 2015
	Manufacturing	September 2014–December 2014
	Mining	September 2014–December 2014
	Construction	September 2014–December 2014
Geographic Area Series	Utilities and Finance	February 2015–November 2015
	Wholesale Trade	February 2015–October 2015
	Services	May 2015–December 2015
	Retail Trade	February 2015–October 2015
	Manufacturing	April 2015–August 2015
	Mining	February 2015–April 2015
	Construction	February 2015–October 2015
Subjects/Series Summary	Industry/Product Analysis (Mining and Manufacturing)	May 2015
	Summary/Subject—Construction	May 2015–July 2015
	Subject/Summary Series—Manufacturing	June 2015–October 2015
	Subject/Summary Series Mining	June 2015–September 2015
	Product Lines—Retail Trade	January 2016
	Establishment and Firms Size—Retail Trade	January 2016
	Product Lines—Services	January 2016–March 2016
	Establishment and Firms Size—Services	January 2016–March 2016
	Product Lines—Wholesale Trade	February 2016
	Establishment and Firms Size—Wholesale Trade	February 2016
	Product Lines—Utilities & Finance	March 2016
	Miscellaneous Subjects—Retail Trade	March 2016
	Misc Subjects—Wholesale Trade	March 2016
	Misc Subjects—Utilities & Finance	June 2016
	Misc Subjects—Services	June 2016
Industry classifications	Bridge	June 2016
	Comparative	June 2016
ZIP Codes	Retail trade	June 2016
	Services	June 2016
Other Economic Census Reports	Franchising	February 2016
	Enterprise Statistics	February 2016

continued

Table 40.1 Continued

Publication Series	*Report Title*	*Release Dates*
Commodity Flow Survey	Preliminary Geographic Area Series: Hazardous Materials, and Exports	December 2013 December 2014
Economic Census of Island Areas	Northern Marianas, Guam, American Samoa, Virgin Island, Puerto Rico	April 2014–September 2015
Survey of Business Owners	Race and ethnicity Veterans	June 2015–October 2015 November 2015
	Company Summary	December 2015
	Characteristics of Businesses and Owners	December 2015

The Economic Census: An Overview

Legal Authority and Confidentiality

The EC is mandated by law under Title 13 of the United States Code (sections 131, 191, and 224) and requires firms to respond, specifying penalties for firms that fail to report. The law also requires the Census Bureau to maintain confidentiality, and individual responses may be used only for statistical purposes. Individual responses may be seen only by people sworn to uphold Title 13. No data are published that could reveal the identity or activity of any individual or business. Confidential information on census forms is exempt from the Freedom of Information Act, and copies retained in respondents' files are immune from legal process.

Reporting Units

In an EC, the Census Bureau collects and publishes data primarily on an "establishment" basis, where an establishment is a business or industrial unit at a single physical location that produces or distributes goods or performs services, such as a single store or factory. The EC features this basis, as opposed to an "enterprise" basis, because many companies own or control more than one establishment, and those establishments may be located in different geographic areas and may be engaged in different industries. By collecting separate information for each establishment, the EC can provide users with comprehensive data for detailed industries and geographic areas.[3] In addition, establishment data provide industry information on the specific inputs and outputs and how they relate to each other. These data enable the Census Bureau to provide measures of value added, which is considered to be the best measure of industry output because value added measures the contribution of each industry to total output by eliminating duplication. The 2012 EC includes a new report that, as described below, aggregates establishment data to the enterprise level.

History[4]

An EC has been taken at regular five-year intervals since 1967; the three previous censuses had been taken in 1954, 1958, and 1963. The 1954 EC was the first census to be fully integrated as it provided comparable data across economic sectors, using consistent time periods, concepts, definitions, classifications, and reporting units. It was the first census to be taken by mail, using lists of firms provided by the administrative records of other federal agencies. Since 1954, administrative records also have been used to provide basic statistics for very small firms, reducing or eliminating the need to send them census questionnaires. Also beginning with the 1954 EC, a distinction is made both in the collection and publication of EC data between "employer" and "nonemployer" businesses. Employer business are defined as firms with one or more paid employees at any time during the year as recorded in the administrative records of other federal agencies; nonemployer businesses are defined as firms subject to federal income tax with no paid employees during the year recorded in these administrative records.

Prior to 1954, individual components of the EC were taken separately at varying intervals. The EC had its origin with the 1810 Decennial Census, when questions on manufacturing were included. Coverage of economic activities was expanded for the 1840 Decennial Census and subsequent censuses to include mining and some commercial activities. The 1905 Manufactures Census was the first time an EC was taken separately from a decennial population census. Censuses covering retail and wholesale trade and construction industries were added in 1930, as were some covering service trades in 1933. Censuses of construction, manufacturing, and the other business service censuses were suspended during World War II.

The industry coverage of the EC has been expanded substantially since 1954, mostly between 1967 and 1992. A census of construction industries was added in 1967, and the scope of service industries was expanded in 1967, 1977, and 1987.[5] Although a few transportation industries were covered as early as 1963, it was not until 1992 that the census was expanded to include transportation except for railroads and passenger air, communications, and utilities. Also in 1992, coverage was expanded to include the financial, insurance, and real estate industries. The most recent change in coverage was in 2007, when scheduled passenger air transportation was added. With these additions, the EC covers roughly 98 percent of the private nonfarm economy. Coverage of the government (public administration) and farm sectors is provided by a census of governments, collected by the Census Bureau, and a census of agriculture, now collected by the US Department of Agriculture.

Beginning with the 1954 EC, data on nonemployer businesses for retail trade and selected services were obtained from tax return records, and these data were integrated where feasible into the EC reports. Since 1972, a separate report on all nonemployer businesses has been issued as part of the EC, and an annual series was added beginning with the 1998 report. After the 1982 EC, nonemployer business data were dropped from the regular EC reports until the 2007 EC, when a report was introduced that includes summary data for both nonemployer and employer businesses.[6]

Uses

The EC is the most comprehensive source of economic information on business establishments available. It provides detailed industry and geographic statistics that are used by businesses, researchers, and government policy makers. In addition, it provides the detailed data used by the Board of Governors, US Federal Reserve System (2012) to benchmark the Index of Industrial Production and Capacity Utilization, by the Bureau of Labor Statistics (2014) to develop weights for the Producer Price Index, and by the Bureau of Economic Analysis to prepare input-output accounts and quarterly GDP.

Universe-level estimates from the EC also are used to benchmark most of the Census Bureau's annual, quarterly, and monthly economic surveys—such as the annual surveys of manufacturing and wholesale trade and the monthly survey of retail trade—and to update their survey sample frames for changes in the composition and organization of the economy. Benchmarking of these series is critical to the reliability of the survey-based estimates.

As previously noted, the estimates from the 2012 EC are not the first estimates for 2012 released by the Census Bureau. For industries covered by its monthly, quarterly, and annual industry surveys, the first estimates for 2012 were released as the sum of the months/quarters for manufacturing, merchant wholesale trade, retail

Table 40.2 Previous release of 2012 estimates

Industry	*Frequency*	*Data Items Covered*	*Industry Detail*	*Release Date for 2012*
Manufacturing	Monthly	Shipments, orders, inventories	Mostly three- and four-digit NAICS industries	February 2013
Manufacturing	Annual[a]	Not conducted in 2012.	Not all six-digit NAICS industries	(x)
Merchant wholesalers	Monthly	Sales, inventories	Mostly three- and four-digit NAICS industries	February 2013
Wholesale trade	Annual[b]	Sales, inventories[c]	Same as monthly survey	March 2014
Retail trade	Monthly	Sales, inventories	Mostly three-and four-digit NAICS industries	February 2013
Retail trade and food services	Monthly	Sales, inventories	Mostly three-and four-digit NAICS industries	January 2013
Retail trade	Annual	Sales, inventories[d]	Same as monthly survey	March 2014
Accommodation and food services	Annual	Sales, inventories[e]	Same as monthly survey	March 2014
Selected services	Quarterly	Revenue and receipts	Mostly three-and four-digit NAICS industries	March 2014
Selected services	Annual	Revenue and receipts[f]	Same as quarterly survey	December 2013

[a]Although not conducted in an EC year, also covers detailed data on type of shipments.

[b]In addition to merchant wholesalers, the annual survey covers manufacturers' sales branches and offices, and agents, brokers, and electronic markets.

[c]In addition to sales and inventories, covers sales taxes, purchases, operating expenses, accounts receivable, e-commerce sales, and inventories held outside United States.

[d]Also covers sales taxes, purchases, operating expenses, accounts receivable, inventories held outside United States, and e-commerce sales.

[e]Same as footnote 4.

[f]Also covers receipts and revenue, inventories, payroll, purchased services, operating expenses, e-commerce sales, and exports.

trade and food services, and selected service industries. For the monthly and quarterly surveys, estimates for 2012 were released at the same time as the release of the estimates for December 2012 (or fourth quarter 2012). For example, the first estimates of sales and inventories for retail trade were released in February 2013. About a year later, estimates from the 2012 annual survey were released and incorporated in the monthly release resulting in revisions into time series back to 2011 and forward from December 2012. (Table 40.2 shows for each of these monthly, quarterly, and annual surveys the items covered, industry detail, and date of release of the first 2012 estimates.) Final and more reliable estimates for 2012 will be released in early 2015 or 2016 when the 2012 EC data are incorporated in the monthly estimates.

The 2012 data from the Census Bureau's monthly, quarterly, and annual sample surveys provide timely estimates that enable users to track short-term trends.[7] However, when compared with the data from the 2012 EC, these data have the following significant limitations: (1) their estimates are based on small samples and subject to significant sampling errors, whereas the EC data, except for the census of construction industries, are based on a complete enumeration; (2) reporting is mandatory in the EC, whereas the data from most of the surveys are reported on a voluntary basis; (3) there are no surveys of construction or mining sectors, which are covered in the EC; (4) for industries covered by the EC, the surveys do not provide data for all six-digit NAICS industries; (5) the surveys provide little or no geographic coverage—only annual state data for manufacturing; and (6) the surveys—especially the monthly and quarterly surveys—have limited data content. (The annual surveys of manufacturing, wholesale and retail trade, and services collect data such as operating expense, purchased services, class of customer, and class of customer data.) By collecting these items on a sample basis, the Census is able to reduce reporting burden on millions of small businesses.

Industry Coverage of the 2012 EC

Industry coverage of the 2012 EC will be the same as the 2007 EC; it will cover almost the entire private nonfarm economy as well as selected government activities. Table 40.3 identifies the industries that will *not* be covered in 2012. EC data also cover government hospitals and government-owned liquor stores, even though the data for the EC do not generally include government-owned establishments.[8] The sectors and industries shown in Table 40.3 reflect the 2012 version of the NAICS. The 2012 EC will cover 1,056 of the 1,065 industries of the 2012 version of US NAICS, as announced in the August 17, 2011 *Federal Register*.

Collecting the 2012 EC

The 2012 EC covered the business activity of about 28 million business establishments. To obtain data for these establishments, the Census Bureau uses both mail questionnaires and administrative records from other federal agencies—the Internal Revenue Service, Social Security Administration, and Bureau of Labor Statistics. Also for the 2012 EC, first-time electronic reporting was formally permitted for firms with a single establishment, and about 30 percent of them filed electronically.

Table 40.3 Industry coverage in the 2012 economic census by NAICS sector and industry

NAICS Code	*Sector*	*NAICS Industries Excluded from 2012 Economic Census*
11	Agriculture, Forestry, Fishing, and Hunting	All
21	Mining	None
22	Utilities	None
23	Construction	None
31–33	Manufacturing	None
42	Wholesale Trade	None
44–45	Retail Trade	None
48–49	Transportation and Warehousing	482, Rail Transportation
		491, Postal Service
51	Information	None
52	Finance and Insurance	5251 Insurance and Employee Benefit Funds
		52591 Open-End Investment Funds
		52592 Trusts, Estates, and Agency Accounts
		52599 Other Financial Vehicles
53	Real Estate and Rental and Leasing	None
54	Professional, Scientific, and Technical Service	None
55	Management of Companies and Enterprises	None
56	Administrative and Support and Waste Management and Remediation Services	None
61	Educational Services	6111, Elementary and Secondary Schools
		6112, Junior Colleges
		6113, Colleges, Universities, and Professional Schools
62	Health Care and Social Assistance	None
71	Arts, Entertainment, and Recreation	None
72	Accommodation and Food Services	None
81	Other Services (Except Public Administration)	8131, Religious Organizations
		81393, Labor Unions and Similar Labor Organizations
		81394, Political Organizations
		814, Private Households
92	Public Administration	All

Note: Although the economic census does not generally include government-owned establishments, some government activities are included. See text for additional details.

Mail questionnaires were used for establishments of large- and medium-size firms, all firms known to operate more than one establishment, all employer firms with payroll above a specified cutoff during 2012 (based on administrative records), and a sample of single-establishment employer firms with payroll below a specified cutoff in classifications for which the need for specialized data preclude reliance solely on administrative records sources. For the 2012 EC, about 4 million census forms were mailed using over 500 different census forms, each customized to particular industries.

Mail questionnaires were not used for single-establishment employer firms with payroll below a specified cutoff and for nonemployer businesses. Data for about 3 million small employers on sales, payroll, and employment, as well as information on location, legal form of organization and industry classification, are derived or estimated from administrative records. These records also are the source of data for about 21 million nonemployer businesses on sales, location, legal form of organization, and industry classification.

The major EC reports now exclude nonemployer businesses, primarily because of the limited information available from administrative records, of their impact on the EC measures of business activity for most industries, and of the cost of collecting additional information from these businesses. (Only the *Economy-Wide Key Statistics Report* provides data for employer and nonemployer businesses.) The Census Bureau has estimated that for 2012, nonemployer businesses accounted for roughly 4 percent of business activity, measured using sales, and 70 percent of all number of businesses. For 2012, the number of these businesses and their sales, receipts, or shipments by industry and geographic area, will be released in the *Nonemployer Statistics* report scheduled to be released in April 2013 on the American Fact Finder on the Census Bureau's website.

Industry and Product Classification

Each establishment covered in an EC is assigned a NAICS industry code based on the primary products shipped, sold, or produced. The product detail for service industries collected in the 2012 EC is based on the North American Product Classification System (NAPCS), the 1999 product classification agreement with Canada and Mexico.[9] For the other industries, the product detail used for the 2012 EC is consistent with NAICS. For the new 2012 EC Enterprise Statistics report, each enterprise or company reporting in the EC will be assigned a special industry code based on the primary industry of its establishments.

Changes for 2012

In an EC, the Census Bureau generally introduces changes to coverage, changes to classification systems, and changes to the data content and reports. For the 2012 EC, there will be no changes in coverage; the following paragraphs describe the changes in other aspects.

New or Updated Classification Systems

The data for the 2012 EC will be presented using the latest classification standards issued by the US Office of Management and Budget (OMB). These standards are the 2012 NAICS, the 2012 NAPCS, and 2013 Metropolitan, Micropolitan, and Combined Statistical Areas.

Industry detail. The 2012 NAICS is very similar to the 2007 system used for the 2007 EC. The most significant revisions are in the manufacturing, utilities, retail trade, and accommodations sectors. For manufacturing, the major changes were collapsing detail that eliminated a net of over 100 industries, primarily to reduce products costs and respondent burden. For utilities, five new electric power generation industries were added. For retail trade, a new industry was created by merging motorcycle, TV, and personal watercraft dealers with all other motor vehicle dealers; another new industry was created by merging heating oil dealers, liquid petroleum gas dealers, and other fuel dealers; and industries in the electronics and appliance store industry was restructured. Lastly, in accommodation and food services, the restaurant industry was restructured.

As part of the 2012 EC Core Business Statistics reports, the Census Bureau will publish two reports on the changes in NAICS: Comparative Statistics will present data for 2012 and 2007 on a 2007 NAICS basis and Bridge Between 2012 NAICS and 2007 NAICS will provide 2012 data for 2012 and 2007 data on the industries that changed since 2007.

Product detail. The Census Bureau has provided data on mining and manufactured products, wholesale and retail trade merchandise lines, and types of service receipts in many past economic censuses. For the 2007 EC, product lines in four service sectors were classified consistent with the NAPCS. For the 2012 EC, selected product categories for wholesale and retail trade have been revised to conform to NAPCS. These data will be published in Product Lines subject reports. In most cases, more product categories will be shown in the affected industries, although there will be some loss of comparability to the prior census product data.[10]

Geographic detail. In the 2012 EC, as in the 2007 EC, the Census Bureau will provide data by state, metropolitan and micropolitan area, county, selected places, and ZIP code.[11] Table 40.4 shows the general availability of data for these geographic areas by sector. For mining, construction, and management, complete establishment detail was not collected in the 2012 EC so that geographic detail will be limited. On the other hand, subnational data for utilities will be available for the first time in 2012.

Metropolitan and micropolitan areas are statistical units determined by OMB. These statistical units are defined in terms of whole counties (or equivalent entities), including in the six New England States. Metropolitan statistical areas have at least one urbanized area of 50,000 or more population, plus adjacent territory that has a high degree of social and economic integration with the core area as measured by commuting patterns. Micropolitan statistical areas, an addition for the 2012 EC, have at least one urban cluster of at least 10,000 but less than 50,000 population, plus adjacent territory that has a high degree of social and economic integration

Table 40.4 Geographic areas in the 2012 economic census

Sector	*States*	*MA's*	*Counties*	*Places*	*Zip Code*
Mining	X				
Utilities	X	X	X	X	
Construction	X				
Manufacturing	X	X	X	X	
Wholesale Trade	X	X	X	X	
Retail Trade	X	X	X	X	X
Transportation and Warehousing	X	X			
Information	X	X	X	X	
Finance and Insurance	X	X			
Real Estate and Rental and Leasing	X	X	X	X	
Professional, Scientific, and Technical Services	X	X	X	X	X
Management of Companies and Enterprises	X				
Administrative and Support and Waste Management and Remediation Services	X	X	X	X	X
Educational Services	X	X	X	X	X
Health Care and Social Assistance	X	X	X	X	X
Arts, Entertainment and Recreation	X	X	X	X	X
Accommodation and Food Services	X	X	X	X	X
Other Services (Except Public Administration)	X	X	X	X	X

MA's—Metropolitan and micropolitan areas determined in 2013 by the Office of Management and Budget for the presentation of geographic area detail by federal statistical agencies.

Places for the 2012 EC are defined by the Census Bureau as places with population or jobs of 2,500 or more. For the 2007 EC, the cutoff was 5,000.

Note: The level of geographic detail varies by sector because of consolidated establishment reporting and data withheld to avoid disclosing information about individual firms. See text for additional details.

with the core area as measured by commuting patterns. Together, metropolitan and micropolitan statistical areas cover about 93 percent of the US population. For the 2012 EC, data will be tabulated for areas defined by OMB as of February 28, 2013. Compared with the areas used for the 2007 EC, a few metropolitan areas have changed boundaries, and there are about 20 new micropolitan areas—areas whose population increased to meet the thresholds. Counties and equivalent entities (boroughs and census areas in Alaska, parishes in Louisiana, and independent cities in Maryland, Missouri, Nevada, and Virginia) to be used for the 2012 EC will be those in existence as of January 1, 2012.

For the selected place detail, the 2012 EC will redefine the places to be shown. These places, which can be either incorporated (legally defined cities, towns, villages, and boroughs), unincorporated, or towns and townships in selected states, will now consist of those with 2,500 or more inhabitants or 2,500 or more workers. The criteria used for the 2012 EC will for the first time introduce the number of workers, primarily from the 2010 Census of Population tabulated by place of work. The change is being made to help make sure that data for all economically important places are published, even if they have few inhabitants.

ZIP codes are administrative units of the US Postal Service, and there were about 40,000 five-digit codes used for 2012. The 2012 EC will show summary data for individual five-digit ZIP codes for retail trade and service sectors. These data will generally be limited to a count of the establishments in each industry or kind of business, further classified by size. ZIP codes generally do not coincide with the Census Bureau's geographic or political areas, and they change according to postal requirements.

Data Content

The 2012 EC will reflect additions to the data items collected in the 2007 EC. These additions have been limited to the collection on the Report of Organization form of data on company-level operating revenues and on net sales, royalties, and license fees for the use of intellectual property and for contract manufacturing provided to others and purchased from others. These items will be published in a new report described in the next section.

Reports

With the exception of the new Enterprise Statistics report, reports for the 2012 EC are essentially the same as in the 2007 EC. The Enterprise Statistics report, which is scheduled to be released in February 2016, is designed to provide periodic comprehensive company-wide data that show data such as enterprise size, extent, and nature of industrial diversification; merger and acquisition activities; foreign operations and foreign ownership; and data items, such as net sales that are best collected at the company level. Its coverage will be essentially be the same as the 2012 EC and consist of private enterprises and their establishments operating in the United States and selected activities of governments.

The 2012 EC Enterprise Statistics report will be based on the "prototype 2007 Enterprise Statistics tables" that include counts of the number of firms, their establishments, sales and receipts, annual payroll, and employment. The data will be cross-tabulated by industry specialization ratio and employment size categories. The 2012 report also will include the new items noted in the previous section such as operating revenues and net sales, royalties and license fees for the use of intellectual property, and contract manufacturing activities.[12]

The new report will be the only comprehensive source of economy-wide company-level statistics and data to relate the activities of companies and their affiliated establishments. These data will be used by the Bureau of Economic Analysis for input-output studies and to calculate the GDP. The Small Business Administration will use the data as part of their process to determine industry size standards for small businesses.

Release Schedule for 2012 Economic Census Data

As shown in Table 40.1, the 2012 EC reports series includes 14 reports, the first of which was released in March 2014 when the *Advance* report and the Economy-Wide

Key Statistics reports will be released. These reports provide preliminary data for broad NAICS categories for all industry sectors and states. More detailed and complete reports will be issued over a two-year period; these reports will replace previously released detail and provide greatly expanded detail for industries, including product lines and size distributions, and for geography, including ZIP codes for selected industries.

In June 2016, 2012 EC reports on *ZIP Code Statistics* are scheduled for release for retail trade and services. The *Comparative Statistics* report that will show United States and state totals classified by 2012 and 2007 NAICS for both 2007 and 2012 and the *Bridge between 2012 NAICS and 2007 NAICS* will show the relationships between 2012 NAICS and 2007 NAICS categories and are scheduled for release in June 2016. The *Franchise Report* that will provide data on franchising and reflect the expanded collection of industry data on franchising in the 2007 EC and the new Enterprise Statistics report are scheduled to be released in February 2016.

The 2012 EC report series also includes several related reports.

- Preliminary data from the *Transportation: Commodity Flow Survey* that report on the origin and destination of commodities shipped from selected industries were released in December 2013, and final reports are scheduled for release at the end of 2014.
- The *Island Area,* which report on the results of special censuses of employer businesses operating in Puerto Rico, U.S. Virgin Islands, Guam, American Samoa, and Commonwealth of the Northern Mariana Islands, will be released beginning in April 2014.
- The *Survey of Business Owners* will provide data for minority- and women-owned businesses, including the number of firms, sales, employment, and payroll by NAICS code, geographic area, size, and legal form of organization. These reports are scheduled to be released from June 2015 to December 2015.

Notes

Originally published in *Business Economics*, Vol. 49, No. 2 (April 2014), pp. 127–135.

1. NAICS is the industry classification system developed by the United States, Canada, and Mexico. It is used by the Census Bureau for the EC and all of its programs. For the United States, the NAICS is prepared by the US Office of Management and Budget's Economic Classification Policy Committee. The complete manual, the North American Industry Classification System Manual 2012, is available from the National Technology Information Service at NTIS.gov.
2. Additional data are available for 2012 from the Census Bureau annual survey programs.
3. For some industries in mining, construction, and utilities, only payroll, employment, and classification information are collected for individual establishments, but the other data items are collected on a consolidated basis. As a result, the extent of geographic detail for these industries, as shown in Table 40.3, is limited.
4. A comprehensive history of the Economic Census may be found in US Bureau of the Census (2014a).

5. Since it was restored in 1967 EC, all data for the construction industries have been collected using a sample survey.
6. For a more detailed discussion of the 2007 EC, see Parker (2008) and US Census Bureau (2007).
7. As discussed in the section on "Uses," they provide most of the key source data for the quarterly estimates of GDP and also provide benchmarks for other key economic statistics.
8. Because of the limited coverage of government activities in the EC, data for some industries are incomplete for some uses. For example, EC data exclude public electric, gas, water and sewer utilities, highway construction performed by government employees, publicly operated buses and subway systems; and public libraries, museums, and zoos.
9. Additional information on NAPCS and its linkages with NAICS can be found on the Census Bureau's website (www.census.gov/naics).
10. Data on manufactured products also is published in the monthly, quarterly, and annual reports of the Current Industrial Reports program.
11. Data for Puerto Rico, the US Virgin Islands, Guam, American Samoa, and the Northern Mariana Islands will be published only as part of the 2012 EC of Puerto Rico and the Island Areas, and are not included in any US totals.
12. More detailed information about the 2007 tables and the 2012 report is available on the Census Bureau website at http://census.gov/econ/esp/about.html.

References

Board of Governors, US Federal Reserve System, 2012. Industrial Production and Capacity Utilization: The 2010 Annual Revision. News Release, March 2012.

National Association for Business Economics, 2012. NABE Speaks Out to Preserve Key Statistical Programs. *NABE News*, August.

Parker, Robert P. 2008. "Focus on Statistics: Detailed Industry, Product, and Geographic Data from the 2007 Economic Census Become Available in 2009." *Business Economics*, 43(3): 69–76.

US Bureau of Labor Statistics, 2014. *BLS Handbook of Methods: Producer Prices*. Chapter 14, http://www.bls.gov/opub/hom/home.htm, accessed February 21, 2014.

US Census Bureau, 2007. *Guide to the 2007 Economic Census*, http://www.census.gov/econ/census02/guide/index.html, accessed February 28, 2014.

———, 2014a. *History of the Economic Census: In Business Since 1810*, http://www.census.gov, accessed February 10, 2014.

———, 2014b. *2012 Economic Census*, http://www.census.gov, accessed February 10, 2014.

CHAPTER 41

2014

ECONOMICS AT WORK

ECONOMICS AT THE AMERICAN CHEMISTRY COUNCIL

Thomas Kevin Swift, American Chemistry Council

The American Chemistry Council (ACC) represents the leading companies in the business of chemistry. Founded in 1872, it is said to be the oldest industrial trade association in North America. It was originally named the Manufacturing Chemists Association, which likely reflected the small-scale manufacturing typical of the nineteenth century. In the 1970s, the name was changed to the Chemical Manufacturers Association, and then in 2000 to the ACC. The ACC membership is over 150 companies. Members range from small enterprises to large multinationals and all are involved in chemical manufacturing, making products that make modern life possible. ACC members are innovative, productive, and responsible—they all have made a voluntary commitment to uphold the highest standards for protecting health, safety, security, and the environment.

The economics function at ACC dates from 1988, when my predecessor, Dr. Allen Lenz, was recruited from the International Trade Administration of the US Department of Commerce to develop an economics team. Prior to that, the association relied on outside consultants to provide analytical support in assessing the economic benefits of the industry, the effects of policy initiatives, and conducting other economic impact studies. In the area of statistics, however, the ACC did publish a statistical publication—*The Chemical Industry Fact Book*—in the late 1950s. This fact book was largely a collection of statistics from various government agencies, but publication ceased during the early 1960s. (In addition to my day job, I fill in as an amateur historian of the chemical industry.) A need was seen to develop in-house analytical capabilities, and the function was created in the late 1980s.

With guidance from a working group of business economists from member companies, Dr. Lenz laid the foundations for the economics function here at the ACC. He recruited me in 1990 as a senior economist, and he built the economics function up to three economists supported by two staff assistants. As an employee of one of our member companies and a consultant to the industry, I had extensive industry knowledge. My first project was to develop an annual statistical publication that would highlight the economic benefits of the industry. This is the typical work of trade association economists. Analysis of policy initiatives is also typical work of a trade association economist, and analysis of energy taxes and other policy initiatives quickly followed. Our portfolio of issues and work with internal clients expanded during the 1990s, and advances in technology improved the way we worked and our ability to provide services.

When Dr. Lenz retired in 1998, I was promoted to lead the department. Around the same time, the ACC underwent a large reorganization into a matrix-type organization of multidisciplinary issue teams, program teams, and shared services. The policy, economics, and risk analysis functions were organized into a shared service that included two economists, a senior policy analyst, and an environmental risk professional, all supported by two staff assistants. Most of our work was policy-oriented support for advocacy purposes, as the ACC is involved in a number of environmental, public health, security, tax, trade, and other public policy issues. The economics function has evolved at the ACC, reflecting the fortunes of the industry as well as the business cycle.

The early 2000s were a rough time for the chemical industry, given the strong US dollar (we are a major exporting sector) and high and volatile natural gas prices that combined to adversely affect the industry's competitiveness. The 2001 recession also hit the industry hard. Between 2000 and early 2008, many facilities were shuttered; and at the ACC there were four different CEOs. A series of restructuring initiatives and downsizings ensued; and during this time I reported to five different people, including two VPs, the Corporate Secretary, the Executive Vice President (twice), and the President and CEO. The staffing of the department shrunk to two at one point, but through this we were able to maintain the value of having economics in-house rather than outsourcing everything, although it was challenging at times. By late 2008 our current President and CEO brought stability; and with a new set of policy and external challenges, our team was able to expand. In a weird way, during the times when our function could seem most vulnerable, these were also the times when executive leadership turned to our team the most. The fluctuating natural gas prices, the hurricane crises, and the Great Recession are prime examples of when leadership wants to be informed by an insider about what is going on, how it is affecting the industry, and what that means for our membership. These are interesting pressures that a trade association economist faces.

The ACC Economics and Statistics Department Today

Now, our team's focus is narrower (we no longer provide environmental risk support nor manage a resin statistics program) and the Economics and Statistics department now includes two economists, a statistician (who is studying to be an economist),

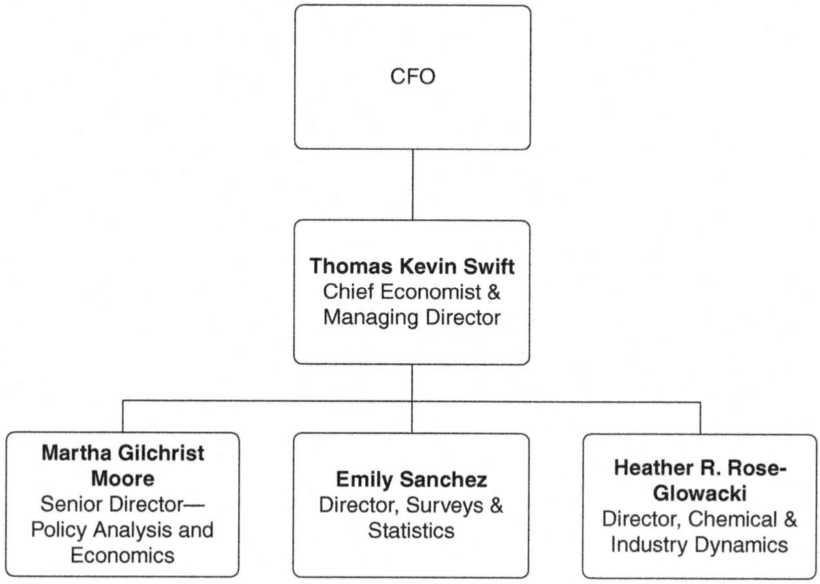

Figure 41.1. ACC Economics and Statistics Department Organization.

and a business research professional. I currently report to the ACC's Chief Financial Officer. We are organized as shown in Figure 41.1.

I had a colleague remark once that I "was the only person not interested in building an empire" at ACC, and it's true. I want to do good economics and have a little fun while doing it. I've always tried to "run lean" with the economics function. I'd rather not be a large target and prefer to keep busy with a nice backlog of projects. Over the years, advances in information technology and automation of business processes have reduced the need for a full-time staff assistant. We have access to one for the hour or so every other week when we need a check request, purchase order, supplies ordered, or assistance with a meeting we are hosting. In doing business economics, the availability of purchased databases and industry-specific publications and software further promote our productivity and enhance our ability to provide economic and other analytical services for our internal clients. During the summer of 2013, we had one position open and one colleague on maternity leave. I recently reflected that the two of us in that time were able to accomplish more (nearly two-fold by my reckoning) than five did 20 years ago! That said, having more support would be very helpful in extending our service offerings, especially with database development.

The current mission of the ACC Economics and Statistics Department is to provide a full range of statistical and economic advice and services for ACC and its members and other partners. The group works to improve overall ACC legislative and regulatory advocacy impact by providing statistics on American chemistry as well as preparing information about the economic value and contributions of chemistry to our economy and society. We function as an in-house consultant, providing survey, economic analysis, and other statistical expertise, as well as monitoring business conditions and changing industry dynamics. The group also offers extensive industry knowledge, a network of leading academic organizations and think tanks, and a dedication to making analysis relevant and comprehensible to a wide audience. The latter is very important, and we strive to present our research findings in as simple a manner as possible. I keep a box of crayons on my desk to remind me of this!

Industry Dynamics

Within the ACC, our team has the most extensive knowledge of our industry and its history, products, markets, and companies. Although none of us are chemists by training, we are often viewed as chemistry experts. To support this, we have developed and maintain a vast repository of information and data on the industry. We subscribe to a number of key services from chemical industry consultants and receive the reports from a number of key chemical equity analysts.

We directly support our senior management. A major member recently announced a decision to spin-off a business, and we were able to quickly prepare an analysis of the impact. We help our membership department in identifying prospective member companies, and we help our panel managers in developing proposals for potential panels that cover a specific chemistry. This represents about one-fifth of our work; and Heather, our business researcher, concentrates on this area. She is developing profiles of chemical companies for senior management. She also maintains our list of new chemical industry investment projects, as well as new projects among our customer industries. The renewed competitiveness of the industry and the wave of new investments are important to the ACC's educational and advocacy outreach. Having an accurate list of projects is essential to this outreach. To better understand the industry's changing dynamics, we participate in many industry conferences and events. Networking is essential, as is keeping on top of the latest analyses conducted by industry consultants and strategy/management consultants.

We are members of the Economic Task Force of the Conseil Européen de l'industrie Chimique, our sister association for Europe. We participate in their meetings, which are held twice a year, and network with our counterparts at various national chemical trade associations. This helps us better understand the changing dynamics of the industry. Often, our colleagues overseas will have a different take on key economic and industry developments; and diversity of thinking is helpful.

Good Numbers Are Foundational

Foundational to good analysis is sound data. We use a variety of government sources (Bureau of Labor Statistics, Bureau of Economic Analysis, Census, and others) for data on employment, capital spending, shipments, inventories, trade, and financial statements. We don't use the data blindly and try very hard to understand how the data are collected, processed, and disseminated as well as their scope. We want to know whether the data are sound, and we will often meet with statistical agencies. At times, adjustments are required or we collect the data ourselves. We have found that NABE's Economic Measurement Seminar gets our new hires up to speed quickly.

For some important metrics, however, the government no longer collects the data or never did. So we survey our member companies in the first quarter (after earnings season) to gather data on company spending on R&D (by type); revenues derived from new products; capital spending (including motivating factor); IT spending; environmental, health and safety spending; and security spending. Data on the latter were needed after 9/11. These are all data points that are essential to our advocacy outreach. Every other year, we solicit data on long-term capital allocations. The survey results are tabulated in-house by Emily, our statistician, and then analyzed and adjusted for our sector. Our member companies account for about 90 percent of the US chemical industry's revenues. Emily also conducts ad hoc benchmark surveys on financial and operational issues for our Council of Small and Medium Enterprises (CSME). Over the years, we have collected some rather unique time-series data.

On example of data services we have developed in-house concerns specialty or performance chemistry, an area where statistical coverage of production or consumption activity never occurred. One result of this effort is specialty chemical market volume indices for the United States. These cover US consumption for nearly 30 functional specialty chemicals markets. The data service pairs annual market research with monthly data and reporting. The inspiration for this was from the DuPont economics team. These market volume indices are used by member companies operating in these businesses to monitor their performance.

We have also developed a service for monitoring downstream end-use customer industry dynamics for the major thermoplastic resins. We compare actual domestic resin sales with implied underlying resin sales that are based on the dynamics of these downstream customer industries. The difference between the two is either build up or drawdown of inventories along the supply chain downstream of resin manufacturing. The need for the service was member-company-driven, and the inspiration for the modeling behind this analytical service was from the steel industry.

The chemical industry is a global industry, and monitoring just the United States is insufficient for most member companies, who truly operate in global markets. As a result, we have also developed a Global Chemical Production Regional Index (Global CPRI) that measures the production volume of the chemical industry in 33 key nations, subregions, and regions, all aggregated to the world total. This index is comparable with the Federal Reserve Board's production indices and features a similar 2007 base year. This monthly series was developed from government industrial production indices for the chemical industry from over 65 nations (Mahapatra and Swift 2012). In a similar manner, my colleague Martha developed the US CPRI, which tracks chemical production in seven major producing regions of the United States. This service is also comparable with the Federal Reserve Board's production indices and allows us to monitor production activity at various levels. The inspiration for all of this was a 1977 documentary film titled *Powers of Ten*. This is an adventure in magnitudes. Starting at a picnic by the lakeside in Chicago, this film expands every ten seconds from ten times farther out until our own galaxy is visible only as a speck of light among many others.

Returning to Earth with breathtaking speed, it moves inward—into the hand of the sleeping picnicker—with ten times more magnification every ten seconds, ending inside a proton of a carbon atom. The Global CPRI and US CPRI facilitate a similar outward and inward view of the industry's fortunes, and we believe we are unique among associations and industries in our ability to examine industry activity at these various levels.

Monitoring Business Conditions

Most NABE members who are familiar with the ACC Economics and Statistics department know us through our weekly economic report. In the 1990s, we published a monthly two-page fact sheet on the industry. This featured minimum text on the first page and a table on the second page. In the wake of 9/11, ACC's president asked me to brief our Monday morning management meeting on developments in the economy. Because of the high uncertainty at that time we developed two potential scenarios—a deepening recession scenario and a recovery scenario—along with indicators to monitor. The recovery scenario did play out. The briefings continued until the president was traveling and asked for an e-mail briefing. Of course, others wanted to be copied, and this weekly e-mail soon evolved into a weekly economic report that now goes out to all ACC staff and to about 1,000 senior level member company decision-makers.

The weekly economic report is a service to our member companies, and for many it consolidates into one publication developments in the economy and the industry. The emphasis is on chemical and energy reports, as well as key macroeconomic reports that affect the industry or its end-use markets. We cover about 25 key economic reports (housing starts and building permits, light vehicle sales, industrial production, and others) that we have deemed important to understanding the industry's demand drivers.

We provide our commentary and insight, and a series of slides is available as well. It is a team effort, and all four of us take a role in covering key indicators and commentary. We meet briefly on Friday mornings to summarize the week's developments. In addition to ACC members, we also share our report with our FOE (Friends of Economics) e-mail list and would be pleased to add any NABE members to the list. Just e-mail the author [kevin_swift@americanchemistry.com].

We are often asked to provide presentations on the economic outlook, the industry outlook, and more recently the implications of the shale gas revolution. The latter has improved the industry's competitiveness and prospects and is leading to over $100 billion in new investment, over half of which is foreign direct investment in the United States. Typical venues include industry conferences, member customer events, member board and planning meetings, industry conferences, and other events. We also provide periodic briefings to ACC staff. We could be doing one or two of these a week and are selective on those we accept. It's not in my DNA to say "no," but I am learning. Of course, we would be more than pleased to speak at a NABE chapter gathering.

Forecasting

For a series of trade and business press briefings in December, we prepare and publish a report that covers the situation and outlook for the chemical industry, the macroeconomy, and key end-use markets. We also forecast R&D and capital spending and imports and exports for the chemical industry. We have developed structural models in order to provide forecasts for the outlook. During the last recession, we prepared reports covering the outlook for the chemical industry and the macroeconomy on a quarterly basis; but in more typical times, we only publish this report at mid-year and year-end. We do, however, make presentations on the economic outlook on a more frequent basis, using the latest data, information, and insight.

In a product that we call the Survey of Economic Forecasters, every month we tabulate and average the macro forecasts of a dozen leading industrial forecasters. The survey covers the variables that we consider to be the key exogenous variables in the models that we develop to forecast the US outlook (GDP, consumer spending, business investment, industrial production, light vehicle sales, housing starts, consumer prices, ten-year Treasury bonds, and the dollar/euro relationship). Though we use the results of the survey to drive our consensus outlook for the macroeconomic environment, we also mention alternative views. We use a similar approach to forecast the outlook for Canada.

For the global outlook we take a similar approach and every quarter tabulate/average the forecasts of GDP, industrial production, and consumer prices for 15 key nations and the euro area. We've also found global GDP and world trade to be important explanatory variables for some of our modeling work. In the past we had developed short-term quarterly models for industry forecasting and longer-term models for policy analysis. This consumed a lot of resources, and in our industry forecasting we now primarily use the services from two prominent forecasting consultancies as well as our own assessment. We continue to use our models for capital spending and R&D spending and for US regional activity.

Because of its position early in the supply chain, the chemical industry is often a sector that leads other sectors at business cycle peaks and troughs. Based on this we developed the Chemical Activity Barometer (CAB), a composite index of chemical industry indicators that produce a leading indicator of broader economy-wide activity. The CAB is comprised of indicators drawn from a range of chemicals, including times series relating to chlor-alkali and other inorganic chemical, pigment, and plastic resins production; hours worked in the chemical industry; chemical company stock data; publicly sourced chemical price data; and several broader economic measures (inventories, building permits and new orders). The CAB provides a long lead for business cycle peaks and troughs and can help identify emerging trends in the wider US economy within sectors closely linked to the business of chemistry, such as housing, retail, and light vehicles. The CAB has been shown to lead business cycle turning points as defined by the National Bureau of Economic Research by three to eight months on average. Moreover, it is timely, as it is released on the Tuesday after the 20th of the month, and is available as a monthly time series back to 1919. Developing the CAB provided an interesting study in economic history and how the structure of American industry has changed. Our communications department maintains a list of over 1,800 that receive the monthly press release, and we would be pleased to add any NABE members to the list. Just e-mail the author.

Using Scenarios

Forecasts tend to be more concerned with accurate prediction. We've learned that single-point forecasts are soon out-of-date, and there are always many factors at play in terms of headwinds and challenges to economic performance. As mentioned before, when we present the consensus point estimates we also explain the risks and potential opportunities and how they could add to or subtract from the consensus outlook.

Particularly, when we are evaluating longer-term trends, we consider various scenarios. In this context, scenarios would be best described as internally consistent and coherent descriptions of potential futures. Our scenario planning involves brainstorming and researching to identify demographic, economic, political, regulatory, and other long-term drivers affecting the industry or segments of the industry. We have conducted scenario exercises concerning the long-term future of the industry as well as for more targeted areas, such as the future of plastics in light vehicles. And we have collaborated with our European colleagues on some of their scenario development.

I am proud that we were able to identify the shale gas revolution and alert our senior management about its implications long before it reached the general business press/media and our trade press. Our most recent exercise examined the possible futures for the economy, the policy environment, and other dynamics through 2030 as they relate to the potential for the US chemical industry. One scenario—*Re-Emerging America*—suggested that development of abundant domestic energy sources would improve industry competitiveness, attract investment, and result in the US chemical industry reemerging as an engine of global growth and innovation. This scenario is playing out.

Analysis of Policy

Policy analysis is our bread and butter. Providing support in this area accounts for more than half our resources. We are often asked to critique regulatory impact analyses (RIAs) from regulatory agencies as well as to provide estimates of our own. For environmental, safety, and security issues many of these analyses entail creating partial equilibrium models and combining them with cost engineering data. For trade and related commercial issues, these are typically partial equilibrium models right out of a managerial economics text. We've developed models that can be used to estimate the impact of certain tax issues, like the Superfund excise taxes. Being able to provide convincing analysis that can be accepted by sometimes critical audiences is critical to our advocacy. For corporate income tax issues we take a different approach. Although we've created microsimulation models for tax analysis, data limitations cause us to rely on "typical taxpayer" models (essentially models calibrated to mimic the chemical industry) based on the *Corporation Sourcebook* data tabulated by the Statistics of Income Division of the Internal Revenue Service.

We each take leadership with our policy issue teams within the ACC. Emily takes leadership on trade and distribution issues in addition to her statistics, survey, and benchmarking work. Martha takes the lead on security and environmental issues, and we jointly provide support for energy issues. I take the lead on tax and related commercial issues. Heather provides much of our support for our separately funded Plastics Division (which advocates opportunities for plastics and promotes their economic, environmental, and societal benefits) and the Chemical Products and Technology Division, which provides comprehensive issue management services for more than 60 self-funded product and sector groups that are focused on specific chemistries and related technologies. These are primarily larger projects that often involve all of us. Health and safety issue support is largely a team effort, as is our support of the ACC's value chain initiatives. These are often analyses of the cost of product de-selection or analyses of the economic benefits of a particular chemistry. This will be subsequently discussed.

As much as we encourage our internal clients to get us involved early and often, we have to be prepared to handle last-minute requests. A typical last-minute request, for example, may be to review a 300-page RIA from an agency, provide an alternative impact estimate, and generate a report or talking points. Sometimes a deadline is only a few hours away, so there is not much that we can do. We have developed a number of internal "on the shelf" information products and services that can provide some answers. Of course, our combined experience and ability to at least provide "back of the envelope" estimates is useful when we don't have much notice. That said, regular, ongoing involvement with our internal clients minimizes any frustration and enables us to provide proactive insight and advice. This involves attending a lot of meetings, but it is worth it.

Economic Benefits of Chemistry

Essential to the work of any trade association economist is to be able to quantify the economic benefits of the industry. The resulting data and insight are used in association advocacy. Within the first week of taking any principles of economics course we've all learned the concept of opportunity costs. This is the basis of about one-fourth of what we do.

We spend about a fourth of our time assessing and communicating the economic benefits of chemistry. We've done this sort of work for the chemical industry at large and for plastics and distinct chemistries. We look at the direct, indirect, and induced effects of the industry. This is typical trade association work and results in the usual job estimates and multipliers, as well as taxes paid. For the chemical industry, for example, we've found that in addition to the 784,000 jobs created directly by the industry, the full impact results in the creation of 6.7 million jobs, a 7.5:1 job multiplier.

To conduct this type of analysis, we use input-output (I-O) modeling. We are heavy users of the technique. We use the IMPLAN modeling software at the national level and for all 50 states to assess the "upstream" impact of the industry, a specific segment of the industry, a family of chemicals, or even individual chemicals. The ACC has a series of self-funded panels that provide targeted research on various chemicals (such as formaldehyde) or families of chemicals (such as solvents). In these "footprint" studies we assess the direct, supplier-induced indirect and payroll-induced effects on economic output, value-added, employment, payrolls, and taxes paid from the shipments of the chemistry. We also use the state-level IMPLAN models to assess the economic footprint for our state fact sheets, which are posted on the ACC website as well as the footprint for the chemistry in a given state. Martha, Emily, and I are versed in using these models, although Martha is the resident expert and took the lead in bringing this expertise in-house.

We also examine downstream uses, assessing the extent to which the chemistry is used in various customer industries and in final goods and services. This involves researching how the chemistry is employed. We delve beyond broad customer industry activity to actual applications. In a recent solvent study, for example, we found that the use of solvents in architectural coatings in new residential construction and remodeling work is much less than the use of solvents in an OEM coating used in appliances or industrial machinery. As result, solvents do not support the entire paint and coatings industry but rather a few segments. One needs to take the uniqueness of the chemistry into account in quantifying the value of output, jobs, and payrolls in these downstream activities in which the chemistry is supportive. For a typical economic footprint study this can involve scores of industries and final goods and services.

In addition to the usual economic footprint (both direct, indirect and induced upstream effects and downstream effects) we are often asked to examine the costs of substitution. This is where the concept of opportunity costs comes into play. In our context of evaluating the socioeconomic benefits of a particular chemistry, it's the cost of the next best alternative. For example, the next best alternative for PVC plumbing in a house is copper plumbing. The installed cost of the latter is four times that of the former. The difference in costs is the opportunity cost or value of the chemistry to society in that particular application. Of course we scale it up for the United States and North America and take into account service life, performance, and other attributes. In evaluating a typical chemistry, we may examine hundreds of applications.

Managing the Department

Over the course of 30+ years and three employers, I've had the privilege of working with scores of economists and analysts, but the team that I've assembled at the ACC is the best. The following are some random thoughts about staff recruitment, having the right mix of staff (in terms of skills and background), management of professionals, department culture, and professional development.

With a small team, new hires really have to fit in! The entire team will interview a candidate. In recruiting we are committed to finding the best person for the position. Having a diverse team fosters our ability to develop solutions for our clients. We endeavor to recruit individuals from a variety of analytical backgrounds and experience. My graduate studies focused on managerial economics, while Martha and Emily are more classically trained economists. Emily is also a statistician. Martha, Heather, and I worked in consulting; and Martha worked for another trade association. Heather did market research and led a marketing team (and is planning to work on her MBA), while we recruited Emily right out of college. In addition to professional/technical knowledge, our human resources department would add accountability, collaboration, results-orientation, initiative, and member/customer focus as key attributes. To this I would add that intellectual curiosity, tenacity (I encourage new team members to read *A Message to Garcia* by Elbert Hubbard), the ability to synthesize information, multitasking, and good writing and speaking skills make for good business economists and analysts.

We aim to provide outstanding services to internal clients and to ACC members. We value excellence and regard integrity and honesty as essential personal qualities. (I post the NABE Professional Conduct Guidelines in my office and have passed them out.) We continuously look for ways to do our work better. Our collegial size—there's just four of us—and our focus facilitate collaboration among the team. We're convinced that teamwork leads to better ideas and better solutions. So, at any given time we may be working on a few projects individually as well as several projects involving two or all of us.

Intellectual capital is important. Everybody on our team shares their time and knowledge with other team members. We support further education opportunities and invest in professional development. I encourage participation in NABE or the National Economists Club (NEC), our local NABE chapter. Participation in other related professional organizations (such as the United States Association for Energy Economics and Strategic and Competitive Intelligence Professionals, for example) as needed is encouraged as well. We actually make this part of our goals and objectives concerning professional development. I am also a big proponent of continuing education, and we work hard to extend our collective knowledge and skill base. We've found the NABE educational opportunities to be targeted and very good. We are looking forward to the development of the NABE Certified Business Economist (CBE) designation as a means of further developing our collective expertise.

Although we value dedication and hard work, we recognize the importance of maintaining a satisfying life outside of the office. To cultivate and support effective employees, we encourage a balance between work and personal life. This includes occasional telecommuting, and we jokingly refer to the various at-home annexes by geography. Commutes in the Washington area can be brutal.

In managing, I do my best to see that my team is equipped with the best tools and to stay out of their way. My thinking is to turn the usual organizational chart/pyramid upside down, and my role is to be supportive of Martha, Emily, and Heather in their front-line work. I want them to succeed, and I work to remove any roadblocks. The leadership style is more participative than authoritarian and begins with serving first, which brings one to aspire to lead.

Conclusion

Working as an economist at the ACC is always interesting. I find the economics of the chemical industry to be fascinating. No two days are the same; and the tax, energy, value chain, economic benefit, and other issues provide new challenges. What makes the job great is my colleagues. They are talented, energetic, full of ideas, and an inspiration. I am honored to work with them.

Note

Originally published in *Business Economics*, Vol. 49, No. 2 (April 2014), pp. 114–121.

Reference

Mahapatra, S. and T. Swift. 2012. "Constructing Global Production Activity Indexes: The Chemical Industry." *Business Economics*, 46(1): 68–81.

CPSIA information can be obtained at www.ICGtesting.com
Printed in the USA
BVOW06*0213290216

438444BV00008B/41/P

9 781137 572509